Loggerhead
Sea Turtles

Loggerhead
Sea Turtles

Edited by
Alan B. Bolten and
Blair E. Witherington

Smithsonian Books
Washington

Copy Editor: Bonnie J. Harmon
Production Editors: E. Anne Bolen and Joanne Reams
Designer: Brian Barth

Library of Congress Cataloging-in-Publication Data

Loggerhead sea turtles / edited by Alan B. Bolten
and Blair E. Witherington.
    p.   cm.
  Includes bibliographical references (p.   ).
  ISBN 1-58834-136-4 (alk. paper)
    1. Loggerhead turtle. I. Bolten, Alan B., 1945–
II. Witherington, Blair E., 1962–
  QL666.C536L65   2003
  597.92′8—dc21   2003045696

British Library Cataloguing-in-Publication Data is
available

Manufactured in the United States of America
10 09 08 07 06 05 04 03   5 4 3 2 1

∞ The paper used in this publication meets the minimum requirements of the American National Standard for Information Sciences—Permanence of Paper
for Printed Library Materials ANSI Z39.48-1984.

Contents

Part One
Biology and Ecology   5

Preface

The number of scientific publications on loggerhead sea turtles, *Caretta caretta*, has increased dramatically during the last twenty years. This period of time followed a major global update on the status of loggerheads at the World Conference in 1979 (Bjorndal 1982) and a thorough species synopsis (Dodd 1988). Therefore, our primary objective for producing this volume was to synthesize the recent advances in our knowledge of loggerhead biology and conservation. This synthesis benefited from the Special Session on the Biology of the Loggerhead Sea Turtle convened during the Twentieth Annual Symposium on Sea Turtle Biology and Conservation, Orlando, Florida (February 2000). As part of this synthesis, the authors have identified the information gaps that must be filled to meet the current and future challenges of conservation and management. This volume is dedicated to the efforts of the many researchers who have provided the baseline information making this synthesis possible, and to future researchers, managers, and conservationists on whom the survival of sea turtles will depend.

We would like to thank the following individuals for reviewing the chapters; in doing so, they have made a significant contribution to this volume: Ralph Ackerman, George Balazs, Karen Bjorndal, Ray Carthy, Peter Dutton, Matthew Godfrey, Brendan Godley, Allen Foley, Neca Marcovaldi, Anne Meylan, Peter Meylan, Jeffrey

Miller, Jeanne Mortimer, Nicholas Mrosovsky, Sally Murphy, Nicholas Pilcher, Brian Riewald, Mike Salmon, Katsufumi Sato, Jeffrey Seminoff, James Spotila, and Jeanette Wyneken.

We would also like to thank Skye White for assistance with the illustrations and Peter Eliazar for assistance with bibliographic data. We thank Karen Bjorndal for suggestions and editorial assistance throughout the production of this volume.

Finally, we would like to thank Vincent Burke and Nicole Sloan from Smithsonian Books, whose patience, guidance, and support have helped to make this volume a reality.

Alan B. Bolten
Archie Carr Center for Sea Turtle Research and Department of Zoology
University of Florida

Blair E. Witherington
Florida Fish and Wildlife Conservation Commission
Florida Marine Research Institute

Literature Cited

Bjorndal, K. A. (ed.). 1982. Biology and conservation of sea turtles. Washington, D.C.: Smithsonian Institution Press.

Dodd, C. K., Jr. 1988. Synopsis of the biological data on the loggerhead sea turtle *Caretta caretta* (Linnaeus 1758). USFWS Biological Report 88(14).

List of Contributors

Osamu Abe
Ishigaki Tropical Station
Seikai National Fisheries Research Institute
148-446, Fukai-Ota, Ishigaki
Okinawa, 907-0451, Japan
turtlea@snf-its.affrc.go.jp

Roberto Argano
Istituto di Zoologia
Università "La Sapienza"
Via dell' Università 32
I-00185 Roma, Italy
argano@axrma.uniroma1.it

Hiroshi Asakawa
Shimoda Aquarium
Shimoda, Shizuoka 415-0001, Japan

Dean A. Bagley
University of Central Florida
Department of Biology
P.O. Box 25000
Orlando, Florida 32816, U.S.A.
de315786@pegasus.cc.ucf.edu

Robert Baldwin
P.O. Box 2531
C.P.O. 111, Oman
wosoman@omantel.net.om

Ibrahim Baran
Dokuz Eylül Üniversitesi
Buca Egitim Fakültesi
Buca-Izmir, Turkey
baran@egtm.bef.deu.edu.tr

Flegra Bentivegna
Stazione Zoologica "Anton Dohrn"
Villa Comunale 1
I-80121 Napoli, Italy
flegra@alpha.szn.it

Karen A. Bjorndal
Archie Carr Center for Sea Turtle Research and
  Department of Zoology
P.O. Box 118525
University of Florida
Gainesville, Florida 32611, U.S.A.
kab@zoology.ufl.edu

Alan B. Bolten
Archie Carr Center for Sea Turtle Research and
  Department of Zoology
P.O. Box 118525
University of Florida
Gainesville, Florida 32611, U.S.A.
abb@zoology.ufl.edu

Brian W. Bowen
Department of Fisheries and Aquatic Sciences
University of Florida
7922 NW 71st Street
Gainesville, Florida 32653, U.S.A.
Current Address:
Hawaii Institute of Marine Biology
University of Hawaii
P. O. Box 1346
Kane'ohe, Hawaii 96744, U.S.A.
bbowen@hawaii.edu

Mohamed N. Bradai
Institut National des Sciences et Technologies
  de la Mer (INSTM)
B. P. 1035
3018 Sfax, Tunisia
mednejmeddine.bradai@instm.rnrt.tn

Juan Antonio Camiñas
Instituto Español de Oceanografía
Centro Oceanografico de Málaga
E-29640 Fuengirola, Spain
jacaminas@ma.ieo.es

Raymond R. Carthy
Florida Cooperative Fish and Wildlife
    Research Unit
P.O. Box 110450
Gainesville, Florida 32611-0450, U.S.A.
Rayc@zoo.ufl.edu

Paolo Casale
Via Antonio Calderara 29
I-00125 Roma, Italy
paolo.casale@tiscalinet.it

Milani Chaloupka
School of Economics
University of Queensland
Brisbane, Queensland 4072, Australia
m.chaloupka@mailbox.uq.edu.au

Deborah T. Crouse
Division of Endangered Species
U.S. Fish and Wildlife Service
4401 Fairfax Drive No. 452
Arlington, Virginia 22203, U.S.A.
debby_crouse@fws.gov

Larry B. Crowder
Duke University Marine Lab
Nicholas School of the Environment
135 Duke Marine Lab Road
Beaufort, North Carolina 28516-9721, U.S.A.
lcrowder@duke.edu

Gregorio De Metrio
University of Bari
DPA, Via Amendola 165/12
Bari, Italy
g.demetrio@tno.it

Andreas Demetropoulos
Cyprus Wildlife Society
Nicosia, Cyprus
andrecws@logos.cy.net

Llewellyn M. Ehrhart
University of Central Florida
Department of Biology
P.O. Box 25000
Orlando, Florida 32816, U.S.A.
lehrhart@pegasus.cc.ucf.edu

Sheryan P. Epperly
Southeast Fisheries Science Center
National Marine Fisheries Service
75 Virginia Beach Drive
Miami, Florida 33149, U.S.A.
Sheryan.Epperly@noaa.gov

Allen M. Foley
Florida Fish and Wildlife Conservation
    Commission
Florida Marine Research Institute
6134 Authority Avenue, Building 200
Jacksonville, Florida 32221, U.S.A.
Allen.Foley@fwc.state.fl.us

Nat B. Frazer
Department of Wildlife Ecology and
    Conservation
University of Florida
P.O. Box 110430
Gainesville, Florida 32611-0430, U.S.A.
FrazerN@wec.ufl.edu

Takashi Fujii
Hiwasa Chelonian Museum
Hiwasaura, Hiwasa, Kaifu
Tokushima 779-2304, Japan

Guido Gerosa
Chelon
Via Val Padana 134/B
I-00141 Roma, Italy
chelon@tin.it

Matthew H. Godfrey
Projeto TAMAR-IBAMA
Caixa Postal 2219
Salvador, Bahia CEP 40210-970, Brazil
Current Address:
Wildlife Resources Commission
307 Live Oak Street
Beaufort, North Carolina 28516, U.S.A.
godfreym@coastalnet.com

Brendan J. Godley
Marine Turtle Research Group
University of Wales Swansea
Swansea SA2 8PP, United Kingdom
mtn@swansea.ac.uk

Kiyoshi Goto
Sea Turtle Association of Japan
Nagao-motomachi 5-17-18-302
Hirakata, Osaka 573-0163, Japan
info@umigame.org

Daw A. Haddoud
Marine Biology Research Center
Tripoli, Libya
Daw_hadod@yahoo.com

Shinya Hagino
Sea Turtle Association of Japan
Nagao-motomachi 5-17-18-302
Hirakata, Osaka 573-0163, Japan
info@umigame.org

Masao Hayami
Sea Turtle Association of Japan
Nagao-motomachi 5-17-18-302
Hirakata, Osaka 573-0163, Japan
info@umigame.org

Selina S. Heppell
Department of Fisheries and Wildlife
Oregon State University
Corvallis, Oregon 97331, U.S.A.
Selina.Heppell@orst.edu

Sally R. Hopkins-Murphy
South Carolina Department of
    Natural Resources
P.O. Box 12559
Charleston, South Carolina 29422-2559, U.S.A.
murphys@mrd.dnr.state.sc.us

Jonathan Houghton
School of Biological Sciences
University of Wales Swansea
Swansea SA2 8PP, United Kingdom
bdhought@swansea.ac.uk

George R. Hughes
KwaZulu-Natal Nature Conservation Service
P.O. Box 13053
Cascades 3202, South Africa
ghughes@kznncs.org.za

Masatoshi Ishii
Wildlife Society of Miyazaki
Higasi-Omiya 3-9-11, Miyazakishi
Miyazaki 880-0825, Japan

Toshitaka Iwamoto
Wildlife Society of Miyazaki
Higasi-Omiya 3-9-11, Miyazakishi
Miyazaki 880-0825, Japan

Takeshi Kamata
Sea Turtle Association of Japan
Nagao-motomachi 5-17-18-302
Hirakata, Osaka 573-0163, Japan
info@umigame.org

Naoki Kamezaki
Sea Turtle Association of Japan
Nagao-motomachi 5-17-18-302
Hirakata, Osaka 573-0163, Japan
JCG03011@nifty.ne.jp

Hiroshi Kato
Sea Turtle Association of Japan
Nagao-motomachi 5-17-18-302
Hirakata, Osaka 573-0163, Japan
info@umigame.org

Jun-ichi Kodama
Wildlife Society of Miyazaki
Higasi-Omiya 3-9-11, Miyazakishi
Miyazaki 880-0825, Japan

Yasuo Kondo
Sea Turtle Association of Japan
Nagao-motomachi 5-17-18-302
Hirakata, Osaka 573-0163, Japan
info@umigame.org

Luc Laurent
BioInsight
Biologie de la Conservation
B.P. 2132
F-69603 Villeurbanne, France
bioinsight@bioinsight.fr

Bojan Lazar
Department of Zoology
Croatian Natural History Museum
Demetrova 1
HR-10000 Zagreb, Croatia
bojan.lazar@hpm.hr

Colin J. Limpus
Queensland Parks and Wildlife Service
P.O. Box 155
Brisbane, Queensland 4002, Australia
col.limpus@env.qld.gov.au

Duncan J. Limpus
Queensland Parks and Wildlife Service
P.O. Box 155
Brisbane, Queensland 4002, Australia

Catherine M. F. Lohmann
Department of Biology
University of North Carolina
Chapel Hill, North Carolina 27599-3280,
    U.S.A.
CLohmann@email.unc.edu

Kenneth J. Lohmann
Department of Biology
University of North Carolina
Chapel Hill, North Carolina 27599-3280,
    U.S.A.
KLohmann@email.unc.edu

Dimitris Margaritoulis
Sea Turtle Protection Society of Greece
Solomou 57
GR-10432 Athens, Greece
margaritoulis@archelon.gr

Yoshimasa Matsuzawa
Archie Carr Center for Sea Turtle Research and
    Department of Zoology
P.O. Box 118525
University of Florida
Gainesville, Florida 32611, U.S.A.
Current Address:
Sea Turtle Association of Japan
Nagao-motomachi 5-17-18-302
Hirakata, Osaka 573-0163, Japan
Ymatsu@umigame.org

Jeffrey D. Miller
Queensland Parks and Wildlife Service
P.O. Box 2066
Cairns, Queensland, Australia
jeff.miller@env.qld.gov.au

Itsuro Miyawaki
Kushimoto Marine Park
Arita, Kushimoto
Wakayama 649-3514, Japan

Kozo Mizobuchi
Sea Turtle Association of Japan
Nagao-motomachi 5-17-18-302
Hirakata, Osaka 573-0163, Japan
info@umigame.org

Thomas M. Murphy
South Carolina Department of
    Natural Resources
585 Donnelley Drive
No. 2 Green Pond, South Carolina 29446,
    U.S.A.
murphyt@pop.scdnr.state.sc.us

Yutaka Nakamura
Wildlife Society of Miyazaki
Higasi-Omiya 3-9-11, Miyazakishi
Miyazaki 880-0825, Japan

Yoshito Nakashima
Wildlife Society of Miyazaki
Higasi-Omiya 3-9-11, Miyazakishi
Miyazaki 880-0825, Japan

Hiroaki Naruse
Sea Turtle Association of Japan
Nagao-motomachi 5-17-18-302
Hirakata, Osaka 573-0163, Japan
info@umigame.org

Kazuyoshi Omuta
Yakushima Sea Turtle Research Group
Nagata, Kamiyakucho, Kumage
Kagoshima 891-4201, Japan

David W. Owens
University of Charleston
Grice Marine Laboratory
205 Fort Johnson Road
Charleston, South Carolina 29412, U.S.A.
owensd@cofc.edu

Robert I. T. Prince
Wildlife Research Centre
Department of Conservation and
    Land Management
P.O. Box 51
Wanneroo, Western Australia 6046, Australia
bobp@calm.wa.gov.au

William E. Redfoot
University of Central Florida
Department of Biology
P.O. Box 25000
Orlando, Florida 32816, U.S.A.
bredfoot@tampabay.rr.com

Masamichi Samejima
Sea Turtle Association of Japan
Nagao-motomachi 5-17-18-302
Hirakata, Osaka 573-0163, Japan
info@umigame.org

Barbara A. Schroeder
National Marine Fisheries Service
Office of Protected Resources
1315 East West Highway
Silver Spring, Maryland 20910, U.S.A.
barbara.schroeder@noaa.gov

Hiroyuki Suganuma
Sea Turtle Association of Japan
Nagao-motomachi 5-17-18-302
Hirakata, Osaka 573-0163, Japan
info@umigame.org

Hiroshi Takeshita
Wildlife Society of Miyazaki
Higasi-Omiya 3-9-11, Miyazakishi
Miyazaki 880-0825, Japan

Teruhiko Tanaka
Sea Turtle Association of Japan
Nagao-motomachi 5-17-18-302
Hirakata, Osaka 573-0163, Japan
info@umigame.org

Tai-ichiro Toji
Sea Turtle Association of Japan
Nagao-motomachi 5-17-18-302
Hirakata, Osaka 573-0163, Japan
info@umigame.org

Masahiro Uematsu
Sea Turtle Association of Japan
Nagao-motomachi 5-17-18-302
Hirakata, Osaka 573-0163, Japan
info@umigame.org

Ikuo Wakabayashi
Sea Turtle Association of Japan
Nagao-motomachi 5-17-18-302
Hirakata, Osaka 573-0163, Japan
info@umigame.org

Blair E. Witherington
Florida Fish and Wildlife Conservation
    Commission
Florida Marine Research Institute
9700 South A1A
Melbourne Beach, Florida 32951, U.S.A.
witherington@cfl.rr.com

Akio Yamamoto
Sea Turtle Association of Japan
Nagao-motomachi 5-17-18-302
Hirakata, Osaka 573-0163, Japan
info@umigame.org

Takanobu Yamato
Sea Turtle Association of Japan
Nagao-motomachi 5-17-18-302
Hirakata, Osaka 573-0163, Japan
info@umigame.org

Abbreviations, Acronyms, and Conventions

AFZ — Australian Fishing Zone

ANCA — Australian Nature Conservation Agency (formerly Australian National Parks and Wildlife Service)

ANOVA — Analysis of variance

Barcelona Convention — Convention for the Protection of the Marine Environment and the Coastal Region of the Mediterranean

Bern Convention — Convention on the Conservation of European Wildlife and Natural Habitats

Bonn Convention — Convention on the Conservation of Migratory Species of Wild Animals

CANDISC — Canonical discriminant analysis

CAP — Caribbean Action Plan

CCC — Caribbean Conservation Corporation

CEEP — Conservatoire Études des Écosystèmes de Provence

CEP — Caribbean Environmental Programme

CHELON — Marine Turtle Conservation and Research Program, Rome, Italy

CIESM — Commission Internationale pour l'Exploration Scientifique de la Mer Méditerranée

CIQRO — Centro de Investigaciones de Quintana Roo

CITES — Convention on International Trade in Endangered Species

CMS — Convention on the Conservation of Migratory Species of Wild Animals (aka the Bonn Convention)

CSC — Centro Studi Cetacei (CSC online publications)

CSIRO — The Commonwealth Science and Industrial Research Organization

CWS — Cyprus Wildlife Society

DCALM — Department of Conservation and Land Management (Western Australia)

DHKD — Dogal Hayati Koruma Dernegi (Society for the Protection of Nature, Turkey)

EC — European Commission

EEC — European Economic Community

FAO — U.N. Food and Agriculture Organization

FCMP — Florida Coastal Management Program

FLOE — Fish LIDAR, Oceanic, Experimental

FMRI — Florida Marine Research Institute

GBR — Great Barrier Reef

GLM — General linear model

HMP — Hatchling related mortality probabilities

ICCAT — International Commission for the Conservation of Atlantic Tunas

ICONA — Instituto Nacional para la Conservatión de la Naturaleza (National Institute for Nature Conservation in Spain)

IEEE	Institute of Electrical and Electronic Engineers
IFREMER	Institut Français de Recherche pour l'Exploitation de la Mer (French Research Institute for Exploitation of the Sea)
INBS	Index Nesting Beach Survey
ISTPM	Institut Spécialisé de Technologie des Pêches Maritimes (Agadir, Morocco)
IUCN	International Union for the Conservation of Nature and Natural Resources/The World Conservation Union
IUCN/EC	IUCN and European Commission
IUCN/SSC	IUCN Species Survival Commission
IUCN/SSC/MTSG	IUCN/SSC Marine Turtle Specialist Group
JMP	Statistical analysis software from SAS Institute
LAE	Least absolute error
LIDAR	Light Direction and Ranging
MANRE	Ministry of Agriculture, Natural Resources, and Environment (Cyprus)
MAP	Mediterranean Action Plan
MED WG	Mediterranean Working Group
MEDASSET	Mediterranean Association to Save the Sea Turtles
MHM	Proxy hatchling mortality estimates
MTSG	Marine Turtle Specialist Group
NGO	Nongovernmental Organizations
NIOF	National Institute for Oceanography and Fisheries (Egypt)
NMFS	National Marine Fisheries Service
NOAA	National Oceanic and Atmospheric Administration (U.S. Department of Commerce)
NRC	National Research Council (United States)
PHPA	Directorate General of Forest Protection and Nature Conservation (Indonesia)
PRINCOMP	Principal component analysis
QDEH	Queensland Department of Environment and Heritage
QDPI	Queensland Department of Primary Industries
QFMA	Queensland Fish Management Authority
QFMA/TrawlMAC	QFMA Trawl Fishery Management Advisory Committee
QPWS	Queensland Park and Wildlife Service
RAC/SPA	Regional Activity Center for Specially Protected Areas
Ramsar Convention	Convention on Wetlands of International Importance
SEAMAP	Southeast Area Monitoring and Assessment Program
SEFSC	Southeast Fisheries Science Center
sGBR	southern Great Barrier Reef
SOPTOM	Station d'Observation et de Protection des Tortues dans le Monde
SPREP	South Pacific Regional Environment Program
SSC	Species Survival Commission
STSSN	Sea Turtle Stranding and Salvation Network
SWFSC	Southwest Fisheries Science Center
TED	Turtle Excluder Device
TEWG	Turtle Expert Working Group
TrawlMAC	Trawl Fishery Management Advisory Committee
UNEP	United Nations Environmental Program
UNEP MAP	UNEP Mediterranean Action Plan
UNEP OCA	UNEP Oceans and Coastal Areas Unit
USACE	U.S. Army Corps of Engineers
USFWS	U.S. Fish and Wildlife Service
WATS	Western Atlantic Turtle Symposium
WECAF	Western Central Atlantic Fisheries Commission
WIDECAST	Wider Caribbean Sea Turtle Conservation Network
WIWO	Working Group for International Waterbird and Wetland Research
WTO	World Trade Organization
WWF	World Wildlife Fund/World Wide Fund for Nature

Introduction

The Loggerhead Sea Turtle—A Most Excellent Fishe[1]

—Alan B. Bolten

> The Atlantic loggerhead is a hardy and adaptable animal, able to make a living
> under all sorts of conditions. Very little is known about the wanderings of indi-
> vidual loggerheads, but the range of situations in which the species occurs is aston-
> ishingly great and implies an unusual ability to take things as they come.
> Carr 1952

A half-century ago, in his classic work *Hand-book of Turtles*, Archie Carr (1952) described the loggerhead sea turtle *(Caretta caretta)* as a generalist species. Not much was known back then about loggerhead sea turtles or, for that matter, any of the sea turtle species. We know a lot more now, and based on our increased knowledge, we would continue to describe the ecology of the loggerhead as that of a generalist species. In fact, the loggerhead is probably the most ecologically generalized sea turtle. Compared to the other sea turtle species, logger-heads have the greatest geographic range in their nesting beaches, which are found in both temperate and tropical latitudes; their foraging range also extends seasonally from temperate to tropical waters. They are globally distributed in all temperate and tropical ocean basins and in-habit open oceanic waters as well as shallow near-shore waters. The diet of loggerheads is also one of the least specialized of all sea turtles.

We know more about the life history of log-gerhead sea turtles than any other sea turtle species. This greater understanding is largely a function of knowing about its early juvenile oceanic stage (formerly referred to as the "lost year"), which is essentially unknown for the six other sea turtle species. It has not always been this way. In the beginning of scientific research on sea turtles, loggerheads were not the stars

---

[1]Author's Note: The use of "*fishe*" is borrowed from Archie Carr's (1967) volume on the natural history of sea turtles: *So Excellent a Fishe.*

1

they are today. Earlier efforts were focused on both the green turtle *(Chelonia mydas)* and hawksbill turtle *(Eretmochelys imbricata)*. These were, and still are, both commercially important species. Tragically, exploitation of green turtles for meat and calipee and of hawksbills for their shell (tortoiseshell or *bekko*) has led to severe population declines. Focus next shifted to the Kemp's ridley *(Lepidochelys kempii)* and the mystery surrounding where it nested, or even if the "bastard turtle" was a legitimate species and not a hybrid. Subsequent alarm for the pending extinction of the species, once its nesting beach at Rancho Nuevo, Mexico, was discovered, led to a flurry of research and the development of conservation and management policies.

Loggerheads are not generally prized for their meat or shell, although they are hunted for food in many regions around the world, and with nesting beaches located in areas with large human populations, their reproductive behavior was not a great mystery. Also, most people would agree that loggerheads do not have the beauty of the green turtle and hawksbill or the unique features of the leatherback *(Dermochelys coriacea)*. So, what is the attraction to loggerhead sea turtles and why has there been so much recent attention given to loggerheads by researchers and conservationists? First, incidental capture in commercial fisheries (trawl fisheries, high seas driftnet fisheries, and longline fisheries) and loss of nesting habitat to coastal development sounded the alarm for the decline in loggerhead populations. This concern has resulted in increased efforts as well as increased funding to study the loggerhead sea turtle to avert disaster. The good news is that we have learned a lot about loggerhead biology, as can be seen in the chapters of this volume. Unfortunately, the bad news is that devastating impacts from commercial fisheries and habitat degradation continue to threaten loggerhead populations.

Second, luck of geography has played a large part in our focus on loggerhead biology and conservation. Loggerheads nest in geographic areas with major research and conservation programs (e.g., Australia, Brazil, Japan, Mediterranean, South Africa, and the southeastern United States). For example, the Archie Carr National Wildlife Refuge, the first National Wildlife Refuge in the United States established for sea turtles, protects a critical nesting beach for what may be the world's largest nesting population of loggerheads.

The extent of our knowledge about a generalist sea turtle species—the loggerhead—is fortuitous. We can develop models (e.g., demographic models, ecogeographic models) for the loggerhead and then extrapolate from these models to the other species of sea turtle. It is usually more appropriate to extrapolate from a generalized species to a specialized species, such as the herbivorous green turtle or the sponge-eating hawksbill, than the other way round. Thus, our knowledge of the life history of the loggerhead provides a framework upon which to develop models and increase our understanding of the biology of the other sea turtle species.

This volume summarizes what we have learned about the biology of loggerhead sea turtles (Part One) and their geographic distribution and population status (Part Two). In Part Three, models are presented that synthesize our knowledge of this species as well as indicate gaps in our knowledge to guide future research. In Part One, the loggerhead is defined from both the genetic perspective (Bowen, Chapter 1) and the morphological perspective (Kamezaki, Chapter 2). The chapters on the ecology and behavior of loggerheads begin with a presentation of orientation mechanisms of hatchlings (Lohmann and Lohmann, Chapter 3); an analysis of the juvenile oceanic stage (Bolten, Chapter 4); and the ecology of juveniles and adults in neritic habitats in the Atlantic (Hopkins-Murphy et al., Chapter 5) and in the Pacific (Limpus and Limpus, Chapter 6). Nesting patterns and reproductive migrations are reviewed (Schroeder et al., Chapter 7); nest site selection, oviposition, and embryonic development are discussed (Miller et al., Chapter 8); and recent research results on the nest environment are presented (Carthy et al., Chapter 9).

Current status of loggerhead populations in the different ocean basins is reviewed in Part two. For the first time since the 1978 World Conference (Bjorndal 1982), Chapters 10 through 14 bring together and synthesize population status and trends for loggerheads in all ocean basins in a single volume and provide an important reference for future studies: Ehrhart et al. (Chapter 10) review population trends in the Atlantic; Margaritoulis et al. (Chapter 11) provide a major overview of loggerheads in the Mediterranean; Limpus and Limpus (Chapter 12) review the decline in the South Pacific populations; Kamezaki et al. (Chapter 13) summarize the nesting populations in Japan; and Baldwin et al. (Chapter 14) review the distribution and abundance of loggerheads in the Indian Ocean.

Conceptual models can help us synthesize what we know about an organism, its habitat, its ecosystem, and interactions among these different levels. In a number of chapters, the authors present conceptual models. The number of these models and the diversity of approaches used are indicative of the wealth of knowledge we have achieved in the last few decades concerning loggerhead sea turtle biology. There are three types of models presented in this volume: ecosystem models, demographic models, and ecogeographic models (e.g., life history models that incorporate ontogenetic habitat shifts). The study of roles and interactions of sea turtles within their ecosystems is a new frontier for sea turtle research. Bjorndal (Chapter 15) presents the foundation of an ecosystem model for loggerhead turtles. Demographic models assess population trends based on the parameters of fecundity, growth, survivorship, and longevity. Heppell and her coauthors (Chapter 16) review the history of demographic models for the At-

lantic, and Chaloupka (Chapter 17) develops a demographic model for the Australian loggerhead population. The volume closes with a discussion of the challenges and opportunities for the conservation of loggerhead sea turtles (Witherington, Chapter 18).

Sea turtle research has benefited greatly from advances in technology. New developments in biotechnology, including molecular genetics and biotelemetry, have provided the tools to study resource utilization, movements, distribution, and dispersal patterns. Computer technologies and statistical applications have improved data management, analysis, and synthesis. Application of these technological advances are illustrated in the chapters of this volume.

This volume summarizes our current knowledge of loggerhead biology and highlights new research and conservation directions. The authors and editors of this volume hope that it will contribute to future efforts to improve the survival outlook for, and our knowledge of, the loggerhead sea turtle.

LITERATURE CITED

Bjorndal, K. A. (ed.) 1982. Biology and conservation of sea turtles. Washington, D.C.: Smithsonian Institution Press.

Carr, A. 1952. Handbook of turtles. Ithaca, N.Y.: Cornell University Press.

Carr, A. 1967. So excellent a fishe. New York: The Natural History Press.

Part One
Biology and Ecology

Chapter 1

What Is a Loggerhead Turtle?

The Genetic Perspective

—Brian W. Bowen

This chapter will review the contributions of molecular genetics to studies of the phylogenetic resolution, phylogeography, population structure, and migratory behavior of loggerhead turtles. To date most of these studies have used mitochondrial DNA (mtDNA) sequence information. Mitochondrial DNA is a double-stranded ring of nucleotides that provides the blueprint for energy production in the cytoplasmic mitochondria. This genome has several features that are advantageous for studies of sea turtles. First, mtDNA is maternally inherited, providing an ideal genetic marker for species with a population structure that is defined by the site fidelity of nesting females (Avise 2000). This mode of mtDNA inheritance also means that a single (haploid) genetic signature is found in each individual, as opposed to two (diploid) genotypes for most nuclear DNA (nDNA) loci. Second, mtDNA sequences evolve rapidly, relative to most nDNA loci, and can provide phylogenetic resolution from the

shallow separations of regional nesting colonies to the deep evolutionary chasms between taxonomic families. Third, mtDNA sequences can serve as natural genetic "tags" to link nesting colonies and distant feeding populations. Fourth, mtDNA studies are less technically demanding than studies of nuclear DNA. Additional contributions from nDNA studies are reviewed where available. However, the vast reservoir of information in the nuclear genome of the loggerhead turtle remains largely untapped.

Evolution

Four families of sea turtles are known from the Cretaceous Period. Three of these survived the extinction at the Cretaceous-Tertiary boundary 63 million years ago (Weems 1988; Zangerl and Sloan 1960), but only two lineages persisted through the Eocene (55–38 million years before present). One was the predecessor of the remarkable leatherback turtle (*Dermochelys*

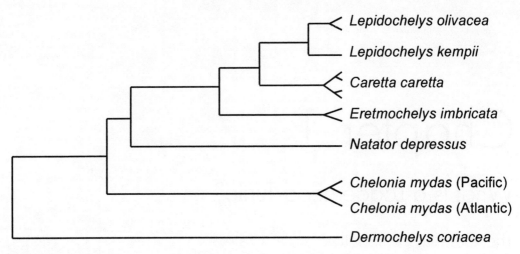

Figure 1.1. Phylogenetic trees for the extant sea turtle species based on mtDNA sequences (adapted from Bowen et al. 1993b; Dutton et al. 1996). Three deep lineages are apparent in the family Cheloniidae, corresponding to the tribes Carettini, Natatorini, and Chelonini. Unbranched terminal twigs in *Lepidochelys kempii*, *Natator depressus*, and *Dermochelys coriacea* indicate low levels of detected mtDNA diversity in rangewide comparisons. Phylogenetic comparisons with nDNA sequences reveal an essentially concordant phylogeny, with unresolved tricotomies for the three tribes (Carettini, Natatorini, and Chelonini) within Cheloniidae and for the three genera *(Caretta, Lepidochelys, and Eretmochelys)* within Carettini (Bowen and Karl 1996).

coriacea; family Dermochelyidae), and the other lineage gave rise to the six species of the family Cheloniidae, including the loggerhead turtle.

From subspecies to subfamilies, relationships within the Cheloniidae have been controversial. Many of these problems are due to the overall similarity among cheloniid sea turtles. Species separated for millions of years are nearly indistinguishable in terms of external morphology (Pritchard 1969), and even separate genera can be difficult to recognize (Frazier 1985; Limpus et al. 1988; Zangerl et al. 1988). In this respect, molecular biology has been a boon to phylogenetic studies of sea turtles, resolving relationships that are refractory to morphological analysis. Researchers have employed albumin proteins (Chen et al. 1980), immunological distances (Frair 1979), serum electrophoresis (Frair 1982), mtDNA sequences (Bowen et al. 1991, 1993b; Dutton et al. 1996), and nDNA sequences (Bowen and Karl 1996). Evolutionary trees based on these methods show broad areas of congruence, and robustly resolve the phylogenetic affiliations of the loggerhead turtle.

Molecular phylogenies show three deep lineages in the family Cheloniidae, corresponding to the tribes Natatorini, Chelonini, and Caret-

tini (Gaffney and Meylan 1988; Zangerl 1958; Zangerl et al. 1988). Fossil evidence indicates that these three tribes differentiated during the Paleocene, Eocene, or Oligocene (63–24 million years before present) (Carr 1942; Weems 1988), a finding that is roughly concordant with the depths of separations in mtDNA sequences (Bowen et al. 1993b; Dutton et al. 1996). While the first two tribes contain single species, the Carettini includes the loggerhead turtle, the two ridley species *(Lepidochelys olivacea* and *L. kempii)*, and the hawksbill turtle *(Eretmochelys imbricata)* (Figure 1.1). The molecular phylogeny indicates that the hawksbill turtle was an early branch of the Carettini lineage. The ridleys subsequently diverged from the loggerhead in the mid-Miocene (perhaps 10 million years before present) based on mtDNA sequence divergences.

The genus *Caretta* is now considered to be monotypic (containing a single species), but in the past this group has been more inclusive (Hay 1908, for example). At one time, the ridley turtles were classified as "loggerheads" (genus *Caretta*), a grouping that subsumes millions of years of independent evolution (Bowen et al. 1991; Carr 1942; Deraniyagala 1934, 1939).

Table 1.1.

Cases of Hybridization or Interspecific Mating between Loggerhead *(Caretta caretta)* and Other Sea Turtle Species

Species	Evidence	Region	Source
Lepidochelys kempii	Mating in captivity	NW Atlantic	1
	Morphology and DNA	NW Atlantic	7
Eretmochelys imbricata	Hatchling morphology	NW Pacific	4
	Electrophoresis	NW Pacific	5
	Hatchling morphology	NW Pacific	3
	Electrophoresis	SW Atlantic	2
	DNA	NW Atlantic	7
Chelonia mydas	DNA	NW Atlantic	7
	Hatchling morphology	NW Pacific	6
	Hatchling morphology	SW Pacific	8

Source Key: 1. Carr 1957. 2. Conceicão et al. 1990. 3. Frazier 1988. 4. Kamezaki 1983. 5. Kamezaki and Namikawa 1984. 6. Kamezaki et al. 1996. 7. Karl et al. 1995. 8. C. J. Limpus, pers. comm.

Note: These crosses include both maternal and paternal contributions from loggerheads (see Karl et al. 1995).

One extinct *Caretta* species has been described from Pliocene (5–2 million years before present) deposits of North Carolina (Zug 2001) and this species may have been sympatric with *Caretta caretta* (Dodd and Morgan 1992).

Deraniyagala (1943, 1945) described putative subspecies based on subtle morphological differences between Atlantic and Indian-Pacific forms (*Caretta caretta caretta* and *C.c. gigas,* respectively), but subsequent reviews have questioned these assignments (Pritchard and Trebbau 1984; Dodd 1988; Kamezaki and Matsui 1997), and genetic assays do not support such divisions (Bowen et al. 1994). The prevailing opinion is that subspecies assignments are not warranted.

Genomic Evolution

The genomes of sea turtles appear to evolve slowly. Chromosomal number and banding patterns are highly conserved across the family Cheloniidae (see Bickham et al. 1981). Kamezaki (1989) resolved the karyotype of loggerhead turtles at $2n = 56$ chromosomes, and other researchers have demonstrated the same number in both Cheloniidae and Dermochelyidae (Bickham et al. 1980; Kamezaki 1990; Medrano et al. 1987). At the level of DNA

sequences, turtles appear to evolve slowly as well. FitzSimmons et al. (1995) discovered that hypervariable nDNA loci are conserved across the oldest divergences in sea turtle evolution. Avise et al. (1992) noted an order-of-magnitude reduction in the rate of mtDNA sequence divergence in turtles relative to other vertebrates. Explanations for this phenomenon remain obscure but could include slow metabolic rate, long generation time, or high accuracy in DNA replication (Avise et al. 1992; Martin 1995).

Loggerhead Hybrids

The earliest known report of marine turtle hybridization is the "McQueggie," alleged by Caribbean fishermen to be a cross between the loggerhead turtle and the green turtle (Garman 1880). More recently, several researchers have identified cases of loggerhead hybridization, based on intermediate conditions in otherwise diagnostic morphological characters (Frazier 1988; Kamezaki 1983). Protein electrophoretic studies have confirmed several hybrid assignments, including an *Eretmochelys* × *Caretta* hybrid in Brazil (Conceicão et al. 1990; Table 1.1).

DNA sequence assays have recently been used to document multiple cases of hybridization involving loggerheads (Karl et al. 1995). One case was discovered during global genetic surveys of green and loggerhead turtles (Bowen et al. 1992, 1994). Four hatchlings from Bahia, Brazil, that were originally identified as green turtles unexpectedly displayed loggerhead mtDNA sequences. Studies of nDNA loci revealed signature patterns of both green and loggerhead turtles. The combination of nDNA and mtDNA evidence indicates that these hatchlings were first generation hybrids between a loggerhead female and a green turtle male (Table 1.1; see also Karl et al. 1995).

The existence of *Caretta* × *Chelonia* hybrids is remarkable because the tribes Carettini and Chelonini represent an ancient division within the family Cheloniidae, dating to perhaps 50+ million years ago. In contrast, the oldest known mammal hybridization involves species separated for about 6 million years (Wilson et al. 1974), and the oldest natural hybridizations known for birds and frogs are estimated to be about 20–25 million years (Prager and Wilson 1975; Wilson et al. 1974). Therefore, *Caretta* and *Chelonia* may be the oldest vertebrate lineages known to hybridize in nature. What could account for the ability of these species to hybridize after tens of millions of years of divergent evolution? The slow rate of genomic and morphological evolution in marine turtles is undoubtedly part of the explanation. A dearth of behavioral barriers to hybridization may also be a factor. Male turtles are notably indiscriminate in mating preferences and have even attempted copulation with hapless scuba divers (W. Witzell, pers. comm.). Such behaviors, coupled with the conserved genomic evolution noted above, undoubtedly increase the likelihood of hybridization.

Future Research

Recent genetic assays have clarified many issues in sea turtle systematics, although there are remaining problems (Bowen and Karl 2000; Karl and Bowen 1999). Perhaps the most fertile ground for further molecular investigations is at the subgeneric and subspecies levels, where fine-scale evolutionary differentiation may be difficult to resolve against a background of ecotypic variation (James 1983). For example, Mediterranean loggerhead turtles are smaller than Atlantic conspecifics, have unique adaptations to the Mediterranean environment (Margaritoulis 1982, 1988; Tiwari and Bjorndal 2000), and are effectively isolated from loggerhead turtles elsewhere in the range (Bowen et al. 1993a). Do these differences merit subspecific status? Probably not. The mtDNA assays demonstrate that Mediterranean turtles diverged recently from Atlantic populations, possibly after the most recent glacial maximum (within 12,000 years; Encalada et al. 1998). Available morphological studies show that the Mediterranean loggerhead is not highly distinct (except in size; Brongersma 1961; Kamezaki, Chapter 2 this volume; Tiwari and Bjorndal 2000). Furthermore, smaller body size is characteristic of a broad array of marine organisms in the Mediterranean and is suspected to be the result of lower primary productivity relative to warm-temperate Atlantic habitats. Hence, the diminutive Mediterranean loggerheads may not require taxonomic recognition, although they should be recognized as a group of specialized and highly isolated populations.

Phylogeography

Cheloniid turtles are primarily tropical in distribution, such that the southern extensions of Africa and South America represent prominent vicariant barriers to dispersal (Bowen et al. 1992, 1994, 1998). By comparison, the loggerhead has a more temperate distribution, including a rookery in the Indian Ocean (Natal, South Africa) within 1,000 km of the South Atlantic Ocean (Hughes 1974a, 1974b). Given this temperate habitat, southern Africa may be less formidable as a barrier to interoceanic gene flow in loggerheads than in the more tropical marine turtle species.

To examine the global phylogeography of loggerhead turtles, Bowen et al. (1994) described mtDNA sequence diversity in eight nesting colonies from across the distribution of loggerhead turtles. The overall topology of a loggerhead mtDNA phylogeny is similar to that observed in a global survey of green turtles (Bowen et al. 1992), with a relatively ancient

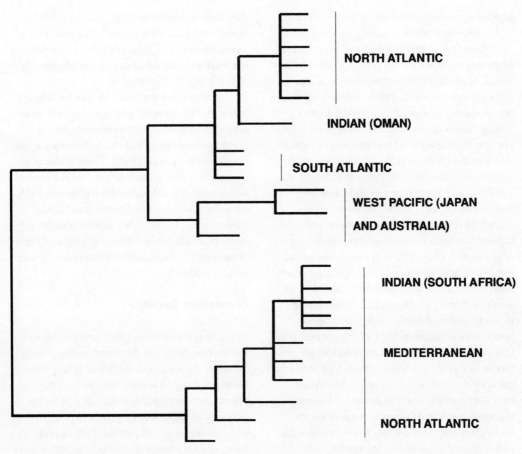

Figure 1.2. Phylogeography of the loggerhead turtle based on mtDNA control region sequence information from FitzSimmons et al. (1996), Encalada et al. (1998), Bolten et al. (1998), and unpublished data by A. L. Bass and N. N. FitzSimmons. Two primary lineages are apparent, indicating an ancient separation between the Indian-Pacific and Atlantic basins, and at least two instances of recent colonization between the Indian-Pacific and Atlantic-Mediterranean basins.

bifurcation and two major branches. One branch is observed primarily in the Indian-Pacific basins, the other primarily in the Atlantic-Mediterranean.

The recent accumulation of mtDNA sequences from the rapidly evolving control region allows a more detailed examination of loggerhead phylogeography. The tree presented in Figure 1.2 is based on control region sequences from FitzSimmons et al. (1996), Encalada et al. (1998), Bolten et al. (1998), and unpublished data from Nancy FitzSimmons (University of Canberra) and Anna Bass (University of South Florida). Based on a molecular clock for control region sequences in sea turtles (2% per million years; Encalada et al. 1996), the divergence between the two primary lineages (d_{max} = 0.063) corresponds to approximately

three million years, indicating a separation of loggerheads in the Atlantic basin from those in the Indian-Pacific basins since the Pliocene. However, this ancient separation has been punctuated by more recent colonizations between the Indian Ocean and the Atlantic-Mediterranean basins. The sole haplotype observed at Oman is nested within a cluster of Atlantic haplotypes and is distinguished by d = 0.005, indicating a colonization event from the Atlantic to the Indian Ocean about a quarter million years ago. The other Indian Ocean haplotype, observed at 100% frequency in Natal, South Africa, is widely distributed in the North Atlantic and the Mediterranean (haplotype B in Encalada et al. 1998). Bowen et al. (1994) suggested that this exchange could have occurred as recently as the current interglacial interval (< 12,000 years before present).

These Indian-Atlantic dispersal events were likely accomplished via the waters around South Africa. Notably, the oldest bifurcation in the mtDNA tree coincides approximately with the beginning of the upwelling of cold water around southern Africa (2.5 million years before present; Shannon 1985) and the onset of glacial cycles in the Pliocene (2.6–2.8 million years before present; Dwyer et al. 1995; Williams et al. 1997). Cold temperate conditions have predominated for most of the last three million years, and these conditions almost certainly curtail opportunities for trans-oceanic colonization of sea turtles. However, such opportunities are not completely eliminated. The Agulhas current flows westward around the continental shelf of southern Africa, feeding Indian Ocean water into an Agulhas-Atlantic mixing area below South Africa (Shannon 1970). This current system promotes the transportation of Indian Ocean biota into the South Atlantic, as indicated by the observation of southern African kelp mats and associated fauna at St. Helena, the southernmost subtropical outpost on the mid-Atlantic ridge (Edwards 1990). Passive dispersal of hatchlings along this route is especially likely to explain the widespread distribution of the South African haplotype in Atlantic-Mediterranean nesting colonies.

The olive ridley sea turtle *(Lepidochelys olivacea)* also recently invaded the Atlantic via southern Africa and has spread up the African coast at least to Guinea-Bissau and up the South American coast to Guyana (Bowen et al. 1998; Pritchard and Trebbau 1984).

Two additional features of the mtDNA control region tree indicate shallow evolutionary partitions within each ocean (Figure 1.2). First, South Atlantic (Brazilian) haplotypes are distinguished from North Atlantic samples by $d = 0.005–0.011$, indicating isolation on a scale of a quarter to a half million years. Nuclear DNA assays are concordant in showing a population separation on this scale (Pearce 2001). Second, the Pacific (Japanese and Australian) haplotypes are distinguished by a minimum of $d = 0.017$ from other conspecifics, indicating isolation on a scale of a million years. Overall the mtDNA

data show evidence of long-distance colonization, but these events appear to be rare. Geography, climate, and natal site fidelity (see below) are predominant influences on the phylogeography of loggerhead turtles.

In contrast to the mtDNA tree for loggerheads, the intraspecific phylogeny for the tropical green turtles shows no intermingling between the Atlantic and the Indian-Pacific oceans (Bowen et al. 1992). These findings are consistent with the expectation that the temperate-adapted loggerhead turtle will more readily transplant between the Atlantic and Indian ocean basins. The mtDNA genealogies demonstrate how differences in the geographic ranges of marine turtle species can influence their evolutionary history.

Population Genetics

In modern sea turtle research, mark-recapture studies have been the dominant methodology for resolving aspects of sea turtle demography. However, tagging studies have not resolved population structure, due in large part to the difficulty of tagging large numbers of hatchlings with markers that will persist to adulthood. Lacking such a tagging system, researchers have turned to molecular genetic markers. The analysis of population structure with protein electrophoresis has met with limited success, due to a low level of detected variation (Gyuris and Limpus 1988; Smith et al. 1978). In contrast, mtDNA analyses have provided information about present-day population structure and natal site fidelity (Allard et al. 1994) as well as historical patterns of dispersal (Bowen et al. 1998; Dutton et al. 1999).

Natal Homing

Do loggerhead females return to nest on their natal beach? Tagging studies demonstrate that the vast majority of nesting females return to the same area in successive nesting seasons, and both sexes return to resident foraging areas between reproductive migrations (Limpus et al. 1992). However, site fidelity as an adult does not require natal homing. Neophyte nesting females could follow experienced breeders to a nesting site and focus on that site for subsequent nesting efforts. This "social facilitation" is a simpler explanation for nesting site fidelity, as it would circumvent the logistic difficulties of locating a natal site decades after departing the beach as a hatchling (Owens et al. 1982). Notably, under social facilitation the nesting beaches in a particular region would be well connected by gene flow, whereas under natal homing the nesting colonies would be genetically isolated by homing behavior.

The nesting beaches of the northwestern Atlantic provide an appropriate forum for examining regional population structure and natal homing in loggerhead turtles. This area hosts one of the largest nesting aggregates in the world, but nesting effort is not evenly distributed, nor is nesting continuous along these coasts (Bjorndal et al. 1983). The Atlantic coast of Florida hosts the vast majority of nesting effort in this region (perhaps 90% of U.S. nesting; Murphy and Hopkins-Murphy 1989), but other important nesting areas are found on the Yucatan peninsula; the Dry Tortugas; Cuba; Georgia, South Carolina, and North Carolina; and the Gulf of Mexico. Most of these nesting locations are separated by open ocean (in the case of Yucatan, Cuba, and the Dry Tortugas) or hundreds of kilometers of coastline (in the case of the southeastern United States).

To elucidate regional population structure, Encalada et al. (1998) analyzed control region sequences from 10 nesting sites in the Atlantic Ocean and Mediterranean Sea (Figure 1.3). Most nesting populations were significantly different in mtDNA haplotype frequencies, and genetic exchange between nesting colonies was low overall, estimated to be on the order of a few individuals per generation. A notable exception to this pattern was the genetic uniformity of samples from the northern part of the U.S. nesting range (see below). Nonetheless, the overall pattern was one of shallow but significant population structure, a finding that is further supported by analyses of heavy metals (Stoneburner et al. 1980) and epibiota (Caine 1986).

Significant population structure has also been reported for the Mediterranean nesting beaches. Schroth et al. (1996) demonstrated fine-scale differentiation of nesting areas along the coasts of Turkey and Greece, based on mtDNA and nDNA markers. A wider survey of mtDNA polymorphisms by Laurent et al. (1998) corroborates these findings, but (as in the western Atlantic) not all nesting areas were genetically distinct. FitzSimmons et al. (1996) demonstrated a genetic distinction between loggerhead nesting colonies in eastern and western Australia, based on mtDNA and nDNA loci, but a low level of diversity precludes a more detailed analysis.

How precise is natal homing behavior in loggerhead turtles? To address this issue, Pearce (2001) and colleagues surveyed mtDNA diversity in 12 rookery sites across the Florida peninsula (n = 274). They found that most adjacent sites were not significantly different in mtDNA haplotype frequencies. However, this survey did resolve three clusters of nesting beaches, corresponding to the Florida panhandle (Gulf of Mexico), southern Florida, and northeastern Florida (see Figure 1.3), with additional management units indicated for the Dry Tortugas and possibly Volusia County (north of Cape Canaveral). Pearce (2001) suggests that population partitions are apparent for loggerhead nesting habitats separated by 100+ km of inappropriate habitat, providing an approximate yardstick for natal site fidelity.

The Historical Perspective

The distinction of regional nesting colonies within the northwestern Atlantic, the Mediterranean Sea, and the Indo-Pacific provides strong evidence in support of natal homing for loggerhead turtles (Bowen et al. 1993a). However, the precision of this homing is a matter of ongoing debate. On one hand, genetic affinities based on mtDNA and nDNA indicate that homing may occur on a scale of 100 km in the Mediterranean (Schroth et al. 1996) and the southeastern United States (Pearce 2001). On the other hand, tagging studies document deviations from nesting site fidelity (Bjorndal et al. 1983; Lebuff 1974; see also Gyuris and Limpus 1988), including at least 11 relocations between Georgia and Florida, U.S.A., over a seven-year period (J. I. Richardson, pers. comm.). The observed population genetic structure appears to

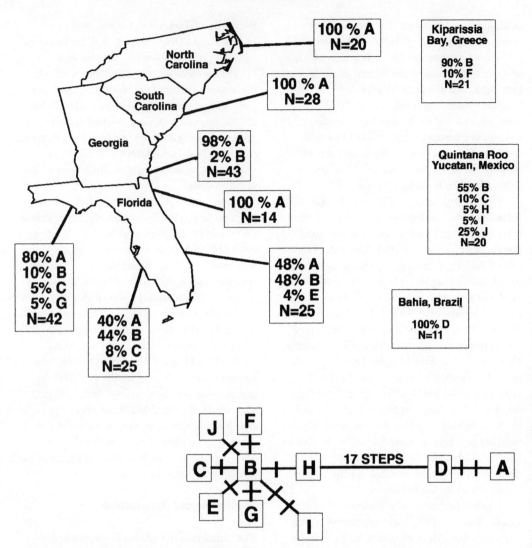

Figure 1.3. *Upper:* Map of sampling areas in the southeastern United States and corresponding haplotype frequencies (adapted from Encalada et al. 1998). Significant partitions are observed between northwestern Florida, southern Florida, and northern sample sites on the Atlantic coast. Haplotype frequencies for other Atlantic-Mediterranean nesting sites are indicated to the right. *Lower:* Parsimony network showing relationships among the 10 haplotypes observed in the Atlantic-Mediterranean basins. Each hash mark indicates a single nucleotide change in mtDNA control region sequences.

be inconsistent with these relocations, because the exchange of even a few migrants per generation is sufficient to prevent population differentiation.

One explanation for this discrepancy involves the geographic scale of observed nesting relocations. Most reported instances of nesting relocations involve adjacent beaches, and long distance relocations are rare. Richardson (1982) reports 20% nesting crossover between adjacent barrier islands in Georgia, but only a 2–4%

crossover involving more distant barrier islands along the Georgia coast. A second explanation invokes the age of nesting colonies on the Atlantic coast of North America (and possibly elsewhere). Climate records indicate that the more northerly nesting areas (including northern Florida, Georgia, South Carolina, and North Carolina) were too cold to support nesting during glacial maxima. Hence, loggerhead turtles must have colonized northward along the Atlantic coast after the most recent ice age (ending about 12,000 years ago). The more northerly nesting areas are almost certainly the product of recent colonization events. One consequence of this colonization process is a progressive loss of genetic diversity at higher latitudes, an expectation that is confirmed in the mtDNA survey (Encalada et al. 1998). Under such dynamic conditions, the consequences of occasional gene flow may not yet be detectable. Finally, temperature-dependent sex determination in marine turtles may influence the transmission of mtDNA genotypes between nesting areas (C. Limpus, pers. comm.). A female moving from a warmer to a cooler nesting colony (from Florida to Georgia, for instance) may leave a predominance of male progeny in the new nesting colony, and this reproductive contribution would not be detected with maternally inherited mtDNA. Nuclear DNA analyses are needed to test these various possibilities and to fully comprehend the population genetic structure of loggerhead turtles.

Nesting habitats are probably ephemeral over evolutionary time, continually arising and disappearing with changes in physical environment (sea level, geography, and beach characteristics), climate (glacial intervals), and biotic environment (nest predation or competition for nesting space). These environmental and ecological changes could promote episodic restructuring of populations through rookery extinctions and colonizations and would explain why some nesting areas in the northwestern Atlantic are not genetically distinct, despite the predominance of natal homing behavior. Given the transient nature of rookeries over evolutionary time scales, absolute natal homing would be a formula for extinction.

Male-Mediated Gene Flow

The population surveys to date have been accomplished primarily with maternally inherited mtDNA sequences. This method is useful for resolving natal homing behavior and nesting site fidelity of females, but what about the male component of population structure? Do males have natal homing behavior, or return to courting areas in the vicinity of their natal beach? To address these questions, research has recently applied hypervariable microsatellite loci. These loci are biparentally inherited in the nuclear genome, and hence will show the influence of both male and female contributions to population structure.

FitzSimmons et al. (1996) found that loggerhead populations in eastern and western Australia showed strong genotype frequency shifts in both mtDNA and microsatellite DNA. These findings indicate population structure and homing by both sexes, at least for breeding aggregates separated by thousands of kilometers. Schroth et al. (1996) found subtle population structure in both mtDNA and nDNA assays on a scale of 100 km in the Mediterranean. Hence the initial surveys indicate that males have the same homing behavior that guides the female-mediated population structure observed with mtDNA. However, a robust test of homing behavior requires populations that overlap on feeding grounds or migratory corridors. If the ranges of eastern and western Australian turtles don't overlap, for example, then opportunities to test homing behavior are greatly diminished.

The southeastern United States, with several nesting populations, provides an appropriate forum for examining male-mediated gene flow. Pearce (2001) surveyed microsatellite loci and mtDNA sequences across this region. As reported above, the mtDNA showed strong population genetic structure, with 30% of genetic variation distributed between nesting colonies (Pearce 2001). However, the microsatellite assays showed no significant population structure. Taken together, the mtDNA data and the nDNA data indicate that females have site fidelity to a particular nesting region in the southeastern United States, while males provide an avenue of gene flow between nesting locations. It is not yet certain whether males conduct this gene flow by reproducing at non-natal breeding areas. Alternately, males may home to a natal region, but mate opportunistically on feeding areas and migratory pathways. For example, females nesting in northern areas may pass a "gauntlet" of males in the vicinity of the large nesting aggregate in southern Florida, effectively homogenizing populations in terms of nDNA genotypes. This phenomenon has been documented for green turtles in eastern Australia (FitzSimmons et al. 1996, 1997). It would be instructive to sample male loggerhead turtles in courting areas, to resolve alternative hypotheses about this reproductive behavior.

This complex population structure (high for mtDNA, low for nDNA) has been recognized previously as a theoretical possibility, but empirical examples are few (Bowen 1997). Only in the marine mammals are there cases of higher population structure in mtDNA relative to nDNA, and this is attributed to the matriarchal structure of social groups (Dizon et al. 1997). Loggerhead turtles of the southeastern United States provide the first black-and-white example, with strong mtDNA structure and essentially no nDNA structure (Pearce 2001). It can be difficult to conceptualize a situation where maternally inherited mtDNA shows population structure and biparentally inherited nDNA shows no structure. The homing by females indicates that each nesting colony is a demographically independent unit, with a distinct sex ratio, age class structure, survivorship, and other demographic characteristics. The gene flow mediated by males does not alter the status of nesting populations as independent management units. In terms of conservation policy, it helps to consider the extreme outcomes: If all the females at a nesting colony were killed, mtDNA data indicate that the nesting colony would cease to exist. If all the males that breed there were killed, nDNA data indicate that other males would soon fill the void. Hence nesting populations remain the fundamental unit of sea turtle management.

Due to male-mediated gene flow, regional nesting colonies of the southeastern United States are well connected in terms of the nuclear genes that mediate disease resistance, response to environmental challenges, and thousands of other traits relevant to survival. This is good news for loggerhead management. Because of this gene flow, the small nesting colonies in Georgia, South Carolina, North Carolina, and the Florida panhandle do not suffer the "bottleneck" effects of reduced genetic diversity (Pearce 2001). Concerns about inbreeding and corresponding loss of genetic diversity are alleviated.

Future Research

The genetic surveys accomplished to date in the western Atlantic, Mediterranean, and Indo-Pacific regions are instructive, but many regions of the world have not been adequately sampled. Furthermore, nDNA studies have not kept pace with the mtDNA surveys, in part because of greater technical challenges, and in part because they require larger sample sizes, a scientific fact that permit agencies have been slow to recognize (Bowen 1992; Bowen and Avise 1994). As a direct result, the most promising new class of nDNA markers, microsatellite polymorphisms, have yet to be fully implemented for sea turtles. However, reports by FitzSimmons et al. (1995, 1996, 1997) and Pearce (2001) indicate that this class of genetic markers will provide many additional insights.

Reproductive Biology

Scattered observations in the wild indicate that sea turtles have a promiscuous mating system, but this hypothesis has been difficult to confirm. With the availability of molecular genetic markers, researchers can now address the question of multiple paternity by observing the number and distribution of genotypes within a nest. In the simplest cases, the presence of more than four genotypes in a nest indicates that at least two fathers contributed gametes, because (diploid) parents can contribute a maximum of two genotypes each. More sophisticated estimates can be made based on the levels of genetic variation (Westneat et al. 1987).

Harry and Briscoe (1988) were the first to assess multiple paternity in loggerhead turtles, based on the distribution of protein electrophoretic markers. The authors presented evidence that about one-third of nests at Mon Repos, Queensland, Australia, had multiple fathers. However, such electrophoretic studies are hampered by low variation, and conclusions were based on inferences about genotype frequency distributions.

Highly variable microsatellite loci are the most robust tool available for assessing multiple paternity. These have now been applied to several sea turtles, and the estimates of multiple paternity range from near zero in Caribbean leatherback turtles (Dutton et al. 2000), to less than 10% in Australian green turtles (FitzSimmons 1998), to greater than 50% at the single nesting site for Kemp's ridley (Kichler et al. 1999). In the only thorough microsatellite survey to date for loggerheads, Moore and Ball (2002) reported that 31% of nests at Melbourne Beach (Florida) had at least two fathers, and 9% had at least three fathers. These findings are concordant with Harry and Briscoe (1988) in indicating that multiple paternity is common in loggerhead turtles.

In theory, the male benefits of multiple mating are straightforward: increased reproductive success. The female benefits of multiple insemination are thought to include greater access to resources (in territorial species), nuptial gifts, increased parental investment by males, and increased genetic diversity. Among these hypothesized benefits, only the genetic aspects are likely to apply to loggerhead turtles (Moore and Ball 2002). These could include greater fertilization rate and higher diversity in hatchlings (Newcomer et al. 1999), increased offspring viability through sperm competition (Olsson and Madsen 1998), or avoidance of genetic incompatibilities (Zeh and Zeh 1996).

Multiple matings (and suspected sperm storage) could also benefit females in cases where males are rare. The temperature-dependent sex determination in sea turtles makes this a tangible possibility, and strong departures from a 1:1 sex ratio have been documented. For example, the sex ratio of loggerhead hatchlings leaving south Florida beaches is highly skewed (93% females; Mrosovsky and Provancha 1989), invoking the possibility that females could far outnumber males on corresponding courting grounds. In this case, the observation of multiple paternity in 31% of nests (Moore and Ball 2002) and the finding of extensive regional gene flow by males (Pearce 2001) alleviate the concern that males may be a limiting resource.

Regardless of the specific advantages of multiple paternity, this behavior is widespread (but not universal) in sea turtles and is commonly observed in freshwater and terrestrial turtles as well (Walker and Avise 2001). The benefits seem to apply across a diverse suite of life history strategies.

Molecular Markers for Tracking Migrations

Loggerhead turtles can navigate across thousands of kilometers, but scientific efforts to track these migrations have met with limited success. Researchers know the locations of major nesting populations in most cases and the location of feeding grounds in some cases (chapters 10 through 14 this volume), but they seldom know which nesting populations use which feeding areas. This gap in loggerhead natural history is the focus of an emerging conservation concern: thousands of loggerheads die every year in driftnets, longlines, trawls, dredges, and related activities, and it is not known which nesting colonies are affected by this mortality. Conservation efforts to date have been stymied by the inability to link marine turtles at sea to their respective nesting populations.

When the genetic distinctiveness of marine turtle nesting populations was discovered, it became apparent that mtDNA sequences could be used as natural genetic tags to assign feeding cohorts to a rookery of origin (Allard et al. 1994; Bowen 1995; Engstrom et al. 2002; Norman et al. 1994). To accomplish this, marine turtle researchers borrowed a technique called mixed stock assessment from fishery biologists, who use differences in genotype frequencies to assess the contribution of riverine salmon stocks to coastal fisheries (Grant et al. 1980). These mixed-stock assessments, based on a maximum likelihood algorithm, are adaptable to mtDNA data (Xu et al. 1994). The distribution of mtDNA haplotypes on nesting beaches can be compared to the haplotype frequencies on the feeding grounds, and this comparison can be used to calculate the most likely contribution from each nesting beach. This information allows wildlife managers to make informed decisions about the impact of human encroachment on marine turtle feeding grounds (Bowen and Avise 1995). Here the author reviews three cases where mixed-stock analyses are used to estimate

Table 1.2.
Estimated Contributions of Atlantic and Mediterranean Rookeries to Juvenile Feeding Grounds in the Western and Eastern Mediterranean

Nesting Colony	Pelagic-feeding		Benthic-feeding	
	Western Mediterranean	Eastern Mediterranean	Western Mediterranean	Eastern Mediterranean
Georgia to North Carolina, USA	0.02	0.02	0.00	0.00
Florida, USA	0.45	0.47	0.00	0.00
Mediterranean	0.53	0.51	1.00	1.00

Source: Laurent et al. 1998.

Note: Estimates are generated for smaller pelagic-feeding juveniles caught in longline fisheries and larger benthic-feeding juveniles caught in bottom trawls, using mtDNA haplotype comparisons with the program UCON (Masuda et al. 1991).

the composition of juvenile feeding grounds. An additional case history, for juvenile loggerheads in the North Atlantic gyre, is presented by Bolten (Chapter 4 this volume; see also Bolten et al. 1998). It would be desirable to survey adult feeding grounds as well, but these are largely unknown, underscoring the desirability of additional lines of evidence, such as satellite telemetry.

Loggerhead Turtles in Mediterranean Fisheries

Researchers have observed that many more juvenile loggerhead turtles occur in the Mediterranean than can be produced by the regional nesting beaches (Laurent 1990). One theory to explain this distribution is that some turtles are derived from the large nesting colonies of the western Atlantic (Groombridge 1990). If true, this would corroborate Archie Carr's postulation of a lengthy oceanic stage (Bolten, Chapter 4 this volume; Carr 1987). However, these juvenile wanderings invoke a strong conservation concern as well, because Mediterranean fisheries capture an estimated 20,000 turtles per year (Groombridge 1990), and perhaps 20–50% of these animals perish (Aguilar et al. 1995).

Nesting beach surveys demonstrate the presence of distinctive mtDNA genotypes in the western Atlantic nesting colonies that are absent from the Mediterranean nesting areas (and vice versa; Bowen et al. 1993a; Encalada et al. 1998; Laurent et al. 1993). Based on these markers,

Laurent et al. (1998) conducted an exhaustive survey of feeding grounds in the eastern and western Mediterranean using specimens from the pelagic longline fisheries and benthic trawl fisheries. These two fisheries impact different stages of loggerhead life history: the pelagic-feeding juvenile stage, with a mean length of about 50 cm (curved carapace length), and the benthic-feeding juvenile stage, with a mean length of about 65 cm. Laurent et al. (1998) reported that approximately 47% ($\pm$ 12% SD) of pelagic-feeding juveniles are derived from western Atlantic nesting colonies, and 53% ($\pm$ 12% SD) from Mediterranean nesting colonies (Table 1.2). However, in the larger size class captured in benthic trawls, no contribution was detected from the western Atlantic. Evidently the western Atlantic turtles depart the Mediterranean prior to switching from pelagic to benthic feeding.

Genetic data demonstrate that turtles from the western Atlantic nesting populations enter the Mediterranean as Archie Carr postulated (see Bolten et al. 1998; Bolten, Chapter 4 this volume). Furthermore, these data indicate that approximately half of the turtles that perish in Mediterranean fisheries are from the western Atlantic nesting beaches, and roughly half are from the Mediterranean rookeries in Greece, Turkey, Libya, Egypt, Israel, Cyprus, and Italy. These findings raise questions about the jurisdiction over endangered species that occupy international waters (see below).

Table 1.3.
Estimated Contributions of Atlantic and Mediterranean Loggerhead Rookeries to Benthic
Feeding Areas of the Northeastern United States

Nesting Colony	Estimated Contribution	
	SHADRACQ	UCON (SD)
Northeastern Florida to North Carolina, USA	0.25	0.25 (0.10)
Southern Florida, USA	0.57	0.59 (0.14)
Northwestern Florida, USA	0.00	0.00
Yucatan, Mexico	0.18	0.16 (0.07)
Bahia, Brazil	0.00	0.00
Kiparissia, Greece	0.00	0.00

Source: Rankin-Baransky et al. 2001.

Note 1: Estimated contributions from northeastern Florida, Georgia, South Carolina, and North Carolina were combined because these nesting areas were not distinguishable with the mtDNA sequence assay (Encalada et al. 1998). Two maximum likelihood programs were employed, SHADRACQ (Kobak 1994) and UCON (Masuda et al. 1991).

Note 2: SD = standard deviation.

Maritime Corridors of the Northeastern United States

Bays and coastal waters along the eastern coast of the United States represent another significant habitat for benthic-feeding juveniles (Hopkins-Murphy et al., Chapter 5 this volume). Many of these same waters are used extensively for recreational and commercial activities; channel dredging, fisheries, and heavy traffic represent growing concerns for juvenile loggerhead turtles. To determine the origin of the turtles that occupy these coastal habitats, Rankin-Baransky et al. (2001) analyzed 82 turtle strandings from Virginia to Massachusetts using mtDNA sequences. Results indicate that regional rookeries contribute to the northern feeding areas in ratios approximately equal to the size of each nesting colony (Table 1.3).

One conclusion that can be drawn from this study is that coastal fisheries and other human activities will impact nesting areas throughout the region. While the southern Florida nesting population is large and seemingly stable, the smaller nesting populations in Quintana Roo (Yucatan Peninsula), northeastern Florida, northwestern Florida, Georgia, South Carolina, and North Carolina are more vulnerable. Some of these nesting colonies have shown evidence

of long-term decline (Richardson 1982), and it is certain that the elevated mortality of advanced juveniles will contribute to this demise. A second conclusion is that the consequences of U.S. coastal activities are not confined to U.S. nesting colonies. In this case an estimated 16–18% of U.S. strandings are from the nesting colony in Yucatan, Mexico (Rankin-Baransky et al. 2001).

The Loggerhead Turtles of Baja California

Loggerhead turtles have been reported sporadically from the eastern Pacific region for decades (Caldwell 1962), but more recent investigations documented a concentration of juvenile loggerhead turtles, estimated at 10,000+ individuals, in the vicinity of Baja California (Pitman 1990; Ramirez et al. 1991). These juveniles represented a biogeographic enigma, because nesting occurs in the western Pacific (primarily in Japan and Australia) but is effectively absent from the central and eastern Pacific. Uchida and Teruya (1991) suggested that the prevailing currents transport hatchlings from Japanese nesting beaches eastward to the feeding areas off Baja California, in a manner analogous to the trans-Atlantic journey postulated by Carr (1987; see Bolten, Chapter 4 this volume). This theory has

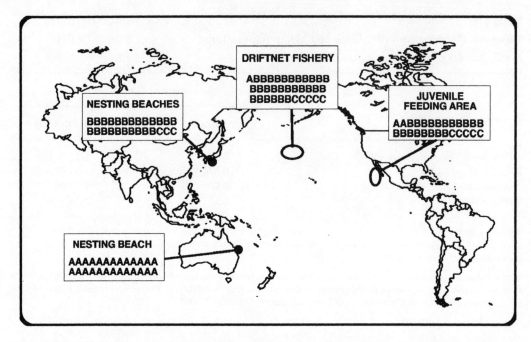

Figure 1.4. Distribution of loggerhead mtDNA markers (Pacific haplotypes A, B, and C) in major Pacific rookeries (in southern Japan and eastern Australia), a driftnet fishery in the central North Pacific, and pelagic feeding areas off Baja California (from Bowen et al. 1995). The mtDNA markers indicate that loggerhead turtles cross the North Pacific Ocean in the course of developmental migrations. Pacific haplotypes A, B, and C are not the same as Atlantic haplotypes A, B, and C.

not been widely accepted because a trans-Pacific migration would exceed 10,000 km.

A piece of the biogeographic puzzle fell into place when juvenile loggerhead turtles were documented in the high seas fisheries of the central North Pacific, north of Hawaii (Nishimura and Nakahigashi 1990; Polovina et al. 2000; Wetherall et al. 1993). The presence of loggerhead turtles in the easterly North Pacific current is consistent with the trans-Pacific migration postulated by Uchida and Teruya (1991).

Do loggerhead turtles traverse the Pacific Ocean? To address this question, samples from the two primary Pacific nesting locations, in Australia and Japan, were compared with samples from turtles drowned in North Pacific driftnet fisheries and with blood or tissue samples from turtles captured off Baja California. In this case, samples from the two candidate nesting areas had a fixed difference in mtDNA haplotypes. Thirty-three of 34 driftnet samples and 24 of 26 Baja California samples matched the haplotypes observed only in Japanese nest samples (Figure 1.4). Genetic data identify Japan as

the primary source of oceanic stage loggerheads and fishery mortalities in the central and eastern Pacific. Loggerhead turtles apparently traverse the entire North Pacific Ocean, approximately one-third of the planet's circumference, in the course of developmental migrations (Bowen et al. 1995; see also Dutton et al. 1998). Subsequently, satellite tagging studies have confirmed this finding and have documented the return voyage from Baja California to Japan (Resendiz et al. 1998).

Conservation Implications

Genetic markers have clear utility in resolving cryptic aspects of loggerhead natural history, including feeding-ground composition and migratory behavior. The resolution of these migratory behaviors has applications under international law. Genetic markers allow wildlife agencies to identify "range states," nations affected by the depletion of natural resources at a distant location. Nations that maintain the developmental habitat for migratory marine species hold exclusive fishing rights for these animals on the high seas, under the 1982 United Nations Convention on the Law of the High Seas (Van Dyke 1993). Furthermore, the 1983 United Nations Convention on the Conservation of Migratory Species (also know as the Bonn Convention) prohibits taking endangered species during migration on the high seas (Hykle 1992). Under the principles outlined in these conventions, the countries where loggerhead turtles nest have some level of jurisdiction over these animals on geographically remote feeding grounds, even if those feeding grounds are within the territorial boundaries of another nation.

Conclusions

What is a loggerhead turtle? The genetic response is diverse:

- From a phylogenetic perspective, this is an animal that diverged from the ridley and hawksbill turtles on the order of 10 million years ago, indicating a long history of independent evolution and adaptation. Loggerheads can produce intergeneric crosses with most other members of the family Cheloniidae, and these may be the oldest lineages known to hybridize in nature.
- In terms of phylogeography, the loggerhead shows evidence of a long separation between Atlantic and Indian-Pacific populations, and regional clusters of genotypes in the western Pacific and South Atlantic. This temperate-adapted species can occasionally transcend geographic boundaries, as indicated by transfer of mtDNA lineages between the Atlantic and Indian oceans via southern Africa. Geography, climate, and natal homing have an indelible influence on the phylogeographic history of the loggerhead.
- In terms of reproductive behavior, mtDNA data demonstrate that females home to the vicinity of their natal beach. Complementary microsatellite data indicate that males may have similar homing migrations, but can also serve as a conduit for gene flow by mating outside their population of origin. Multiple paternity in loggerhead clutches has been verified in both Atlantic and Pacific populations.
- Molecular markers demonstrate that loggerheads conduct incredible developmental migrations. Juvenile movements across the Atlantic and Pacific oceans are perhaps the longest aquatic migrations known to science.

The genetic perspective is diverse, but these are just the first tenuous steps in understanding the genetic constitution and the corresponding life history features of the loggerhead turtle. Many aspects of population genetics and reproductive behavior remain to be explored with genetic assays, and these findings have direct application to conservation issues for loggerhead turtles. As whole-genome studies continue to expand their taxonomic grasp, it is probable that a turtle genome will be sequenced in the coming decade, opening up a vast library of genetic information. Future researchers may directly study the genes that guide natal homing, vast migrations, and other remarkable adaptations in loggerhead turtles. The loggerhead genome is still a mystery for the most part, a call to men and women who can put one foot in the lab, one foot in the water, and one foot on the beach.

ACKNOWLEDGMENTS

Loggerhead genetic studies were made possible by the people who spent innumerable hours with sand in their shoes, including A. Abreu-Grobois, D. Atentio, K. Bjorndal, A. Bolten, R. Carthy, M. Camhi, P. Castenada, C. Coogan, M. Duffy, L. Ehrhart , R. Ferris, L. Fisher, G. Garris, K. Goto, R. Herrera, S. Hopkins-Murphy, N. Kamezaki, L. Letson, C. Limpus, G. Marcovaldi, M. Marcovaldi, D. Margaritoulis, R. Mezich, J. I. Richardson, N. Richardson, J. P. Ross, K. Sato, S. Shea, G. Smith, J. Thome, B. Witherington, M. Zacks, and J. Zurita. For invaluable contributions and advice I thank J. C. Avise, E. Almira, D. Amorocho, A. L. Bass, R. Briseno-Duenas, P. Dutton, S. Encalada, S. Epperly, E. Ezcurra, R. Ferl, N. FitzSimmons, J. Frazier, A. Foley, M. Harris, K. Horikoshi, J. A. Huff, S. A. Karl, R. C. Klinger, C. J. Kobak, R. Marquez, H. Martins, M. Masuda, A. B. Meylan, C. Moritz, J. A. Musick, J. Norman, L. Ogren, F. Percival, R. Pitman, P. Pritchard, K. Rankin-Baransky, S. Reynolds, S. Sadove, C. Sears, S. Shanker, B. Schroeder, J. Spotila, M. Swingle, C. J. Williams, W. Witzell, Archie Carr Center for Sea Turtle Research, Broward County Environmental

Quality Control Board, Centro de Investigaciones El Colegio de la Frontera Sur (CIQRO, Mexico), The Conservancy, DNA Sequencing Core at University of Florida, Florida Department of Natural Resources, Florida Cooperative Fish and Wildlife Research Unit, Georgia Deparatment of Natural Resources, Instituto Nacional de Pesca (Mexico), Natal Parks Board (South Africa), Projeto Tartaruga Marinha (TAMAR, Brazil), Queensland Department of Environment and Heritage, Sea Turtle Association of Japan, Sea Turtle Protection Society of Greece, South Carolina Wildlife and Marine Resources Department, the Sultanate of Oman, and the Volusia County Turtle Patrol. Nancy FitzSimmmons and Anna Bass generously contributed unpublished DNA sequences. Special thanks to Kathy Moore, Alan Bolten, and an anonymous reviewer for comments that improved the manuscript. The author's research was funded by the U.S. National Science Foundation, the National Marine Fisheries Service, the U.S. Fish and Wildlife Service, the National Geographic Society, the Turner Foundation, and private contributions.

DEDICATION

This chapter is dedicated to the author's father, Dr. John Robert Bowen, who was born in 1922, was raised on a farm in New Hampshire, practiced medicine for over half a century, taught compassion to his children and students, and continues to study the intricacies of humanity.

LITERATURE CITED

Aguilar, R., J. Mas, and X. Pastor. 1995. Impact of Spanish swordfish longline fisheries on the logger-head sea turtle *Caretta caretta* population in the western Mediterranean. *In* T. H. Richardson and J. I. Richardson (compilers). Proceedings of the 12th annual symposium on sea turtle biology and conservation, 91–96. NOAA Technical Memorandum NMFS-SEFC-361.

Allard, M. W., M. M. Miyamoto, K. A. Bjorndal, A. B. Bolten, and B. W. Bowen. 1994. Support for natal homing in green turtles from mitochondrial DNA sequences. Copeia 1994:34–41.

Avise, J. C. 2000. Phylogeography: The history and formation of species. Cambridge, Mass.: Harvard University Press.

Avise, J. C., B. W. Bowen, T. Lamb, A. B. Meylan, and E. Bermingham. 1992. Mitochondrial DNA evolution at a turtle's pace: Evidence for low genetic variability and reduced microevolutionary rate in the Testudines. Molecular Biology and Evolution 9:457–473.

Bickham, J. W., K. A. Bjorndal, M. W. Haiduk, and W. E. Rainey. 1980. The karyotype and chromosomal banding patterns of the green turtle *(Chelonia mydas)*. Copeia 1980:540–543.

Bjorndal, K. A., A. B. Meylan, and B. J. Turner. 1983. Sea turtle nesting at Melbourne Beach, Florida, I. Size, growth, and reproductive biology. Biological Conservation 26:65–77.

Bolten, A. B., K. A. Bjorndal, H. R. Martins, T. Dellinger, M. J. Biscoito, S. E. Encalada, and B. W. Bowen. 1998. Trans-Atlantic developmental migrations of loggerhead sea turtles demonstrated by mtDNA sequence analyses. Ecological Applications 8:1–7.

Bowen, B. W. 1992. CITES and scientists: Conservation in conflict. Marine Turtle Newsletter 58:5–6.

———. 1995. Tracking marine turtles with genetic markers; voyages of the ancient mariners. BioScience 45:528–534.

———. 1997. Complex population structure and the conservation genetics of migratory marine mammals: Lessons from sea turtles. *In* A. E. Dizon, S. J. Chivers, and W. F. Perrin (eds). Molecular genetics of marine mammals, 77–84. Journal of Marine Mammalogy, Special Publication 3.

Bowen, B. W., and J. C. Avise. 1994. Conservation research and the legal status of PCR products. Science 266:713.

———. 1995. Conservation genetics of marine turtles. *In* J. C. Avise and J. L. Hamrick (eds.). Conservation genetics: Case histories from nature, 190–237. New York: Chapman and Hall.

Bowen, B. W., and S. A. Karl. 1996. Population structure, phylogeography, and molecular evolution. *In* P. L. Lutz and J. A. Musick (eds). The biology of sea turtles, 29–50. Boca Raton, Fla.: CRC Press.

———. 2000. Meeting report: Taxonomic status of the East Pacific green turtle (*Chelonia agassizii*). Marine Turtle Newsletter 89:20–22.

Bowen, B. W., A. B. Meylan, and J. C. Avise. 1991. Evolutionary distinctiveness of the endangered Kemp's ridley sea turtle. Nature 352:709–711.

Bowen, B. W., A. B. Meylan, J. P. Ross, C. J. Limpus, G. H. Balazs, and J. C. Avise. 1992. Global population structure and natural history of the green turtle *(Chelonia mydas)* in terms of matriarchal phylogeny. Evolution 46:865–881.

Bowen, B. W., J. C. Avise, J. I. Richardson, A. B. Meylan, D. Margaritoulis, and S. R. Hopkins-Murphy. 1993a. Population structure of loggerhead turtles *(Caretta caretta)* in the northwestern Atlantic Ocean and Mediterranean Sea. Conservation Biology 7:834–844.

Bowen, B. W., W. S. Nelson, and J. C. Avise. 1993b. A molecular phylogeny for marine turtles: Trait mapping, rate assessment, and conservation relevance. Proceedings of the National Academy of Sciences 90:5574–5577.

Bowen, B. W., N. Kamezaki, C. J. Limpus, G. H. Hughes, A. B. Meylan, and J. C. Avise. 1994. Global phylogeography of the loggerhead turtle *(Caretta caretta)* as indicated by mitochondrial DNA haplotypes. Evolution 48:1820–1828.

Bowen, B. W., F. A. Abreu-Grobois, G. H. Balazs, N. Kamezaki, C. J. Limpus, and R. J. Ferl. 1995. Trans-Pacific migrations of the loggerhead sea turtle demonstrated with mitochondrial DNA markers. Proceedings of the National Academy of Sciences 92:3731–3734.

Bowen, B. W., A. M. Clark, F. A. Abreu–Grobois, A. Chavez, H. Reichart, and R. J. Ferl. 1998. Global phylogeography of the ridley sea turtles (*Lepidochelys* spp.) inferred from mitochondrial DNA sequences. Genetica 101:179–189.

Brongersma, L. D. 1961. Notes upon some sea turtles. Zoologische Verhandelingen, Leiden 51:1–46.

Caine, E. A. 1986. Carapace epibionts of nesting loggerhead sea turtles: Atlantic coast of U.S.A. Journal of Experimental Marine Biology and Ecology 95:15–26.

Caldwell, D. K. 1962. Sea turtles in Baja California waters (with special reference to those of the Gulf of California), and the description of a new subspecies of northeastern Pacific green turtle. Contributions to Science, Los Angeles County Museum 61:1–31.

Carr, A. F. 1942. Notes on sea turtles. Proceedings of the New England Zoological Club 21:1–16.

———. 1957. Notes on the zoogeography of the Atlantic sea turtles of the genus *Lepidochelys*. Revista de Biologica Tropical 5:45–61.

———. 1987. New perspectives on the pelagic stage of sea turtle development. Conservation Biology 1:103–121.

Chen, B.-Y., S.-H. Mao, and Y.-H. Ling. 1980. Evolutionary relationships of turtles suggested by immunological cross-reactivity of albumins. Comparative Biochemistry and Physiology 66B:421–425.

Conceicão, M. B., J. A. Levy, L. F. Marins, and M. A. Marcovaldi. 1990. Electrophoretic characterization of a hybrid between *Eretmochelys imbricata* and *Caretta caretta* (Cheloniidae). Comparative Biochemistry and Physiology 97B:275–278.

Deraniyagala, P. E. P. 1934. Relationships among loggerhead turtles (Carettidae). Ceylon Journal of Science (B) 28:207–209.

———. 1939. The Mexican loggerhead in Europe. Nature 144:156.

———. 1943. Subspecies formation in loggerhead turtles (Carettidae). Spolia Zeylanica 23:79–92.

———. 1945. Some subspecies characters of the loggerhead *Caretta caretta*. Spolia Zeylanica 24:95–98.

Dizon, A. E., S. J. Chivers, and W. F. Perrin, editors. 1997. Molecular genetics of marine mammals. Journal of Marine Mammalogy, Special Publication 3.

Dodd, C. K., Jr. 1988. Synopsis of the biological data on the loggerhead sea turtle *Caretta caretta* (Linnaeus 1758). U.S. Fish and Wildlife Service Biological Report 88(14): 1–110.

Dodd, C. K., Jr., and G. S. Morgan. 1992. Fossil sea turtles from the early Pliocene Bone Valley Formation, Central Florida. Journal of Herpetology 26:1–8.

Dutton, P. H., S. K. Davis, T. Guerra, and D. Owens. 1996. Molecular phylogeny for marine turtles based on sequences of the ND4-leucine tRNA and control regions of mitochondrial DNA. Molecular Phylogenetics and Evolution 5:511–521.

Dutton, P. H., G. H. Balazs, and A. E. Dizon. 1998. Genetic stock identification of sea turtles caught in the Hawaii-based pelagic longline fishery. *In* S. P. Epperly and J. Braun (compilers). Proceedings of the 17th annual sea turtle symposium, 43–44. NOAA Technical Memorandum NMFS-SEFSC-415.

Dutton, P. H., B. W. Bowen, D. W. Owens, A. Barragan, and S. K. Davis. 1999. Global phylogeography of the leatherback turtle, *Dermochelys coriacea*. Journal of Zoology 248:397–409.

Dutton, P. H., E. Bixby, and S. K. Davis. 2000. Tendency towards single paternity in leatherbacks detected with microsatellites. *In* F. A. Abreu-Grobois, R. Briseno-Duenas, R. Marquez, and L. Sarti (compilers). Proceedings of the 18th international symposium on sea turtle biology and conservation, 156. NOAA Technical Memorandum NMFS-SEFSC-436.

Dwyer, G. S., T. M. Cronin, P. A. Baker, M. E. Raymo, J. S. Buzas, and T. Correge. 1995. North Atlantic deepwater temperature change during late Pliocene and late Quaternary climatic cycles. Science 270:1347–1351.

Edwards, A. 1990. Fish and fisheries of Saint Helena Island. University of Newcastle upon Tyne, U.K.: Center for Tropical Coastal Management Studies.

Encalada, S. E., P. N. Lahanas, K. A. Bjorndal, A. B. Bolten, M. M. Miyamoto, and B. W. Bowen. 1996. Phylogeography and population structure of the green turtle *(Chelonia mydas)* in the Atlantic Ocean and Mediterranean Sea: A mitochondrial DNA control region sequence assessment. Molecular Ecology 5:473–484.

Encalada, S. E., K. A. Bjorndal, A. B. Bolten, J. C. Zurita, B. Schroeder, E. Possardt, C. J. Sears, and B. W. Bowen. 1998. Population structure of loggerhead turtle *(Caretta caretta)* nesting colonies in the Atlantic and Mediterranean regions as inferred from mtDNA control region sequences. Marine Biology 130:567–575.

Engstrom, T. N., P. A. Meylan, and A. B. Meylan. 2002. Origin of juvenile loggerhead turtles (*Caretta caretta*) in a tropical developmental habitat in Caribbean Panama. Animal Conservation 5:125–133.

FitzSimmons, N. N. 1998. Single paternity of clutches and sperm storage in the promiscuous green turtle *(Chelonia mydas)*. Molecular Ecology 7:575–584.

FitzSimmons, N. N., C. Moritz, and S. S. Moore. 1995. Conservation and dynamics of microsatellite loci over 300 million years of marine turtle evolution. Molecular Biology and Evolution 12:432–440

FitzSimmons, N. N., C. Moritz, C. J. Limpus, J. D. Miller, C. J. Parmenter, and R. Prince. 1996. Comparative genetic structure of green, loggerhead, and flatback populations in Australia based on variable mtDNA and nDNA regions. *In* B. W. Bowen and W. N. Witzell (eds). Proceedings of the international symposium on sea turtle conservation genetics, 25–32. NOAA Technical Memorandum NMFS-SEFSC-396.

FitzSimmons, N. N., C. J. Limpus, J. A. Norman, A. R. Goldizen, J. D. Miller, and C. Moritz. 1997. Philopatry of male marine turtles inferred from mitochondrial DNA markers. Proceedings of the National Academy of Sciences 94:8912–8917.

Frair, W. 1979. Taxonomic relations among sea turtles elucidated with serological tests. Herpetologica 35:239–244.

———. 1982. Serum electrophoresis and sea turtle classification. Comparative Biochemistry and Physiology 72B:1–5.

Frazier, J. 1985. Misidentification of sea turtles in the eastern Pacific: *Caretta caretta* and *Lepidochelys olivacea*. Journal of Herpetology 19:1–11.

———. 1988. Sea turtles in the land of the dragon. Sanctuary (Asia) 8:15–23.

Gaffney, E. S., and P. A. Meylan. 1988. A phylogeny of turtles. *In* M. J. Benton (ed.). The phylogeny and classification of tetrapods. Vol. 1. Amphibians, reptiles, and birds, 157–219. Systematics Association Special Volume No. 35A. Oxford, U.K.: Clarendon Press.

Garman, S. 1880. On certain species of Chelonioidae. Bulletin of the Museum of Comparative Zoology Harvard 8:4–8.

Grant, W. S., G. B. Milner, P. Krasnowski, and F. M. Utter. 1980. Use of biochemical genetic variants for identification of sockeye salmon *(Oncorhynchus nerka)* stocks in Cook Inlet, Alaska. Canadian Journal of Fisheries and Aquatic Sciences 37:1236–1247.

Groombridge, B. 1990. Marine turtles in the Mediterranean; distribution, population status, conservation. Report to the Council of Europe, Environment Conservation and Management Division, Nature and Environment Series 48. Strasbourg, France.

Gyuris, E., and C. J. Limpus. 1988. The loggerhead turtle *Caretta caretta* in Queensland: Population breeding structure. Australian Journal of Wildlife Research 15:197–209.

Harry, J. L., and D. A. Briscoe. 1988. Multiple paternity in the loggerhead turtle *(Caretta caretta)*. Journal of Heredity 79:96–99.

Hay, O. P. 1908. On three existing species of sea-turtles, one of them *(Caretta remivaga)* new. Proceedings of the U.S. National Museum 1605:183–198.

Hughes, G. R. 1974a. The sea turtles of Southeast Africa I. Investigational Report no. 35 of the Oceanographic Research Institute, Durban, South Africa.

———. 1974b. The sea turtles of Southeast Africa II. Investigational Report no. 36 of the Oceanographic Research Institute, Durban, South Africa.

Hykle, D. J. 1992. The migratory species (Bonn) convention and marine turtle conservation. *In* M. Salmon and J. Wyneken (compilers). Proceedings of the 11th annual workshop on sea turtle biology and conservation, 61–63. NOAA Technical Memorandum NMFS-SEFC-302.

James, F. C. 1983. Environmental component of morphological differentiation in birds. Science 221:184–186.

Kamezaki, N. 1983. The possibility of hybridization between the loggerhead turtle, *Caretta caretta*, and the hawksbill turtle, *Eretmochelys imbricata*, in specimens hatched from eggs collected in Chita Peninsula. Japan Journal of Herpetology 10:52–53.

———. 1989. Karyotype of the loggerhead turtle, *Caretta caretta*, from Japan. Zoological Science (Tokyo) 6:421–422.

———. 1990. Karyotype of the hawksbill turtle, *Eretmochelys imbricata*, from Japan, with notes on a method for preparation of chromosomes from liver cells. Japan Journal of Herpetology 13:111–113.

Kamezaki, N., and M. Matsui. 1997. Allometry in the loggerhead turtle, *Caretta caretta*. Chelonian Conservation and Biology 2:421–425.

Kamezaki, N., and T. Namikawa. 1984. Electrophoretic evidence for a case of natural hybridization between the loggerhead turtle, *Caretta caretta*, and the hawksbill turtle, *Eretmochelys imbricata*. Japan Journal of Herpetology 10:108.

Kamezaki, N., Y. Nakajima, and M. Ishii. 1996. Rapid communication: Hybrids between *Caretta caretta* × *Chelonia mydas* from the Horinouchi Beach, Miyazaki. Umigame Newsletter 30:7–9.

Karl, S. A., and B. W. Bowen. 1999. Evolutionary significant units versus geopolitical taxonomy: molecular systematics of an endangered sea turtle (genus *Chelonia*). Conservation Biology 13: 990–999.

Karl, S. A., B. W. Bowen, and J. C. Avise. 1995. Hybridization among the ancient mariners: Identification and characterization of marine turtle hybrids with molecular genetic assays. Journal of Heredity 86:262–268.

Kichler, K., M. T. Holder, S. K. Davis, R. Marquez-M., and D. W. Owens. 1999. Detection of multiple paternity in the Kemp's ridley sea turtle with limited sampling. Molecular Ecology 8:819–830.

Kobak, C. 1994. SHADRACQ ver. 1060 software. Used with permission of the author. New Brunswick, N. J.: Rutgers University,

Laurent, L. 1990. L'origine des tortues caouannes, *Caretta caretta* (Linnaeus 1758) de Méditerranée Occidentale. Rapports de la Commission Internationale pour la Mer Méditerranée 32:240

Laurent, L., J. Lescure, L. Excoffier, B. W. Bowen, M. Domingo, M. Hadjichristophorou, L. Kornaraki, and G. Trabuchet. 1993. Etude genetique des relations entre les populations mediterraneenne et atlantique d'une tortue marine *(Caretta caretta)* a l'aide d'un marqueur mitochondrial. Comptes Rendus de l'Academie des Sciences, Paris 316:1233–1239.

Laurent, L., P. Casale, M. N. Bradai, B. J. Godley, G. Gerosa, A. C. Broderick, W. Schroth, B. Schierwater, A. M. Levy, D. Freggi, E. M. Abd El-Mawla, D. A. Hadoud, H. E. Gomati, M. Domingo, M. Hadjichristophorou, L. Kornaraki, F. Demirayak, and C. Gautier. 1998. Molecular resolution of the marine turtle stock composition in fishery bycatch: A case study in the Mediterranean. Molecular Ecology 7:1529–1542.

LeBuff, C. R., Jr. 1974. Unusual nesting relocation in the loggerhead turtle, *Caretta caretta*. Herpetologica 30:29–31.

Limpus, C. J., E. Gyuris, and J. D. Miller. 1988. Reassessment of the taxonomic status of the sea turtle genus *Natator* McCulloch, 1908, with redescription of the genus and species. Transactions of the Royal Society of South Australia 112:1–9.

Limpus, C. J., J. D. Miller, C. J. Parmenter, D.

Reimer, N. McLachland, and R. Webb. 1992. Migration of green *(Chelonia mydas)* and loggerhead *(Caretta caretta)* turtles to and from eastern Australian rookeries. Wildlife Research 19:347–358.

Margaritoulis, D. 1982. Observations on loggerhead sea turtle, *Caretta caretta*, activity during three nesting seasons (1977–1979) in Zakynthos, Greece. Biological Conservation 24:193–204.

———. 1988. Post-nesting movements of loggerhead sea turtles tagged in Greece. Rapports de la Commission International pour la Mer Mériterranée 31:284.

Martin, A. P. 1995. Metabolic rate and directional nucleotide substitution in animal mitochondrial DNA. Molecular Biology and Evolution 12:1124–1131.

Masuda, M., S. Nelson, and J. Pella. 1991. User manual for GIRLSEM, GIRLSYM, and CONSQRT. USA-DOC-NOAA-NMFS. Program and users manual available from U.S.-Canada Salmon Program, 11305 Glacier Hwy., Juneau, Alaska.

Medrano, L., M. Dorizzi, F. Rimblot, and C. Pieau. 1987. Karyotype of the sea turtle *Dermochelys coriacea* Vandelli 1761. Amphib-Reptilia 8:171–178.

Moore, M. K., and R. M. Ball, Jr. 2002. Multiple paternity in loggerhead turtle *(Caretta caretta)* nests on Melbourne Beach, Florida: A microsatellite analysis. Molecular Ecology 11:281–288.

Mrosovsky, N., and J. Provancha. 1989. Sex ratio of loggerhead sea turtles hatching on a Florida beach. Canadian Journal of Zoology 67:2533–2539.

Murphy, T. M., and S. R. Hopkins-Murphy. 1989. Sea turtle and shrimp fishing interactions: A summary and critique of relevant information. Washington D.C.: Center for Marine Conservation.

Newcomer, S. D., J. A. Zeh, and D. W. Zeh. 1999. Genetic benefits enhance the reproductive success of polyandrous females. Proceedings of the Royal Society of London 96:10236–10241.

Nishimura, W., and S. Nakahigashi. 1990. Incidental capture of sea turtles by Japanese research and training vessels: Results of a questionnaire. Marine Turtle Newsletter 51:1–4.

Norman, J. A., C. Moritz, and C. J. Limpus. 1994. Mitochondrial DNA control region polymorphisms: genetic markers for ecological studies of marine turtles. Molecular Ecology 3:363–373.

Olsson, M., and T. Madsen. 1998. Sexual selection and sperm competition in reptiles. *In* T. R. Birkhead and A. P. Moller (eds.). Sperm competition and sexual selection, 503–578. San Diego, Calif.: Academic Press.

Owens, D. W., M. A. Grassman, and J. R. Hendrickson. 1982. The imprinting hypothesis and sea turtle reproduction. Herpetologica 38:124–135.

Pearce, A. F. 2001. Contrasting population structure of the loggerhead turtle *(Caretta caretta)* using mitochondrial and nuclear DNA markers. Master's Thesis, University of Florida, Gainesville.

Pitman, R. 1990. Pelagic distribution and biology of sea turtles in the eastern tropical Pacific. *In* T. H. Richardson, J. I. Richardson, and M. Donnelly (compilers). Proceedings of the 10th annual workshop on sea turtle biology and conservation, 143–148. NOAA Technical Memorandum NMFS-SEFC-278.

Polovina, J. J., D. R. Kobayashi, D. M. Parker, M. P. Seki, and G. H. Balazs. 2000. Turtles on the edge: Movement of loggerhead turtles *(Caretta caretta)* along ocean fronts, spanning longline fishing grounds in the central North Pacific, 1997–1998. Fisheries Oceanography 9:71–82.

Prager, E. M., and A. C. Wilson. 1975. Slow evolutionary loss of the potential for interspecific hybridization in birds: A manifestation of slow regulatory evolution. Proceedings of the National Academy of Sciences 72:200–204.

Pritchard, P. C. H. 1969. Studies of the systematics and reproductive cycles of the genus *Lepidochelys*. Ph.D. Dissertation, University of Florida, Gainesville.

Pritchard, P. C. H., and P. Trebbau. 1984. The turtles of Venezuela. Contributions to Herpetology 2. Caracas, Venezuela: Society for the Study of Amphibians and Reptiles.

Ramirez Cruz, J. C., I. Pena Ramirez, and D. Villanueva Flores. 1991. Distribution y abundancia de la tortuga perica, *Caretta caretta* Linnaeus (1758), en la costa occidental de Baja California Sur, Mexico. Archelon 1:1–4. (Available from BITMAR: Banco de Information sobre Tortugas Marinas, Instituto de Ciencias del Mar y Limnologia, Apartado Postal 811, Mazatlan, Sinaloa, Mexico 82000)

Rankin-Baransky, K., C. J. Williams, A. L. Bass, B. W. Bowen, and J. R. Spotila. 2001. Origin of loggerhead turtles stranded in the northeastern United States as determined by mitochondrial DNA analysis. Journal of Herpetology 35:638–646.

Resendiz, A., B. Resendiz, W. J. Nichols, J. A. Seminoff, and N. Kamezaki. 1998. First confirmed east-west trans-Pacific movement of a loggerhead turtle *(Caretta caretta)*, released in Baja California, Mexico. Pacific Science 52:151–153.

Richardson, J. I. 1982. A population model for adult female loggerhead sea turtles *(Caretta caretta)* nesting in Georgia. Ph.D. Dissertation, University of Georgia, Athens.

Schroth, W., B. Streit, and B. Schierwater. 1996. Evolutionary handicap for turtles. Nature 384:521–522.

Shannon, L. V. 1970. Ocean circulation off South Africa. Fishery Bulletin of South Africa 6:27–33.

———. 1985. The Benguela ecosystem. Part. I. Evolution of the Benguela physical features and processes. Oceanography and Marine Biology Annual Reviews 23:105–182.

Smith, M. H., H. O. Hillstad, M. N. Manlove, D. O. Straney, and J. M. Dean. 1978. Management implications of genetic variability in loggerhead and green sea turtles. *In* Proceedings of the 13th international congress of game biologists, 302–312.

Stoneburner, D. L., M. N. Nicora, and E. R. Blood. 1980. Heavy metals in loggerhead sea turtle eggs *(Caretta caretta):* Evidence to support the hypothesis that demes exist in the western Atlantic population. Journal of Herpetology 14:171–175.

Tiwari M., and K. A. Bjorndal. 2000. Variation in morphology and reproduction in loggerheads *(Caretta caretta)* nesting in the United States, Brazil, and Greece. Herpetologica 56:343–356.

Uchida, S., and H. Teruya. 1991. Transpacific migration of a tagged loggerhead, *Caretta caretta*, and tag-return results of loggerheads released from Okinawa, Japan. *In* I. Uchida (ed.). International Symposium on Sea Turtles 1988 in Japan, 171–182. Hemeji City, Japan: Hemeji City Aquarium.

Van Dyke, J. M. 1993. International governance and stewardship of the high seas and its resources. *In* J. M. Van Dyke, D. Zaelke, and G. Hewison (eds.). Freedom for the seas in the 21st century: Ocean governance and environmental harmony, 13–20. Washington D.C.: Island Press.

Walker, D. E., and J. C. Avise. 2001. Turtle mating systems: Behavior, sperm storage, and genetic paternity. Journal of Heredity 92:206–211.

Westneat, D. F., P. C. Frederick, and R. H. Wiley. 1987. The use of genetic markers to estimate the frequency of successful alternate reproductive tactics. Behavioral Ecology and Sociobiology 21:35–45.

Wetherall, J. A., G. H. Balazs, R. A. Tokunaga, and M. Y. Y. Yong. 1993. Bycatch of marine turtles in North Pacific high-seas driftnet fisheries and impacts on the stocks. *In* J. Ito, W. Shaw and R. L. Burgner (eds.). Symposium on biology, distribution, and stock assessment of species caught in the high seas driftnet fisheries in the North Pacific Ocean, 519–538. Bulletin Number 53(III) International North Pacific Fisheries Commission, Vancouver, Canada.

Weems, R. E. 1988. Paleocene turtles from the Aquia and Brightseat formations, with a discussion of their bearing on sea turtle evolution and phylogeny. Proceedings of the Biological Society, Washington 101:109–145.

Williams, D. F., J. Peck, E. B. Karabanov, A. A. Prokopenko, V. Kravchinsky, J. King, and M. I. Kuzmin. 1997. Lake Baikal record of continental climate response to orbital insolation during the past five million years. Science 278:1114–1117.

Wilson, A. C., L. R. Maxson, and V. M. Sarich. 1974. Two types of molecular evolution: Evidence from studies of interspecific hybridization. Proceedings of the National Academy of Sciences 71:2843–2847.

Xu, S., C. J. Kobak, and P. E. Smouse. 1994. Constrained least squares estimation of mixed population stock composition from mtDNA haplotype frequency data. Canadian Journal of Fisheries and Aquatic Sciences 51:417–425.

Zangerl, R. 1958. Die oligozanen Meerschildkroten von Glarus. Schweizerische Palaeontologische Abhandlungen 73:1–56.

Zangerl, R., and R. E. Sloan. 1960. A new specimen of *Desmatochelys lowi* Williston, a primitive Cheloniid sea turtle from the Cretaceous of South Dakota. Fieldiana Geology 14:7–40.

Zangerl, R., L. P. Hendrickson, and J. R. Hendrickson. 1988. A redescription of the Australian flatback sea turtle, *Natator depressus*. Bishop Museum Bulletin of Zoology 1:1–69.

Zeh, J.A., and D.W. Zeh. 1996. The evolution of polyandry I: Intragenomic conflict and genetic incompatibility. Proceedings of the Royal Society of London 263:1711–1717.

Zug, G. R. 2001. Turtles of the Lee Creek Mine (Pliocene: North Carolina). *In* C. E. Ray and D. J. Bohaska (eds.). Geology and paleontology of the Lee Creek Mine, North Carolina, III, 203–218. Smithsonian Contributions to Paleobiology no. 90.

Chapter 2

What Is a Loggerhead Turtle?

The Morphological Perspective

—Naoki Kamezaki

Reptiles arose in the Paleozoic Era, about 300 million years ago, and reached a peak of diversity in the Mesozoic Era. Reptiles were among the earliest terrestrial vertebrates, but over their long evolutionary history, this group has repeatedly invaded marine habitats as well. Marine reptiles were notably abundant in the Jurassic and Cretaceous Periods (263–205 million years ago). Today, only four groups of reptiles rely primarily on marine habitats: specialized members of the crocodiles, snakes, iguanas, and turtles. Among these, only two families of living turtles have ancient marine ancestors; the marine snakes and iguanas and one saltwater crocodile all represent relatively recent adaptations to the marine environment, dating to the Pliocene or Pleistocene. In contrast, the sea turtles of the families Dermochelyidae and Cheloniidae represent a marine lineage that traces back to the early Cretaceous, about 110 million years ago (Hirayama 1998).

Cheloniid turtles are characterized by a suite of morphological adaptations to life in an aquatic medium. The objective of this chapter is to describe this morphology and osteology for the loggerhead turtle. Where possible this is done in a comparative approach, by bringing in parallel data sets from other cheloniid sea turtles. In essence, the anatomy and osteology of loggerhead turtles (and other marine turtles) can be understood in terms of adaptation to a marine environment, superimposed on the constraints of living in an organic box.

Morphology of Cheloniidae

The family Cheloniidae includes five living genera and six species of sea turtles: loggerhead turtle *(Caretta caretta)*, green turtle *(Chelonia mydas)*, hawksbill turtle *(Eretmochelys imbricata)*, flatback turtle *(Natator depressus)*, olive ridley turtle *(Lepidochelys olivacea)*, and Kemp's ridley turtle *(L. kempii)*.

The carapace of cheloniid turtles has 12–13

28

pairs of marginal scutes, 4–9 pairs of costal scutes, and 5–7+ vertebral scutes. The oval to heart-shaped carapace retains the embryonic spaces between the ribs at their distal ends adjacent to the peripheral elements. The carapace and the plastron are connected by ligaments, and neither is hinged. The bones of the carapace are rather thick, although fontanels persist in the carapace and plastron. The carapace is composed of a nuchal bone, 7–15 neural bones, 8 pairs of pleural bones, 11–13 pairs of peripheral bones, two suprapygals, and one pygal bone. The pleural bones make contact with the peripherals via the free ends of the ribs, which fit into pits in most of the peripheral bones. The nuchal bone is relatively large and has sutural connections with the first neural bone and the first pair of peripheral bones.

The plastron is covered by an intergular scute, a pair of gular scutes, humeral scutes, pectoral scutes, abdominal scutes, femoral scutes, anal scutes, and an interanal scute. Sometimes, the intergular and interanal scutes are absent, especially in the loggerhead. Three or four pairs of inframarginal scutes are present along the bridge. The plastron is composed of nine bones: a pair of epiplastra, an entoplastron, a pair of hyoplastra, a pair of hypoplastra, and a pair of xiphiplastra. There are persistent fontanels along the midline.

The limbs and head are generally larger than those of other turtles and are covered by scutes. Prefrontal and postorbital scutes of the head are commonly used to identify loggerheads. The orbits occupy a rather dorsal position, as is typical of many freshwater turtles. The forelimbs are paddlelike with elongated digits, and the hind limbs are rudderlike. The neck is short. All the cheloniid turtles have lost the ability to completely retract the head and limbs, presumably during adaptation to marine existence.

The skull of cheloniid turtles provides more protection those of other turtles. The temporal region of the skull has a complete roof in which the parietal contacts the squamosal. The premaxillae are not fused and meet the vomer, which separates the internal nares and contacts the palatines. A secondary palate is present, but posterior palatine fenestrae are not present. The pterygoid bones separate the basisphenoid from the palatines. Bony trabeculae of the beak are fused. The quadrate bone never encloses the stapes, and the maxilla bone does not contact the quadratojugal bone. The dentary is confined to the anterior half of the lower jaw. The comparative morphology of the skull in the Cheloniidae containing the loggerhead is well described in Gaffney (1979).

Morphological Features of Loggerheads

Color

In adults, the dorsal color of the carapace and head is reddish brown. The plastron is lighter than the carapace, with diffuse dark margins. There are descriptions of loggerhead coloration from Sri Lanka (Deraniyagala 1930, 1939, 1953), the western Atlantic (Carr 1952), West Africa (Villiers 1958), South Africa (Hughes 1974), Australia (Cogger 1983), the Mediterranean (Fretey 1986) and Japan (Nishimura 1967). However, geographic variation in coloration is difficult to assess, because no quantitative or qualitative standards have been established for comparison.

In hatchlings, the color of the dorsum is dark brown or reddish brown. The plastron may vary in color from creamy white to reddish to dark brown. Caldwell (1959) reported considerable variation in the coloration of loggerhead hatchlings, even within the same clutch. As with adults, these differences have not been objectively measured or compared among populations.

Scutes

The loggerhead carapace has five vertebral scutes (Figure 2.1). The first vertebral is rather short. The second and fourth vertebrals are elongate, and fifth vertebral is large and wide. There are usually five pairs of costals, but four pairs and other anomalous scute arrangements are occasionally observed (e.g., left-right asymmetry). The first costal is the smallest and the third is the largest. The nuchal scute is very wide, and contacts the first coastal on each side. The marginal scutes are typically 12 (sometimes

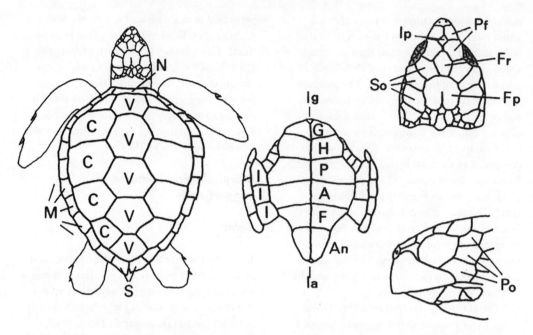

Figure 2.1. External morphology and scutellation of the loggerhead turtle. V: vertebral scute; C: coastal scute; M: marginal scute; N: nuchal scute; S: supracaudal scute; I: inframarginal scute; Ig: intergular scute; G: gular scute; H: humeral scute; P: pectoral scute; A: abdominal scute; F: femoral scute; An: anal scute; Ia: interanal scute; Ip: interprefrontal scute; Pf: prefrontal scute; Fr: frontal scute; So: supraocular scute; Fp: frontoparietal scute; Po: postoculars.

13) pairs including the supracaudal scute. There are usually three pairs of inframarginal scutes, which are not perforated by pores, as is observed in *Lepidochelys*, the closest genus to *Caretta*, phylogenetically. A small intergular and a small anal scute, are sometimes present on the anterior and posterior of the plastron respectively.

The crown of the head includes a rather large and polygonal frontoparietal scute. There are two pairs of prefrontals, often with an additional scute at their common border. The frontoparietal scute is surrounded by three supraoculars on each side and three parietal scutes behind. There are three or four postoculars, followed by two transverse rows of three temporal scales. There are three or four preoculars, but they are reduced in adults. The mandibular rhamphotheca is commonly bordered by three inframandibular scutes.

Scute formation has traditionally been regarded as an important character for sea turtle taxonomy and classification. However, variations in scute pattern are common in the log-

gerhead turtles. Kamezaki (1989) examined the relationships between the scute anomaly ratio of hatchlings and the incubation period, which is a function of incubation temperature. In this survey, long incubation period (or low incubation temperature) corresponded to an increase in the number of scute anomalies in the costals, marginals, nuchals, interprefrontals, intergulars, and mandibulars.

Although the number of marginal scutes was formerly used as a diagnostic character in marine turtle taxonomy (Deraniyagala 1933), variation in this character is higher than previously suspected, and it should not be used as a criterion for classification.

Body Proportions

Body proportions of the loggerhead turtle are well documented and are described in detail elsewhere (e.g., Dodd 1988; Pritchard and Trebbau 1984). However, there are few comparative studies of body features among che-

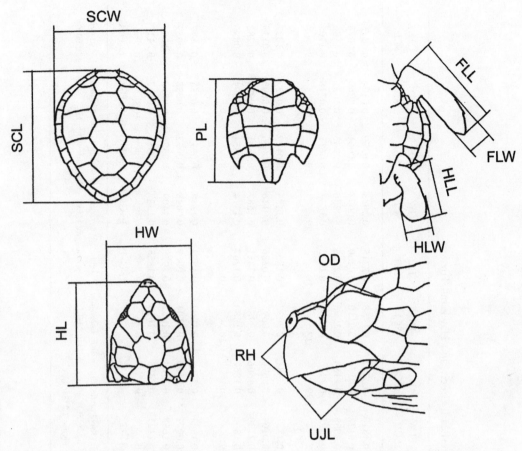

Figure 2.2. Measurements of the loggerhead turtle. SCL: standard carapace length along a straight line; SCW: carapace width along a straight line; PL: plastron length; FLL: forelimb length; FLW: forelimb width; HLL: hind limb length; HLW: hind limb width; HL: head length; HW: head width; RH: rostrum height; OD: orbital diameter; UJL: upper jaw length.

loniid species. In this section, the body proportions of three species, the loggerhead, green, and hawksbill turtles, are compared . These comparisons are based on 11 meristic characters (Figure 2.2) in relation to the straight carapace length (SCL, measured from the nuchal notch to the tip of the posterior marginal) of turtles.

To allow comparison of body proportions among the three species, ratios of straight carapace length (SCL) to straight carapace width (SCW), plastron length (PL), forelimb length (FLL), forelimb width (FLW), hind limb length (HLL), hind limb width (HLW), head length (HL), head width (HW), rostrum height (RH), orbital diameter (OD), and upper jaw length (UJL) are listed in Table 2.1. Statistically signif-

icant differences ($p < 0.01$, t-test) among species are found in the relative PL, FLW, HL, HW, RH, OD, and UJL. Relative PLs in the loggerhead and hawksbill are shorter than in the green. FLW in the loggerhead is relatively wider than in the hawksbill, but there is no difference in the FLL. Larger forelimb size in the loggerhead is thought to be an adaptation for longer distance migration, compared to the hawksbill turtle, which does not routinely migrate across ocean basins (Bowen et al. 1995; Pritchard and Trebbau 1984; Wyneken 1997).

A distinctive feature of the loggerhead turtle is the relatively large head (Pritchard and Trebbau 1984). Accordingly, the relative HL and HW are larger in loggerhead than in green

Table 2.1.
Comparisons of Relative Morphometric Characters among Loggerhead, Green, and Hawksbill Turtles

Species			SCL (cm)	SCW SCL	PL SCL	FLL SCL	FLW SCL	HLL SCL	HLW SCL	HL SCL	HW SCL	RH SCL	OD SCL	UJL SCL
Caretta caretta (Loggerhead)	Mean		829	0.7807	0.7571	0.5022	0.1810	0.3792	0.1753	0.2215	0.2035	0.0759	0.0804	0.1275
	SD		55	0.0283	0.0266	0.0363	0.0128	0.0176	0.0110	0.0160	0.0097	0.0061	0.0060	0.0078
	Max.		960	0.8344	0.8091	0.5534	0.2055	0.4180	0.1995	0.2716	0.2236	0.0905	0.1031	0.1406
	Min.		719	0.7343	0.6977	0.4244	0.1591	0.3426	0.1488	0.1933	0.1847	0.0615	0.0718	0.1105
	n		29	29	29	29	27	29	27	28	29	29	29	29
Chelonia mydas (Green)	Mean		882	0.8072	0.8343	0.5189	0.1758	0.3581	0.2038	0.1867	0.1435	0.0429	0.0727	0.1027
	SD		102	0.0572	0.0341	0.0460	0.0164	0.0690	0.0697	0.0286	0.0116	0.0055	0.0095	0.0135
	Max.		976	0.9627	0.9010	0.6072	0.2130	0.4606	0.3983	0.2351	0.1687	0.0531	0.0924	0.1282
	Min.		723	0.7702	0.7807	0.4589	0.1538	0.1867	0.1580	0.1207	0.1314	0.0354	0.0594	0.0886
	n		10	10	9	10	9	10	10	10	9	8	9	7
Eretmochelys imbricata (Hawksbill)	Mean		581	0.7809	0.7482	0.4753	0.1564	0.3706	0.1762	0.1952	0.1318	0.0517	0.0754	0.1177
	SD		86	0.0196	0.0186	0.0230	0.0077	0.0150	0.0104	0.0069	0.0048	0.0052	0.0053	0.0039
	Max.		784	0.8048	0.7819	0.5230	0.1658	0.3903	0.1952	0.2079	0.1409	0.0576	0.0827	0.1257
	Min.		502	0.7380	0.7171	0.4505	0.1421	0.3485	0.1613	0.1855	0.1257	0.0386	0.0663	0.1118
	n		10	10	10	10	10	9	10	9	10	10	10	10
Significant Difference			—	—	L=H<G	—	L>H	—	—	L>G=H	L>G>H	L>H>G	L>H=G	L>H>G

Note : L = Loggerhead turtle, *Caretta caretta*; G = Green turtle, *Chelonia mydas*; H = Hawksbill turtle, *Eretmochelys imbricata*; SD = standard deviation. Column head abbreviations: SCL = straight carapace length; SCW = straight carapace width; PL = plastron length; FLL = forelimb length; FLW = forelimb width; HLL = hind limb length; HLW = hind limb width; HL = head length; HW = head width; RH = rostrum height; OD = orbital diameter; UJL = upper jaw length (see Figure 2.2).

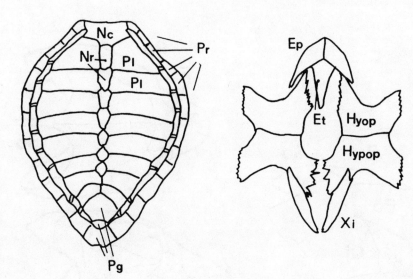

Figure 2.3. Bone structure of the shell in the loggerhead turtle. Nc: nuchal bone; Nr: neural bone; Pl: pleural bone; Pr: peripheral bone; Pg: pygal bone; Ep: epiplastra; Et: entoplastron; Hyop: hyoplastra; Hypop: hypoplastra; Xi: xiphiplastra.

and hawksbill turtles. Furthermore, the loggerhead has a relatively large beak compared with other species, as indicated by relative RH and UJL. The larger head and the corresponding muscle mass and large beak are thought to be adaptations for feeding on hard-bodied organisms such as mollusks or crustaceans.

To characterize allometric growth, Kamezaki and Matsui (1997) presented the relationships, at four life stages, of 11 characters relative to carapace length and 8 characters relative to head length. HL and HW were negatively allometric to SCL in all life stages; FLL and FLW were negatively allometric in most stages. Ratios of some characters appear to change with life stage (Kamezaki and Matsui 1997).

Bones of the Shell

The carapace of the loggerhead is composed of a nuchal, neural, pleural, peripheral, suprapygal, and pygal bones (Figure 2.3). These bones are rather thick in this species, although fontanels persist between the ends of the ribs and peripherals. The nuchal bone is relatively large, is concave anteriorly, and is connected with the first neural and the first pair of peripherals. The neural bones are rather narrow and form a continuous series, each with a concave anterior edge and short anterolateral edges that contact the preceding pair of pleurals. There are usually 7–11 neural bones. Each neural bone has a vertebral centrum attached to the ventral surface. When seven neural bones are present, vertebrae 1 and 2 attach to neural 1; if there are more than a total of seven neurals, some share a vertebral centrum.

There are eight pairs of pleural bones in the loggerhead turtle, a number that is constant in living turtles. There are usually 12 pairs of peripheral bones in loggerheads, while the green and the hawksbill turtles have 11 pairs. Peripherals I–X are long and narrow, while peripherals XI and XII are increasingly wide and thick. Peripherals, except I, II, III, and X, bear a deep pit for reception of rib end.

The plastron consists of nine bony elements, including a pair of epiplastra, an entoplastron, a pair of hyoplastra, a pair of hypoplastra, and a pair of xiphiplastra (Figure 2.3). The epiplastra are reduced and are broader anteriorly than posteriorly. The entoplastron is elongate and dagger-shaped. The hyoplastra and hypoplastra are similar in shape, with projections on the anterolateral faces of the hyoplastra and the posterolateral faces of the hypoplastra. The xiphiplastra are elongate, simple, and nearly straight.

Skull

The bone structure of the loggerhead skull (Figure 2.4) is described in detail by Pritchard and Trebbau (1984). The skull of the logger-

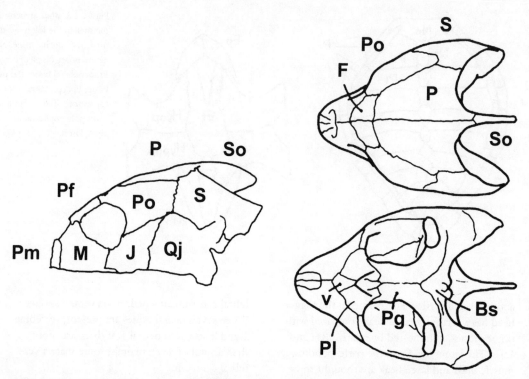

Figure 2.4. Bone structure of the skull in the loggerhead turtle. Pm: premaxilla; M: maxilla; Pf: prefrontal; F: frontal; P: parietal; Po: postorbital; J: jugal; Qj: quadratojugal; S: squamosal; So: supraoccipital; V: vomer; Pl: palatal; Pg: pterygoid; Bp: basisphenoid.

head turtle has a rather heavy and large construction relative to the other cheloniid species.

The orbits are large and laterally facing with some dorsal protection offered by a lateral flange of the postorbital bone. The frontal bones are usually excluded from the orbit by the prefrontal and postorbital contact above the eye. The parietals are very large and are posteriorly expanded. The nasal opening is somewhat dorsally directed. A moderate secondary palate is present and is perforated by numerous nutritive foramina. The maxillae are in contact medially between the premaxillae and the vomer. Other cheloniids do not normally have this contact; instead, the vomer divides the maxillae. There is a median ridge at the junction of the pterygoids. The external process of the pterygoid is small and curved upward.

The mandible, U-shaped in most turtles, is V-shaped in the loggerhead. The crushing surface is narrow in subadults and broader in adults. It forms an extensive crushing surface at the sym-physis, which is slightly concave in profile.

To compare the skulls of loggerheads, greens, and hawksbills, the author measured 17 characters in the three species and calculated a ratio of each to cranial length (LC2) (Table 2.2; Figure 2.5). The ratio LC1/LC2 suggests that the posterior projection of the supraoccipital is reduced in the loggerhead turtle relative to those of the green and hawksbill. The upper jaw length (UJL), which includes the premaxilla, maxilla, and jugal, is shorter in the loggerhead than in green or hawksbill turtles. The width of the condylus mandibularis (WCM) and the height of premaxilla (HPM) in are largest loggerheads, among the three species. Furthermore, the loggerhead has a shorter and stronger mandible than the green or hawksbill, as indicated by the relative sizes of the LM, the LJA, and the HM (Table 2.2). The hard structure of the loggerhead mandible is adapted for foraging its behavior: crushing hard-shelled organisms such as snails or crustaceans.

Table 2.2.

Comparisons of Relative Morphometric Characters of Skulls among Loggerhead (L), Green (G), and Hawksbill (H) Turtles

Species		LC2	LC1/LC2	UJL/LC2	HC/LC2	OD/LC2	OH/LC2	WN/LC2	HPM/LC2	WPO/LC2	WZ/LC2	WC/LC2	WCM/LC2	LSP/LC2	WM/LC2	LM/LC2	LJA/LC2	HM/LC2
Caretta caretta (Loggerhead)	Mean	178.59	1.35	0.49	0.79	0.39	0.32	0.18	0.25	0.32	1.01	0.90	0.21	0.40	0.86	0.96	0.33	0.32
	SD	13.58	0.04	0.04	0.04	0.02	0.02	0.01	0.02	0.02	0.06	0.04	0.03	0.02	0.04	0.02	0.02	0.02
	Max.	213.00	1.44	0.61	0.86	0.43	0.35	0.21	0.29	0.36	1.14	1.02	0.32	0.43	0.96	1.02	0.36	0.37
	Min.	160.00	1.26	0.37	0.71	0.35	0.28	0.15	0.20	0.25	0.85	0.83	0.18	0.37	0.79	0.90	0.28	0.28
	n	43	43	43	43	43	43	43	43	43	43	43	43	43	43	43	43	43
Chelonia mydas (Green)	Mean	132.27	1.46	0.53	0.77	0.46	0.35	0.20	0.21	0.33	0.95	0.87	0.19	0.39	0.85	1.00	0.24	0.28
	SD	9.02	0.13	0.03	0.06	0.05	0.03	0.02	0.03	0.03	0.07	0.07	0.02	0.03	0.09	0.05	0.05	0.02
	Max.	153.00	1.67	0.60	0.87	0.55	0.42	0.24	0.27	0.38	1.12	0.97	0.22	0.44	1.56	1.09	0.39	0.33
	Min.	120.00	1.22	0.42	0.64	0.38	0.29	0.15	0.15	0.26	0.73	0.66	0.15	0.28	0.64	0.86	0.19	0.22
	n	114	114	114	113	112	114	114	113	114	110	114	113	114	113	113	114	113
Eretmochelys imbricata (Hawksbill)	Mean	131.86	1.53	0.54	0.79	0.48	0.36	0.21	0.20	0.34	0.95	0.87	0.19	0.40	0.86	1.03	0.22	0.28
	SD	7.45	0.10	0.02	0.05	0.04	0.03	0.02	0.02	0.02	0.06	0.06	0.02	0.03	0.07	0.03	0.03	0.02
	Max.	146.00	1.63	0.57	0.84	0.52	0.39	0.23	0.23	0.39	1.03	0.94	0.22	0.43	0.93	1.08	0.31	0.31
	Min.	123.00	1.28	0.51	0.67	0.38	0.31	0.16	0.17	0.29	0.81	0.71	0.16	0.31	0.70	0.96	0.19	0.25
	n	14	14	14	14	14	14	14	14	14	14	14	14	14	13	14	14	14
Significant Difference		L<G=H	L<G=H	L<G=H	L>G=H	L<G=H	L<G=H	L<G=H	L>G=H	L<G=H	L>G=H	L>G=H	L>G=H	L=G=H	L=G=H	L<G=H	L>G=H	L>G=H

Note: L = Loggerhead turtle, *Caretta caretta;* G = Green turtle, *Chelonia mydas;* H = Hawksbill turtle, *Eretmochelys imbricata;* SD = standard deviation. Column head abbreviations are as follows: LC2 = cranial length, from anterior tip of the premaxilla to the posterior tip of the condylus mandibularis of the quadrate; LC1 = cranial length, from the anterior tip of the premaxilla to the posterior tip of the supraoccipital; UJL = upper jaw length; HC = height of cranium; OD = maximum orbit diameter; OH = orbit height; WN = width of nasal opening; HPM = height of premaxilla; WPO = width of preorbital; WZ = width of zygomatic; WC = width of cranium; WCM = width of condylus mandibularis; LSP = length of secondary palate; WM = width of mandible; LM = length of mandible from anterior tip to lateral posterior tip; LJA = length of mandibular symphysis; HM = height of mandible (see Figure 2.4).

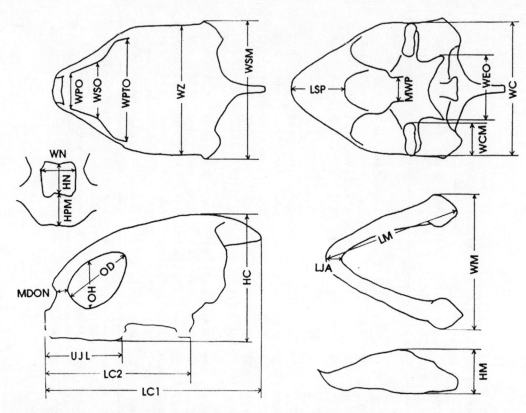

Figure 2.5. Skull measurements of the loggerhead turtle. LC1: cranial length, measured from the anterior tip of the premaxilla to the posterior tip of the supraoccipital; LC2: cranial length, measured from the anterior tip of the premaxilla to the posterior tip of the condylus mandibularis of the quadrate; UJL: upper jaw length; HC: height of cranium; OH: orbital height; OD: orbital diameter; MDON: minimum distance between orbit and nasal opening; HPM: height of premaxilla; HN: height of nasal opening; WN: width of nasal opening; WPO: width of preorbital; WSO: width of supraorbital; WPTO: width of postorbital; WZ: Width of zygomatic; WSM: width between squamosals; LSP: length of secondary palate; MWP: minimum width across pterygoid; WEO: width of exoccipital; WC: width of cranium; WCM: width of condylus mandibularis; LJA: length of mandibular symphysis; LM: length of mandible from anterior tip to lateral posterior tip; WM: width of mandible; HM: height of mandible.

The nasal and orbital openings of the loggerhead are smaller than in the green and hawksbill, but there is no difference between the latter species, as shown in the relative size of the OD, OH, and WN. Relative width of cranium across the postorbitals (WZ), which indicates overall cranium width, is larger in loggerheads than in the green and hawksbill turtles.

Sexual Dimorphism

In all cheloniid species, the mature male differs from the female in having a longer tail and a single enlarged, strongly curved claw on each forelimb (Figure 2.6). However, these differences only appear in mature individuals. Furthermore, the male tends to be larger than the female and has a relative larger head in relation to the body (Deraniyagala 1939). The carapace shape of the male is rather elongated in some populations, with a smoother margin than in the female (Deraniyagala 1939). Geldiay et al. (1982) presented regression lines for meristic characters relative to carapace length in loggerhead turtles from Turkey. The relationship between straight carapace length and width is rather similar for both sexes. However, the plastron length is markedly longer in mature females than in mature males (Geldiay et al. 1982).

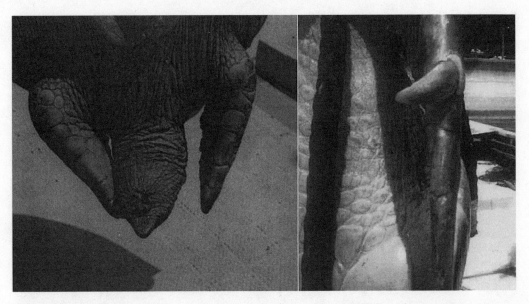

Figure 2.6. Morphological features of male loggerhead turtle. *Left:* longer tail. *Right:* curved claw of forelimb.

Pritchard and Trebbau (1984) presented Richardson's observation about sexual dimorphism of Atlantic loggerheads; males have a longer carapace than females, on average, and also have a disproportionately larger head. Unusually large skulls invariably are found on males. By contrast, for loggerhead turtles measured at Yakushima Island, the largest nesting site in the North Pacific Ocean, straight carapace length of mature males is 86.2 ± 6.9 cm (n = 10) (Kamezaki, unpubl. data) and is not statistically different from that of nesting females in the same locality (85.6 ± 4.68; n = 690).

Geographic Variation

Subspecies

Deraniyagala (1933) described the Indo-Pacific loggerheads as a separate species, *Caretta gigas*, to distinguish it from the Atlantic loggerheads, *C. caretta*. Diagnostic characters were believed to include 13 pairs of marginal scutes in *C. gigas* as opposed to 12 pairs in *C. caretta*. *C. gigas* was reported to have 7–12 neural bones, which is highly variable, in contrast to 7–8 neural bones in *C. caretta*. After examining a series of museum specimens, Deraniyagala (1939) revised his opinion and declared the Indo-Pacific

form to be a subspecies of *C. caretta*. Carr (1952) approved of this taxonomic opinion.

However, the diagnostic characters used to distinguish *C. c. gigas* from *C. c. caretta* have not held up under further scrutiny. Brongersma (1961) showed that the average number of marginal scutes varied as follows: western Atlantic, 12.62; western Europe, 12.71; Senegal, 12.83; Mediterranean, 12.57; and Indo-Pacific, 12.78. Pritchard (1979) reported an average count of 11.07 (excluding a supracaudal scute) for Mexican Pacific loggerheads (which are speculated to be migrants from Japan; Bowen et al. 1995) and 11.44 for Japanese specimens. Pritchard (1979) and Pritchard and Trebbau (1984) concluded that such slight variations could not justify subspecies recognition, and the name *gigas* was rejected in the checklist of Wermuth and Mertens (1977). As discussed above, marginal scute number is influenced by environmental factors, such as incubation temperature, and should not be used as a diagnostic character.

Size

The size of sea turtles is commonly indicated as the straight-line carapace length (SCL; usually measured from the nuchal notch to the tip of the posterior marginal). The measurements for

Table 2.3.
Geographic Comparison of Straight Carapace Length in Nesting Loggerhead Turtles

Localities	SCL	SD	Min.–Max.	N	Source
Atlantic					
North Carolina	92.5	—	85.0–98.0	13	12
Georgia	92.4	—	80.5–107.0	52	12
Florida	92.5	—	77.5–106.7	164	3
	90.5	—	81–109	50	1
	92.3	—	81–110	110	2
	93.1	—	83.0–105.0	137	12
	90.9	5.0	—	51	13
Mexico	90.5	—	73–109	423	11
Brazil	92.9	3.0	—	28	13
Colombia	87.7	—	70.0–102.0	65	8
Senegal	105.3	—	—	3	11
Mediterranean					
Greece	79.4	4.4	—	14	13
Greece	73.7[a]	6.1	—	27	10
Northern Cyprus	65.4[a]	15.2	—	11	4
Indian					
Oman	93.6	—	81.8–107.0	200	5
South Africa	87.6	4.1	76.0–98.0	320	6
Pacific					
Queensland	88.7[a]	—	73.2–106.9	2,207	9
Yakushima(Japan)	85.6	4.68	73.5–101.5	690	7
Miyazaki(Japan)	84.5	5.64	70.0–97.0	183	7
Minabe(Japan)	83.2	5.25	69.2–103.1	281	7

Source Key: 1. Davis and Whiting 1977. 2. Ehrhart and Yoder 1978. 3. Gallagher et al. 1972. 4. Godley and Broderick 1992. 5. Hirth and Hollingworth 1973. 6. Hughes 1975. 7. Kamezaki et al. 1995. 8. Kaufmann 1975. 9. Limpus 1985. 10. Margaritoulis 1982. 11. Marquez 1990. 12. Stoneburner 1980. 13. Tiwari and Bjorndal 2000.

Note: CCL = curved carapace length; SCL = straight carapace length; SD = standard deviation; N = number.

[a]Converted from CCL to SCL by SCL = 0.98CCL − 5.14 (Frazer and Ehrhart 1983).

nesting female are listed in Table 2.3. The largest and smallest SCLs are recorded from Senegal, Africa (Marquez 1990), and northern Cyprus in the Mediterranean Sea (Godley and Broderick 1992), respectively. In general, the loggerhead rookeries with the largest individuals are found in the Atlantic Ocean. In the Indian and Pacific oceans, the nesting females are intermediate in size between the Mediterranean and Atlantic populations. These differences are thought to be caused by the unique trophic conditions of each ocean basin. In contrast, green turtle skulls are larger in the southern hemisphere than in the northern hemisphere or near the equator (Kamezaki and Matsui

1995). That is, the size differences in *C. mydas* are not sorted by ocean basins, but by latitudinal differences.

The sizes of marine turtles are thought to be affected by genetics, energy consumption, food quality and abundance, and age. In terms of genetics, phylogenetic analyses with mtDNA reveal two distinctive matrilineages in the loggerhead. These two primary loggerhead mtDNA lineages were observed in both Atlantic-Mediterranean and Indo-Pacific samples (Bowen et al. 1994). One lineage contains nesting beach samples from Queensland (SCL = 88.7 cm), Japan (SCL = 83.2–85.6 cm), Greece (SCL = 73.7–79.4 cm), South Africa (SCL =

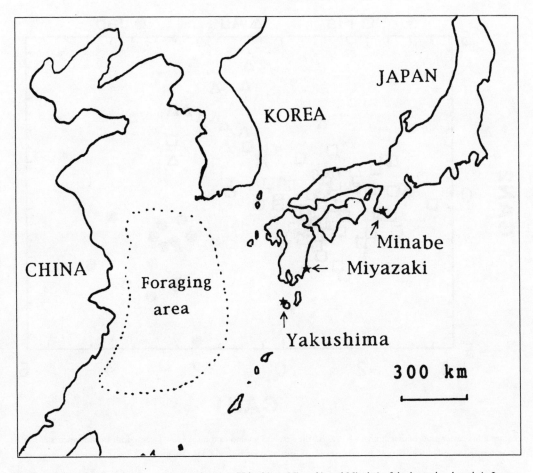

Figure 2.7. Map showing the three major nesting sites (Yakushima, Miyazaki, and Minabe) of the loggerhead turtle in Japan.

87.6 cm), and the southeastern United States (SCL = 90.5–92.5 cm); another lineage includes Oman (SCL = 93.6 cm), Brazil (SCL = 92.9 cm), and the southeastern United States (SCL = 90.5–92.5 cm). If the area of overlap in the southeastern United States is removed, the two lineages are characterized by relatively smaller and larger carapace lengths, respectively. So there is a possibility that the geographic difference in carapace length can be explained in part by genetic factors.

Carapace lengths of Japanese loggerheads differ statistically among three nesting areas: Yakushima, Miyazaki, and Minabe (Figure 2.7; Kamezaki et al. 1995). The largest carapaces are found in Yakushima (SCL = 85.6 cm), the smallest in Minabe (SCL = 83.2 cm) (Table 2.3). Foraging areas for these turtles are primar-

ily in the East China Sea (Iwamoto et al. 1985; Kamezaki et al. 1997).

It is notable that carapace length differences found in Japanese nesting turtles correspond with the distance between the foraging area and the nesting site. The reproductive migrations between nesting and foraging sites may influence body size in two ways. First, the effort required for a longer migration may divert energy that would otherwise be channeled into growth. Second, a longer migration may entail a greater risk of mortality. Specifically, survival ratios in Minabe are believed to be lower than in Yakushima because the females nesting in Minabe migrate through the coastal water of Shikoku and Kyushu, where many set nets and trawling fisheries operate. Lower survival rate may reduce the mean age (and size) of nesting females. If

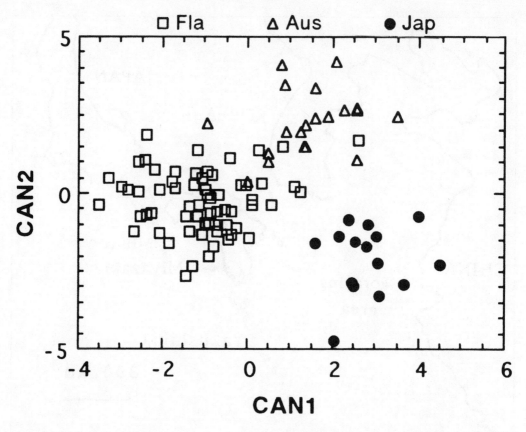

Figure 2.8. Scatter plots of discriminant scores on the first and second canonical axes. Twenty-four measurements of skulls (cranium and mandible) were used for analyses. Aus: Australia; Fla: Florida; Jap: Japan.

this is true, Minabe should have younger females on average than Yakushima, a hypothesis that may be testable in the future. Based on the carapace length difference among Japanese loggerheads rookeries, the author provisionally concludes that carapace size is affected by the energy consumption of migration and/or survival rate.

Skull

Comparative morphometric study is useful for determining taxonomic relationships within an animal group, but few such data are available for loggerheads. This stems from the difficulty in obtaining adequate samples, both because of the loggerhead's worldwide distribution and because few collections have adequate material from this very large animal. Here the author shows the geographic variation in skull mor-

phometrics among rookeries from Australia, Florida, and Japan, which includes both the Pacific and the Atlantic populations. A similar comparison for green turtles is also available (Kamezaki and Matsui 1995).

Twenty cranial and four mandibular measurements (as diagrammed in Figure 2.5) were examined for a total of 105 skulls from three populations. The skulls from Australia (n = 25), Florida (n = 63), and Japan (n = 17) are deposited in Queensland Museum, University of Central Florida, Chelonian Research Institute, in Dr. P. C. H. Pritchard's private collection, and in the author's private collection, respectively. Analyses were made without discrimination of sex because of the lack of information regarding the sex of each specimen.

Multiple-group principal components analysis was conducted using the general linear model (GLM) and principal component analysis (PRINCOMP) procedures of SAS for 24 skull measurements, including the mandible, and 20 cranial measurements, excluding the four mandibular measurements. For visualization of geographic differences between local samples, the first principal component scores that represented overall size variation were removed, and the remaining scores were then used for canonical discriminate analysis using the canonical discriminant analysis (CANDISC) procedure.

In the canonical discriminate analyses, the first and second canonical axes accounted, respectively, for 58.3 and 41.7% of the among-locality variation in 24 skull measurements. The Japanese sample was completely separated from the other samples on the first and second canonical axis of both analyses (Figure 2.8). On the other hand, the Australian sample partly overlapped with the sample from Florida.

These results showed that the Japan sample is notably distinct from the Australia and Florida samples. However, there is no single skull character that perfectly distinguishes one region from the others. Based on these data, the author regards this species as monotypic. That is, the presence of two subspecies (Indo-Pacific and Atlantic population) in *C. caretta* is not supported.

Conclusions

Morphological examinations of the loggerhead has revealed many adaptations to the marine habitat. Over deep evolutionary time, morphological changes such as an enlarged flipper and a reduced carapace are clear adaptations for long aquatic migrations. On a shorter evolutionary time scale, the heavy skull of the loggerhead, with massive maxillae meeting on the midline, distinguishes it from other cheloniid turtles and is an obvious adaptation for handling hard-shelled prey items. Over very recent evolutionary time, loggerhead turtles show morphometric distinctions among rookeries on separate continents, and these are probably adaptations to the conditions of different ocean basins. The success of these adaptations is readily apparent,

because the loggerhead lineage traces back to the Miocene Epoch (Bowen et al. 1993), and the broader cheloniid lineage traces back to the Cretaceous Period. However, the successful history and remarkable adaptations of the loggerhead turtle do not equip it for the most recent hazards of human-induced mortality. In particular, fishing nets pose a grave danger to loggerhead survival, and it is not clear that this species, which has survived since the age of dinosaurs, will survive the age of man.

ACKNOWLEDGMENTS

I thank B. W. Bowen for critically reviewing this manuscript and two anonymous reviewers for their extensive comments. I also thank P. C. H. Pritchard, L. M. Ehrhart, and P. Couper for allowing me to examine their skull collections. I am is grateful to M. Matsui for his encouragement in this study.

LITERATURE CITED

Bowen, B. W., W. S. Nelson, and J. C. Avise. 1993. A molecular phylogeny for marine turtles: Trait mapping, rate assessment, and conservation relevance. Proceedings of the National Academy of Sciences 90:5574–5577.

Bowen, B. W., N. Kamezaki, C. J. Limpus, G. R. Hughes, A. B. Meylan, and J. C. Avise. 1994. Global phylogeography of the loggerhead turtle *(Caretta caretta)* as indicated by mitochondrial DNA haplotypes. Evolution 48:1820–1828.

Bowen, B. W., F. A. Abreu-Grobois, G. H. Balazs, N. Kamezaki, C. J. Limpus, and R. J. Ferl. 1995. Trans-Pacific migrations of the loggerhead turtle *(Caretta caretta)* demonstrated with mitochondrial DNA markers. Proceedings of the National Academy of Sciences 92:3731–3734.

Brongersma, L. D. 1961. Notes upon some sea turtles. Zoologische Verhandelingen, Leiden 51:1–46.

Caldwell, D. K. 1959. The loggerhead turtles of Cape Romain, South Carolina. Bulletin of the Florida State Museum, Biological Sciences 4:319–348.

Carr, A. F., Jr. 1952. Handbook of turtles. Ithaca, N.Y.: Cornell University Press.

Cogger, H. G. 1983. Reptiles and amphibians of Australia, 3rd ed. Frenchs Forest, New South Wales, Australia: Reed Books Pty. Ltd.

Deraniyagala, P. E. P. 1930. The Testudinata of Ceylon. Ceylon Journal of Science (B) 16:43–88.

———. 1933. The loggerhead turtles (Carettidae) of Ceylon. Ceylon Journal of Science (B) 18:61–72.

———. 1939. The tetrapod reptiles of Ceylon. Vol. 1. Testudinates and crocodilians. Colombo, Ceylon: Colombo Museum.

———. 1953. A colored atlas of some vertebrates from Ceylon. Vol. 2. Tetrapod reptilia. Ceylon National Museum Publication, Colombo, Ceylon.

Davis, G. E., and M. C. Whiting. 1977. Loggerhead sea turtle nesting in Everglades National Park, Florida, U.S.A. Herpetologica 33:18–28.

Dodd, C. K., Jr. 1988. Synopsis of the biological data on the loggerhead sea turtle *Caretta caretta* (Linnaeus 1758). U.S. Fish and Wildlife Service Biological Report 88(14): 1–110.

Ehrhart, L. M., and R. G. Yoder. 1978. Marine turtles of Merritt Island National Wildlife Refuge, Kennedy Space Center, Florida. Florida Marine Research Publication 33:25–30.

Fretey, J. 1986. Les reptiles des France metropolitaine et des iles satellites: Tortues et lezards. Paris: Hatier.

Gaffney, E. S. 1979. Comparative cranial morphology of recent and fossil turtles. Bulletin of the American Museum of Natural History 164:65–376.

Gallagher, R. M., M. L. Hollinger, R. M. Ingle, and C. R. Futch. 1972. Marine turtle nesting on Hutchinson Island, Florida, in 1971. Florida Department of Natural Resources Marine Research Laboratory Special Science Report 37:1–11.

Geldiay, T., T. Koray, and S. Balik. 1982. Status of sea turtle populations (*Caretta c. caretta* L. and *Chelonia m. mydas* L.) in the northern Mediterranean Sea, Turkey. *In* K. A. Bjorndal (ed.). Biology and conservation of sea turtles, 426–436. Washington, D.C.: Smithsonian Institution Press.

Godley, B. J., and A. C. Broderick (eds). 1992. Glasgow University turtle conservation expedition to northern Cyprus. Glasgow, U.K.: People's Trust for Endangered Species.

Hirayama, R. 1998. Oldest known sea turtle. Nature 392:705–708.

Hirth, H. F., and S. L. Hollingworth. 1973. Report to the Government of the People's Democratic Republic of Yemen on marine turtle management. United Nations Development Program no. TA3178. Rome: FAO.

Hughes, G. R. 1974. The sea turtles of southeast Africa I. Investigational Report no. 35 of the Oceanographic Research Institute, Durban, South Africa.

Hughes, G. R. 1975. The marine turtles of Tongaland, VIII. Lammergeyer 22:9–18.

Iwamoto, T., M. Ishii, Y. Nakashima, H. Takeshita, and A. Itoh. 1985. Nesting cycles and migrations of the loggerhead sea turtle in Miyazaki, Japan. Japanese Journal of Ecology 35:505–511.

Kamezaki, N. 1989. Relation between scutellation and incubation period in *Caretta caretta*. Japanese Journal of Herpetology 13:53.

Kamezaki, N., and M. Matsui. 1995. Geographic variation in skull morphology of the green turtle, *Chelonia mydas,* with a taxonomic discussion. Journal of Herpetology 29:51–60.

Kamezaki, N., and M. Matsui. 1997. Allometry in the loggerhead turtle, *Caretta caretta*. Chelonian Conservation and Biology 2:421–425.

Kamezaki, N., K. Goto, Y. Matsuzawa, Y. Nakashima, K. Omuta, and K. Sato. 1995. Carapace length and width of the loggerhead turtle, *Caretta caretta,* nested in the coast of Japan. Umigame Newsletter of Japan 26:12–13.

Kamezaki, N., I. Miyawaki, H. Suganuma, K. Omuta, Y. Nakashima, K. Goto, K. Sato, Y. Matsuzawa, M. Samejima, M. Ishii, and T. Iwamoto. 1997. Post-nesting migration of Japanese loggerhead turtle, *Caretta caretta*. Wildlife Conservation Japan 3:29–39.

Kaufmann, R. 1975. Studies on the loggerhead sea turtle *Caretta caretta caretta* in Colombia, South America. Herpetologica 32:323–326.

Limpus, C. J. 1985. A study of the loggerhead sea turtle, *Caretta caretta,* in eastern Australia. Ph.D. Dissertation, University of Queensland, St. Lucia, Australia.

Margaritoulis, D. 1982. Observations on loggerhead sea turtle *Caretta caretta* activity during three nesting seasons (1977–1979) in Zakynthos, Greece. Biological Conservation 24:193–204.

Marquez M., R. 1990. Sea turtles of the world. FAO Fisheries Synopsis 11(125). Rome: FAO.

Nishimura, S. 1967. The loggerhead turtles in Japan and neighboring waters (Testudinata: Cheloniidae). Publications of the Seto Marine Biological Laboratory 15:19–35.

Pritchard, P. C. H. 1979. Encyclopedia of turtles. Neptune, N.J.: T. F. H. Publications.

Pritchard, P. C. H., and P. Trebbau. 1984. The turtles of Venezuela. Society for the Study of Amphibians and Reptiles, Contributions to Herpetology no. 2.

Stoneburner, D. L. 1980. Body depth: An indicator of morphological variation among nesting groups of adult loggerhead sea turtles *(Caretta caretta)*. Journal of Herpetology 14:205–206.

Tiwari, M., and K. A. Bjorndal. 2000. Variation in morphology and reproduction in loggerheads, *Caretta caretta,* nesting in the United States, Brazil, and Greece. Herpetologica 56:343–356.

Villiers, A. 1958. Tortues et crocodiles de l'Afrique

noire francaise. Initiations Etudiennes Africaines, Institut Francais d'Afrique Noire, Dakar 15:1–354.

Wermuth, H., and R. Mertens. 1977. Liste der rezenten Amphibien und Reptilien. Testudines, Crocodylia, Rhynchocephalia. Das Tierreich 100:1–174.

Wyneken, J. 1997. Sea turtle locomotion: Mechanics, behavior, and energetics. *In* P. L. Lutz and J. A. Musick (eds). The biology of sea turtles, 165–198. Boca Raton, Fla.: CRC Press.

Chapter 3

Orientation Mechanisms of Hatchling Loggerheads

—Kenneth J. Lohmann and Catherine M. F. Lohmann

Loggerhead turtles migrate intermittently throughout their lives. As hatchlings, the turtles swim from their natal beaches into the open ocean (Salmon and Wyneken 1987), often taking refuge in circular current systems (gyres) that serve as moving, open-sea nursery grounds (Bolten et al. 1998; Carr 1986). As juveniles, many take up residence in coastal areas but migrate seasonally between summer and winter habitats (Musick and Limpus 1997). Finally, as adults, turtles periodically leave their feeding grounds and migrate to mating and nesting areas, after which most return to individual feeding sites (Limpus et al. 1992; Musick and Limpus 1997). This itinerant lifestyle depends on a sophisticated suite of orientation cues and guidance mechanisms that enable the turtles to maintain consistent headings and navigate accurately across vast expanses of ocean.

At no point in the life cycle are orientation abilities more vividly displayed, or more crucial to survival, than during the hatchling stage. For hatchlings, minimizing time on the beach reduces exposure to environmental extremes and terrestrial predators. Similarly, rapid and direct movement through shallow, near-shore waters reduces exposure to fish and avian predators that are concentrated in coastal areas. It is therefore not surprising that natural selection has favored orientation mechanisms that guide young turtles quickly and reliably to the relative safety of the open ocean along paths that approximate straight lines.

The migration of hatchling loggerheads differs from the first migration of birds and other terrestrial animals in two important ways. First, turtles migrate through an underwater environment where visual landmarks are absent and celestial cues often cannot be perceived (Ehrenfeld and Koch 1967; Luschi et al. 1996). Second, whereas most young birds have the opportunity to practice or refine at least some orientation skills during short forays prior to migration (Baker 1984, 1993; Wiltschko and

Wiltschko 1998), turtles remain in an underground nest chamber until the moment they emerge to migrate. Thus, young turtles must somehow guide themselves through a completely unfamiliar environment even as they experience it for the first time.

This chapter begins with a summary of the orientation mechanisms that guide hatchling loggerheads, first on land as they move from their nests to the sea, then in the ocean as they migrate offshore. The experimental evidence that hatchlings can exploit positional information in the earth's magnetic field to help them remain within a gyre or other oceanic region is then reviewed. The chapter concludes with a discussion of the need to incorporate these findings into conservation practices.

Orientation during the Offshore Migration

Sea-Finding Behavior

Hatchlings usually emerge from their nests at night and begin to crawl seaward almost immediately (Mrosovsky 1968; Witherington et al. 1990). Carr and Ogren (1960) demonstrated that green turtle hatchlings (*Chelonia mydas*) use cues specific to their location to guide themselves to the sea rather than following a specific compass heading that is independent of local conditions. When hatchling green turtles were translocated from the east coast of Costa Rica to the west coast, they crawled westward toward the sea in the new location, even though such headings would have led inland at the original emergence site (Carr and Ogren 1960). Although such a translocation experiment has not yet been done with loggerheads, sea-finding cues used by hatchling loggerheads and green turtles appear to be similar in most regards.

Stranded debris and irregularities in the beach surface frequently obstruct the view of hatchlings at the nest site. Thus, turtles must often ascertain the seaward direction without having a direct view of the ocean (Limpus 1971; Mrosovsky 1972; Parker 1922). Visual cues are nevertheless of primary importance in sea finding (reviewed by Witherington 1997;

Lohmann et al. 1997). Hatchlings released on a beach with one or both eyes covered either crawled in circles or moved along circuitous, seemingly random paths (Carr and Ogren 1960; Daniel and Smith 1947; Mrosovsky and Shettleworth 1968). Some hatchlings responded to beach slope when tested in darkness under laboratory conditions, but such nonvisual cues appear to exert little or no influence on directional movement if visual cues are present (Salmon et al. 1992).

Although visual cues are apparently crucial in enabling hatchlings to reach the sea, it has proven challenging to identify the precise visual stimulus or stimuli to which turtles respond. During the past century, a number of slightly different explanations for sea finding have been proposed (Table 3.1).

One of the first hypotheses was based on the fact that water reflects more light than does land. As a consequence, the oceanic horizon is usually brighter than the landward horizon. This consideration, along with evidence that hatchlings prefer brighter lights to dimmer ones, led to the hypothesis that hatchlings locate the ocean by crawling toward the brightest horizon (Daniel and Smith 1947; Ehrenfeld 1968; Mrosovsky 1972; Mrosovsky and Shettleworth 1968).

In a study involving hundreds of natural loggerhead emergences in Australia, however, Limpus (1971) investigated conditions under which hatchlings failed to locate the sea. He concluded that hatchlings moved towards that part of the horizon line that was at the lowest angle of elevation from the turtles' position, even if this area was not the most brightly illuminated. The lowest-horizon hypothesis also accurately predicted both the movement of hatchlings released at various locations along the beach and the orientation of turtles tested in an arena in which horizon elevation could be manipulated.

Additional evidence that horizon elevation is important in sea-finding was obtained by Salmon et al. (1992), who tested turtles inside a circular arena where black paper could be used to obscure various regions of an otherwise illuminated background. Loggerhead hatchlings consistently moved away from elevated silhou-

Table 3.1.
Summary of Eight Hypotheses Proposed to Explain Sea-Finding in Hatchling Sea Turtles

Significant Refs.	Explanation of Sea-Finding
10	Hatchlings move toward regions in which the horizon is open and clear, and away from those in which the horizon is interrupted by masses such as trees and shrubbery.
1, 2[a], 5[a], 6[a], 9[a]	Hatchlings move toward the brightest direction. A turtle finds this direction by turning until the brightness input to each eye is equal and balanced, then moves straight ahead to maintain the balance.
4	Hatchlings move toward that part of the horizon line that is at the lowest angle of elevation from their position; if all horizons are at the same angle of elevation, turtles choose the brightest.
14[a]	Hatchlings move toward the brightest direction. They determine this direction by assessing light that falls within an "input cone" with a large horizontal angle of acceptance (perhaps approximately 180°).
13[a]	Hatchlings find the sea using a system of redundant orientation mechanisms that includes both optic and nonoptic components. Brightness and form vision both play a role; beach slope might also be used under some conditions.
7[a], 3[a], 8[a]	Hatchlings find the sea by relying on a complex phototropotaxis, in which the turtle turns until brightness inputs to specific regions of the retina are balanced. Hatchlings then move straight ahead to maintain the balance, a response that leads them to the brightest, most open horizon.
11, 12	Hatchlings move away from elevated silhouettes of dunes and vegetation (or toward the lowest horizon); they also crawl toward bright regions, but if brightness and horizon elevation conflict, elevation is used.
15, 16, 17	Hatchlings have a strong tendency to move toward the brightest direction as assessed with a cone of acceptance approximately 180° wide and 10–30° high. However, responses to shapes and objects perceived with form vision can override brightest direction in some cases.

Reference Key: 1. Daniel and Smith 1947. 2. Ehrenfeld 1968.[a] 3. Kingsmill and Mrosovsky 1982.[a] 4. Limpus 1971. 5. Mrosovsky 1967.[a] 6. Mrosovsky 1972.[a] 7. Mrosovsky 1978.[a] 8. Mrosovsky and Kingsmill 1985.[a] 9. Mrosovsky and Shettleworth 1968.[a] 10. Parker 1922. 11. Salmon and Wyneken 1994. 12. Salmon et al. 1992. 13. van Rhijn 1979.[a] 14. Verheijen and Wildschut 1973.[a] 15. Witherington 1992. 16. Witherington 1997. 17. Witherington and Martin 2000.

Note: This list is not comprehensive, and subtle differences exist between some papers that are grouped together. The hypotheses proposed by Limpus (1971) and Salmon et al. (1992) are functionally similar, although the terminology used in the two papers differs.

[a]Papers based on sea turtles other than loggerheads.

ettes and toward the lowest illuminated horizon, even when doing so meant moving toward an area of dimmer, lower light instead of toward an area where the light was brighter but higher. The authors concluded that hatchlings find the sea by moving away from elevated silhouettes, a response that also takes them toward the lowest horizon.

Experiments on the beach have confirmed that loggerhead hatchlings do not always move in the direction that human optical measure-ments indicate is brightest (Adamany et al. 1997; Salmon and Witherington 1995). Does this mean that the brightest-direction hypothesis is incorrect? The question is not easily answered because turtles may assess brightest direction using different rules than human instruments employ. Hatchling turtles appear to integrate brightness measurements over only a limited part of the visual field that falls within a specific "cone of acceptance" (Verheijen and Wildschut 1973; Witherington 1992). For both photometers and hatchlings, the height and breadth of the acceptance cone critically influence assessments of what direction is brightest. Experiments suggest that the acceptance cone of loggerhead hatchlings spans about 180° in horizontal breadth but extends no more than 30° upward or downward from the horizon (Witherington 1992, 1997). This restricted vertical dimension suggests that light close to the horizon influences hatchlings more strongly than does light higher up in the visual field.

Viewed in the context of acceptance cones, the tendency of hatchlings to orient away from silhouettes (or toward the lowest horizon) might plausibly be interpreted as an epiphenomenon of brightest-direction orientation (Witherington 1997). Dune silhouettes darken areas near the horizon that fall within a hatchling's cone of acceptance; thus, a turtle orienting away from an elevated silhouette might do so because it perceives little light in that direction and brighter illumination elsewhere.

On the other hand, the same results can potentially be explained without invoking brightest-direction orientation at all. As discussed previously, hatchlings might simply assess the angle of horizon elevation and crawl towards that part of the horizon that is lowest (Limpus 1971), a process that would not require any assessment of brightness. Another possibility is that hatchlings rely on form vision to directly perceive the trees and dunes that line the beach on the landward side and then move away from these objects (Witherington 1992, 1997). Although form vision in sea turtles has not yet been studied in detail, laboratory experiments suggest that hatchling loggerheads can perceive darkened vertical stripes and other shapes, an ability that might assist them in distinguishing the landward and seaward horizons under some conditions (Witherington 1992). Thus, several different visual stimuli, as well as several different modes of neural processing, might potentially be involved in sea finding.

In summary, it seems reasonable to conclude that visual cues are of primary importance in sea-finding. From a functional perspective, the elevation of the horizon and the brightness of the light also appear to be important factors under at least some conditions. Less clear is precisely which feature or features of the visual environment turtles discern (horizon elevation, brightness within the cone of acceptance, the shape of silhouettes, other as yet unidentified visual cues, or some combination). Disentangling the various potential cues will be challenging because altering any one can change others.

Orientation to Oceanic Waves

Immediately after entering the ocean, loggerhead hatchlings establish an offshore course by swimming into waves (Lohmann 1992; Lohmann and Lohmann 1996a; Salmon and Lohmann 1989). In the laboratory, turtles tethered in a wave tank oriented randomly in still water but swam into waves when waves were present (Wyneken et al. 1990). In the ocean, hatchlings swam into approaching waves when tethered in floating arenas placed offshore (Salmon and Lohmann 1989). At times when no waves were present, hatchlings either swam in circles or established courses in apparently random directions (Lohmann 1992; Salmon and Lohmann 1989).

Similar results have been obtained with hatchling green turtles and leatherbacks (Dermochelys coriacea) (Lohmann and Lohmann 1992; Lohmann et al. 1990). Thus, hatchlings of at least three sea turtle species appear to maintain seaward orientation early in the offshore migration by using wave propagation direction as an orientation cue. Because waves and swells entering shallow, coastal areas are refracted until they approach a beach directly, swimming into waves reliably guides turtles away from land and toward the open sea.

Detecting Waves while Underwater

The ability of hatchlings to detect wave direction while swimming underwater at night suggests that turtles do not detect waves visually. Experiments in a wave tank have confirmed that visual cues are not necessary for wave orientation; hatchlings oriented into waves even in the absence of visible light (Lohmann et al. 1990; Wyneken et al. 1990).

The environmental stimuli that hatchlings use to determine wave direction may vary with the depth of the water. In shallow water imme-

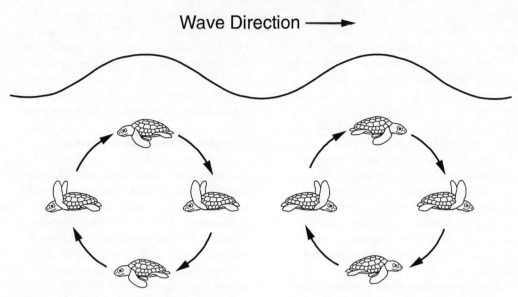

Figure 3.1. The motion of a hatchling turtle swimming with *(right)* and against *(left)* the direction of wave propagation (modified from Lohmann and Lohmann 1992). See text for details.

diately adjacent to shore, waves approaching the beach induce water near the ocean floor to move toward and away from shore in a rhythmic, horizontal motion known as wave surge. In deeper water, particles near the surface of the ocean describe an orbital (circular) pattern of movement as waves propagate (Denny 1988). Hatchlings can apparently use both surge motion and orbital movements to guide themselves seaward (Lohmann et al. 1995; Wang et al. 1998).

Evidence that hatchlings orient to wave surge was obtained by testing turtles on a surge simulator, a machine that produces movements closely resembling those that small, oceanic waves generate near the ocean floor (Wang et al. 1998). Because the swimming behavior of a hatchling is activated when its ventral surface fails to contact substrate (Carr 1963, 1982), turtles could be tested while "swimming" in air on the simulator (Lohmann et al. 1995; Manning et al. 1997). Hatchlings subjected to simulated surge approaching from their right or left sides spent significantly more time attempting to turn than did turtles aligned parallel with the surge axis. These results demonstrate that turtles can detect surge motion and respond by attempting to orient along its axis. Because turtles normally enter the ocean already oriented seaward, remaining aligned with the

surge axis while swimming presumably leads hatchlings offshore. Such a response may play a brief but important role in enabling turtles to maintain offshore headings as they swim through shallow water on their way to the open sea.

In deeper water, hatchlings can determine the direction of wave movement by sensing the orbital motion produced as waves propagate (Lohmann et al. 1995). The sequence of accelerations occurring within wave orbits provides hatchlings with a way to determine how they are aligned relative to the direction of wave propagation (Cook 1984; Lohmann and Lohmann 1992). For example, a hatchling facing into approaching waves is accelerated upward, backward, downward, and then forward with each wave cycle, whereas a turtle oriented in the direction of wave movement is accelerated upward, forward, downward, and then backward (Figure 3.1). In principle, a turtle need only distinguish between these two sequences to differentiate orientation against and with wave propagation direction.

That hatchlings can indeed detect wave direction in this way has been demonstrated using a wave motion simulator, a machine that reproduces in air the circular movements that turtles normally encounter while swimming beneath small oceanic waves (Figure 3.2; Lohmann et al.

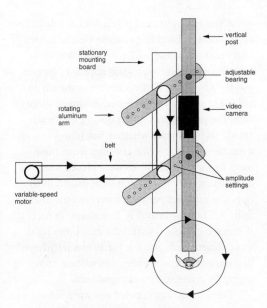

Figure 3.2. Diagram of the wave motion simulator used to produce orbital movements similar to those experienced by hatchling loggerheads migrating offshore. A variable-speed motor turns a belt, which in turn drives two identical acrylic arms coupled together by a second belt. As the arms rotate, they remain parallel to each other. Bearings connect a wooden post to the arms in such a way that the post remains vertical as the arms rotate. Thus, a hatchling attached to the bottom of the post is subjected to circular movements simulating those that occur near the ocean surface as waves propagate. The diagram is modified from Lohmann et al. (1995).

1995). Hatchlings subjected to orbital movements that simulated waves approaching from their right sides attempted to turn right, whereas movements that simulated waves from the left elicited left-turning behavior. Movements simulating waves from directly in front of the turtles elicited little turning in either direction. Additional experiments with the wave simulator revealed that loggerhead hatchlings from eastern Florida responded most strongly to wave orbits with amplitudes and periods closely resembling those of typical waves at their natal beach (Manning et al. 1997).

Magnetic Compass Orientation

Hatchlings that have just entered the ocean appear to orient exclusively on the basis of waves; no evidence presently exists for the involvement of other directional cues at this early stage of the offshore migration. Because waves entering shallow water refract until they approach the beach directly, swimming into waves leads turtles seaward.

In deeper water farther from land, waves no longer provide a reliable indicator of offshore direction. Nevertheless, hatchling loggerheads tracked from a Florida beach continued on the same offshore headings even after entering areas where wave direction no longer coincided with their established courses (Witherington 1995). The ability to maintain headings seemingly independent of wave direction implies that, after they have distanced themselves from land, hatchlings use one or more alternative sources of directional information to guide their movements.

Laboratory experiments have demonstrated that loggerhead (Light et al. 1993; Lohmann 1991; Lohmann and Lohmann 1994a) and leatherback (Lohmann and Lohmann 1993) hatchlings can orient to the earth's magnetic field. Thus, one possibility is that magnetic compass orientation supplants wave orientation as hatchlings distance themselves from shore.

Two functionally different types of magnetic compasses are known to exist in animals (Wiltschko and Wiltschko 1988, 1995). Inclination or axial compasses, unlike traditional manmade compasses, do not detect the polarity of the field (i.e., north vs. south). Instead, such compasses define "poleward" as the direction along the earth's surface in which the angle formed between the magnetic field vector and the gravity vector is smallest (Wiltschko and Wiltschko 1972). For an animal with an inclination compass, inverting the vertical component of the field has the same behavioral effect as reversing the horizontal component, whereas reversing the horizontal and vertical components together (so that the polarity of the total field vector is reversed) has no effect (Wiltschko and Wiltschko 1988). In contrast, animals with polarity compasses determine north using the polarity of the horizontal field component. Thus, inverting the vertical component has no effect on orientation, but reversing the vertical and horizontal components together leads to a reversal of orientation direction.

Loggerhead hatchlings reversed their direction of orientation when the vertical component of the magnetic field was inverted, but not when the vertical and horizontal components were reversed together (Light et al. 1993). These data provide evidence that the loggerhead compass is an inclination compass rather than a polarity compass and that it is functionally similar to the magnetic compass of birds. The physiological mechanisms that underlie magnetic field detection in sea turtles and other animals remain to be determined (reviewed by Lohmann and Johnsen 2000).

Acquisition of Magnetic Directional Preference

If the magnetic compass functions in the offshore migration of hatchlings, then turtles must inherit or acquire a preference for swimming toward the magnetic direction that coincides with the seaward direction. In initial experiments (Light et al. 1993; Lohmann 1991), hatchling loggerheads were permitted to swim toward a dim light in the east (their normal migratory direction) before they were tested in darkness. These animals subsequently swam east to northeast in the geomagnetic field. To determine whether the initial course of the turtles influenced their subsequent magnetic orientation, turtles in one experiment were exposed to light from either magnetic east or west before being tested in darkness (Lohmann and Lohmann 1994a). Hatchlings that had been exposed to light in the east oriented eastward, whereas those that had been exposed to light in the west swam approximately westward. Reversing the magnetic field resulted in a corresponding shift in orientation, demonstrating that the turtles were indeed orienting magnetically in the dark. An additional group of turtles tested in darkness without prior exposure to light cues was not significantly oriented.

These results indicate that the position of light cues, or perhaps just the experience of maintaining a course toward a specific direction, can influence subsequent magnetic orientation behavior. Moreover, because hatchlings without prior light exposure oriented randomly, the results suggest that turtles do not emerge from their nests with a preferred magnetic bearing, but instead must acquire one.

Although light cues play a critical role in the orientation of hatchlings on the beach, turtles that enter the ocean under natural conditions initially orient into waves and appear to ignore visual cues. Thus, if light cues are normally involved in setting the preferred magnetic direction, the process may occur during the beach crawl. To investigate whether hatchlings can set a magnetic course while crawling from their nests to the ocean, turtles were placed into one end of a runway with a dim light placed in the opposite end and permitted to crawl toward the light (C. Lohmann and K. Lohmann, in prep.). When a hatchling finished the crawl, the light was extinguished, and the turtle was transferred in darkness to a water-filled orientation arena, where its orientation was monitored.

Turtles that had crawled eastward subsequently swam eastward in darkness, whereas hatchlings that had crawled westward swam west. Reversing the magnetic field around the swimming hatchlings resulted in a corresponding shift in orientation, demonstrating that the turtles were orienting to the earth's magnetic field. Other hatchlings placed into the runway in darkness and permitted to crawl with no light present were not significantly oriented. These results are consistent with the hypothesis that turtles emerge from their nests without an established directional preference; they may, however, acquire one while crawling a short distance across the beach.

Hatchlings can also establish a magnetic directional preference on the basis of wave cues (Goff et al. 1998). Loggerhead hatchlings that had never crawled across a beach were tethered inside a wave tank and allowed to swim into waves for 30 minutes. The waves were then terminated. Half the turtles were allowed to continue swimming in the local geomagnetic field; the other half were subjected to a field with a reversed vertical component, a treatment that has the same effect on the turtle magnetic compass as reversing the horizontal component (Light et al. 1993; see above). Hatchlings that swam in the earth's magnetic field continued to swim in the direction from which waves had previously approached. Turtles tested in the reversed field, however, swam in the opposite direction. A third group of turtles that swam without previ-

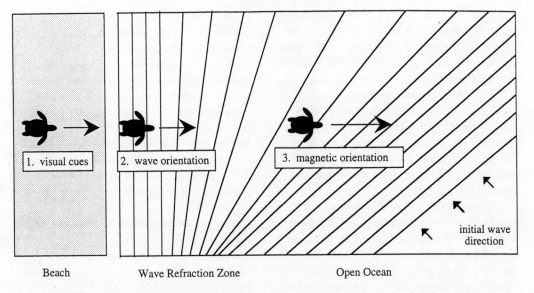

Beach   Wave Refraction Zone   Open Ocean

Figure 3.3. Diagram summarizing the orientation cues hypothesized to guide hatchling Florida loggerheads from their nests to the Gulf Stream current. The beach is to the left, and progressively deeper water is to the right. Lines represent oceanic waves moving toward the beach; as they enter shallow coastal areas, waves refract until they approach the beach directly. Visual cues guide hatchlings from their nests to the sea. Near shore, turtles orient into refracted waves, which provide a reliable cue for swimming seaward. In deeper water, waves no longer provide a consistent cue for offshore orientation, and hatchlings are hypothesized to transfer their seaward courses to their magnetic compasses. The diagram is adapted from Lohmann and Lohmann (1996a).

ous exposure to waves was not significantly oriented. These results provide additional evidence that turtles do not inherit a magnetic preference for the offshore direction, but instead acquire one that is based on other directional cues.

Under laboratory conditions, then, hatchlings can establish a magnetic directional preference in at least three different ways: by swimming towards a light source, by crawling towards a light source, or by swimming into waves. Taken together, the results suggest that the experience of maintaining a course, either on land or in water, is sufficient to establish a magnetic directional preference. Under natural conditions, hatchlings use visual cues to guide themselves as they crawl across the beach to the sea, then continue offshore by orienting into waves. Thus, it appears that the seaward course a turtle initiates while crossing the beach and swimming away from land is transferred to the magnetic compass, so that a hatchling can continue on the same heading after swimming beyond the wave refraction zone and into the open sea.

Sequential Orientation Mechanisms Used during the Offshore Migration

In summary, hatchling loggerheads from eastern Florida appear to use three different types of orientation cues sequentially during their offshore migration (Figure 3.3). On the beach, hatchlings crawl seaward using visual information that might include brightness, horizon elevation, and perception of objects such as dunes and trees. Once in the ocean, turtles initially swim offshore by orienting into waves, apparently without regard to visual cues. While crawling across the beach, swimming offshore, or both, hatchlings probably transfer the initial seaward heading to their magnetic compasses, enabling them to maintain offshore courses after passing beyond the wave refraction zone.

Oriented Movements in the Open Ocean

The offshore migration of hatchling Florida loggerheads is just the first step in a much longer transoceanic journey. Young loggerheads evidently remain for at least several years in the North Atlantic gyre, the circular current system that encircles the Sargasso Sea (Bolten, Chapter 4 this volume; Carr 1986; Hays and Marsh 1997). During this time many young loggerheads cross to the eastern side of the Atlantic Ocean (Bolten et al. 1994, 1998) before returning to the vicinity of the southeastern United States to take up residence in coastal feeding grounds (Carr 1987; Musick and Limpus 1997; Sears et al. 1995).

Young loggerheads in the open sea may benefit from oriented movements that serve to keep them within oceanic regions favorable for growth and development. For example, whereas the warm waters of the Gulf Stream provide a suitable environment for young turtles, straying beyond the latitudinal extremes of the North Atlantic gyre can be fatal. As the northern edge of the gyre approaches Portugal, the east-flowing current divides. The northern branch continues past Great Britain, and the water temperature decreases rapidly. Loggerheads swept north in this current soon die from the cold (Carr 1986, 1987; Hays and Marsh 1997). Similarly, turtles that venture south of the gyre may be swept into the South Atlantic current system and transported far from their normal range. An ability to recognize the latitudinal extremes of the gyre and to respond by orienting in an appropriate direction might therefore have considerable adaptive value.

Positional Information in the Earth's Magnetic Field

Several features of the earth's magnetic field vary in a predictable way across the surface of the earth and might, in principle, be used in position finding (Skiles 1985). For example, at each location on the globe, the geomagnetic field lines intersect the earth's surface at a specific angle of inclination (Figure 3.4). Because inclination angles vary with latitude, an animal able to distinguish between different field inclinations might be able to approximate its latitude (Lohmann et al. 1999; Skiles 1985).

In addition to inclination angle, at least three other magnetic parameters could hypo-

thetically be used in assessing position (Figure 3.4). These include the intensity (strength) of the total field, the intensity of the horizontal field, and the intensity of the vertical field. Additional magnetic features such as declination potentially exist for an animal that can detect geographic north as well as magnetic north (Gould 1985; Quinn 1984). For sea turtles, however, limited visual abilities probably preclude the use of star patterns and other celestial cues that might conceivably be used to determine geographic north (Ehrenfeld and Koch 1967).

Detection of Magnetic Inclination Angle

The geomagnetic parameter most strongly correlated with latitude is field line inclination (Skiles 1985). To determine if loggerheads can distinguish between different inclination angles, hatchlings were tethered in a water-filled arena surrounded by a computerized coil system (Figure 3.5) that was used to generate earth-strength fields with different inclinations (Lohmann and Lohmann 1994b). Hatchlings exposed to a field with an inclination angle found along the northern boundary of the North Atlantic gyre swam south-southwest (Figure 3.6). In contrast, hatchlings exposed to an inclination angle found near the southern boundary of the gyre swam in a northeasterly direction (Figure 3.6). Turtles exposed to inclination angles they do not normally encounter (i.e., from north or south of the North Atlantic gyre) or to field inclinations found well within the northern and southern extremes of the gyre were not significantly oriented.

These results demonstrate that loggerheads can distinguish between different magnetic inclination angles. In addition, inclination angles found near the northern and southern gyre boundaries elicited orientation that would direct turtles approximately toward the gyre center. The results are therefore consistent with the hypothesis that specific inclination angles in effect warn turtles that they have reached the latitudinal extremes of the gyre and must swim toward the gyre center to avoid straying out of the warm-water current system (Lohmann and Lohmann 1994b). For turtles that are safely within the gyre, drifting passively presumably poses no danger of displacement into undesir-

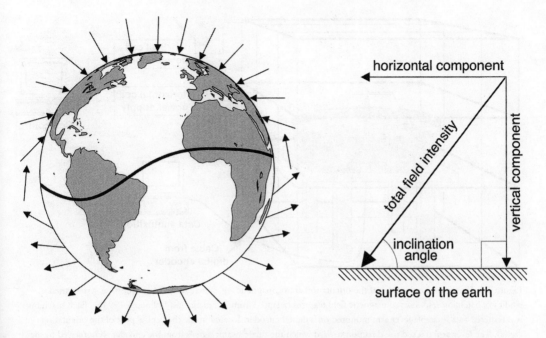

Figure 3.4. *Left:* Diagram of the earth's magnetic field illustrating how field lines (represented by arrows) intersect the earth's surface and how inclination angle (the angle formed between the field lines and the earth) varies with latitude. At the magnetic equator (the curving line across the earth), field lines are parallel to the earth's surface and the inclination angle is 0°. An animal migrating north from the magnetic equator to the magnetic pole encounters progressively steeper inclination angles along its journey. At the magnetic poles, the inclination angle is 90°. *Right:* Diagram illustrating four elements of geomagnetic field vectors that might, in principle, provide sea turtles or other long-distance migrants with positional information. The field present at each location on the earth can be described in terms of total field intensity and inclination angle. The total intensity of the field can be resolved into two vector components: the horizontal field intensity and the vertical field intensity.

able areas. The absence of a directional preference among turtles exposed to an inclination angle found near the gyre's latitudinal center is consistent with this interpretation.

Detection of Magnetic Field Intensity

A second geomagnetic feature that varies across the surface of the earth is field intensity. To determine if hatchling loggerheads can perceive differences in intensity, the coil system was used to produce fields with different intensities but the same inclination angle. Hatchlings were exposed to one of two intensities that they normally encounter during their first months at sea (Lohmann and Lohmann 1996b). Turtles tested in a field of 52,000 nano-Tesla (nT) swam eastward (Figure 3.7). This field is 10.6% stronger than the natal beach field and corresponds to the intensity that hatchlings en-

counter near North and South Carolina. Turtles exposed to a 43,000 nT field (a field 8.5% weaker than the natal beach field, and one first encountered on the eastern side of the Atlantic near Portugal) swam westward (Figure 3.7).

These results demonstrate that hatchlings can distinguish between field intensities that occur in different locations along their migratory route. Moreover, because both eastward orientation near South Carolina and westward orientation near the coast of Portugal would function to keep young turtles within the gyre, the results imply that turtles can derive positional information from field intensity.

Detection of Region-Specific Magnetic Fields

In the initial experiments involving inclination and intensity, one of the two parameters was

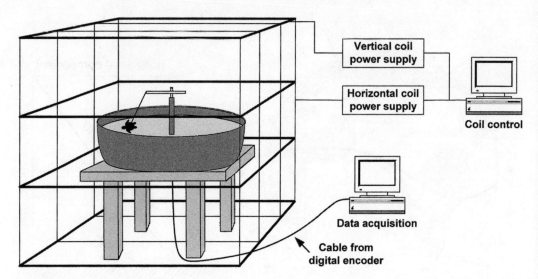

Figure 3.5. Diagram (not to scale) of the orientation arena, magnetic coil system, and data acquisition system used in studies of hatchling responses to magnetic field features (adapted from Lohmann and Lohmann 1994b). Each hatchling was tethered to a rotatable lever arm mounted on a digital encoder (located inside the central post of the orientation arena). The lever arm tracked the direction toward which the turtle swam; signals from the encoder were relayed to the data acquisition computer, which recorded the orientation of the turtle every 10 seconds. The arena was enclosed by a magnetic coil system consisting of two different coils arranged orthogonally. One coil controlled the horizontal component of the field while the other controlled the vertical component. Each coil measured 2.27 m on a side and was constructed in accordance with the four-coil design of Merritt et al. (1983). The turtles were tethered in the center of the coil with the tank positioned so that the surface of the water was within a few centimeters of the horizontal plane halfway between the top and bottom coils. The turtles were restricted by the tether to a horizontal area defined by a circle of radius 25 cm or less; the range of vertical movement was restricted to 5 cm or less. In the region where the turtles swam, the field generated by the coil was highly uniform (Kirschvink 1992; Merritt et al. 1983).

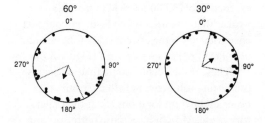

Figure 3.6. Orientation of hatchling loggerheads tested in magnetic fields of the same intensity but different inclinations (data from Lohmann and Lohmann 1994b). Turtles exposed to a 60° inclination angle (an angle found near the northern edge of the North Atlantic gyre) were significantly oriented toward the south-southwest, whereas those exposed to an inclination angle of 30° (found near the southern border of the gyre) swam in a northeasterly direction. Each dot represents the mean angle of a single hatchling. The arrow in the center of each circle indicates the mean angle of the group, and the dashed lines represent the 95% confidence interval.

held constant while the other was varied. Although this approach was necessary to demonstrate that turtles could detect each feature, both field elements actually vary in different directions across the earth's surface. As a consequence, most pairings of inclination and intensity used in the initial experiments did not result in fields that match precisely those that exist in the North Atlantic. To determine whether loggerheads can distinguish between the magnetic fields that actually occur in different oceanic regions, hatchlings were subjected to fields replicating those found in three widely separated locations along the perimeter of the North Atlantic gyre (Lohmann et al. 2001).

Turtles tested in a magnetic field replicating one that exists offshore near northern Florida swam east-southeast (Figure 3.8). Those exposed to a field replicating one found near the

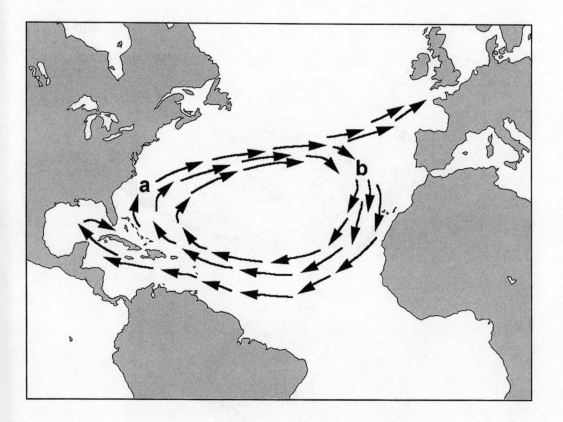

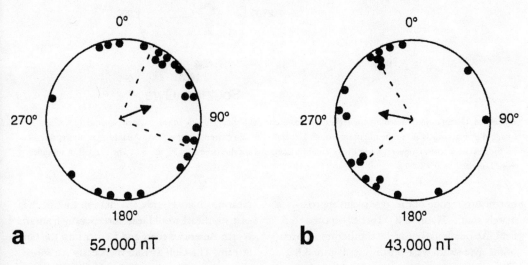

a   52,000 nT   **b**   43,000 nT

Figure 3.7. *Top:* Generalized diagram of the North Atlantic gyre (after Carr 1986; Gross 1977) indicating the only location (a) within the gyre where the field intensity is 52,000 nT and the location (b) where Florida loggerheads in the gyre presumably first encounter a field intensity of 43,000 nT. *Bottom:* Orientation of hatchling loggerheads tested in a magnetic field of 52,000 nT (left) and 43,000 nT (right). Diagrams are modified from Lohmann and Lohmann (1996b) and Lohmann et al. (1999). Conventions in the orientation diagrams are the same as in Figure 3.6.

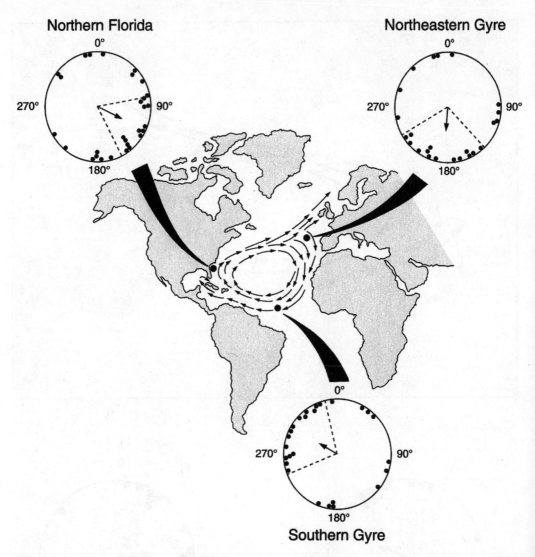

Figure 3.8. Orientation of hatchling loggerheads in magnetic fields characteristic of three widely separated locations (marked by black dots) along the migratory route. Generalized main currents of the North Atlantic gyre are represented on the map by arrows. Conventions in the orientation diagrams are the same as in Figure 3.6. The diagram is modified from Lohmann et al. (2001).

northeastern edge of the gyre swam approximately south (Figure 3.8). Turtles exposed to a field like one found near the southernmost part of the gyre swam west-northwest (Figure 3.8). Thus, the results demonstrate that loggerhead turtles can distinguish among magnetic fields that exist in widely separated oceanic regions.

In addition, the orientation behavior elicited by each of the three fields is consistent with the interpretation that these responses have functional significance in the migration.

Near northern Florida, orientation toward the east-southeast would lead turtles away from the North American coast and farther into the Gulf Stream. The Gulf Stream veers eastward soon after passing Florida; when it does, turtles positioned safely away from the gyre perimeter are presumably less likely to stray into the fatally cold water that lies to the north. In the northeastern region of the gyre, the Gulf Stream divides. Southward orientation in this area is likely to help turtles remain in the gyre and avoid the

North Atlantic drift, the north-flowing current that can carry turtles into the cold oceanic regions of Great Britain and Scandinavia (Carr 1986, 1987; Hays and Marsh 1997). Near the southernmost boundary of the gyre, orientation to the west-northwest is consistent with the migratory route of the turtles. Such orientation may prevent turtles from straying too far south and may also help them remain in favorable currents that facilitate movement back toward the North American coast, where most Florida loggerheads spend their late juvenile years (Musick and Limpus 1997).

Thus, specific magnetic fields characteristic of widely separated oceanic regions elicit orientation responses that are likely to help turtles remain safely within the gyre and progress along the migratory route. The results imply that young loggerheads exploit such fields as navigational markers.

Secular Variation and Responses of Hatchlings

The results just described indicate that specific magnetic fields elicit orientation responses in hatchlings on the first occasion that turtles encounter them. These responses therefore appear to be fully functional when the turtles first emerge from their nests. Indeed, this may be essential because young turtles swept out of the warm waters of the gyre usually die before they can regain entry (Carr 1986; Hays and Marsh 1997). Thus, turtles probably cannot learn to recognize dangerous geographic areas because entering such regions is, in itself, fatal. Instead, responses that help young turtles avoid perilous areas probably must be inherited.

Courtillot et al. (1997) suggested that functionally useful responses to specific regional fields are unlikely to evolve because of secular variation (the change in field elements such as inclination and intensity that occurs over time). This argument, however, fails to consider how evolutionary processes sculpt behavior as an environment changes. The earth's field does indeed change, but strong selective pressure presumably acts to ensure a continuous match between the responses of hatchlings and the fields that mark critical boundaries at any point in time

(Lohmann and Lohmann 1998; Lohmann et al. 1999, 2001). For example, under present conditions in the North Atlantic, natural selection presumably removes from the population those young Florida loggerheads that stray out of the gyre, while favoring those with orientation responses that keep them safely inside. As the magnetic values marking the gyre boundaries change, turtles that fail to respond "correctly" to the new field conditions will be quickly eliminated and replaced by other turtles with slightly different responses that enhance the likelihood of survival under the new conditions. Only the genes of the surviving turtles will be passed on, and in this way the responses of hatchlings may evolve in parallel with the continuously changing field.

Several similar elements of orientation and migratory behavior are under genetic control and have been shown to evolve rapidly. For example, part of the central European population of a migratory bird, the blackcap *Sylvia atricapilla*, evolved an entirely new migration route to the British Isles within only three decades (Berthold et al. 1992). The direction of first migration appears to be encoded by at most a few genes (Helbig 1991, 1996), and the new route appears to be based on a genetically programmed west-northwesterly orientation preference that is spreading rapidly through the population (Berthold et al. 1992; Helbig 1996). Crossbreeding experiments with blackcaps from nonmigratory and migratory populations have also demonstrated that both the urge to migrate and the direction of orientation can be transmitted quickly and easily into a nonmigratory population (Berthold et al. 1990). These examples, and many others (Brower 1996; Dingle 1996; Terrill 1991), highlight the evolutionary flexibility of migratory adaptations and the rapidity with which changes in orientation behavior can arise.

These considerations aside, responses to region-specific magnetic fields might be rendered useless during the limited periods of exceedingly rapid field change that sometimes accompany polarity reversals of the earth's field. Such transient periods of rapid change, however, do not preclude the evolution of magnetic responses during the intervening and usually longer intervals (Skiles 1985) when the earth's field changes slowly and is relatively stable. In the same way, numerous periods of rapid climate change over evolutionary time have not prevented animals from evolving adaptations to specific climates, even though such adaptations may be rendered useless or harmful when the climate changes again. Thus, nothing intrinsic in secular variation, and nothing about polarity reversals, precludes sea turtles or other long-distance migrants from evolving behavioral responses that exploit the positional information inherent in the earth's magnetic field.

Conservation Implications

The responses of hatchling loggerheads to regional magnetic fields have presumably been favored by natural selection because they increase survivorship in the specific geographic regions in which the turtles live and migrate. For young Florida loggerheads, the warm waters of the North Atlantic gyre provide an open-ocean refuge favorable for growth and survival. Loggerheads in different parts of the world, however, have different developmental habitats and follow different migratory routes. Those that hatch in Japan, for example, enter the Pacific gyre system and are thought to complete a circuit around the Pacific Ocean during their developmental years (Bowen et al. 1995). Thus, if regional magnetic fields function as open-sea navigational markers, then such markers are likely to be specific to particular oceanic basins and to particular migratory routes. Populations in different parts of the world should therefore be expected to have evolved different responses to different regional magnetic fields that mark critical boundaries unique to the migratory route of each group.

These considerations have clear implications for conservation practices. For example, one should not be surprised if hatchlings from one part of the world are unable to adopt an appropriate migratory route when introduced to another location far away. Hatchlings translocated from the geographic region in which their recent ancestors evolved will presumably lack inherited orientation responses that coincide with the magnetic landmarks of the new area. This deficit in inherited navigational information may prevent young turtles from remaining in appropriate developmental areas or from moving reliably along a suitable migratory route.

In this context, the authors note that an extensive effort to reestablish a nesting colony of green turtles in Bermuda failed, even though thousands of eggs and hatchlings were transported to Bermuda from Costa Rica over a period of years (Eliazar et al. 1998; Mrosovsky 1983). Although numerous factors might have contributed to the failure, one that has not been considered before is that the Costa Rican hatchlings might have inherited navigational instructions specific for the Caribbean region and therefore were poorly suited for a geographic area so far from their normal range. If so, then similar efforts to reestablish an eradicated nesting colony by transplanting eggs or hatchlings from one location to another may fail whenever the normal migratory route of the introduced turtles differs significantly from that of the eradicated group.

Conclusions

Considerable progress has been made in unraveling the directional cues that guide hatchling loggerheads from the eastern coast of Florida to the Gulf Stream. An important caveat, however, is that detailed studies have been carried out only with hatchlings from southern Florida. Thus, whether the mechanisms outlined in this chapter are generally applicable to loggerhead populations in other parts of the world is not known. Different mechanisms, or perhaps different uses of the same cues, appear likely to exist among sea turtles that nest in different ecological settings. For example, whereas Florida hatchlings need to maintain only a single, consistent heading from the nest to the Gulf Stream, a different pattern might exist among populations that nest on island beaches. In such settings, following a straight-line course away from the beach would lead hatchlings emerging on opposite sides of an island toward very different directions and might result in at least some turtles moving away from appropriate developmental habitats. How hatchlings that emerge on islands guide themselves has not yet been investigated.

In comparison to our knowledge of the mechanisms guiding offshore migration, our understanding of open-ocean navigation in sea turtles is still in its infancy. Young turtles can distinguish between different regional magnetic fields and apparently exploit the positional information inherent in such cues. However, given that all migratory animals studied to date use multiple sources of information to orient and navigate (Able 1991, 1993; Gould 1998), additional directional or positional cues might also play a role in guiding young loggerheads along their open-sea migratory route.

ACKNOWLEDGMENTS

We thank Mike Salmon and Jeanette Wyneken for their stimulating collaboration and discussion and for making their laboratory facilities in Florida available to us. We are also grateful to our many graduate and undergraduate student assistants for their help in all aspects of the work, and to Jay Callaway for his expertise in electronics. Research on threatened and endangered species was authorized under Florida DEP special permit TP 065. The work has been supported by grants from the National Science Foundation (IBN-9120338, IBN-9419993, and IBN-9816065) and by funding from the University of North Carolina.

LITERATURE CITED

Able, K. P. 1991. Common themes and variations in animal orientation systems. American Zoologist 31:157–167.

Able, K. P. 1993. Orientation cues used by migratory birds: A review of cue-conflict experiments. Trends in Ecology and Evolution 8:367–371.

Adamany, S. L., M. Salmon, and B. E. Witherington. 1997. Behavior of sea turtles at an urban beach. III. Costs and benefits of nest caging as a management strategy. Florida Scientist 60:239–253.

Baker, R. R. 1984. Bird navigation: The solution of a mystery? London: Hodder and Stoughton.

———. 1993. The function of post-fledging exploration: A pilot study of three passerines ringed in Britain. Ornis Scandinavica 24:71–79.

Berthold, P., W. Wiltschko, H. Miltenberger, and U. Querner. 1990. Genetic transmission of migratory behavior into a nonmigratory bird population. Experientia 46:107–108.

Berthold, P., A. J. Helbig, G. Mohr, and U. Querner. 1992. Rapid microevolution of migratory behaviour in a wild bird species. Nature 360:668–670.

Bolten, A. B., H. R. Martins, K. A. Bjorndal, and J. Gordon. 1994. Size distribution of pelagic-stage loggerhead sea turtles (Caretta caretta) in the waters around the Azores and Madeira. Arquipelago 11A:49–54.

Bolten, A. B., K. A. Bjorndal, H. R. Martins, T. Dellinger, M. J. Biscoito, S. E. Encalada, and B. W. Bowen. 1998. Transatlantic developmental migrations of loggerhead sea turtles demonstrated by mtDNA sequence analysis. Ecological Applications 8:1–7.

Bowen, B. W., F. A. Abreu-Grobois, G. H. Balazs, N. Kamezaki, C. J. Limpus, and R. J. Ferl. 1995. Trans-Pacific migrations of the loggerhead turtle (Caretta caretta) demonstrated with mitochondrial DNA markers. Proceedings of the National Academy of Sciences 92:3731–3734.

Brower, L. P. 1996. Monarch butterfly orientation: Missing pieces of a magnificent puzzle. Journal of Experimental Biology 199:93–103.

Carr, A. 1963. Orientation problems in the high seas travel and terrestrial movements of marine turtles. In L. E. Slater (ed.). Bio-telemetry, 179–193. New York: MacMillan Company.

———. 1982. Notes on the behavioral ecology of sea turtles. In K. A. Bjorndal (ed.). Biology and conservation of sea turtles, 19–26. Washington, D.C.: Smithsonian Institution Press.

———. 1986. Rips, FADS, and little loggerheads. Bioscience 36:92–100.

———. 1987. New perspectives on the pelagic stage of sea turtle development. Conservation Biology 1:103–121.

Carr, A., and L. Ogren. 1960. The ecology and migrations of sea turtles. 4. The green turtle in the Caribbean Sea. Bulletin of the American Museum of Natural History 121:7–48.

Cook, P. H. 1984. Directional information from surface swell: Some possibilities. In J. D. McLeave, G. P. Arnold, J. J. Dodson, and W. H. Neill (eds.). Mechanisms of migration in fishes, 79–101. New York: Plenum Press.

Courtillot, V., G. Hulot, M. Alexandrescu, J.-L. LeMouel, and J. L. Kirschvink. 1997. Sensitivity and evolution of sea-turtle magnetoreception: Observations, modelling and constraints from geomagnetic secular variation. Terra Nova 9:203–207.

Daniel, R. S., and K. U. Smith. 1947. The sea-approach of the neonate loggerhead turtle

(Caretta caretta). Journal of Comparative Physiology and Psychology 40:413–420.

Denny, M. W. 1988. Biology and the mechanics of the wave-swept environment. Princeton, N.J.: Princeton University Press.

Dingle, H. 1996. Migration. New York: Oxford University Press.

Ehrenfeld, D. W. 1968. The role of vision in the sea-finding orientation of the green turtle *(Chelonia mydas)*. 2. Orientation mechanism and range of spectral sensitivity. Animal Behaviour 16:281–287.

Ehrenfeld, D. W., and A. L. Koch. 1967. Visual accommodation in the green turtle. Science 155:827–828.

Eliazar, P. J., K. A. Bjorndal, and A. B. Bolten. 1998. Operation Green Turtle revisited. *In* R. Byles and Y. Fernandez (compilers). Proceedings of the 16th annual symposium on sea turtle biology and conservation, 43. NOAA Technical Memorandum NMFS-SEFSC-412.

Goff, M., M. Salmon, and K. J. Lohmann. 1998. Hatchling sea turtles use surface waves to establish a magnetic compass direction. Animal Behavior 55:69–77.

Gould, J. L. 1985. Are animal maps magnetic? *In* J. L. Kirschvink, D. S. Jones, and B. J. MacFadden (eds.). Magnetite biomineralization and magnetoreception in organisms, 257–268. New York: Plenum Press.

Gould, J. L. 1998. Sensory bases of navigation. Current Biology 8:R731–R738.

Gross, M. G. 1977. Oceanography. Englewood Cliffs, N.J.: Prentice Hall, Inc.

Hays, G. C., and R. Marsh. 1997. Estimating the age of juvenile loggerhead sea turtles in the North Atlantic. Canadian Journal of Zoology 75:40–46.

Helbig, A. J. 1991. Inheritance of migratory direction in a bird species: A cross-breeding experiment with SE- and SW-migrating blackcaps *(Sylvia atricapilla)*. Behavioral Ecology and Sociobiology 28:9–12.

———. 1996. Genetic basis, mode of inheritance and evolutionary changes of migratory directions in palearctic warblers (Aves: Sylviidae). Journal of Experimental Biology 199:49–55.

Kingsmill, S. F., and N. Mrosovsky. 1982. Sea-finding behaviour of loggerhead hatchlings: The time course of transient circling following unilateral and asynchronous bilateral blindfolding. Brain Behavior and Evolution 20:29–42.

Kirschvink, J. L. 1992. Uniform magnetic fields and double-wrapped coil systems: Improved techniques for the design of bioelectromagnetic experiments. Bioelectromagnetics 13:401–411.

Light, P., M. Salmon, and K. J. Lohmann. 1993. Geomagnetic orientation of loggerhead sea turtles: Evidence for an inclination compass. Journal of Experimental Biology 182:1–10.

Limpus, C. J. 1971. Sea turtle ocean finding behaviour. Search 2:385–387.

Limpus, C. J., J. D. Miller, C. J. Parmenter, D. Reimer, N. McLachland, and R. Webb. 1992. Migration of green *(Chelonia mydas)* and loggerhead *(Caretta caretta)* turtles to and from eastern Australian rookeries. Wildlife Research 19:347–358.

Lohmann, K. J. 1991. Magnetic orientation by hatchling loggerhead sea turtles *(Caretta caretta)*. Journal of Experimental Biology 155:37–49.

———. 1992. How sea turtles navigate. Scientific American 266:100–106.

Lohmann, K. J., and S. Johnsen. 2000. The neurobiology of magnetoreception in vertebrate animals. Trends in Neuroscience 23:153–159.

Lohmann, K. J., and C. M. F. Lohmann. 1992. Orientation to oceanic waves by green turtle hatchlings. Journal of Experimental Biology 171:1–13.

———. 1993. A light-independent magnetic compass in the leatherback sea turtle. Biological Bulletin 185:149–151.

———. 1994a. Acquisition of magnetic directional preference in hatchling loggerhead sea turtles. Journal of Experimental Biology 190:1–8.

———. 1994b. Detection of magnetic inclination angle by sea turtles: A possible mechanism for determining latitude. Journal of Experimental Biology 194:23–32.

———. 1996a. Orientation and open-sea navigation in sea turtles. Journal of Experimental Biology 199:73–81.

———. 1996b. Detection of magnetic field intensity by sea turtles. Nature 380:59–61.

———. 1998. Migratory guidance mechanisms in marine turtles. Journal of Avian Biology 29:585–596.

Lohmann, K. J., M. Salmon, and J. Wyneken. 1990. Functional autonomy of land and sea orientation systems in sea turtle hatchlings. Biological Bulletin 179:214–218.

Lohmann, K. J., A. W. Swartz, and C. M. F. Lohmann. 1995. Perception of ocean wave direction by sea turtles. Journal of Experimental Biology 198:1079–1085.

Lohmann, K. J., B. E. Witherington, C. M. F. Lohmann, and M. Salmon. 1997. Orientation, navigation, and natal beach homing in sea turtles. *In* P. L. Lutz, and J. A. Musick (eds.). The biology of sea turtles, 107–135. Boca Raton, Fla.: CRC Press.

Lohmann, K. J., J. T. Hester, and C. M. F. Lohmann. 1999. Long-distance navigation in sea turtles. Ethology, Ecology, and Evolution 11:1–23.

Lohmann, K. J., S. D. Cain, S. A. Dodge, and C. M. F. Lohmann. 2001. Regional magnetic fields as navigational markers for sea turtles. Science 294:364–366.

Luschi, P., F. Papi, H. C. Liew, E. H. Chan, and F. Bonadonna. 1996. Long-distance migration and homing after displacement in the green turtle (Chelonia mydas): A satellite tracking study. Journal of Comparative Physiology A 178:447–452.

Manning, E. L., H. S. Cate, and K. J. Lohmann. 1997. Discrimination of ocean wave features by hatchling sea turtles. Marine Biology 127:539–544.

Merritt, R., C. Purcell, and G. Stroink. 1983. Uniform magnetic fields produced by three, four, and five square coils. Review of Scientific Instruments 54:879–882.

Mrosovsky, N. 1967. How turtles find the sea. Science Journal 3:2–7.

———. 1968. Nocturnal emergence of sea turtles: Control by thermal inhibition of activity. Nature 220:1338–1339.

———. 1972. The water-finding ability of sea turtles; behavioral studies and physiological speculations. Brain Behavior and Evolution 5:202–225.

———. 1978. Orientation mechanisms of marine turtles. In K. Schmidt-Koenig and W. T. Keeton (eds.). Animal migration, navigation, and homing, 413–419. Berlin: Springer-Verlag.

———. 1983. Conserving sea turtles. London: British Herpetological Society.

Mrosovsky, N., and S. F. Kingsmill. 1985. How turtles find the sea. Zeitschrift fuer Tierpsychologie 67:237–256.

Mrosovsky, N., and S. J. Shettleworth. 1968. Wavelength preferences and brightness cues in the water finding behavior of sea turtles. Behaviour 32:211–257.

Musick, J. A., and C. J. Limpus. 1997. Habitat utilization and migration in juvenile sea turtles. In P. L. Lutz and J. A. Musick (eds.). The biology of sea turtles, 137–163. Boca Raton, Fla.: CRC Press.

Parker, G. H. 1922. The crawling of young loggerhead turtles toward the sea. Journal of Experimental Zoology 36:323–331.

Quinn, T. P. 1984. An experimental approach to fish compass and map orientation. In J. D. McLeave, G. P. Arnold, J. J. Dodson, and W. H. Neill (eds.). Mechanisms of migration in fishes, 113–123. New York: Plenum Press.

Salmon, M., and K. J. Lohmann. 1989. Orientation cues used by hatchling loggerhead sea turtles (Caretta caretta) during their offshore migration. Ethology 83:215–228.

Salmon, M., and B. E. Witherington. 1995. Artificial lighting and seafinding by loggerhead hatchlings: Evidence for lunar modulation. Copeia 1995:931–938.

Salmon, M., and J. Wyneken. 1987. Orientation and swimming behavior of hatchling loggerhead turtles (Caretta caretta L.) during their offshore migration. Journal of Experimental Marine Biology and Ecology 109:137–153.

———. 1994. Orientation by hatchling sea turtles: Mechanisms and implications. Herpetological Natural History 2(1): 13–24.

Salmon, M., J. Wyneken, E. Fritz, and M. Lucas. 1992. Seafinding by hatchling sea turtles: Role of brightness, silhouette and beach slope as orientation cues. Behaviour 122:56–77.

Sears, C. J., B. W. Bowen, R. W. Chapman, S. B. Galloway, S. R. Hopkins-Murphy, and C. M. Woodley. 1995. Demographic composition of the feeding population of juvenile loggerhead sea turtles (Caretta caretta) off Charleston, South Carolina: Evidence from mitochondrial DNA markers. Marine Biology 123:869–874.

Skiles, D. 1985. The geomagnetic field: Its nature, history, and biological relevance. In J. L. Kirschvink, D. S. Jones, and B. J. MacFadden (eds.). Magnetite biomineralization and magnetoreception in organisms, 43–102. New York: Plenum Press.

Terrill, S. B. 1991. Evolutionary aspects of orientation and migration in birds. In P. Berthold (ed.). Orientation in birds, 180–201. Basel, Switzerland: Birkhäuser Verlag.

van Rhijn, F. A. 1979. Optic orientation in hatchlings of the sea turtle (Chelonia mydas). 1. Brightness: Not the only optic cue in sea-finding orientation. Marine Behaviour and Physiology 6:105–121.

Verheijen, F. J., and J. T. Wildschut. 1973. The photic orientation of hatchling sea turtles during water finding behaviour. Netherlands Journal of Sea Research 7:53–67.

Wang, J. H., J. K. Jackson, and K. J. Lohmann. 1998. Perception of wave surge motion by hatchling sea turtles. Journal of Experimental Marine Biology and Ecology 229:177–186.

Wiltschko, R., and W. Wiltschko. 1995. Magnetic orientation in animals. Berlin: Springer.

———. 1998. The navigation of birds and its development. In R. P. Balda, I. M. Pepperberg, and A. C. Kamil (eds.). Animal cognition in nature, 155–199. San Diego: Academic Press.

Wiltschko, W., and R. Wiltschko. 1972. Magnetic compass of European robins. Science 176:62–64.

———. 1988. Magnetic orientation in birds. *In* R. F. Johnston (ed.). Current ornithology, vol. 5, 67–121. New York: Plenum Press.

Witherington, B. E. 1992. Sea-finding behavior and the use of photic orientation cues by hatchling sea turtles. Ph.D. dissertation, University of Florida, Gainesville.

———. 1995. Observations of hatchling loggerhead turtles during the first few days of the lost year(s). *In* J. I. Richardson and T. H. Richardson (compilers). Proceedings of the 12th annual sea turtle workshop on sea turtle biology and conservation, 154–157. NOAA Technical Memorandum NMFS-SEFSC-361.

———. 1997. The problem of photopollution for sea turtles and other nocturnal animals. *In* J. R. Clemmons and R. Buchholz (eds.). Behavioral approaches to conservation in the wild, 303–328. Cambridge, U.K.: Cambridge University Press.

Witherington, B. E., and R. E. Martin. 2000. Understanding, assessing, and resolving light-pollution problems on sea turtle nesting beaches, rev. 2nd ed. Florida Marine Research Institute Technical Report TR-2.

Witherington, B. E., K. A. Bjorndal, and C. M. McCabe. 1990. Temporal pattern of nocturnal emergence of loggerhead turtle hatchlings from natural nests. Copeia 1990:1165–1168.

Wyneken, J., M. Salmon, and K. J. Lohmann. 1990. Orientation by hatchling loggerhead sea turtles *Caretta caretta* L. in a wave tank. Journal of Experimental Marine Biology and Ecology 139:43–50.

Chapter 4

Active Swimmers—Passive Drifters:

The Oceanic Juvenile Stage of Loggerheads in the Atlantic System

—Alan B. Bolten

The life history of loggerhead sea turtles can be studied as a series of ontogenetic habitat shifts. These ecological and geographic shifts, sometimes spanning thousands of kilometers, have at best been a challenge and at times an obstacle to our understanding of sea turtle biology. This is particularly true for posthatchling sea turtles. Loggerhead hatchlings (5 cm carapace length) leave nesting beaches in the western Atlantic (primarily in the southeastern United States), enter the ocean, and are not seen again in coastal waters of the western Atlantic until they are about half grown at 50 cm in carapace length. This life stage from hatching to the 50 cm juvenile has been called the "lost year" (Bolten and Balazs 1995; Carr 1986) and is the focus of this chapter. The chapter will concentrate on the North Atlantic loggerhead population(s); examples from the Mediterranean, the Indian Ocean, and the Pacific will be presented when available.

Tremendous progress has been made in un-

derstanding the "lost year" life stage since Archie Carr's classic publication "Rips, FADS, and Little Loggerheads" in 1986. Our progress has been a result of both increased research efforts in the natural history of this life stage and development of new research tools. The most important tools have come from the fields of biotechnology (e.g., genetic markers to identify populations and movements); biotelemetry (e.g., remote tracking and sensing technologies to evaluate movements and distribution patterns); and computer science (e.g., development of the personal computer has facilitated statistical modeling and demographic and ecological analyses).

Terminology

There is inconsistency in the use of oceanographic terms in the sea turtle literature. This is particularly evident in the discussions of the oceanic juvenile stage. I have been among those guilty of misuse of terms (e.g., Bjorndal et al. 2000a; Bolten and Balazs 1995; Bolten et al. 1993). As more research is conducted in the ocean away from nesting beaches, researchers should be consistent in their descriptive terms and should use accepted oceanographic terminology.

To describe the early juvenile stage of sea turtles as the pelagic stage or the older juvenile stage as the benthic stage does not correctly communicate the ecological and physical oceanographic associations for these life stages. According to standard oceanographic terminology (Lalli and Parsons 1993), the terms "oceanic stage" and "neritic stage" should be used.

The oceanic zone is the vast open ocean environment where bottom depths are greater than 200 m. The neritic zone describes the inshore marine environment (from the surface to the bottom) where bottom depths do not exceed 200 m. The neritic zone generally includes the continental shelf, but in areas where the continental shelf is very narrow or nonexistent, the neritic zone conventionally extends to areas where bottom depths are less than 200 m (Lalli and Parsons 1993).

Organisms are pelagic if they occupy the water column, but not the bottom, in either the neritic zone or the oceanic zone. Organisms are epipelagic if they occupy the upper 200 m in the oceanic zone. Organisms on the bottom in either the neritic zone or the oceanic zone are described as benthic or demersal. Therefore, organisms can be pelagic in shallow coastal (neritic) waters or in the deep open ocean (oceanic). Likewise, organisms can be benthic in shallow coastal waters as well as in the deep ocean. Descriptions of sea turtle life stages should be consistent. The early juvenile stage found in the open ocean should be the oceanic stage, not the pelagic stage, and the later juvenile stage found in coastal waters should be the neritic stage, not the benthic stage.

Life Stages

As with the terminology used to describe the association of sea turtles with the ocean realm, there has been inconsistency in the use of terms to describe the life stages of the loggerhead sea turtle. Some of this confusion has resulted from mixing the use of habitat descriptions with life stages and the use of imprecise terms to describe life stages.

The general life stages of the Atlantic loggerhead sea turtle and the habitats they occupy are diagrammed in Figure 4.1 and discussed below. A comparison of Figure 4.1 with earlier life history diagrams (Carr 1986; Musick and Limpus 1997) demonstrates how much has been learned about the early developmental stages of loggerhead sea turtles.

Eggs, Embryos, and Hatchling Stage—Terrestrial Zone

The life cycle begins with oviposition on the nesting beach—the habitat for the egg, embryo, and early hatchling stage. Characteristics of the nesting beach environment have been reviewed by Ackerman (1997) and Carthy et al. (Chapter 9 this volume), and nest site selection has been reviewed by Miller et al. (Chapter 8 this volume). Bjorndal (Chapter 15 this volume) and Bouchard and Bjorndal (2000) present data on the flow of nutrients between the nest and the beach environment and on the effects of loggerhead nesting on the nesting beach ecosystem. After embryonic development, little turtles hatch from eggs, emerge from the nest (Moran et al. 1999), and actively orient and move rapidly to the sea (Lohmann and Lohmann, Chapter 3 this volume).

Hatchling Swim Frenzy Stage—Neritic Zone

The hatchling stage (or neonate stage) continues in the near-shore waters and is of short duration (days). The hatchlings go through an active swimming period known as the "swim frenzy" (Wyneken and Salmon 1992), orient relative to wave direction, and maintain orientation relative to the earth's magnetic field (Lohmann and Lohmann, Chapter 3 this volume). The "swim frenzy" is thought to bring the hatchlings to the major offshore currents.

The hatchling stage describes recently hatched individuals that are in the nest chamber prior to emergence from the nest, on the beach, or in the sea (hatchling swim frenzy stage). Hatchlings are nutritionally dependent on the

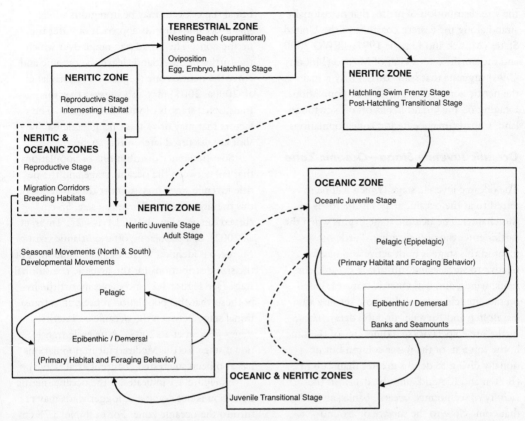

Figure 4.1. Life cycle diagram of the Atlantic loggerhead sea turtle. Boxes represent life stages and the corresponding ecosystems. Solid lines represent movements between life stages and ecosystems; dotted lines are speculative.

remains of their yolk; this is primarily a prefeeding stage. The hatchling stage ends when the turtles begin to feed.

Post-hatchling Transitional Stage— Neritic Zone

The posthatchling transitional stage begins when the turtles begin to feed, often while still in the neritic zone. Turtles in this stage live at or near the surface. This transitional stage ends when the turtles enter the oceanic zone. The posthatchling transitional stage may not be marked by a major behavioral shift or a functional change in ecological role, but rather by a change in location—from the neritic to the oceanic zone. In the western Atlantic, this would be where the Gulf Stream–Azores current system leaves the continental shelf. Off the coast of South Africa, it is the Agulhas current (Hughes 1974). This transitional stage can take

days, weeks, or months depending on the stochasticity of surface currents and winds that either facilitate or inhibit the posthatchlings from reaching the oceanic zone (Witherington 2002, in review a). Although the resultant geographic movements of the turtles may be primarily passive relative to the currents and winds, the posthatchlings actively swim and orient within the currents, increasing their chances of survival and the probability of reaching the oceanic zone (Lohmann and Lohmann, Chapter 3 this volume; Witherington, in review a).

There may be a small percentage of the population that never leaves the neritic zone (Figure 4.1). The existence of this phenomenon is speculative. For one reason or another, probably by pure stochastic events, these individuals may never enter the major current systems and, if they survive, may go through their juvenile development entirely within the neritic zone. There is no direct evidence for this except that the size distribution of turtles that occasionally strand along the eastern coastline of the United States (Musick and Limpus 1997; TEWG 2000) and the northwestern Gulf of Mexico (Plotkin 1996) suggests that some turtles may remain in the neritic zone. Also, the juvenile populations foraging on the Grand Banks off of Newfoundland, Canada, may be neritic zone populations.

Oceanic Juvenile Stage—Oceanic Zone

The oceanic juvenile stage (which will be referred to as the oceanic stage) is the focus of this chapter. The oceanic stage begins when the turtles enter the oceanic zone. Turtle movement in this stage is both active and passive relative to surface and subsurface oceanic currents, winds, and bathymetric features (based on satellite telemetry and remote sensing studies; Bolten and Riewald, unpubl. data). These turtles are epipelagic, spending 75% of the time in the top 5 m of the water column but occasionally diving to depths greater than 200 m (Bolten and Riewald, unpubl. data). In the vicinity of seamounts, oceanic banks, and ridges that come close to the surface or around oceanic islands, loggerheads may become epibenthic/demersal by feeding or spending time on the bottom. In the Atlantic, turtles leave the oceanic zone over a wide size range, and as a result, the duration of the oceanic juvenile stage ranges between 6.5 and 11.5 years (Bjorndal et al. 2000a). The causes for the variation in duration of this stage are not known, but may depend on the location of the turtles in the oceanic zone and available currents, food resources, or other cues.

Juvenile Transitional Stage—Oceanic and Neritic Zones

The ontogenetic shift from the oceanic to the neritic zone is a dramatic one, and as such, there is probably a period of transition, perhaps in both behavior and morphology. Kamezaki and Matsui (1997) discuss specific allometric relationships that change during the juvenile transitional stage that they suggest are related to changes in foraging behavior (epipelagic vs. benthic).

The geographic regions where the transitional stages occur may be in regions where major oceanic currents approach or enter the neritic zone. The broad size range over which the turtles in the Atlantic leave the oceanic and enter the neritic zone (Figure 4.2; Bjorndal et al. 2000a, 2001) may also suggest that this transitional stage is of variable duration. The factors that may drive this ontogenetic habitat shift are discussed later in this chapter.

Size-frequency distributions of populations that fall between the oceanic stage and the neritic juvenile stage may support the existence of this transitional stage. The mean size, 53 cm curved carapace length (CCL) (n = 27; Tiwari et al. 2002), of a population off the Atlantic coast of Morocco is identical to the estimated midpoint of the size distributions for the juvenile transitional stage (see Figure 4.2) and may support the hypothesis that this population represents a transitional stage between the oceanic and neritic stages (Tiwari et al. 2002). A juvenile transitional stage for the Mediterranean populations has also been suggested (Laurent et al. 1998).

As Figure 4.1 indicates, if the oceanic-neritic transition is not complete, loggerheads may return to the oceanic zone. For example, a 78 cm loggerhead tagged along the eastern coast of Florida was recaptured in the Azores (Eckert and Martins 1989). Also, if juvenile loggerheads make multiple loops in the Atlantic gyre system rather than a single developmental loop, this could result in periodic movements between the oceanic and neritic zones.

Neritic Juvenile Stage and Adult Foraging Stage—Neritic Zone

The neritic juvenile stage and adult foraging stage occur in the neritic zone. The turtles are active and feed primarily on the bottom (epibenthic/demersal), although they do capture prey throughout the water column (Bjorndal, Chapter 15 this volume). In temperate areas there may be seasonal movements among foraging grounds, but in tropical areas the turtles may not show distinct temporal movement patterns. Depending on geographic region and population, the neritic juvenile stage and the adult foraging stage may occupy the same habitats, or different size classes may be

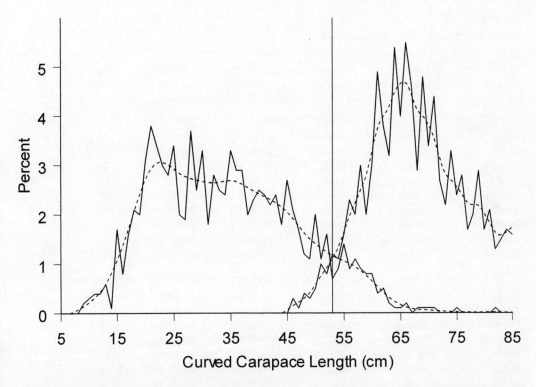

Figure 4.2. Size-frequency distributions of oceanic stage loggerheads captured in waters around the Azores (left-hand curves, n = 1692) and neritic stage loggerheads stranded in the southeastern United States (right-hand curves, n = 1803) (modified from Bjorndal et al. 2000a, 2001). Percentages were calculated for each population. Dashed lines are the cubic smoothing splines (df = 15); vertical reference line at the intersection of the two smooth curves at 53 cm curved carapace length (CCL).

distributed differentially by water depth. This life stage is reviewed for the Atlantic by Schroeder et al. (Chapter 7 this volume) and for the Pacific by Limpus and Limpus (Chapter 6 this volume).

Reproductively mature adults leave these foraging habitats to migrate to breeding habitats and may use specific migratory corridors. Depending on geographic region, these migratory corridors may take the turtles out of the neritic zone and through the oceanic zone before returning to the neritic zone in the vicinity of the nesting beach. In other geographic regions, the migratory corridors may be entirely within the neritic zone.

Oceanic Juvenile Stage Loggerheads

Identification of Source Rookeries

The question asked by sea turtle biologists, "Where do the hatchling turtles go when they leave the nesting beach?" is the reciprocal of the question asked by early explorers and sailors: "Where do the little loggerheads found in the open ocean come from?" In the late 19th century, Prince Albert the First of Monaco (1898) wrote that Azorean turtles (oceanic stage) must have come from the "Antilles ou Floride," transported by the Gulf Stream. Brongersma (1972) also suggested that the little turtles in the eastern Atlantic came from the western Atlantic rookeries. Carr (1986) and later Bolten et al. (1993) used the comparison of size-frequency distributions to suggest that the little loggerheads found in the oceanic zone around the Azores were an earlier life stage of the larger turtles in the neritic waters of the western Atlantic. The relationship between the little loggerheads in the oceanic zone and the larger sized neritic loggerheads in the western Atlantic was further supported by a flipper tagging program managed by the Archie Carr Center for

Table 4.1.
Locations of Recaptured Loggerheads

Tag Number	Capture Location	Recapture Location	Capture Date (DD-MM-YY)	Recapture Date (DD-MM-YY)	CCL 1 (cm)	CCL 2 (cm)
A. Turtles Initially Captured and Recaptured in the Oceanic Zone in the Waters around the Azores						
BP701	Azores	Azores	12-06-89	27-08-89	45.8	—
BP624	Azores	Azores	15-06-89	21-09-91	41.0	52.0
A3913	Azores	Azores	20-07-90	16-11-90	52	52.5
BP683	Azores	Azores	28-08-91	21-12-94	60.4	70.9
BP2764	Azores	Azores	30-01-93	15-07-94	69.1	—
BP2774	Azores	Azores	06-08-93	04-08-95	53.5	—
A6001	Azores	Azores	08-07-94	12-08-96	35	—
N8082	Azores	Azores	30-06-97	28-08-97	53	—
BP3092	Azores	Azores	22-09-97	07-10-97	48.1	—
B. Turtles Initially Captured in the Oceanic Zone and Recaptured in a Different Geographic Location						
K5583[a]	Azores	Sicily	14-07-86	26-08-91	19.3	42.0
K5781[b]	Canaries	Cuba	13-06-87	14-11-87	—	—
BP2267[c]	Madeira	Canaries	29-06-90	04-02-93	40.5	49.8
AW3803	Mediterranean	FL, USA	28-07-90	15-05-94	—	—
A7951	Azores	NC, USA	14-05-91	17-11-95	45.0	74.0
A8006	Azores	Nicaragua	15-06-91	23-01-00[d]	56	—
A7710	Azores	Cuba	18-06-91	26-02-94	46	—
BP2151	Azores	Nicaragua	11-07-91	13-12-96[d]	50.5	—
A4821	Azores	NC, USA	10-05-92	23-06-96	28.0	48.0
A4837	Azores	Spain	30-06-92	15-11-95	26.0	42.0
N7869	Azores	Morocco	26-06-96	28-07-00	23	—
N5921	Azores	FL, USA	08-08-96	06-19-98	64.0	69.6

Note 1: CCL 1 and CCL 2 refer to curved carapace length at initial capture and recapture, respectively. Turtles are listed in order by initial capture date. NC = North Carolina; FL = Florida.

Note 2: The following institutions and individuals assisted with tag return information: Archie Carr Center for Sea Turtle Research, University of Florida, U.S.A. (K. Bjorndal, P. Eliazar); Azorean commercial fishing fleets; Centro Oceanografico de Canarias, Spain (C. Santana); Centro Oceanografico de Malaga, Spain (J. Caminas); Donana National Park, Spain; Fernandina Beach, Florida Stranding Network; Fort Macon State Park, North Carolina, U.S.A. (R. Neuman); Greenpeace (Mediterranean Program); Instituto Espanol de Oceanografia, La Coruna, Spain (J. Mejuto); International Fund for Animal Welfare ("Song of the Whale," J. Gordon); Miskitu and Creole communities in Nicaragua; U.S. National Marine Fisheries Service, Beaufort, North Carolina, U.S.A. (J. Braun, S. Epperly); University of the Azores, Department of Oceanography and Fisheries, Horta, Portugal (H. Martins, C. Leal); University of Central Florida Turtle Research Group (L. Ehrhart, D. Bagley); World Wildlife Fund, Progetto Tartarughe, Roma, Italy (M. Cocco, G. Gerosa); K. Abdelkhalek; J. and G. Franck ("Shanghai"); S. Forman ("Cajun Girls"); C. Lagueux (Wildlife Conservation Society); L. Steiner; and S. Viallelle.

[a]Bolten et al. 1992a.

[b]Bolten et al. 1992b.

[c]Bjorndal et al. 1994

[d]Exact recapture date is not known; these are the last possible dates.

Sea Turtle Research at the University of Florida (Table 4.1; Bjorndal et al. 1994; Bolten et al. 1992a, 1992b). A number of turtles captured and tagged in the oceanic zone have been recaptured in the neritic zone of the western Atlantic (Table 4.1, B).

With the development of molecular genetic tools (e.g., mitochondrial DNA sequence analyses), the relative contributions of rookeries to mixed stocks of oceanic stage loggerheads could be evaluated (Bowen 1995, Chapter 1 this volume). After the Atlantic rookeries were genetically characterized (Encalada et al. 1998), Bolten et al. (1998) were able to demonstrate that the oceanic stage loggerheads in the waters around the Azores and Madeira were primarily from rookeries in the southeastern United States (90%) and Mexico (10%). Studies are currently under way with significantly larger sample sizes from the mixed oceanic stage populations (Bolten et al., unpubl. data), more complete rookery sampling (e.g., Cape Verde Islands; Luis Felipe et al., unpubl. data), and increased sampling of rookeries in the southeastern United States (Bjorndal et al., unpubl. data; Pearce 2001). These additional data will likely result in changes to the percentages of contributions from the specific rookeries, but the conclusion that the primary source rookeries for the Azorean-Madeiran populations are from the western Atlantic (primarily the southeastern United States) will probably continue to be supported (Bolten et al., unpubl. data). In addition, recent developments in statistical models for analyzing mixed stock composition will likely result in broader, and more realistic, confidence intervals for the point estimates of rookery contributions to foraging populations (Bolker et al., in press). Studies in the Pacific (Bowen et al. 1995) and Mediterranean (Laurent et al. 1993, 1998) also demonstrate the use of genetic markers as a tool to estimate contributions from rookeries to mixed foraging stocks in the oceanic zone.

The classic diagram of the oceanic currents and the movements of loggerhead turtles in the North Atlantic (Carr 1986, 1987a) leaving the rookeries of the western Atlantic, becoming entrained in the Gulf Stream–Azores current, traveling eastward to the Azores, Madeira, and the Canary Islands, and circling back to the western Atlantic in the North Atlantic gyre is well known. However, this scenario is an oversimplification of what is known of movements of loggerheads. Oceanic stage loggerheads spend 7–12 years in the waters around the Azores (see below; Bjorndal et al. 2000a) and may make only one transit rather than multiple loops. Also, based on flipper tag returns (Bolten et al. 1992a) and molecular genetic studies (Laurent et al. 1993, 1998), movement of small loggerheads from western Atlantic rookeries and Azorean waters into the western Mediterranean

is probably more common than originally thought. These loggerheads from the western Atlantic apparently leave the Mediterranean before they mature and reproduce (Laurent et al. 1998).

Genetic studies of other populations of oceanic stage loggerheads in the Atlantic are currently under way and will soon provide additional details to Carr's classic diagram. For example: What are the rookery sources of the aggregation of small loggerheads in the Grand Banks off Newfoundland, Canada, and in the Canary Islands? What are the relationships of these populations to the Azorean-Madeiran population? In addition, studies are underway to identify the rookery sources for the hypothesized oceanic-neritic transitional population off the coast of Morocco (Tiwari et al. 2002, unpubl. data).

Size-Frequency Distribution and Demography

Research conducted in the waters around the Azores during the last decade has provided the most thorough data on the size range, somatic growth rates, and duration of the oceanic stage. The size-frequency distribution of loggerheads in the waters around the Azores ranges from 8.5 to 82 cm curved carapace length (CCL) (see Figure 4.2; Bjorndal et al. 2000a). The size distribution is not significantly different from another nearby oceanic zone aggregation in the waters around Madeira (Bolten et al. 1993). Using length-frequency analyses with Multifan software, Bjorndal et al. (2000a) estimated the duration of the oceanic stage to be 6.5–11.5 years, depending on the size of the turtles when they leave the oceanic zone (46–64 cm CCL). Based on a skeletochronology study of neritic stage loggerheads, Snover et al. (2000) concluded that loggerheads are 52 cm straight carapace length (SCL) when they settle in the neritic zone off the eastern coast of the United States. This value of 52 cm SCL is similar to the value of 53 cm CCL at the intersection of the cubic smoothing splines of the size-frequency distributions of the oceanic and the neritic stages (see Figure 4.2), which is equivalent to 8.2 years duration in the oceanic stage (Bjorndal et al. 2000a).

The length-frequency analyses generated the following estimates of the von Bertalanffy growth model: K = 0.072 ± 0.003 yr^{-1} and asymptotic CCL (Linf) = 105.5 ± 2.7 cm (Bjorndal et al. 2000a). The size-specific growth rate function from length-frequency analyses is consistent with growth rates calculated from recaptures of tagged turtles (summarized in Bjorndal et al. 2000a).

Bjorndal et al. (in press a) have recently completed a skeletochronology analysis of oceanic stage loggerhead turtles from the waters around the Azores and Madeira and have found that the growth rates closely match the results from the length-frequency analyses. An important contribution of their study is the presentation of a size-at-age relationship for oceanic stage loggerheads. In addition, the skeletochronology analyses of the oceanic stage provide evidence for the first time of the phenomenon of compensatory growth in sea turtles. That is, turtles that are small for their age grow more rapidly and "catch up," resulting in reduced coefficients of variation for size-at-age with increasing age (Bjorndal et al., in press a). The authors conclude that compensatory growth may be a response to living in a stochastic environment.

Zug et al. (1995) evaluated the somatic growth rates of oceanic stage loggerheads in the Pacific using skeletochronology. The age-specific growth function for the Pacific was similar in shape to that for the Atlantic, but the growth rate was slower (Bjorndal et al., in press a). Using the same data set as Zug et al. (1995) but a different modeling approach, Chaloupka (1998) presented a polyphasic growth function for the Pacific oceanic stage.

The duration of the oceanic stage in the Pacific may be longer than that in the Atlantic based on the slower growth rates in the Pacific and the larger size (67 cm CCL) of the loggerheads that begin to recruit to the western Pacific neritic zone (Limpus and Limpus, Chapter 6 this volume) compared with the size (46 cm CCL) of those that begin to recruit to the western Atlantic neritic zone (see Figure 4.2; Bjorndal et al. 2000a, 2001). However, recent data from the eastern Pacific may suggest that the size at recruitment to the neritic zone in the Pacific may be similar to that in the Atlantic. Seminoff (2000) reports that loggerheads as small as 44 cm SCL begin to recruit to a neritic zone

foraging ground in the Gulf of California. The size reported by Seminoff (2000) is similar to the size (46 cm CCL) at which the Atlantic population begins to recruit to the neritic zone (see Figure 4.2; Bjorndal et al. 2000a, 2001). Are differences in individual sizes at recruitment to the neritic zone between eastern and western Pacific populations real, or do they reflect gaps in our knowledge of the Pacific loggerhead neritic juvenile populations? Extensive neritic foraging habitats in the western Pacific need to be surveyed to answer this question.

At present, there is not a good explanation for the differences in growth functions and growth rates between the oceanic stage loggerhead populations in the Atlantic and those in the Pacific. These differences, if real, may be based on nutritional differences between the two ocean basins. Interestingly, Atlantic-Pacific differences in growth function and size at recruitment to neritic habitats have also been reported for green turtles (Bjorndal et al. 2000b).

Estimates for survival probabilities for the oceanic stage are vital for the development of demographic models. Survival probabilities for the oceanic stage have been generated as fitted values in demographic models rather than as direct estimates (this volume: Chaloupka, Chapter 17; Heppell et al., Chapter 16). Catch-curve analyses can be used to estimate survival probabilities, but emigration and mortality are confounded. Bjorndal et al. (in press b) used catch-curve analyses to estimate survival probabilities of oceanic stage loggerheads in the waters around the Azores. At ages before loggerheads begin to emigrate from the oceanic zone (two to six years of age), the estimate of annual survival probability is 0.911; after emigration begins at seven years of age, the estimate of survival probability is 0.643.

In recent publications, Bjorndal et al. (2000a, in press a, in press b) have begun to derive some critical demographic values for the oceanic stage (e.g., size-at-age, somatic growth, survival probabilities, and stage duration) that can be used in the development of population models of loggerhead turtles. Prior to these publications, the duration of the "lost year" was unknown and was a serious gap for model development. Both demographic chapters in this volume incorporate these recent results (Chaloupka, Chapter 17; Heppell et al., Chapter 16). There is a great need for the quantification of sources of mortality from natural and anthropogenic (e.g., longline bycatch) causes. There may be differences in mortality between turtles from the nesting beaches in the northern region of the eastern coast of the United States and those from the southern region, as hypothesized by Hopkins-Murphy et al. (Chapter 5, this volume) and Heppell et al. (Chapter 16, this volume). To develop appropriate management and conservation plans, methods to assess relative population abundance and population trends for the oceanic stage are needed (Bjorndal and Bolten 2000).

Distribution, Movements, and Diving Behavior

In 1994, Bolten et al. (1996) and Bolten and Riewald (unpubl. data) began to use satellite telemetry to evaluate movement patterns of oceanic stage loggerheads. The primary objective at that time was to determine if oceanic stage loggerheads make multiple loops in the Atlantic gyre system or stay in the waters around the Azores until they reach the age or size to return to the neritic zone of the western Atlantic. That question has not been answered directly, but patterns of movement observed using satellite telemetry are consistent with residency in the oceanic zone around the Azores, not movement out of the region. In addition, long-term recaptures (see Table 4.1, A) of tagged oceanic stage loggerheads in Azorean waters suggest that in general, turtles do not make multiple loops in the Atlantic gyre during their oceanic stage but rather spend that developmental period in the waters around the Azores. The movement patterns reported for loggerheads in Madeiran waters (Dellinger and Freitas 2000) suggest that turtles in Madeira may be doing something different. This would not be surprising when one considers the differences in the oceanic currents and bathymetric features between the two regions.

Since 1994, Bolten and Riewald (unpubl. data) have instrumented 38 turtles with transmitters to determine patterns of movement and distribution relative to environmental features observed from remote sensing data (e.g., altimetry to evaluate currents, chlorophyll to assess areas of productivity, and sea surface temperature). In addition, transmitters with depth sensors were used to record diving behavior. Oceanic stage loggerheads spend 75% of the time in the top 5 m of the water column; 80% of dives are 2–5 m, and the remainder of the dives are distributed throughout the top 100 m of the water column; occasionally dives are greater than 200 m (Bolten and Riewald, unpubl. data). Turtles in Azorean waters travel at sustained speeds of about 0.2 m/s (Bolten and Riewald, unpubl. data).

In 1998 a satellite telemetry program was begun in Madeira (Dellinger and Freitas 2000). Dive parameters were recorded that were similar to those observed for turtles in Azorean waters by Bolten and Riewald (unpubl. data, see above). No correlation was observed between maximum dive depth and body size (Dellinger and Freitas 2000); however, the range of body size of the turtles instrumented with transmitters may not have been large enough to show this relationship.

The significant difference between the Dellinger study and the data collected by Bolten and Riewald is in the movement patterns of the turtles after release. Rather than demonstrating movements consistent with residency, as observed in Azorean waters, the turtles in the Madeiran study "actively swam long distances against prevalent currents" and moved away from the point of release primarily to the north and west (Dellinger and Freitas 2000). However, the conclusion that turtles swam against the current must be evaluated further because it is based on mean current movement patterns. Currents are highly variable at any location, and mean movement patterns may not be indicative of the current direction for a given location at a given time. Additionally, altimetry data used to describe mean current patterns do not have sufficient resolution to permit identification of smaller, local features (e.g., countercurrents). Major currents are often associated with adjacent countercurrents that may influence turtle movement. Countercurrents associated with the Azores current have been identified (Alves and de Verdiere 1999).

In the Pacific, George Balazs and colleagues have instrumented oceanic stage loggerheads with satellite transmitters primarily to determine the behavior and survivorship of turtles caught in longline fisheries. In a recent report they conclude that nine juvenile loggerheads caught in the longline fishery in the central North Pacific all traveled westward against prevailing currents (Polovina et al. 2000). This conclusion requires further examination because, as discussed above, satellite altimetry data do not have the resolution that this conclusion requires. Major currents may have countercurrents associated with them, and because of the accuracy of turtle positions and the resolution of the remote sensing data, one cannot rule out the possibility that the turtles were swimming/moving with the countercurrent.

Although there are differences in interpretation of results from satellite tracking data, it is clear that oceanic stage turtles may behave differently in different areas. In the Azores, turtle tracking data and flipper tag returns suggest a long period of residency, whereas turtles appear to be moving through Madeiran waters and are also nonresident in the regions of the Hawaiian study. This may not be surprising when one considers the physical oceanographic aspects of the regions. The Azorean region is characterized by a complexity of sea mounts, banks, and the Mid-Atlantic Ridge, which results in a complexity of eddies and convergent zones—prime habitats for the oceanic stage loggerheads.

Ontogenetic Habitat Shifts: Why Do Loggerheads Leave the Oceanic Zone?

As the "mystery of the lost year" unravels and researchers begin to understand where small loggerheads in the oceanic zone come from and how long they stay in that zone, the next questions are: Why (and how) do they leave the oceanic zone? Why does an animal that is finding food, growing, and surviving leave its habitat for a habitat with which it is almost totally unfamiliar—where it must learn to find new food sources and avoid a new suite of predators?

Werner and Gilliam (1984) reviewed the theoretical basis for ontogenetic habitat shifts and hypothesized that a species will shift habitats to maximize growth rates. Can this hypothesis be applied to the Atlantic loggerhead population living in the oceanic zone? If the size-specific growth function for the oceanic stage (Bjorndal et al. 2000a) is extrapolated and compared to that of the size-specific growth function for the neritic stage (Bjorndal et al. 2001), the lines intersect (slopes of each line are significantly different, $p < 0.001$; Figure 4.3). That is, for a given carapace length greater than approximately 64 cm (a size by which almost all of the loggerheads have left the oceanic zone; see Figure 4.2), growth rates will be greater in the neritic zone than in the oceanic zone. Additional support for this hypothesis comes from a skeletochronology study that demonstrated an increase in growth rates after the turtles moved from the oceanic stage to the neritic juvenile stage (Snover et al. 2000). Thus, reduced growth rates in the oceanic zone relative to those for turtles of the same size in the neritic zone may be an evolutionary explanation for why turtles leave the oceanic zone. Now it would be exciting to determine the "how" of this feedback system; research is needed to address this question.

One may also ask the reciprocal question of ontogenetic habitat shifts: Why do hatchlings leave the neritic zone and enter the oceanic zone? This question is particularly interesting in light of the evidence that the Australian flatback turtle, *Natator depressus*, apparently does not have an oceanic stage (Walker 1994; Walker and Parmenter 1990). The tradeoff may be between increased food resources and increased predation risk in the neritic zone (see Walker 1994). For loggerheads, there must be strong selection for hatchlings to leave neritic waters, possibly to avoid increased predation risk, which may be significantly lower in the open ocean.

The question of ontogenetic habitat shifts in the life history of sea turtles is fertile ground for speculation and research. A good place to pursue this question would be off Australian nesting beaches where there are flatback turtles that apparently stay in coastal waters and do not have an oceanic stage and where there are also loggerhead turtles that apparently do have an oceanic stage in the Pacific (e.g., Queensland; Limpus 1995). Predation risks and food re-

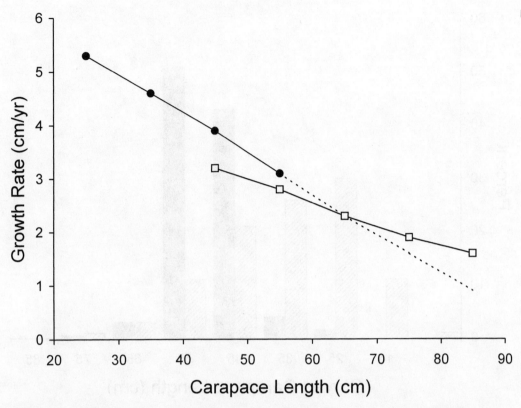

Figure 4.3. Size-specific growth functions of oceanic stage (solid circles) and neritic stage loggerheads (open boxes) based on length-frequency analyses (data from Bjorndal et al. 2000a, 2001). Dashed line is an extrapolation of the growth function for the oceanic stage loggerheads. The slopes of the lines are significantly different (p < 0.001).

sources may be similar for both species, although the flatback hatchling is larger, which may reduce its predation risk and/or facilitate exploitation of different food resources.

Anthropogenic Impacts on the Oceanic Stage

A major threat to the survival of loggerhead turtles during the oceanic stage is the risk of incidental capture in commercial fisheries. The bycatch of oceanic juveniles has been well documented for the high seas driftnet fishery (Wetherall et al. 1993). Incidental take of oceanic stage loggerheads in the swordfish longline fisheries has recently received a lot of attention (Aguilar et al. 1995; Balazs and Pooley 1994; Bolten et al. 1994, 2000; Laurent et al. 1998).

The mean size CCL (plus or minus the standard deviation) for loggerheads captured in the swordfish fishery in the Azores during an experiment conducted in 2000 was 49.8 ± 6.2 cm CCL (n = 224; Figure 4.4; Bolten et al., unpubl. data), which is significantly larger (p < 0.001; Kolmogorov-Smirnov Test, ks = 0.6528) than the baseline for the oceanic stage population, 34.5 ± 12.6 cm CCL (n = 1692; calculated from Bjorndal et al. 2000a). The largest size classes in the oceanic stage are the ones impacted by the swordfish longline fishery (Figure 4.4). Earlier studies in Azorean waters documenting swordfish longline captures show similar size classes impacted by that fishery (Bolten et al. 1994; Ferreira et al. 2001). The demographic consequences of the increased mortality of these size classes relative to population recovery have been discussed (Crouse et al. 1987; see also this volume: Chaloupka, Chapter 17; Heppell et al., Chapter 16).

Similar size classes are impacted by longline

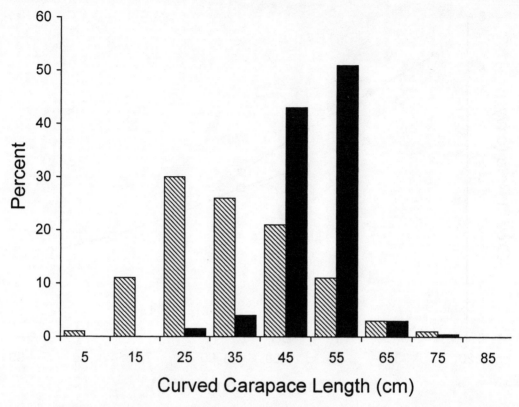

Figure 4.4. Size-frequency distribution of oceanic stage loggerheads (hatched bars; mean CCL 34.5 ± 12.6 cm; n = 1692; from Bjorndal et al. 2000a) and loggerheads caught in a swordfish longline fishery in the waters around the Azores July–December 2000 (solid bars; mean CCL 49.8 ± 6.2 cm; n = 224; Bolten et al., unpubl. data). The size distribution of the longline captures is significantly larger (p < 0.001; Kolmogorov-Smirnov Test, ks = 0.6528) than the baseline oceanic stage population.

fisheries in other regions. In the western Mediterranean the mean size of loggerheads caught in drifting longline fisheries was 47.4 ± 10.4 cm CCL (n = 62), and in the eastern Mediterranean it was 45.9 ± 7.5 cm CCL (n = 53) (Laurent et al. 1998). Witzell (1999) reported a mean size of 55.9 ± 6.5 cm CCL (n = 98) for loggerheads caught in the longline fishery from the western North Atlantic, primarily the Grand Banks, Newfoundland, Canada. In the Pacific the mean size of loggerheads caught by longlines is 57.7 ± 11.5 cm SCL (n = 163; Balazs and Parker, unpubl. data).

Results from satellite telemetry with satellite-linked time-depth recorders have demonstrated the potential negative impacts of longline hooking on the dive behavior and movement patterns of oceanic juveniles. Following release, hooked turtles have a signifi-

cantly reduced diving behavior (e.g., shallower dive depths), and their movements appear to be influenced to a greater extent by ocean current movements—the turtles drift with the current (Bolten and Riewald, unpubl. data). Researchers in Hawaii report different results for movement patterns for longline hooked turtles (Polovina et al. 2000), but see the discussion above.

There are numerous fisheries that impact oceanic stage loggerhead populations, and new ones continue to be developed. For example, the fishery for black scabbard *(Aphanopus carbo)* in Madeira has a significant bycatch of oceanic stage loggerheads (Dellinger and Encarnacao 2000). This fishery is currently being developed in the Azores.

The open ocean is full of debris, and small loggerheads frequently ingest plastics, tar, styrofoam, and monofilament (Carr 1987b; Witherington, in review b). This ingestion (as well as entanglement) is often lethal. The sublethal effects from marine debris ingestion may also have severe consequences, but they are difficult to quantify. Laboratory feeding trials have documented that posthatchling loggerheads were not able to adjust their intakes to counter nutrient-dilute diets that were similar to what turtles would experience when ingesting debris (McCauley and Bjorndal 1999). However, the authors suggest that with increasing size, turtles may be better able to adjust their intakes.

Conclusions—Where Do We Go from Here?

We have come a long way since "Rips, FADS, and Little Loggerheads" (Carr 1986), but we have only begun to unlock the "mystery of the lost year." These are exciting times. Multidisciplinary approaches—with expertise in physical and biological oceanography, population genetics, statistical modeling, demography, and ecosystem analyses—are needed for the study of sea turtle biology, especially the study of the oceanic stage.

To develop more complete demographic and geographic models for oceanic stage loggerhead sea turtles, we need to understand the relationships among the various populations within an ocean basin. For the Atlantic, we need to know the relationships between what we believe is the main oceanic stage population in the waters around the Azores and other populations on the Grand Banks of Canada, in the Mediterranean, and along the western coast of Africa. Molecular genetic tools and more sophisticated statistical analyses of mixed stocks will be needed to help us answer these questions.

What is the fate of the small loggerheads that never become entrained in the main ocean currents? Are these "lost" in the evolutionary sense, or do they have an entirely neritic development?

Developing methods for assessing population trends is another research area requiring high priority. Having spent many a day in the open ocean looking for little loggerheads, I can personally attest to the challenges of this goal. Population trends in this oceanic stage will allow us to predict trends in the nesting population 20 plus years ahead of time—maybe enough time to reverse/avert potential disasters!

Finally, quantifying the role of oceanic stage loggerheads in their ecosystem(s) may be one of the most exciting directions for research. Collaborations with other disciplines will be necessary to understand these system processes. Researchers have only begun to identify qualitatively the interactions of loggerheads with other species in the oceanic zone. For example, what are the prey and food items of loggerheads and what are the main predators of loggerheads? Quantifying these relationships is an important objective. Bjorndal (Chapter 15 this volume) explores these interactions, but the data are sparse.

Several ecosystem models are being developed for marine ecosystems. To incorporate oceanic stage loggerheads into these models will require a better understanding of their trophic status and food web interactions. Simple gut content studies as well as studies utilizing newer technologies (e.g., stable isotope analyses) are needed to evaluate the trophic status of oceanic stage loggerheads.

ACKNOWLEDGMENTS

I have been extraordinarily fortunate to have had the opportunity to pursue the "mystery of the lost year." Archie Carr stimulated my interest in this question, and my collaboration with Karen Bjorndal made it happen. To Karen I will always be indebted for the development of ideas, companionship in the field, and support during those frustrating times trying to solve a "mystery." My work in the Azores has given me the opportunity to develop a lasting friendship with Helen Martins, without whom this work would never have been accomplished. In addition, work in the Azores would not have been possible without the collaboration of my many friends and colleagues in "equipa tartaruga" and the collegiality of all of the faculty, staff, and students of the Department of Oceanography and Fisheries, University of the Azores, Horta. In 1990, a collaboration developed with Joseph Franck and Greet Wouters from the M/V Shanghai that began an important working relationship with the sport fishing industry in Horta. I have benefited from the collaborations with Brian Riewald, who was developing a model of oceanic stage movements and distribution patterns.

Funding for the research has been provided by

the U.S. National Marine Fisheries Service. Additional funding has been received from the Disney Wildlife Conservation Fund.

Karen Bjorndal, Brian Riewald, and Jeffrey Seminoff have commented on earlier drafts of this chapter. Peter Eliazar assisted with the literature cited and mark-recapture data.

DEDICATION

This chapter is dedicated to the memory of Brian Riewald (1972–2001), a brilliant student and great colleague. Brian was making significant contributions to our understanding of the distribution and movements of small loggerheads in the open ocean. Brian is greatly missed.

LITERATURE CITED

Ackerman, R. A. 1997. The nest environment and the embryonic development of sea turtles. *In* P. L. Lutz and J. A. Musick (eds.). The biology of sea turtles, 83–106. Boca Raton, Fla.: CRC Press.

Aguilar, R., J. Mas, and X. Pastor. 1995. Impact of Spanish swordfish longline fisheries on the loggerhead sea turtle *Caretta caretta* population in the western Mediterranean. *In* J. L. Richardson and T. H. Richardson (compilers). Proceedings of the 12th annual workshop on sea turtle biology and conservation, 1–6. NOAA Technical Memorandum NMFS-SEFSC-361.

Albert the First. 1898. Sur le developpement des tortues *T. caretta. Societe* de Biologie 50:10–11.

Alves, M., and de C. de Verdiere. 1999. Instability dynamics of a subtropical jet and applications to the Azores current system: Eddy driven mean flow. Journal of Physical Oceanography 29:837–864.

Balazs, G. H., and S. G. Pooley (eds.). 1994. Research plan to assess marine turtle hooking mortality: Results of an expert workshop held in Honolulu, Hawaii, November 16–18, 1993. NOAA Technical Memorandum NMFS-SWFSC-201.

Bjorndal, K. A., and A. B. Bolten (eds.). 2000. Proceedings of a workshop on assessing abundance and trends for in-water sea turtle populations. NOAA Technical Memorandum NMFS-SEFSC-445.

Bjorndal, K. A., A. B. Bolten, J. Gordon, and J. Caminas. 1994. *Caretta caretta* (loggerhead): Growth and pelagic movement. Herpetological Review 25:23–24.

Bjorndal, K. A., A. B. Bolten, and H. R. Martins. 2000a. Somatic growth model of juvenile loggerhead sea turtles *Caretta caretta:* Duration of

pelagic stage. Marine Ecology Progress Series 202:265–272.

Bjorndal, K. A., A. B. Bolten, and M. Y. Chaloupka. 2000b. Green turtle somatic growth model: Evidence for density dependence. Ecological Applications 10:269–282.

Bjorndal, K. A., A. B. Bolten, B. Koike, B. A. Schroeder, D. J. Shaver, W. G. Teas, and W. N. Witzell. 2001. Somatic growth function for immature loggerhead sea turtles in southeastern U.S. waters. Fishery Bulletin 99:240–246.

Bjorndal K. A., A. B. Bolten, T. Dellinger, C. Delgado, and H. R. Martins. In press a. Compensatory growth in oceanic loggerhead sea turtles: Response to a stochastic environment. Ecology.

Bjorndal, K. A., A. B. Bolten, and H. R. Martins. In press b. Estimates of survival probabilities for oceanic-stage loggerhead sea turtles *(Caretta caretta)* in the North Atlantic Fishery Bulletin.

Bolker, B., T. Okuyama, K. Bjorndal, and A. Bolten. In press. Stock estimation for sea turtle populations using genetic markers: Accounting for sampling error of rare genotypes. Ecological Applications.

Bolten, A. B., and G. H. Balazs. 1995. Biology of the early pelagic stage—the "lost year." *In* K. A. Bjorndal (ed.). Biology and conservation of sea turtles, rev. ed., 579–581. Washington D.C.: Smithsonian Institution Press.

Bolten, A. B., H. R. Martins, K. A. Bjorndal, M. Cocco, and G. Gerosa. 1992a. *Caretta caretta* (loggerhead). Pelagic movement and growth. Herpetological Review 23:116.

Bolten, A. B., J. C. Santana, and K. A. Bjorndal. 1992b. Transatlantic crossing by a loggerhead turtle. Marine Turtle Newsletter 59:7–8.

Bolten, A. B., H. R. Martins, K. A. Bjorndal, and J. Gordon. 1993. Size distribution of pelagic-stage loggerhead sea turtles *(Caretta caretta)* in the waters around the Azores and Madeira. Arquipélago 11A:49–54.

Bolten, A. B., K. A. Bjorndal, and H. R. Martins. 1994. Life history model for the loggerhead sea turtle *(Caretta caretta)* population in the Atlantic: Potential impacts of a longline fishery. *In* G. H. Balazs and S. G. Pooley (eds.). Research plan to assess marine turtle hooking mortality: Results of an expert workshop held in Honolulu, Hawaii, November 16–18, 1993, 48–54. NOAA Technical Memorandum NMFS-SWFSC-201.

Bolten, A. B., K. A. Bjorndal, H. R. Martins, and G. H. Balazs. 1996. Satellite telemetry of pelagic-stage juvenile loggerheads in the eastern Atlantic. *In* J.A. Keinath, D.E. Barnard, J. A. Musick, and B. A. Bell (compilers). Proceedings of the 15th annual symposium on sea turtle biology and conservation, 39–41. NOAA Technical Memorandum NMFS-SEFSC-387.

Bolten, A. B., K. A. Bjorndal, H. R. Martins, T. Dellinger, M. J. Biscoito, S. E. Encalada, and B. W. Bowen. 1998. Transatlantic developmental migrations of loggerhead sea turtles demonstrated by mtDNA sequence analysis. Ecological Applications 8:1–7.

Bolten, A. B., H. R. Martins, and K. A. Bjorndal (eds.). 2000. Proceedings of a workshop to design an experiment to determine the effects of longline gear modification on sea turtle bycatch rates [Workshop para a elaboração de uma experiência que possa diminuir as capturas acidentais de tartarugas marinhas nos Açores], 2–4 September 1998, Horta, Azores, Portugal. NOAA Technical Memorandum NMFS-OPR-19.

Bouchard, S. S., and K. A. Bjorndal. 2000. Sea turtles as biological transporters of nutrients and energy from marine to terrestrial ecosystems. Ecology 81:2305–2313.

Bowen, B. W. 1995. Tracking marine turtles with genetic markers: Voyages of the ancient mariners. Bioscience 45:528–534.

Bowen, B. W., F. A. Abreu-Grobois, G. H. Balazs, N. Kamezaki, C. J. Limpus, and R. J. Ferl. 1995. Trans-Pacific migrations of the loggerhead turtle (Caretta caretta) demonstrated with mitochondrial DNA markers. Proceedings of the National Academy of Sciences 92:3731–3734.

Brongersma, L. D. 1972. European Atlantic turtles. Zoologische Verhandelingen (Leiden) 121:1–318.

Carr, A. F. 1986. Rips, FADS, and little loggerheads. Bioscience 36:92–100.

———. 1987a. New perspectives on the pelagic stage of sea turtle development. Conservation Biology 1:103–121.

———. 1987b. Impact of nondegradable marine debris on the ecology and survival outlook of sea turtles. Marine Pollution Bulletin 18:352–356.

Chaloupka, M. 1998. Polyphasic growth in pelagic loggerhead sea turtles. Copeia 1998:516–518.

Crouse, D. T., L. B. Crowder, and H. Caswell. 1987. A stage-based population model for loggerhead sea turtles and implications for conservation. Ecology 68:1412–1423.

Dellinger, T., and H. Encarnacao. 2000. Accidental capture of sea turtles by the fishing fleet based at Madeira Island, Portugal. In H. Kalb and T. Wibbels (compilers). Proceedings of the 19th international symposium on sea turtle biology and conservation, 218. NOAA Technical Memorandum NMFS-SEFSC-443.

Dellinger, T., and C. Freitas. 2000. Movements and diving behaviour of pelagic stage loggerhead sea turtles in the North Atlantic: Preliminary results obtained through satellite telemetry. In H. Kalb and T. Wibbels (compilers). Proceedings of the 19th international symposium on sea turtle biology and conservation, 155–157. NOAA Technical Memorandum NMFS-SEFSC-443.

Eckert, S. A., and H. R. Martins. 1989. Transatlantic travel by juvenile loggerhead turtle. Marine Turtle Newsletter 45:15.

Encalada, S. E., K. A. Bjorndal, A. B. Bolten, J. C. Zurita, B. Schroeder, E. Possardt, C. J. Sears, and B. W. Bowen. 1998. Population structure of loggerhead turtle (Caretta caretta) nesting colonies in the Atlantic and Mediterranean as inferred from mitochondrial DNA control region sequences. Marine Biology 130:567–575.

Ferreira, R. L., H. R. Martins, A. A. da Silva, and A. B. Bolten. 2001. Impact of swordfish fisheries on sea turtles in the Azores. Arquipélago 18A:75–79.

Hughes, G. R. 1974. The sea turtles of Southeast Africa, II. Investigational Report no. 36 of the Oceanographic Research Institute, Durban, South Africa.

Kamezaki, N., and M. Matsui. 1997. Allometry in the loggerhead turtle, Caretta caretta. Chelonian Conservation and Biology 2:421–425.

Lalli, C. M., and T. R. Parsons. 1993. Biological oceanography: An introduction. New York: Pergamon Press.

Laurent, L., J. Lescure, L. Excoffier, B. Bowen, M. Domingo, M. Hadjichristophorou, L. Kornaraki, and G. Trabuchet. 1993. Etude genetique des relations entre les populations mediterraneenne et atlantique d'une tortue marine (Caretta caretta) a l'aide d'un marqueur mitochondrial. Comptes Rendus De L'Academie Des Sciences (Paris), Serie III Sciences de la Vie, Biologie et Pathologie Animale 316:1233–1239.

Laurent, L., P. Casale, M. N. Bradai, B. J. Godley, G. Gerosa, A. C. Broderick, W. Schroth, B. Schierwater, A. M. Levy, D. Freggi, E. M. Abd El-Mawla, D. A. Hadoud, H. El-Gomati, M. Domingo, M. Hadjichristophorou, L. Kornaraki, F. Demirayak, and C. Gautier. 1998. Molecular resolution of marine turtle stock composition in fishery bycatch: A case study in the Mediterranean. Molecular Ecology 7:1529–1542.

Limpus, C. J. 1995. The status of Australian sea turtle populations. In K. A. Bjorndal (ed.). Biology and conservation of sea turtles, rev. ed., 297–303. Washington D.C.: Smithsonian Institution Press.

McCauley, S. J., and K. A. Bjorndal. 1999. Conservation implications of dietary dilution from debris ingestion: Sublethal effects in post-hatchling log-

gerhead sea turtles. Conservation Biology
13:925–929.

Moran, K. L., K. A. Bjorndal, and A. B. Bolten. 1999.
Effects of the thermal environment on the temporal pattern of emergence of hatchling loggerhead
turtles (Caretta caretta). Marine Ecology Progress
Series 189:251–261.

Musick, J. A., and C. J. Limpus. 1997. Habitat utilization and migration in juvenile sea turtles. In
P. L. Lutz and J. A. Musick (eds.). The biology of
sea turtles, 137–164. Boca Raton, Fla.: CRC Press.

Pearce, A. F. 2001. Contrasting population structure
of the loggerhead turtle (Caretta caretta) using
mitochondrial and nuclear DNA markers. Master's
Thesis, University of Florida, Gainesville.

Plotkin, P. T. 1996. Occurrence and diet of juvenile
loggerhead sea turtles, Caretta caretta, in the
Northwestern Gulf of Mexico. Chelonian Conservation and Biology 2:78–80.

Polovina, J. J., D. R. Kobayashi, D. M. Parker,
M. P. Seki, and G. H. Balazs. 2000. Turtles on the
edge: Movement of loggerhead turtles (Caretta
caretta) along oceanic fronts, spanning longline
fishing grounds in the central North Pacific,
1997–1998. Fisheries Oceanography 9:71–82.

Seminoff, J. A. 2000. Biology of the East Pacific
green turtle (Chelonia mydas agassizii) at a warm
temperate foraging area in the Gulf of California,
Mexico. Ph.D. Dissertation, University of Ari-
zona, Tucson.

Snover, M. L., A. A. Horn, and S. A. Macko. 2000.
Detecting the precise time at settlement from
pelagic to benthic habitats in the loggerhead sea
turtle. In H. Kalb and T. Wibbels (compilers).
Proceedings of the 19th international symposium
on sea turtle biology and conservation, 174. NOAA
Technical Memorandum NMFS-SEFSC-443.

TEWG. 2000. Assessment update for the Kemp's ridley and loggerhead sea turtle populations in the
western North Atlantic. NOAA Technical Memorandum NMFS-SEFSC-444.

Tiwari, M., K. A. Bjorndal, A. B. Bolten, and
A. Moumni. 2002. Morocco and Western Sahara:
Sites of an early neritic stage in the life history of
loggerheads? In A. Mosier, A. Foley, and B. Brost
(compilers). Proceedings of the 20th annual symposium on sea turtle biology and conservation,
9. NOAA Technical Memorandum NMFS-
SEFSC-477.

Walker, T. A. 1994. Post-hatchling dispersal of sea
turtles. In R. James (compiler). Proceedings of the
Australian marine turtle conservation workshop,
79–94. Held at Sea World Nara Resort, Gold
Coast, 14–17 November 1990. Canberra, Australia: Queensland Department of Environment
and Heritage, and Australian Nature Conservation
Agency.

Walker, T. A., and C. J. Parmenter. 1990. Absence of
a pelagic phase in the life cycle of the flatback
turtle, Natator depressa (Garman). Journal of Biogeography 17:275–278.

Werner, E. E., and J. F. Gilliam. 1984. The ontogenetic niche and species interactions in size-
structured populations. Annual Review of Ecology
and Systematics 15:393–425.

Wetherall, J. A., G. H. Balazs, R. A. Tokunaga, and
M. Y. Y. Yong. 1993. Bycatch of marine turtles in
North Pacific high-seas driftnet fisheries and im-
pacts on the stocks. International North Pacific
Fisheries Commission Bulletin 53:519–538.

Witherington, B. E. 2002. Ecology of neonate loggerhead turtles inhabiting lines of downwelling
near a Gulf Stream front. Marine Biology
140:843–853.

———. In review a. A test of a "smart drifter" hypothesis describing the distribution of neonate
loggerhead turtles in the open ocean.

———. In review b. Frequency of tar and plastics
ingestion by neonate loggerhead turtles captured
from the western Gulf Stream off Florida, U.S.A.

Witzell, W. N. 1999. Distribution and relative abundance of sea turtles caught incidentally by the U.S.
pelagic longline fleet in the western North Atlantic
Ocean, 1992–1995. Fishery Bulletin 97:200–211.

Wyneken, J., and M. Salmon. 1992. Frenzy and post-
frenzy swimming activity in loggerhead, green,
and leatherback hatchling sea turtles. Copeia
1992:478–484.

Zug, G. R., G. H. Balazs, and J. A. Wetherall. 1995.
Growth in juvenile loggerhead sea turtles (Caretta
caretta) in the North Pacific pelagic habitat.
Copeia 1995:484–487.

Chapter 5

Ecology of Immature Loggerheads on Foraging Grounds and Adults in Internesting Habitat in the Eastern United States

—Sally R. Hopkins-Murphy, David W. Owens, and Thomas M. Murphy

The focus of this chapter is the ecology of loggerheads during two phases of their life history: immature loggerheads on their neritic foraging grounds and adult females that inhabit coastal waters (internesting habitat) during the nesting season. Most adult females observed in internesting habitat of the eastern United States do not feed and are generally not considered to be on foraging grounds. Schroeder et al. (Chapter 7 this volume) provide information on females during nonnesting years at resident feeding areas.

Size Classes and Distribution

Unlike other sea turtle species that seem to have more specific habitat requirements (Hendrickson 1980), loggerheads that have matured beyond the oceanic juvenile stage show exceptional variability in depth utilization, latitude of occurrence, and general habitat preferences. Of the 40 countries/regions in the wider

Caribbean that participated in the first Western Atlantic Turtle Symposium (WATS I), 29 reported some level of foraging activity by loggerheads (Bacon 1981; Carr et al. 1982). However, only six countries list foraging loggerheads as "frequent" (Honduras, Martinique, and Mexico-Gulf), "common" (Belize, Panama, and Mexico-Caribbean), or "abundant" (United States). The most detailed information on loggerhead size distribution comes from the U.S. Atlantic and Gulf of Mexico (Ehrhart 1989; Ehrhart et al., Chapter 10 this volume).

In the eastern United States, neritic juvenile-sized loggerheads (generally 45–80 cm straight carapace length, SCL) are common to abundant in coastal inlets, sounds, bays, estuaries, and lagoons during the spring, summer, and fall months from Long Island Sound south to Florida and into the Gulf of Mexico (Butler et al. 1987; Fritts et al. 1983; Lutcavage and Musick 1985; Morreale et al. 1992; see also Ehrhart et al., Chapter 10 this volume). Log-

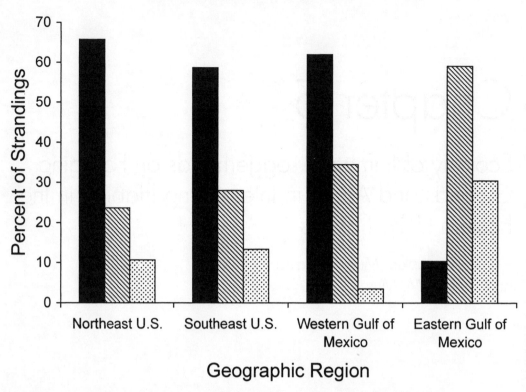

■ 40.0-69.9 cm ▨ 70.0-91.9 cm ⊡ >92.0 cm

Figure 5.1. Percentage distribution by size class of loggerhead turtle strandings, 1986–1994 (TEWG 1998).

gerheads remain abundant through the winter in Florida (Ehrhart et al. 1996; Schroeder et al. 1998). In most of these shallow, partially enclosed coastal waters, large immatures and adults are seldom found. The largest size immature loggerheads are most commonly found in open shelf waters. Open shelf waters where large immatures and adults are observed range out to hundreds of kilometers offshore onto the broader reaches of the continental shelf.

Immatures commonly recruit from the oceanic environment at about 40 cm SCL in the western Atlantic (Carr 1987). To examine the distribution of neritic immatures and adults, the authors looked at three size classes within four regions: the northeastern and southeastern United States and the western and eastern Gulf of Mexico. These data are based on stranded carcasses from the Sea Turtle Stranding and Salvage Network (STSSN) as compiled by the Turtle Expert Working Group (TEWG 1998). When the percentage representation of the

three size classes within the four regions is given (Figure 5.1), two patterns that stand out are the lack of adults in the western Gulf of Mexico and the apparent overrepresentation of larger immatures in the eastern Gulf of Mexico. However, when the actual numbers of animals are examined (Figure 5.2), there are more of the larger immatures in the southeast than elsewhere. Because these data are based on strandings, they could be influenced by fishing effort as well as turtle abundance. Epperly et al. (1995) report that loggerheads were generally smaller in Long Island Sound, New York, than in three other estuarine systems farther south. The mean size in Long Island Sound was 54 cm curved carapace length (CCL) compared with 66 cm CCL in Pamlico and Core sounds, North Carolina; 74 cm CCL in the Chesapeake Bay; and 71 cm CCL in Indian River, Florida (Epperly et al. 1995). Schroeder et al. (1998) report mean size of loggerheads in Florida Bay as 80 cm SCL (approximately 87 cm CCL). This overall distri-

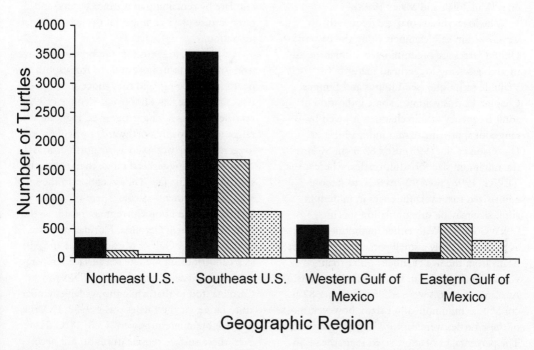

Figure 5.2. Size frequency of neritic immatures and adult loggerheads that stranded in four U.S. regions during 1986–1994 (TEWG 1998).

bution suggests a developmental movement south along the east coast and into the southeastern Gulf of Mexico.

To develop management strategies for channels maintained by hopper dredges, the U.S. Army Corps of Engineers (USACE) initiated a multifaceted sea turtle research program (Dickerson et al. 1995). As part of these studies, monthly trawling surveys were conducted in six channels along the southeastern Atlantic coast from June 1991 through March 1993 to evaluate species composition, population structure, and spatial and seasonal distribution. The six channels selected were Canaveral and St. Mary's River, Florida; Brunswick and Savannah, Georgia; Charleston, South Carolina; and Morehead City, North Carolina. There were 645 loggerheads captured, and all but 13 were measured. None was under 40 cm SCL. Nineteen were between 40 and 50 cm; 209 between 50 and 60 cm; 217 between 60 and 70 cm; 56 between 70 and 80 cm; 55 between 80 and 90 cm; and 76 greater than 90 cm SCL.

These size classes are nearly identical to those in Figure 5.1 of the stranding data. When the 632 measured loggerheads are combined into the three size classes shown in Figure 5.1, the percentages for the size classes are the following: 40.0–69.9 cm = 70%; 70.0–91.9 cm = 17.5%; and > 92.0 cm = 12.0%. When compared with data for stranded loggerheads, these percentages are most similar to the northeastern U.S. region, somewhat similar to the southeastern U.S. region, and not at all like the two regions within the Gulf of Mexico.

A comparison of catch rates with Southeast Area Monitoring and Assessment Program (SEAMAP) data suggests that loggerheads congregate in channel habitats along the southeastern United States during summer and fall. SEAMAP data are collected by the South Carolina Department of Natural Resources, with extensive trawl surveys based on a stratified random sampling design in near-shore waters between Cape Hatteras and central Florida, and have been conducted seasonally since 1989. It is also apparent that loggerheads are most abundant in mud- and hard-bottom areas, not sandy ones (VanDolah and Maier 1993).

The loggerheads that are frequently observed within ship channels along the eastern United States are predominately immature. Although assessing loggerhead maturity by size is a fallible technique (see Limpus and Limpus, Chapter 12 this volume), some indication of adult frequency at ship channels is given by ranges of approximate minimum adult size. Dickerson et al. (1995) used 82.5 cm SCL as the minimum size for adult turtles, whereas the TEWG (1998) used 92 cm SCL to denote adult-sized turtles. Differences in minimum adult size may be subpopulation specific (TEWG 2000). With either minimum adult size as a criterion, only a small percentage of loggerheads from the five channels, other than Canaveral channel, can be identified as adults. At Canaveral, 36% were adult size (using 82.5 cm SCL as minimum adult size); however, most of these turtles were captured April though July. The percentages of adult-sized loggerheads in the other channels (using the 82.5 cm criterion) were St. Mary's, 4.3%; Brunswick, 5.4%; Savannah, 2.8%; Charleston, 4.4%; and there were no data for Morehead City. Clearly, the Cape Canaveral ship channel, with its proximity to the major nesting beaches of central Florida, is a unique habitat.

Although neritic stage immatures and adult loggerheads utilize the entire continental shelf along the eastern U.S. seaboard and into the Gulf of Mexico, they appear not to be randomly mixed. Average size is smaller in the more northerly areas, whereas larger immatures are more common in the south. Adults tend to be found in deeper, more offshore areas. Based on stranded animals, Florida, Georgia, South Carolina, and North Carolina have the largest number of individuals in all size classes.

Seasonality

Sea turtles live in an environment that is thermally stable in any given place, but that can vary in temperature with both depth and season and with geographic location. The rapid heat transfer between a turtle and seawater strongly limits the warming effect of metabolism (Spotila et al. 1997). Thus, loggerheads behaviorally thermoregulate by remaining in warmer waters, and temperature plays an important role in seasonal migrations.

In general, loggerheads can be said to move from offshore to inshore and/or from south to north in the spring, and they move the opposite direction in the fall. Shoop and Kenney (1992) reported that as spring progresses, loggerheads range more broadly northward. By September, loggerheads are observed as far north as Massachusetts. The loggerhead range then contracts southward in the fall. The exception to these seasonal movements occurs where the Gulf Stream and the Loop Current are nearer to the coast, as in North Carolina, Florida, and areas of the southern Gulf of Mexico. Coles and Musick (2000), using satellite sea surface temperature data and aerial survey data off North Carolina, found that while the available temperature range for the turtles was 4.9–32.2°C, the preferred temperatures were 13.3–28°C. However, these surface temperatures do not necessarily describe the true temperature range that a turtle would experience at various depths when feeding or resting. Water temperatures recorded by satellite transmitters attached to postnesting females were found to be several degrees lower than sea surface temperatures (Hopkins-Murphy, unpubl. data).

In the North Atlantic, circulation and thermodynamics are complex. As the western edge of the Gulf Stream passes south of the Grand Banks and turns eastward toward Europe, it spins off warm-core rings onto the cooler northeastern slope. Pelagic longline data indicate that loggerhead turtle distribution (mean CCL = 55.9 cm) in the summer and fall months extends from coastal waters to beyond the edge of the continental shelf from Cape Hatteras, North Carolina, to Georges Bank and the Grand Banks. These turtles are apparently able to move out of critically cold winter slope water to more southern waters (Witzell 1999).

Sometimes, cold fronts can move through the northeast and cold-stun loggerheads in "blind pockets" such as Cape Cod Bay and Long Island Sound (Morreale et al. 1992). There have been cold-stunning events in

Florida in Mosquito Lagoon (Witherington and Ehrhart 1989), a shallow water system, and in the Laguna Madre in Texas, as well.

Between early May and November in Chesapeake Bay, Lutcavage and Musick (1985) and Byles (1988) found loggerheads to be common well up into the Potomac River area. Loggerheads commonly go into pound nets in this region and in North Carolina's Pamlico Sound. Loggerheads seem to learn and reuse productive foraging areas, sometimes going into the same pound net repeatedly. Epperly et al. (1995) used both aerial surveys and surveys of commercial pound net fishermen, recreational anglers, and the general public to study the seasonal distribution and size classes of loggerheads in North Carolina. They occurred year-round in the ocean but were only seasonally present in the sounds (April through December). Winter temperatures averaged 8°C, the temperature below which cold-stunning occurs (Spotila et al. 1997; Witherington and Ehrhart 1989), and approaches the lower lethal tolerance limit (Schwartz 1978) in the sounds. Based on strandings and pound net captures (Lutcavage and Musick 1985), aerial surveys (Shoop and Kenney 1992), and the results of various tracking technologies (Byles 1988; Renaud and Carpenter 1994), it is clear that water temperature is a critical environmental cue that loggerheads use to guide their movements in and out of shallow coastal waters.

During the unusually cold winters of 1978 and 1979, large numbers of loggerheads that showed evidence of being buried in the mud were captured by trawl fishermen in the Canaveral ship channel (Carr et al. 1980). The authors concluded that these loggerheads were brumating in the channel. Richardson and Hillestad (1979) reported no evidence of overwintering in South Carolina and Georgia channels. In the study of channel use in the southeast (Dickerson et al. 1995), 95.6% of the captures were in water temperatures > 16°C. From these studies, brumation is still poorly documented and appears to be a rare event (Ogren and McVea 1982).

Although loggerheads are seen to sharply increase in abundance at the Canaveral channel during January, they are only infrequently found or are absent in the channels of Georgia and the Carolinas during midwinter (Dickerson et al. 1995). In Charleston Harbor, loggerheads were more abundant in summer than in fall. Tagging data from Charleston Harbor indicate that immature loggerheads migrate annually. Immatures tagged in the fall were absent during the winter, but were recaptured the following spring (VanDolah and Maier 1993).

The adult loggerheads found in the Canaveral channel were seen by Dickerson et al. (1995) to be highly seasonal with regard to sex. Of the 60 adult-sized turtles captured there from March through May, there were 24 males and one female. From June through August there were 32 females and one male, and from September through November there were only two males and no females. These numbers coincide with the spring migratory breeding season for males, the summer nesting season for females, and the fall when only juveniles are present and both adult males and adult females have left coastal waters for their resident feeding areas.

Spatial Distribution and Habitats

The foraging grounds for neritic immature and adult loggerheads are essentially the entire continental shelf. There are especially wide areas of the shelf along the eastern seaboard of the United States, in the Gulf of Mexico, and around Cuba. On the east coast, loggerheads occupy all areas of the shelf from the coast out to the western wall of the Gulf Stream. Shoop and Kenney (1992) found that loggerheads had a propensity to stay in waters < 200 m deep and were seen usually at depths of < 60 m. Whereas large immature loggerheads, greater than about 85 cm CCL, are rare in most confined coastal waters, aerial surveys indicate that they are quite common on the continental shelf, particularly along the east coast and the eastern Gulf of Mexico (Fritts et al. 1983).

The near-shore ecosystems that loggerheads inhabit are highly variable. The Chesapeake Bay is essentially an arm of the Atlantic Ocean in that it is both deep and wide (80 km) near its mouth. It is a plankton-based system with large numbers of fishes that provide food material for an equally large benthic community. In contrast, the sounds in North Carolina are large, shallow areas with only small inlets to the ocean. They receive large quantities of freshwater, are generally brackish, and have large sea grass beds. The sounds in South Carolina and Georgia are large, open bodies of water that are also extensions of the ocean, but they are shallow. Florida's east coast Indian River lagoon system (including Mosquito Lagoon) lacks major sounds and bays, but does have narrow inlets connecting it to the Atlantic Ocean. The Gulf of Mexico can be divided oceanographically into two halves. The eastern half is influenced strongly by Caribbean inflow and has relatively clear water, whereas the western half is influenced more by the turbid Mississippi River, incurs tremendous shrimp trawling pressure, and has hundreds of man-made gas and oil production structures. These areas vary greatly in habitat type, but all are important to loggerheads.

Large immatures and adults tend to be seen in association with hard substrates such as reefs and petroleum production structures. Based on aerial surveys, Lohoefener et al. (1989) found an association of loggerheads with platforms off the Chandeleur Islands in the Gulf of Mexico. However, the association did not seem as clear in other areas of high oil-rig density to the west, but there were also fewer turtles there.

Well-known loggerhead resting areas such as Grays Reef off Georgia, the extensive live bottom areas off east-central Florida, and the Flower Gardens coral reefs 150 km off the Louisiana/ Texas border almost always have loggerheads present (Hickerson and Peccini 2000). Rosman et al. (1987) used video systems to observe the behavior of sea turtles on hard substrates in the Gulf of Mexico. In most cases the animals appeared to use the hard substrates only for resting.

Renaud and Carpenter (1994) satellite tracked four loggerheads captured while sleeping at night on oil production platforms off eastern Texas. The turtles were immatures (28–98 kg) and were monitored over periods of 5–10.5 months. The calculated core areas for each of the four turtles ranged from 90 to 4,297 km^2 with home ranges of 954–28,833 km^2. During 10.5 months of tracking, one of the turtles stayed in a small core area for more than three months before a severe cold front

passed, after which it moved to the east and occupied three additional areas before the transmitter signal was lost.

There is a lack of hard-bottom habitat for loggerheads near shore from northern Florida to Winyah Bay, South Carolina. There are two factors that probably contribute to this. One, there are large rivers emptying into this part of the coast, resulting in lower salinities and higher turbidity near shore, which is not conducive to the growth of live bottom organisms. Second, this same area of the coast is where shrimp trawling gear negatively impacts live bottom areas for at least six months of the year.

It is not clear how loggerheads use structured, hard-bottom habitats or whether loggerheads favor them over softer substrates. Because aerial surveys and other observations are done during the day, it is possible that turtles use the structures as regular resting areas, often at night, and forage over many kilometers of habitat during the day. While they are seen sleeping and foraging at various times on these substrates, these same areas are where divers also tend to congregate. Thus it cannot be ruled out that there are just as many turtles on soft substrates. Nevertheless, the impression is that loggerheads prefer habitats with hard substrates, including man-made materials. Because of their apparent importance to loggerheads, the locations of hard-bottom areas and their size and status are important also.

Diet

Information on the diet of loggerheads foraging within the neritic zone of the eastern United States and Gulf of Mexico has come principally from analyses of fecal samples from live turtles or from gut contents of dead stranded turtles. Loggerheads in these waters feed mostly on large, benthic, slow-moving or sessile invertebrates and occasionally on carrion from fisheries bycatch (Burke et al. 1990, 1993; Burke and Standora 1993; Lutcavage and Musick 1985; Plotkin et al. 1993; Ruckdeschel and Shoop 1988; Shoop and Ruckdeschel 1982; Youngkin 2001). At a majority of sites in the region, hard-shelled arthropods and mollusks predominate in loggerhead gut contents.

Diet studies in the region report food items that vary among geographic areas and among seasons. In Long Island Sound, New York, loggerheads were found to have fed mostly on spider crabs *(Libinia emarginata),* followed by rock crab*s (Cancer irroratus),* lady crabs *(Ovalipes ocellatus),* and hermit crabs *(Pagurus pollicaris)* (Burke and Standora 1993; Burke et al. 1990, 1993). To the south, loggerheads in Chesapeake Bay, Virginia, were reported by Lutcavage and Musick (1985) to have fed principally on horseshoe crabs *(Limulus polyphemus).* Near the dredged ship channel off Cumberland Island, Georgia, the highest proportion of gut contents from dead loggerheads contained arthropods (crabs and hermit crabs), followed by gastropod mollusks, then by fish (presumed to be trawl bycatch), echinoderms, and various other invertebrates (Ruckdeschel and Shoop 1988; Shoop and Ruckdeschel 1982; Youngkin 2001). In the northwestern Gulf of Mexico, Plotkin et al. (1993) found loggerheads to have fed mostly on sea pens *(Pennatula aculeata),* followed by various species of crabs and mollusks. In the extensive 20-year survey of gut contents from Cumberland Island loggerheads by Youngkin (2001), turtles showed seasonal shifts in diet, with frequency of spider crabs *(Libinia* spp.) peaking in the spring and the frequency of whelks *(Busycon* spp.) peaking in the fall.

Sex Ratios of Neritic Immatures

The sex ratio of immature loggerheads foraging along the eastern United States and in the Gulf of Mexico is decidedly biased toward females. Wibbels et al. (1987) reported a 1.0:1.9 female-biased sex ratio for 256 live-captured immature loggerheads along the Atlantic coast, and using dead stranded sea turtles in Texas, Stabenau et al. (1996) determined a nearly identical 1.0:1.9 male to female sex ratio for 103 loggerheads. A similar 1:2 male to female sex ratio for neritic immatures has been shown consistently at foraging grounds from Virginia through Florida Bay (Owens 1997; Wibbels et al. 1991).

Present sex ratios of neritic immatures are the product of the thermal environment of their natal beaches, more than a decade in the past,

and of sex-specific survivorship over the same developmental period. To compare the observed sex ratio of neritic immatures in the eastern United States to an expected sex ratio based on their sex ratio at hatching, the authors used hatchling sex ratio data published in the literature and compiled in the TEWG report (1998). They divided sex ratios of hatchlings between a northern nesting subpopulation, distributed from the North Carolina/Virginia line to northeastern Florida (37.5–29° N), and a southern Florida nesting subpopulation, distributed from 29° N on the eastern coast to 28° N on the western coast (Table 5.1). Other subpopulations have been identified, but they were not included in this analysis because of incomplete data and small population size. The southern Florida nesting subpopulation is approximately an order of magnitude larger than the northern one (TEWG 2000). The authors used different clutch sizes because in a t-test of clutch size between South Carolina and central Florida, the northern turtles laid significantly more eggs per clutch than did the Florida females. A hatching success rate of 0.60 was assumed for each subpopulation (NMFS and USFWS 1991). Based on these data, the expected male to female sex ratio of hatchlings entering the ocean is 1:6. However, the observed male to female ratio in loggerheads recovered from the neritic foraging grounds is 1:2 (Owens 1997; Stabenau et al. 1996; Wibbles et al. 1987, 1991).

At least two hypotheses might explain the disparity between observed neritic immature sex ratios and expected sex ratios based on hatchlings leaving their natal beaches. One hypothesis is that hatchlings from the strongly female-biased southern Florida subpopulation, or specifically the females from this population, incur a much greater rate of mortality than hatchlings from the northern subpopulation, or male hatchlings in general. Another hypothesis is that foraging grounds in the Bahamas, the northern Caribbean, and the southern Gulf of Mexico, as yet poorly surveyed for immature loggerhead sex ratio, may be found to have the strongly female-biased sex ratio predicted here (Table 5.1). From the four studies mentioned above, foraging grounds along the eastern coast of the

Table 5.1.

Hypothesized Sex Ratios of Loggerheads from the Northern Subpopulation and the Southern Florida Nesting Subpopulation

| | | | | Hatchlings to the Ocean | | | Female |
Subpopulation	Nests	Eggs/Clutch	Total Eggs	Male	Female	Total	Proportion
Northern	6,220[a]	126[b]	781,200	234,360	234,360	468,720	0.50[c]
Southern Florida	64,000[a]	110[d]	7,040,000	422,400	3,801,600	4,224,000	0.90[e]
Total	70,220	—	7,821,200	656,760	4,035,960	4,692,720	0.86

Note: Ratios based on annual hatchling production.

[a]Turtle Expert Working Group 1998.

[b]Caldwell 1959; Hopkins-Murphy et al. 1999.

[c]Mrosovsky et al. 1984.

[d]Dodd 1988.

[e]Mrosovsky and Provancha 1989.

United States do seem to be the primary foraging areas for neritic immature loggerheads, with no other major areas described. A study to explain this apparent shift in sex ratios is needed.

Genetic Ratios of Neritic Immatures

Genetic analyses indicate that turtles from several subpopulations mix on foraging grounds (TEWG 2000). Based on hatchling productivity (Table 5.1), the expected ratio of hatchlings entering the ocean from the northern subpopulation to those entering from the southern Florida subpopulation is 1:9. Assuming an even mix during and after the oceanic stage, this ratio should be present on the feeding grounds. However, mitochondrial DNA samples from neritic juvenile loggerheads in South Carolina (Sears 1994), Georgia (Sears et al. 1995), and the Chesapeake Bay (Norrgard 1995) all show approximately equal representation from the northern subpopulation and the southern Florida subpopulation.

Some of the disparity between observed and expected genetic ratios can be explained by nonrandom mixing of subpopulations. The proportional contributions of the larger southern Florida subpopulation increase along the east coast in a general north-south gradient,

with increasing representation by the Florida subpopulation from 46% in Chesapeake Bay to 84% in Florida Bay (TEWG 2000). However, when all studies are considered, the combined ratio is still far from the expected 1:9 northern to southern ratio based on production of hatchlings (Table 5.1).

In regard to both sex ratio and genetic composition, the northern subpopulation appears to be disproportionately represented in surveyed foraging assemblages compared with the southern Florida subpopulation. If there is a differentially higher mortality of the southern Florida hatchlings, which is one hypothesis supported by the data, then the effects should be already apparent by the time loggerheads are oceanic immatures in the Azores. Bolten et al. (1998) found 20% of the loggerheads there were from the northern subpopulation, 70% from southern Florida, and 10% from Mexico (n = 131), ratios that do not approach the expected representation by each of the subpopulations. Does the northern subpopulation have higher oceanic survivorship than the southern Florida subpopulation? Or are the southern Florida subpopulation immatures distributed within the more poorly surveyed Caribbean? Given the strong Gulf Stream current that runs close to most of Florida's east-coast nesting beaches, it is doubtful that hatchlings entrained in this current would wind up in the Caribbean prior to reaching the Azores.

Adult Females during the Nesting Season

Very few studies have documented the internesting habitat use of adult female loggerheads in the western Atlantic. The authors are aware of only three areas where these studies have been conducted: northern South Carolina (Murphy and Hopkins 1981), southern Georgia (Stoneburner 1982), and southern Virginia (Bartol and Musick 1998). The most complete study, with the largest sample size, was conducted in South Carolina and is described here in more detail than the other two.

South Carolina

Movement patterns and internesting habitat use by adult females was intensively studied in the late 1970s in South Carolina (Murphy and Hopkins 1981). The study used sonic and radio telemetry to measure habitat use. The study was conducted in three stages during three nesting seasons.

The study area, where the turtles were monitored, was approximately 67 km straight-line distance along the coast from North Inlet, South Carolina (33.324° N, 79.168° W), to Raccoon Key, South Carolina (33.001° N, 79.492° W), and extended out 67 km seaward to approximately the western edge of the Gulf Stream. This area covered approximately 4,500 km². The near-shore waters were generally shallow (< 10 m) with shoals and sand bars near the nesting beaches.

The intensity of telemetric monitoring varied within the study area. The primary area was < 5 km from shore east of Sand Island and South Island (the nesting beach). The secondary area was from Winyah Bay to Cape Romain Shoals and < 8 km from shore. The remaining portion of the study area was monitored periodically, primarily at night or during continuous tracking of individual turtles. Locations were based on LORAN C coordinates of the vessel location when in the immediate vicinity of an instrumented turtle.

The transmitters weighed 0.8 kg and were attached with plastic-coated stainless steel wire through two holes drilled in posterior left marginal scutes. The range of sonic transmitters was variable, depending on water turbulence and turbidity, with an effective minimum range of 1.5 km near shore and 2.5 km in the clear waters offshore.

After nesting, one loggerhead turtle was equipped with a sonic transmitter in early August 1977 and continuously monitored for 66.5 hours. She moved 8.3 km from the beach and remained there until sunrise, when she moved at a constant heading for 11 hours. This movement averaged 2.35 km/h, covered a distance of 25.8 km, and resulted in a location 34 km from the nesting beach. She then stayed at an offshore live bottom reef until monitoring was discontinued due to failure of the receiving unit. Her movements appeared typical of a loggerhead that has laid her final nest of the season (Hopkins-Murphy, unpubl. data; Schroeder, pers. comm.).

In 1978, seven loggerhead turtles equipped with sonic transmitters, including four that also had radio transmitters, resulted in 826 telemetric locations on five of the seven turtles. All turtles went to the East Bank shoal after nesting. Of these, two took a course to the southeast along the general configuration of the depth contours to Cape Romain Shoals, 3 km east of Cape Island. A single individual traveled at a 120° heading for 15 km over a period of 8.5 hours (1.8 km/h). She then turned almost due north, covered 12 km in 10.5 hours (1.1 km/h), and maintained this heading from 1025 hours until dark (2100 hours). The change in bearing was a clear and precise shift in direction. She continued a slow meandering movement during daylight for several days. Another turtle left the East Bank Shoal and then moved into the Winyah Bay ship channel. Three of the units provided no discernable data on direction of movements.

The final stage of the study, conducted in 1979, was designed to increase the sample size of turtles monitored and to evaluate internesting habitat use as well as individual movements. Twenty-nine turtles on nesting beaches were instrumented with both sonic and radio transmitters to monitor both land and sea movements. Only movements at sea are reported here.

A 72-foot trawler, the R/V Atlantic Sun, was used during four cruises for a total of 19 days. During these 19 days, search patterns were conducted 24 hours a day. Additional sonic monitoring was conducted during 21 days from small boats. Sixty-seven individual locations for 22 of the 29 turtles (no more than two locations per day for any individual turtle) revealed that most internesting turtles used high relief areas 1–10 m in depth. These included the area around the end of the southern Winyah Bay jetty (a dredge spoil disposal site), East Bank Shoals, the shoal waters off of Cedar Island, and the Cape Romain Shoals. The movements of turtles were also found to parallel high relief contour lines, but no patterns were identified for depth or bottom type during the nesting season. Turtles were regularly located more than 10 km north or south of the nesting beach. These locations were, however, within 10 km of shore. Movements were parallel to the coast and not directly out to sea. As the nesting season was ending in August, the frequency of sonic contacts declined, and no further contacts were recorded by 15 August.

Movements at sea fell into two categories. The first involved long distance directional movements, and the second was unpatterned activity in a limited area. The directional movements were typified by speeds of 1–3 km/h and involved remarkably straight paths. Changes in direction sometimes occurred and were also abrupt about a point, as opposed to gradual alterations of the course. The second movement type involved concentrated activity in limited areas referred to as core areas. Core area movements were unpatterned movements during daylight hours that resulted in less than a 5 km displacement between night areas. Core area activity often was interspersed with periods of no discernable movement. The duration of this type of activity was generally one to three days for any area.

Internesting activities were almost exclusively diurnal. Whether it was a long distance movement or movement in a core area, activity was initiated at sunrise each morning. No correlation between activity and time during daylight

hours was observed, but by late evening activity became greatly reduced.

Nocturnal activities of turtles were limited except for those associated with nesting. Turtles were not displaced by wind or currents at night and could be left after dark and relocated in the same area before dawn the following morning. Nocturnal periods of inactivity away from the nesting beach and extended periods of inactivity in core areas during the first few days following nesting most likely represent resting activity associated with ovulation of the next clutch of eggs (Owens 1997).

In the South Carolina study, nesting loggerhead turtles remained in near-shore waters during the entire nesting season. Internesting movements tended to be parallel to the coast and were primarily to the south of the nesting beach. Shoals and areas of high relief were found to receive concentrated use by turtles during the internesting period, while the areas immediately adjacent to the nesting beaches had high use only by turtles about to nest or following a night when egg deposition was not accomplished. Turtles were inactive at night, and daylight activity involved either long, straight-line movements or unpatterned activities in core areas.

The high use of near-shore waters by adult female loggerheads throughout the nesting season clearly demonstrates the potential for conflict with commercial shrimping activities. This potential may be reduced somewhat by the turtles utilizing areas around shoals where trawler operation is not possible. Finally, concentration areas do occur around obvious physical features that can be considered to be essential internesting habitats.

Georgia

In a study by Stoneburner (1982), eight adult female loggerhead turtles on nesting beaches were instrumented with satellite transmitters in 1979 and 1980 (four each year). There were two problems associated with the data set of this study. In both years, persons in boats removed and/or destroyed transmitters, and at least one transmitter is believed to have indicated aberrant swimming speeds. Three were interfered with during 1979, and all four transmitters were prematurely removed in 1980. Reliable internesting habitat use was only obtained for one turtle in 1979 and one in 1980, and the information on this latter turtle is questionable since it was not known when the transmitter was removed.

Following nesting on Cumberland Island National Seashore, Georgia, both turtles swam in a northerly direction and entered the estuarine waters behind the island. After one to three days, the turtles then left the estuary for the open ocean of the Georgia Bight. They did not wander randomly while at sea prior to renesting, but moved directly to small isolated areas of stable substrates, such as shipwrecks, maritime waste disposal sites, artificial reefs, and limerock outcroppings.

Virginia

Bartol and Musick (1998) used satellite transmitters to track the movements of loggerheads that had nested at Back Bay National Wildlife Refuge, Virginia. In 1998, two turtles were instrumented on 14 and 20 July, respectively. One turtle traveled into the Chesapeake Bay, Virginia, during the two-week internesting interval. She nested again on 31 July, which was confirmed by the refuge personnel. After laying this nest, which appears to have been the final one of the season, her postnesting movement took her into Delaware Bay, where she remained until the second week of October.

The other turtle did not go north into Chesapeake Bay, but continued to reside off the Virginia/North Carolina coast. Because of her close proximity to the shoreline, Bartol and Musick (1998) were unable to determine if she laid a second nest. She remained in this area until 18 October, when signal was lost.

Conclusions

In his status report at WATS II, Ehrhart (1989) posed several questions, all of which are relevant today: What are the sizes or densities of foraging populations and how stable are they? What is the stage-class composition of these populations? How contiguous or homogeneous are

these populations to which researchers have arbitrarily given national or regional identities? Future research should revisit these questions, especially in the areas of the Atlantic basin that are not well studied. New techniques in genetics and telemetry have generated additional questions, but some of the answers to these may be found in the basic research of past decades. The authors suggest the following research topics:

- Gather empirical abundance and genetic data to determine distributions of subpopulations throughout the Atlantic basin.
- Determine sex ratios in combination with genetics of subpopulation survivorship for different age classes in different areas of the Atlantic basin.
- Use remote sensing techniques to elucidate internesting habitat use by adult females in the southern Florida subpopulation.
- Conduct a study of juvenile habitat use by loggerheads in the Caribbean.
- Collect additional life-history data (sex, reproductive status, genetic identity) from stranded carcasses.

ACKNOWLEDGMENTS

Thanks are expressed to J. Seithel and K. Swanson for administrative and graphics support, respectively. Section 6 Grant-in-Aid funding under the Endangered Species Act from the U.S. Fish and Wildlife Service and the National Marine Fisheries Service supported this work. This is contribution number 188 of the Grice Marine Biological Laboratory, College of Charleston.

LITERATURE CITED

Bacon, P. R. 1981. The status of sea turtle stocks management in the western central Atlantic. Western Central Atlantic Fishery Commission Studies no. 7.

Bartol, S. M., and J. A. Musick. 1998. Movements of adult female loggerhead sea turtles found nesting in Virginia. Final Report to USACE, Norfolk, Va.

Bolten, A. B., K. A. Bjorndal, H. R. Martins, T. Dellinger, M. J. Biscoito, S. E. Encalada, and B. W. Bowen. 1998. Transatlantic developmental migrations of loggerhead sea turtles demonstrated by mtDNA sequence analysis. Ecological Applications 8:1–7.

Burke, V. J., and E. A. Standora. 1993. Diet of juvenile Kemp's ridley and loggerhead sea turtles from Long Island, New York. Copeia 1993:1176–1180.

Burke, V. J., S. J. Morreale, and E. A. Standora. 1990. Comparisons of diet and growth of Kemp's ridley and loggerhead turtles from the Northeastern U.S. In T. H. Richardson, J. I. Richardson, and M. Donnelly (compilers). Proceedings of the 10th annual workshop on sea turtle biology and conservation, 135. NOAA Technical Memorandum NMFS-SEFC-278.

Burke, V. J., S. J. Morreale, and E. A. Standora. 1993. Diet of the Kemp's ridley sea turtle, Lepidochelys kempii, in New York. Fishery Bulletin 92:26–32.

Butler, R. W., W. A. Nelson, and T. A. Henwood. 1987. A trawl survey method for estimating loggerhead turtles, Caretta caretta, abundance in five eastern Florida channels and inlets. Fishery Bulletin 85:447–453.

Byles, R. A. 1988. behavior and ecology of sea turtles from Chesapeake Bay, Virginia, Ph.D. dissertation, College of William and Mary, Williamsburg, Va.

Caldwell, D. K. 1959. The loggerhead turtles of Cape Romain, South Carolina (abridged and annotated manuscript of W. P. Baldwin, Jr., and J. P. Loftin, Jr.). Bulletin of the Florida State Museum of Biological Sciences 4:319–348.

Carr, A. 1987. New perspectives on the pelagic stage of sea turtle development. Conservation Biology 1:103–121.

Carr, A., L. Ogren, and C. McVea. 1980. Apparent hibernation by the Atlantic loggerhead turtle, Caretta caretta, off Cape Canaveral. Biological Conservation 19:7–14.

Carr, A., A. Meylan, J. Mortimer, K. Bjorndal, and T. Carr. 1982. Surveys of sea turtle populations and habitats in the western Atlantic. NOAA NMFS-SEFC Technical Memorandum 91.

Coles, W. C., and J. A. Musick. 2000. Satellite sea surface temperature analysis and correlation with sea turtle distribution off North Carolina. Copeia 2000:551–554.

Dickerson, D. D., K. J. Reine, D. A. Nelson, and C. E. Dickerson, Jr. 1995. Assessment of sea turtle abundance in six South Atlantic U.S. channels. USACE Miscellaneous Paper EL-95-5.

Dodd, C. K., Jr. 1988. Synopsis of the biological data on the loggerhead sea turtle Caretta caretta (Linnaeus 1758). USFWS Biological Report 88.

Ehrhart, L. M. 1989. Status report of the loggerhead turtle. In L. Ogren, (ed.). Proceedings of the second western Atlantic turtle symposium, October 12–16, 1987, Mayaguez, Puerto Rico, 122–144.

NOAA Technical Memorandum NOAA NMFS-SEFSC-226.

Ehrhart, L. M., W. E. Redfoot, and D. A. Bagley. 1996. A study of the population ecology of in-water marine turtle populations on the east-central Florida coast from 1982–1996. Comprehensive final report to the National Marine Fisheries Service, Purchase Order 40GENF500155.

Epperly, S. P., J. Braun, and A. Veishlow. 1995. Sea turtles in North Carolina waters. Conservation Biology 9:384–394.

Fritts, T. H., A. B. Irvine, R. D. Jennings, L. A. Collum, W. Hoffman, and M. A. McGehee. 1983. Turtles, birds and mammals in the northern Gulf of Mexico and nearby Atlantic waters. USFWS, FWS/OBS-82/65. Washington, D.C.: U.S. Department of the Interior.

Hendrickson, J. R. 1980. The ecological strategies of sea turtles. American Zoologist 20:597–608.

Hickerson, E. L., and M. B. Peccini. 2000. Using GIS to study habitat use by subadult loggerhead sea turtles (Caretta caretta) at the Flower Garden Banks National Marine Sanctuary in the northwest Gulf of Mexico. In H. Kalb, and T. Wibbles (compilers). Proceedings of the 19th annual symposium on sea turtle biology and conservation, 179–181. NOAA Technical Memorandum NMFS-SEFSC-443.

Hopkins-Murphy, S. R., C. P. Hope, and M. E. Hoyle. 1999. A history of research and management of the loggerhead turtle (Caretta caretta) on the South Carolina coast. Final Report to the U.S. Fish and Wildlife Service.

Lohoefener, R., W. Hoggard, K. Mullin, C. Roden, and C. Rogers. 1989. Are sea turtles attracted to petroleum platforms? In S. Eckert, K. Eckert, and T. Richardson (compilers). Proceedings of the ninth annual workshop on sea turtle conservation and biology, 103–104. NOAA Technical Memorandum NMFS-SEFSC-232.

Lutcavage, M., and J. A. Musick. 1985. Aspects of the biology of sea turtles in Virginia. Copeia 1985:449–456.

Morreale, S. J., A. B. Meylan, S. S. Sadove, and E. A. Standora. 1992. Annual occurrence and winter mortality of marine turtles in New York waters. Journal of Herpetology. 26:301–308.

Mrosovsky N., and J. A. Provancha. 1989. Sex ratio of loggerhead sea turtles hatching on a Florida beach. Canadian Journal of Zoology 67:2533–2539.

Mrosovsky, N., S. R. Hopkins-Murphy, and J. I. Richardson. 1984. Sex ratio of sea turtles: Seasonal changes. Science 225:739–741.

Murphy, T. M., and S. R. Hopkins. 1981. Sonic and

radio tracking of nesting *Caretta caretta*. *In* Reproductive ecology of *Caretta caretta* in South Carolina, 5–38. Study Completion Report to U.S. Fish and Wildlife Service.

NMFS and USFWS. 1991. Recovery plan for U.S. population of loggerhead turtle. Washington, D.C.: National Marine Fisheries Service.

Norrgard, J. 1995. Determination of stock composition and natal origin of a juvenile loggerhead turtle population *(Caretta caretta)* in Chesapeake Bay using mitochondrial DNA analysis. M.S. Thesis, College of William and Mary, Gloucester Point, Va.

Ogren, L., and C. McVea, Jr. 1982. Apparent hibernation by sea turtles in North American waters. *In* K. Bjorndal (ed.). Biology and conservation of sea turtles, 127–132. Washington, D.C.: Smithsonian Institution Press.

Owens, D. W. 1997. Hormones in the life history of sea turtles. *In* P. Lutz and J. Musick (eds.). The biology of sea turtles, 315–341. Boca Raton, Fla.: Chemical Rubber Company Press.

Plotkin, P. T., M. K. Wicksten, and A. F. Amos. 1993. Feeding ecology of the loggerhead sea turtle *Caretta caretta* in the Northwestern Gulf of Mexico. Marine Biology 115:1–15.

Renaud, M. L., and J. A. Carpenter. 1994. Movements and submergence patterns of the loggerhead turtles *(Caretta caretta)* in the Gulf of Mexico determined through satellite telemetry. Bulletin of Marine Science 55:1–15.

Richardson, J. I., and H. O. Hillestad. 1979. Survey for wintering turtles in South Carolina and Georgia. Final report to the National Marine Fisheries Service, Miami, Fla., Contract no. 03-78-D08-0062.

Rosman, I., G. S. Boland, L. R. Martin, and C. Chandler. 1987. Underwater sightings of sea turtles in the northern Gulf of Mexico. U.S. Department of Interior Minerals Management Service, Outer Continental Shelf Study MMS87/0107.

Ruckdeschel, C. A., and C. R. Shoop. 1988. Gut contents of loggerheads: Findings, problems, and new questions. *In* B. A. Schroeder (compiler). Proceedings of the eighth annual workshop on sea turtle biology and conservation, 98–98. NOAA Technical Memorandum NMFS-SEFC-214.

Schroeder, B. A., A. M. Foley, B. E. Witherington, and A. E Mosier. 1998. Ecology of marine turtles in Florida Bay: Population structure, distribution, and occurrence of fibropapilloma. *In* S. P. Epperly and J. Braun (compilers). Proceedings of the 17th annual sea turtle symposium, 265–267. NOAA Technical Memorandum NMFS-SEFSC-415.

Schwartz, F. J. 1978. Behavioral and tolerance responses to cold water temperatures by three species of sea turtles *(Reptilia, Cheloniidae)* in North Carolina. Florida Marine Resources Publication 33:16–18.

Sears, C. J. 1994. Preliminary genetic analysis of the population structure of Georgia loggerhead sea turtles. NOAA Technical Memorandum NMFS-SEFSC-351:135–138.

Sears, D. J., B. W. Bowen, R. W. Chapman, S. B. Galloway, S. R. Hopkins-Murphy, and C. M. Woodley. 1995. Demographic composition of the juvenile loggerhead sea turtle *(Caretta caretta)* feeding population off Charleston, South Carolina: Evidence from mitochondrial DNA markers. Marine Biology 123:869–874.

Stabenau, E. K., K. S. Stanley, and A. M. Landry, Jr. 1996. Sex ratios from stranded sea turtles on the upper Texas coast. Journal of Herpetology 30:427–430.

Shoop, C. R., and R. D. Kenney. 1992. Seasonal distribution and abundances of loggerhead and leatherback sea turtles in waters of the northeastern United States. Herpetological Monographs 6:43–67.

Shoop, C. R., and C. A. Ruckdeschel. 1982. Increasing strandings in the southeast United States: A complicating factor. Biological Conservation 23:213–215.

Stoneburner, D. L. 1982. Satellite telemetry of loggerhead sea turtle movement in the Georgia Bight. Copeia 1982:400–408.

Spotila, J. R., M. P. O'Connor, and F. V. Paladino. 1997. Thermal biology. *In* P. Lutz and J. Musick (eds.). The biology of sea turtles, 297–314. Boca Raton, Fla.: Chemical Rubber Company Press.

TEWG. 1998. An Assessment of the Kemp's ridley *(Lepidochelys kempii)* and loggerhead *(Caretta caretta)* sea turtle populations in the western North Atlantic. NOAA Technical Memorandum NMFS-SEFSC-409.

———. 2000. Assessment update for the kemp's ridley and loggerhead sea turtle populations in the Western North Atlantic. NOAA Technical Memorandum NMFS-SEFSC-444.

VanDolah, R. F., and P. P. Maier. 1993. The distribution of loggerhead turtles *(Caretta caretta)* in the entrance channel of Charleston Harbor, South Carolina, U.S.A. Journal of Coastal Research 9:1004–1012.

Wibbels, T., D. W. Owens, Y. A. Morris, and M. S. Amoss. 1987. Sexing techniques and sex ratios for immature loggerhead sea turtles captured along the Atlantic coast of the United States. *In* W. N.

Witzell (ed.). Ecology of east Florida sea turtles, 65–74. NOAA Technical Report, National Marine Fisheries Service 53.

Wibbels, T., R. E. Martin, D. W. Owens, and M. S. Amoss, Jr. 1991. Female-biased sex ratio of immature loggerhead sea turtles inhabiting the Atlantic coastal waters of Florida. Canadian Journal of Zoology 69:2973–2977.

Witherington, B. E., and L. M. Ehrhart. 1989. Hypothermic stunning and mortality of marine turtle in the Indian River Lagoon system, Florida. Copeia 1989:696.

Witzell, W. N. 1999. Distribution and relative abundance of sea turtles caught incidentally by the U.S. pelagic longline fleet in the western North Atlantic Ocean, 1992–1995. Fishery Bulletin 97:200–211.

Youngkin, D. 2001. A long-term dietary analysis of loggerhead sea turtles (Caretta caretta) based on strandings from Cumberland Island, Georgia. M.S. Thesis, Florida Atlantic University, Boca Raton.

Chapter 6

Biology of the Loggerhead Turtle in Western South Pacific Ocean Foraging Areas

—Colin J. Limpus and Duncan J. Limpus

The loggerhead turtle is one of six species of marine turtles that have been widespread and abundant within the South Pacific Ocean region. However, it was poorly documented in the region prior to the latter half of the 20th century (Dodd 1988). This contrasts with the considerable amount of information that exists in the older literature for the region's green turtles *(Chelonia mydas)* and hawksbills *(Eretmochelys imbricata)* (Barrett 1919; Ellis 1937; Jukes 1847; Parsons 1962; Saville-Kent 1893; Thompson 1849, in Moore 1979). The difference in attention was largely because of the significance of these latter species in harvests for food and tortoiseshell. Certainly within the western South Pacific region, where green turtles have been abundant, there seems to have been a bias against hunting loggerhead turtles, with the species often being ignored by indigenous and other hunters in favor of the preferred green and hawksbill turtles (Johannes and Mac-Farlane 1991; Smith 1987; Thompson 1849, in Moore 1979; Thomson 1934). In eastern Australia, the turtle soup factories in Brisbane and the southern Great Barrier Reef, that operated from the late 1800s until 1950 and supplied turtle soup to Australian and overseas markets, appear to have harvested only green turtles. This applied even at harvest sites such as Moreton Bay and Bundaberg where loggerhead turtles were more abundant than green turtles in the mid-1900s (Limpus 1985; Limpus et al. 1994a, 1994b). A corollary of this is that there appear to have been no large-scale anthropogenic impacts on loggerhead turtle populations in the South Pacific region prior to World War II.

Commencing with nesting beach studies in the 1960s, loggerhead turtles have been the focus of continuing systematic nesting beach and foraging area research and monitoring studies in eastern Australia. Little emphasis has been given to studies of loggerhead turtles in the South Pacific Ocean basin outside of the Australia studies. As a consequence, the following account of the biology and ecology of logger-head turtles in South Pacific Ocean foraging areas is biased largely to results from the Australian region. There is a distinct possibility that apart from the young loggerhead turtles in their oceanic life stage, the species is scarce in the southern central and eastern Pacific Ocean. This account includes previously unpublished observations and data from the authors' studies.

Long-Term Studies of Loggerheads in Eastern Australia

Mark-Recapture Studies

Mark-recapture studies of loggerhead turtles in foraging areas of eastern Australia commenced in 1974. These in-water studies developed in parallel to the Queensland nesting beach studies, which commenced at Mon Repos in 1968 (Limpus 1985). Initially the in-water studies were conducted on the coral reefs adjacent to Heron Island (23.43° S, 151.92° E) in the southern Great Barrier Reef (GBR) (Limpus 1985; Limpus et al. 1984). Annual sampling of these reefs has continued to the present except during 1993. Loggerhead turtles have been captured opportunistically during numerous additional parallel studies of green and hawksbill turtles elsewhere in the Great Barrier Reef since 1987. Commencing in 1990, a second loggerhead turtle foraging population in Moreton Bay (27.35° S, 153.40° E) has been sampled annually (Limpus et al. 1994a).

Loggerhead turtles were captured as they were encountered during systematic searches of the various accessible habitats. Most turtles were captured by day using the turtle rodeo capture method (Limpus 1978; Limpus and Read 1985). In addition, nighttime turtle rodeo captures were made over the reef flat adjacent to Heron Island with the aid of a 12-volt flood-light mounted beneath the catch boat. Some turtles were captured by approaching them on foot and leaping to grasp them by the carapace. This beach-jump capture method (Limpus and Read 1985) was used only adjacent to islands, at high tide along the beach by night and on the reef flats at low tide by day. Small numbers of loggerhead turtles were also captured by snorkeling and by SCUBA diving along reef margins by both day and night.

In the early years of the study, turtles were tagged with monel cattle ear tags applied to the trailing margin of the front flipper (Limpus 1992a). Since 1982, loggerhead turtles in eastern Australia have been tagged with self-locking standard titanium turtle tags (Stockbrands Company, Pty. Ltd., Perth, Western Australia). The reverse side of tags was inscribed: "Return Wildlife Box 155 Brisbane 4002 Qld Australia." The titanium tags have been applied through or immediately adjacent to the enlarged scale closest to the body on the posterior edge of the left and right front flippers (Limpus 1992a). If the animal already carried tags, the condition of the tags was assessed, and if a tag was insecure, an additional tag was applied. In the majority of cases, each turtle was released with a minimum of two securely attached titanium tags, one in each front flipper. Because of a high tag loss rate with monel tags (Limpus 1992a), data from tagging prior to 1982 are unreliable for analysis for many demographic parameters. Data from studies of foraging turtles are supplemented with data reported through the Queensland Parks and Wildlife Service marine wildlife stranding and mortality database network. Some tag recoveries, particularly relating to breeding migration, have been reported by the public.

Turtle Measurements, Sex, and Maturity

Following their capture, most turtles were landed on a nearby beach or boat for gonad examination. They were released usually within five hours of being brought ashore. Other turtles were released where captured, usually within 10 minutes of capture, after having been tagged and measured.

Curved carapace length (CCL) was measured using a flexible fiberglass tape (± 0.1 cm) laid over the curve of the midline of the carapace from the junction of the skin and carapace above the neck to the most posterior margin of the junction of the supracaudal scutes. The calibration of fiberglass tape measures was checked regularly against steel rules. Use of a tape measure was discontinued when length changes exceeded ± 0.2 cm within 100.0 cm. Any large barnacles on the carapace likely to interfere with a measurement were removed.

Tail length from carapace (TLC) was measured to the tip of the straightened tail from the posterior midline junction of the supracaudal scutes using a steel tape measure (± 0.5 cm). A negative sign for this measurement indicates a distance short of the carapace margin.

Because most immature male turtles cannot be distinguished from females using external sexual characteristics, turtles were sexed by visual examination of gonads and associated ducts, using a laparoscope with live turtles (Limpus 1992b; Limpus et al. 1994a, 1994b), or during necropsies of freshly dead stranded turtles. The standard laparoscope used was a 5 mm diameter scope inserted through a 7 mm diameter cannula. The cannula was inserted through the inguinal area anterior and lateral to the right hind flipper. To facilitate the insertion of the cannula, a 1 cm incision was made in the skin with a scalpel. Passage of the cannula through the underlying muscle and connective tissue and penetration of the peritoneum was facilitated with the trochar supplied with the cannula. On removal of the cannula, the skin incision was closed with a water-soluble suture. To minimize infection, the instruments were maintained in a 70% ethanol bath in preparation for and following each surgical examination and were scrubbed and boiled on a regular basis.

Gonad biopsies were taken during some laparoscopic examinations using punch biopsy forceps passed through a 5 mm cannula inserted adjacent to the cannula for the endoscope. Gonad samples were prepared for microscopic examination using the periodic acid (Schiff) technique (fixed in 10% formalin, wax embedded, cut to 8 mm sections and dyed with hematoxylin, eosin, and periodic acid).

Within this study, a turtle was defined as mature (adult) if its gonads and associated ducts were fully developed. This does not imply that the turtle has already bred, only that it has the structural potential to breed.

The following key was applied for assessing the sex and maturity status of loggerhead turtles (modified from Limpus 1992b and based on the results of examining > 2,000 gonads of foraging and nesting loggerhead turtles):

Turtles whose gonads cannot be examined.
- Female: Nesting turtles are obviously adult females. Short-tailed (TLC < 5 cm) turtles in courtship groups are probably, but not always, adult females.
- Male: Any turtle with TLC > 5 cm can be accepted as male (the longest tail recorded on a nesting female was TLC = 4 cm; Limpus 1985). Long-tailed turtles in courtship groups are accepted as adult males.
- Unsexed (sex not determined): Any other turtle.
- Maturity: Any turtle with an undifferentiated tail and with CCL < 80 cm (the minimum breeding size for loggerhead turtles in eastern Australia; Limpus 1985) was recorded as immature. For males (TLC > 5 cm), those with TLC < 19.0 cm were recorded as immature, and those with TLC > 19.0 cm were recorded as adult, regardless of CCL. The maturity status of unsexed turtles with CCL > 80.5 cm and TLC < 5 cm was recorded as "undetermined."

Turtles whose gonads are examined.
- Mature females: Females recorded as mature had ovaries with an expanded stroma. Each oviduct was pink, convoluted and straplike, and at least 1.5 cm in cross-section width adjacent to the ovary. Yellow, vascularized, vitellogenic follicles (0.3–3.0 cm diameter), corpora lutea, corpora albicantia (scars from healed corpora lutea), or atretic follicles may be present in the ovary. Eggs may be present in the oviduct.
- Immature, pubescent females: Females recorded as pubescent immature had ovaries with an expanding or approximately fully expanded stroma. Each oviduct was partly convoluted, oval in cross section, and 0.3–1.5 cm in diameter adjacent to the ovary. No corpora albicantia, corpora lutea, developing follicles, or atretic follicles will be present in the ovaries.
- Immature, prepubescent females: Females recorded as pubescent immature had ovaries with a nonexpanded stroma. Each oviduct was white, straight, or slightly convoluted,

cylindrical to oval in cross section, and < 0.3 cm wide opposite the ovary. No vitellogenic follicles, corpora lutea, corpora albicantia, or atretic follicles will be present in the ovary.

- Mature males: Males recorded as mature had cylindrical testes with each epididymis distinctly enlarged and pendulous.
- Immature, pubescent males: Males recorded as pubescent immature had testes approximately elliptical in cross section. Each epididymis formed a nonpendulous ridge on the body wall. These turtles should also be characterized by TLC = 9–19 cm, claws elongating and recurving, and the penis distinguishable from clitoris.
- Immature, prepubescent males: Males recorded as prepubescent immature had testes that were flat or ellipsoidal in cross section, each with an epididymis that was not bulging from the body wall.

Because a corpus albicans is a healed corpus luteum and a corpus luteum is formed by the release (ovulation) of a mature follicle from the ovary, the presence of corpora albicantia indicates that a female has bred in a past nesting season. Similarly the absence of corpora albicantia on the ovaries of a female with oviducal eggs indicates that she is in her first breeding season. Therefore, the absence of corpora albicantia in the ovaries of females that have recently ovulated can be used to identify those females that are new recruits to the breeding population. When gonads could not be identified unambiguously as either ovary or testis, the turtle was defined as an intersex animal for the purposes of the present study. Laparoscopic examination of gonads to assess sex, maturity, and breeding status has been a routine procedure performed on the vast majority of turtles sampled in the annual monitoring of foraging populations in Queensland since 1982.

Ecology, Behavior, Threats, and Status

Foraging Habitat

Migration recaptures of adult female loggerhead turtles that breed at eastern Australian rookeries indicate that these turtles inhabit widely dispersed foraging habitats in coastal waters from Montague Island (35.25° S) in southern New South Wales to as far north as the Solomon Islands (5.33° S) and from New Caledonia (22.33° S, 166.50° E) in the east to the Arnhem Land coast (13.60° S, 136.42° E) in the western Gulf of Carpentaria (Bustard 1972; Limpus et al. 1992). Adult and large immature loggerhead turtles are year-round residents of a wide range of marine habitats inside the continental shelf waters of eastern Australia north of at least 30° S. To the south, loggerhead turtles are rare waifs within the coastal waters of the southeastern Australian states of Victoria and Tasmania (37–44° S; Green 1971; Viridans 2000).

Although small posthatchling loggerheads from oceanic habitats dominate the strandings in New Zealand, some adult-sized loggerheads have been reported intermittently from the coastal waters of northern New Zealand, between 34 and 38° S (McCann 1966; Gill 1997). There is no indication that these loggerhead turtles have anything but a transient association with these New Zealand waters. Foraging adult and large immature loggerhead turtles are regularly encountered on the reefs of New Caledonia, especially in the Isles des Pines region (P. Beloff, pers. comm.). In Fiji, foraging large-sized loggerhead turtles are widespread, but they are uncommon at any particular location (Guinea 1993). Loggerhead turtles appear to be an uncommon foraging species in the coastal waters of the South Pacific island nations outside of the region bounded by tropical and warm temperate eastern Australia, Papua New Guinea, New Caledonia, and Fiji (Pritchard 1982).

At a finer local scale of distribution, adult and large immature loggerhead turtles can be found foraging at any coral reef, rocky reef, bay, or estuary throughout the tropical and warm temperate waters of eastern Australia. In coral reef habitats, loggerhead turtles are sympatric with green turtles and hawksbill turtles (Limpus 1992b). In shallow seagrass pastures, loggerhead turtles are regularly encountered feeding among the more abundant green turtles (Limpus et al. 1994b). Based on loggerhead turtle captures in eastern and northern Australian prawn trawl fisheries, the species also forages over the extensive soft-bottomed habitats at less than 40 m depth throughout coastal waters of the inner continental shelf (Poiner and Harris 1996; Robins 1995). In these continental shelf waters, loggerhead, flatback *(Natator depressus)* and olive ridley *(Lepidochelys olivacea)* turtles occupy similar habitats.

Based on postnesting migration tag recoveries and the authors' observations across many coastal waters throughout eastern Australia, the largest numbers of foraging loggerhead turtles appear to occur within the intertidal and subtidal waters in the region of Moreton Bay, Hervey Bay, and Sandy Straits and the coral reefs of the Capricorn-Bunker groups of the southern Great Barrier Reef (23–28° S).

Although there has been no direct study of these turtles with respect to their body temperature, each winter loggerhead turtles are captured foraging along with green turtles over the intertidal banks of Moreton Bay where winter water temperatures can be as low as 15°C (Read et al. 1996). Even at these temperatures there is no evidence that any eastern Australian loggerhead turtle population undertakes north-south, summer-winter, nonbreeding migrations such as occur with the species in the higher latitudes of the eastern United States (Musick and Limpus 1997). At water temperatures approaching 15°C, the loggerhead turtles foraging on the Moreton Banks are quite lethargic in their swimming. There are unconfirmed reports from local fishermen indicating that during winter some of the loggerhead turtles move from feeding over the intertidal banks of eastern Moreton Bay to rest in the bottom of adjacent channels.

Although they may be aggregated for feeding at some localities, foraging loggerhead turtles are solitary animals. They do not swim in groups, and they are not territorial in the sense of driving other turtles out of their home range. Many individuals may share overlapping home ranges to be feeding within sight of one another, and different individuals may even alternate in the use of a particular refuge under a coral ledge. However, feeding or resting individuals have been observed to defend a personal space. The behavior shown by these turtles is a posturing with the anterior body and head raised and the mouth gaping towards the intruding individual. On rare occasions, loggerhead turtles have been observed attempting to bite other turtles that approached too closely. The resulting bite often results in the removal of a triangular piece of keratin, 1–2 cm in diameter, that exposes bone on the dorsal surface of a posterior marginal scute. The regular occurrence of these white "bite marks" on wild loggerhead turtles suggests that there are social interactions within the species that keep foraging individuals apart. These aggressive displays can even be directed towards other species. In two instances, moribund immature green turtles were found in the Moreton Bay area with compressed fractures to the head that matched the shape and size of loggerhead turtle jaws marks.

While loggerhead turtles are commonly seen foraging by day, some individuals are also active at night. In the clear calm waters over the coral reefs surrounding the islands of the southern Great Barrier Reef, loggerhead turtles can be seen foraging on most nights in the shallows adjacent to the islands during the higher levels of the tidal cycle. The nighttime foraging area is not necessarily the same as the daytime foraging area. At Heron Island, tagged loggerhead turtles captured foraging within tens of meters of the island at night included many turtles that had never been captured by day within several kilometers of the island. In Shoalwater Bay (22.33° S, 150.20° E) during 1990 and 1991, a local fisherman (Bill Chippendale) tagged the turtles captured in an arrowhead fish trap in intertidal waters. This trap captured large numbers of green turtles by day and by night (n = 159). However, all loggerhead turtle captures (n = 7) occurred at night.

Recruitment from Oceanic Habitats

Each year new untagged loggerhead turtles with a distinctly different appearance than that of the long-term residents of coastal inshore waters arrive to live in the study areas. The size of these turtles ranges from that of large immatures to small adults. These newly arrived turtles have bright colors (yellow plastron, orange skin on neck and shoulders, brown carapace); dark-colored jaw sheaths inside the mouth (dark pigment is restricted to surface layers while deeper layers are white); large (up to 1.5 cm diameter) burrowing barnacles, *Stephanolepas muricata*, on the leading edge of the flippers; keeling on the vertebral scutes; a sharp serrated carapace margin; and a sharp trailing edge to the distal portion of each front flipper. It is not uncommon for these newly arrived turtles also to be carrying the commensal Columbus crab *(Planes minutus)*. The crab usually retreats to the top of the tail under the carapace when the turtle is captured. These crabs are lost within a few weeks of the turtle's arrival. In contrast, commensal Columbus crabs are commonly found on loggerhead turtles in the oceanic environment (Davenport 1994; Dellinger et al. 1997; McMillan 1967). Loggerhead turtles when recaptured after about one year of residency are characterized by never carrying Columbus crabs; by algal discoloration of the plastron, skin, and carapace; by yellow skin on the neck and shoulders; by loss of dark pigment from the surface of jaw sheaths; by reduced sharpness to the edges of the carapace; by reduced serration of the carapace margin; and by worn trailing edges to the distal end of the front flippers. *S. muricata* on the flippers are usually dead within the first year, but scars from these barnacles may be discernible for up to two years. These barnacles appear to be killed when the leading edges of the flippers dig into the substrate while the turtles forage and rest on the bottom.

Loggerhead turtles with the above characteristics are presumed to be turtles that have recently recruited to residency in coastal inshore foraging areas from the oceanic habitats and are recorded as such in the research database. The dark coloration of the inner surfaces of the jaw sheaths are presumed to result from eating pigmented prey such as janthinid snails in the oceanic habitats, and this pigmented layer is abraded off by the course food items of the coastal benthic environment. The *Planes* crabs are probably removed by predatory fish such as remora (Echeneidae) and trevally (Carangidae) that are regularly associated with foraging loggerhead turtles in coastal waters (Limpus 1978).

There is a pronounced absence from eastern Australian coastal waters of small immature loggerhead turtles in the size range between hatchling (4–5 cm CCL) and approximately 70 cm CCL. There is no knife-edge effect for

Table 6.1.

Sizes of Loggerheads Recently Recruited from Oceanic Habitats to Southern Queensland Coastal Foraging Areas

	Curved Carapace Length (cm)			
Foraging Area	Mean	SD	Range	N
Capricornia	79.05	4.336	68.0–93.9	53
Hervey Bay	78.63	1.863	76.0–80.0	3
Moreton Bay	78.18	3.746	66.7–85.1	52
Combined	78.62	4.013	66.7–93.9	108

Note: SD = standard deviation; N = number.

the size at which these immature turtles leave the oceanic environment. Rather, they recruit to coastal foraging habitats across a wide range of sizes from 66.7 to 93.9 cm (mean CCL = 78.62 cm; Table 6.1; Figure 6.1). There is no detectable difference in size of turtles recruiting to residency within the southern Great Barrier Reef, Hervey Bay, and Moreton Bay foraging areas (Table 6.1; one-way analysis of variance, $p > 0.25$). Loggerhead turtles recruit to coastal residency in eastern Australia at a much larger size than do green turtles or hawksbills (Figure 6.1). If the growth of loggerhead turtles in the oceanic habitats of the South Pacific Ocean is similar to that of those in the North Pacific Ocean (turtles of known age to 46 cm CCL; Chaloupka 1998), then young loggerhead turtles recruiting to coastal habitats in eastern Australia are considerably older than 10 years.

Since systematic recording of recent recruits began in 1994, 24% (n = 84) of these recently recruited loggerheads have had scars from recent shark bites. In contrast, healing wounds from recent shark bites are encountered at a low frequency (< 1%) with turtles that have an established residency within eastern Australian coastal foraging areas. Recruitment to coastal residency appears to be an event associated with an elevated risk of shark attack and death.

Diet

Loggerhead turtles in eastern Australia are carnivorous, exhibiting a range of feeding behav-

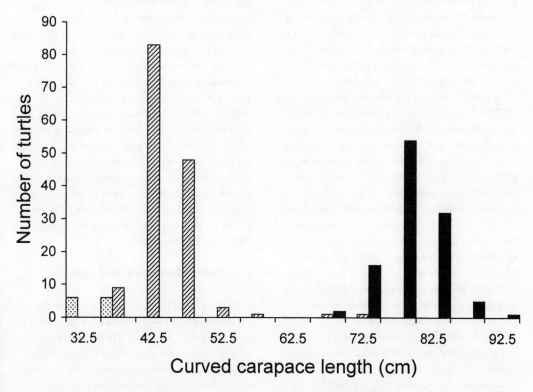

Figure 6.1. Size of marine turtles that have recently recruited to residency in coastal foraging areas of central and southern Queensland.

iors and ingesting a wide variety of prey items (> 100 taxa; Limpus et al. 2001; Moodie 1979). Large immature and adult loggerhead turtles are specialized for feeding on slow-moving, hard-bodied invertebrate prey. The most commonly consumed taxa are gastropod and bivalve mollusks and portunid (swimming) crabs and pagurids (hermit crabs). However, soft-bodied prey including holothurians, jelly-fish, and sea anemones are also consumed to a lesser extent. The specific prey species selected are a function of the turtle's feeding area rather than its sex or size. As individuals, even within the one area, their diet is unpredictable, with some variability in the diet being attributed to individual preference.

Loggerhead turtles in soft-bottom habitats such as Moreton Bay may locate buried infaunal prey items by mining for them (Limpus et al. 1994a; Preen 1996): the turtles dig shallow meandering trenches ≅ 1.5 m wide, with the advancing edge 0.3–0.45 m deep, using sweeps of their front flippers. The exposed infaunae, which include a range of thick- and thin-shelled bivalves and polychaetes (Preen 1996), are picked up in the mouth and ingested. In the southern Great Barrier Reef, loggerhead turtles bite into the loose sandy substrate to feed on rhinoclavid gastropods living within the top few centimeters of sand in coral reef lagoon habitat (Moodie 1979). Some loggerhead turtles feed by picking visible prey items off the substrate surface (Limpus et al. 2001). These prey items include large clams *(Tridacna maxima)*, portu-nid and pagurid crabs and sea anemones. Log-gerhead turtles are occasionally captured when they ingest anglers' hooks baited with fish that are lying on the substrate surface. Loggerhead turtles will cease feeding at the bottom to pluck available food such as jellyfish, *Pelagia noctiluca*, from within the water column. They will also feed at or near the surface on suspended or floating prey such as gooseneck barnacles, *Lepas* sp., and on discarded trawl bycatch.

Even though turtles in this life stage are described as benthic feeding, they readily revert to feeding at the water surface or within the water column, as they did during their previous oceanic life stage (Limpus et al. 2001).

Contrary to the hypothesis of Limpus (1973), loggerhead turtles either do not feed or do so infrequently during their internesting period. Limpus (1973) did not consider water uptake when accounting for weight changes in the nesting females throughout the breeding season. Recently ingested food rarely has been found in gastrointestinal tracts during necropsy of the large series of stranded carcasses of internesting loggerhead turtles from the vicinity of Queensland rookeries. Internesting status was established by the presence of oviducal eggs or mature follicles in association with full-sized corpora lutea. In addition, gastrointestinal tracts of hundreds of female loggerhead turtles on nesting beaches during all stages of the breeding season have been examined during laparoscopic examination of the ovaries. These observations have consistently shown that the breeding female has a largely empty gut for the duration of the nesting season. Therefore, it is concluded that breeding loggerhead turtles do not use the internesting habitat as a foraging area and that at this time they live off fat reserves accumulated before they began their breeding migrations from distant home foraging areas.

Basking

Low numbers of loggerhead turtles are encountered basking with the numerous basking green turtles within the region from the southern Great Barrier Reef to Hervey Bay (23–25° S). Basking turtles were first recorded in the southern Great Barrier Reef in 1910 (Barrett 1919). While this basking behavior is most obvious by day, animals exhibiting similar behavior also can be observed at the same locations by night. The term "basking" is applied also to turtles that haul out at night and appear to be sleeping near or below the high-tide line. Most basking has been observed during spring and summer (October–January). This period coincides with the eastern Australian breeding season for green and loggerhead turtles. At Sandy Cape on Fraser Island (25.25° S, 153.17° E) in northern Hervey Bay, there has been annual tagging of many of the basking turtles since 1995. Here, the basking loggerhead turtles have included male and female breeding migrants and locally resident adults and immature turtles. As an extreme example of fidelity to a basking area, an unsexed adult-sized loggerhead turtle (T92860; CCL = 85 cm) was encountered basking at night near Sandy Cape 15 times during the period from 29 October 1996 to 20 January 1997; 12 times from 16 November 1997 to 11 January 1998; and 8 times from 16 December 1998 to 30 January 1999.

Population Structure and Function

Data shown in Figure 6.2 are typical for the annual sampling of loggerhead foraging populations in eastern Australia. There are effectively no small immature loggerhead turtles in this region comparable to those in coastal waters of the western Atlantic (Musick and Limpus 1997). Loggerhead turtles resident in eastern Australian foraging areas range in size from medium-sized immature turtles to large adults (CCL = 62.5–113.0 cm; Limpus 1985; Limpus et al. 1984, 1994a; Figure 6.2a).

At both Moreton Bay and the southern Great Barrier Reef foraging areas and for all years since routine gonad examination began in 1982, the population has been strongly biased to males with a male to female sex ratio of 1:0.41 in the southern Great Barrier Reef (Limpus 1985; Figure 6.2a) and 1:0.54 in in Moreton Bay (Limpus et al. 1994a). However, within the Moreton Bay population the sex ratio varies with maturity and size class. There the proportion of females decreases with advancing maturity and increasing CCL (Limpus et al. 1994a). A small proportion (< 1%) of loggerhead turtles have gonads that cannot be clearly identified as either male or female (intersex) (Limpus et al. 1994a). These gonads are usually ovitestes with seminiferous tubules in the medulla and scattered small previtellogenic follicles in the cortex. Several of these intersex turtles have had their gonads reexamined repetitively over periods of up to 15 years, and none have displayed any evidence of changing sex.

To address growth and maturation period, the authors have considered data from a series of female loggerheads resident in the southern Great Barrier Reef that have been part of the mark-recapture project from the time they recruited to the time they were recognized as adults (Table 6.2). The mean duration of the growth phase from coastal recruitment to first breeding was 13 years (SD = 3.7; range = 9–23 years; n = 15). This is a more direct measure of the duration of growth within this neritic, benthic-feeding phase than are values hypothesized from mathematical modeling of size (Frazer et al. 1994).

For the wider population of loggerhead turtles that are residents of these coral reefs of the southern Great Barrier Reef (23° S), the CCL growth rate is usually 1–2 cm per year for large immature individuals and slows to a few millimeters per year for young adults. Growth effectively stops in old adults. However, growth rate can vary significantly both between years and between feeding areas. In Moreton Bay (27° S), immature loggerhead turtles have been growing an order of magnitude slower, 2–3 mm per year, than similar-sized immature individuals resident in the southern Great Barrier Reef.

During the latter stages of the immature growth phase, the ovaries and oviduct enlarge, resulting in a turtle that is structurally indistinguishable from an adult. The first vitellogenic cycle to form large numbers of mature-sized follicles usually occurs about two to four years after gonads and ducts appear to be fully developed. However, ovulation rarely occurs in the season of first vitellogenesis, and the enlarged follicles are resorbed. Most young adults ovulate for the first time in their second season of vitellogenesis, which occurs two to three years after first vitellogenesis (Limpus 1990). The mean size at first breeding recorded for the group followed from recruitment to adulthood was CCL = 94.4 cm (SD = 3.45 cm; range = 90.5–101.5 cm; n = 14; see Table 6.2).

The minimum breeding size recorded for eastern Australian loggerhead turtles recorded at nesting beaches has been 80.0 cm (Limpus

1985). However, commencement of breeding at this minimum size is rare for the population. Indeed this is approximately the same size at which they recruit as young immature turtles from the oceanic environment. There is no knife-edge size effect for first breeding in this population (Table 6.2; Figure 6.2b). On average, females that grow to maturity in the southern Great Barrier Reef commence breeding at a size (CCL = 94.4 cm) only slightly smaller than the average size of breeding females within the entire population (Mon Repos, CCL = 95.1 cm; Limpus 1985, 1990) (Heron Island, CCL = 95.7 cm; Limpus et al. 1984). Similarly, most male loggerhead turtles reach maturity at approximately the average size of adult males (Figure 6.2c; Limpus 1985; Limpus et al. 1994a).

Based on analysis of the mark-recapture studies within southern Great Barrier Reef coral reefs, there was no sex-specific difference in annual survival probability for immature or adult loggerhead turtles (Chaloupka and Limpus 2002). The mean annual survival for adult loggerhead turtles was 0.875 (95% confidence interval = 0.84–0.91), which was lower than the mean annual survival for adult green turtles resident in the same southern Great Barrier Reef waters (Chaloupka and Limpus, in press). Mean annual survival for immature loggerhead turtles was 0.859 (95% confidence interval = 0.83–0.89), but when possible transients were accounted for, the mean annual survival for resident immature turtles was 0.918 (95% confidence interval = 0.88–0.96). The survivorship of immature loggerhead turtles was similar to that of immature green turtles resident in the same southern Great Barrier Reef waters (Chaloupka and Limpus, in press).

During the eight-year period 1985–1992, the reference loggerhead population on Heron Island Reef declined by ≅ 3% per year (Chaloupka and Limpus 2001). It was hypothesized that the population decline within these protected coral reef habitats of the southern Great Barrier Reef could be the result of declining rates of recruitment of young turtles from the oceanic environment. The measured rate of tagging of new individuals into this population is in agreement with this hypothesis (Figure 6.3). In the context of a 21-year time frame since

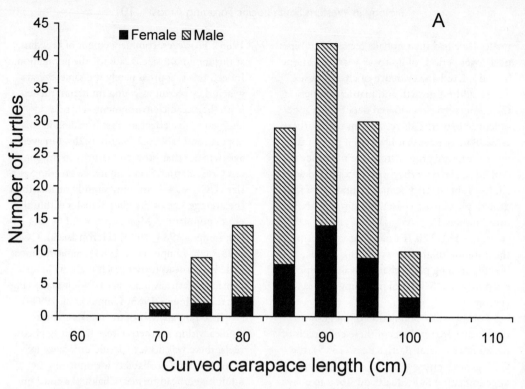

Figure 6.2. Size distribution by sex and maturity for resident foraging loggerheads captured on Heron and Wistari reefs, southern Great Barrier Reef (sGBR), Queensland, during March–April 1992. A. All turtles (n = 136). B. Females (n = 40). C. Males (n = 96). D. All turtles: sex × maturity (n = 136).

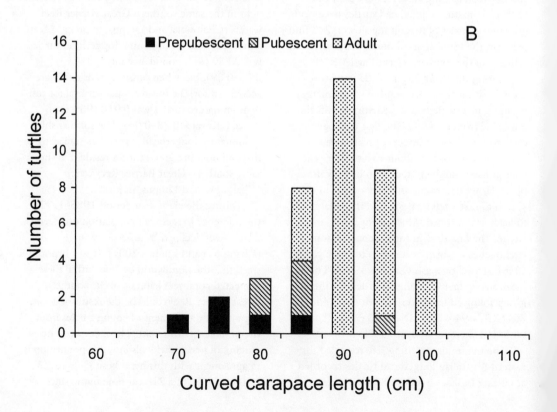

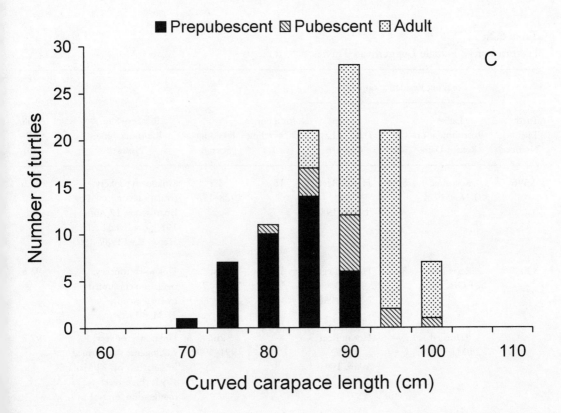

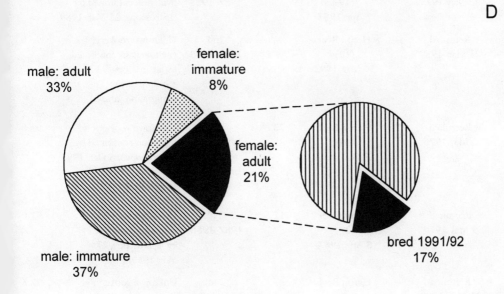

Table 6.2.
Histories of 17 Female Loggerhead Turtles

| Turtle Tag Number | Foraging Residency on Reef | | | Recruitment to First Breeding (years) | Breeding Season | Rookery Site, Reproduction, Notes | Adult CCL (cm) |
	Latest Recruitment or Return Date	CCL (cm)	Site (n) Date of Last Capture				
X596	Recruited 1 Nov. 1974	80.5	Heron Reef (56) 11 Mar. 1988	15	1st 1988–1989	Unknown rookery; ovulation confirmed by laparoscopy, 17 Apr. 1989; observed back on Heron Reef 1989–1991.	94.0
X2009	Recruited 31 Oct. 1974	80.5	Heron Reef (34) 7 Mar. 1988	15	1st 1988–1989	Unknown rookery; ovulation confirmed by laparoscopy, 28 Mar. 1989	95.5
	Returned 28 Mar. 1989	—	Heron Reef (5) 6 Apr. 1991	—	2nd 1991–1992	Unknown rookery; vitellogenesis confirmed by laparoscopy, 22 Mar. 1991; three-year remigration interval.	97.5
X2065	Recruited 13 May 1975	87.0	Heron Reef (49) 7 Apr. 1987	13	1st 1987–1988	Unknown rookery; ovulation confirmed by laparoscopy, 21 Mar. 1989.	95.5
	Returned 21 Mar. 1989	—	Heron Reef (10) 24 Mar. 1992	—	2nd 1992–1993	Unknown rookery; vitellogenesis confirmed by laparoscopy, 23 Mar. 1992; five-year remigration interval.	96.0
X2342	Recruited 5 May 1976	77.5	Heron Reef (49) 17 Oct. 1998	23	1st 1998–1999	Unknown rookery; ovulation confirmed by laparoscopy, 16 Oct. 1999; observed back on Heron Reef 1999.	91.0
X2385	Recruited 9 May 1976	83.5	Heron Reef (27) 3 Apr. 1987	12	1st 1987–1988	Unknown rookery; ovulation confirmed by laparoscopy, 27 Mar. 1989.	91.0
	Returned 27 Mar. 1989	—	Heron Reef (3) 22 Mar. 1991	—	2nd 1991–1992	Unknown rookery; ovulation confirmed by laparoscopy, 22 Mar. 1992; four-year remigration interval; observed back on Heron Reef 1992.	92.5

Table 6.2. continued:

X2392	Recruited 9 May 1976	85.0	Heron Reef (51) 1 Apr. 1986	11	1st 1986–1987	Unknown rookery; ovulation confirmed by laparoscopy, 13 Mar. 1987.	94.5
	Returned 13 Mar. 1987	—	Heron Reef (12) 7 Apr. 1991	—	2nd 1991–1992	Unknown rookery; vitellogenesis confirmed by laparoscopy, 23 Mar. 1991; five-year remigration interval.	96.0
X2757	Recruited 19 May 1997	80.0	Heron Reef (33) 6 Apr. 1990	14	1st 16 Dec. 1990 to 03 Jan. 1991	Lady Musgrave Island (migration distance 69 km); aid at least two clutches (incomplete tagging census)	92.0
	Returned 23 Mar. 1991	—	Heron Reef (4) 27 Apr. 1992	—	2nd 26 Dec. 1993 to 11 Jan. 1994	Lady Musgrave Island; laid at least two clutches incomplete tagging census); three-year remigration interval.	93.8
	Returned 13 Oct. 1995	—	Heron Reef (3) 20 Oct. 1995	—	3rd 1 Jan. 1996	Lady Musgrave Island; laid at least one clutch (incomplete tagging census); two-year remigration interval; observed back on Heron Reef 1996.	93.8
X2764	Recruited 20 May 1977	83.0	Heron Reef (2) Wistari Reef (5) 26 Aug 1985	10	1st 1986–1987	Unknown rookery; ovulation confirmed by laparoscopy, 17 Mar. 1987.	90.5
	Returned 17 Mar. 1987	—	Heron Reef (4) 09 Apr 1987	—	2nd 1989–1990	Unknown rookery; ovulation confirmed by laparoscopy, 11 Apr. 1990; three-year remigration interval; observed back on Wistari and Heron Reefs 1990–1992.	91.5
X9334	Recruited 4 Nov. 1977	<87.5[a]	Heron Reef (28) 8 Apr. 1991	15	1st 7 Jan. 1992	Isles des Pines, New Caledonia (migration distance 1594 km); laid at least one clutch (no tagging census)	98.3
	Returned 20 Mar. 1992	—	Heron Reef (3) 17 Oct. 1994	—	2nd 1995–1996	Nesting not recorded; ovulation confirmed by laparoscopy, 13 Aug. 1996; four-year remigration interval; observed back on Heron Reef 1996–1998.	99.6

Table 6.2. continued:

X9343	Recruited 5 Nov. 1977	82.5	Wistari Reef (4) 24 Oct. 1980	?	1st before 1990	Unknown rookery; ovulation confirmed by laparoscopy, 23 Mar. 1992.	?
	Returned 25 Mar. 1992	—	Wistari Reef (3) 3 Mar. 1992	—	2nd 1992–1993	Unknown rookery; ovulation confirmed by laparoscopy, 29 Oct. 1995.	91.6
	Returned 29 Oct. 1995	—	Wistari Reef (4) 4 Aug. 1998	—	3rd 1998–1999	Unknown rookery; vitellogenesis confirmed by laparoscopy, 04 Aug. 1998; six-year remigration interval; observed back on Wistari Reef 1999.	92.2
X9374	Recruited 6 Feb. 1978	86.0	Heron Reef (14) 9 Apr 1987	10	1st 26 Dec. 1987 to 10 Jan. 1988	Wreck Rock Beach (migration distance 96 km); laid at least two clutches (incomplete tagging census)	95.0
	Returned 7 Mar. 1988	—	Heron Reef (1) 7 Apr. 1992	—	2nd 1993–1994	Nesting not recorded; vitellogenesis confirmed by laparoscopy, 27 Mar. 1992; six-year remigration.	?
	Returned 18 Oct. 1994	—	Heron Reef (2) 1 Nov. 1995	—	3rd 25 Dec. 1995 to 08 Jan. 1996	Wreck Rock Beach; laid at least two clutches (incomplete tagging census); two-year remigration interval.	97.5
X22755	Recruited 24 Oct. 1980	<91.5[a]	Wistari Reef (3) 19 July 1985	? (> 8)	1st 1987–1988	Unknown rookery; ovulation confirmed by laparoscopy, 11 Apr. 1989.	?
	Returned 11 Apr. 1989	—	Wistari Reef (2) 2 Apr. 1990	—	2nd ? Unknown	Probable unrecorded breeding season during 1990–1992.	?
	Returned ?	—	? (no recaptures)	—	3rd ? 1993–1994	Unknown rookery; ovulation confirmed by laparoscopy, 29 Oct .1995; observed back on Wistari Reef 1995–1996.	?
T703	Recruited 15 Oct. 1982	85.0	Heron Reef (14) 5 Aug. 1998	17	1st 1998-1999	Unknown rookery; ovulation confirmed by laparoscopy, 18 Aug. 1999; observed back on Heron Reef 1999.	101.5
T732	Recruited 17 Oct. 1982	78.5	Heron Reef (13) 16 Oct. 1994	13	1st 22 Dec. 1994 to 02 Feb. 1995	Mon Repos (migration distance 159 km); laid four clutches.	92.4

Table 6.2. continued:

				n			
	Returned 18 Oct. 1995	—	Heron Reef (13) 10 Aug. 1998	—	2nd 22 Nov. 1998 to 15 Jan. 1999	Mon Repos; laid five clutches; four-year remigration interval; observed back on Heron Reef 1999.	95.1
T4422	Recruited 8 Feb. 1984	83.0	Heron Reef (8) 25 Mar. 1991	9	1st 1992–1993	Unknown rookery; ovulation confirmed by laparoscopy, 16 Oct. 1994.	?
	Returned 16 Oct. 1994	—	Heron Reef (1)	—	2nd 1994–1995	Unknown rookery; ovulation confirmed by laparoscopy, 06 Aug. 1996; two-year remigration interval.	92.9
	Returned 6 Aug. 1996	—	Heron Reef (1)	—	3rd 1996–1997	Unknown rookery; ovulation confirmed by laparoscopy, 11 Aug. 1997; two-year remigration interval.	95.0
	Returned 11 Aug. 1997	—	Heron Reef (3) 28 Oct. 1998	—	4th 1998–1999	Unknown rookery; vitellogenesis confirmed by laparoscopy, 28 Oct. 1998; two-year remigration; observed back on Heron Reef 1999.	95.4
T16312	Recruited 26 Sept. 1985		Heron Reef (15) 31 Mar. 1992	9	1st 27 Nov. 1993	Sandy Cape, Fraser Island (migration distance 210 km); necropsy confirmed of oviducal eggs; killed by tiger shark during internesting.	91.0
T38229	Recruited 16 Apr. 1989	77.0	Heron Reef (17) 16 Oct. 1998	10	1st 9 Jan. 1999	Rules Beach (migration distance 115 km); laid at least one clutch (incomplete tagging census); observed back on Heron Reef 1999.	99.6

Note 1: Turtles were identified when they recruited to feeding ground residency on the Heron Island Reef, southern Great Barrier Reef, and when they reached sexual maturity. Recruitment and return dates are when turtles were first observed and are the latest dates for these events.

Note 2: CCL = curved carapace length; n = number of captures.

[a]Turtle had not recently recruited to residency in the coral reef habitat when she was first measured.

1978, these changes in recruitment rate should reflect long-term changes within the dynamics of the total broader population rather than a population decline in response to mortality within this localized study site, which is relatively free of anthropogenic impacts on turtles.

Annual Breeding Rates

In any one year only a portion of the available adult females in a foraging area prepares for breeding (see Figure 6.2d) and hence undertakes breeding migrations to the rookeries.

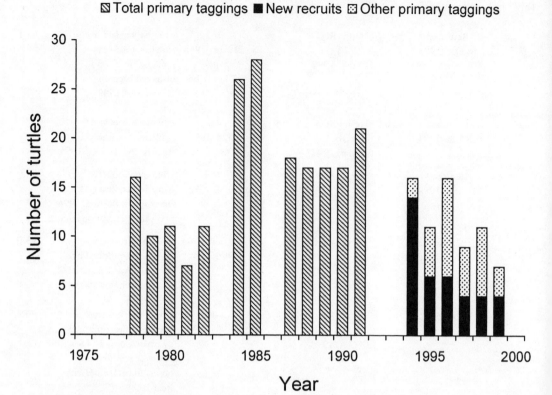

Figure 6.3. Annual frequency of encountering primary tagged loggerhead turtles on Heron Reef, southern Great Barrier Reef. A primary tagged turtle is one tagged for the first time in its life. There have been systematic mark-recapture studies of these turtles since 1974, and in excess of 95% of all resident turtles have been tagged since 1977. Since 1994 there has been systematic examination of untagged turtles to identify recent recruits from the oceanic environment. A few turtles are not captured soon after they recruit from the oceanic environment; others move between adjacent reefs. These are collectively identified as "other primary taggings."

There are large fluctuations in the proportion of breeding adult females in the population across the years ranging from 0 to 0.73 (Figure 6.4). Breeding rates over the years have not fluctuated in synchrony at these two feeding sites. This contrasts with the synchronous fluctuations in annual breeding rates of eastern Australian green turtles as measured in their foraging areas (Limpus and Nicholls 2000). While the synchrony of fluctuations in green turtle breeding rates has been closely linked to regional climate fluctuations, no similar underlying environmental factor has been found to provide a unifying explanation for the annual fluctuations in loggerhead turtle breeding rates.

Given the bias to males, the high proportion of immature turtles in the population, and the low proportion of adult females breeding in any one year, a large feeding population is needed in eastern Australia to support even a modest nesting population (see Figure 6.2d).

Breeding Migration and Foraging-Area Fidelity

When a turtle eventually reaches adulthood and its ovaries enlarge to form mature yolky follicles, she can be expected to leave her foraging area and migrate to breed at a site within the region of her birth (Bowen et al. 1994). Adult female loggerhead turtles depart from southern Great Barrier Reef foraging areas (23° S) to commence their breeding migrations in late October to early November, whereas females from Moreton Bay (27° S) depart in early to mid-November (Limpus and Limpus 2001). When

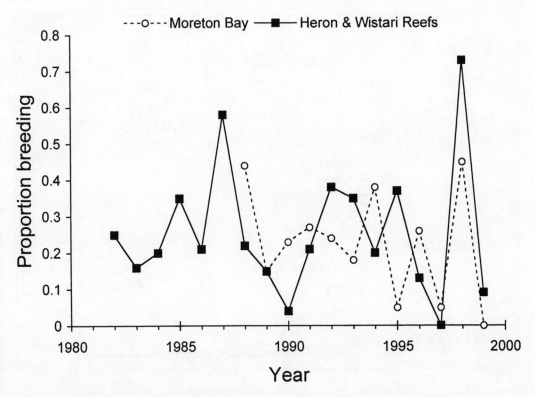

Figure 6.4. Annual proportion of adult female loggerhead turtles resident in eastern Australian foraging areas that prepared for breeding.

loggerhead turtles make breeding migrations, they do not normally breed at the closest available nesting beach. Instead, resident turtles from the one foraging area disperse to breed at widely scattered beaches. Loggerhead turtles resident on the coral reef surrounding Heron Island have been recorded migrating 8–1,600 km to their respective nesting beach (see Table 6.2; Figure 6.5a; Limpus 1989; Limpus et al. 1992). These migrations occur even though these turtles live within sight of the Heron Island loggerhead rookery. Similarly, loggerhead turtles resident in Moreton Bay have been recorded migrating some 30–1,600 km to their respective nesting beaches (Figure 6.5b; Limpus and Limpus 2001).

At the completion of her first breeding season, the young adult female returns to the foraging area where she grew to maturity (see Table 6.2; Limpus and Limpus 2001). With successive breeding migrations throughout the remainder of her life, the adult female continues

to return with high fidelity to her particular foraging area (Table 6.2; Limpus 1989; Limpus et al. 1992). An example of this extreme fidelity to a localized foraging area is illustrated by X2031: she was first recorded on the Heron Island Reef in May 1975 as an adult; she has been recorded on 52 occasions on this reef over 24.5 years up to November 1999; during this time she has made multiple breeding migrations to the Swain Reefs some 192 km distant. See Limpus (1989) for other case histories.

The distribution of loggerhead turtle courtship areas relative to the foraging areas, and hence the distribution of breeding males, is poorly documented (Limpus 1985). Unlike green turtles, mating pairs of loggerhead turtles are rarely observed in the immediate vicinity of the eastern Australian nesting beaches.

There are no indications that nonbreeding adults or immature turtles depart from their foraging areas during the breeding season. While there has been a small proportion of tag

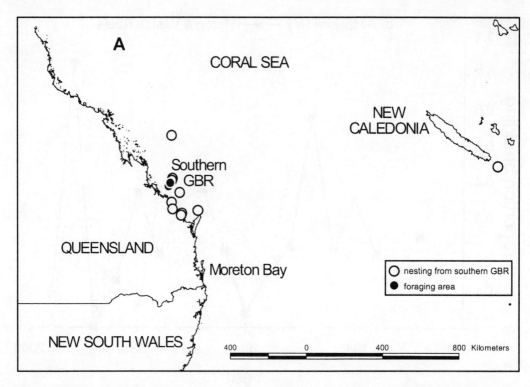

Figure 6.5. Dispersal of adult female loggerheads from shared foraging areas to their respective nesting beaches. Solid circles denote foraging areas; open circles denote nesting beaches. A. Dispersal from a subtropical coral reef foraging area adjacent to Heron Island in the southern Great Barrier Reef. B. Dispersal from a warm temperate foraging area in Moreton Bay.

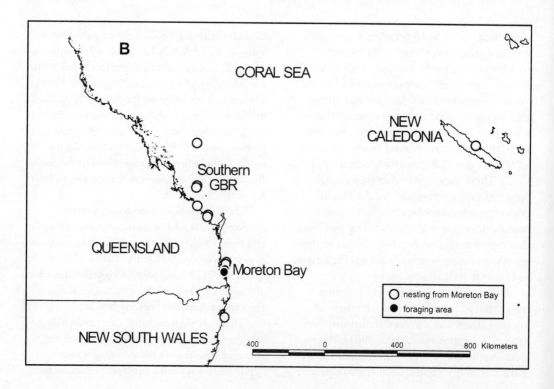

recoveries that demonstrate that individual turtles may interchange between adjacent reefs for foraging (Limpus 1985; Limpus 1989; Limpus et al. 1992), there is only one tag recovery from the 26 years of mark-recapture studies to support the hypothesis of developmental migration through a succession of coastal foraging areas for eastern Australian loggerhead turtles.

Threats within Foraging Areas

An annual mortality rate of several hundred loggerhead turtles during the early 1990s was attributable to capture in prawn trawl fisheries in northern and eastern Australian foraging areas (Poiner and Harris 1996; Robins 1995) and has been identified as contributing to the recent decline in the eastern Australian nesting population (Chaloupka and Limpus 1997; Heppell et al. 1996; Limpus and Reimer 1994). The Woongarra Marine Park, declared in 1991, regulates a seasonal closure to trawling within the waters immediately offshore from Mon Repos and adjacent beaches during the summer turtle nesting season. The voluntary use of turtle excluder devices (TEDs) in the trawl fisheries of eastern and northern Australia has been encouraged and implemented to varying degrees in recent years. There has been compulsory turtle excluder device use within the northern prawn fishery since April 2000 and within the east coast prawn fisheries since December 2000. Discussions are continuing between the fishing industry and the conservation agencies with a view to further reducing turtle mortality from trawl captures in additional areas off Queensland and New South Wales.

The number of stranded loggerhead carcasses recovered in Queensland and New South Wales indicates a combined mortality approaching 100 turtles per year from boat-strike and propeller cuts, entanglement in crab pots and float lines, and ingestion of or entanglement in fishing line (Queensland Parks and Wildlife Service [QPWS] stranding database). Based on tag returns and the frequency of tagged postbreeding migrant turtles in foraging areas, an estimated tens of loggerhead turtles per year are taken by indigenous harvests in neighboring countries and in northern Australia (Limpus and Reimer 1994). Less than 10 loggerhead turtles per year have been killed in shark control programs off surf beaches in Queensland and New South Wales since 1993 (QPWS stranding database).

Loggerhead turtle mortality from anthropogenic sources throughout the coastal foraging areas of the western South Pacific region appears to be of the order of several hundreds of turtles per year.

Modeling

Demographic data from the eastern Australian foraging populations of loggerhead turtles have been used to develop mathematical models for investigating population performance (Chaloupka and Limpus 1997; Heppell et al. 1996). These models indicate that with the current nesting population of a few hundred females annually, the loss of hundreds of adult and large immature turtles per year in coastal habitats represents a significant threat to the survival of loggerhead turtles in the South Pacific region.

Status

The loggerhead turtle is scheduled as endangered under the 1992 Australian Endangered Species Act and the 1992 Queensland Nature Conservation Act. A major part of the foraging habitat utilized by the eastern Australian loggerhead turtle stock is contained within the waters of the Great Barrier Reef World Heritage Area (listed 1981; Wachenfeld et al. 1998). A major part of the Great Barrier Reef World Heritage Area is managed via multiple-use zoning within the Great Barrier Reef Marine Park administered by the Australian Government. The Moreton Bay Marine Park also is managed via multiple-use zoning by the Queensland Government. Shoalwater and Corio bays, Sandy Strait, and Moreton Bay have been declared Ramsar sites in accordance with the Ramsar Convention on Wetlands.

ACKNOWLEDGMENTS

This study was conducted as part of the Queensland Turtle Conservation Project of the Queensland Parks and Wildlife Service (QPWS), the Queensland government wildlife conservation agency. Transport of the study team, turtle catch boats, and other equipment to Heron Island from Gladstone was donated by P&O Australian Resorts. Seaworld Research and Rescue Foundation and Trevor Long have annually provided *Seaworld I* as a mother ship and research platform for a week each year in Moreton Bay. Field assistance in capturing, handling, and measuring the turtles was provided by numerous QPWS staff and volunteers. Milani Chaloupka collaborated in the analysis of aspects of the demographic data for these turtles. This assistance is gratefully acknowledged.

LITERATURE CITED

Barrett, C. 1919. In Australian wilds. The gleanings of a naturalist. Melbourne, Australia: Melbourne Publishing Company.

Bowen, B. W., N. Kamezaki, C. J. Limpus, G. H. Hughes, A. B. Meylan, and J. C. Avis. 1994. Global phylogeography of the loggerhead turtle *(Caretta caretta)* as indicated by mitochondrial DNA haplotypes. Evolution 48:1820–1820.

Bustard, H. 1972. Australian sea turtles: Their natural history and conservation. London: Collins.

Chaloupka, M. 1998. Polyphasic growth in pelagic loggerhead sea turtles. Copeia 1998:516–518.

Chaloupka, M., and C. J. Limpus. 1997. Heuristic simulation modeling of trawl fishery impacts on sGBR loggerhead population dynamics. *In* S. P. Epperly, J. Braun (compilers). Proceedings of the 17th annual sea turtle symposium, 26–29. NOAA Technical Memorandum NMFS-SEFSC-415.

———. 2001. Trends in the abundance of sea turtles resident in southern Great Barrier Reef waters. Biological Conservation 102:235–249.

———. 2002. Survival probability estimates for the endangered loggerhead sea turtle resident in southern Great Barrier Reef waters. Marine Biology 140:267–277.

———. In press. Estimates of sex- and stage-specific survival probabilities for green sea turtles resident in southern Great Barrier Reef waters. Marine Ecology Progress Series.

Davenport, J. 1994. A cleaning association between the oceanic crab *Planes minutus* and the loggerhead turtle *Caretta caretta*. Journal of Marine Biological Association, U.K. 74:735–737.

Dellinger, T., J. Davenport, and P. Wirtz. 1997. Comparisons of social structure of Columbus crabs living on loggerhead sea turtles and inanimate flotsam. Journal of Marine Biological Association, U.K. 77:185–194.

Dodd, C. K., Jr. 1988. Synopsis of the biological data on the loggerhead sea turtle *Caretta caretta* (Linnaeus 1758). USFWS Biological Report 88.

Ellis, A. F. 1937. Adventures in coral seas. Sydney, Australia: Angus and Robertson.

Frazer, N. B., C. J. Limpus, and J. L. Green. 1994. Growth and estimated age at maturity of Queensland loggerhead turtles. *In* K. A. Bjorndal, A. B. Bolten, D. A. Johnson, and P. J. Eliazar (compilers). Proceedings of the 14th annual symposium on sea turtle biology and conservation, 42–46. NOAA Technical Memorandum NMFS-SEFSC-351.

Gill, B. J. 1997. Records of turtles and sea snakes in New Zealand, 1837–1996. New Zealand Journal of Marine and Freshwater Research 31:477–486.

Green, R. H. 1971. Sea turtles round Tasmania. Records of the Queen Victoria Museum 38:1–4.

Guinea, M. L. 1993. The sea turtles of Fiji. SPREP Reports and Studies Series 65:1–48.

Heppell, S. S., C. J. Limpus, D. T. Crouse, N. B. Frazer, and L. B. Crowder. 1996. Population model analysis for the loggerhead sea turtle, *Caretta caretta*, in Queensland. Wildlife Research 23:143–159.

Johannes, R. E., and J. W. MacFarlane. 1991. Traditional fishing in the Torres Strait Islands. Hobart, Australia: CSIRO Division of Fisheries.

Jukes, J. B. 1847. Narrative of the surveying voyage of HMS Fly, commanded by Captain F. P. Blackwood, R. N., in Torres Strait, New Guinea, and other islands of the eastern Archipelago, during the years 1842–1846, vol. 1. London: Boone.

Limpus, C. J. 1973. Loggerhead turtles in Australia: Food resources while nesting. Herpetologica 29:42–45.

———. 1978. The reef. *In* H. J. Lavery (ed.). Exploration north: Australia's wildlife from desert to reef, 187–222. Richmond, Australia: Richmond Hill Press.

———. 1985. A study of the loggerhead sea turtle, *Caretta caretta*, in eastern Australia. Ph.D. Thesis, Zoology Department, University of Queensland, Australia.

———. 1989. Forage area fidelity following breeding migrations in *Caretta caretta*. *In* S. A. Eckert, K. L. Eckert, and T. H. Richardson (compilers). Proceedings of the ninth annual workshop on sea turtle conservation and eiology, 97–99. NOAA Technical Memorandum NMFS-SEFC-232.

———. 1990. Puberty and first breeding in *Caretta caretta*. *In* T. H. Richardson, J. I. Richardson, and M. Donnelly (compilers). Proceedings of the 10th annual workshop on sea turtle biology and conservation, 81–83. NOAA Technical Memorandum NMFS-SEFC-278.

———. 1992a. Estimation of tags loss in marine turtle research. Wildlife Research 19:457–469.

———. 1992b. The hawksbill turtle, *Eretmochelys im-*

bricata, in Queensland: Population structure within a southern Great Barrier Reef feeding ground. Wildlife Research 19:489–506.

Limpus, C. J., and D. J. Limpus. 2001. The loggerhead turtle, Caretta caretta, in Queensland: Breeding migrations and fidelity to a warm temperate feeding area. Chelonian Conservation and Biology 4:142–153.

Limpus, C., and N. Nicholls. 2000. ENSO regulation of Indo-Pacific green turtle populations. In G. Hammer, N. Nicholls, and C. Mitchell (eds.). Applications of seasonal climate forecasting in agricultural and natural ecosystems, 399–408. Dordrecht, The Netherlands: Kluwer Academic Publishers.

Limpus, C. J., and P. C. Read. 1985. The loggerhead turtle, Caretta caretta, in Queensland: Observations on internesting behaviour. Australian Wildlife Research 12:535–540.

Limpus, C., and D. Reimer. 1994. The loggerhead turtle, Caretta caretta, in Queensland: A population in decline. In R. James (compiler). Proceedings of the Australian marine turtle conservation workshop, 39–59. Queensland Department of Environment and Heritage and Australian Nature Conservation Agency.

Limpus, C. J., P. J. Couper, and M. A. Read. 1994a. The loggerhead turtle Caretta caretta, in Queensland: Population structure in a warm temperate feeding area. Memoirs of the Queensland Museum 37:195–204.

———. 1994b. The green turtle, Chelonia mydas, in Queensland: Population structure in a warm temperate feeding area. Memoirs of the Queensland Museum 35:139–154.

Limpus, C. J., D. L. de Villiers, M. A. de Villiers, D. J. Limpus, and M. A. Read. 2001. The loggerhead turtle, Caretta caretta in Queensland: Feeding ecology in warm temperate waters. Memoirs of the Queensland Museum 46:631–645.

Limpus, C. J., A. Fleay, and M. Guinea. 1984. Sea turtles of the Capricornia Section, Great Barrier Reef Marine Park. In W. T. Ward and P. Saenger (eds). The Capricornia section of the Great Barrier Reef, 61–78. Brisbane: Royal Society of Queensland and Australian Coral Reef Society.

Limpus, C. J., J. D. Miller, C. J. Parmenter, D. Reimer, N. McLachlan, and R. Webb. 1992. Migration of green (Chelonia mydas) and loggerhead (Caretta caretta) turtles to and from eastern Australian rookeries. Wildlife Research 19:347–358.

McCann, C. 1966. The marine turtles and snakes occurring in New Zealand. Records of the Dominion Museum 5:201–215.

McMillan, R. P. 1967. The crab Planes minutus asso-

ciating with a turtle. West Australian Naturalist 10:194.

Moodie, E. G. 1979. Aspects of the feeding biology of the loggerhead turtle (Caretta caretta). B.Sc. Honors Thesis, James Cook University of North Queensland, Townsville, Australia.

Moore, D. R. 1979. Islanders and Aborigines at Cape York. Canberra: Australian Institute of Aboriginal Studies.

Musick, J. A., and C. J. Limpus. 1997. Habitat utilization and migration in juvenile sea turtles. In P. L. Lutz and J. A. Musick (eds.). The biology of sea turtles, 137–163. Boca Raton, Fla.: CRC Press.

Parsons, J. J. 1962. The green turtle and man. Gainesville: University of Florida Press.

Poiner, I. R., and A. N. M. Harris. 1996. Incidental capture, direct mortality and delayed mortality of sea turtles in Australia's northern prawn fishery. Marine Biology 125:813–825.

Preen, A. R. 1996. Infaunal mining: A novel foraging method of loggerhead turtles. Journal of Herpetology 30:94–96.

Pritchard, P. C. H. 1982. Marine turtles of the South Pacific. In K. A. Bjorndal (ed.). Biology and conservation of sea turtles, 253–274. Washington, D.C.: Smithsonian Institution Press.

Read, M. A., G. C. Grigg, and C. J. Limpus. 1996. Body temperature and winter feeding in immature green turtles, Chelonia mydas, in Moreton Bay, southeastern Queensland. Journal of Herpetology 30:262–265.

Robins, J. B. 1995. Estimated catch and mortality of sea turtles from the east coast otter trawl fishery of Queensland, Australia. Biological Conservation 74:157–167.

Saville-Kent, W. 1893. The Great Barrier Reef of Australia: Its products and potentialities. Melbourne, Australia: John Currey, O'Neil.

Smith, A. 1987. Usage of marine resources by aboriginal communities on the east coast of Cape York Peninsula. Report to the Great Barrier Reef Marine Park Authority, Townsville, Australia.

Thomson, D. F. 1934. The dugong hunters of Cape York. Journal Royal Anthropological Institute 64:237–264.

Wachenfeld, D. R., J. K. Oliver, and J. I. Morrissey. 1998. State of the Great Barrier Reef World Heritage Area 1998. Townsville, Australia: Great Barrier Reef Marine Park Authority.

Viridans Pty. Ltd. 2000. Wild animals of Victoria. Melbourne, Australia: Department of Natural Resources and Environment.

Chapter 7

Nesting Patterns, Reproductive Migrations, and Adult Foraging Areas of Loggerhead Turtles

—Barbara A. Schroeder, Allen M. Foley,
and Dean A. Bagley

Monitoring trends in loggerhead turtle populations is critical to assessing population status and to developing and assessing conservation strategies. Presently, the most reliable estimates of sea turtle population size come from counts on nesting beaches. In addition to providing population estimates, nesting beach data also provide information on how reproductive effort is focused spatially and temporally. Several measured parameters are key to describing reproductive effort and to estimating the number of nesting females from nest count data. Among these parameters are clutch frequency, remigration interval, and nesting site fidelity (collectively referred to here as nesting patterns). These three key measures are intimately linked and have great bearing on the accuracy of the simple calculations used to derive nesting population estimates from numbers of nests. Although numerous authors have reported clutch frequency and remigration interval values for loggerheads at nesting beaches around the world, information on nesting site fidelity is less frequent in the literature, perhaps because of the difficulty of obtaining this measure.

Effective conservation programs for sea turtles require more than an understanding of nesting patterns and nesting population size. With regard to the adult life stage, information on migratory routes and foraging areas is also needed. The purpose of this chapter is to outline the loggerhead reproductive data necessary for guiding conservation programs. Here, the authors review available data on loggerhead nesting patterns, reproductive migrations, and adult foraging areas, and they evaluate deficiencies in understanding these aspects of loggerhead life history.

Nesting Patterns

For most of their lives, sea turtles are difficult, if not impossible, to census. However, one segment of each population predictably presents itself for counting, when adult females crawl from the water to nest. On some beaches, "saturation tagging" of all nesting females can lead to direct counts of individuals, but on other beaches that cover large expanses, these direct counts are not practical because of the difficulties in successfully intercepting all nesting turtles.

It is logistically feasible on most beaches to count the number of nests made each night during an early morning survey of the nesting beach (Schroeder and Murphy 1999). This count can then be used to determine both the number of adult females nesting annually and the number of breeding females in the population, provided two key parameters are known: (1) clutch frequency, defined as the number of nests deposited by a female during one reproductive season, and (2) remigration interval, defined as the number of years between reproductive seasons (Carr et al. 1978; Limpus 1985). Clutch frequency is sufficient to derive an estimate of annual numbers of breeding females, but remigration intervals are also needed to estimate the total number of breeding females in the population.

The tendency of a turtle to return to nest near the area where she nested previously, either within a season or in a previous season, is referred to as nesting site fidelity (also referred to as site fixity). Carr (1975) recommended the term "philopatry" for discussing the return to a broader geographic place (e.g., an island or a broad stretch of coastline) and the term "site fixity" (herein referred to as "nesting site fidelity") for discussing finer scale discrimination. Although nesting site fidelity is not a parameter that is directly used to calculate breeding female population size, knowledge of this parameter is necessary to evaluate the validity of values for clutch frequency and remigration intervals (Did a survey effort encompass enough beach to locate all of a turtle's nests?).

Clutch Frequency

Loggerheads deposit from one to seven clutches during a single nesting season (Table 7.1; Dodd 1988; Lenarz et al. 1981; Lund 1986; Talbert et al. 1980). This wide range may reflect both true variation and survey error. Error is ex-

pected to result when some nesting females are either not observed or not recognized every time they nest within a particular year on the survey beach.

Accurate determinations of clutch frequency require that every female on the survey beach be intercepted and documented each time she nests within a nesting season. This is seldom accomplished. Because a loggerhead can nest in approximately one hour, at any time during the night, and up to seven times over a span of three to four months (Dodd 1988) and hundreds of kilometers of beach (Encalada et al. 1998), it is reasonable to assume that some nesting attempts by each female might be missed. The accuracy of a clutch frequency determination will depend heavily upon survey completeness and on nest site fidelity among the turtles studied. Even if surveyed areas are large and nesting site fidelity is strong, females that have a nesting area centered near the edge of the surveyed area may still nest outside the surveyed area. This "edge effect" (Murphy and Hopkins 1984) will result in clutch frequencies that are biased low.

Determinations of clutch frequency rely upon the collection of information from uniquely marked individuals. Marking is most commonly accomplished through the use of various types of external flipper tags (Balazs 1999). With a typical internesting interval of about 14 days (Dodd 1988) and a maximum clutch frequency of six to seven nests (Lenarz et al. 1981; Lund 1986; Talbert et al. 1980), flipper tags must be retained for at least three to four months in order to assure that individual females are recognized each time they nest within a season. The loss of flipper tags over the course of a typical nesting season (several months) is low (0.5–1.3%; Limpus 1992) and is not likely to impede repeat identification of nesting females.

Several published methods to measure clutch frequency do not require that females be intercepted every time they nest. Some of these methods assume a predictable internesting interval and interpolate the number of "missed" nests per female based on observed nesting events during a nesting season (Frazer and Richardson 1985; Hughes 1974). Addison

Table 7.1.

The Mean Number of Clutches per Female (Clutch Frequency) per Reproductive Season at Various Loggerhead Rookeries around the World

Location	Number of Females	Observed Clutches per Season	Mean Clutch Frequency		Source
			Observed	Corrected	
Little Cumberland Island, GA, USA	427	—	—	4.1	10
Little Cumberland Island, GA, USA	36–62[a]	—	2.39–3.42[a]	2.81–4.18[a]	3
South Brevard County, FL, USA	236	1–3	2.05	3.24	2
Key Island, FL, USA	521	1–7	1.84	3.9	1
Cape San Blas, FL, USA	111	1–4	1.35	—	7
Colombia (Caribbean coast)	80	1–4	1.12	—	6
Zakynthos, Greece	148	1–3	1.18	—	9
Tongaland, Natal, Africa	241–321[b]	1–5	1.81–2.29[b]	3.65–4.21[b]	4
Miyazaki, Japan	199	1–2	1.10	—	5
Yakushima Island, Japan	358	1–6	2.06	—	11
Mon Repos, Australia	1,207	1–6	2.91	3.41	8

Source Key: 1. Addison 1996a, 1996b. 2. L. M. Ehrhart, unpublished data. 3. Frazer and Richardson 1985. 4. Hughes 1974. 5. Iwamoto et al. 1985. 6. Kaufmann 1975. 7. M. M. Lamont, unpublished data. 8. Limpus 1985. 9. Margaritoulis 1982, 1983. 10. Murphy and Hopkins 1984. 11. Nishimura 1994.

Note 1: The corrected frequencies adjust for turtles that were either known or suspected to have nested both inside and outside of the study site.

Note 2: FL = Florida; GA = Georgia.

[a]Range of annual values over a 10-year period.

[b]Range of annual values over a four-year period.

(1996b) used only nesting turtles that were intercepted more than once to estimate a "corrected" clutch frequency. Addison's corrected clutch frequency of 3.9 nests/season/female was substantially higher than the empirically measured frequency of 1.8 nests/season/female (Table 7.1). Murphy and Hopkins (1984) created a stochastic frequency distribution of nesting based on the date of initial nesting in a season and the average internesting interval for all females encountered over a period of many years on one nesting beach. The trend of a steadily rising number of nests that was created as this simulated nesting season progressed was then reversed at the typical midpoint of the season. A clutch frequency of 4.1 nests/season/female was determined by dividing the total number of nests generated from the stochastic frequency distribution by the number of females used to create it. Although these methods are helpful in overcoming the logistic difficulties of intercepting females every time they nest, the assumptions on which they are based and the resulting data need to be periodically assessed and verified.

Several other methods of determining clutch frequency warrant further investigation or experimentation. Rostal et al. (1991, 1997) approached the question in a two-fold manner—by examining the reproductive tracts of gravid Kemp's ridleys via ultrasonography and by monitoring reproductive hormones over the course of the nesting season. Both methods resulted in a higher estimated clutch frequency for Kemp's ridleys than that previously reported from mark-recapture studies and may well represent a more accurate determination. Recent advances in satellite telemetry potentially hold promise as tools for assessing clutch frequency. Satellite transmitters with appropriate sensors, similar to time-depth recorders used to gather data on haul-out behavior of walruses and pinnipeds, could be developed (Bengston and Stewart 1992; Jay et al. 2001). Deployed at the

Table 7.2.

Years between Successive Nesting Seasons (Remigration Intervals) for Various Loggerhead Rookeries around the World

| Location | Number of Remigrations | Remigration Interval | | | Source |
		Range	Observed Mean	Corrected Mean	
Little Cumberland Island, GA, USA	242	1–6	2.54		5
South Brevard County, FL, USA	161	1–7	2.71		1
South Brevard County, FL, USA	187	1–15	3.69		2
Tongaland, Natal, South Africa	740	1–9	2.58		3
Queensland, Australia	1,112	1–9	2.98	3.48	4

Source Key: 1. Bjorndal et al. 1983. 2. L. M. Ehrhart, unpublished data. 3. Hughes 1982. 4. Limpus 1985. 5. Richardson et al. 1978.

Note 1: The corrected mean was adjusted to account for tag loss.

Note 2: FL = Florida; GA = Georgia.

start of the nesting season, these tags would generate remotely sensed data that could yield information on the number of emergences over the course of the nesting season.

In addition to varying between beaches (see Table 7.1), clutch frequency is also likely to vary between years (Frazer and Richardson 1985). Clutch frequencies also vary among individuals, with remigrants having higher clutch frequencies than recruits (Limpus 1985; Lund 1986). Thus, interannual variation in the proportion of remigrants and recruits is likely to result in annual variation in clutch frequency. Events not related to a physiological reproductive capability can cause nesting turtles to fall short of their potential complement of clutch deposits, thus decreasing clutch frequency. These events could include mortality of females during the internesting period and disturbances on nesting beaches (e.g., human activity, beachfront lighting, coastal armoring; Lutcavage et al. 1997).

The importance of obtaining accurate estimates of clutch frequency, with appropriate error statistics, cannot be overstated. This value is the divisor used to convert the number of nests to the number of nesting females and can have profound effects on the estimate of nesting females. For these reasons, and for the reasons noted above with regard to shifts in clutch frequency, the authors believe that comprehensive monitoring programs should incorporate periodic assessments of clutch frequency in order to ensure accuracy.

Remigration Interval

Long-term mark-recapture studies on most of the world's principal loggerhead nesting beaches have shown that loggerhead remigration intervals range from one to nine years (Dodd 1988). The mean observed remigration interval ranges from 2.5 to about 3.0 years (Table 7.2). Limpus (1985) applied a correction factor to his data to account for tag loss and reported a 3.48-year remigration interval for Australian loggerheads. Richardson et al. (1978) and Hughes (1982) reported a high proportion of turtles that were never documented to nest in a subsequent season. However, Hughes (1982) cautions that a major cause of the uncertainty in assessing remigration intervals is likely to be tag loss (see below for further discussion).

Mortality also plays an important role in determining whether females will return to nest in a subsequent season. High mortality in the adult female portion of the population (e.g., extensive fishing pressure near nesting beaches, along migratory routes, or at resident foraging areas) can dramatically affect the proportion of the population that is available (alive) to remigrate and nest in subsequent nesting seasons. Population modeling efforts for the intensively studied eastern Australian loggerhead population indicate that population stability requires high adult survivorship over an extended period of time and breeding over multiple nesting seasons (C. Limpus, pers. comm.). Thus, the low remigration rates observed at a number of important loggerhead rookeries may be an artifact of unnaturally high levels of mortality combined with the practical difficulties of long-term marking of individuals.

Remigration intervals are most commonly determined by flipper-tagging nesting females and by conducting multiyear nesting beach surveys in order to intercept and identify tagged females at least once each season they nest. The onus of intercepting individual females every time they nest over the course of the nesting season (as required for determining clutch frequency) is not necessary when determining remigration intervals. Flipper tag loss over the average remigration period (two to three years) ranges from 10 to 50% (Limpus 1985) and becomes a greater source of error in determining remigration intervals than it is in determining clutch frequency. Tag loss is likely to result in underestimated remigration intervals (by excluding long-interval turtles more likely to lose tags) and overestimated numbers of breeding females. The increasing use and success of subdermal passive integrated transponder (PIT) tags as a permanent marker in sea turtles should allow researchers to overcome the tag loss factor; however, problems with the compatibility of available PIT tag readers and PIT tags could affect research results.

Remigration intervals are not fixed for individuals. Nesting females may shift from one cycle (e.g., two years) to another (e.g., three or four years) and may shift multiple times during the course of their breeding lifetime (Hughes 1974; Limpus 1985). The proportion of recruits and remigrants that nest during a given year and the remigration intervals characteristic of the population may change over time. Varia-

tion in mortality rates at nesting beaches, on foraging grounds, or along migratory routes plays a role in determining what proportion of adult females nest during one season and what proportion eventually remigrates (Frazer 1984). Annual variation in the quality of forage may lengthen or shorten remigration intervals (Limpus and Nicholls 1988). Just as periodic evaluation of clutch frequency is needed, periodic evaluation of remigration interval is also needed to ensure accurate estimates of the total number of breeding females in a population.

Nesting Site Fidelity

Nesting site fidelity is most commonly measured in terms of the mean distance between nest sites of individual turtles, either within or between seasons. Whereas there are a number of long-distance within- and between-season movements documented in the literature (see e.g., Iwamoto et al. 1985; LeBuff 1974; Sea Turtle Protection Society of Greece 1995; Stoneburner and Ehrhart 1981), the typical distance between nest sites is 5 km or less. Loggerheads can exhibit strong site fidelity (Table 7.3). Ehrhart (1980) reported that 21% of turtles observed returning at multiyear intervals were less than 1.0 km away from their first observed nesting site. Mean distance between nest sites of individual loggerheads, within and between seasons, is similar between loggerhead populations (Table 7.3).

Nesting site fidelity can vary among females, with some individuals always nesting on a relatively small section of a particular nesting beach (stronger nesting site fidelity) and others spreading their nests over a larger section of beach (weaker nesting site fidelity). Turtles with weaker nesting site fidelity can contribute to inaccuracy in determining either clutch frequencies or remigration intervals. For example, at Potamakia Beach, Greece, loggerheads that were documented nesting more than once during one year (stronger nesting site fidelity) were significantly more likely to be documented as remigrants in subsequent years than were individuals either observed nesting only once (weaker nesting site fidelity) or observed during abandoned nesting emergences (Hays and

Table 7.3.

Distances between the Nest Sites of Individual Loggerheads from Various Rookeries around the World

Location	Number of Observations	Mean (km)	Range (km)	Source
Tongaland, Natal, South Africa[a]	505	< 4.0	0–12	2
Hutchinson Island, FL, USA[a]	21	17.48	0.2–95.2	5
Cape Canaveral, FL, USA[a]	394	6.89	0–32.3	1
Mon Repos, Australia[a]	150	0.382	0.025–1.25	4
Jupiter Island, FL, USA[a]	803	3.0	0–14.0	3
Tongaland, Natal, South Africa[b]	85	3.47	0–11.6	2
Cape Canaveral, FL, USA[b]	39	5.47	0–27.94	1

Source Key: 1. Ehrhart 1980. 2. Hughes 1974. 3. Lund 1986. 4. Limpus 1985. 5. Worth and Smith 1976.

Note: FL = Florida.

[a]Nest sites within a nesting season.

[b]Nest sites between seasons.

Sutherland 1991). Similarly, Richardson et al. (1978) calculated a 49% remigration rate for recruits (turtles not previously tagged when first observed at Little Cumberland Island, Georgia) and a 70% remigration rate for loggerheads with an established remigration pattern. The lower remigration rate for previously untagged turtles may indicate that some portion of these turtles had nested elsewhere previously and/or nested elsewhere following the observed nesting at this particular beach.

Logistic difficulties in intercepting nesting females (even during comprehensive surveys) and the added problem of tag loss both introduce bias in the evaluation of nesting site fidelity. Cooperation and data sharing among projects on adjoining beaches can help reduce some of these biases.

Anthropogenic factors also complicate the evaluation of nesting site fidelity. Nesting turtles that are continuously thwarted by disturbances may (1) move to another nesting site, (2) emerge more frequently, or (3) attempt to nest in unsuitable areas (Murphy and Hopkins-Murphy, unpubl. data). Thus, the mean nesting site fidelity of a population could change with increasing disturbances such as development and human activity. The potential for variation in nesting site fidelity over time reemphasizes

the need to periodically assess clutch frequency and remigration intervals to ensure accuracy.

Reproductive Migrations and Adult Foraging Areas

Much of what researchers have learned about the life history and behavior of adult loggerheads has been gleaned from the brief period when adult females are present on nesting beaches. However, conserving loggerheads requires additional information extending beyond the nesting beach to include aspects of their life at sea. Of particular importance is an understanding of where adult loggerheads reside during the nonbreeding season and how they move between foraging areas, courtship areas, and nesting beaches. Most research in this regard has been to identify areas that females inhabit during the nonnesting season and the routes they take to reach these areas (e.g., Bell and Richardson 1978; Hughes 1974; LeBuff 1990; Margaritoulis 1988; Meylan et al. 1983). More recently, research has broadened to include studies of females and males migrating to mating and nesting grounds, and studies of resident adults, both males and females, at their foraging sites (e.g., Limpus et al. 1992; Sakamoto et al. 1997).

The classical means of elucidating sea turtle migrations is to tag nesting females and record the distant recovery of those tags when turtles strand or are captured. These tag return data are available from virtually all the major loggerhead nesting populations. Results of these studies indicate that adult females make both short- and long-distance postnesting migrations. No breeding loggerheads appear to be "nonmigratory" (Limpus 1992).

Recapture data provide point-to-point movement information but offer little insight into travel routes or into whether the point of recovery is an actual destination. As a result, recaptures of tagged turtles may not provide a complete picture of the range of foraging areas (Limpus 1985). Additionally, tag recaptures away from the nesting beach should be interpreted with an understanding that recapture rates and locations are frequently biased by variable recapture methods (e.g., reporting of flipper-tagged turtles captured in U.S. shrimp trawls dropped significantly during the years of controversy over the implementation of turtle excluder devices). Despite the limitations, flipper tag data are important in formulating hypotheses that can be further evaluated using additional techniques.

The advent of satellite telemetry has dramatically increased knowledge of loggerhead migratory behavior. Research efforts using satellite telemetry to determine loggerhead reproductive migrations are under way in the Mediterranean, South Africa, Japan, Australia, Brazil, Bahamas, and the United States (A. Bolten, pers. comm.; Hays et al. 1992; C. S. Hopkins-Murphy, pers. comm.; Limpus, pers. comm.; B. Schroeder, unpubl. data; Sakamoto et al. 1997). The principal focus of these studies has been to identify postnesting migration routes and adult foraging areas.

Approximately 100 postnesting female loggerheads have been satellite tracked worldwide. Data acquired through the use of satellite tags may include various diving measures, dive profiles, and water temperature, as well as standard data such as latitude/longitude, time, and a measure of the accuracy of the transmitted location. Ideally, satellite telemetry and flipper-tagging programs should work to complement each other.

Based on published and unpublished satellite telemetry data and flipper tag return data, a number of conclusions can be drawn with regard to loggerhead postnesting migratory behavior and loggerhead adult foraging areas.

- Postnesting females depart from the nesting beach immediately following deposition of the last clutch, in most cases within 24 hours.
- Postnesting females typically make directed migrations. Random wandering does not appear to be a characteristic behavior. This evidence contradicts the conclusion of Hendrickson (1980) that loggerheads did not appear to exhibit directed movements during reproductive migrations.
- The migratory route taken may be coastal or may involve crossing deep oceanic waters; an oceanic route may be taken even when a coastal route is an option.
- All females dispersing from a rookery do not necessarily follow the same migratory path, even if the foraging destinations are similar.
- Ocean currents may affect migration routes, resulting in temporary course adjustments. Postnesting females sometimes swim against prevailing currents.
- Postnesting loggerheads take up residence in discrete foraging areas. These areas are relatively small in size, on the order of tens of square kilometers, and are located on continental shelves.
- Postnesting females may move among a few preferred foraging sites within the larger foraging area.
- Adult females exhibit strong site fidelity to foraging areas and have been observed to return to these sites over the course of many breeding seasons.
- Some U.S. loggerheads migrate to two successive, seasonally dependent foraging areas. For these turtles, initial postnesting migration is north, and a second migration is directed south as northern waters cool.
- Foraging areas may be located relatively near the nesting beach or thousands of kilometers distant and may be located within a different nation than the nesting beach.
- The migratory route may be wholly contained within the waters of one nation or

Table 7.4.

Locations of Principal Foraging Areas of Postnesting Loggerheads

Nesting Beach	Principal Resident Foraging Areas	Source
Japan	East China Sea, South China Sea	6, 7, 16
Eastern Australia	Eastern Australia, Coral Sea, southern and eastern Papua New Guinea, Gulf of Carpentaria	9
Southeast Africa	Mozambique, Tanzania (mainland), Zanzibar, Madagascar	4, 5
Florida east coast, USA	Bahamas, Cuba, Mexico, Florida coastal waters, Gulf of Mexico	3, 12, 17
Florida west coast, USA	Florida West Coast, Cuba, Mexico, Gulf of Mexico	17
Georgia and South Carolina, USA	USA, southeast and mid-Atlantic coast	1, 13, 14
Masirah Island, Oman	Arabian Gulf, southern Arabian peninsula westward to Yemen, Gulf of Oman east to Pakistan	15
Cay Sal, Bahamas	Southern Bahamas	2
Brazil	Coast of Brazil	10
Greece	Tunisia, Adriatic Sea, eastern and western Mediterranean	8, 11

Source Key: 1. Bell and Richardson 1978. 2. A. Bolten and K. Bjorndal, unpubl. data. 3. L. Ehrhart, unpubl. data. 4. Hughes 1995. 5. Hughes et al. 1967. 6. Iwamoto et al. 1985. 7. Kamezaki et al. 1997. 8. Lazar et al. 2000. 9. Limpus 1985, 1992. 10. Marcovaldi et al. 2000. 11. Margaritoulis 1988. 12. Meylan et al. 1983. 13. S. Murphy, unpubl. data. 14. Plotkin and Spotila 2000. 15. P. Ross, pers. comm. 16. Sakamoto et al. 1997. 17. B. Schroeder, unpubl. data.

Note: From various rookeries around the world, as identified from tag returns and satellite telemetry data.

may involve travel through the waters of other nations.

- Loggerheads do not necessarily nest at the nesting beach located closest to their home foraging area.
- Foraging areas of female loggerheads from different nesting beaches (including genetically distinct subpopulations) within a region may overlap.

Information on the location of foraging areas is available for many of the major loggerhead rookeries (Table 7.4). Although researchers are beginning to understand migratory routes and destinations of postnesting loggerheads, detailed habitat characterization of adult foraging areas is lacking. It does not appear that adult loggerheads from regional rookeries converge at a few discrete sites; rather, their resident foraging areas are widespread (Table 7.4). This dispersal of foraging areas challenges efforts to ensure their protection. Limpus (1992), in describing the situation for eastern Australia adult loggerheads, said, "Even the Great Barrier Reef Marine Park, the largest marine conservation area in the world, is not large enough to contain an entire population of *C. caretta*." Geographically extensive feeding areas for the adult segment of the population are undoubtedly characteristic of all major loggerhead rookeries.

Long-term tagging studies of large immature loggerheads on foraging grounds in eastern Australia are providing evidence that long-term fidelity to a resident foraging area has its origins in an imprinting to the feeding ground where a turtle reaches sexual maturity (Limpus 1994). This underscores the need to ensure that these habitats are protected and that threats at these sites are addressed.

While data regarding migratory behavior of adult females are accumulating, studies of reproductive migratory behavior of adult males are rare, and the published literature is lacking in this regard. Limpus's recent studies in Australia of loggerheads on their foraging grounds indicate that males migrate to courtship and mating areas and then return with high site fidelity to their foraging areas, while females continue on to nesting beaches (C. Limpus, pers. comm.). In the western Atlantic, Henwood (1987) documented seasonal differences in the abundance of adult males in the near-shore waters off central Florida, with males present in significantly higher numbers in the months immediately preceding the onset of the nesting season. This is similar to what Limpus reported for male loggerheads on the other side of the globe. Henwood (1987) suggested that the presence of the same individual males in the vicinity of nesting beaches during consecutive reproductive seasons may indicate annual breeding, although the reproductive condition of the males was not verified through laparoscopy or other means.

A significant assemblage of adult male loggerheads resides year-round in Florida Bay at the southern terminus of the Florida peninsula, and studies of the migratory behavior of these turtles are under way (Schroeder, unpubl. data). The Florida Bay data suffer from the same lack of confirmation of individual reproductive condition. Clearly, more work is needed to understand the behavior of the male component of the population, especially relative to reproductive periodicity.

Conclusions

Information relative to nesting patterns, reproductive migrations, and adult foraging areas is critical to understanding and conserving global loggerhead populations. Clutch frequency, remigration interval, and nesting site fidelity are key variables that need to be regularly evaluated to ensure that population estimates derived from nesting beach data are accurate. Limitations in measuring clutch frequencies and remigration intervals can result in profound overestimates of abundance of breeding females. There are few recent assessments of these key measures at the principal loggerhead rookeries around the world. Increased focus on the reproductive periodicity and migratory movements of adult male loggerheads is needed for all the major nesting assemblages. Comprehensive studies similar to the long-term in-water studies on log-

gerheads in eastern Australia are needed at all of the other major regional foraging sites for this species. The integration of data on migratory routes and foraging areas, as part of an ecosystem-based assessment, is also needed to ensure long-term habitat protection.

ACKNOWLEDGMENTS

Much of the information in this paper is the result of research efforts by our colleagues who are working to conserve loggerhead turtles worldwide. In particular, we wish to acknowledge the long-term studies of loggerheads led by Llew Ehrhart, George Hughes, Colin Limpus, Dimitris Margaritoulis, and Jim Richardson. Ken Dodd's excellent 1988 Synopsis of the Biological Data on the Loggerhead Sea Turtle served as a valuable reference and starting point and we acknowledge his efforts. The paper was improved by two anonymous reviewers.

LITERATURE CITED

Addison, D. S. 1996a. Mean annual nest frequency for renesting loggerhead turtles (*Caretta caretta*) on the southwest coast of Florida. Marine Turtle Newsletter 75:13–15.

———. 1996b. *Caretta caretta* (Loggerhead sea turtle). Nesting frequency. Herpetological Review 27:76.

Balazs, G. H. 1999. Factors to consider in the tagging of sea turtles. *In* K. L. Eckert, K. A. Bjorndal, F. A. Abreu-Grobois, and M. Donnelly (eds.). Research and management techniques for the conservation of sea turtles, 101–109. IUCN/SSC Marine Turtle Specialist Group Publication no. 4.

Bell, R., and J. I. Richardson. 1978. An analysis of tag recoveries from loggerhead sea turtles (*Caretta caretta*) nesting on Little Cumberland Island, Georgia. *In* G. E. Henderson (ed.). Proceedings of the Florida and interregional conference on sea turtles, 24–25 July 1976, Jensen Beach, Florida, 20–24. Florida Marine Research Publications no. 33.

Bengston, J. L., and B. S. Stewart. 1992. Diving and haulout behavior of crabeater seals in the Weddell Sea, Antarctica, during March 1986. Polar Biology 12:635–644.

Bjorndal, K. A., A. B. Meylan, and B. J. Turner. 1983. Sea turtles nesting at Melbourne Beach, Florida, I. Size, growth and reproductive biology. Biological Conservation. 26:65–77.

Carr, A. 1975. The Ascension Island green turtle colony. Copeia 1975:547–555.

Carr, A., M. H. Carr, and A. B. Meylan. 1978. The ecology and migrations of sea turtles, 7. The west Caribbean green turtle colony. Bulletin of the American Museum of Natural History 162:1–46.

Dodd, C. K. 1988. Synopsis of the biological data on the loggerhead sea turtle *Caretta caretta* (Linnaeus 1758). USFWS Biological Report 88(14).

Encalada, S. E., K. A. Bjorndal, A. B. Bolten, J. C. Zurita, B. Schroeder, E. Possardt, C. J. Sears, and B. W. Bowen. 1998. Population structure of loggerhead turtle *(Caretta caretta)* nesting colonies in the Atlantic and Mediterranean as inferred from mitochondrial DNA control region sequences. Marine Biology 130:567–575.

Ehrhart, L. M. 1980. A continuation of base-line studies for environmentally monitoring space transportation systems (STS) at John F. Kennedy Space Center. Vol. 4. Threatened and endangered species of the Kennedy Space Center. Part 1: Marine turtle studies. Final report 1976–1979.

Frazer, N. B. 1984. A model for assessing mean age-specific fecundity in sea turtle populations. Herpetologica 40:281–291.

Frazer, N. B., and J. I. Richardson. 1985. Annual variation in clutch size and frequency for loggerhead turtles, *Caretta caretta*, nesting at Little Cumberland Island, Georgia, U.S.A. Herpetologica 41:246–251.

Hays, G. C., and J. M. Sutherland. 1991. Remigration and beach fidelity of loggerhead turtles nesting on the island of Cephalonia, Greece. Journal of Herpetology 25:232–233.

Hays, G. C., P. I. Webb, J. P. Hayes, I. G. Priede, and J. French. 1992. Satellite tracking of a loggerhead turtle *(Caretta caretta)* in the Mediterranean. *In* M. Salmon and J. Wyneken (compilers). Proceedings of the 11th annual workshop on sea turtle biology and conservation, 53–55. NOAA Technical Memorandum NMFS-SEFSC-302.

Hendrickson, J. R. 1980. Ecological strategies of sea turtles. American Zoologist 20:597–608.

Henwood, T. A. 1987. Movements and seasonal changes in loggerhead turtle *Caretta caretta* aggregations in the vicinity of Cape Canaveral, Florida (1978–84). Biological Conservation 40:191–202.

Hughes, G. R. 1974. The sea turtles of southeast Africa. II. The biology of the Tongaland loggerhead turtle *Caretta caretta* with comments on the leatherback turtle *Dermochelys coriacea* L. and the green turtle *Chelonia mydas* L. in the study region. Oceanographic Research Institute Investigational Report no. 36.

Hughes, G. R. 1976. Irregular reproductive cycles in the Tongaland loggerhead sea turtle, *Caretta*

caretta L. *(Cryptodira: Chelonidae)*. Zoologica Africana 11:285–291.

Hughes, G. R. 1982. Nesting cycles in sea turtles—typical or atypical? *In* K. Bjorndal (ed.). Biology and conservation of sea turtles, 81–89. Washington, D.C.: Smithsonian Institution Press.

Hughes, G. R. 1995. Conservation of sea turtles in the southern African region. *In* K. Bjorndal (ed.). Biology and conservation of sea turtles, rev. ed., 397–404. Washington, D.C.: Smithsonian Institution Press.

Hughes, G. R., A. J. Bass, and M. T. Mentis. 1967. Further studies on marine turtles in Tongaland, I. Lammergeyer 3:7–53.

Iwamoto, T., M. Ishii, Y. Nakashima, H. Takeshita, and A. Itoh. 1985. Nesting cycles and migrations of the loggerhead sea turtle *Caretta caretta* in Miyazaki, Japan. Japanese Journal of Ecology 35:505–512.

Jay, C. V., S. D. Farley, and G. W. Garner. 2001. Summer diving behavior of male walruses in Bristol Bay, Alaska. Marine Mammal Science 17:617–631.

Kamezaki, N., I. Miyawaki, H. Suganuma, K. Omuta, Y. Nakajima, K. Goto, K. Sate, Y. Matsuzawa, M. Samejima, M. Ishii, and T. Iwamoto. 1997. Post-nesting migration of Japanese loggerhead turtle, *Caretta caretta*. Wildlife Conservation Japan 3:29–39.

Kaufmann, R. 1975. Studies on the loggerhead sea turtle, *Caretta caretta caretta* (Linne) in Colombia, South America. Herpetologica 31:323–326.

Lazar, B., D. Margaritoulis, and N. Tvrtkovic. 2000. Migrations of the loggerhead sea turtle *(Caretta caretta)* into the Adriatic Sea. *In* F. A. Abreu-Grobois, R. Briseno, R. Marquez, F. Silva, and L. Sarti (compilers). Proceedings of the 18th annual workshop on sea turtle biology and conservation, 180. NOAA Technical Memorandum NMFS-SEFSC-436.

LeBuff, C. R., Jr. 1974. Unusual nesting relocation in the loggerhead turtle, *Caretta caretta*. Herpetologica 30:29–31.

———. 1990. The loggerhead turtle in the eastern Gulf of Mexico. Sanibel, Fla.: *Caretta* Research, Inc.

Lenarz, M. S., N. B. Frazer, M. S. Ralston, and R. B. Mast. 1981. Seven nests recorded for loggerhead turtle *(Caretta caretta)* in one season. Herpetological Review 12:9.

Limpus, C. J. 1985. A study of the loggerhead sea turtle, *Caretta caretta*, in Eastern Australia. Ph.D. Thesis, University of Queensland, St. Lucia, Queensland, Australia.

———. 1992. Estimation of tag loss in marine turtle research. Wildlife Research 19:457–469.

———. 1994. The loggerhead turtle, *Caretta caretta*,

in Queensland: Feeding ground selection following her first nesting season. *In* K. A. Bjorndal, A. B. Bolten, D. A. Johnson, and P. Eliazar (compilers). Proceedings of the 14th annual workshop on sea turtle biology and conservation, 78–81. NOAA Technical Memorandum NMFS-SEFSC-351.

Limpus, C. J. and N. Nicholls. 1988. The southern oscillation regulates the annual numbers of green turtles *Chelonia mydas* breeding around northern Australia. Australian Journal of Wildlife Research 15:157–161.

Limpus, C. J., J. D. Miller, C. J. Parmenter, D. Reimer, N. McLachlan, and R. Webb. 1992. Migration of green *(Chelonia mydas)* and loggerhead *(Caretta caretta)* to and from eastern Australian rookeries. Wildlife Research 19:347–358.

Lund, F. 1986. Nest production and nesting site tenacity of the loggerhead turtle, *Caretta caretta*, on Jupiter Island, Florida. M.S. Thesis, University of Florida, Gainesville.

Lutcavage, M. E., P. Plotkin, B. Witherington, and P. L. Lutz. 1997. Human impacts on sea turtle survival. *In* P. L. Lutz and J. A. Musick (eds.). The biology of sea turtles, 387–409. Boca Raton, Fla.: CRC Press.

Marcovaldi, M. A., A. C. C. D. da Silva, B. M. G. Gallo, C. Baptistotte, E. P. Lima, C. Bellini, E. H. S. M. Lima, J. C. de Castilhos, J. C. A. Thome, L. M. de P. Moreira, and T. M Sanches. 2000. Recaptures of tagged turtles from nesting and feeding grounds protected by Projeto TAMAR-IBAMA, Brasil. *In* H. Kalb and T. Wibbles (compilers). Proceedings of the 19th annual workshop on sea turtle biology and conservation, 164–166. NOAA Technical Memorandum NMFS-SEFSC-443.

Margaritoulis, D. 1982. Observations on loggerhead sea turtle *Caretta caretta* activity during three nesting seasons (1977–1979) in Zakynthos, Greece. Biological Conservation 24:193–204.

———. 1983. The inter-nesting interval of Zakynthos loggerheads. *In* N. S. Margaris, M. Arianoutsou-Faraggitaki, and R. J. Reiter (eds.). Adaptations to Terrestrial Environments, 135–144. New York: Plenum Press.

———. 1988. Post-nesting movements of loggerhead sea turtles tagged in Greece. Rapports Commission Internationale de la Mer Méditerranée 31:284.

Meylan, A. B., K. A. Bjorndal, and B. J. Turner. 1983. Sea turtles nesting at Melbourne Beach, Florida, II. Post-nesting movements of *Caretta caretta*. Biological Conservation 26:79–80.

Murphy, T. M., and S. R. Hopkins. 1984. Aerial and ground surveys of marine turtle nesting beaches in the Southeast region, U.S. Final Report to the

National Marine Fisheries Service, NMFS Contract No. NA83-GA-C-00021.

Nishimura, W. 1994. Internesting interval and nest frequency for loggerhead turtles on Inakahama Beach, Yakushima Island, Japan. Marine Turtle Newsletter 67:21–22.

Plotkin, P. T., and J. R. Spotila. 2002. Post-nesting migrations of loggerhead turtles *Caretta caretta* from Georgia, U.S.A.: Conservation implications for a genetically distinct subpopulation. Oryx 36(4): 396–399.

Richardson, J. I., T. H. Richardson, and M. W. Dix. 1978. Remigration patterns of loggerhead sea turtles *(Caretta caretta)* nesting on Little Cumberland and Cumberland Islands, Georgia. Florida Marine Research Publications. 33:39–44.

Rostal, D., J. Grumbles, and D. Owens. 1991. Physiological evidence of higher fecundity in wild Kemp's ridleys: Implications to population estimates. *In* M. Salmon and J. Wyneken, compilers. Proceedings of the 11th annual workshop on sea turtle biology and conservation, 180. NOAA Technical Memorandum NMFS-SEFSC-302.

Rostal, D. C., J. S. Grumbles, R. A. Byles, R. Marquez-M., and D. W. Owens. 1997. Nesting physiology of Kemp's ridley sea turtles, *Lepidochelys kempi*, at Rancho Nuevo, Tamaulipas, Mexico, with observations on population estimates. Chelonian Conservation and Biology 2:538–547.

Sakamoto, W., T. Bando, N. Arai, and N. Baba. 1997. Migration paths of the adult female and male loggerhead turtles *Caretta caretta* determined through satellite telemetry. Fisheries Science 63:547–552.

Sea Turtle Protection Society of Greece. 1995. Long distance inter-nesting travel. Marine Turtle Newsletter 70:27.

Schroeder, B., and S. Murphy. 1999. Population surveys (ground and aerial) on nesting beaches. *In* K. L. Eckert, K. A. Bjorndal, F. A. Abreu-Grobois, and M. Donnelly (eds.). Research and management techniques for the conservation of sea turtles, 45–55. IUCN/SSC Marine Turtle Specialist Group Publication no. 4.

Stoneburner, D. L., and L. M. Ehrhart. 1981. Observations on *Caretta caretta caretta*: A record internesting migration in the Atlantic. Herpetological Review 12:66.

Talbert, O. R., Jr., S. E. Stancyk, J. M. Dean, and J. M. Will. 1980. Nesting activity of the loggerhead turtle *(Caretta caretta)* in South Carolina. 1. A rookery in transition. Copeia 1980:709–718.

Worth, D. F., and J. B. Smith. 1976. Marine turtle nesting on Hutchinson Island, Florida, in 1973. Florida Marine Research Publication 18:1–17.

Chapter 8

Nest Site Selection, Oviposition, Eggs, Development, Hatching, and Emergence of Loggerhead Turtles

—Jeffrey D. Miller, Colin J. Limpus,
and Matthew H. Godfrey

As with all sea turtles, the production of the next generation of loggerhead turtles results from a synergism of the effects of the ecological conditions in the foraging area on the energetics of the female parent and of beach environmental conditions on development of the embryos. To be successful, reproduction must occur when environmental conditions support adult activity (e.g., sufficient quality and quantity of food in the foraging area, suitable beach structure for digging, nearby internesting habitat) (Georges et al. 1993). Further, the environmental conditions of the nesting beach must favor embryonic development and survival (i.e., modest temperature fluctuation, low salinity, high humidity, well drained, well aerated; Mortimer 1990, 1995). Additionally, the hatchlings must emerge to onshore and offshore conditions that enhance their chance of survival (e.g., less than 100% depredation, appropriate offshore currents for dispersal) (Georges et al. 1993).

General Reproductive Cycle and Nesting Distribution

All marine turtles prepare for reproduction in their foraging areas during the period (usually several years) before they migrate, at least short distances, to mating areas. The mating period precedes nesting and may last more than six weeks. After several weeks of mating, the males return to their foraging areas, and the females proceed to the nesting areas (Limpus 1985; Limpus and Miller 1993; Miller 1997). After producing several clutches of eggs during a reproductive period of several months, the females return to their feeding areas to recover from the effort of reproduction and migration. Following a quiescent period lasting a few to several years, females migrate to the mating areas, and the cycle continues (Limpus 1985; Limpus and Miller 1993; Miller 1997; Owens et al. 1989).

The cycle of energy accumulation, deposition, reorganization, and utilization in the foraging areas that support reproduction by loggerhead turtles has not been studied in detail; however, studies of other marine turtles provide the information for a general account. Following its reproductive effort, the female returns to the foraging area, where she is reproductively quiescent over a variable period of years (one to several years), and during this time she accumulates the energy to support her next reproductive effort (vitellogenesis, migration, egg production, oviposition, and return migration). Neophyte breeders are already in their foraging areas, having completed puberty (Limpus 1990; Limpus and Limpus, Chapter 6, this volume). Only when the right mix of endogenous (e.g., hormone levels and/or fat reserves) and exogenous (e.g., photoperiod) factors interact (Licht 1980; Licht et al. 1982; Owens 1980; Wibbels et al. 1990, 1992) does vitellogenesis begin. Vitellogenesis requires 10–12 months for completion. The duration of each phase in the foraging area depends, in part, on the quality and quantity of food available (Bjorndal 1997). Loggerheads are carnivorous, feeding mainly on benthic invertebrates, especially mollusks (see Table 28 in Dodd 1988). Although the timing of reproduction in herbivorous green turtles has been linked to fluctuations in major weather patterns (Limpus and Nicholls 2000), reproduction in carnivores (e.g., loggerheads) does not appear to have a direct connection to climate fluctuations (Limpus and Miller 1993).

The loggerhead turtle is the exception to the tropical nesting pattern exhibited by the other sea turtles (Gasperetti et al. 1993; Hirth 1997; Limpus et al. 1988; Marquez 1994; Marquez et al. 1976; Sternberg 1981; Witzell 1983). The major portion of loggerhead nesting occurs in warm temperate and subtropical areas, with the exception of Masirah Island, Oman (Gasperetti et al. 1993; Ross and Barwani 1995), several small nesting aggregations in the Caribbean (Dodd 1988) and minor, scattered nesting locations elsewhere in tropical areas (Dodd 1988). The nesting aggregation at Masirah Island is located inside the tropics, but its use is consistent with the general pattern of extratropical nesting by the species because the upwelling from the cold Indian Ocean currents makes the area warm temperate to subtropical.

Loggerhead turtles spread their reproductive effort both temporally and spatially. Because they nest near or outside the tropics, loggerhead turtles must respond to a temporally limited nesting season. In the Northern Hemisphere the nesting season is between May and August, whereas in the Southern Hemisphere nesting occurs between October and March (Dodd 1988). The timing of nesting at specific sites may be more restricted, particularly toward the northern or southern extent of the nesting range. Spatial clumping occurs because loggerhead turtles concentrate their nesting at a few primary locations that are augmented by lower density, satellite nesting sites; in addition, a few isolated, low density nesting sites are known (Dodd 1988; Sternberg 1981).

Maturation, Courtship, and Mating

The straight carapace length of nesting loggerhead turtles ranges from approximately 70 to 109 cm (curved carapace lengths are slightly larger; see Table 7 in Dodd 1988). Minimum breeding size varies among populations of nesting loggerhead turtles and is not a good indicator of reproductive maturity because not all individuals begin to breed at the minimum size (Limpus 1985; Limpus et al. 1994). Individual turtles begin and finish puberty at different sizes (Limpus 1990); some individuals may be 10 cm or more longer than the minimum breeding size and still be immature or just starting puberty (Limpus et al. 1994; Limpus and Limpus, Chapter 6, this volume). Based on gonad examination, the duration of puberty (morphological and functional maturation of the oviduct and ovaries or testis and epididymis) in loggerheads is on the order of 10 years for turtles in the western South Pacific (Limpus 1990).

After becoming reproductively ready, female and male loggerheads migrate from their foraging areas to copulate in the general vicinity of the nesting area (Limpus et al. 1992). Typically, female loggerhead turtles do not reproduce every year (Dodd 1988; Hirth 1980); however, male loggerheads may breed every year (Wibbels et al. 1990).

Remigration intervals (period between reproductive seasons, *sensu* Limpus 1985) for loggerhead turtles vary from one to nine or more years (Dodd 1988; Limpus 1985), with the majority of females having two-, three-, or four-year cycles. The determination of the remigration interval for a population can be affected by the duration of the study, tag loss (Limpus 1992), partial coverage of a potential nesting area (Hughes 1982), long reproductively quiescent periods (Limpus 1985), or a change in annual survivorship that removes the turtles from the reproductive population.

Only a few studies provide the foundation for the current understanding of courtship and mating in loggerheads (Caldwell 1959; Caldwell et al. 1959; Ehrhart 1995; Limpus 1985; Wood 1953). Much more in-water observational research is needed to elucidate the details of the process. As with other species, the behaviors that comprise courtship are poorly described (Ehrhart 1995; Miller 1997). The few behaviors that have been recorded indicate that head movements, nuzzling/biting, or flipper movements, among others, may be used by the male to determine the receptiveness of the female. It is not known whether or not females exude a pheromone that signals her reproductive status, but field observations suggest this may be the case (Limpus, unpubl. observ.).

The male attempts to mount the female, while the female seemingly tries to avoid being mounted. Individuals may circle each other; the female may turn to face the male or attempt to leave the area while one or more males interact with her and each other. The female receives bites, mostly to her neck and shoulders, from the male before she is mounted. She also acquires damage to the shoulders of her carapace margin from the male's curved claws. The progressive healing of the mating damage during the nesting season indicates that mating occurs in the weeks just preceding the ovulatory cycle, and it follows that sperm are stored in the oviducts for use during the nesting season.

Insemination is achieved with the male's tail curled under the female's tail to bring the penis and cloaca into apposition. The penis is inserted into the female's cloaca, but details of this process are lacking. Mounting, and possibly sperm transfer, may last for several hours, but the rate of transfer is not known. Data for green turtles suggest that the duration of penile insertion is related to the rate of fertilization, but this work was done in a captive situation and may not be completely applicable in the wild (Simon et al. 1975; Ulrich and Owens 1974; Witham 1970).

In the mating areas, mounted pairs are regularly seen at the surface of the water, but they may be seen anywhere in the water column. The male has little control of the position in the water because he uses his clawed front flippers to hang onto the carapace of the female; the female does the swimming and determines when the couple will surface for a breathe. The male may be able to influence the upward direction by raising his head and creating drag.

Philopatry and Nesting Site Fidelity

Philopatry (i.e., migration from nesting areas to foraging areas and return, *sensu* Carr 1975) among loggerhead turtles is relatively high. Based on returns of tagged turtles, for example, 1,404 of 1,433 loggerhead turtles (98%, data collected over nine seasons) were recaptured at the original tagging location in Australia (Limpus 1985). In Tongaland, South Africa, 93.1% (mode 800 m) and 91.1% (mode 400 m) returned to within 9.6 km of the original tagging site (Hughes 1974b). At Little Cumberland Island, Georgia, 51% (22 of 43) returned to within 16.6 km, 7% (3) returned to within 50 km, and 42% (18) returned at greater distances from the original tagging site (Bell and Richardson 1978). Besides being examples of philopatry, these data illustrate that thorough coverage of the local nesting site and adjacent areas is very important in obtaining appropriate data. Particularly in the Bell and Richardson study, coverage over distances greater than 50 km contributed valuable data on the distribution of nesting. More recently, genetic data have defined strong links between breeding turtles and the region of their birth (Bowen et al. 1993, 1994, 1995) rather than with the specific beach where hatching occurred.

Loggerhead turtles show a high degree of nesting site fidelity (*sensu* Carr 1975). Once it has returned to the region of its birth and selected a nesting beach, a loggerhead turtle will tend to renest in relatively close proximity (0–5 km) during successive nesting attempts within the same and subsequent breeding season, although a small percentage of turtles will utilize more distant nesting sites in the general area (Bjorndal et al. 1983; Limpus 1985; Limpus et al. 1984a). Records of intra-seasonal nesting movements suggest that loggerhead turtles are capable of moving long distances but the proportion of individuals doing so is low (Limpus 1985). In general, loggerhead turtles return to the same beach to lay subsequent clutches following successful oviposition (Limpus 1985).

Nesting Site Selection

Typical loggerhead nesting beaches tend to be sandy, wide, open beaches backed by low dunes and fronted by a flat sandy approach from the sea, although specific characteristics vary from rookery to rookery. For instance, in South Africa loggerheads are found on beaches with adjacent reefs or rocky outcrops (Hughes 1974a, 1974b), while in the Mediterranean loggerheads emerge primarily on beaches fronted by mostly sandy areas (Le Vin et al. 1998). In Japan, an analysis of 300 nesting beaches revealed that of the 23 factors studied, the most important was the softness of the sand, followed by distance from the nearest human settlement (Kikukawa et al. 1998, 1999).

Once a female has selected a beach on which to lay her eggs, she must choose where on the beach to dig the nest. There are serious outcomes from this choice. For instance, the eggs must be placed far enough from the tidal zone to avoid being eroded or excessively washed by high tides, which may be lethal to the developing embryos (Whitmore and Dutton 1985). At the same time, the eggs must not be placed so far from the ocean that the emerging hatchlings are at a greater risk to land predators (Blamires and Guinea 1998) or are unable to find the sea due to visual obstructions (Godfrey and Barreto 1995).

The place where the eggs are deposited will determine the developmental microenvironment of the nest and can affect many characteristics of the hatchlings, including hatching and emergence success, sex ratio, fitness, vulnerability to nest predators, and so on. Because the character of the beach, including elevation, temperature, moisture, and humus content, changes with distance from the sea (Spotila et al. 1987), there is ample opportunity for females to select a particular type of environment into which to deposit their eggs. The research challenge is to identify the characteristics of the beach to which the turtle is responding, positively or negatively, and which she is ignoring.

More is known about cues that discourage nesting than about those that encourage nesting, principally as a result of the number of studies conducted on urban or developed beaches. For instance, artificial lighting on the beachfront reduces the number of nesting loggerheads, relative to those on beach areas free of lighting (Ehrhart et al. 1996; Witherington 1992). In the Florida Keys, nesting turtles seem to avoid areas backed by tall Australian pines (*Casuarina* sp.) (Schmelz and Mezich 1988), while loggerhead nests on an urban beach in Boca Raton, Florida, tended to be clustered in front of tall buildings, possibly because their silhouettes block the artificial light of the city (Salmon et al. 1995). Smaller structures on the beach, such as exposed pilings used to counter erosion, result in lower numbers of clutches being laid (Bouchard et al. 1998), and sand introduced as part of beach "renourishment" programs can lower the number of successful clutches laid, due to increased compaction or hardness (Crain et al. 1995).

In the absence of disturbance, loggerhead turtles tend to lay their eggs in nonrandom patterns (Martin et al. 1989; Hays and Speakman 1993; Mellanby et al. 1998). The challenge has been to discover the forces behind the pattern of nesting site selection. In general, the methodology of these studies has been to look for correlations between successful nesting attempts and environmental measures (e.g., sand temperature or moisture content, slope, distance from the high tide line or the vegetation line, etc.). Interestingly, many of the studies focused only on successful nests, ignoring unsuccessful

Table 8.1.

Factors That Have Been Related to Nest Site Selection in Loggerhead Turtles

Source	Site	Slope	Temp.	Distance	Sand Type	Moisture	Compaction	Erosion	pH	Salinity
3	Florida, USA						NS			
7	Florida, USA			NS						
6	Greece			NR						
4	Florida, USA	SC			SC	NS			NS	
5	Florida, USA							NS		
8	Florida, USA		SC							
9	Florida, USA	SC	NS			NS				NS
2	S. Carolina, USA	SC	SC		SC	SC				
1	N. Carolina, USA			NS						

Source Key: 1. Brooks 1989. 2. Cardinal et al. 1998. 3. Foote and Sprinkel 1995. 4. Garmestani et al. 1998. 5. Grant and Beasley 1998. 6. Hays and Speakman 1993. 7. Hays et al. 1995. 8. Stoneburner and Richardson 1981. 9. Wood and Bjorndal 2000.

Note: Temp. = temperature; NS = not significant; NR = nonrandom; SC = significant correlation.

nesting attempts in which a female emerged onto a nesting beach but did not lay any eggs. From 10 to 75% of loggerhead nesting attempts are unsuccessful on many beaches (Dodd 1988); perhaps much could be learned from studying unsuccessful nesting behavior in conjunction with successful behavior.

Unfortunately, most results from studies of nesting site selection were inconclusive or contradicted the findings of other studies (Table 8.1). For instance, whereas Stoneburner and Richardson (1981) found that an abrupt rise in sand temperature was associated with the onset of nesting in turtles that crawled up the beach, Wood and Bjorndal (2000) found no relation between temperature changes and successful nesting events. Overall, although nest placement on the beach is largely nonrandom (but see Hays et al. 1995), it remains unclear what forces are behind the nesting site selection process in loggerhead turtles. If the multiple regression approach used by Kikukawa et al. (1998, 1999) were applied in other nesting areas to assess the relative importance of the factors influencing nesting site selection, perhaps an unambiguous picture would emerge.

Given that anthropogenic alteration of the beach environment can discourage nesting (e.g., through increased lighting, removal of vegetation, or placement of structures on the beach),

it would be interesting to design an experiment that manipulated the beach environment to stimulate nesting. For instance, Caillouet (1995) suggested the use of sea turtle decoys to stimulate turtles to nest on a particular beach. Perhaps this could be taken further by manipulating specific local environmental features of the beach while a sea turtle is choosing a nesting site in order to discover what factors drive the selection process. Although logistically challenging, the results of such a study might reveal far more about the selection process than traditional descriptive studies.

Nesting Beach Characteristics

Although it is not entirely clear why some beaches are used by sea turtles to deposit eggs and others are not, a potential nesting beach must meet several minimum requirements. It must be easily accessible from the ocean, be high enough to avoid being inundated frequently by high tides, and have enough sand cohesion to allow nest construction, and its sand must facilitate gas diffusion and have temperatures conducive to egg development (Mortimer 1990).

Because variability of physical and chemical characteristics was high in beach sand collected from 50 nesting areas from around the world,

Mortimer (1990) suggested that "factors other than physiognomy of sand on nesting beaches may be as important, or more important, in nest[ing] site selection" than the characteristics of the sand.

The result of beach and nesting site selection is that the eggs incubate in a low salinity, high humidity, well-ventilated substrate that is not inundated during development and provides insulation from the high beach surface temperatures while being in the temperature range that facilitates development (Ackerman 1980, 1997; Miller 1985; Maloney et al. 1990). Given the level of investigation concerning the nesting process, it seems odd that no one has been able to define the process by which the turtle (any species) selects its nesting beach or the site for the nest on the beach.

Nesting Process

All species of sea turtles share a core set of nesting behaviors (Bustard and Greenham 1969; Bustard et al. 1975; Ehrenfeld 1979; Schulz 1975). The process has been subdivided into 7–11 steps (Bustard and Greenham 1969; Bustard et al. 1975; Carr and Ogren 1960; Hendrickson 1982; Kaufmann 1968; Tufts 1972). Regardless of the number of steps, the general pattern includes emerging from the surf, ascending the beach, excavating the body pit, digging the egg chamber, oviposition, filling in the egg chamber, filling the body pit, and returning to the sea.

There are two types of gaits, alternating and simultaneous, used by sea turtles to move on the beach; they leave asymmetrical or symmetrical tracks, respectively, in the sand (Pritchard et al. 1983). The loggerhead uses an alternating gait and moves one front flipper and the hind flipper on the opposite side forward at the same time, moving only two flippers at a time. In many populations, the resulting track is approximately 90 cm wide and asymmetrical, with the marks made by the front flippers obviously offset and extending beyond the hind flipper marks.

Typically, loggerheads require between one and two hours to complete the nesting process (Hirth 1980). The description of the nesting process of the loggerhead by Pritchard and

Trebbau (1984) is both descriptive and comparative (see also Bustard et al. 1975; Miller 1997). Using the nesting process of loggerhead turtles as the model, Hailman and Elowson (1992) described 50 separate action patterns derived from the gait.

When the turtle first emerges from the waves, it may pause at the water's edge and be washed over by several waves before starting up the beach. For the most part, the turtle continues uphill while it is on the hard, sloping part of the beach. The turtle crawls a few meters, then pauses to rest, breathe, and possibly scrutinize its surroundings (Pritchard and Trebbau 1984). During this phase, loggerhead turtles, like all marine turtles, are easily disturbed by activity on the beach. Lighting, movement, and/or obstacles may cause a change in direction or may even cause the turtle to abandon the nesting effort. Several authors have been unable to identify the reason for the aborted nesting attempt; sometimes the female is deterred from nesting by "factors known only to the turtle" (Dodd 1988).

The occurrence rate of aborted nesting attempts varies among populations (e.g., it is high in the southeastern United States, low in Queensland, Australia; Dodd 1988; Limpus 1985). Whatever the cause(s), a loggerhead usually returns the same night or a following night for a further nesting attempt (e.g., 1.08 days; Limpus 1985), and the majority return to the same beach (87.5%; Limpus 1985).

Loggerhead turtles prepare the nesting site before digging the egg chamber by clearing away surface debris, using either simultaneous or alternating sweeps of the front flippers. The turtle "swims" forward as the area in front is cleared. Loose, dry substrate immediately under or behind the turtle may be cleared by its hind flippers (Hailman and Elowson 1992). Although the digging action obviously moves the turtle forward into the "body pit," the cue to stop excavating the body pit is unknown. In very dry or loose sand conditions a turtle will excavate a deeper body pit; digging a deeper body pit places the turtle at the level of firmer, possibly more cohesive, sand that will hold the shape of the egg chamber.

The hind flippers are used to excavate the

egg chamber (Schulz 1975). The shape of the egg chamber has been described as "flask shaped" (Schulz 1975) or as other similar shapes; however, Carthy et al. (in review) found that the nest shape had a thicker neck and a less round chamber than previously described. The nest measurements correlated well with several measurements of the size of the female (e.g., neck width × straight carapace length, nest depth × straight carapace width) and her reproductive output (e.g., number of eggs × nest depth and minimum egg depth), but not with the length of bones in the hind flipper (hand) (Carthy et al., in review). The digging action creates a chamber with a narrower neck and a wider bottom (diameter of neck ≅ 16–21 cm; chamber diameter ≅ 23–26 cm; depth to top of eggs ≅ 35 cm; depth to bottom of chamber ≅ 60 cm; Carthy et al., in review) unless the dryness and particle size of the sand or buried debris causes the shape to alter (Bustard and Greenham 1968). Loggerhead turtles construct nests that are larger and deeper than those made by hawksbill turtles, which are smaller turtles (Carr et al. 1966), and smaller and shallower nests than those constructed by green turtles, which are larger turtles (Hirth 1997).

The alternating use of the hind flippers removes about a cup of sand at a time. The sand is placed by the digging flipper to the side of the chamber. As the turtle takes its weight on this flipper, some newly excavated sand falls on top of it. The alternate flipper throws the sand on top of it forward and extends into the nest chamber for another scoop. With occasional pauses to rest, the alternating process continues until the turtle's hind flippers cannot touch the walls or bottom of the chamber (Hailman and Elowson 1992). When a turtle missing one hind flipper attempts to dig, it uses the one good limb properly and moves the stump of the other in sequence as if it were actually removing sand. A turtle missing one hind flipper digs an improperly shaped nest that usually is not large enough to hold the entire clutch of eggs.

During oviposition both hind flippers of a loggerhead are extended outwards behind the turtle on the sand. When the cloaca contracts, the tip of the tail points downward and slightly forward; then as the eggs drop, the tail relaxes backward. With each contraction, the outer edges of the rear flippers curl. The eggs are laid singly or in small groups (two or three, sometimes four).

Loggerhead turtles are relatively tolerant of external stimuli during egg laying. However, the level of indifference to disturbing stimuli varies among individuals; some may cease oviposition when tagged, while others may attempt to bite the tag area or the sand in front of them, and still others may show no response at all. Part of this variation is a function of the number of eggs already laid. As a general rule, turtles become more tolerant as they lay more eggs. Turtles are even more tolerant of disturbing stimuli while filling the egg chamber and covering the nesting site.

The nest chamber is filled by scraping sand into the hole with the hind flippers (Hailman and Elowson 1992); this sand was the last removed and is typically the moistest. When the neck of the chamber has been filled higher than the floor of the body pit, the sand is compacted by alternating use of the hind limbs. After compaction, the turtle resumes front flipper action like that used to excavate the body pit. Sand is thrown backwards along the carapace over the nesting site; as the turtle moves forward it continues throwing sand backwards. At the end of the process, the turtle has moved at least 1 m forward of the actual site of the egg chamber so that the remnant of the body pit is not above the eggs (Hailman and Elowson 1992). The primary outcome of this behavior is the reestablishment of insulating sand over the eggs to a depth approximating that of the beach surface, thus facilitating the rapid reestablishment of temperature and moisture in the sand above the eggs. Because most predators can locate a nest within a few days of oviposition or near emergence (Hopkins et al. 1979), camouflaging the nest is of secondary importance only, if it is important at all.

Endocrine Regulation of Reproduction

There is continuing growth in the understanding of the role of the endocrine system in regulation of reproduction in the loggerhead turtle (Owens 1980, 1997). For adult female loggerheads in the foraging area, estrodial 17β (E_2) appears to be the stimulus for vitellogenesis in the months leading up to migration (Wibbels et al. 1990). As E_2 increases during vitellogenesis, so too does testosterone. At the completion of the vitellogenic phase, the dramatic decrease in E_2 in synchrony with the rise in testosterone to its highest level appears to initiate migration to the breeding areas (Owens 1997). In addition, elevated testosterone levels may also influence courtship and mating behaviors (Wibbels et al. 1990).

Following successful courtship, ovulation may be stimulated by elevated levels of luteinizing hormone (LH) approximately two weeks prior to the first clutch being laid and within 48 hours after nesting for each successive clutch (Wibbels et al. 1992; Owens 1997). These elevated LH levels may also stimulate progesterone production by the ovary (Wibbels et al. 1992). Wibbels et al. (1992) hypothesized that elevated testosterone levels in the postmating female may sensitize follicles and corpora lutea to LH stimulation.

Females come ashore with undetectable levels of arginine vasotocin (AVT). When body pit construction begins, AVT levels increase, possibly via a neuroendocrine mechanism associated with the behavior. AVT levels reach their peak during early to midoviposition, and plasma concentrations of AVT decrease to baseline levels as the turtle returns to the water. AVT, which is produced in the neurohypophysis, is transported by the bloodstream to the oviducts, where it is believed to stimulate the synthesis of prostaglandin F (PGF) (Owens 1997). PGF and prostaglandin E_2 (PGE$_2$) are hypothesized to play active roles during oviposition; PGF stimulates oviducal contractions to move eggs through the oviducts in concert with PGE$_2$, which promotes vaginal relaxation (Guillette et al. 1991). The level of PGE$_2$ increases during construction of the body pit and increases rapidly up to middle of oviposition. By late oviposition the levels have decreased sharply; they then decrease more slowly until the turtle is covering the nest, after which the levels approach the baseline before the turtle reenters the water (Guillette et al. 1991). The stimuli for PGE$_2$

synthesis and release are unknown and may involve AVT.

Whittier et al. (1997) hypothesize that testosterone and corticosterone interact over the period of successive nestings and may be involved in reproductive functions such as the mobilization of lipid reserves for egg production in loggerheads. The linkage between endocrine function and the stimulus to initiate postnesting migration to the home feeding area remains to be elucidated.

Reproductive Output

Loggerhead turtles follow the standard pattern of reproduction for sea turtles: "large clutches of relatively small eggs; multiple clutches produced during a well-defined nesting season; communal nesting in well-defined ancestral nesting areas; [and] careful construction of [a] covered nest" (Moll 1979). The potential negative impact of infrequent environmental perturbations (i.e., heavy rain, waves causing erosion) on the reproductive output for the season is reduced by laying sequential clutches of eggs at approximately two-week intervals in different places in the beach environment. This strategy enhances the probability of success of incubation by optimizing among the size and shape of the eggs, the number of eggs, the number of clutches laid in a nesting season, and when in the season the eggs are laid, in the context of the factors that influence the conditions of the beach.

Loggerhead turtles lay white, spherical, cleidoic eggs with flexible, aragonite shells (Miller 1985; Packard and DeMarco 1991) that are medium sized (4.0 cm, 36 g) compared with those of other species, which range from the small eggs of *Lepidochelys olivacea* (3.9 cm, 35 g) and *L. kempii* (3.8 cm, 30 g) to the large eggs of *Dermochelys coriacea* (5.3 cm, 90 g) and *Natator depressus* (5.1 cm, 80 g) (Ewert 1979; Van Buskirk and Crowder 1994). *Chelonia mydas* lays eggs that are slightly larger (4.5 cm, 48 g) and *Eretmochelys imbricata* lays eggs that are slightly smaller (3.8 cm, 28 g) than those of loggerhead turtles (Ewert 1979; Van Buskirk and Crowder 1994).

The number of eggs laid in each clutch

varies between clutches as well as within and between populations (Dodd 1988; Hirth 1980; Limpus 1985). The overall range is 23–198, with a mean of 112.4 per clutch (mean of 19 populations; Van Buskirk and Crowder 1994). Some of the lower values are probably the result of counting eggs in clutches that were the remainder of disturbed nesting attempts (Limpus 1985); some may be real, albeit from females that were not functioning properly. Similarly, the very large clutch counts may result from counting eggs in two clutches laid in juxtaposed nests.

Like all other sea turtles, loggerhead turtles lay several clutches of eggs during a nesting season (Hirth 1980; Miller 1997; Van Buskirk and Crowder 1994). The number of clutches produced results from several factors (Moll 1979), including (1) the energetics required to support reproduction, (2) the physiological control of ovulation that allows groups of eggs to be separated in space and time, and (3) the risks of mortality associated with the nesting beach and internesting habitat.

The extremes of the typical range vary from one to six clutches per season; the maximum number reported is seven (Lenarz et al. 1981). The mean number of clutches laid per season varies within populations (i.e., between seasons) and among populations (Hughes 1974a, 1974b; Limpus 1985); mean values are usually in the range of two to four. Unfortunately, determining the number of times a turtle nests during a reproductive season is difficult because of incomplete coverage of the nesting season or nesting area or loss of individuals from the nesting group (Hughes 1982). Further, remigrant turtles (i.e., those that have previously nested) may lay one or two more clutches per season than maiden nesting turtles (Lund 1986). Although nearly every nesting beach study reports the number of clutches laid per turtle, it is clear that the reproductive subtleties that impact on the number of clutches laid require better definition before the data are used to estimate the number of female turtles in the population (Marquez 1994) or other parameters of the population.

The internesting interval (*sensu* Limpus 1985) is the interval between when a turtle returns to the sea after laying a clutch of eggs and when she next emerges to lay, whether or not that attempt is successful. Given this definition, the internesting period of loggerheads varies from about 12 to 16 days (Caldwell 1962; Dodd 1988; Hughes and Mentis 1967; Limpus 1985). Extremely short "internesting" intervals represent second attempts at laying a clutch following a disturbance, not new clutches (Miller 1985, 1997).

Fecundity is the product of the clutch count, the number of clutches per breeding season, and the number of breeding seasons in the life of the turtle (Limpus et al. 1984b). Unfortunately, the number of times a loggerhead turtle reproduces during its life is unknown.

Egg Composition and Ovulation

A normal egg is composed of an aragonite shell attached to a shell membrane inside of which is albumen, which surrounds the vitelline membrane enclosing the yolk; the embryonic disk is contained on the vitelline membrane (Miller 1985; Packard and DeMarco 1991). The energy and chemical components of the eggs come from the food eaten and stored by the female while in her foraging area, not the nesting area. The follicles result from the metabolic processes of digestion of food, and the shell is constructed from calcium carbonate in the form of aragonite (orthorhombic $CaCO_3$). If the foraging area is known, studies of the energy and chemical transfer from the environment to the follicles and the impact on the turtle's reproductive success can be enhanced; without this linkage, biochemical analysis of eggs from the nesting beach is of limited value (e.g., Sakai et al. 1995).

When producing an average clutch of 110 eggs, loggerhead turtles infrequently fabricate eggs that are not normal, including yolkless eggs (*sensu* Hughes et al. 1967), multiyolked eggs, chain-form eggs, and shell-less eggs (*sensu* Limpus 1985). Yolkless eggs contain small granules of yolk material surrounded by albumen but have no vitelline membrane. In addition, they do not contain a zygote or embryo and have no propensity for development.

Therefore, the yolkless egg is not strictly an "egg" and should not be included in clutch counts. Yolkless eggs are seldom larger than 50% of the diameter of normal eggs and result from ovulatory debris or fragments of a ruptured yolk entering the oviduct and being layered with albumen and a shell (Miller 1985).

Multiyolked eggs occur in loggerhead turtle clutches on an irregular basis (Limpus 1985). Multiyolked eggs contain two or more yolks within a single shell with varying degrees of constriction between the yolks. As a general rule, the greater the constriction is between yolks, the greater the possibility that the embryo(s) will hatch. Chain-form eggs are an extreme form of the multiyolked egg; they are linked together by small connections of shell material in a chain so that each yolk and its surrounding albumen are separate. Shell-less eggs also occur infrequently; the yolk and albumen are usually encased in the shell membrane without the outer shell structure. The occurrence of multiyolked eggs, chain-form eggs, or shell-less eggs indicates a problem with the oviduct, the cause of which remains undefined (Miller 1985).

The ovary is comprised of a stroma (ovarian tissue) and previtellogenic follicles (diameter range 1–5 mm). The ovary may also contain evidence of ovulation; if ovulation has occurred recently, the corpora hemorrhagica are approximately 15–10 mm in diameter and are situated on postovulatory, fluid-filled vesicles in the stroma where the follicle was ovulated. If ovulation occurred some time in the past, corpora lutea or corpora albicantia will be present; the diameter will depend on the time since ovulation (range 2–8 mm). The oviduct is a long tube (> 4 m) containing a lining of specialized secretory cells that produce the albumen, shell membrane, and shell (Aitken and Solomon 1976; Solomon and Baird 1976). The female turtle arrives at her nesting area with more than enough mature follicles present in her ovaries to supply yolks for all the eggs to be laid during the season. The mature follicles will absorb water before ovulation and increase slightly in diameter from about 2.5 cm to about 3.0 cm. The unused follicles will be resorbed (become corpora atretica) in the months following the nesting season (Limpus and Miller, unpubl. data).

The hormonal control of ovulation has not been described in detail for loggerhead turtles; it is assumed to be similar to the general cycle described for green turtles by Licht (1980) and Owens (1980). Ovulation coincides with a surge in the levels of luteinizing hormone and progesterone. The details that allow for the selective release of approximately 110 follicles from the two ovaries containing a total of several hundred other mature follicles await elucidation.

When ovulated, each follicle travels through the coelom from the ovary to the infundibulum of the oviduct, where it is fertilized by sperm presumably located in the folds of the infundibulum. Because the sperm from all inseminating males are mixed in the folds, the sperm from several different males are available to fertilize the ova that will form a clutch (Harry and Briscoe 1988).

Fertility and Development

Most eggs laid by loggerhead turtles are fertile. Combined counts of eggshell remnants and unhatched eggs opened to determine if any development had occurred indicate fertility is typically greater than 80% (Blanck and Sawyer 1981; Hughes 1970, 1974a, 1974b; Hughes and Mentis 1967; Hughes et al. 1967; Limpus 1985; Miller 1985, 1999). The level of fertility probably exceeds 95%; however, distinguishing between intraoviducal death and early embryonic death (before the formation of blood isles) within eggs that have been in the nest chamber for 60 or more days is difficult (Miller 1997). In eastern Australia, 100% of many hundreds of loggerhead eggs specifically examined for the presence of an embryo at oviposition contained an embryo, that is, all had been fertilized (Miller and Limpus, unpubl. observ.).

The fertilized ovum continues down the oviduct, where special cells in the lining of the anterior glandular region of the oviduct secrete albumen (Aitken and Solomon 1976). Once the yolk has been coated with albumen, the inner shell membrane is secreted from special cells in the shell-forming segment (Owens 1980; Solomon and Baird 1976, 1979). Following formation of the shell membrane, aragonite crystals begin to form the outer portion of the shell (Packard and Hirsch 1986; Packard et al. 1982; Schleich and Kastle 1988; Solomon and Baird 1976, 1979). The shell is not fully formed until at least the seventh day following ovulation (Miller 1985).

First cleavage begins within hours of fertilization, but development is suspended at middle gastrulation until oviposition (Bellairs 1991; Miller 1985). However once oviposited, development resumes within a few hours (four to eight hours, depending on temperature). Rough handling (movement involving rotation and/or jarring) of the eggs after development resumes causes rupturing of delicate membranes and results in the death of the embryo (Limpus et al. 1979; Miller 1985); the embryos remain susceptible to movement-induced mortality until the embryo and its membranes have developed through 20–25 days (about 50%) of incubation (Parmenter 1980).

The morphological changes that occur during development of marine turtles, including loggerheads, have been described for the Cheloniidae and Dermochelyidae (Miller 1985). In general terms, development involves three primary themes: (1) structural differentiation of body and organs (organogenesis), (2) functional development of organs and systems, and (3) embryonic growth.

Six stages of development, extending from first cleavage to middle gastrulation, are completed within the oviduct before the embryo enters a short diapause prior to oviposition (Miller 1985). At oviposition (stage 6; Miller 1985), the edges of the groove blastopore on the blastodisc curve slightly to the anterior. Shortly thereafter (stages 7–11), the neural groove forms, the head fold forms, the amnion arises and extends posteriorly to the vicinity of the first somite, and the number of somites increases to six. During stages 12–16, somites increase from 8 to 27, the first pharyngeal cleft opens, the mouth is shaped into a deep V, amnion covers the entire body, and the caudal amniotic tube has formed. By stage 14, blood islands appear around the periphery of the "yolk-sac" membrane, and the heart is S-shaped and beating. During stages 17–21, the pharyngeal clefts open, and the limb buds appear as small ridges on the lateral body and extend to become paddle shaped. The limb paddles twist to orient parallel with body. Late in this series the carapace margin is indicated as a ridge on the lateral body wall, but the inframarginal scutes are not defined.

During stages 22–27 (middle third of development), species-specific characteristics become increasingly evident as the shape of the scales and the pigmentation of the carapace progress. Initially, the carapace is indicated as a lateral ridge before the anterior portion completes across the neck. The central, lateral, and marginal scales differentiate, and the claw is present on the first digit (stage 25). Pigmentation of the scales expands and darkens, while the scales of skin develop and become pigmented. The volume of extra-embryonic yolk is still greater than the volume of the embryo.

During the final third of development (stages 28–31), the scales of the carapace finish differentiation, and embryonic pigmentation is complete. The structure and pigmentation of the embryo look increasingly like those of a hatchling. The volume of the extra-embryonic yolk reduces to be approximately 50% the volume of the embryo.

Pipping (stage 31) occurs as the embryo ruptures the extra-embryonic membranes and the shell. At this time the embryo takes its first breath and membranous circulation shuts down. As the embryo struggles out of the shell (stage 32), the embryonic curvature of the body flattens, causing the internalization of the remnant yolk and a reduction in the transverse plastronal fold. During hatching, the extra-embryonic fluids of the amnion and allantois drain away; the activity in the nest chamber and in the climb to the beach surface abrades the extra-embryonic membranes.

Nest Environment

Embryos are vulnerable to extremes in environmental conditions in three areas: (1) moisture (including substrate humidity and salinity), (2) gas exchange, and (3) temperature (Ackerman 1980, 1991, 1997; Georges et al. 1993; Maloney et al. 1990; Miller 1985; Mortimer 1990; Packard and Packard 1988). Each of these variable conditions experienced by the developing embryo during incubation has an impact. However, they may not operate independently. The potential for synergism among moisture, gas exchange, and temperature within the nest may change the impacts. For example, as temperature increases so does embryonic oxygen demand and the potential for environmental water vapor exchange.

Loggerhead turtle eggs become turgid soon after oviposition by absorbing water vapor from the surrounding sand; eggs usually increase in weight by 5–10%. Hatching success appears be little affected by egg water exchange in the range of –10 to +30% of the initial egg mass (Ackerman 1997). However, excessive weight loss (water loss) is critical; eggs cannot lose more than 40% of their initial mass if they are to survive to hatching. The hydrologic conditions of the beach that influence change in the weight of the eggs include salt and organic material, and substrate (Ackerman 1997; Packard and Packard 1988).

Because of the structure of the eggshell and of the beach, small differences in the partial pressure of gases occur between the eggs in the nest and the surrounding sand (Ackerman 1980, 1997), facilitating adequate gas exchange to support the demands of the developing embryos (Ackerman 1980, 1997; Prange and Ackerman 1974). Unfortunately, gas diffusion is affected by the water content (e.g., excessive rainfall) and particle size of the sand (Ackerman 1980, 1991; Kraemer and Bell 1980; Prange and Ackerman 1974; Ragotzkie 1959). Although the developing embryos usually receive adequate ventilation, inundation of the nest for several hours near the end of incubation may kill the entire clutch (Miller and Limpus, unpubl. observ.), presumably by reducing oxygen availability at the prepipping stages, when the oxygen demand is higher than during early developmental stages (Maloney et al. 1990). Beaches exposed to high tidal ranges have the potential for fluctuation of the water table below nests in response to tidal cycles to enhance flushing of CO_2 from and replenishment of O_2 to the nest environment from the atmosphere (Maloney et al. 1990).

Nesting beach temperatures are typically between 24 and 33°C, although short periods outside this range may occur occasionally (Bustard 1972; Caldwell 1959; Ewert 1979; Limpus et al. 1985; Miller 1985, 1997). Eggs that incubate at temperatures lower than 22°C for the last third of incubation and those held at temperatures greater than 33°C for extended periods seldom hatch. Incubation period is an inverse function of temperature (Limpus et al. 1985; Miller 1985).

The sexual differentiation of loggerhead embryos is determined by temperature (Limpus et al. 1985; Mrosovsky 1980; Mrosovsky and Yntema 1980; Yntema and Mrosovsky 1979). The pivotal temperature varies between populations within a species (Limpus et al. 1985). Even though the generality that cooler temperatures produce males and warmer temperatures produce females holds, within fluctuating beach temperatures, the sex of the hatchlings is determined by the proportion of development at a temperature, not by the duration of exposure to the temperature (Georges et al. 1994).

Incubation Period, Hatching, and Emergence

Incubation period is defined as the time from oviposition to the hatchling leaving the eggshell. In constant temperature incubation studies with loggerheads, the minimum temperature for successful incubation is approximately 25°C; at this temperature development is normal but slow, taking approximately 13 weeks (Limpus et al. 1985; McGehee 1979; Miller 1985; Yntema and Mrosovsky 1980, 1982). The maximum temperature for successful incubation is 33°C in eastern Australia (Limpus et al. 1985) and 34°C in the eastern United States (McGehee 1979; Yntema and Mrosovsky 1980, 1982), with resulting incubation periods of approximately 6.5 weeks. At the upper extremes of temperature, development is rapid and the possibility of developmental abnormalities is higher. With constant temperature incubation in the 26–32°C range, a change of 1°C adds increases or decreases the incubation period by about five days (Mrosovsky 1980). In nesting beach studies, it has been more common to quantify the incubation-to-emergence period (IEP), which is the period from oviposition to hatchling emergence to the beach surface. The authors' observations indicate that in extremely loose dry sand, hatchling emergence to the beach surface can take up to two weeks longer than the incubation period (Limpus and Miller, unpubl. observ.).

In the nest chamber embryos use their caruncle to cut through the amnion, chorioallantoic membranes, and shell (Miller 1985). There is a reduction in natural nest volume as embryos hatch and extra-embryonic fluids (amnion and allantoic) drain away to leave space within the nest cavity (Kraemer and Richardson 1979). As a result of its struggles, the curled hatchling wiggles out of the eggshell and begins to flatten, with resulting internalization of the remaining yolk (Miller 1985). The residual eggshells are shuffled downward by the actions of the hatchlings (socially facilitated digging; *sensu* Carr and Hirth 1961). In cohesive sand, the hatchlings move the space in nest created by the fluid drainage upwards to the surface of the beach. Digging hatchlings pause when O_2 levels drop and CO_2 levels reach critical (albeit undefined) thresholds in the context of their ability to function anaerobically. As digging continues, the sand above the hatchlings is scratched away and settles down past them. Near the surface, the drier sand collapses into the chamber so that the hatchlings emerge out of a depression in the sand.

Loggerhead turtle eggs typically have 80% (or higher) hatching success (i.e., number of hatchlings leaving their eggs), unless external factors (e.g., depredation, environmental conditions, microbial infection, etc.) interfere (National Research Council 1990).

Hatchlings typically emerge onto the beach surface more than two days after hatching from their eggs. The time between hatching and emergence is a function of the depth of the nest and the compaction of the sand. Emergence usually occurs during the early part of the night (Limpus 1985) and is controlled, at least in part, by the difference in the sand temperature experienced by the hatchlings as they approach the surface (Bustard 1967; Mrosovsky 1968). Recently, Moran et al. (1999) examined the theories advanced to explain the behavior. Their results indicate that the cue for emergence onto

the beach surface by hatchlings paused several centimeters below is controlled by a critical threshold temperature above which hatchlings do not emerge. As hatchlings dig toward the surface they reach the lower limit of the heat absorbed by the sand. At sunset, the gradient of latent heat contained in the sand reverses. An hour or more after the temperature at the level of the hatchlings has dropped below the threshold level, the hatchlings begin to dig toward the surface, arriving on the beach in the early evening. The drop in temperature below the threshold also causes clutches of hatchlings to emerge on cool, cloudy, and/or rainy days.

As a general rule, emergence success (number of hatchlings reaching the beach surface) is slightly lower than hatching success because not all hatchlings that struggle out of their eggshells actually make the climb to the beach surface. Some are malformed and cannot climb, and others die within the nest chamber (Miller 1985).

Hatchling loggerhead turtles are about 45 mm (range, 35–49 mm) in straight carapace length and weigh about 21 g (range, 17–27 g) (see Tables 22–25 in Dodd 1988). The size of the hatchlings is reasonably consistent around the world; the hatchlings weigh slightly less than 50% of their ovipositional egg weight (Hirth 1980).

If they emerge during the day, hatchlings face two significant problems: (1) potentially lethal temperatures and (2) predators. At some nesting beaches the surface temperature of the sand during midday may exceed 45°C; under direct sun, hatchlings die or receive severe burns from the sand, causing them to die later or be unable to swim (Miller and Limpus, unpubl. observ.). Day or night, before reaching the relative safety of deep offshore water, hatchlings potentially face a wide range of terrestrial and aquatic predators including both invertebrates (i.e., ants, crabs, etc.) and vertebrates (i.e., fish: sharks and teleosts; reptiles: *Varanus* sp. and others; birds: gulls, crows, egrets, raptors, and many others; and mammals: raccoons, rats, cats, dogs, foxes, bears, and others; see Table 21 in Dodd 1988). Depredation may or may not be less while crossing the beach at night when surface sand temperatures are sublethal. Darkness may afford hatchlings the best chance of successful dispersal from the nesting site to the open ocean.

Conclusions

Reproduction in loggerhead turtles follows the same general pattern that is found in other sea turtles. Loggerhead turtles gather the energy necessary for reproduction over several years, while in their foraging areas, before they migrate to mate and then move to subtropical nesting areas. Loggerhead turtles return to beaches in the region in which they were hatched (philopatry), typically after intervals of two to four years (although much longer intervals have been recorded). They return to nesting sites with a high degree of accuracy (high nesting site fidelity) within the reproductive season. The nesting beaches they use facilitate embryonic development by having low salinity, high humidity, and a well ventilated substrate that is not inundated during development. Loggerhead turtles lay clutches containing about 110 eggs that are round and medium sized compared with those of other sea turtles. The duration of incubation varies inversely with temperature. Sex is determined by nest temperature. Hatching and emergence success of loggerhead turtles are typically high (greater than 80%). Emergence is typically nocturnal and is controlled by a threshold temperature above which the hatchling do not emerge.

Although some aspects of the reproductive biology are well known (e.g., sequential nesting behavior, number of eggs in a clutch), others are not. The control of ovulation, energy conversion metabolism, and nesting site selection cues, all require detailed investigation.

ACKNOWLEDGMENTS

We would like to thank the editors for inviting us to participate in the loggerhead special session at the 20th Annual Symposium on Sea Turtle Biology and Conservation. We also wish to thank the reviewers for their helpful comments on the manuscript.

LITERATURE CITED

Ackerman, R. A. 1980. Physiological and ecological aspects of gas exchange by sea turtle eggs. American Zoologist 20:575–583.

————. 1991. Physical factors affecting the water exchange of buried reptile eggs. *In* D. C. Demming and M. W. J. Ferguson (eds.). Egg incubation; its effects on embryonic development in birds and reptiles, 193–211. Cambridge, U.K.: Cambridge University Press.

————. 1997. The nest environment and the embryonic development of sea turtles. *In* P. L. Lutz and J. Musick (eds.). The biology of sea turtles, 83–106. Boca Raton, Fla.: CRC Press.

Aitken, R. N., and S. E. Solomon. 1976. Observations on the ultrastructure of the oviduct of the Costa Rican green turtle (*Chelonia mydas* L.). Journal Experimental Marine Biology Ecology 21:75–90.

Bell, R., and J. I. Richardson. 1978. Analysis of tag recoveries from loggerhead sea turtles *(Caretta caretta)* nesting on Little Cumberland Island, Georgia. Florida Marine Research Bulletin 33:20–24.

Bellairs, R. 1991. Overview of early stages of avian and reptilian development. *In* D. C. Demming and M. W. J. Ferguson (eds.). Egg incubation: Its effects on embryonic development in birds and reptiles, 371–383. Cambridge, U.K.: Cambridge University Press.

Bjorndal, K. A. 1997. Foraging ecology and nutrition of sea turtles. *In* P. L. Lutz and J. Musick (eds.). The biology of sea turtles, 199–231. Boca Raton, Fla.: CRC Press, Boca Raton.

Bjorndal, K. A, A. B. Meylan, and B. J. Turner. 1983. Sea turtles nesting at Melbourne Beach, Florida. I. Size, growth and reproductive biology. Biological Conservation 26:65–77.

Blamires, S. J., and M. L. Guinea. 1998. Implications of nest site selection on egg predation at the sea turtle rookery at Fog Bay. *In* R. Kennett, A. Webb, G. Duff, M. Guinea, and G. Hill (eds.). Marine turtle conservation and management in Northern Australia, 20–24. Proceedings of a workshop held at the Centre for Indigenous Natural and Cultural Resource Management and Centre for Tropical Wetlands Management, Northern Territory University, Darwin, Australia.

Blanck, C. E., and R. H. Sawyer. 1981. Hatchery practices in relation to early embryology of the loggerhead sea turtle, *Caretta caretta* (Linne). Journal of Experimental Marine Biology and Ecology 49:163–177.

Bouchard, S., K. Moran, M. Tiwari, D. Wood, A. Bolten, P. Eliazar, and K. Bjorndal. 1998. Effects of exposed pilings on sea turtle nesting activity at Melbourne Beach, Florida. Journal of Coastal Research 14:1343–1347.

Bowen, B. W., J. C. Avise, J. I. Richardson, A. B. Meylan, D. Margaritoulis, and S. R. Hopkins-Murphy. 1993. Population structure of loggerhead turtles, *Caretta caretta*, in northwestern Atlantic Ocean and Mediterranean Sea. Conservation Biology 7:834–844.

Bowen, B. W., N. Kamezaki, C. J. Limpus, G. R. Hughes, A. B. Meylan, and J. C. Avise. 1994. Global phylogeography of the loggerhead turtle *(Caretta caretta)* as indicated by mitochrondrial DNA haplotypes. Evolution 48:1820–1828.

Bowen, B. W., F. A. Abreu-Grobois, G. H. Balazs, N. Kamezaki, C. J. Limpus, and R. J. Ferl. 1995. Trans-Pacific migrations of the loggerhead turtle *(Caretta caretta)* demonstrated with mitochrondrial DNA markers. Proceedings of the National Academy Sciences 92:3731–3734.

Brooks, W. B. 1989. Nesting activity of the loggerhead sea turtle *(Caretta caretta)* on Bald Head Island, North Carolina. *In* S. A. Eckert, K. L. Eckert, and T. H. Richardson (compilers). Proceedings of the ninth annual workshop on sea turtle biology and conservation, 211–213. NOAA Technical Memorandum NMFS-SEFSC-232.

Bustard, H. R. 1967. Mechanism of nocturnal emergence from the nest in green turtle hatchlings. Nature 214:317.

———. 1972. Sea turtles: Their natural history and conservation. London: Collins.

Bustard, H. R., and P. Greenham. 1968. Physical and chemical factors affecting hatching in the green sea turtle, *Chelonia mydas* (L.). Ecology 49:269–276.

———. 1969. Nesting behaviour of the green sea turtle on a Great Barrier Reef island. Herpetologica 25:93–102.

Bustard, H. R., P. Greenham, and C. J. Limpus. 1975. Nesting behaviour of loggerhead and flatback turtles in Queensland, Australia. Proceedings of the Koninklijke Nederlandse Akademie van Wetenschappen, Series C 78:111–122.

Caillouet, C. W., Jr. 1995. Sea turtle decoys—could they be used to establish nesting colonies? Marine Turtle Newsletter 68:22–23.

Cardinal, J. L., B. Willis, B. Weaver, and E. T. Koepfler. 1998. Influence of meteorological and beach sand physical characteristics upon nest location of the loggerhead sea turtle *(Caretta caretta)*. *In* R. Byles and Y. Fernandez (compilers). Proceedings of the 16th annual symposium on sea turtle biology and conservation, 30. NOAA Technical Memorandum NMFS-SEFSC-412.

Caldwell, D. K. 1959. The loggerhead turtles of Cape Romain, South Carolina (abridged and annotated manuscript of W. P. Baldwin, Jr., and J. P. Loftin, Jr.). Bulletin of the Florida State Museum, Biological Series 4:319–349.

———. 1962. Comments on the nesting behavior of Atlantic loggerhead sea turtles, based primarily on tagging returns. Quarterly Journal Florida Academy of Sciences 25:287–302.

Caldwell, D. K., A. F. Carr, and L. Ogren. 1959. The Atlantic loggerhead sea turtle. 1. Nesting and migration. Bulletin of the Florida State Museum, Biological Series 4:295–308.

Carr, A. F. 1975. The Ascension Island green turtle colony. Copeia 1975:547–555.

Carr, A. F., and H. Hirth 1961. Social facilitation in green turtle siblings. Animal Behavior 9:68–70.

Carr, A. F., and L. Ogren. 1960. The ecology and migrations of sea turtles. 4. The green turtle in the Caribbean Sea. Bulletin of the American Museum of Natural History 121:1–48.

Carr, A., H. Hirth, and L. Ogren. 1966. Ecology and migrations of sea turtles. 6. The hawksbill turtle in the Caribbean Sea. American Museum Novitates 2248:1–29.

Carthy, R. R., K. A. Bjorndal, and A. B. Bolten. In review. Nest morphology of the loggerhead sea turtle *(Caretta caretta)*.

Crain, D. A., A. B. Bolten, and K. A. Bjorndal. 1995. Effects of beach renourishment on sea turtles: Review and research initiatives. Restoration Ecology 3:95–104.

Dodd, C. K., Jr. 1988. Synopsis of the biological data on the loggerhead sea turtle *Caretta caretta* (Linnaeus 1758). USFWS Biological Report 88:1–110.

Ehrhart, L. M. 1995. A review of sea turtle reproduction. *In* K. A. Bjorndal (ed.). Biology and conservation of sea turtles, rev. ed., 29–39. Washington, D.C.: Smithsonian Institution Press.

Ehrhart, L. M., D. A. Bagley, L. T. Uong, and R. D. Owen. 1996. Marine turtle nesting at Archie Carr National Wildlife Refuge in 1994: Another record-breaking year for loggerhead and green turtle nest production. *In* J. A. Keinath, D. E. Barnard, J. A. Musick, and B. A. Bell (compilers). Proceedings of the 15th annual symposium on sea turtle biology and conservation, 79–83. NOAA Technical Memorandum NMFS-SEFSC-387.

Ehrenfeld, D. 1979. Behavior associated with nesting. *In* M. Harless and H. Morlock (eds.). Turtles: Perspectives and research, 417–434. New York: J. Wiley and Sons.

Ewert, M. 1979. The embryo and its egg: Development and natural history. *In* M. Harless and H. Morlock (eds.). Turtles: Perspectives and research, 333–413. New York: J. Wiley and Sons.

Foote, J., and J. Sprinkel. 1995. Beach compactness as a factor affecting turtle nesting on the west coast of Florida. *In* K. A. Bjorndal, A. B. Bolten, D. A. Johnson, and P. J. Eliazar (compilers). Proceedings of the 14th annual symposium on sea turtle biology and conservation, 217–220. NOAA Technical Memorandum NMFS-SEFSC-351.

Garmestani, A. S., H. F. Percival, K. M. Portier, and K. G. Rice. 1998. Evaluation of physical parameters as indicators of nesting beach selection for the loggerhead sea turtle in the Ten Thousand Islands of Florida. *In* S. P. Epperly and J. Braun (compilers). Proceedings of the 17th annual symposium on sea turtle biology and conservation, 53–54. NOAA Technical Memorandum NMFS-SEFSC-415.

Gasperetti, J., A. F. Stimson, J. D. Miller, J. P. Ross, and P. Gasperetti. 1993. Turtles of Arabia. *In* W. Buttiker and F. Krump (eds.). Fauna of Saudi Arabia, vol. 13, 170–367. Jeddah, Saudi Arabia: National Commission for Wildlife Conservation and Development and Meteorology and Environmental Protection Administration.

Georges, A., C. J. Limpus, and C. J. Parmenter. 1993. Natural history of the *Chelonia. In* C. J. Glasby, G. J. B. Ross, and P. L. Beesley (eds.). Fauna of Australia. Vol. 2A, Amphibia and reptilia, 120–128. Canberra: Australian Government Publishing Service.

Georges, A., C. J. Limpus, and R. Stoutjesijk. 1994. Hatchling sex in the marine turtle *Caretta caretta* is determined by proportion of development at a temperature, not daily duration of exposure. Journal of Experimental Zoology 270:432–444.

Godfrey, M. H., and R. Barreto. 1995. Beach vegetation and sea-finding orientation of turtle hatchlings. Biological Conservation 74:29–32.

Grant, G. S., and J. Beasley. 1998. Correlations of loggerhead turtle nesting activities with beach erosion rates on Topsail Island, North Carolina. *In* S. P. Epperly and J. Braun (compilers). Proceedings of the 17th annual symposium on sea turtle biology and conservation, 182–183. NOAA Technical Memorandum NMFS-SEFSC-415.

Guillette, L. J., Jr., K. A. Bjorndal, A. B. Bolten, T. S. Gross, B. D. Palmer, B. Witherington, and J. M. Matter. 1991. Plasma estrodiol-17β, progesterone, prostaglandin F, and prostaglandin E$_2$ concentrations during natural oviposition in the loggerhead turtle *(Caretta caretta)*. General and Comparative Endocrinology 82:121–130.

Harry, J. L., and D. A. Briscoe. 1988. Multiple paternity in the loggerhead turtle *(Caretta caretta)*. Journal of Heredity 79:96–99.

Hailman, J. P., and A. M. Elowson. 1992. Ethogram of the nesting female loggerhead *(Caretta caretta)*. Herpetologica 48:1–30.

Hays, G. C., and J. R. Speakman. 1993. Nest placement by loggerhead turtles, *Caretta caretta.* Animal Behaviour 45:47–53.

Hays, G. C., A. Mackay, C. R. Adams, J. A. Mortimer, J. R. Speakman, and M. Boerema. 1995. Nest site selection by sea turtles. Journal of Marine Biological Association of the United Kingdom 75:667–674.

Hendrickson, J. R. 1982. Nesting behavior of sea turtles with emphasis on physical and behavioral determinants of nesting success or failure. *In* K. A. Bjorndal (ed.). Biology and conservation of sea turtles, 53–57. Washington, D.C.: Smithsonian Institution Press.

Hirth, H. F. 1980. Some aspects of the nesting behavior and reproductive biology of sea turtles. American Zoologist 20:507–523.

———. 1997. Synopsis of biological data on the green turtle, *Chelonia mydas* (Linnaeus 1758). USFWS Biological Report 97(1):1–120.

Hopkins, S. R., T. M. Murphy, Jr., K. B. Stansell, and P. M. Wilkinson. 1979. Biotic and abiotic factors affecting nest mortality in the Atlantic loggerhead turtle. Proceedings of the annual conference of the Southeastern Association of Fish and Wildlife Agencies 32:213–223.

Hughes, G. R. 1970. Further studies on marine turtles in Tongaland, 3. Lammergeyer 12:7–25.

———. 1974a. The sea turtles of South-east Africa. I. Status, morphology, and distribution. Investigational Report no. 35 of the Oceanographic Research Institute, Durban, South Africa.

———. 1974b. The sea turtles of South-east Africa. II. Investigational Report no. 36 of the Oceanographic Research Institute, Durban, South Africa.

———. 1982. Nesting cycles in sea turtles—typical or atypical? *In* K. A. Bjorndal (ed.). Biology and conservation of sea turtles. Washington, D.C.: Smithsonian Institution Press.

Hughes, G. R., and A. Mentis. 1967. Further studies on marine turtles in Tongaland, 2. Lammergeyer 3:55–72.

Hughes, G. R., A. Bass, and M. Mentis. 1967. Further studies on marine turtles in Tongaland. Lammergeyer 7:4–54.

Kaufmann, R. 1968. Zur brutbiolooguie der meeresschildkrote, *Caretta caretta caretta* L. Mitt. Instituto Colombo-Aleman de Investigaciones Cientificas 2:45–56.

Kikukawa, A., N. Namezaki, K. Hirate, and H. Ota. 1998. Factors affecting nesting beach selection by sea turtles: A multivariate approach. *In* S. P. Epperly and J. Braun (compilers). Proceedings of the 17th annual symposium on sea turtle biology and conservation, 65–66. NOAA Technical Memorandum NMFS-SEFSC- 415.

———. 1999. Factors affecting nesting beach selection

by loggerhead turtles *(Caretta caretta):* A multivariate approach. Journal of Zoology 249:447–454.

Kraemer, J. E., and R. Bell. 1980. Rain-induced mortality of eggs and hatchlings of loggerhead sea turtles *(Caretta caretta)* on the Georgia coast. Herpetologica 36:72–77.

Kraemer, J .E., and J. I. Richardson. 1979. Volumetric reduction in nest contents of loggerhead sea turtles *(Caretta caretta)* (Reptilia, Testudines, Cheloniidae) on the Georgia coast. Journal of Herpetology 13:255–260.

Lenarz, M. S., N. B. Frazer, M. S. Rolston, and R. B Mast. 1981. Seven nests recorded for loggerhead turtle *(Caretta caretta)* in one season. Herpetological Review 12:9.

Le Vin, D. A., A. C. Broderick, and B. J. Godley. 1998. Effects of offshore features on the emergence point of marine turtles in Northern Cyprus. *In* R. Byles and Y. Fernandez (compilers). Proceedings of the 16th annual symposium on sea turtle biology and conservation, 91–92. NOAA Technical Memorandum NMFS-SEFSC-412.

Licht, P. 1980. Evolutionary and functional aspects of pituitary gonadotropins in the green turtles, *Chelonia mydas.* American Zoologist 20:565–574.

Licht, P., D. Owens, K. Cliffton, and C. Penaflores. 1982. Changes in LH and progesterone associated with nesting cycle and ovulation in the olive ridley sea turtle, *Lepidochelys olivacea.* General and Comparative Endocrinology 48:247–253.

Limpus, C. J. 1985. A study of the loggerhead sea turtle, *Caretta caretta,* in eastern Australia. Ph.D. Dissertation, University of Queensland, St Lucia, Australia.

———. 1990. Puberty and first breeding in *Caretta caretta. In* T. H. Richardson, J. I. Richardson, and M. Donnelly (eds.). Proceedings of the 10th annual workshop on sea turtle biology and conservation, 81–84. NOAA Technical Memorandum NMFS-SEFSC-278.

———. 1992. Estimation of tag loss in marine turtle research. Wildlife Research 19:457–469.

Limpus, C. J., and J. D. Miller. 1993. Family Cheloniidae. *In* C. J. Glasby, G. J. B. Ross, and P. L. Beesley (eds.). Fauna of Australia. Vol. 2A. Amphibia and Reptilia, 113–138. Canberra: Australian Government Publishing Service.

Limpus, C., and N. Nicholls. 2000. ENSO regulation of Indo-Pacific green turtle populations. *In* G. Hammer, N. Nicholls, and C. Mitchell (eds.). Applications of seasonal climate forecasting in agricultural and natural ecosystems, 339–408. Dordrecht, The Netherlands: Kluwer Academic Publishers.

Limpus, C. J., V. Baker, and J. D. Miller. 1979. Movement induced mortality of loggerhead eggs. Herpetologica 35:335–338.

Limpus, C. J., P. J. Couper, and M. A. Read. 1994. The loggerhead turtle, *Caretta caretta,* in Queensland: Population structure in a warm temperate feeding area. Memoirs of the Queensland Museum 37:195–204.

Limpus, C. J., A. Fleay, and M. Guinea. 1984a. Sea turtles of the Capricorn Section, Great Barrier Reef. *In* W. T. Ward and P. Saenger (eds.). The Capricorn Section of the Great Barrier Reef: Past, present and future, 61–78. Brisbane: Royal Society of Queensland and Australian Coral Reef Society.

Limpus, C. J., A. Fleay, and V. Baker. 1984b. The flatback turtle, *Chelonia depressa,* in Queensland: Reproductive periodicity, philopatry, and recruitment. Australian Wildlife Research 11:579–587.

Limpus, C. J., P. Reed, and J. D. Miller. 1985. Temperature dependent sex determination in Queensland sea turtles: intraspecific variation in *Caretta caretta. In* G. Grigg, R. Shine, and H. Ehmann (eds.). Biology of Australian Frogs and Reptiles, 343–351. Sydney, Australia: Surrey Beatty and Sons.

Limpus, C. J., E. Gyuris, and J. D. Miller. 1988. Reassessment of the taxonomic status of the sea turtle genus *Natator* McCulloch 1908, with a redescription of the genus and species. Transactions of the Royal Society of South Australia 112:1–9.

Limpus, C. J., J. D. Miller, C. J. Parmenter, D. Reimer, N. McLachlan, and R. Webb. 1992. Migration of green *(Chelonia mydas)* and loggerhead *(Caretta caretta)* turtles to and from eastern Australian rookeries. Wildlife Research 19:347–358.

Lund, F. 1986. Nest production and nesting-site tenacity of the loggerhead turtle, *Caretta caretta,* on Jupiter Island, Florida. Master's Thesis, University of Florida, Gainesville.

Maloney, J. E., C. Darian-Smith, Y. Takahashi, and C. J. Limpus. 1990. The environment for development of the embryonic loggerhead turtle *(Caretta caretta)* in Queensland. Copeia 1990:378–387.

Martin, R. E., R. G. Ernest, N. Williams-Walls, and J. R. Wilcox. 1989. Long-term trends in sea turtle nesting on Hutchinson Island, Florida. *In* S. A. Eckert, K. L. Eckert, and T. H. Richardson (compilers). Proceedings of the ninth annual workshop on sea turtle biology and conservation, 111–113. NOAA Technical Memorandum NMFS-SEFSC-232.

Marquez M., R. 1994. Synopsis of biological data on the Kemp's ridley turtle, *Lepidochelys kempi* (Garman 1880). NOAA Technical Memorandum NMFS-SEFSC-343.

Marquez M., R., O. A. Villanueva, S. C. Penaflores. 1976. Sinopsis de datos biologicos sobre la tortuga golfina *Lepidochelys olivacea* (Eschscholtz 1829). Sinopsis sobre la Pesca (INP/S2, SAT), INP 2.

McGehee, M. A. 1979. Factors affecting the hatching success of loggerhead sea turtle eggs *(Caretta caretta caretta)*. Master's Thesis, University of Central Florida, Orlando.

Mellanby, R. J., A. C. Broderick, and B. J. Godley. 1998. Nest site selection in Mediterranean marine turtles at Chelones Bay, Northern Cyprus. *In* R. Byles and Y. Fernandez (compilers). Proceedings of the 16th annual symposium on sea turtle biology and conservation, 103–104. NOAA Technical Memorandum NMFS-SEFSC-412.

Miller, J. D. 1985. Embryology of marine turtles. *In* C. Gans, F. Billett, and P. F. A. Maderson (eds.). Biology of the Reptilia, vol. 14A, 269–328. New York: Wiley-Interscience.

———. 1997. Reproduction in sea turtles. *In* P. L. Lutz and J. A. Musick (eds.). The biology of sea turtles, 51–80. Boca Raton, Fla.: CRC Press.

———. 1999. Determining clutch size and hatching success. *In* K. L. Eckert, K. A. Bjorndal, F. A. Abreu-Grobois, and M. Donnelly (eds.). Research and management techniques for the conservation of sea turtles, 124–129. IUCN/SSC Marine Turtle Specialist Group Publication 4, Gland, Switzerland.

Moll, E. O. 1979. Reproductive cycles and adaptations. *In* M. Harless and H. Morlock (eds.). Turtles: Perspectives and research, 305–331. New York: J. Wiley and Sons.

Moran, K. L., K. A. Bjorndal, and A. B. Bolten. 1999. Effects of the thermal environment on the temporal pattern of emergence of hatchling loggerhead turtles *Caretta caretta*. Marine Ecology Progress Series 189:251–261.

Mortimer, J. A. 1990. The influence of beach sand characteristics on the nesting behavior and clutch survival of green turtles *(Chelonia mydas)*. Copeia 1990:802–817.

———. 1995. Factors influencing beach selection by nesting sea turtles. *In* K. A. Bjorndal (ed.). Biology and conservation of sea turtles, 45–51. Washington, D.C.: Smithsonian Institution Press.

Mrosovsky, N. 1968. Nocturnal emergence of hatchling sea turtles: Control by thermal inhibition of activity. Nature 220:1338–1339.

———. 1980. Thermal biology of sea turtles. American Zoologist 20:531–547.

Mrosovsky, N., and C. L. Yntema. 1980. Temperature dependence of sexual differentiation in sea turtles: Implications for conservation practices. Biological Conservation 18:271–280.

National Research Council. 1990. The decline of the sea turtles: Causes and prevention. Washington, D.C.: National Academy Press.

Owens, D. W. 1980. The comparative reproductive physiology of sea turtles. American Zoologist 20:549–563.

———. 1997. Hormones in the life history of sea turtles. *In* P. L. Lutz and J. A. Musick (eds.). The biology of sea turtles, 315–341. Boca Raton, Fla.: CRC Press.

Owens, D. W., T. Wibbels, D. Comuzzie, D. Rostal, and C. Limpus. 1989. Sea turtle reproductive chronology: The model and the questions. *In* S. A. Eckert, K. L. Eckert, and T. H. Richardson (compilers). Proceedings of the ninth annual workshop on sea turtle biology and conservation, 135–137. NOAA Technical Memorandum NMFS-SEFSC-232.

Packard, G. C., and M. J. Packard. 1988. The physiological ecology of reptilian eggs and embryos. *In* C. Gans and R. Huey (eds.). Biology of the reptilia. Vol. 16, Ecology B, 525–607. New York: Alan R. Liss Press.

Packard, M. J., and K. F. Hirsch. 1986. Scanning electron microscopy of eggshells of contemporary reptiles. Scanning Electron Microscopy 1986:1581–1590.

Packard, M. J., and V. G. DeMarco. 1991. Eggshell structure and formation in eggs of oviparous reptiles. *In* D. C. Deeming and M. W. J. Ferguson (eds.). Egg incubation: Its effects on embryonic development in birds and reptiles, 53–69. Cambridge, U.K.: Cambridge University Press.

Packard, M. J., G. C. Packard, and T. J. Boardman. 1982. Structure of eggshells and water relations of reptilian eggs. Herpetologica 38:136–155.

Parmenter, C. J. 1980. Incubation of the eggs of the green sea turtle, *Chelonia mydas*, in Torres Strait, Australia: The effect of movement on hatchability. Australian Wildlife Research 7:487–491.

Prange, H. D., and R. A. Ackerman. 1974. Oxygen consumption and mechanism of gas exchange of green turtle *(Chelonia mydas)* eggs and hatchlings. Copeia 1974:758–763.

Pritchard, P. C. H., and P. Trebbau. 1984. The turtles of Venezuela. Society Study Amphibian Reptiles Contributions to Herpetology 2.

Pritchard, P. C. H., P. Bacon, A. Berry, A. Carr, J. Fletemeyer, R. Gallagher, S. Hopkins, R. Lankford, M. Marquez, L. Ogren, W. Pringle, H. Reichart, and R. Witham. 1983. *In* K. A. Bjorndal and G. H. Balazs (eds.). Manual of sea turtle research and conservation techniques, 2nd ed. Washington, D.C.: Center for Environmental Education.

Ragotzkie, R. 1959. Mortality of loggerhead turtle eggs from excessive rainfall. Ecology 40:303–305.

Ross, J. P., and M. A. Barwani. 1995. Review of sea turtles in the Arabian area. *In* K. A. Bjorndal (ed.). Biology and conservation of sea turtles, rev. ed., 373–383. Washington, D.C.: Smithsonian Institution Press.

Sakai, H., H. Ichihashi, H. Suganuma, and R. Tatsukawa. 1995. Heavy metal monitoring in sea turtles using eggs. Marine Pollution Bulletin 30:347–353.

Salmon, M., R. Reiners, C. Lavin, and J. Wyneken. 1995. Behavior of loggerhead sea turtles on an urban nesting beach. I. Correlates of nest placement. Journal of Herpetology 29:560–567.

Schleich, H. H., and W. Kastle. 1988. Reptile eggshells SEM atlas. Stuttgart: Gustav Fischer.

Schmelz, G. W., and R. R. Mezich. 1988. A preliminary investigation of the potential impact of Australian pines on the nesting activities of the loggerhead turtle. *In* B. A. Schroeder (compiler). Proceedings of the eighth annual workshop on sea turtle biology and conservation, 63–66. NOAA Technical Memorandum NMFS-SEFSC-214.

Schulz, J. P. 1975. Sea turtles nesting in Surinam. Zoologische Verhandelingen 143:1–144.

Simon, M. H., G. F. Ulrich, and A. S. Parkes. 1975. The green sea turtle *(Chelonia mydas):* Mating, nesting, and hatching on a farm. Journal of Zoology 177:411–423.

Solomon, S. E., and T. Baird. 1976. Studies on the eggshell (oviductal and oviposited) of *Chelonia mydas* L. Journal of Experimental Marine Biology and Ecology 22:145–160.

———. 1979. Aspects of the biology of *Chelonia mydas* L. Oceanography Marine Biology Annual Reviews 17:347–361.

Spotila, J. R., E. A. Standora, S. J. Morreale, and G. J. Ruiz. 1987. Temperature dependent sex determination in the green turtle *(Chelonia mydas):* Effects on the sex ratio on a natural nesting beach. Herpetologica 43:74–81.

Sternberg, J. 1981. The worldwide distribution of sea turtle nesting beaches. Washington, D.C.: Center for Environmental Education.

Stoneburner, D. L., and J. I. Richardson. 1981. Observations on the role of temperature in loggerhead turtle nest site selection. Copeia 1981:238–231.

Tufts, C. E. 1972. Report on the Buritaca Marine Turtle Nesting Reserve with emphasis on biological data from "Operacion Tortuga 1972" and recommendations for the future. Mimeographed report, Inderena, Bogota.

Ulrich, G. F., and D. W. Owens. 1974. Preliminary note on reproduction of *Chelonia mydas* under farm conditions. Proceedings of the World Mariculture Society 5:205–214.

Van Buskirk, J., and L. B. Crowder. 1994. Life-history variation in marine turtles. Copeia 1994:66–81.

Whittier, J. M., F. Corrie, and C. Limpus. 1997. Plasma steroid profiles in nesting loggerhead turtles *(Caretta caretta)* in Queensland, Australia: relationship to nesting episode and season. General and Comparative Endocrinology 106:39–47.

Whitmore, C. P., and P. H. Dutton. 1985. Infertility, embryonic mortality, and nest-site selection in leatherback and green sea turtles in Suriname. Biological Conservation 34:251–272.

Wibbels, T., D. W. Owens, C. J. Limpus, P. C. Reed, and M. S. Amoss, Jr. 1990. Seasonal changes in serum gonadal steroids associated with migration, mating and nesting in the loggerhead sea turtle *(Caretta caretta)*. General and Comparative Endocrinology 79:154–164.

Wibbels, T., D. W. Owens, P. Licht, C. J. Limpus, P. C. Reed, and M. S. Amoss, Jr. 1992. Serum gonadotropins and gonadal steroids associated with ovulation and egg production in sea turtles. General and Comparative Endocrinology 87:71–78.

Witham, R. 1970. Breeding of a pair of pen-reared green turtles. Quarterly Journal of the Florida Academy of Sciences 33:288–290.

Witherington, B. E. 1992. Behavioral response of nesting turtles to artificial lighting. Herpetologica 48:31–39.

Witzell, W. N. 1983. Synopsis of biological data on the hawksbill turtle, *Eretmochelys imbricata* (Linnaeus 1766). FAO Fisheries Synopsis 137.

Wood, F. G. 1953. Mating behavior of captive loggerhead turtles. Copeia 1953:184–186.

Wood, D. W., and K. A. Bjorndal. 2000. Relation of temperature, moisture, salinity, and slope to nest site selection in loggerhead sea turtles. Copeia 2000:119–128.

Yntema, C. L., and N. Mrosovsky. 1979. Incubation temperature and sex ratio in hatchling loggerhead turtles: A preliminary report. Marine Turtle Newsletter 11:9–10.

———. 1980. Sexual differentiation in hatchling loggerheads *(Caretta caretta)* incubated at different controlled temperatures. Herpetologica 36:33–36.

———. 1982. Critical periods and pivotal temperatures for sexual differentiation in loggerhead sea turtles. Canadian Journal of Zoology 60:1012–1016.

Chapter 9

Incubation Environment of Loggerhead Turtle Nests:

Effects on Hatching Success and Hatchling Characteristics

—Raymond R. Carthy, Allen M. Foley, and Yoshimasa Matsuzawa

By nesting on oceanic beaches, a dynamic natural system with a wide range of environmental characteristics, female loggerheads expose their clutches to a range of physical parameters that affect incubation (Foley 1998). Although the eggs will develop only under certain conditions, they can withstand some variations in temperature, moisture, and concentrations of respiratory gases. However, even these tolerable variations have an effect because both hatching success and many of characteristics of the hatchlings can vary, depending on the incubation environment (Carthy 1996; Foley 1998; McGehee 1990).

Loggerhead eggs are coupled to the incubation environment. The developing eggs exchange heat, water, and gas with the nesting medium (Ackerman 1997). Whether or not development is completed and the eggs hatch depends on the degree and direction of these exchanges. Eggs incubated at constant temperatures lower than 24.0°C or greater than 33.0°C

seldom hatch (McGehee 1979; Miller 1982; Yntema and Mrosovsky 1980). The eggs initially contain more than enough water to complete incubation and can tolerate some loss of water during incubation (Ackerman 1997; Foley 1998). Nevertheless, the eggs will not develop when incubation environments are too dry (Ackerman 1997). The sand at the nest site must also allow for sufficient gas exchange. For example, too much water in the sand around the nest will preclude egg development by restricting gas exchange (Ackerman 1997; Packard et al. 1977).

In this chapter, some of the factors that determine the characteristics of the incubation environment and how the incubation environment influences hatching success and the expression of hatchling phenotypic plasticity are discussed. Human-related alterations of nesting environments are also reviewed, and their possible effect on the reproductive output of nesting females is addressed. Lastly, the authors provide recommendations on future research directions that need to be addressed to fulfill conservation goals for loggerheads.

Factors Determining the Incubation Environment

The degree and direction of exchanges of heat, water, and gas between the eggs and the nesting medium depend on the incubation environment, which is determined by a combination of at least three factors: (1) the characteristics of the sand, (2) other characteristics of the nesting site, and (3) the dimensions of the nesting cavity. The characteristics of the sand that may influence the incubation environment include water content, matric potential (how tightly the sand particles hold water), osmotic potential (related to the salinity of the water in the sand), particle-size distribution, mean particle size, albedo (reflectivity), sorting, porosity, compaction, shear strength, and thermal and hydraulic properties (how quickly heat and water move through the sand particles). Other characteristics of the nesting site that influence the incubation environment include distance from the ocean, elevation, amount and type of vegetation, and climate (e.g., air temperature, exposure to solar radiation, frequency of storms and rainfall). The dimensions of the nesting cavity influence the incubation environment by determining the depth at which the clutch will incubate, the number of eggs that will be on the periphery of the clutch and in direct contact with the sand, and the number of eggs that will be in the center of the egg mass and not in direct contact with the sand (Carthy 1996).

Characteristics of the Nesting Medium

Loggerheads most commonly nest in sands with a mean particle diameter of 0.25–0.5 mm, but they also nest in finer and coarser media (Foley 1998; Hughes 1974; Mann 1979). The particle size of the sand on loggerhead nesting beaches has been positively correlated with the total porosity, air-filled pore space, and hydraulic properties of the nesting medium (Foley 1998). Consequently, as particle size increases, gas and water tend to move more easily through the

nesting medium, resulting in increasing gas exchange and a potentially decreasing sand water content. Particle size has also been related to how quickly thermal energy can move through the medium. As the mean particle size of the sand decreases, heat may move more easily through the medium (Speakman et al. 1998), potentially resulting in more widely fluctuating incubation temperatures. On green turtle nesting beaches, the sorting of the sand particles has been thought to influence the exchange of respiratory gases and water between the eggs and the nesting medium (Mortimer 1990), and the same is probably true on loggerhead nesting beaches.

The water content of the sand (by mass) at loggerhead nesting sites typically ranges from 2 to 10% (Ackerman 1997; Caldwell et al. 1959; Foley 1998; McGehee 1990). The water content, matric potential, and osmotic potential of the sand all influence the exchange of water between the egg and the nesting medium. As the matric or osmotic potential of the sand increases (usually with decreasing sand water content or increasing sand water salinity, respectively), the eggs become more likely to lose water during incubation. Sand water content also affects exchanges of gas and heat between the eggs and the nesting medium because the ability of gas and heat to move through the nesting medium decreases with increasing sand water content.

Some of the solar radiation reaching the surface of the sand is reflected into the atmosphere, but the rest is absorbed into the sand and converted into heat energy. How much radiation is reflected and how much is absorbed depends on the albedo of the sand. Accordingly, darker colored sands are warmer than lighter colored sands when both are exposed to the same intensity of radiation (Hanson et al. 1998; Limpus et al. 1983; Milton et al. 1997).

Other Nesting Site Characteristics

Whether or not a nest is inundated and the frequency and extent of any inundations depend on how far the nesting site is from the ocean, the frequency and magnitude of tidal fluctuations, how high the clutch sits above the groundwater, the frequency of storms, and how

Figure 9.1. Decline of sand temperature due to inundation and the following latent heat loss. As a typhoon approached Senri Beach, Wakayama, Japan, the sea surges washed over the beach, and it rained heavily. The temperature at 50 cm dropped steeply by about 5°C during the inundation. After the water receded, the temperature began to decrease further, reaching a low of 17°C (from Matsuzawa et al., in prep.).

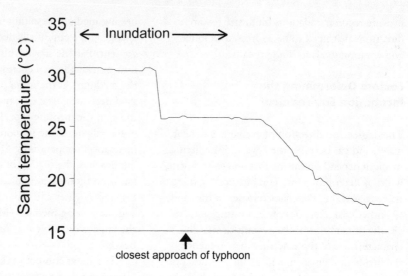

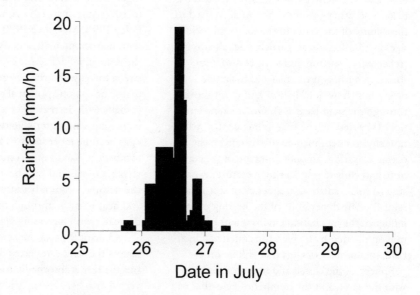

quickly the nesting medium drains. Nesting site inundation affects water content and salinity. Both sand water content and salinity increase as inundations increase in frequency (Foley 1998). Rain, which may be the most common source for the water in the sand where loggerhead clutches incubate (Ackerman 1997), increases the water content of the sand and decreases its salinity. In addition, sand with a large mean particle size may aid the rain in reducing the salinity of the sand water by allowing salt to be more effectively flushed from the surface layers of the sand (Foley 1998).

Sand temperatures can be lowered by inundation or heavy rainfall and by heat loss through regular infrared reradiation. After the initial decrease, sand temperature at the surface can be depressed by evaporation. On Senri Beach, Wakayama, Japan, the sand temperature at the depth of incubating loggerhead clutches continued to decrease long after inundation (Figure 9.1).

Solar radiation (shortwave) heats the nesting medium. The latitude of the nesting site affects the intensity of the solar radiation because solar radiation (and thus sand temperature) generally decreases with increasing latitudes. These decreases in sand temperature with increasing latitude probably account for the longer incubation periods of loggerhead clutches on beaches in Georgia and North Carolina when compared to those on Florida beaches during the same part of the nesting season (Mrosovsky 1988). Latitudinal declines in incubation period are also found in Brazil (Marcovaldi et al. 1997).

Loggerheads usually nest in the open sand, but they may also nest in the vegetated areas behind the beach (Foley 1998; Hughes 1974). Because vegetated areas experience more root infiltration than open areas (Witherington 1986), they may contain less available water for use by incubating eggs. Vegetation at the nesting site can also lower incubation temperatures through shading (Foley et al. 2000).

The Nesting Cavity

The depth at which the female buries her clutch affects the incubation environment. For example, the sand water content can increase with depth (Foley 1998). Furthermore, incubation temperatures and the amplitude of their fluctuations can also decrease with depth on loggerhead nesting beaches (Foley et al. 2000; Maloney et al. 1990).

The incubation environment can differ between the periphery and the center of the clutch. Eggs on the periphery of the clutch can gain more water (or lose less water) during incubation (Carthy 1996; Foley 1998; Hotaling et al. 1985; Packard et al. 1981) and experience lower incubation temperatures (Foley et al. 2000; Godfrey et al. 1997; Maloney et al. 1990) than do adjacent eggs in the center of the clutch. Peripheral eggs may also be exposed to higher concentrations of O_2 and lower concentrations of CO_2 than central eggs (Ackerman 1980). The proportions of eggs on the periphery and in the center of the clutch depend on the size and shape of the nesting cavity and the number of eggs (Carthy 1996). As these proportions vary, the overall incubation environment varies, as more or fewer eggs are exposed to either a peripheral or a central incubation environment.

The characteristics of the sand can exert substantive effects on the size, shape, and depth of the chamber a nesting female prepares for her eggs (Carthy 1996). The shear strength of the sand (i.e., resistance to digging) at nesting sites is determined by the mean particle size, particle type, sorting, compaction, and water content. Loggerheads construct a nesting cavity with specific proportions, but variations in the shear strength of the sand can cause a loggerhead to dig a nesting cavity that is atypical in shape (Carthy 1996).

Effects on Hatching Success

Changes in hatching success are the most noticeable effect of various incubation environments. Near its lethal limit, incubation temperature accounts for decreases in hatching success (Yntema and Mrosovsky 1980). On some Japanese nesting beaches, many eggs and preemergent hatchlings were found dead in clutches that were exposed to higher temperatures (Figure 9.2). The hatching success of loggerhead clutches decreases when sand water content is too high (Ackerman 1997; Foley 1998; Packard et al. 1977) or too low (McGehee 1990). Very dry conditions may also inhibit adequate eggshell dissolution during incubation and reduce the chances of successful pipping (Carthy 1996). The salinity of the sand water is believed to lower the hatching success of green turtle clutches (Mortimer 1990), but loggerhead clutches appear to tolerate higher sand water salinities better (Foley 1998).

Effects on Hatchling Characteristics

Sex Determination

The characteristics of loggerhead hatchlings can be modified to some degree by the incubation environment. This susceptibility of hatchlings to the influences of the incubation environment is an example of phenotypic plasticity (Roff 1992; Rollo 1995). Perhaps the best-known influence of the incubation environment on a loggerhead hatchling characteristic is the influence of incubation temperature on hatchling sex. Like many other reptiles, loggerhead turtles exhibit temperature-dependent sex determination (TSD): the sex of the offspring is influenced by the incubation temperature of the eggs (Yntema

Figure 9.2. The influence of temperature on emergence percentage and incubation duration. The upper graph shows the relationship between mean sand temperature for four days before first emergence (T) and emergence percentage (E) for 18 clutches. Emergence percentage is the ratio of emerging hatchlings to hatching eggs. The curve was fitted by least-squares regression; E = 100/{1 + exp[1.9 (T − 31.6)]}; r^2 = 0.960 (adapted from Matsuzawa et al. 2002).

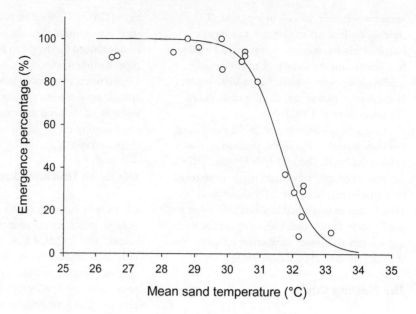

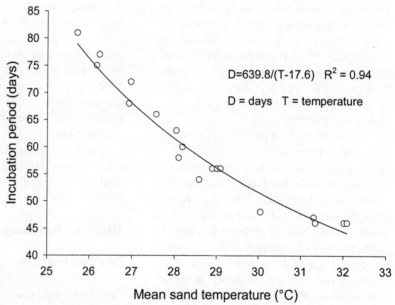

and Mrosovsky 1980). An incubation environment of approximately 29.0°C produces an equal number of male and female hatchlings (Limpus et al. 1983; Marcovaldi et al. 1997; Mrosovsky 1988). Cooler incubation temperatures produce more males, and warmer incubation temperatures produce more females. The amplitude of the fluctuation of sand temperature also has an effect on sex determination. Under widely fluctuating thermal regimes, more females are produced than under more stable

temperature regimes having the same mean temperature (Georges et al. 1994).

Other Hatchling Characteristics

Incubation temperature can also influence characteristics of loggerhead hatchlings other than gender. Warmer incubation temperatures produce hatchlings with greater body mass (Kuroyanagi and Kamezaki 1993; Matsuzawa et al., in prep.), greater activity levels, and faster

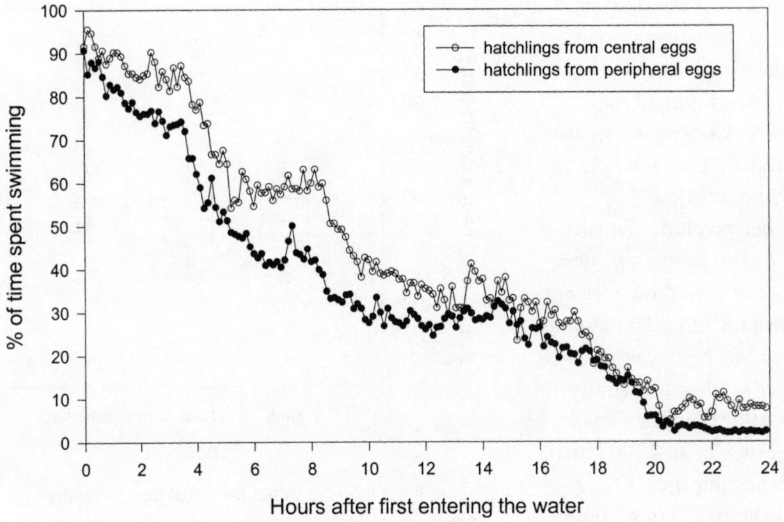

Figure 9.3. The mean swimming activity (percent time spent power-stroking) during the first 24 hours in the water of loggerhead hatchlings from peripheral eggs (n = 70) and central eggs (n = 27) of 10 clutches from the northern half of the Ten Thousand Islands, Florida, during 1994. Peripheral eggs were in direct contact with the soil surrounding the clutch. Central eggs were at least one egg away from the periphery of the clutch. The swimming activity of each hatchling was scored every eight minutes.

growth rates than do cooler incubation temperatures (Kuroyanagi and Kamezaki 1993). The direction and degree of water exchanges between loggerhead eggs and the incubation environment may affect loggerhead hatchling characteristics such as size (McGehee 1990), hydration, early swimming behavior, and early growth (Foley 1998). Utilization of yolk resources by the developing embryo has been linked to egg hydration: greater water availability allows for greater use of yolk, yielding more robust hatchlings (Carthy 1996; Thompson 1987).

Gas exchange affects embryonic development, eggshell dynamics, emergence from the egg, and hatching success (nest emergence). All eggs must exchange gases with the environment during incubation because developing embryos need to take in O_2 and get rid of CO_2. The sensitivity of loggerhead eggs to reduced gas exchange may be greater near the end of incubation, when the consumption of O_2 and the production of CO_2 peak (Ackerman 1977). Nevertheless, some restriction of gas exchange between the clutch and the surrounding medium may be beneficial because levels of CO_2 are thought to play an important role in establishing acid/base balances in the blood of developing hatchlings (Ackerman 1977). The build-up of CO_2 in the nesting chamber is also critical to the formation of carbonic acid on the surface of the egg. The acid aids in dissolution of the eggshell during incubation, making additional calcium available to the embryo and thinning the shell to facilitate pipping (Bustard and Greenham 1968; Carthy 1996).

The dimensions of the nesting cavity also influence characteristics of the hatchlings by influencing the incubation environment. Variations in the vertical dimensions of the nesting cavity change the depth at which eggs incubate. Variations in the horizontal dimensions of the nesting cavity change the number of eggs that incubate in the center of the nest and the number that incubate at the periphery (Carthy 1996). Loggerhead hatchlings from eggs that were at the center of clutches have been found to be larger, to be more active during the swimming frenzy period (Figure 9.3), and to grow faster than hatchlings from peripheral eggs (Foley 1998). Loggerhead hatchlings from center eggs likely emerge from the nesting cavity more dehydrated than hatchlings from peripheral eggs, as evidenced by the greater decrease [dilution] in serum total protein in hatchlings from center eggs after the first 24 hours in the water (Foley 1998). It follows that drier nesting sites might produce hatchlings that are more dehydrated than those from wetter nesting sites.

Anthropogenic Influences

Human-related activities on loggerhead nesting beaches potentially alter incubation environments in a myriad of ways. The characteristics of the sand, other characteristics of the nesting site, and the dimensions of the nesting cavity may be affected by coastal armoring, beach nourishment, beachfront development, and even conservation activities. Consequently, anthropogenic influences can alter both hatching success and hatchling characteristics.

Coastal armoring either precludes females from nesting altogether or forces them to nest at lower elevations than they would on adjacent, unarmored beaches (Mosier 1998). The sand at lower beach nesting sites has a higher water content (Foley 1998), greater sand water salinity (Bustard and Greenham 1968; Hughes 1974), and lower temperature (Foley et al. 2000) than the sand at higher beach nesting sites. Other man-made structures on the beach (e.g., buildings, beach chairs, boats, picnic tables, boardwalks, fences) may have the same effect as coastal armoring by limiting the area of nesting.

In the absence of rainfall, the water content of the sand in the area where loggerhead clutches are buried might depend primarily on the upward movement of water from the water table (De Jong 1979; Olsson-Seffer 1909). Armoring structures that are partially or completely buried (e.g., step revetments, waffle revetments) could alter the sand water content because these structures sit between the groundwater and the nesting cavity.

The amount of shading at nesting sites can be either decreased or increased by human-related activities. The removal of beach vegetation can increase the exposure of nesting sites to solar radiation, thus increasing incubation temperature. The introduction of nonnative plants, which can produce a greater degree of shading than native vegetation, can lower incubation temperatures (Schmelz and Mezich 1988). On some Florida beaches, tall condominiums stand close to the shore and shade areas of the sand during the day. In Boca Raton, Florida, the sand in shaded areas averaged 1–2°C cooler than that in unshaded areas (Mrosovsky et al. 1995).

Beach nourishment may have the single greatest effect on incubation environments because it attempts to re-create a nesting beach. The sand used in nourishment can be darker or lighter in color than the original sand, resulting

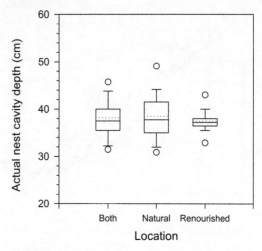

Figure 9.4. Observed values for actual nest cavity depth (full cavity depth less body pit depth) of loggerhead turtles at a natural (n = 35) and a renourished (n = 15) beach. Values are combined in "both." Variances are significantly different between sites. Levene's F = 0.01 (α = 0.05). Dotted line: mean; solid line: median; box: 50% of observed values; bars: 80% of observed values; outliers: 90% of observed values (adapted from Carthy 1996).

in either higher (Ackerman 1997) or lower (Milton et al. 1997) incubation temperatures. Nourished beaches can have higher sand water contents than natural beaches (Ackerman 1997; Parkinson et al. 1994; Rimkus and Ackerman 1993), possibly increasing water availability and decreasing temperature fluctuations and gas exchange. By creating a beach with a more compact matrix (Crain et al. 1995) and changing other characteristics of the sand, beach nourishment also affects the architecture of the loggerhead nesting cavity. Compared to those on natural beaches, nesting cavities on nourished beaches exhibit skewed variations in nest depth (Figure 9.4), potential air space, and several shape parameters that are influenced by the mechanics of excavation (Carthy 1996).

Human-related activities performed solely to promote the recovery of loggerheads can also alter incubation environments. To increase hatching success, loggerhead clutches are relocated from areas where hatching success is lower to areas where hatching success is greater. This often involves moving clutches from areas that are low on the beach to areas that are high on the beach (Blanck and Sawyer 1981; Dutton and Whitmore 1983; Wyneken et al. 1988). Nest relocation can create substantial changes in the incubation environment and in the characteristics of hatchlings (Foley 1998; Foley et al. 2000). Even if a clutch is relocated to a site with characteristics that are identical to the original site, the incubation environment can still be altered if the depth and shape of the new nesting cavity does not match that of the original nesting cavity.

Moderate movement or rotation does not adversely affect eggs for approximately the first 12 hours after they are laid. After that time, moving the eggs may disrupt embryonic membranes, causing decreased hatching success (Blanck and Sawyer 1981; Limpus et al. 1979). In older eggs that are not as susceptible to movement-induced mortality, a change in the orientation of the egg (i.e., rotating the top of the egg downward) may prevent fluid drainage during pipping (R. R. Carthy, pers. observ.).

Conservation strategies that involve leaving nests in situ probably affect incubation environments the least. Nevertheless, even methods such as screening or caging nests in situ to protect eggs from predators may affect hatchling behavior by modifying magnetic orientation (K. Lohmann, pers. comm.) or by increasing incubation temperatures (the latter via heating of any exposed portions of the cage or screen by the sun).

Female loggerheads nest at various distances from the water and at various sites along the beach. This behavior results in the exposure of clutches to a variety of incubation environments and helps avoid complete loss of reproductive effort if some of the incubation environments preclude development. By concentrating clutches on one area of the beach (e.g., low beach areas because of armoring or development, or high beach areas or hatcheries because of conservation activities), anthropogenic influences often reduce the variety of incubation environments. If the remaining incubation environments are inappropriate for development, then all the clutches fail.

Because the characteristics of hatchlings vary with incubation environments, a scattered nesting pattern also increases the variation of hatchling characteristics. This may ensure that at all times at least some hatchlings have characteristics that are appropriate for survival, when the exact characteristics that are best suited for survival vary unpredictably over space and time (Foley 1998). Human-related activities that reduce the variety of incubation environments reduce the variety of hatchling characteristics that are produced. If the specific characteristics produced by the limited incubation environments do not enhance survival (compared to other possible characteristics), then the overall survival rate of hatchlings may be less than it would have been had the full spectrum of incubation environments and, consequently, the full spectrum of hatchling characteristics been maintained.

Conclusions

Work by many researchers has revealed some of the nuances of the incubation environment of marine turtle nests, the factors that influence it, and the effects of that environment on hatching success and hatchling characteristics. However, the complexity of all the interactions does limit the critical factors biologists and conservationists have the time and resources to study. In that light, there are several informational needs that the authors feel are priorities.

Researchers need to know more about hatchling sex ratios, especially within-year and between-year variations. Standardized methodologies for monitoring nesting beach temperatures to determine hatchling sex ratios (such as those outlined by Godfrey and Mrosovsky 1999) should become a component of nesting beach surveys. Researchers also need to know how variations in hatchling sex ratios affect the population and how these ratios are affected by climate change.

Researchers should review the criteria for determining whether or not human-related changes to the nesting beaches adversely affect the reproductive efforts of loggerheads. Most often, only decreases in hatching success are used to distinguish adverse effects. This methodology does not address other potential impacts, such as the altering of hatchling characteristics (i.e., fitness or sex). Researchers should increase their understanding of these "suboptimizing" effects to aid loggerhead populations in their struggle to cope with the accelerated rate of anthropogenic change.

LITERATURE CITED

Ackerman, R. A. 1977. The respiratory gas exchange of sea turtle nests *(Chelonia, Caretta)*. Respiratory Physiology 31:19–38.

———. 1980. Physiological and ecological aspects of gas exchange by sea turtle eggs. American Zoologist 20:575–583.

———. 1997. The nest environment and the embryonic development of sea turtles. *In* P. L. Lutz and J. A. Musick (eds.). The biology of sea turtles, 83–106. Boca Raton, Fla.: CRC Press.

Blanck, C. E., and R. H. Sawyer. 1981. Hatchery practices in relation to early embryology of the loggerhead sea turtle, *Caretta caretta* (Linné). Journal of Experimental Marine Biology and Ecology 49:163–177.

Bustard, R. H., and P. Greenham. 1968. Physical and chemical factors affecting hatching in the green sea turtle. Ecology 49:269–276.

Caldwell, D. K., A. Carr, and L. H. Ogren. 1959. The Atlantic loggerhead sea turtle, *Caretta caretta* (L.), in America. I. Nesting and migration of the Atlantic loggerhead turtle. Bulletin of the Florida State Museum 4:295–308.

Carthy, R. R. 1996. The role of the eggshell and nest chamber in loggerhead turtle *(Caretta caretta)* egg incubation. Ph.D. Dissertation, University of Florida, Gainesville.

Crain, D. A., A. B. Bolten , and K. A. Bjorndal. 1995. Effects of beach nourishment on sea turtles: Review and research initiatives. Restoration Ecology 3:95–104.

De Jong, T. M. 1979. Water and salinity relations of California beach species. Journal of Ecology 67:647–663.

Dutton, P. H., and C. P. Whitmore. 1983. Saving doomed eggs in Suriname. Marine Turtle Newsletter 24:8–10.

Foley, A. M. 1998. The nesting ecology of the loggerhead turtle *(Caretta caretta)* in the Ten Thousand Islands, Florida. Ph.D. Dissertation, University of South Florida, St. Petersburg.

Foley, A. M., S. A. Peck, G. R. Harman, and L. W. Richardson. 2000. Loggerhead turtle *(Caretta caretta)* nesting habitat on low-relief mangrove islands in southwest Florida and consequences to hatchling sex ratios. Herpetologica 56:433–445.

Georges, A., C. Limpus, and R. Stoutjesdijk. 1994. Hatchling sex in the marine turtle *Caretta caretta* is determined by proportion of development at a temperature, not daily duration of exposure. Journal of Experimental Zoology 200:432–444.

Godfrey, M., and N. Mrosovsky. 1999. Estimating hatchling sex ratios. *In* K. L. Eckert, K. A. Bjorndal, F. A. Abreu-Grobois, and M. Donnelly (eds.). Research and management techniques for the conservation of sea turtles, 136–138. IUCN/SSC Marine Turtle Specialist Group Publication 4. Gland, Switzerland.

Godfrey, M. H., R. Barreto, and N. Mrosovsky. 1997. Metabolically generated heat of developing eggs and its potential effect on the sex ratio of sea turtle hatchlings. Journal of Herpetology 31:616–619.

Hanson, J., T. Wibbels, and E. Martin. 1998. Predicted female bias in sex ratios of hatchling loggerhead sea turtles from a Florida nesting beach. Canadian Journal of Zoology 76:1850–1861.

Hotaling, E. C., D. C. Wilhoft, and S. B. McDowell. 1985. Egg position and weight of hatchling snapping turtles, *Chelydra serpentina*, in natural nests. Journal of Herpetology 19:534–536.

Hughes, G. R. 1974. The sea turtles of South-east Africa. I. Status, morphology and distributions. Investigational Report no. 35. Durban, South Africa: Oceanographic Research Institute.

Kuroyanagi, K., and N. Kamezaki. 1993. Growth of loggerhead hatchlings incubated at different temperatures [In Japanese]. Echolocation 14:5–6.

Limpus, C. J., V. Baker, and J. D. Miller. 1979. Movement induced mortality of loggerhead eggs. Herpetologica 35:335–338.

Limpus, C. J., P. Reed, and J. D. Miller. 1983. Islands and turtles: The influence of choice of nesting beach on sex ratio. *In* Proceedings of the inaugural Great Barrier Reef conference, 397–402. Townsville, Queensland, Australia: James Cook University Press.

Maloney, J. E., C. Darian-Smith, Y. Takahashi, and C. J. Limpus. 1990. The environment for development of the embryonic loggerhead turtle *(Caretta caretta)* in Queensland. Copeia 1990:378–387.

Mann, T. M. 1979. Impact of developed coastline on nesting and hatchling sea turtles in Southeastern Florida. Florida Marine Research Publications 33:53–55.

Marcovaldi, M. A., H. Godfrey, and N. Mrosovsky. 1997. Estimating sex ratios of loggerhead turtles in Brazil from pivotal incubation durations. Canadian Journal of Zoology 75:755–770.

Matsuzawa, Y., K. Sato, W. Sakamoto, and K. A. Bjorndal. 2002. Seasonal fluctuations in sand temperature: Effects on the incubation period and mortality of loggerhead sea turtle *(Caretta caretta)* pre-emergent hatchlings in Minabe, Japan. Marine Biology 140:639–646.

McGehee, M. A. 1979. Factors affecting the hatching success of loggerhead sea turtle eggs *(Caretta caretta)*. Master's Thesis, University of Central Florida, Orlando.

———. 1990. Effects of moisture on eggs and hatchlings of loggerhead sea turtles *(Caretta caretta)*. Herpetologica 46:251–258.

Miller, J. D. 1982. Development of marine turtles. Ph.D. Dissertation, University of New England, Armidale, New South Wales.

Milton, S. L., A. S. Schulman, and P. L. Lutz. 1997. The effects of beach nourishment with aragonite versus silicate sand on beach temperature and loggerhead sea turtle nesting success. Journal of Coastal Research 13:904–915.

Mortimer, J. A. 1990. The influence of beach sand characteristics on the nesting behavior and clutch survival of green turtles *(Chelonia mydas)*. Copeia 1990:802–817.

Mosier, A. E. 1998. The impact of coastal armoring structures on sea turtle nesting behavior at three beaches on the east coast of Florida. Master's Thesis, University of South Florida, St. Petersburg.

Mrosovsky, N. 1988. Pivotal temperatures for loggerhead turtles from northern and southern nesting beaches. Canadian Journal of Zoology 66:661–669.

Mrosovsky, N., C. Lavin, and M. H. Godfrey. 1995. Thermal effects of condominiums on a turtle beach in Florida. Biological Conservation 74:151–156.

Olsson-Seffer, P. 1909. Hydrodynamic factors influencing plant life on sandy seashores. New Phytologist 8:39–49.

Packard, G. C., M. J. Packard, and T. J. Boardman. 1981. Patterns and possible significance of water exchange by flexible-shelled eggs of painted turtles *(Chrysemys picta)*. Physiological Zoology 54:165–178.

Packard, G. C., C. R. Tracy, and J. J. Roth. 1977. The physiological ecology of reptilian eggs and embryos, and the evolution of viviparity within the class Reptilia. Biological Review 52:71–105.

Parkinson, R. W., J. White, and M. Perez-Bedmar. 1994. Effects of beach nourishment on compaction, grain size, moisture and temperature: Sebastian Inlet. *In* K. A. Bjorndal, A. B. Bolten, D. A. Johnson, and P. J. Eliazar (compilers). Proceedings of the 14th annual symposium on sea turtle biology and conservation, 112–114. NOAA Technical Memorandum NMFS-SEFSC-351.

Rimkus, T. A., and R. A. Ackerman. 1993. The impact of beach renourishment on the hydric climate of sea turtle nesting beaches along the Atlantic coast of Florida. *In* J. I. Richardson and T. H. Richardson (compilers). Proceedings of the 12th annual symposium on sea turtle biology and conservation, 97–102. NOAA Technical Memorandum NMFS-SEFSC-361.

Roff, D. A. 1992. The evolution of life histories. New York: Chapman and Hall.

Rollo, C. D. 1995. Phenotypes: Their epigenetics, ecology, and evolution. London: Chapman and Hall.

Schmelz, G. W., and R. R. Mezich. 1988. A preliminary investigation of the potential impact of Australian pines on the nesting activities of the loggerhead turtle. *In* B. A. Schroeder (compiler). Proceedings of the eighth annual workshop on sea turtle conservation and biology, 63–66. NOAA Technical Memorandum NMFS-SEFC-214.

Speakman, J. R., G. C. Hays, and E. Lindblad. 1998. Thermal conductivity of sand and its effect on the temperature of loggerhead sea turtle *(Caretta caretta)* nests. Journal of the Marine Biological Association of the United Kingdom 78:1337–1352.

Thompson, M. B. 1987. Water exchange in reptilian eggs. Physiological Zoology 60:1–8.

Witherington, B. E. 1986. Human and natural causes of marine turtle clutch and hatchling mortality and their relationship to hatchling production on an important Florida nesting beach. Master's Thesis, University of Central Florida, Orlando.

Wyneken, J., T. J. Burke, M. Salmon, and D. K. Pederson. 1988. Egg failure in natural and relocated sea turtle nests. Journal of Herpetology 22:88–96.

Yntema, C. L., and N. Mrosovsky. 1980. Sexual differentiation in hatchling loggerheads incubated at different controlled temperatures. Herpetologica 36:33–36.

Part Two

Geographic Distribution, Abundance, and Population Status

Chapter 10

Loggerhead Turtles in the Atlantic Ocean:

Geographic Distribution, Abundance, and Population Status

—Llewellyn M. Ehrhart, Dean A. Bagley, and William E. Redfoot

The status of the loggerhead in certain subregions of the Atlantic was reviewed by Brongersma (1972), Bacon (1981), Carr et al. (1982), Mager (1985), Márquez (1990), and Ehrhart (1989), among others. The Ehrhart review dealt with loggerhead nesting and foraging in the western Atlantic; it used data from the national reports of the first Western Atlantic Turtle Symposium (WATS I) (Bacon et al. 1984) and was part of the proceedings of the second Western Atlantic Turtle Symposium (WATS II) (Ogren et al. 1989). The WATS II review is used here as a starting point for the treatment of the status of loggerheads in the western Atlantic. Also of salient relevance here is the recent work of Fretey (1998), an exhaustive compilation of the literature concerning marine turtles of Macaronesia (the Azores, Madeira, Canary Islands, and the Cape Verde Islands), and the western coast of Africa. The importance of that work and that it goes far beyond the scope of the synopsis presented here is recog-

nized and acknowledged. There have been changes in the status of loggerheads in the Atlantic, or in our understanding of it, since WATS II; it is the authors' intent to provide an update through perusal of the recent literature and from direct communication with colleagues on the western rim of the Atlantic. Also provided is a compendium of the information in Fretey's thorough compilation of the literature relevant to the eastern Atlantic, augmented with references from the past three to four years and with personal communication with workers in the region.

Nesting Distribution

Any attempt to rank national or regional coastlines as major, intermediate, or minor loggerhead nesting grounds is necessarily arbitrary and will fail to accommodate some geographic areas accurately. The authors have chosen to designate as "minor" those areas where nesting is

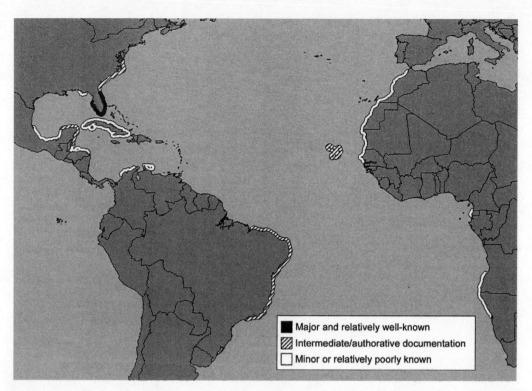

Figure 10.1. Geographic distribution and abundance of loggerhead nesting throughout the Atlantic and the Caribbean. A white border along a continental or insular shoreline depicts "minor" nesting areas where nesting is infrequent or where scant information suggests that fewer than 1,000 nests are deposited per season. A border of diagonal lines conveys nesting assemblages of "intermediate" size, approximating 1,000–5,000 nests per season, for which there is better information than there was 10 years ago. A black coastal margin indicates a major nesting assemblage, supporting more than 5,000 nests per season, where documentation is relatively thorough.

infrequent or where scant information suggests that fewer than about 1,000 nests are deposited per season, throughout the region (Figure 10.1). Assemblages producing 1,000–5,000 nests per year regionwide for which better information is available now than there was 10 years ago are regarded as "intermediate" in size (Figure 10.1). Major nesting assemblages are defined as those supporting more than 5,000 nests per year for which the documentation of nesting is relatively thorough (Figure 10.1).

The Eastern Atlantic

Oceanic Islands

There is no loggerhead nesting in the Canary Islands (L. F. López-Jurado, pers. comm.), in the Azores (Santos et al. 1995), or in the Madeira archipelago (Groombridge 1982). The Cape Verde Islands, however, are now known to support a nesting assemblage of at least intermediate size (L. F. López-Jurado, E.U. Project Cabo Verde Natura 2000, pers. comm.). Over 1,000 nesting females were tagged on just 5 km of beaches on Boavista Island during the 2000 nesting season. There may be as many as 5,000 nesting females per year in the entire archipelago, but this needs to be confirmed. These turtles seem to constitute a morphologically distinct nesting population (Cejudo et al. 2000). The mean straight carapace length of the Cape Verde nesting females is noticeably smaller (77.1 cm) than that of the southeastern U.S. nesting aggregation (approximately 92 cm).

African Mainland

Minor levels of nesting occur on the coast of Morocco (Brongersma 1995; Márquez 1990) and the coast of Senegal (Brongersma 1995; Dupuy 1986–87; Márquez 1990). Although other species of marine turtles have been reported to nest in the Gulf of Guinea region down to Angola, it has been generally believed that loggerheads do not (Butynski 1996; Castroviejo et al. 1994; Hughes 1988; Taylor and Weyer 1958; Tomas et al. 1999). Recently, however, Fretey (1998) reported loggerhead nesting in Cameroon at Nagae'. There is a minor level of nesting in southern Angola (Márquez 1990) and along the coast of Namibia (Brongersma 1995; IUCN 1993; Márquez 1990), but nesting does not occur along the Atlantic coast of South Africa or on the island of St. Helena (Fretey 1998).

The Western Atlantic

The Atlantic Coast of South America

Loggerheads apparently do not nest on Uruguayan beaches (Achaval et al. 2000; de Padua Almeida et al. 2000; Fallabrino et al. 2000; Gudynas 1980), but there is much more information about loggerhead nesting in Brazil available now than there was in 1989. At that time Ehrhart (1989) questioned Bullis' (1984) inference that more than 2,000 females nested on the Brazilian coast and that it should be recognized as a major nesting aggregation. Now, based on the work of Projeto Tamar, since its creation in 1980, significant nesting concentrations have been documented along the coast from northern Sergipe to northern Bahia state and from southern Bahia to the northern coast of Rio de Janiero state. There are references in the literature to scattered nesting from the states of Maranhao and Ceara on the north to Santa Catarina in the south (Bacon 1981; Márquez 1990; Soto et al. 1997). Published and unpublished accounts provide an estimate of 4,000 nests per year countrywide (Baptistotte et al. 1999; M. Godfrey, pers. comm.; Marcovaldi, in press; Marcovaldi and Laurent 1996; Marcovaldi and Marcovaldi 1999; Marcovaldi et al. 1997; Projeto Tamar Data Bank, unpubl.). The greatest concentration of nesting appears to be on the northern coast of the state of Bahia. Recent analysis of nesting data from Praia do Forte, one of the important beaches in the region, reveals that the level of nesting has been stable for the period 1987–1999 (Santos et al. 2000).

On a global scale, based wholly on the estimated annual nest production figures, the Brazilian coast ranks as an intermediate level loggerhead nesting ground. However, haplotype frequency comparisons have shown that the Brazilian loggerheads constitute a demographically independent subpopulation (Bowen et al. 1994; Encalada et al. 1998); it is therefore of major importance from the point of view of conservation and management. Marine turtles have been protected by federal regulations in Brazil since 1986, and judging by the record at Praia do Forte (Santos et al. 2000), nesting activity has been stable for more than a decade.

Loggerhead nesting in French Guiana, Suriname ("observed nesting only once"; Reichart and Fretey 1993), and Guyana is apparently negligible.

The Caribbean Sea

In general terms, the loggerhead is considerably more rare in Caribbean waters than either the green turtle or the hawksbill (K. Eckert, pers. comm.). There is little loggerhead nesting in the Caribbean.

The Southern Caribbean

There is just a smattering of nesting on the Venezuelan coast, mostly at Los Roques atoll (Carr et al. 1982; CCC 1980; Pritchard and Trebbau 1984) and on the Peninsula de Paria, Sucre State (Guada and Vernet 1992). Bacon (1975) reported little if any nesting in Curaçao. The first loggerhead nest, verified by hatchlings, was documented there in 1991 (Sybesma and Hoetjes 1992). There is also recent documentation of successful nesting by loggerheads on the small northeastern coast beaches, which may be the most important remaining nesting beaches on the island and in the Netherlands Antilles (Debrot and Pors 1995). Sparse nesting activity is also known from Aruba (Barmes et al. 1993). Bonaire supports a handful of loggerhead nests per season, with an estimated five nesting females (T. van Eijck, pers. comm.).

The situation in Colombia continues to be dire. Whereas Kaufmann (1971) estimated an annual nesting population of 400–600 loggerheads 30 years ago, the slaughter of nesting turtles has decimated the population so severely that in 1987 only eight nests were observed on the beaches between the Buritaca and Dibulla rivers in the regions of Magdalena and Guajira (Munoz et al. 1989). A survey in the same region in 1997 (Amorocho et al. 1999) found slightly greater nesting activity (25 nests), but it is likely that nesting is negligible all along the entire northern coast, including the good beaches east of Santa Marta.

New information from the San Andres archipelago (D. Amorocho, pers. comm.) reveals that there is still some slight loggerhead nesting activity on the islands of Serranilla (five nests), Roncador (two nests), and Serrana (six nests). The paucity of nesting suggested by these small numbers suggests that the statement of Carr et al. (1982) that "as nesting territory, San Andres is finished" still applies.

The Western Caribbean

Loggerhead nesting in southern Central America (Panama, Costa Rica, Nicaragua) is so infrequent (Bacon 1981; Carr et al. 1982; Engstrom et al. 2002) as to be considered negligible. There is unquantified nesting on the Guatemalan coast between Cabo Tres Puntas and Rio Montagua and perhaps slightly more in Honduras between Puerto Cortes and La Ceiba (Bacon 1981). Approximately 20 nests are produced per year at the most active beach on the Honduran coast (C. Diez, pers. comm.). Not surprisingly (because of its proximity to Quintana Roo, Mexico), Belize supports more loggerhead nesting than any of the other countries in the region. The most recent report estimates 40–70 nests per year on Ambergris Cay ("clearly the most important site"; Smith et al. 1992) and some additional nesting on Glover's Reef, Half-Moon Cay on Lighthouse Reef, Nicolas Cay, Ranguana Cay, and other smaller cays of the area. Nevertheless, the region as a whole can be regarded as a minor loggerhead nesting site, and there is no information available from which to decipher a trend.

The greatest level of loggerhead nesting activity in Mexico occurs on the Caribbean coast of Quintana Roo, especially at Isla Cozumel and Boca Paila (Márquez 1990). Smaller numbers nest on the northeastern coast of the Yucatan peninsula, from Cabo Catoche and Isla Contoy to Ascencion Bay (Márquez 1990), and there is scattered nesting along the Gulf of Mexico coast as far north as Tamaulipas (e.g., Miranda 2000).

Haplotype frequency comparisons have shown that the Quintana Roo assemblage is a genetically distinct subpopulation (Encalada et al. 1998). Estimates of nest production and population trends have fluctuated somewhat over the past 20 years, but the information available by 1990 suggested a slight upturn (about 200 nests) in the Quintana Roo colony, to a total of approximately 1,200 nests per year (R. Márquez, pers. comm.). The estimate rises to 1,500–2,300 for the entire Caribbean coast (Zurita-Gutierrez et al. 1993). The fact that a survey in 1997 found 1,391 loggerhead nests at Xcaret beach, alone (Arenas et al. 2000), makes the upper figure of the estimate (2,300) seem quite reasonable. On the basis of numbers alone, the Yucatan-Quintana Roo colony ranks as one of intermediate size, but as in the case of Brazil, its genetic distinction conveys major importance insofar as conservation and management are concerned.

The Northern Caribbean

Regarding Cuba, Bacon (1981) reported that there was "some nesting all around the island." Information provided at WATS I (Márquez 1984) indicated that the principal nesting beaches are found on the cays and islands of the southern coast of the Cuban archipelago, but no quantitative estimates were given at that time or at WATS II. In his review, Márquez (1990) reported minor nesting beaches "on some islands of the Caribbean region," principally on the south-central coast of Cuba. Currently there are approximately 250–300 loggerhead nests per year in all of Cuba, including the small cays (F. Moncada-Gavilán, pers. comm.), and nesting areas on the southwestern coast of Cuba account for about 63% of all loggerheads nesting in the country.

For the Cayman Islands, Bacon (1981) referenced Lewis (1940), who reported loggerhead nesting as rare, even 60 years ago. Data presented by Ottenwalder (1989) at the WATS II meeting stated that the number of loggerhead nests had been reduced to two to three per year. From 1971 until 1991, 43 loggerhead nests were verified on Grand Cayman Island and one on Little Cayman Island (Wood and Wood 1994). More recently, there seems to have been an upswing in nesting. There were 18 confirmed loggerhead nests on Grand Cayman in 1999 (J. Aiken, pers. comm.).

Historically in Jamaica, one-third of the nesting beaches included loggerheads (R. Kerr, pers. comm.), but both Bacon (1981) and Carr et al. (1982) considered loggerhead nesting there to be rare. New information presented at WATS I (Royer 1984) gave a figure of 210 nesting females. At WATS II, Ehrhart (1989) included this figure because no new information could be found. There have been no confirmed recent reports of loggerhead nesting, and it is believed that the species has been extirpated from Jamaican beaches (R. Kerr, pers. comm.). Additionally, there are no recent reports of loggerhead nesting from Pedro Cays, which were noted to have nesting in the 1940s.

The decline of loggerhead nesting in Jamaica seems to be mirrored on the island of Hispaniola. Although marine turtles once abounded in Haitian waters, there were no confirmed nesting records for loggerheads in Haiti during surveys made in 1982–1983 (Ottenwalder 1996) or in 1997–1998 (C. Diez, pers. comm.). Bacon (1981) and Carr et al. (1982) reported "occasional" nesting on the northeastern and northwestern coasts of the Dominican Republic and noted, "when nesting turtles are encountered, they are regularly killed and their eggs taken." The level of loggerhead nesting was reported to be about 60 (30–90) nesting females at WATS I (Inchaustegui 1984), an estimate based solely on interviews with fishermen. At the WATS II meeting, however, Ottenwalder (1989) estimated that there were about 52 nesting females in the Dominican Republic and Cayman Islands. Today it is believed that there is no loggerhead nesting in the Dominican Republic (F. Moncada-Gavilán, pers. comm.).

Bacon (1981) reported occasional nesting by loggerheads on mainland Puerto Rico as well as nesting on Culebra Island. However, it is believed that today there is no loggerhead nesting either in Puerto Rico or on adjacent islands

(C. Diez, pers. comm.). The nesting and stranding records kept by the Department of Natural and Environmental Resources confirm this (H. Horta, pers. comm.).

The Eastern Caribbean

Loggerheads are not known to nest in the U.S. Virgin Islands and are rarely observed offshore (K. Eckert, pers. comm.), nor are they known to nest in the British Virgin Islands (Eckert et al. 1992). No nesting is known from Anguilla, Saint Martin, Saint Barthelemy, or Saba (Meylan 1983), or from Antigua and Barbuda (Fuller et al. 1992). It is generally held that loggerheads do not nest in St. Kitts–Nevis, but "an occasional nesting loggerhead" on the southeastern peninsula was reported in 1989 (Eckert et al. 1992).

Early reviewers believed that loggerhead nesting was rare in Guadeloupe (Bacon 1981; Carr et al. 1982), and there are no recent reports of any nesting there (J. Chevalier, pers. comm.). Neither is there any nesting at Dominica or Martinique (Carr et al. 1982).

In St. Lucia, loggerheads formerly nested infrequently on beaches such as Pigeon Island, Cas-en-Bas and Pitton Sivons (Carr et al. 1982; Dodd 1988), but the St. Lucia Department of Fisheries has no evidence of recent nesting (d'Auvergne and Eckert 1993). No loggerhead nesting occurs today in Barbados (Horrocks 1992, pers. comm.).

Earlier reviewers believed that no loggerheads nested on Grenadine beaches and that they nested rarely on Grenada. At WATS II, the national representative of Grenada stated that loggerheads did not nest in Grenada (Finlay 1989). The Sea Turtle Action Recovery Plan for St. Vincent and the Grenadines (Scott and Horrocks 1993) reports two documented nests on Palm Island in the Grenadines and verbal reports of nesting on Mahault beach in Canouan. During the creation of the Recovery Plan, however, it could not be confirmed that loggerheads of any size had ever been common in St. Vincent and the Grenadines waters. At the present time, loggerheads are rarely seen in the Grenadines (Scott and Horrocks 1993). A 1991 survey of nesting turtles failed to identify any loggerhead nests on Trinidad or Tobago (Godley 1993).

Bermuda

Loggerheads used to nest occasionally in Bermuda (Bacon 1981). However, Ottenwalder (1989) reported that there had been no nesting there in over a decade.

The Bahama Islands and the Turks and Caicos Islands

In the Bahamas, loggerhead nesting was reported to be common and occurred on the islands of Great Inagua, Little Inagua, Andros, and Abaco (Bacon 1981). There were small numbers of loggerheads nesting on Walker's Cay, Grand Bahama, Bimini, and Eleuthera, although nesting had decreased greatly in the previous 50 years (Carr et al. 1982). Both Ehrhart (1989) and Márquez (1990) believed that nesting no longer occurs in the Bahamas, but recent information confirms that loggerhead nesting still exists at low levels on Grand Bahama, Great and Little Abaco, Great Inagua, Andros, and Jimento Cays (K. Bjorndal and A. Bolten, unpubl. data).

The Cay Sal Bank is a six-island group located between Florida and Cuba and is considered to be part of the Bahamas. Brief surveys conducted in recent years on Cay Sal Bank and the Anguilla Cays revealed previously unknown nesting by loggerheads. A conservative estimate based on a low-nesting year suggests that this island group may produce 500–600 nests in a 90-day season (Addison and Morford 1996; Addison 1997).

There is occasional nesting by loggerheads in the Turks and Caicos islands (Bacon 1981). In the Caicos Islands, Carr et al. (1982) reported that loggerhead nesting took place in smaller numbers than hawksbill nesting (no numbers given for either species). Fifty females nested there in 1982 (Mager 1985), but no recent information could be found.

The Southeastern United States and the Gulf of Mexico

The loggerhead population of the U.S. Atlantic and Gulf coasts produces approximately 53,000–92,000 nests per year and numbers about 32,000–56,000 adult females (assuming a mean of 4.1 nests per female and an average

remigration interval of 2.5 years; TEWG 2000). It is one of only two or three major assemblages in the world and is the only one in the Atlantic Basin (Figure 10.1). The most important recent work relating to the distribution and abundance of Atlantic loggerheads is the 1998 assessment of populations in the western North Atlantic by the U.S. National Marine Fisheries Service's Turtle Expert Working Group (TEWG). As the result of their consideration of the work of Bowen et al. (1993), Bowen (1995), and Encalada et al. (1998), they recognized four demographically independent loggerhead subpopulations (TEWG 1998). These include the "Yucatan nesting subpopulation," discussed above, and the "northern nesting subpopulation," which produces about 6,200 nests per year on the southeastern U.S. coast between North Carolina and northeastern Florida. Loggerheads are also known to nest infrequently a little farther north, from Maryland (Graham 1973) to New Jersey (Brandner 1983).

Also included is the southern Florida nesting subpopulation, which produces about 49,000–83,000 nests per year (TEWG 2000). By far the greatest proportion of that nesting is on the Florida Atlantic coast, below 29° N latitude, but it also includes about 2,200–8,500 nests per year on the Florida Gulf coast (TEWG 2000). A much smaller assemblage, the Florida panhandle nesting subpopulation, produces about 600 nests per year on beaches of the northern Gulf coast (TEWG 2000).

The TEWG argues persuasively that because of the known fidelity of nesting females to their natal beaches and the low gene flow between nesting assemblages, these genetically distinct entities are vulnerable to extinction. That is to say, their demographic independence must be recognized and dealt with for purposes of conservation and management.

The TEWG used data from the first six years of the Index Nesting Beach Survey (INBS) program (a standardized survey that began in 1989) to examine trends in the northern subpopulation and the southern Florida subpopulation. An earlier independent analysis of statewide data in South Carolina showed a 5% per year decline between 1980 and 1987

(Hopkins-Murphy and Murphy 1988). That trend has continued: loggerhead nest production in South Carolina had fallen to about 3,000 per season by the end of the 1990s, compared with about 5,600 as recently as 20 years ago (S. Murphy, pers. comm.). Also, a long-term independent study at Little Cumberland Island, Georgia, showed a 2.6% per year decline (J. Richardson, pers. comm.). Nevertheless, the TEWG detected no statistically valid trend in the 1989–1995 data for this subpopulation.

Long-term studies on beaches within the southern Florida subpopulation show collective increases of 3.6% annually for the period 1989–1998 (TEWG 2000). About 25% of the annual nesting by this subpopulation occurs at what is now called the Archie Carr National Wildlife Refuge, in southern Brevard County. The data derived from nest surveys carried out there from 1982 through 2000 show a clear upward trend in loggerhead nest production, with $r^2 = 0.754$ and $p < 0.0001$ (Ehrhart, unpubl. data). Recently, Witherington and Koeppel (2000) analyzed nesting data from Florida index beaches through 1998 and concluded that "loggerhead nesting in Florida appears to be stable or increasing" at most, but not all, beach sites within the southern Florida subpopulation range. The apparent prosperity of the southern Florida subpopulation in the modern era stands in stark contrast to the troubling decline that the authors believe is shown clearly by the northern assemblage.

Foraging Distribution

Researchers' understanding of loggerhead foraging aggregations in Atlantic coastal waters is generally superficial and, on the whole, only a modicum of new information has come to light in the past decade. For many regions of the western Atlantic, the authors found no new information and had to base decisions about the relative importance of foraging areas on earlier reviews (Bacon 1981; Carr et al. 1982), the WATS I national reports, and reports that are essentially anecdotal. For the eastern Atlantic the authors have gleaned information from Fretey's (1998) work, but there too, most references to foraging loggerheads are anecdotal. The distribution map of foraging within neritic habitats (Figure 10.2) constitutes an update of the one in the WATS II review, with the addition of the western coast of Africa. Designation of the importance of foraging areas as "minor," "intermediate," or "major" is far more subjective here than it is with regard to the nesting distribution, where estimated or actual nest production figures could be used as criteria. What follows, then, is the authors' best judgment as to the relative importance of foraging areas around the rim of the Atlantic, based on information derived from the literature and a great deal of personal communication with researchers in the field. Elsewhere in this volume, Bolten (Chapter 4) describes the oceanic foraging distribution of Atlantic loggerheads, and Hopkins-Murphy et al. (Chapter 5) treat feeding and foraging habitats in the region.

The Eastern Atlantic

Although there are records of loggerhead carcass strandings along the Atlantic coast of Europe (Brongersma 1972), the authors have not found evidence to suggest that this area is foraging habitat. Loggerheads, both oceanic stage juveniles and adults, are commonly found foraging in the waters around and north of the Azores to about 42° N latitude, eastward to the Atlantic coast of Spain, and in the waters around the Madeira, Canary, and Cape Verde islands (Bolten et al. 1993; Brongersma 1972; Groombridge 1982; Márquez 1990; Santos et al. 1995). The oceanic stage juveniles are from the Americas, carried east by the North Atlantic gyre (Bolten et al. 1993, 1998; Brongersma 1972; Márquez 1990). The adult loggerheads are probably from the Moroccan and Cape Verde Islands nesting populations (Brongersma 1972; López-Jurado et al. 2000; Schleich 1979).

The African Mainland

Along the tropical western coast of Africa, loggerheads are known to forage in the near-shore and offshore waters of Senegal (Dupuy 1986–87). The large size of these loggerheads was noted, indicating that they were adults, but

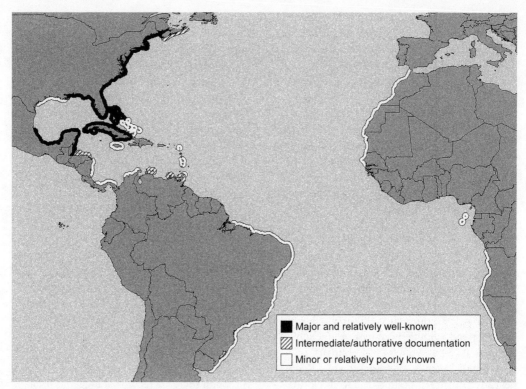

Figure 10.2. Map of loggerhead foraging within neritic habitats in the Atlantic and the Caribbean. A white margin along a continental or insular shoreline depicts "minor" foraging areas where information is scant or anecdotal and where there is no reason to suspect moderate or great abundance. A border of diagonal lines conveys "intermediate" abundance, evidenced by published work or recent personal communications. A black border depicts areas where there is adequate documentation to discern an abundance of foraging animals.

an estimate was not made of the number of turtles in this area. Loggerheads are occasionally seen in the Gulf of Guinea (Butynski 1996).

There are reports of loggerheads in Angolan waters (Brongersma 1995; Hughes et al. 1973); however, Carr and Carr (1991) could not find loggerheads despite surveys by plane and boat and interviews with fishermen. Brongersma (1995) noted stranding records of loggerheads on the coast of Namibia but did not discuss either size classes or abundance.

The Western Atlantic

The Atlantic Coast of South America
Across the Atlantic, it is mostly by reference to the WATS I National Report for Brazil and information in Gudynas (1980), Fallabrino et al. (2000), and de Padua Almeida et al. (2000) and by inference from the nesting distribution that the authors designate the entire coast of Brazil south of Maranhao to northern Uruguay as a minor foraging area (see Figure 10.2). Further investigations along that coast may very well identify greater aggregations in localized areas.

References to loggerheads in Suriname (Reichart and Fretey 1993) and Guyana (Pritchard 1989) are so few and brief that the authors have not designated any areas on the northeastern coast of South America, except Trinidad and Tobago (see below), as even minor foraging areas (see Figure 10.2).

The Caribbean Sea
The most recent information provided in most areas of the Caribbean is from Mager (1985) and Ehrhart (1989). Since that time, new information in the literature is seriously lacking. Thanks to the efforts of the Wider Caribbean Sea Turtle Conservation Network (WIDE-

CAST), many of the Caribbean Islands have created recovery plans and begun pilot projects. While much of that information is not yet in the literature, many of those involved in these projects have been willing to share their data. Although communication with individuals has allowed the authors to provide some recent but unpublished information, limitations have forced the authors to make some arbitrary decisions about how to depict loggerhead foraging in the Caribbean as a whole. The term "foraging area" brings to mind "many" animals, that is, an aggregation, not just occasional sightings here and there. For most islands where there were references to loggerheads, they were almost always immature animals captured in deeper waters offshore or in deep channels, or the record involved only one or two animals. The paucity of information regarding loggerheads in the Caribbean is reflective of the fact that there just are not many there. Therefore, the authors designate as "minor foraging areas" only those areas where loggerheads have been seen occasionally or more frequently. Some conflicting reports could not be resolved, and these are included below.

The Southern Caribbean

Loggerheads are "observed often" in waters of the Venezuelan states of Sucre and Nueva Esparta (at Isla Margarita) (Flores 1969), observed "sometimes" in the waters of Aruba (Barmes et al. 1993), and observed "regularly" in the waters around the island of Curaçao (Sybesma and Hoetjes 1992). Immature loggerheads are not commonly seen in Bonaire, and adults are seen only seasonally (T. van Eijck, pers. comm.). As a result, the authors have designated that region as a foraging area of intermediate importance (see Figure 10.2), recognizing that this decision is subject to further study and review. Clearly, this aggregation is not well studied, and no size class or population information is available.

The recent literature appears to be devoid of references to loggerhead foraging along the northern Colombian coast. The authors have, nevertheless, recognized it as a minor foraging area (see Figure 10.2) on the basis of Bacon's (1981) contention that adult loggerheads for-

aged there frequently and on the observation of Carr et al. (1982) that loggerheads were encountered more commonly than green turtles in the foraging habitats.

The Western Caribbean

There is new information available about the use of foraging habitats by loggerheads along the Panamanian coast. Engstrom et al. (2002) have shown that juveniles are common over the grass beds and coral reefs of Chiriqui Lagoon, thus confirming the observations of 20 years ago by Bacon (1981) and Carr et al. (1982). Mitochondrial DNA markers were used to show that these Chiriqui Lagoon loggerheads originate from the nesting beaches of southern Florida and Mexico (Engstrom et al. 2002). Similarly, it is becoming clear that loggerheads forage over the seagrass beds, coral reefs, and offshore cays on the Nicaraguan coast (Lagueux 1998).

There is virtually no new information concerning loggerhead foraging on the Honduran and Guatamalan coasts. The assessment of that area as a foraging ground of intermediate importance (see Figure 10.2) may be overly optimistic, but it is based on information in the two older but quite reliable reviews (Bacon 1981; Carr et al. 1982). There is, however, relatively new information concerning loggerhead foraging in Belize (Smith et al. 1992), and it corroborates the earlier assessments of Bacon (1981) and Carr et al. (1982) that juveniles were numerous along the southern coast and that larger loggerheads occurred there year-round. Understanding, once again, that the matter is greatly in need of further study, the authors have designated the Belizean coast as a major foraging area for loggerheads (see Figure 10.2).

Virtually the same circumstances prevail all along the Mexican coast. The earlier reviewers (Bacon 1981; Carr et al. 1982) left no doubt that juvenile and adult loggerheads foraged abundantly along the shorelines of the states of Vera Cruz, Tabasco, Campeche, and especially, Yucatan and Quintana Roo. Nevertheless, and in spite of the fact that there are many nesting beach projects ongoing in this area, there is an apparent dearth of information relating to foraging aggregations and developmental habitats in the previous two decades. The authors have adhered to the assessments of the earlier reviewers, designating the coastlines on all three sides of the Yucatan Peninsula as major foraging areas (see Figure 10.2), and they suggest that this is an area ripe for further investigation.

The Northern Caribbean

There were no data regarding foraging by loggerheads in Cuba in either the Bacon (1981) or the Carr et al. (1982) account. Mager (1985) noted harvesting but did not give size class information, and the WATS II report indicated that adult foraging is frequent (Ehrhart 1989). From 1976 to 1980 the fishery in Cuba landed an average of 860 metric tons of sea turtles, 36% of which consisted of loggerheads (Moncada-Gavilán and Nodarse 1983). In recent years, the total catch has increased to more than 900 tons per year, representing an estimated 2,500 loggerheads. Tags taken from captured animals indicate that adult loggerheads caught in Cuba come from nesting beaches in Florida (Ottenwalder and Ross 1992). Information on subadults/juveniles remains unavailable.

The National Report for the Cayman Islands (Parsons 1984) stated that loggerheads were netted in George Town Harbor (no size class or number given) and that in 1977 seven loggerheads were reported in the landing records. Accounts from older residents suggest that there used to be a foraging population of loggerheads in Grand Cayman. There were two reports in 1999 of adult loggerheads in the water, and crushed queen conch shells are commonly seen (J. Aiken, pers. comm.).

Early in the 20th century, adult loggerheads foraged occasionally in Jamaica (Bacon 1981). Adults were also occasionally captured in drift lines in deeper water, and there were reports of loggerheads far offshore that may have been migrating (Carr et al. 1982). R. Kerr (pers. comm.) believes there are adult foraging populations in the Port Royal cays, south of Kingston Harbor; in Old Harbor Bay; in Portland Bight; and on the northern coast at Runaway Bay. The 1982 survey done for WATS I suggested that foraging loggerheads occurred throughout the coastal shelf, yet the scarcity of recent confirmed reports suggests a different scenario today (R. Kerr, pers. comm.).

Although marine turtles once abounded in Haitian waters (Carr et al. 1982), there is no abundance of turtles there now. Only two loggerhead carapaces could be found during aerial surveys and in markets, hotels, and tourist shops during 1982–1983 (Ottenwalder 1996). In-water surveys conducted in 1997–1998 provided no loggerhead encounters or sightings (C. Diez, pers. comm.). In the Dominican Republic, Bacon (1981) made reference to occasional foraging by adults. Today the only reports are of subadult carcasses (F. Moncada-Gavilán, pers. comm.).

Foraging adults were reported from mainland Puerto Rico, Mona Island, and Vieques, but there were no population estimates (Bacon 1981). Aerial surveys conducted in 1977 showed loggerheads in foraging habitat, but not in concentrated numbers (Carr et al. 1982). Today it appears that there is no loggerhead foraging in Puerto Rican waters. Every few years there are one or two subadult strandings, presumably young loggerheads traveling the southern extent of the North Atlantic gyre (C. Diez, pers. comm.).

The Eastern Caribbean

There is no mention of loggerheads in the unpublished Sea Turtle Action Recovery Plan for the U.S. Virgin Islands, and there is apparently no information regarding loggerheads from the U.S. Virgin Islands (K. Eckert, pers. comm., unpubl. data).

Loggerheads are sporadically captured by net in the British Virgin Islands, generally off the island of Anegada. Three loggerheads were reportedly captured in 1984 and four in 1985. There have been no additional sightings, and no foraging areas had been identified through 1992 (Eckert et al. 1992).

Information about foraging at Anguilla is fragmentary, and identification is not always reliable, but loggerheads occur at least occasionally in these waters as one was net-captured during Meylan's (1983) survey. Anguillan fishermen consider loggerheads to be rare. In Saint Martin and St. Barthelemy, loggerheads are present but are rarely encountered (Meylan 1983).

In Barbuda, loggerheads are not common but are well known to fishermen. The turtles are most often found at the northwestern end of Barbuda in shallow water where there are large numbers of queen conch (Fuller et al. 1992). At St. Kitts and Nevis, loggerheads are seen only rarely (Meylan 1983). Nevis fishermen periodically report "strange turtles," which may be loggerheads (Eckert and Honebrink 1992).

Most of the juvenile loggerheads observed in Antigua are approximately 18–45 kg and are observed occasionally both inshore and offshore. Adults have not been seen (Meylan 1983). Several confirmed sightings have occurred in recent years east of the island in deep water and most often in spring and early summer (Fuller et al. 1992). Loggerheads are rarely encountered in Monserrat (Meylan 1983).

In Guadeloupe, loggerheads forage occasionally in near-shore waters and are also occasionally sighted in deeper offshore waters (Bacon 1981). They are fairly well known to fishermen on the eastern coast near Goyave and may be even more common around the St. Francois–Moule area of Grande Terre, but they are uncommon in Basse Terre (Carr et al. 1982). Fishermen from Îles des Saintes (islands southwest of Guadeloupe) occasionally find loggerheads basking at the surface offshore (O. Lorvelec, pers. comm.).

Foraging by both adults and juveniles is rare in Dominica (Bacon 1981), and although seldom seen, they are best known by people who fish the deep channels between the islands (Carr et al. 1982). The loggerhead is frequently called "channel turtle." Bacon (1981) reported frequent foraging by both adults and juveniles on the eastern coast of Martinique. Although Carr et al. (1982) reported that loggerheads ranging in size from subadult to adult are fairly common further offshore, no juveniles were known from this area.

In St. Lucia, occasional foraging by both adults and juveniles has been reported (Bacon 1981), and small loggerheads were occasionally found in the area of Gros Islet (Carr et al. 1982). In recent years there have been some unconfirmed reports of sightings at sea by fishermen, but there is no information regarding size class (d'Auvergne and Eckert 1993). Earlier reviews did not address Barbados. In this area

there have been only two confirmed captures in the previous 20 years (J. Horrocks, pers. comm.). No foraging grounds have been identified (Horrocks 1992).

Loggerheads are sometimes sighted in the offshore waters of St. Vincent and the Grenadines. Bacon (1981) reported that loggerhead foraging takes place all around the islands and that loggerheads are third in abundance in the Grenadines foraging habitat (Carr et al. 1982). In Grenada, loggerheads are typically of subadult size, nearly all greater than 18 kg (Carr et al. 1982), and foraging by juveniles occurs only occasionally (Bacon 1981). During the creation of the regional sea turtle recovery plan it could not be confirmed that loggerheads of any size had ever been common in St. Vincent and the Grenadines waters (Scott and Horrocks 1993).

Fishermen in Trinidad catch loggerheads only in deep water (Carr 1956). Bacon (1981) reported frequent foraging by adults in Trinidad, but they are rare in Tobago.

Bermuda

Earlier in the 20th century adult loggerheads foraged frequently in Bermuda (Bacon 1981), but today there is apparently no foraging there by adult or subadult loggerheads. Juvenile loggerheads are known from strandings during the winter months and are usually associated with washed-up *Sargassum* (J. Gray, pers. comm.).

The Bahama Islands and the Turks and Caicos Islands

In the Bahamas, adult loggerhead foraging occurred at Great Inagua, Andros, and the Abacos (Bacon 1981), but there were no population estimates. At the Abacos, one of the most commonly encountered adult turtles was the loggerhead, and they were present year-round (Carr et al. 1982). At WATS II, adult foraging was regarded as frequent (Ehrhart 1989). No recent information could be found, but there is apparently still foraging by adults, as indicated by two adult females that returned to the area of the middle cays in 1999 after they had nested and been fitted with satellite transmitters at the Archie Carr National Wildlife Refuge in Melbourne Beach, Florida (S. MacPherson, pers. comm.). Tag returns from the 1980s showed that nesting females used the Bahamas as foraging grounds, but few recent returns have been received (L. Ehrhart, unpubl. data).

Foraging by both adults and juveniles occurred occasionally in the Turks and Caicos islands (Bacon 1981). In the Caicos Islands, there were small numbers of loggerheads of all sizes, and there were juveniles in shoal grass along the fringing reef (Carr et al. 1982). The authors could find no recent information.

Atlantic North America and the Gulf of Mexico

The large foraging population of the U.S. Gulf and Atlantic coasts is better known than any of the others, and some of the essentials of their population biology and life history are beginning to be understood. Generally speaking, immature loggerheads are found in the estuarine and near-shore waters along the Canadian Maritime, New England, mid-Atlantic, and upper southeastern coasts during the warmer months of the year (Epperly et al. 1995; Hillestad et al. 1978; Keinath et al. 1987; Lazell 1980; Morreale et al. 1992; Squires 1954), and in the lagoonal and near-shore waters of central and southern Florida year-round (Ehrhart 1983; Ernest et al. 1989; Henwood 1987; Mendonca and Ehrhart 1982; Schroeder et al. 1998; Wells and Bellmund 1990). Even in the United States, however, there are few systematic, extended studies that can elucidate long-term trends in population density and structure. The primary new information concerning this assemblage is the TEWG's (1998) estimates, by two slightly different methods, of 224,000 and 234,000 loggerheads in the post–oceanic stage population.

Conclusions

Loggerheads are the only marine turtles that nest predominately outside of the Tropics. For many years the general perception of the species' nesting range in the Atlantic has been that it is "antitropical," marked by a curious discontinuity on the eastern and western rims of the Caribbean and by a broader discontinuity along the equatorial western African coast (particularly the Gulf of Guinea region). Certainly nothing in this review contradicts the Caribbean and equatorial African gaps, but it may be said that the "antitropical" label does not fit quite so well as it did 20–30 years ago. The fact that we now know of significant nesting in the Cape Verde Islands, the coast of Brazil north of Bahia, Quintana Roo in Mexico, and perhaps Cameroon, all situated between the tropics of Cancer and Capricorn (see Figure 10.1), makes it reasonable to modify the generalized picture of loggerhead nesting biogeography to include some parts of the Tropics.

Some specific modifications of previously held ideas that have come to light during the course of this review include the following:

- The discovery of a moderately large nesting aggregation in the Cape Verde Islands, especially the previously unrecognized beach on the island of Boavista.
- The discovery of a significant new nesting area (500–600 nests per year) in the eastern Bahamas, at Cay Sal Bank.
- The understanding that loggerhead nesting is concentrated in two areas along the Brazilian coast, from northern Sergipe to northern Bahia and from southern Bahia to northern Rio de Janeiro.
- The understanding that loggerhead nesting is essentially finished in Jamaica and Hispaniola.
- A better understanding of the extent of loggerhead nesting in Cuba: about 250–300 nests per year, approximately 63% of them along the southwestern coast.

One of the more disturbing issues that came to light is the apparent decline of the northern subpopulation of the southeastern U.S. loggerhead aggregation. It is especially egregious when contrasted with the apparent prosperity of the southern Florida subpopulation in the last 20 years. The causes of this disparity are undoubtedly many and complex, but at the risk of seeming to oversimplify, the authors suggest that because of its proximity to the shrimping grounds and because it was a much smaller group to begin with, the pre–turtle-excluder-

Table 10.1.

Summary of Nesting Information for the Loggerhead Turtle in the Atlantic Basin, by Subregion

Location	Nest Numbers	Data Time Period	Estimation Methods and Assumptions	Trends	Source
Cape Verde Islands					
Boavista Island	> 1,000 nesting females/year	2000	Tagging on nesting beach	Unknown	17
African mainland					
Morocco	Not quantified	Unknown	Unknown	Unknown	8, 20
Senegal	Not quantified	Unknown	Unknown	Unknown	8, 11, 20
Cameroon	Not quantified	Unknown	Unknown	Unknown	13
Angola	Not quantified	Unknown	Unknown	Unknown	20
Namibia	Not quantified	Unknown	Unknown	Unknown	8, 15, 20
Brazil					
Sergipe and northern Bahia	2,400 nests/year	1987–1999	Limited nest counts	Stable	19
Southern Bahia to Rio de Janerio	1,600 nests/year	1987–1999	Limited nest counts	Stable	19
Caribbean					
Southern					
Venezuela	Not Quantified	1988–1991	Limited surveys	Unknown	14
Colombia (mainland)	25 nests	1997	Limited nest counts	Decreasing	4
Colombia (San Andres Archipelago)	< 15 nests/year	1998–1999	Limited reconnaissance	Decreasing	3
Aruba	<10 nests/year	2000	Verified hatchlings	Unknown	6, 29
Curaçao	< 10 nests/year	1991, 1993	Nesting surveys	Unknown	9, 25
Western					
Guatemala	Not quantified	Unknown	Unknown	Unknown	5
Honduras	< 30 nests/year	Unknown	Unknown	Unknown	10
Belize	< 100 nests/year	Unknown	Limited nest counts	Unknown	24
Mexico (Quintana Roo and Yucatan)	1,431–2,266 nests/year	Unknown	Unknown	Problematic	21, 26
Northern					
Cuba	= 300 nests/year	Unknown	Unknown	Unknown	22
Jamaica	Probably extirpated	Unknown	Unknown	Unknown	16
Eastern					
St. Kitts and Nevis	< 10 nests/year	1989	Unknown	None	12
St. Vincent and Grenadines	< 10 nests/year	1982	Unknown	None	23
Bahamas	Not Quantified	Unknown	Unknown	Unknown	7
Cay Sal Banks	500–600 nests/year	1995, 1996	Limited surveys/ estimated	Unknown	1, 2
Turks and Caicos islands	50 nests/year	1982	Unknown	Unknown	18
Gulf of Mexico					
Mexico	< 100 nests/year	Unknown	Unknown	Unknown	26
Florida Panhandle	600 nests/year	1989–1998	Total nest counts	Unknown	27
Southwestern Florida	5,100 nests/year	1989–1998	Total nest counts	Increasing	27, 28
Southeastern USA					
Southern Florida	62,000 nests/year	1989–1998	Total nest counts	Stable or increasing	27, 28
Northern Florida to North Carolina	6,200 nests/year	1989–1998	Total nest counts	Stable or declining	22, 27

Source Key: 1. Addison 1997. 2. Addison and Morford 1996. 3. D. J. Amorocho, pers. comm. 4. Amorocho et al. 1999. 5. Bacon 1981. 6. Barmes et al. 1993. 7. K. Bjorndal and A. Bolten, pers. comm. 8. Brongersma 1995. 9. Debrot and Pors 1995. 10. C. Diez, pers. comm. 11. Dupuy 1986–87. 12. Eckert et al. 1992. 13. Fretey 1998. 14. Guada and Vernet 1990. 15. IUCN 1993. 16. R. Kerr, pers. comm. 17. L. F. López-Jurado (EU Project Cabo Verde Natura 2000), pers. comm. 18. Mager 1985. 19. Marcovaldi, in press. 20. Márquez 1990. 21. R. Márquez, pers. comm. 22. S. Murphy, pers. comm. 23. Scott and Horrocks 1993. 24. Smith et al. 1992. 25. Sybesma and Hoetjes 1992. 26. TEWG 1998. 27. TEWG 2000. 28. Witherington and Koeppel 2000. 29. L. Zeinstra, pers. comm.

device loss of adult and subadult loggerheads had a much greater impact on the northern group. It is clear that the southern Florida group has responded positively to good management and basic protection under U.S. law. It seems possible that, after a longer lag period, the northern group may respond to those same practices and protection and begin to recover.

Another disconcerting feature brought out by this review is the great lack of research progress made in understanding the distribution, status, and biology of foraging populations of loggerheads. Except for a few studies in the United States, there are precious few ongoing investigations of population structure and seasonal and long-term trends in densities of in-water populations. It has been nearly impossible to find systematically gathered, relevant new data upon which to build the foraging aspect of this review, but there are one or two bright spots. The work of Engstrom et al. (2002) in Chiriqui Lagoon, Panama, demonstrates the possibilities that may exist elsewhere along the Central American coast and at places like Trinidad and the extensive coastline of Brazil. On the other side of the Atlantic, the recent work of Tiwari et al. (2002) on the coast of Morocco and Western Sahara suggests that there may be many opportunities for rewarding in-water investigations all along the western coast of Africa. An eminent sea turtle conservationist once said that sea turtles spend 0.0001% of their lives on nesting beaches, but sea turtle biologists spend 99.9999% of their time and effort studying them there. The call for more in-water work is not original here; it appears in recovery plans and action plans all over the world. A review such as this one points up how little progress we have made in this field since the days of Bacon (1981), Carr et al. (1982), and WATS I. The cause of marine turtle conservation and management will benefit greatly from systematic, long-term studies of foraging populations.

ACKNOWLEDGMENTS

Putting together information of this scope required the help of many who had personal knowledge where there was a lack of recent literature. We gratefully acknowledge the following individuals for their contributions: Jonathan Aiken, Diego Amorocho, Anna Bass, Karen Bjorndal, Boyd Blihovde, Johan Chevalier, Ann Cook, Carlos Diez, Karen Eckert, Matthew Godfrey, Jennifer Gray, Kathy Hall, Julia Horrocks, Hector Horta, Janina Jakubowska, Rhema Kerr, Chris Koeppel, Luis Felipe López-Jurado, Olivier Lorvelec, Félix Moncada-Gavilán, Jeanne Mortimer, Mario Mota, Sally Murphy, Peter Pritchard, Saskia Renshoff, Claire Shirley, Tom van Eijck, and Lidy Zeinstra.

We would also like to acknowledge the tremendous assistance of the Sea Turtle Online Bibliography (Bolten, Bjorndal, and Eliazar) and the (online) Bibliography of the Loggerhead Sea Turtle (Dodd), the extensive resources and generosity of the Chelonian Research Institute, Dr. John Weishampel of the University of Central Florida GAMES (Geospatial Analysis and Modeling of Ecological Systems) Lab and Winnie Tyler and Deidra Campbell of the University of Central Florida Interlibrary Loan Department.

LITERATURE CITED

Achaval, F. Y., H. Marin, and L. C. Barea. 2000. Incidental capture of turtles with pelagic longline. In F. A. Abreu-Grobois, R. Briseno-Duenas, R. Márquez, and L. Sarti (compilers). Proceedings of the 18th international sea turtle symposium, 261. NOAA Technical Memorandum NMFS-SEFSC-436.

Addison, D. S. 1997. Sea turtle nesting on Cay Sal, Bahamas, recorded June 2–4, 1996. Bahamas Journal of Science. 5:34–35.

Addison, D. S., and B. Morford. 1996. Sea turtle nesting activity on the Cay Sal Bank, Bahamas. Bahamas Journal of Science. 3:31–36.

Amorocho, D., J. A. Cordoba B., and S. Miklin H. 1999. Current status of nesting sea turtles in the northern Colombian Caribbean. Marine Turtle Newsletter 85:6–7.

Arenas, A., R. Villavicencio, A. D'Amiano, L. Gomez, and R. Raigoza. 2000. The sea turtle program of Xcaret, 97 nesting season results. In F. A. Abreu-Grobois, R. Briseno-Duenas, R. Márquez, and L. Sarti (compilers). Proceedings of the 18th international sea turtle symposium, 172–174. NOAA Technical Memorandum NMFS-SEFSC-436.

Bacon, P. R. 1975. Review of research, exploitation and management of the stocks of sea turtles in the Caribbean region. FAO Fisheries Circular 334.

———. 1981. The status of sea turtle stocks management in the western central Atlantic. WECAF Studies no. 7.

Bacon, P., F. Berry, K. Bjorndal, H. Hirth, L. Ogren,

and M. Weber (eds.). 1984. Proceedings western Atlantic turtle symposium, San Jose, Costa Rica, July 1983. Miami, Fla.: University of Miami Press.

Baptistotte, C., J. T. Scalfoni, and N. Mrosovsky. 1999. Male-producing thermal ecology of a southern loggerhead turtle nesting beach in Brazil: Implications for conservation. Animal Conservation 2:9–13.

Barmes, T., K. L. Eckert, and J. Sybesma. 1993. WIDECAST sea turtle recovery action plan for Aruba. In K. L. Eckert (ed.). CEP Technical Report no. 25. Kingston, Jamaica: UNEP/CEP.

Bolten, A. B., H. R. Martins, K. A. Bjorndal, and J. Gordon. 1993. Size distribution of pelagic-stage loggerhead sea turtles (Caretta caretta) in the waters around the Azores and Madeira. Arquipelago. Life and Marine Sciences 11A:49–54.

Bolten, A. B., K. A. Bjorndal, J. R. Martins, T. Dellinger, M. J. Biscoito, S. E. Encalada, and B. W. Bowen. 1998. Transatlantic developmental migrations of loggerhead sea turtles demonstrated by mtDNA sequence analysis. Ecological Applications 8:1–7.

Bowen, B. W. 1995. Molecular genetic studies of marine turtles. In K. A. Bjorndal (ed.). Biology and conservation of sea turtles, rev. ed., 585–587. Washington, D.C.: Smithsonian Institution Press.

Bowen, B. W., J. C. Avise, J. I. Richardson, A. B. Meylan, D. Margaritoulis, and S. R. Hopkins-Murphy. 1993. Population structure of loggerhead turtles (Caretta caretta) in the northwestern Atlantic Ocean and Mediterranean Sea. Conservation Biology 7:834–844.

Bowen, B. W., N. Kamezaki, C. J. Limpus, G. H. Hughes, A. B. Meylan, and J. C. Avise. 1994. Global phylogeography of the loggerhead turtle (Caretta caretta) as indicated by mitochodrial DNA haplotypes. Evolution 48:1820–1828.

Brandner, R. L. 1983. A sea turtle nesting at Island Beach State Park, Ocean County, New Jersey. Herpetological Review 14:110.

Brongersma, L. D. 1972. European Atlantic turtles. Zoologische Verhandelingsen, Leiden 121:1–318.
———. 1995. Marine turtles of the eastern Atlantic Ocean. In K. A. Bjorndal (ed.). Biology and conservation of sea turtles, rev. ed., 407–416. Washington, D.C.: Smithsonian Institution Press.

Bullis, H. R. 1984. A summary of numerical and other quantitative data derived from descriptive materials in the WATS national reports for fisheries, foraging, and nesting, by species. In P. Bacon, F. Berry, K. Bjorndal, H. Hirth, L. Ogren, and M. Weber (eds.). Proceedings of the western Atlantic turtle symposium, San Jose, Costa Rica, July 1983, vol. 3, app. 7, 65–74. Miami, Fla.: University of Miami Press.

Butynski, T. M. 1996. Marine turtles on Bioko Island, Equatorial Guinea. Oryx 30:143–149.

Carr, A. 1956. The windward road. New York: Alfred A. Knopf.

Carr, A. F., A. Meylan, J. Mortimer, K. Bjorndal, and T. Carr. 1982. Surveys of sea turtle populations and habitats in the western Atlantic. NOAA Technical Memorandum NMFS-SEFC-91.

Carr, T., and N. Carr. 1991. Surveys of the sea turtles of Angola. Biological Conservation 58:19–29.

Castroviejo, J., J. Juste B., J. P. del Val, R. Castelo, and R. Gil. 1994. Diversity and status of sea turtle species in the Gulf of Guinea islands. Biodiversity and Conservation 3:828–836.

CCC (Caribbean Conservation Corporation). 1980. Survey and preliminary census of marine turtle populations in the western Atlantic. Final Report to the National Marine Fisheries Service.

Cejudo, D., I. Cabrera, L. F. López-Jurado, C. Évora, and P. Alfama. 2000. The reproductive biology of Caretta caretta on the Island of Boavista (Republic of Cabo Verde, West Africa). In H. J. Kalb and T. Wibbels (compilers). Proceedings of the 19th annual symposium on sea turtle biology and conservation, 244–245. NOAA Technical Memorandum NMFS-SEFSC-433.

D'Auvergne, C., and K. L. Eckert. 1993. WIDECAST sea turtle recovery action plan for St. Lucia. K. L. Eckert (ed.). CEP Technical Report no. 26. Kingston, Jamaica: UNEP/CEP.

Debrot, A. O., and L. P. J. Pors. 1995. Sea turtle nesting activity on northeast coast beaches of Curacao, 1993. Caribbean Journal of Science 31:333–338.

de Padua Almeida, A., C. Baptistotte, and J. A. P. Schineider. 2000. Loggerhead turtle tagged in Brazil found in Uruguay. Marine Turtle Newsletter 87:10.

Dodd, C. K., Jr. 1988. Synopsis of the biological data on the loggerhead sea turtle Caretta caretta (Linnaeus 1758). USFWS Biological Report 88.

Dupuy, A. R. 1986–87. Donnees nouvelles sur les tortues marines au Senegal. Bulletin de l'Institut Fondamental d'Afrique Noire Ser. A, Sciences Naturelles 46:403–411.

Eckert, K. L., and T. D. Honebrink. 1992. WIDECAST sea turtle recovery action plan for St. Kitts and Nevis. K. L. Eckert (ed.). CEP Technical Report no. 17. Kingston, Jamaica: UNEP/CEP.

Eckert, K. L., J. A. Overing, and B. B. Lettsome. 1992. WIDECAST sea turtle recovery action plan for the British Virgin Islands. K. L. Eckert (ed.). CEP Technical Report no. 15. Kingston, Jamaica: UNEP/CEP.

Ehrhart, L. M. 1983. Marine turtles of the Indian River Lagoon system. Florida Scientist 46:337–346.

———. 1989. A status review of the loggerhead turtle, *Caretta caretta,* in the western Atlantic. *In* L. Ogren, F. Berry, K. Bjorndal, H. Kumpf, R. Mast, G. Medina, H. Reichart, and R. Witham (eds.). Proceedings of the second western Atlantic turtle symposium (WATS II), 122–135. NOAA Technical Memorandum NMFS-SEFC-226.

Encalada, S. E., K. A. Bjorndal, A. B. Bolten, J. C. Zurita, B. Schroeder, E. Possardt, C. J. Sears, and B. W. Bowen. 1998. Population structure of loggerhead turtle *(Caretta caretta)* nesting colonies in the Atlantic and Mediterranean as inferred from mitochondrial DNA control region sequences. Marine Biology 130:567–575.

Engstrom, T. N., P. A. Meylan, and A. B. Meylan. 2002. Origin of juvenile loggerhead turtles *(Caretta caretta)* in a tropical developmental habitat in Caribbean Panamá. Animal Conservation 5:125–133.

Epperly, S. P., J. Braun, and A. Veishlow. 1995. Sea turtles in North Carolina waters. Conservation Biology 9:384–394.

Ernest, R. G., R. E. Martin, N. Williams-Walls, and J. R. Wilcox. 1989. Population dynamics of sea turtles utilizing shallow coastal waters off Hutchinson Island, Florida. *In* S. A. Eckert, K. L. Eckert, and T. H. Richardson (compilers). Proceedings of the ninth annual workshop on sea turtle biology and conservation, 57–59. NOAA Technical Memorandum NMFS-SEFC-232.

Fallabrino, A., A. Bager, A. Estrades, and F. Achaval. 2000. Current status of marine turtles in Uruguay. Marine Turtle Newsletter 87:4–5.

Finlay, J. 1989. *In* L. Ogren, F. Berry, K. Bjorndal, H. Kumpf, R. Mast, G. Medina, H. Reichart, and R. Witham (eds.). Proceedings of the second western Atlantic turtle symposium (WATS II), 86. NOAA Technical Memorandum NMFS-SEFC-226.

Flores, C. 1969. Notas sobre reptiles acuaticas de Venezuela y su importancia economica. Lagena 21–22:1–19.

Fretey, J. 1998. Marine turtles of the Atlantic coast of Africa. UNEP/CMS Technical Publication no. 1.

Fuller, J. E., K. L. Eckert, and J. I. Richardson. 1992. WIDECAST sea turtle recovery action plan for Antigua and Barbuda. K. L. Eckert (ed.). CEP Technical Report no. 16. Kingston, Jamaica: UNEP/CEP.

Godley, B. 1993. 1991 survey of marine turtles nesting in Trinidad and Tobago. Marine Turtle Newsletter 61:15–18.

Graham, S. 1973. The first record of *Caretta caretta caretta* nesting on a Maryland beach. Bulletin of the Maryland Herpetological Society 9:24–26.

Groombridge, B. 1982. The IUCN Amphibia-Reptilia red data book. Part 1. Testudines, Crocodylia, Rhynchocephalia. Gland, Switzerland: IUCN.

Guada, H. J., and P. Vernet. 1992. New nesting areas for sea turtles on the Peninsula de Paria, Sucre State, Venezuela. Marine Turtle Newsletter 57:18–19.

Gudynas, E. 1980. Notes on the sea turtles of Uruguay. Association for the Study of Reptiles and Amphibians Journal 1:69–76.

Henwood, T. A. 1987. Movements and seasonal changes in loggerhead turtle *Caretta caretta* aggregations in the vicinity of Cape Canaveral, Florida (1978–84). Biological Conservation 40:191–202.

Hillestad, H. O., J. I. Richardson, and G. K. Williamson. 1978. Incidental capture of sea turtles by shrimp trawlermen in Georgia. *In* Proceedings of the 32nd annual conference of the Southeast Association of Fish and Wildlife Agencies, 167–178.

Hopkins-Murphy, S. R., and T. M. Murphy. 1988. Status of the loggerhead turtle in South Carolina. *In* B. A. Schroeder (compiler). Proceedings of the eighth annual workshop on sea turtle conservation and biology, 35–37. NOAA Technical Memorandum NMFS-SEFC-214.

Horrocks, J. A. 1992. WIDECAST sea turtle recovery action plan for Barbados. K. L. Eckert (ed.). CEP Technical Report no. 12. Kingston, Jamaica: UNEP/CEP.

Hughes, B. 1988. Herpetology in Ghana (West Africa). British Herpetological Society Bulletin no. 25.

Hughes, G. R., B. Huntley, and D. Wearne. 1973. Sea turtles in Angola. Biological Conservation 5:58–59.

IUCN (World Conservation Union). 1993. Environmental synopsis: Namibia. Gland, Switzerland: IUCN/EC.

Inchaustegui, S. 1984. National report for the country of Dominican Republic. *In* P. Bacon, F. Berry, K. Bjorndal, H. Hirth, L. Ogren, and M. Weber (eds.). Proceedings western Atlantic turtle symposium, San Jose, Costa Rica, July 1983, vol. 3, app. 7, 169–176. Miami, Fla.: University of Miami Press.

Kaufmann, R. 1971. Report on status of sea turtles in Columbia. *In* IUCN New Series Supplemental Paper 31, 75–78.

Keinath, J. A., J. A. Musick, and R. A. Byles. 1987. Aspects of the biology of Virginia's sea turtles: 1979–1986. Virginia Journal of Science 38:229–236.

Lagueux, C. J. 1998. Demography of marine turtles harvested by Miskitu Indians of Atlantic Nicaragua. *In* R. Byles and Y. Fernandez (compilers). Proceedings of the 16th annual symposium on sea turtle biology and conservation, 90. NOAA Technical Memorandum NMFS-SEFSC-412.

Lazell, J. D. Jr. 1980. New England waters: Critical habitat for marine turtles. Copeia 1980:290–295.

Lewis, C. B. 1940. The Cayman Islands and marine turtles. *In* C. Grant (ed.) The herpetology of the Cayman Islands, 56–65. Bulletin Institute Jamaica Science Series 2.

López-Jurado, L., I. Cabrera, D. Cejudo, C. Evora, and P. Alfama. 2000. Distribution of marine turtles in the Archipelago of Cape Verde, Western Africa. *In* H. Kalb and T. Wibbles (compilers). Proceedings of the 19th annual symposium on sea turtle conservation and biology, 245–247. NOAA Technical Memorandum NMFS-SEFSC-443.

Mager, A., Jr. 1985. Five-year status reviews of sea turtles listed under the Endangered Species Act of 1973. St. Petersburg, Fla.: NMFS.

Marcovaldi, M. A. In press. Projeto Tamar-Ibama: An experience of 20 years conserving sea turtles in Brazil. Proceedings of the 21st annual symposium on sea turtle biology and conservation.

Marcovaldi, M. A., and A. Laurent. 1996. A six season study of marine turtle nesting at Paria do Forte, Bahia, Brazil, with implications for conservation and management. Chelonian Conservation and Biology 2:55–59.

Marcovaldi, M. A., and G. G. dei Marcovaldi. 1999. Marine turtles of Brazil: The history and structure of Projeto Tamar-Ibama. Biological Conservation 91:35–41.

Marcovaldi, M. A., M. H. Godfrey, and N. Mrosovsky. 1997. Estimating sex ratios of loggerhead turtles in Brazil from pivotal incubation durations. Canadian Journal of Zoology 75:755–770.

Márquez, R. 1984. National report for the country of Cuba. *In* P. Bacon, F. Berry, K. Bjorndal, H. Hirth, L. Ogren, and M. Weber (eds.). Proceedings western Atlantic turtle symposium, San Jose, Costa Rica, July 1983, vol. 3, app. 7, 143–160. Miami, Fla.: University of Miami Press.

———. 1990. Sea turtles of the world. An annotated and illustrated catalogue of sea turtle species known to date. FAO Species Catalogue. Vol. 11. FAO Fisheries Synopsis 125. FAO: Rome, Italy.

Meylan, A. B. 1983. Marine turtles of the Leeward Islands, Lesser Antilles. Smithsonian Institution Atoll Research Bulletin no. 278.

Mendonca, M. T., and L. M. Ehrhart. 1982. Activity, population size and structure of immature *Chelonia mydas* and *Caretta caretta* in Mosquito Lagoon, Florida. Copeia 1982:161–167.

Miranda, J. L. 2000. Sea turtles in southern Vera Cruz, Mexico: A proposal. *In* F. A. Abreu-Grobois, R. Briseno-Duenas, R. Márquez, and L. Sarti (compilers). Proceedings of the 18th international sea turtle symposium, 261. NOAA Technical Memorandum NMFS-SEFSC-436.

Moncada-Gavilán, F., and G. Nodarse Andreu. 1983. Informe Nacional sobre la actividad desarrollada por Cuba en el estudio y conservación de las tortugas marinas. Centro de Investigaoiones Pesqueras, Departamento Cría Experimental, MIP, Julio 1983.

Morreale, S. J., A. B. Meylan, S. S. Sadove, and E. A. Standora. 1992. Annual and winter mortality of marine turtles in New York waters. Journal of Herpetology 26:301–308.

Munoz, D., M. Alfaro, L. Ma. Blain, N. Anzola, and G. Gomez. 1989. Sea turtles in Buritaca-Don Diego, Colombia. Marine Turtle Newsletter 45:9–11.

Ogren, L., F. Berry, K. Bjorndal, H. Kumpf, R. Mast, G. Medina, H. Reichart, and R. Witham (eds.). 1989. Proceedings of the second western Atlantic turtle symposium (WATS II). NOAA Technical Memorandum NMFS-SEFC-226.

Ottenwalder, J. A. 1989. Report on Subregion Greater Antilles. *In* L. Ogren, F. Berry, K. Bjorndal, H. Kumpf, R. Mast, G. Medina, H. Reichart, and R. Witham (eds.). Proceedings of the second western Atlantic turtle symposium (WATS II), 84–85. NOAA Technical Memorandum NMFS-SEFC-226.

———. 1996. The current status of sea turtles in Haiti. Contributions to Herpetology 12:381–393.

Ottenwalder, J. A., and J. P. Ross. 1992. The Cuban sea turtle fishery: Description and needs for management. *In* M. Salmon and J. Wyneken (compilers). Proceedings of the 11th annual workshop on sea turtle biology and conservation, 90–92. NOAA Technical Memorandum NMFS-SEFC-302.

Parsons, J. 1984. National report for the country of Cayman Islands. *In* P. Bacon, F. Berry, K. Bjorndal, H. Hirth, L. Ogren, and M. Weber (eds.). Proceedings western Atlantic turtle symposium, San Jose, Costa Rica, July 1983, vol. 3, app. 7, 118–122. Miami, Fla.: University of Miami Press.

Pritchard, P. C. H. 1989. Geographic distribution, *Caretta caretta* (loggerhead). Herpetological Review 20:13–14.

Pritchard, P. C. H., and P. Trebbau. 1984. The turtles of Venezuela. SSAR Contributions to Herpetology no. 2. Caracas, Venezuela: Society for the Study of Amphibians and Reptiles.

Reichart, H. A., and J. Fretey 1993. WIDECAST sea turtle recovery action plan for Surinam. K. L. Eckert (ed.). CEP Technical Report no. 24. Kingston, Jamaica: UNEP/CEP.

Royer, E. 1984. National report for the country of Jamaica. *In* P. Bacon, F. Berry, K. Bjorndal, H. Hirth,

L. Ogren, and M. Weber (eds.). Proceedings western Atlantic turtle symposium, San Jose, Costa Rica, July 1983, vol. 3, app. 7, 225–295. Miami, Fla.: University of Miami Press.

Santos, R. S., S. Hawkins, L. R. Monteiro, M. Alves, and E. J. Isidro. 1995. Marine research, resources and conservation in the Azores. Aquatic Conservation: Marine and Freshwater Ecosystems 5:311–354.

Santos, A. S., M. A. Marcovaldi, and M. H. Godfrey. 2000. Update on the nesting population of loggerhead sea turtles in Praia do Forte, Bahia, Brazil. Marine Turtle Newsletter 89:8–11.

Schleich, H. H. 1979. Sea turtle protection needed at the Cape Verde Islands. Marine Turtle Newsletter 12:12.

Schroeder, B. A., A. M. Foley, B. E. Witherington, and A. E. Mosier. 1998. Ecology of marine turtles in Florida Bay: Population structure, distribution, and occurrence of fibropapilloma. In S. P. Epperly and J. Braun (compilers). Proceedings of the 17th annual sea turtle symposium, 265–267. NOAA Technical Memorandum NMFS-SESFC-415.

Scott, N., and J. A. Horrocks, J. A. 1993. Sea turtle recovery action plan for St. Vincent and the Grenadines. K. L. Eckert (ed.). CEP Technical Report no. 27. Kingston, Jamaica: UNEP/CEP.

Smith, G. W., K. L. Eckert, and J. P. Gibson. 1992. WIDECAST Technical Report no. 18. Kingston, Jamaica: UNEP/CEP.

Soto, J. M. R., R. C. P. Beheregaray, and R. A. R. de P. Rebello. 1997. Range extension: Nesting by Dermochelys and Caretta in southern Brazil. Marine Turtle Newsletter 77:6–7.

Squires, H. J. 1954. Records of marine turtles in the Newfoundland area. Copeia 1954:68.

Sybesma, J., and P. C. Hoetjes. 1992. First record of the olive ridley and of nesting by the loggerhead turtle in Curaçao. Caribbean Journal of Science 28:103–104.

Taylor, E. H., and D. Weyer. 1958. Report on a collection of amphibians and reptiles from Harbel, Republic of Liberia. The University of Kansas Science Bulletin 38:1191–1229.

TEWG. 1998. An assessment of the Kemp's ridley (Lepidochelys kempii) and loggerhead (Caretta caretta) sea turtle populations in the western North Atlantic. NOAA Technical Memorandum NMFS-SEFSC-409.

——— 2000. Assessment update for the Kemp's ridley and loggerhead sea turtle populations in the western North Atlantic. NOAA Technical Memorandum NMFS-SEFSC-444.

Tiwari, M., K. A. Bjorndal, A. B. Bolten, and A. Moumni. 2002. Morocco and Western Sahara: Sites of an early neritic stage in the life history of loggerheads? In A. Mosier, A Folley, and B. Brost (compilers). Proceedings of the 20th annual symposium on sea turtle biology and conservation, 9. NOAA Technical Memorandum NMFS-SEFSC-477.

Tomas, J., J. Castroviejo, and J. A. Raga. 1999. Sea turtles in the south of Bioko Island (Equatorial Guinea). Marine Turtle Newsletter 84:4–6.

Wells, P., and S. Bellmund. 1990. Sea turtle activity in the Florida Keys 1980–1989. In T. H. Richardson, J. I. Richardson, and M. Donnelly (compilers). Proceedings of the 10th annual workshop on sea turtle biology and conservation, 25–27. NOAA Technical Memorandum NMFS-SEFC-278.

Witherington, B. E., and C. M. Koeppel. 2000. Sea turtle nesting in Florida, U.S.A., during the decade 1989–1998: An analysis of trends. In H. Kalb and T. Wibbles (compilers). Proceedings of the 19th annual symposium on sea turtle conservation and biology, 94–96. NOAA Technical Memorandum NMFS-SEFSC-443.

Wood, F. E., and J. R. Wood. 1994. Sea turtles of the Cayman Islands. In M. A. Brunt and J. E. Davies (eds.). The Cayman Islands: Natural history and biogeography, 229–236. The Netherlands: Kluwer Academic Publishers.

Zurita-Gutierrez, J. C., R. Herrera, and B. Prezas. 1993. Tortugas marinas del Caribe. In S. I. Salazar-Vallejo and N. E. Gonzalez (eds.). Biodiversidad Marine y Costera de Mexico, 735–751. Comisión Nacional Bioversidad y CIQRO, Mexico.

Chapter 11

Loggerhead Turtles in the Mediterranean Sea:

Present Knowledge and Conservation Perspectives

—Dimitris Margaritoulis, Roberto Argano, Ibrahim Baran,
Flegra Bentivegna, Mohamed N. Bradai, Juan Antonio Camiñas,
Paolo Casale, Gregorio De Metrio, Andreas Demetropoulos,
Guido Gerosa, Brendan J. Godley, Daw A. Haddoud,
Jonathan Houghton, Luc Laurent, and Bojan Lazar

The Mediterranean Sea covers an area of about 2.5 million km², with a coastline of approximately 46,000 km, of which 19,000 km belong to islands. Natural communication with other seas is restricted to that with the Atlantic at the Straits of Gibraltar, where a narrow (approximately 12 km) passage is formed, across which lies a shallow sill. From an oceanographic point of view, the Mediterranean is an evaporation basin, and the resulting water deficit and salinity differences sustain a permanent strong incoming surface current and a weaker subsurface countercurrent across the Straits of Gibraltar. The Mediterranean Sea is roughly divided into two basins, the western and the eastern, connected by the shallow (approximately 400 m deep) Channel of Sicily and the narrow Straits of Messina. The two basins have different hydrological conditions, the eastern being more saline and warmer. Because of lack of nutrients, the Mediterranean is one of the less productive seas in the world (Miller 1983).

The loggerhead turtle is the most abundant sea turtle species in the Mediterranean, having evolved local populations. It seems that the latest colonization occurred about 12,000 years ago from stocks in the western Atlantic (Bowen et al. 1993). Marine turtles in the Mediterranean have only relatively recently attracted the interest of researchers and conservationists (Argano 1979; De Metrio et al. 1983; Demetropoulos and Hadjichristophorou 1982; Geldiay et al. 1982; Margaritoulis 1982; Mayol and Castello Mas 1983).

This chapter presents a synthesis of the current knowledge, including the largely unpublished data gathered to date (1999), regarding the biology and conservation status of this regional population.

Nesting Habitats and Breeding Populations

Nesting Areas and Nesting Activity

Nesting in the Mediterranean is confined almost exclusively to the eastern basin. The main

Table 11.1.
Annual Nesting Effort in Cyprus

| Nesting Area | Number of Seasons | Number of Nests/Season | | | Sources |
		Average	Min.	Max.	
Akrotiri/Episkopi	6	22.7	10	32	6, 7
Chrysochou Bay	5	119.8	109	152	3
Northern beaches	7	372.0	245	519	1, 2, 4, 5
Western beaches	7	57.1	40	72	3
Total		571.6	404	775	

Source Key: 1. Broderick and Godley 1996. 2. Broderick et al. 1997, 1999. 3. A. Demetropoulos and M. Hadjichristophorou, pers. observ. 4. Godley and Kelly 1996. 5. Godley et al. 1998c. 6. MacLean et al. 1998. 7. I. Williamson, pers. comm.

Note: Data derived from monitoring projects.

nesting concentrations are found in Cyprus, Greece, and Turkey where long-term monitoring projects are in operation (Tables 11.1–11.3; Figure 11.1). Recently, nesting grounds were revealed in Libya, but their nesting potential needs quantification (Laurent et al. 1995). Current information on nesting areas and nesting effort is summarized by country below.

Algeria
No tracks were found during a 1989 survey of 16 beach samples, totaling 73.9 km, distributed throughout the main sandy zones, and surveyed one to seven times (Laurent 1990).

Croatia
A survey of the southern coasts showed no nesting (Lazar et al. 1997). Nonetheless, according to local people, eggs have been used in the past for domestic consumption (Lazar and Tvrtkovic in RAC/SPA 1998).

Cyprus
The first surveys of turtle nesting were conducted in 1976–77, and an annual conservation project was initiated in 1978, concentrating mainly on the beaches of the western coast and Chrysochou Bay (Demetropoulos and Hadjichristophorou 1989; Table 11.1). In 1988 a brief field study of marine turtle nesting was carried out on the northern beaches (Groombridge and Whitmore 1989), highlighting their regional importance, and an annual monitoring project was initiated in 1992 (see Table 11.1).

Egypt
Little nesting has been recorded along the Mediterranean shores of Egypt. In a single survey over 249 km of sandy coastline from Alexandria to the Libyan border, few signs of nesting were found (Kasparek 1993). Negligible nesting in this part of the Egyptian coastline was confirmed in 1998 by Clarke et al. (2000). A single survey along the Nile delta (166 km of sandy beach) found no nesting, but 200 km of sandy coastline, from the Suez Canal to the Israeli border, surveyed three times in one season, revealed 20 loggerhead turtle clutches (Clarke et al. 2000).

France
No nesting has been recorded on the Mediterranean coasts of France, including Corsica (Delaugerre 1987; Laurent 1991).

Greece
Nesting was first recorded in 1977 on the island of Zakynthos (Margaritoulis 1982). Nesting here was subsequently shown to constitute the single most important nesting concentration in the Mediterranean, reaching average nesting densities of more than 230 nests/km/season. The greater part of the 16,000 km Greek coastline has been investigated through aerial and ground surveys, and other nesting areas have been found, mainly along the western and southern coasts and on the island of Crete (Margaritoulis 1987, 1998; Margaritoulis et al. 1995a). Nesting areas have been classified as "major areas," "areas of moderate nesting," and

Table 11.2.
Annual Nesting Effort in Greece

Nesting Area	Number of Seasons	Number of Nests/Season			Sources
		Average	Min.	Max.	
"Major" Areas					
Bay of Chania, Crete	6	114.9	77	192	12, 17, 21, 23, 34
Kyparissia Bay, Peloponnesus[a]	15	580.7	286	927	7, 9, 11, 13 22, 27, 29, 31, 35, 36
Lakonikos Bay, Peloponnesus	7	191.9	107	239	24, 27, 29, 31, 37
Rethymno, Crete	8	387.3	315	516	11, 12, 17, 21, 23, 34
Zakynthos (Bay of Laganas)	16	1,301.3	857	2,018	7, 8, 13–16, 20, 25, 26, 30, 32, 33
"Moderate" Areas					
Bay of Messara, Crete	8	53.5	15	80	12, 17, 21, 23, 34
Beaches adjacent to Kyparissia	2	64.0	60	68	10, 35
Ipirus coast[b]	1	40.0	40	40	28
Kefalonia (Mounda beach)	6	28.8	17	45	3–6
Kerkyra[b]	1	20.0	20	20	28
Koroni	5	55.0	35	66	19
Kos[b]	1	60.0	60	60	28
Kotychi	3	50.3	32	80	10, 31
Lefkas[b]	1	50.0	50	50	28
Rhodes	5	10.6	4	21	1, 2, 13
Romanos	3	22.3	17	30	10, 18
SE Peloponnesus (incl. Kythira)[b]	1	20.0	20	20	28
Total		3,050.6	2,012	4,472	

Source Key: 1. Gerosa et al. 1998. 2. G. Gerosa and M. Aureggi, pers. observ. 3. Houghton 1996. 4. Houghton et al. 1997. 5. Houghton et al. 1998. 6. J. Houghton , pers. observ. 7. Margaritoulis 1987. 8. Margaritoulis 1988a. 9. Margaritoulis 1988d. 10. Margaritoulis 1989. 11. Margaritoulis 1993. 12. Margaritoulis 1996. 13. Margaritoulis and Arapis 1990. 14. Margaritoulis and Dimopoulos 1993. 15. Margaritoulis and Dimopoulos 1994. 16. Margaritoulis and Dimopoulos 1995. 17. D. Margaritoulis and M. Dretakis, pers. observ. 18. D. Margaritoulis and G. Hiras, pers. observ. 19. D. Margaritoulis and C. Johnston, pers. observ. 20. D. Margaritoulis and K. Katselidis, pers. observ. 21. D. Margaritoulis and A. Panagopoulou, pers. observ. 22. D. Margaritoulis and A. F. Rees, pers. observ. 23. Margaritoulis and Sioris 1997. 24. D. Margaritoulis and K. Teneketzis, pers. observ. 25. Margaritoulis et al. 1991. 26. Margaritoulis et al. 1992. 27. Margaritoulis et al. 1994. 28. Margaritoulis et al. 1995a. 29. Margaritoulis et al. 1995b. 30. Margaritoulis et al. 1996a. 31. Margaritoulis et al. 1996b. 32. Margaritoulis et al. 1997. 33. Margaritoulis et al. 1998a. 34. Margaritoulis et al. 1998b. 35. Margaritoulis et al. 1999. 36. Margaritoulis et al. 2000. 37. Teneketzis 1997.

Note: Data derived from monitoring projects, unless otherwise specified.

[a]Extrapolated, in some seasons, to the whole bay length from the monitored core area.

[b]Estimate after a number of surveys in one season.

"areas of occasional or diffuse nesting" (Margaritoulis 2000). All major areas and several areas of moderate nesting are monitored annually (see Table 11.2).

Israel

Little nesting is recorded along the 190 km coastline of Israel. It seems that nesting is greatly reduced, probably due to heavy past ex-

Table 11.3.
Annual Nesting Effort in Turkey

| Nesting Area | Number of Seasons | Number of Nests/Season | | | Sources |
		Average	Min.	Max.	
Akyatan	4	15.3	1	29	4, 5, 10
Anamur	2	191.0	187	195	10, 11
Belek	3	129.7	68	168	2, 8, 10
Cirali (Olympos)	1	34.0	34	34	10
Dalaman	1	73.0	73	73	10
Dalyan	9	165.0	52	269	2, 3, 9, 10
Demirtas	1	98.0	98	98	2
Fethiye	7	124.1	88	158	1, 2, 7, 9, 10
Gazipasa	1	110.0	110	110	2
Göksu Delta	5	64.6	36	117	2, 6, 10
Kale	1	39.0	39	39	10
Kizilot	4	107.2	50	146	10
Kumluca	2	162.5	75	250	2, 10
Patara	6	52.5	33	85	2, 9, 10
Total		1,365.9	944	1,771	

Source Key: 1. Baran and Türkozan 1996. 2. I. Baran, pers. observ. 3. Erk'akan 1993. 4. Gerosa et al. 1995. 5. G. Gerosa and M. Aureggi, pers. observ. 6. Glen et al. 1997. 7. Türkozan and Baran 1996. 8. Türkozan et al. 1998. 9. Other references in Türkozan et al. 1998. 10. Yerli and Demirayak 1996. 11. Yerli and Dolezel 1998.

Note: Data derived from monitoring projects.

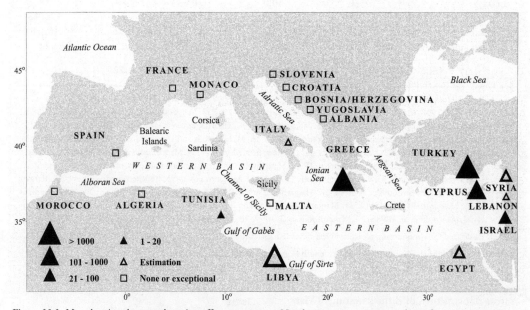

Figure 11.1. Map showing the annual nesting effort per country. Numbers represent average values of nests per season. Solid triangles feature values derived from monitoring projects; open triangles are estimates.

Table 11.4.
Overall Nesting Effort in the Mediterranean

| Country | Number of Nests/Season | | | |
	Average	Min.	Max.	Sources
Cyprus	571.6	404	775	Table 11.1
Greece	3,050.6	2,012	4,472	Table 11.2
Israel [a]	32.7	10	52	2, 3
Tunisia (Kuriat Islands) [b]	10.2	5	15	1
Turkey	1,365.9	944	1,771	Table 11.3
Total	5,031.0	3,375	7,085	

Source Key: 1. Bradai 1996. 2. Kuller 1999. 3. Z. Kuller, pers. comm.

Note: Data derived from monitoring projects.

[a]Data over seven seasons.

[b]Data over four seasons.

ploitation and the degradation of beaches (Sella 1982; Kuller 1999). Since 1993 almost the entire coast is surveyed annually, and all nests are relocated to beach hatcheries (Kuller 1999; Table 11.4).

Italy
Nesting is only recorded in southern Italy and is mostly confined to the islands of Lampedusa and Linosa, with occasional nests in Sicily and on the Ionian coasts and the Adriatic-Apulian coasts (Basso 1996; Cocco and Gerosa 1990; Di Palma 1978; Freggi 1997; Gerosa et al. 2000; Gramentz 1989; Ragonese and Jereb 1992). The maximum annual number of nests is estimated at 15.

Lebanon
Although no specific survey has been conducted, some nesting is reported (Ramadan-Jaradi in RAC/SPA 1998).

Libya
Nesting was first reported from the area of the Kouf National Park (Schleich 1987) and from the Gulf of Sirte and the eastern coasts (Haddoud and Assigier, in press; Meininger et al. 1994). In 1995, a single survey of 50 beach segments, totaling 142 km spread between the Egyptian border and Sirte (744 km of sandy coastline), revealed 176 nests, suggesting a nesting population of regional importance (Laurent et al. 1995). Further surveys (Haddoud and El Gomati, in press; Laurent et al. 1999) from Sirte to the Tunisian border demonstrated that nesting activity, although spread over the entire coast, may be less dense in western areas.

Morocco
No nesting was recorded during a 1989 survey of four beach samples, totaling 24 km, distributed throughout the main sandy zone and surveyed one to four times (Laurent 1990).

Spain
No nesting is known along the Mediterranean coast, except a fully developed loggerhead embryo found in Ebro Delta (Llorente et al. 1992/93).

Syria
Eighteen nests (presumably of loggerheads) were found during a single survey over 79.5 km of sandy coastline (Kasparek 1995).

Tunisia
Little nesting has been recorded on the main-

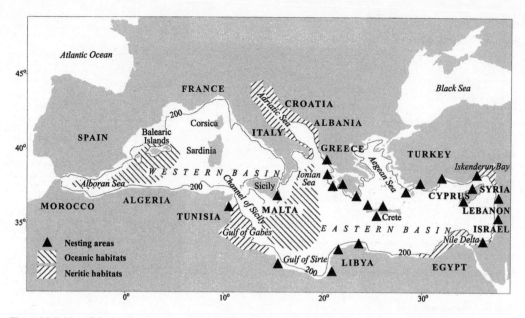

Figure 11.2. Map of the Mediterranean region showing approximate locations of nesting areas and of known oceanic and neritic habitats. The 200 m isobath delimits the continental shelf. Schematic presentation of nesting areas does not imply similar nesting levels.

land (Bradai 1995, 1996; Laurent et al. 1990). Nesting on Kuriat Islands, the most important Tunisian nesting site, is monitored annually (see Table 11.4).

Turkey

Preliminary work in the late 1970s revealed loggerhead nesting from the region of Marmaris east to Mersin (Geldiay et al. 1982). In a systematic 1988 survey, 17 important nesting areas, for both loggerhead and green turtles, were identified (Baran and Kasparek 1989a). Thereafter, specific monitoring projects have been conducted at some of these areas (see Table 11.3).

Other Countries

Although no systematic beach surveys have yet been undertaken, loggerheads may nest in Albania where tracks have been reported (Haxhiu and Uruci in RAC/SPA 1998), and along the sandy coast of Montenegro, in Yugoslavia. No nesting has been documented in Bosnia-Herzegovina, Slovenia, or Monaco. Although, there are historical records on egg laying in the Maltese islands (Despott 1915), no nesting has been recorded there since 1930 (Gramentz 1989).

Summary for the Region

Based on the recorded annual numbers in Cyprus, Greece, Israel, Tunisia, and Turkey, the total nesting effort in the Mediterranean ranges from 3,375 to 7,085 nests per season (see Table 11.4). These are minimum numbers, as a proportion of clutches (in Greece 15%, after Margaritoulis 2000) are laid at sites other than monitored beaches. In addition, these numbers do not include nests in countries where monitoring has not yet been completely instigated. Future monitoring, particularly in Libya, is expected to substantially increase these figures. The distribution of nesting sites in the Mediterranean is illustrated in Figure 11.2.

Reproductive Parameters

The vast majority of loggerhead nesting in the Mediterranean occurs between beginning of June and early August, with sparse nesting from mid-May to early September. Tables 11.5–11.10 summarize baseline data on several reproductive parameters. It is known that nesting loggerheads in the Mediterranean are significantly smaller than those in other parts of the world (Broderick and Godley 1996; Margari-

Table 11.5.
Carapace Measurements of Nesting Females

Country, Area	Number of Seasons	Mean (cm)	Range of Individual Values (cm)	Sample Size	Sources
Straight Length					
Greece, Kefalonia	5	76.8–80.1	63.5–87.0	11–15	10, 11, 17, 19
Greece, Kyparissia Bay	3	78.6–79.1	66.0–95.0	13–97	13, 14
Greece, Zakynthos	3	78.3–79.2	68.5–90.0	195–343	14, 15
Libya	1	78.7	62.3–83.2	9	9
Turkey, Dalyan	1	73.1	60.2–83.9	49	6
Turkey, Fethiye	1	73.2	66.0–87.5	22	1
Turkey [a]	1	72.0	58.0–87.0	58	20
Straight Width					
Greece, Kefalonia	5	57.1–59.2	45.0–77.0	11–15	10, 11, 17, 19
Greece, Kyparissia Bay	3	59.1–59.4	46.0–72.0	12–99	13, 14
Greece, Zakynthos	3	58.6–59.3	49.0–68.5	194–343	14, 15
Turkey, Dalyan	1	53.5	46.8–62.3	49	6
Turkey, Fethiye	1	54.4	47.5–65.5	22	1
Turkey [a]	1	52.0	43.0–67.0	58	20
Curved Length					
Cyprus, Alagadi	8	71.1–77.9	64.5–90.0	6–39	3, 4, 7, 8
Cyprus, western beaches	20	66.5–79.8	60.0–90.0	2–11	5
Greece, Kefalonia	5	81.6–84.7	71.9–93.0	11–15	10, 11, 17, 19
Greece, Kyparissia Bay	3	83.1–83.8	70.0–99.0	28–101	13, 14
Greece, Lakonikos Bay	2	84.1–84.6	78.0–92.0	11–12	16, 18
Greece, Zakynthos	4	82.7–83.8	70.0–96.5	146–345	14, 15
Libya	1	78.0	71.0–86.3	11	12
Tunisia	1	79.7	73.0–85.0	3	2
Turkey, Fethiye	1	77.3	68.0–91.0	27	1
Turkey [a]	1	76.0	63.0–91.0	58	20
Curved Width					
Cyprus, Alagadi	8	63.8–68.2	54.5–82.0	6–39	3, 4, 7, 8
Cyprus, western beaches	20	50.0–69.8	50.0–77.0	2–11	5
Greece, Kefalonia	5	71.3–76.2	52.0–79.0	11–15	10, 11, 17, 19
Greece, Kyparissia Bay	3	73.9–75.2	57.0–88.0	27–102	13, 14
Greece, Zakynthos	4	73.5–74.6	60.0–87.0	35–345	14, 15
Turkey, Fethiye	1	69.2	61.0–79.0	27	1
Turkey [a]	1	68.0	50.0–79.0	58	20

Source Key: 1. Baran and Türkozan 1996. 2. M. N. Bradai and I. Jribi, pers. observ. 3. Broderick and Godley 1996. 4. Broderick et al. 1997, 1999. 5. A. Demetropoulos and M. Hadjichristophorou, pers. observ. 6. Erk'akan 1993. 7. Godley and Kelly 1996. 8. Godley et al. 1998c. 9. Haddoud and El Gomati, in press. 10. Houghton 1996. 11. Houghton et al. 1997, 1998. 12. Laurent et al. 1995. 13. Margaritoulis 1988b. 14. D. Margaritoulis, pers. observ. 15. D. Margaritoulis and K. Katselidis, pers. observ. 16. D. Margaritoulis and K. Teneketzis, pers. observ. 17. Stringell et al. 1996. 18. Teneketzis 1997. 19. White 1998. 20. Yerli and Demirayak 1996.

Note: Lengths measured from notch to tip and widths at the widest point.

[a] Anamur, Fethiye, Göksu Delta, Kale, Kizilot, Kumluca.

Table 11.6.
Clutch Size

Country, Area	Number of Seasons	Mean	Range of Individual Values or (SD)	Sample Size	Sources
Cyprus, Alagadi	8	74.8–82.7	9–159	27–194	3, 4, 10, 11
Cyprus, western beaches and Chrysochou Bay	19	74.2–97.2	25–164	20–94	6
Greece, Bay of Chania	3	110.3–117.1	2–177	92–103	24, 25, 30
Greece, Bay of Messara	1	108.1	62–150	49	24
Greece, Kefalonia	6	99.8–120.4	39–176	23–32	13–15, 33, 36
Greece, Kyparissia Bay	9	105.2–126.8	6–211	33–506	18, 21, 28, 29, 31
Greece, Lakonikos Bay	5	107.1–126.1	7–197	24–208	22, 26, 28, 34
Greece, Rethymno	5	102.0–124.6	1–190	160–378	19, 20, 24, 25, 30
Greece, Rhodes	3	78.0–108.3	45–152	2–6	8
Greece, Zakynthos	16	111.4–130.4	11–199	49–598	17, 21, 22, 23, 27
Israel[a]	—	76.3	(15.2)	31	1
Israel[a]	—	82.0	55–149	—	32
Libya	1	95.2	72–128	14	12, 16
Tunisia, Kuriat Islands	3	81.5–105.5	59–145	5–11	5
Turkey, Akyatan	2	68.0–87.5	35–108	4–7	8, 9
Turkey, Anamur	1	89.0	(20.9)	20	38
Turkey, Dalyan	1	73.4	24–148	235	7
Turkey, Fethiye	2	82.9–86.0	29–203	156–156	2, 35
Turkey[b]	1	65–101	40–139	5–156	37

Source Key: 1. Ashkenazi and Sofer 1988. 2. Baran and Türkozan 1996. 3. Broderick and Godley 1996. 4. Broderick et al. 1997, 1999. 5. M. N. Bradai and I. Jribi, pers. observ. 6. A. Demetropoulos and M. Hadjichristophorou, pers. observ. 7. Erk'akan 1993. 8. G. Gerosa and M. Aureggi, pers. observ. 9. G. Gerosa and P. Casale, pers. observ. 10. Godley and Kelly 1996. 11. Godley et al. 1998c. 12. Haddoud and El Gomati, in press. 13. Hays and Speakman 1991, 1992. 14. Houghton 1996. 15. Houghton et al. 1997, 1998. 16. Laurent et al. 1995. 17. Margaritoulis 1987, 1988a. 18. Margaritoulis 1988b. 19. Margaritoulis 1993. 20. Margaritoulis 1996. 21. D. Margaritoulis, pers. observ. 22. Margaritoulis and Arapis 1990. 23. D. Margaritoulis and K. Katselidis, pers. observ. 24. D. Margaritoulis and A. Panagopoulou, pers. observ. 25. Margaritoulis and Sioris 1997. 26. D. Margaritoulis and K. Teneketzis, pers. observ. 27. Margaritoulis et al. 1991, 1992. 28. Margaritoulis et al. 1994, 1995b. 29. Margaritoulis et al. 1996b. 30. Margaritoulis et al. 1998b. 31. Margaritoulis et al. 1999, 2000. 32. Silberstein and Dmi'el 1991. 33. Stringell et al. 1996. 34. Teneketzis 1997. 35. Türkozan and Baran 1996. 36. White 1998. 37. Yerli and Demirayak 1996. 38. Yerli and Dolezel 1998.

Notes: Clutch size measured during clutch relocations or posthatch excavations of nondepredated nests. SD = standard deviation.

[a]Data from several seasons.

[b]Anamur, Belek, Cirali, Dalaman, Dalyan, Fethiye, Gazipasa, Göksu Delta, Kale, Kizilot, Kumluca, Patara.

toulis 1982, 1988b; Table 11.5). Furthermore, there seem to be substantial differences, particularly in nesting female size and clutch size, among the Mediterranean colonies (Tables 11.5 and 11.6). Other differences among sites may appear in the duration of re-nesting intervals (Table 11.9); however, insufficient data have as yet been gathered to undertake robust statistical analysis. Incubation durations (Table 11.8) are generally short in the Mediterranean. When comparison is made with studies of other conspecific populations, this is highly suggestive of

female-biased sex ratios in hatchling production (Godley et al. 2001). First attempts to estimate the sex ratio of hatchlings, in relation to nest temperatures, were undertaken in Cyprus and Turkey; the results suggest a pivotal temperature of approximately 29°C (Kaska et al. 1998).

Population Structure

In addition to the apparent morphological and biological differences, substructuring of breeding stocks within Mediterranean has been con-

Table 11.7.
Mass and Diameter of Eggs

Country, Area	Number of Seasons	Mean	Range of Individual Values	Sample Size	Sources
Mass (g)					
Cyprus, Alagadi	1	32.4	26.4–38.6	12	1
Cyprus, western beaches	2	26.9–31.9	22.8–36.5	13–30	2
Greece, Zakynthos	1	29.8	23.0–35.4	45	8
Turkey, Dalyan	1	27.5	15.9–36.5	173	3
Diameter (mm)					
Cyprus, Alagadi	1	37.4	32.9–39.6	12	1
Cyprus, western beaches	2	38.0–38.6	34.9–40.2	13–26	2
Greece, Kefalonia	5	36.1–38.7	27.0–42.6	12–30	5–7, 9, 10
Greece, Zakynthos	1	36.7	33.0–41.9	45	8
Turkey, Akyatan	1	34.5	31–37	15	4
Turkey, Dalyan	1	37.0	33.0–41.0	65	3
Turkey [a]	1	40.4–42.1	37.0–45.0	5–8	11

Source Key: 1. A. Broderick and B. Godley, pers. observ. 2. A. Demetropoulos and M. Hadjichristophorou, pers. observ. 3. Erk'akan 1993. 4. G. Gerosa and M. Aureggi, pers. observ. 5. Houghton 1996. 6. J. Houghton, pers. observ. 7. Houghton et al. 1997, 1998. 8. D. Margaritoulis, pers. observ. 9. Stringell et al. 1996. 10. White 1998. 11. Yerli and Demirayak 1996.

[a]Cirali, Gazipasa, Kumluca.

Table 11.8.
Duration of Incubation Measured in Nondepredated, Noninundated and/or Nonrelocated Nests

Country, Area	Number of Seasons	Mean (days)	Range of Individual Values or (SD)	Sample Size	Sources
Cyprus, Alagadi	7	47.3–48.7	42–60	17–58	3, 4, 7
Greece, Bay of Chania	2	53.3–54.3	43–74	73–76	14
Greece, Kefalonia	1	54.9	47–64	26	9, 10
Greece, Kyparissia Bay	3	48.1–53.9	43–67	35–302	11, 16
Greece, Lakonikos Bay	4	52.1–59.3	43–84	35–150	12, 15
Greece, Rethymno	3	51.7–55.2	40–77	105–156	14
Greece, Rhodes	2	49.0–55.0	44–55	1–3	6
Greece, Zakynthos	4	57.6–62.3	42–97	14–185	11, 13
Israel	—	—	50–55	—	1
Libya	1	55.0	48–62	5	8
Turkey, Akyatan	1	52.0	48–55	5	6
Turkey, Anamur	1	51.3	(5.6)	26	18
Turkey, Dalyan	1	59.3	51–71	47	5
Turkey, Fethiye	2	55.0–56.9	—	—	2, 17

Source Key: 1. Ashkenazi and Sofer 1988. 2. Baran and Türkozan 1996. 3. Broderick and Godley 1996. 4. Broderick et al. 1997, 1999. 5. Erk'akan 1993. 6. G. Gerosa and M. Aureggi, pers. observ. 7. Godley and Kelly 1996. 8. Haddoud and El Gomati, in press. 9. J. Houghton, pers. observ. 10. Houghton and Hays 2002. 11. D. Margaritoulis, pers. observ. 12. Margaritoulis and Arapis 1990. 13. D. Margaritoulis and K. Katselidis, pers. observ. 14. D. Margaritoulis and A. Panagopoulou, pers. observ. 15. D. Margaritoulis and K. Teneketzis, pers. observ. 16. Margaritoulis et al. 1999, 2000. 17. Türkozan and Baran 1996. 18. Yerli and Dolezel 1998.

Table 11.9.

Renesting Interval Calculated from Subsequently Observed Nestings of the Same Individuals

Country, Area	Number of Seasons	Mean (days)	Range of Individual Values	Sample Size	Sources
Cyprus, Alagadi	7	12.7–13.7	10–18	7–34	2–5
Greece, Kefalonia	4	15.8–17.0	13–20	9–20	6–9
Greece, Kyparissia Bay	2	15.2–19.3	12–24	6–14	11, 13
Greece, Rethymno	1	13.6	12–18	17	14
Greece, Zakynthos	9	14.6–19.9	11–28	14–181	10–12, 14–16
Turkey, Fethiye	1	16.2	12–34	6	1

Source Key: 1. Baran and Türkozan 1996. 2. Broderick and Godley 1996. 3. Broderick et al. 1997, 1999. 4. Godley and Kelly 1996. 5. Godley et al. 1998c. 6. Hays and Speakman 1991, 1992. 7. Houghton 1996. 8. J. Houghton, pers. observ. 9. Houghton et al. 1997, 1998. 10. Margaritoulis 1983. 11. Margaritoulis 1987. 12. Margaritoulis 1988a. 13. Margaritoulis 1988b. 14. D. Margaritoulis, pers. observ. 15. Margaritoulis and Arapis 1990. 16. Margaritoulis et al. 1991.

firmed by genetic studies. Indeed, although loggerheads nesting in the Mediterranean share common haplotypes with those nesting in the western Atlantic, they have diverged genetically (Bowen et al. 1993; Laurent et al. 1993, 1998). Genetic divergence appears more prominent in nesting colonies in Turkey (Laurent et al. 1998). Other genetic analyses from different nesting areas in Turkey showed differentiation among rookeries (Schroth et al. 1996), providing evidence of subpopulations.

Table 11.10.

Size and Mass of Hatchlings

Country, Area	Number of Seasons	Mean	Range of Individual Values or (SD)	Sample Size	Sources
Straight Carapace Length (mm)					
Cyprus, Alagadi	1	40.0	24.9–49.3	2064	2
Cyprus, western beaches	2	40.3–41.5	36–45	180–325	1
Greece, Zakynthos	1	40.4	(0.7)	20	3
Turkey, Fethiye	1	39.8	28–45	302	5
Turkey, Göksu Delta	1	39.1	36–42	37	4
Straight Carapace Width (mm)					
Cyprus, Alagadi	1	30.4	20.0–39.7	2064	2
Greece, Zakynthos	1	33.9	(0.7)	20	3
Turkey, Fethiye	1	30.1	24–35	302	5
Mass (g)					
Cyprus, Alagadi	1	15.3	9.4–21.4	1482	2
Cyprus, western beaches	2	15.9–16.7	12.0–21.5	180–325	1

Source Key: 1. A. Demetropoulos and M. Hadjichristophorou, pers. observ. 2. Loughran et al. 2000. 3. Margaritoulis 1982. 4. Peters et al. 1994. 5. Türkozan and Baran 1996.

Note: Data taken from hatchlings that emerged naturally from nests in situ.

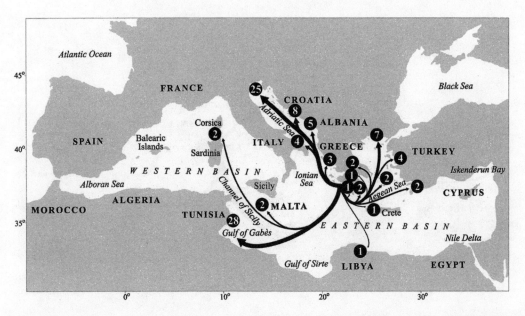

Figure 11.3. Postnesting movements of loggerheads, tagged in Greece from 1982 to 1999, adapted from Margaritoulis (1988c) with the inclusion of unpublished data. From a total of 2,868 females, tagged from 1982 until 1999 at the nesting beaches of Zakynthos and Kyparissia Bay, 100 individuals (3.5%) were recovered at distances longer than 150 km from the respective nesting areas. Of the recovered animals, 28% were found in the Gulf of Gabès, 42% in the Adriatic Sea. Arrows are indicative and do not suggest migratory paths.

Migrations and Marine Habitats

Migrations within the Mediterranean

Postnesting movements of turtles tagged in Greece show a wide dispersion in the eastern basin, with marked clusters of recaptures at the Gulf of Gabès and the Adriatic Sea; only two females were recovered in the western basin (Margaritoulis 1988c; Figure 11.3). An Italian project (Argano et al. 1992) was operated in collaboration with fishermen from 1981 until 1990. During this period, 1,047 loggerheads, mostly juveniles, were tagged after their capture (mostly in longlines). Of these, 51 (4.9%) have been recovered at both the eastern and western basins, showing active passage in both directions through the Channel of Sicily and the Straits of Messina. Some individuals were recaptured in the same area after one, two, or four years, suggesting a possibility of site fidelity. As in the postnesting females from Greece, a proportion of juveniles, tagged after their capture in a particular longline fishery in the north Ionian Sea, showed similar clusters of recaptures in the re-

gion of the Gulf of Gabès and in the Adriatic Sea (Figure 11.4). One individual from this group was recovered outside the Mediterranean (Portugal).

Analyses of tag recoveries in the Adriatic provide evidence of a possible postnesting pathway along the eastern coast (Lazar et al. 2000). The use of satellite telemetry, which has already been undertaken on a small scale in the Mediterranean (Bentivegna and Paglialonga 1998; Hays et al. 1991), will play an important role in future determination of migratory routes.

Analyzing information on incidental catch, solicited through inquiries in the longline fishery of Alicante (Spain), Camiñas and de la Serna (1995) developed a seasonal migration model for the western basin (Figure 11.5). According to the model, juvenile stocks, originating from both the Mediterranean and the Atlantic, increase in spring and reach their highest number in July (spring migration). After that, part of the stock gradually moves towards the Alboran Sea, where it stays until December, then disappears. Another part follows the Algerian current to the warmer waters of the eastern Mediter-

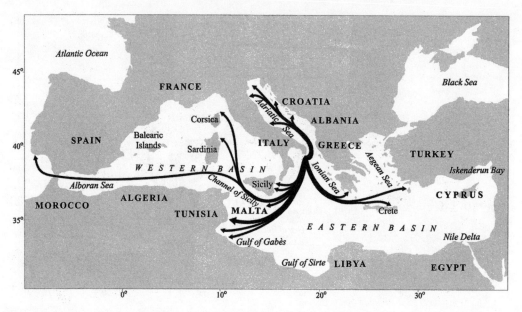

Figure 11.4. Tag returns of mostly juvenile loggerheads, tagged (and released) after capture in northern Ionian Sea, adapted from Argano et al. (1992). Arrows are indicative and do not suggest migratory routes.

ranean (autumn migration). During winter few turtles remain around the Balearic Islands. Furthermore, data analysis in the Gibraltar area shows the entry of Atlantic specimens during the spring and an exit at the end of the summer (Camiñas 1997a).

The wider dispersal of juvenile loggerheads, in comparison with green turtles, has been noted in the eastern Mediterranean through analysis of size distribution in stranding data (Baran and Kasparek 1989b; Godley et al. 1998a).

Oceanic Zone

High incidental captures in pelagic fisheries, that is, drifting longlines and drift nets, and analysis of size class distribution (see Laurent 1998a and references therein), as well as recaptures of tagged juvenile specimens (Argano et al. 1992) provide evidence that both Mediterranean basins are exploited by oceanic stage juveniles (see Figure 11.2).

Neritic Zone

The benthic habitats in the neritic zone are used as foraging grounds by both juveniles and adults (Musick and Limpus 1997). Analyses of size distribution in Mediterranean turtle by-catch, notably in shallow waters, as through bottom trawling (Laurent 1998a and references therein), have revealed that benthic foraging habitats are found mainly in the eastern basin (Laurent and Lescure 1994; Laurent et al. 1996). This is consistent with studies of tag recoveries (Argano et al. 1992; Lazar et al. 2000; Margaritoulis 1988c).

Following the high percentage of tag returns (see Figure 11.3), the Gulf of Gabès, an intensively fished shallow area of about 77,000 km², was originally thought to be a wintering area for the adult loggerhead population nesting in Greece (Margaritoulis 1988c). However, analysis of recaptures by the Italian tagging project (Argano et al. 1992), as well as research results in Tunisia (Bradai 1992; Laurent and Lescure 1994), revealed that juveniles also frequent this area. Dietary analyses of 31 digestive tract samples showed that loggerheads were actively feeding on benthic invertebrates, mostly gastropods, hermit crabs, holothurians, and lamellibranchs, at sea water temperatures between 16.3°C and 17.1°C (Laurent and Lescure 1994).

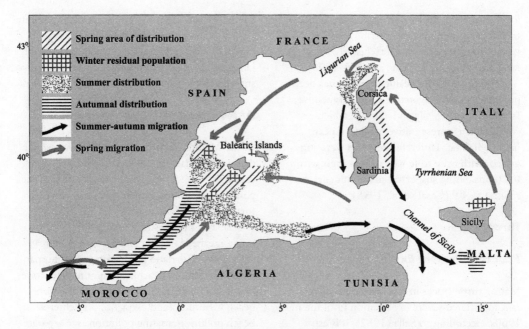

Figure 11.5. Model of loggerhead migrations in the western Mediterranean Sea, adapted from Camiñas and de la Serna (1995).

A similar phenomenon seems to occur in the Adriatic Sea (Argano et al. 1992; Lazar 1995; Lazar and Tvrtkovic 1995; Lazar et al. 2000; Margaritoulis 1988c), where a high incidence of turtle bycatch in the winter, through bottom trawling, has been recorded (Lazar and Tvrtkovic 1995). Preliminary data on stomach contents of turtles in a shallow (< 50 m) continental shelf of the northern Adriatic revealed echinoids and crustaceans as major prey groups (Lazar et al. 2002).

Other large continental shelf areas where large-sized loggerheads interact with bottom trawling activities, namely the bays of Mersin and Iskenderun in Turkey (Laurent et al. 1996; Oruç et al. 1997) and the Nile Delta in Egypt (Laurent et al. 1996, 1998) might also contain important neritic habitats (see Figure 11.2).

Stock Composition at Marine Habitats

Since the western Mediterranean holds no nesting grounds, the relatively large number of juvenile loggerheads caught incidentally in pelagic fisheries raised the question as to their origin. It was initially suggested that the juveniles were derived mostly from populations nesting in the eastern Mediterranean and, in part, from the Atlantic (Argano and Baldari 1983). On the other hand, while comparing loggerhead sizes in the western Atlantic, the Azores, and the Balearic islands, Carr (1987) hypothesized that loggerheads originating from beaches in the western Atlantic follow a transatlantic migration and that some of them enter the Mediterranean. This has been corroborated by recoveries in the Mediterranean of loggerheads tagged in the western Atlantic (Basso and Cocco 1986; Bolten et al. 1992; Manzella et al. 1988).

Genetic markers, identified recently for nesting populations in the Mediterranean, confirmed the suspected demographic link between nesting colonies in the eastern basin and oceanic juvenile feeding aggregates in the western Mediterranean. Indeed, from analysis of cytochrome b and control region haplotype frequencies, it was estimated that 53–55% of the oceanic loggerheads in both the western and eastern basins were derived from Mediterranean nesting populations, and the rest were derived from the western Atlantic (Laurent et al. 1998). On the other hand, genetic identification of large juvenile and adult loggerheads caught by bottom trawlers (and therefore, presumably, in a neritic stage) revealed that they originated exclusively from Mediterranean stocks (Laurent et al. 1998).

The sex ratio of oceanic juveniles has been preliminarily investigated around Lampedusa Island, between Sicily and Tunisia, which is considered a representative Mediterranean oceanic habitat. Different scenarios were suggested, with male to female ratios ranging from 0.8 (considering suspected stress influence on results) to 4.9 (Casale et al. 1998).

Threats

Past and Present Exploitation

Marine turtle stocks in the eastern Mediterranean suffered severe exploitation until the mid 1960s. According to Sella (1982), it is estimated that from the end of the First World War until the mid-1930s at least 30,000 turtles, both green turtles and loggerheads, were caught offshore of what is now Israel. A similar situation developed in the 1950s at Iskenderun Bay, where a slaughterhouse operated. Although that turtle harvest was primarily aimed at green turtles, it is thought that loggerhead stocks were also affected. In Italy, Di Palma (1978) noted that before 1980 a specialized fishery operated in the Isole Eolie, north of Sicily, catching an estimated 500–600 turtles annually. Even though fishing of turtles has been prohibited in Italy since 1980, the exploitation of accidentally caught turtles allows the existence of some local traditions connected with the consumption of turtle meat (Argano et al. 1990; Basso and Cocco 1986) and the illegal selling of turtle shells (Argano et al. 1990; Vallini, in press). Turtles were also sold until recently in Malta (Gramentz 1989), Spain (Mayol and Castello Mas 1983), and Algeria and Morocco (Laurent 1990). In Tunisia, although selling of turtles in fish markets was stopped in 1990, there is still a clandestine trade for local consumption (Laurent et al. 1996) as well as occasional consumption by fishermen onboard their vessels (M. N. Bradai, pers. observ.).

Today, exploitation of turtles is still undertaken openly in Egypt, where both loggerheads and green turtles are sold in fish markets, despite legislation forbidding the practice. It is estimated that several thousand turtles are probably killed annually in Egypt, with loggerheads constituting 68% of the total (Laurent et al. 1996).

At Nesting and Internesting Areas

In the Mediterranean, a general anthropogenic degradation has been noted at almost all significant nesting sites, and some areas known in the past to host nesting activity have been lost to turtles (e.g., Malta) or severely degraded (e.g., Israel). The main anthropogenic threats affecting loggerhead nesting and internesting areas include vehicular and pedestrian traffic, human presence at night, beachfront lighting and noise, uncontrolled development and construction, beach furniture, sand extraction, beach erosion, beach pollution, marine pollution (see separate section below), planting of vegetation, boat strikes (see separate section below), near-shore fishing, and use of underwater explosives. The Mediterranean is the destination of millions of tourists during summer months, coinciding with the nesting season. The extensive urbanization of the coastline, especially in areas with sandy beaches, largely aimed at tourism and recreation, is probably the most serious threat.

The assumed decline in turtle populations and reduction of nesting habitats has triggered management programs to address the seemingly natural loss due to nest predation. Loggerhead nests in the Mediterranean are subject to predation by wild canids, feral/domestic dogs and, to a lesser extent, ghost crabs. Wild canids are absent from the islands of Zakynthos, Crete, and Kefalonia. The loss of loggerhead clutches to predators has been recorded as 48.4% at Kyparissia Bay, Greece (Margaritoulis 1988b), 70–80% in Dalyan, Turkey (Erk'akan 1993), 36.0% (including green turtle clutches) in Cyprus (Broderick and Godley 1996), and 44.8% in Libya (Laurent et al. 1995).

Incidental Catch and Mortality

There is a significant bycatch of sea turtles in various Mediterranean fisheries. The most severe catch occurs around the Balearic Islands where it is estimated that between 1,950 and more than 35,000 juveniles are caught annually in the drifting longline fishery (Aguilar et al. 1995; Camiñas 1988, 1997b; Mayol and Castello Mas 1983). Total bycatch also seems to be high in "less industrialized" fisheries such as those using gill nets and bottom longlines, which are widespread and difficult to assess. Furthermore, data on the turtle bycatch of several non-Mediterranean fleets fishing in the Mediterranean (Aguilar et al. 1995) are lacking. A description of fisheries in the Mediterranean and a review of incidental captures of marine turtles are found in Gerosa and Casale (1999).

Direct mortality is generally low in trawlers and highest in gill nets and trammel nets (Gerosa and Casale 1999; Laurent 1998a; and references therein). Although captures in drifting longlines seem to be low in direct mortality, their subsequent effect has not been adequately documented. Aguilar et al. (1995) have reported a delayed mortality of 24.4%, which is alarming, considering the thousands of juvenile loggerheads caught annually in this fishery. Although some turtles caught incidentally are used for local consumption, a number of turtles are killed by fishermen for various and rather obscure reasons such as antagonism, prejudice, and ignorance (Gerosa and Casale 1999; Godley et al. 1998b). A stranding data analysis in Cyprus revealed that over 40% of the sample had skull injuries (Godley et al. 1998c), whereas from a sample of 524 strandings (90% loggerheads) along the coasts of Greece, over 23% had injuries presumably inflicted intentionally after capture (Kopsida et al. 2002).

Boat Strike

The effect of speedboats is of great concern in turtle-frequented waters with dense tourist activities. Losses of nesting females were documented at Zakynthos in 1993 (Margaritoulis and Dimopoulos 1994) and, more recently, in Rethymno, Crete (D. Margaritoulis and T. Belalidis, pers. observ.). From a sample of 42 loggerheads recovered in the Gulf of Naples, 28.1% had injuries attributed to boat strikes (Bentivegna and Paglialonga 1998), and from a total of 524 strandings (90% loggerheads) along

the coasts of Greece, 9% had injuries caused by boat strikes (Kopsida et al. 2002).

Marine Pollution

Although parts of the Mediterranean are profoundly polluted, little is known of the effects of contaminants on marine turtles. Twenty out of 99 loggerheads examined in the Maltese islands were contaminated, mostly with crude oil (Gramentz 1988). However, a similar examination in Turkey and Cyprus showed that very few animals were affected (Godley et al. 1998a). As loggerhead turtles are long-lived animals, they have been shown to be bioaccumulators of heavy metals (Storelli et al. 1998a, 1998b). Heavy metal burdens in loggerhead turtles are similar to or lower than corresponding concentrations in turtles from Japan (Godley et al. 1999), and a study to determine chlorobiphenyls and organochlorine pesticide residues in tissues collected from green and loggerhead turtles in the Mediterranean found burdens to be low but higher in the omnivorous loggerheads (McKenzie et al. 1999). Marine debris has been found to affect Mediterranean loggerheads (Basso 1992; Gramentz 1988). In the Gulf of Naples, over a period of four years (1993–1996), about 3% of the juvenile loggerheads recovered had swallowed various marine litter (Bentivegna and Paglialonga 1998). In a digestive tract analysis in the Adriatic, a juvenile loggerhead was found with plastic, nylon ropes, and Styrofoam pieces in its gut (Lazar et al. 2002).

Conservation

Legal and Regulatory Aspects

There are several international conventions containing provisions applicable to marine turtles in the Mediterranean region. The one with the highest regional importance is the Convention for the Protection of the Marine Environment and the Coastal Region of the Mediterranean (Barcelona Convention), to which all Mediterranean countries (except the former Yugoslavia) are parties. In the context of the convention, the parties adopted in 1989 and revised in 1999 the Action Plan for the Conservation of

Mediterranean Marine Turtles (see RAC/SPA 1998). Coordination of activities for the implementation of the Action Plan is undertaken by the RAC/SPA, based in Tunis. Furthermore, priority actions for implementing the Action Plan have been adopted by the parties at both regional and national levels (RAC/SPA 1999). Another important supranational instrument is the Convention on the Conservation of European Wildlife and Natural Habitats (Bern Convention), which has taken a leading role (with an effective administrative structure) in establishing specific recommendations for countries hosting nesting habitats. More recently, the Convention on the Conservation of Migratory Species of Wild Animals (CMS, the Bonn Convention) became active in the region.

Other instruments originate from the European Union, whose member states must comply with various regulations and directives, decided by the European Parliament. The Habitats Directive (no. 92/43), featuring the loggerhead turtle among "priority" species, aims at the establishment of a coherent network of protected sites, known as Natura 2000.

Most Mediterranean countries have developed national legislation to protect sea turtles. Species-specific protective legislation generally prohibits intentional killing, harassment, possession, trade, or attempts at these. Furthermore, some countries have taken steps towards introducing site-specific legislation for turtle habitats. The nesting areas at Zakynthos have been protected since 1984 under a presidential decree that restricts building and development behind the nesting beaches. These regulations have been recently (December 1999) incorporated into new legislation establishing a National Marine Park in the area, including maritime restrictions. In Turkey, the nesting beaches of Belek, Dalyan, Fethiye, Göksu Delta, and Patara were designated a Specially Protected Area (SPA), in the context of the Barcelona Convention. In Cyprus, the nesting beaches of Lara and Toxeftra (about 10 km of coastline), including a maritime zone extending to the 20 m isobath, have been protected since 1989 under the Fisheries Regulation. In Italy, a reserve for the protection of the nesting beach on Lampedusa was established in 1984.

Protection of Populations and Habitats

In the case of nesting areas, usual management practices involve mitigating abiotic, biotic, and anthropogenic factors that may adversely affect incubation and hatching. These have been in effect for several years in most Mediterranean nesting areas. In some countries (e.g., Cyprus, Israel) competent state agencies undertake this responsibility, while in other countries (e.g., Greece, Italy) this is mostly done by nongovernmental organizations with varying support from the state. Universities and research institutes, in the course of their research programs, have also taken up management responsibilities.

Protection of marine habitats, both oceanic and neritic, is at an early stage. This is apparently a combined result of the relative paucity of data on these habitats, the difficulty in their delineation, and above all, the high-value economic activities involved (e.g., fisheries). The revised Action Plan for the Conservation of Mediterranean Marine Turtles contains several provisions regarding the identification of, the assessment of threats to, and the protection of marine habitats (RAC/SPA 1998). A priority for Mediterranean populations should be the reduction of human impacts (especially fishing-induced mortality) affecting the large-sized classes, which are more important for the population's viability (Laurent et al. 1992), in the neritic habitats of the eastern Mediterranean (Laurent 1998b).

The relatively high degree of public sensitization, noted the last few years in the Mediterranean, has required the development of an appropriate infrastructure to rehabilitate injured or sick turtles. This need is currently covered either in existing aquaria or in specially established rescue centers (Bentivegna et al. 1993; Corsini 1996; Gerosa and Cocco 1990; Pont and Alegre 2000; Schofield and Kopsida 2000). However, hospitalizing sea turtles should not be considered as a solution to the serious problem of intentional and incidental mortality at sea.

Public Awareness, Education, and Capacity Building

At a regional level, the RAC/SPA promotes capacity building on sea turtle conservation techniques by organizing or supporting practical courses and training seminars. Furthermore, it supports field surveys, production of informative material, and elaboration of specific reports and manuals (Demetropoulos and Hadjichristophorou 1995; Gerosa 1996; Gerosa and Casale 1999). Public awareness projects on behalf of sea turtles, either aiming at specific target groups or at the general public, are conducted in several Mediterranean countries (Dimopoulos 1995; Kuller 1999; Lazar and Tvrtkovic in RAC/SPA 1998; Margaritoulis 1998). Present trends, in line with the IUCN Global Strategy for the Conservation of Marine Turtles (Donnelly 1995), advocate that local stakeholders be incorporated in any conservation plan. Inhabitants and visitors of nesting areas are sensitized on site and, in several cases, through involvement of the tourist industry (Gerosa 1992; Margaritoulis 1998). Children comprise an important target group. Using the sea turtle as a "flagship" species, presentations by talented animators, specially designed traveling kits to be deployed by teachers, and guided visits to nesting areas and rescue centers sensitize children and prepare the ground for participation in future conservation practices (Bentivegna 1998; Kremezi-Margaritouli 1992; Kuller 1999).

Conclusions

The Mediterranean holds a remarkable loggerhead breeding population, with morphological and genetic differentiation. The noted population substructuring makes the Mediterranean population as a whole more vulnerable, and breeding colonies must be considered as separate management units.

Although progress has been made in the protection of some nesting areas, providing adequate protection to additional significant nesting beaches is a priority action. The implementation and enforcement of legal measures specified for nesting beaches and the improvement of the effectiveness of beach management are also priority issues.

At the same time there is a need to identify the different management units and assess the anthropogenic impacts affecting them, across all habitats. Fisheries interaction should be of special concern, taking into account that early juveniles use oceanic habitats in both Mediterranean basins, while large juveniles and adults exploit neritic habitats confined to the eastern basin.

Conservation of marine turtles in the Mediterranean is a complicated endeavor involving many nations and a diversity of human activities on land and at sea, requiring both a regional approach and considerable effort at the national level. The provisions of the Action Plan, in the context of the Barcelona Convention, and the ensuing priorities for its implementation are a great step towards this goal.

ACKNOWLEDGMENTS

The authors would like to acknowledge the generous help of their coworkers in the free provision of unpublished data for this review. Although regional, supranational, governmental, and nongovernmental bodies and organizations support work on Mediterranean marine turtles, much of this information would not have been collected without the vast volunteer effort that is mobilized in the region each year. Lenio Karatzas kindly prepared the figures.

LITERATURE CITED

Aguilar, R., J. Mas, and X. Pastor. 1995. Impact of Spanish swordfish longline fisheries on the loggerhead sea turtle *Caretta caretta* population in the western Mediterranean. *In* J. I. Richardson and T. H. Richardson (compilers). Proceedings of the 12th annual workshop on sea turtle biology and conservation, 1–6. NOAA Technical Memorandum NMFS-SEFSC-361.

Argano, R. 1979. Preliminary report on western Mediterranean sea turtles. Annual report on WWF project 1474. Rome.

Argano, R., and F. Baldari. 1983. Status of western Mediterranean sea turtles. Rapports et procès-verbaux des réunions de la Commission Internationale pour l'Exploration Scientifique de la Mer Méditerranée 28:233–235.

Argano, R., M. Cocco, G. Gerosa, and C. Jacomini. 1990. Relazione attività 1988/89. Progetto tartarughe marine. Rome: WWF–Italy and University "La Sapienza."

Argano, R., R. Basso, M. Cocco, and G. Gerosa. 1992. New data on loggerhead *(Caretta caretta)* movements within Mediterranean. Bollettino del Museo dell' Istituto di Biologia dell' Università di Genova 56–57:137–164.

Ashkenazi, S., and A. Sofer. 1988. Conservation of the endangered sea turtles *Chelonia mydas* and *Caretta caretta* in Israel. Rapports et procès-verbaux des réunions de la Commission Internationale pour l'Exploration Scientifique de la Mer Méditerranée 31:286.

Baran, I., and M. Kasparek. 1989a. Marine turtles Turkey. Status survey 1988 and recommendations for conservation and management. Heidelberg, Germany: WWF.

———. 1989b. On the whereabouts of immature sea turtles (*Caretta caretta* and *Chelonia mydas*) in the eastern Mediterranean. Zoology in the Middle East 3:31–36.

Baran, I., and O. Türkozan. 1996. Nesting activity of the loggerhead turtle, *Caretta caretta*, on Fethiye beach, Turkey, in 1994. Chelonian Conservation and Biology 2:93–96.

Basso, R. 1992. Osservazioni e ricerce sulle tartarughe marine presenti nei mari italiani. Lecce, Italy: Edizione del Grifo.

———. 1996. Primi documentati casi di schiusa sul litorale del mare Adriatico di tartaruga comune *(Caretta caretta)* con l' ausilio di unità cinofile. *In* Atti del Convegno su la fauna degli Iblei, 153–157. Noto, Italy: Ente Fauna Siciliana.

Basso, R., and M. Cocco. 1986. Il progetto nazionale tartarughe marine. Thalassia Salentina 16:65–72.

Bentivegna, F. 1998. Loggerhead sea turtle conservation in the Gulf of Naples. *In* S. P. Epperly and J. Braun (compilers). Proceedings of the 17th annual sea turtle symposium, 10. NOAA Technical Memorandum NMFS-SEFSC-415.

Bentivegna, F., and A. Paglialonga. 1998. Status of the sea turtles in the Gulf of Naples and preliminary study of migration. *In* S. P. Epperly and J. Braun (compilers). Proceedings of the 17th annual sea turtle symposium, 141–144. NOAA Technical Memorandum NMFS-SEFSC-415.

Bentivegna, F., P. Cirino, and A. Toscano. 1993. Care and treatment of loggerhead sea turtles from the Gulf of Naples, Italy. Marine Turtle Newsletter 61:6–7.

Bolten, A. B., H. R. Martins, K. A. Bjorndal, M. Cocco, and G. Gerosa. 1992. *Caretta caretta* (loggerhead). Pelagic movement and growth. Herpetological Review 23:116.

Bowen, B. W., J. C. Avise, J. I. Richardson, A. B. Meylan, D. Margaritoulis, and S. R. Hopkins-Murphy. 1993. Population structure of loggerhead turtles *(Caretta caretta)* in the northwestern Atlantic Ocean and Mediterranean Sea. Conservation Biology 7:834–844.

Bradai, M. N. 1992. Les captures accidentelles de *Caretta caretta* au chalut benthique dans le Golfe de Gabès. Rapports et procès-verbaux des réunions de la Commission Internationale pour l'Exploration Scientifique de la Mer Méditerranée 33:285.

———. 1995. Nidification de la caouanne *Caretta caretta* sur les plages sud-est de la Tunisie. Rapports et Procès-verbaux des réunions de la Commission Internationale pour l'Exploration Scientifique de la Mer Méditerranée 34:237.

———. 1996. La nidification de la tortue marine *Caretta caretta* aux îles Kuriates. Bulletin de l'Institut National des Sciences et Technologies de la Mer, numéro spécial 3:68–71.

Broderick, A. C., and B. J. Godley. 1996. Population and nesting ecology of the green turtle, *Chelonia mydas*, and the loggerhead turtle, *Caretta caretta*, in northern Cyprus. Zoology in the Middle East 13:27–46.

Broderick, A. C., B. J. Godley, A. Kelly, and A. McGowan. 1997. Glasgow University turtle conservation expedition to northern Cyprus 1995. Expedition report. Swansea: Marine Turtle Research Group, University of Wales.

Broderick, A. C., F. Glen, and B. J. Godley. 1999. Marine turtle conservation project, northern Cyprus project report 1999. Swansea, U.K.: Marine Turtle Research Group, University of Wales.

Camiñas, J. A. 1988. Incidental captures of *Caretta caretta* (L.) with surface long-lines in the western Mediterranean. Rapports et Procès-verbaux des réunions de la Commission Internationale pour l'Exploration Scientifique de la Mer Méditerranée 31:285.

———. 1997a. Relación entre las poblaciones de la tortuga boba *(Caretta caretta)* procedentes del Atlántico y del Mediterráneo y efecto de la pesca sobre las mismas en la región del Estrecho de Gibraltar. *In* Serie Congresos 9, Universidad de Murcia, Aulas del Mar, Biologia Pesquera (1995–1996), 131–146.

———. 1997b. Captura accidental de tortuga boba *(Caretta caretta)* en el Mediterráneo con palangre de superficie. Colección de Documentos Científicos, ICCAT 44:446–455.

Camiñas, J. A., and J. M. de la Serna. 1995. The loggerhead distribution in the western Mediterranean Sea as deducted from captures by the Spanish long line fishery. Scientia Herpetologica 1995:316–323.

Carr, A. 1987. New perspectives on the pelagic stage of sea turtle development. Conservation Biology 1:103–121.

Casale, P., G. Gerosa, R. Argano, S. Barbaro, and G. Fontana. 1998. Testosterone titers of immature loggerhead sea turtles *(Caretta caretta)* incidentally caught in the central Mediterranean: A preliminary sex ratio study. Chelonian Conservation and Biology 3:90–93.

Clarke, M., A. C. Campbell, W. S. Hameid, and S. Ghoneim. 2000. Preliminary report on the status of marine turtle nesting populations on the Mediterranean coast of Egypt. Biological Conservation 94:363–371.

Cocco, M., and G. Gerosa. 1990. Progetto tartarughe marine. Rapporto attività 1990. WWF–Italy. Rome: Dipartimento di Biologia Animal e dell'Uomo, University "La Sapienza."

Corsini, M. 1996. Notes on the efforts to treat sea turtles. Biologia Gallo-Hellenica 23:3–12.

Delaugerre, M. 1987. Status of marine turtles in the Mediterranean (with particular reference to Corsica). Vie Milieu 37:243–264.

De Metrio, G., G. Petrosino, A. Matarese, A. Tursi, and C. Montanaro. 1983. Importance of the fishery activities with drift lines on the populations of *Caretta caretta* (L.) and *Dermochelys coriacea* (L.) (Reptilia, Testudines) in the Gulf of Taranto. Oebalia 9:43–53.

Demetropoulos, A., and M. Hadjichristophorou. 1982. Turtle conservation in Cyprus. Bulletin of Biological Society of Cyprus 2:23–26.

———. 1989. Sea turtle conservation in Cyprus. Marine Turtle Newsletter 44:4–6.

———. 1995. Manual on marine turtle conservation in the Mediterranean. Nicosia, Cyprus: UNEP(MAP), RAC/SPA, IUCN, CWS, Fisheries Department/MANRE.

Despott, G. 1915. The reptiles of the Maltese islands. The Zoologist 19:821–827.

Dimopoulos, D. 1995. Aspects of sea turtle conservation efforts in Greece with emphasis on the island of Zakynthos. *In* J. I. Richardson and T. H. Richardson (compilers). Proceedings of the 12th annual workshop on sea turtle biology and conservation, 26–27. NOAA Technical Memorandum NMFS-SEFSC-361.

Di Palma, M. G. 1978. Notizie sulle tartarughe marine in Sicilia. Naturalista Siciliano, ser. 4, 2(1–2):1–6.

Donnelly, M. 1995. A global strategy for marine turtles. Marine Turtle Newsletter 71:17.

Erk'akan, F. 1993. Nesting biology of loggerhead turtles *Caretta caretta* L. on Dalyan Beach, Mugla-Turkey. Biological Conservation 66:1–4.

Freggi, D. 1997. Tartarughe marine a Lampedusa: Osservazioni sulle stagioni riproduttive 1994–1996. *In* Fauna del Mediterraneo: Immagini e note di ecologia marina, 12–48. Quaderni dell'Acquario di Livorno 3. Livorno, Italy: Acquario di Livorno.

Geldiay, R., T. Koray, and S. Balik. 1982. Status of sea

turtle populations *(Caretta c. caretta* and *Chelonia m. mydas)* in the northern Mediterranean Sea, Turkey. *In* K. A. Bjorndal (ed.). Biology and conservation of sea turtles, 425–434. Washington, D.C.: Smithsonian Institution Press.

Gerosa, G. 1992. Relazione sullo stato attuale della "Spiaggia dei Conigli," Lampedusa (AG) (giugno–ottobre 1991). Rome: CHELON, WWF–Italy.

———. 1996. Manual on marine turtle tagging in the Mediterranean. Tunis: UNEP (MAP), RAC/SPA.

Gerosa, G., and P. Casale. 1999. Interaction of marine turtles with fisheries in the Mediterranean. Tunis: UNEP (MAP), RAC/SPA.

Gerosa, G., and M. Cocco. 1990. "Progetto Tartarughe" Handbook. Rome: WWF–Italy.

Gerosa, G., P. Casale, and S. V. Yerli. 1995. Report on a sea turtle nesting beach study (Akyatan, Turkey), 1994. *In* Proceedings of international congress of chelonian conservation, 173–180. Gonfaron, France: Editions SOPTOM.

Gerosa, G., E. Daelli, M. Aureggi, and F. Mazzella. 1998. Marine turtle survey at Rhodes island, Greece, 1997–1998. Rome: CHELON.

Gerosa, G., M. Aureggi, G. Montinaro, and V. Cotroneo. 2000. Identificazione di tre nidi di *Caretta caretta* (Linnaeus 1758) in litorali antropizzati della Calabria Ionica. *In* Atti del 4° Convegno Nazionale sui Cetacei e sulle Tartarughe marine, 23. Milan: Museo Civico di Storia Naturale di Milano. CSC online publications, work 74.

Glen, F., B. J. Godley, A. K. Broderick, and A. C. Broderick. 1997. Marine turtle nesting in the Göksu Delta, Turkey, 1996. Marine Turtle Newsletter 77:17–19.

Godley, B. J., and A. Kelly. 1996. Glasgow University turtle conservation expedition to northern Cyprus 1996. Expedition report. Swansea: Marine Turtle Research Group, University of Wales.

Godley, B. J., R. W. Furness, and S. E. Solomon. 1998a. Patterns of mortality in marine turtles in the eastern Mediterranean. *In* R. Byles and Y. Fernandez (compilers). Proceedings of the 16th annual symposium on sea turtle biology and conservation, 59–61. NOAA Technical Memorandum NMFS-SEFSC-412.

Godley, B. J., A. C. Gücü, A. C. Broderick, R. W. Furness, and S. E. Solomon. 1998b. Interaction between marine turtles and artisanal fisheries in the eastern Mediterranean: A probable cause for concern? Zoology in the Middle East 16:49–64.

Godley, B. J., R. Thomson, and A. C. Broderick. 1998c. Glasgow University turtle conservation expedition to northern Cyprus 1998. Expedition report. Swansea: Marine Turtle Research Group, University of Wales.

Godley, B. J., D. R. Thompson, and R. W. Furness. 1999. Do heavy metal concentrations pose a threat to marine turtles from the Mediterranean Sea? Marine Pollution Bulletin 38:497–502.

Godley, B. J., A. C. Broderick, and N. Mrosovsky. 2001. Estimating hatchling sex ratios of logger-head turtles in Cyprus from incubation durations. Marine Ecology Progress Series 210:159–201.

Gramentz, D. 1988. Involvement of loggerhead turtle with the plastic, metal, and hydrocarbon pollution in the central Mediterranean. Marine Pollution Bulletin 19:11–13.

———. 1989. Marine turtles in the central Mediterranean Sea. Centro 1:41–56.

Groombridge, B., and C. Whitmore. 1989. Marine turtle survey in northern Cyprus. Marine Turtle Newsletter 47:5–8.

Haddoud, D. A., and F. Assigier. In press. Survey of sea turtle in eastern part of Libya. In Proceedings of the premier congrès magrébin des sciences de la mer. Hammamet, Tunisia.

Haddoud, D. A., and H. El Gomati. In press. The coast survey of marine turtle activity along the coast of Libya. Phase 2. Between Sirte and Mis-ratah. Deuxièmes Journées Maghrébines des Sciences de la Mer. Aghezdis, Agadir, Morocco: ISTPM.

Hays, G. C., and J. R. Speakman. 1991. Reproductive investment and optimum clutch size of loggerhead sea turtles (Caretta caretta). Journal of Animal Ecology 69:455–462.

———. 1992. Clutch size for Mediterranean logger-head turtles (Caretta caretta). Journal of Zoology 226:321–327.

Hays, G. C., P. I. Webb, J. P. Hayes, I. G. Priede, and J. French. 1991. Satellite tracking of a loggerhead turtle (Caretta caretta) in the Mediterranean. Journal of Marine Biological Association of the U.K. 71:743–746.

Houghton, J. D. R. 1996. Reasons for egg failure and neonate mortality in the loggerhead turtle (Caretta caretta) on the Greek island of Kefalonia. Thesis, University of Southampton, U.K.

Houghton, J. D. R., and G. C. Hays. 2002. Asyn-chronous emergence by loggerhead turtle (Caretta caretta) hatchlings as a result of in-nest thermal differences. In A. Mosier, A. Foley, and B. Brost (compilers). Proceedings of the 20th annual symposium on sea turtle biology and conserva-tion, 174–177. NOAA Technical Memorandum NMFS-SEFSC-477.

Houghton, J. D. R., D. J. Suggett, and K. T. Hudson. 1997. The Kefalonian marine turtle project: Expe-dition report 1997. Isle of Wight: Kefalonian Ma-rine Turtle Project.

Houghton, J. D. R., D. J. Suggett, S. J. Maynard, S. Sharpe, and M. White. 1998. The Kefalonian marine turtle project: Expedition report 1998. Isle of Wight: Kefalonian Marine Turtle Project.

Kaska, Y., R. Downie, R. Tippett, and R. W. Furness. 1998. Natural temperature regimes for loggerhead and green turtle nests in the eastern Mediter-ranean. Canadian Journal of Zoology 76:723–729.

Kasparek, M. 1993. Marine turtle conservation in the Mediterranean. Marine turtles in Egypt. Phase I. Survey of the Mediterranean coast between Alexandria and El-Salum. Report funded by MEDASSET, RAC/SPA, and NIOF (Egypt), London, U.K.

———. 1995. The nesting of marine turtles on the coast of Syria. Zoology in the Middle East 11:51–62.

Kopsida, H., D. Margaritoulis, and D. Dimopoulos. 2002. What marine turtle strandings can tell us. In A. Mosier, A. Foley, and B. Brost (compilers). Proceedings of the 20th annual symposium on sea turtle biology and conservation, 207–209. NOAA Technical Memorandum NMFS-SEFSC-477.

Kremezi-Margaritouli, A. 1992. Sea turtles stimulate environmental education in Greece. Marine Turtle Newsletter 57:21–22.

Kuller, Z. 1999. Current status and conservation of marine turtles on the Mediterranean coast of Is-rael. Marine Turtle Newsletter 86:3–5.

Laurent, L. 1990. Les tortues marines en Algérie et au Maroc (Méditerranée). Bulletin de la Société Herpétologique de France 55:1–23.

———. 1991. Les tortues marines des côtes françaises Méditerranéennes continentales. Faune de Provence (CEEP) 12:76–90.

———. 1998a. Review and analysis of the available knowledge of marine turtle nesting and popula-tion dynamics in the Mediterranean. UNEP (OCA) MED WG 145/3. Tunis: RAC/SPA (UNEP).

———. 1998b. Conservation management of Mediter-ranean loggerhead sea turtle Caretta caretta popu-lations. Scientific basis for establishing a marine turtle conservation strategy for the Mediterranean. Report on WWF project 9E0103. Rome: WWF International Mediterranean Program.

Laurent, L., S. Nouira, A. Jeudy de Grissac, and M. N. Bradai. 1990. Les tortues marines de Tunisie: Pre-mières données. Bulletin de la Société Herpéto-logique de France 53:1–17.

Laurent, L., J. Lescure, L. Excoffier, B. Bowen, M. Domingo, M. Hadjichristophorou, L. Kor-naraki, and G. Trabuchet. 1993. Genetic studies of relationships between Mediterranean and Atlantic populations of loggerhead turtle *Caretta caretta* with a mitochondrial marker. Compte Rendu de l' Académie des Sciences, Paris 316:1233–1239.

Laurent, L., and J. Lescure. 1994. L'hivernage des tortues caouannes *Caretta caretta* (L.) dans le sud Tunisien. Revue d' Ecologie (Terre et Vie) 49:63–85.

Laurent, L., J. Clobert, and J. Lescure. 1992. The demographic modeling of the Mediterranean loggerhead sea turtle population: First results. Rapports et procès-verbaux des réunions de la Commission Internationale pour l'Exploration Scientifique de la Mer Méditerranée 33:300.

Laurent, L., M. N. Bradai, D. A. Hadoud, and H. E. Gomati. 1995. Marine turtle nesting activity assessment on Libyan coasts. Phase 1. Survey of the coasts between the Egyptian border and Sirte. Tunis: RAC/SPA (UNEP).

Laurent, L., E. M. Abd El-Mawla, M. N. Bradai, F. Demirayak, and A. Oruç. 1996. Reducing sea turtle mortality induced by Mediterranean fisheries: Trawling activity in Egypt, Tunisia and Turkey. Report on WWF project 9E0103. Rome: WWF International Mediterranean Program.

Laurent, L., P. Casale, M. N. Bradai, B. J. Godley, G. Gerosa, A. C. Broderick, W. Schroth, B. Schierwater, A. M. Levy, D. Freggi, E. M. Abd El-Mawla, D. A. Hadoud, H. E. Gomati, M. Domingo, M. Hadjichristophorou, L. Kornaraky, F. Demirayak, and Ch. Gautier. 1998. Molecular resolution of marine turtle stock composition in fishery by-catch: A case study in the Mediterranean. Molecular Ecology 7:1529–1542.

Laurent, L., M. N. Bradai, D. H. Hadoud, H. M. El Gomati, and A. A. Hamza. 1999. Marine turtle nesting activity assessment on Libyan coasts. Phase 3. Survey of the coasts between the Tunisian border and Misratah. Tunis: RAC/SPA (UNEP).

Lazar, B. 1995. Analyses of incidental catch of marine turtles (Reptilia, Cheloniidae) in the eastern part of the Adriatic Sea: Existence of over-wintering areas? *In* N. Ljubesic (ed.). Proceedings of the symposium in honour of Zdravko Lorkovic, 97. Zagreb, Croatia.

Lazar, B., and N. Tvrtkovic. 1995. Marine turtles in the eastern part of the Adriatic Sea: Preliminary research. Natura Croatica 4:59–74.

Lazar, B., N. Tvrtkovic, G. Gerosa, D. Holcer, and I. Grbac. 1997. Adriatic marine turtle program: Results of research on potential marine turtle nesting beaches along the southern coast of Croatia. UNEP/MAP Report 5/97. Tunis: RAC/SPA (UNEP).

Lazar, B., D. Margaritoulis, and N. Tvrtkovic. 2000. Migrations of the loggerhead sea turtle *(Caretta caretta)* into the Adriatic Sea. *In* F. A. Abreu-Grobois, R. Briseño-Dueñas, R. Márquez-Millán and L. Sarti-Martínez (compilers). Proceedings of the 18th international sea turtle symposium, 101–102. NOAA Technical Memorandum NMFS-SEFSC-436.

Lazar, B., D. Zavodnik, I. Grbac, and N. Tvrtkovic. 2002. Diet composition of the loggerhead sea turtle, *Caretta caretta*, in the northern Adriatic Sea: A preliminary study. *In* A. Mosier, A. Foley, and B. Brost (compilers). Proceedings of the 20th annual symposium on sea turtle biology and conservation, 146–147. NOAA Technical Memorandum NMFS-SEFSC-477.

Llorente, G. A., M. A. Carretero, X. Pascual, and A. Perez. 1992/93. New record of a nesting loggerhead turtle *Caretta caretta* in western Mediterranean. British Herpetological Society Bulletin 42:14–17.

Loughran, A. L., A. C. Broderick, B. J. Godley, and R. W. Furness. 2000. Factors affecting size of loggerhead and green turtle hatchlings in northern Cyprus, eastern Mediterranean. *In* F. A. Abreu-Grobois, R. Briseño-Dueñas, R. Márquez-Millán and L. Sarti-Martínez (compilers). Proceedings of the 18th international sea turtle symposium, 200–201. NOAA Technical Memorandum NMFS-SEFSC-436.

MacLean, A., J. Crane, S. Freeman, D. Lundie, and J. Mendum. 1998. Loggerhead nesting on Akrotiri Peninsula, Cyprus. Marine Turtle Newsletter 79:23–24.

Manzella, S. A., C. T. Fontaine, and B. A. Schroeder. 1988. Loggerhead sea turtle travels from Padre Island, Texas to the mouth of the Adriatic Sea. Marine Turtle Newsletter 42:7.

Margaritoulis, D. 1982. Observations on loggerhead sea turtle *Caretta caretta* activity during three nesting seasons (1977–1979) in Zakynthos, Greece. Biological Conservation 24:193–204.

———. 1983. The inter-nesting interval of Zakynthos loggerheads. *In* N. S. Margaris, M. Arianoutsou-Faraggitaki, and R. J. Reiter (eds.). Adaptations to terrestrial environments, 135–144. New York: Plenum Press.

———. 1987. Nesting activity and factors affecting breeding of the loggerhead sea turtle *Caretta caretta* (L.) in Greece. Report to the EEC on project ENV-790-GR. Athens: Ministry of Environment.

———. 1988a. Nesting activity of the loggerhead turtle on Zakynthos island during 1986 and 1987 nesting seasons. Athens: Ministry of Environment.

———. 1988b. Nesting of the loggerhead sea turtle *Caretta caretta* on the shores of Kyparissia Bay, Greece, in 1987. Mésogée 48:59–65.

———. 1988c. Post-nesting movements of loggerhead sea turtles tagged in Greece. Rapports et Procès-verbaux des réunions de la Commission Internationale pour l'Exploration Scientifique de la Mer Méditerranée 31:284.

———. 1988d. Monitoring of loggerhead sea turtle nesting in the Bay of Kyparissia, during 1988. Athens: Sea Turtle Protection Society.

———. 1989. Determination of nesting habitats of *Caretta caretta* in Greece, 1989: Western Peloponnesus. Report to the EEC on project 6610/89/39. Athens: Sea Turtle Protection Society.

———. 1993. Monitoring and conservation of the loggerhead turtle in Greece during 1990–1992: Zakynthos, western Peloponnesus, Lakonikos Bay, Crete. Report to the EEC on project MedSPA-90-1/GR/28/GR/05. Athens: Sea Turtle Protection Society.

———. 1996. Recovery of the loggerhead sea turtle populations nesting on Crete. Report to the EEC on project LIFE95/GR/A22/GR/01115/KRI. Athens: Sea Turtle Protection Society.

———. 1998. On the island of Crete: A new nesting area of the loggerhead turtle in the Mediterranean. *In* R. Byles and Y. Fernandez (compilers). Proceedings of the 16th annual symposium on sea turtle biology and conservation, 98–100. NOAA Technical Memorandum NMFS-SEFSC-412.

———. 2000. An estimation of the overall nesting activity of the loggerhead turtle in Greece. *In* F. A. Abreu-Grobois, R. Briseño-Dueñas, R. Márquez-Millán and L. Sarti-Martínez (compilers). Proceedings of the 18th international sea turtle symposium, 48–50. NOAA Technical Memorandum NMFS-SEFSC-436.

Margaritoulis, D., and T. Arapis. 1990. Monitoring and conservation of the loggerhead sea turtle *Caretta caretta* in Greece. Report to WWF International on project 3825. Athens: Sea Turtle Protection Society.

Margaritoulis, D., and D. Dimopoulos. 1993. The loggerhead sea turtle *Caretta caretta* on Zakynthos. An update of monitoring and conservation work. Athens: Sea Turtle Protection Society.

———. 1994. The loggerhead sea turtle on Zakynthos. Population status and conservation efforts during 1993. Report to WWF–Greece on project 0034.03. Athens: Sea Turtle Protection Society.

———. 1995. The loggerhead sea turtle on Zakynthos. Population status and conservation efforts during 1994. Report to WWF–Greece on project 0034.03. Athens: Sea Turtle Protection Society.

Margaritoulis, D., and J. Sioris. 1997. The loggerhead sea turtle on Crete. An update of conservation work during 1996. Report to the EC on project LIFE95/GR/A22/GR/01115/KRI. Athens: Sea Turtle Protection Society.

Margaritoulis, D., D. Dimopoulos, and L. Kornaraki. 1991. Monitoring and conservation of *Caretta caretta* on Zakynthos during 1990. Athens: Sea Turtle Protection Society.

———. 1992. The loggerhead sea turtle on Zakynthos. An update of monitoring and conservation work during 1991. Athens: Sea Turtle Protection Society.

Margaritoulis, D., M. Dretakis, and A. Kotitsas. 1995a. Discovering new nesting areas of *Caretta caretta* in Greece. *In* J. I. Richardson and T. H. Richardson (compilers). Proceedings of the 12th annual workshop on sea turtle biology and conservation, 214–217. NOAA Technical Memorandum NMFS-SEFSC-361.

Margaritoulis, D., D. Dimopoulos, and C. Irvine. 1996a. The loggerhead sea turtle on Zakynthos. Population status and conservation efforts during 1995. Report to WWF–Greece on project 0034.03. Athens: Sea Turtle Protection Society.

Margaritoulis, D., C. Pappa, and G. Hiras. 1996b. Conservation work at the nesting areas of *Caretta caretta* on Peloponnesus during 1995 (Kyparissia Bay, Lakonikos Bay, Strophilia-Kotychi). Report to WWF–Greece on project 0034.03. Athens: Sea Turtle Protection Society.

Margaritoulis, D., D. Dimopoulos, and K. Katselidis. 1997. The loggerhead sea turtle on Zakynthos. Population status and conservation efforts during 1996. Athens: Sea Turtle Protection Society.

———. 1998a. The loggerhead sea turtle on Zakynthos. Monitoring and conservation work during 1997. Athens: Sea Turtle Protection Society.

Margaritoulis, D., C. Pappa, and K. Teneketzis. 1994. Monitoring and conservation of the *Caretta caretta* populations at Kyparissia Bay and Lakonikos Bay, during 1993. Report to WWF–Greece on project 0034.03. Athens: Sea Turtle Protection Society.

———. 1995b. Monitoring and conservation of the *Caretta caretta* populations at Kyparissia Bay and Lakonikos Bay, during 1994. Report to WWF–Greece on project 0034.03. Athens: Sea Turtle Protection Society.

Margaritoulis, D., A. F. Rees, M. Michalopoulos, and Y. Dracopoulos. 1999. Monitoring and conservation of the loggerhead nesting population in southern Kyparissia Bay, during 1998. Athens: Sea Turtle Protection Society.

Margaritoulis, D., A. F. Rees, M. Michalopoulos, H. Olsen, and A. Sahinidis. 2000. Monitoring and conservation of the loggerhead nesting population in southern Kyparissia Bay, during 1999. Athens: Sea Turtle Protection Society.

Margaritoulis, D., J. Sioris, and Th. Belalidis. 1998b. The loggerhead sea turtle on Crete. An update of conservation work during 1997. Report to the EC on project LIFE95/GR/A22/GR/01115/KRI. Athens: Sea Turtle Protection Society.

Mayol, J., and M. Castello Mas. 1983. Contribuion al conocimiento de la Tortuga Boba en las Baleares. Palma de Mallorca, Spain: ICONA.

McKenzie, C., B. J. Godley, R. W. Furness, and D. E. Wells. 1999. Concentrations and patterns of organochlorine contaminants in marine turtles from Mediterranean and Atlantic waters. Marine Environmental Research 4:117–135.

Meininger, L., P. A. Wolf, D. A. Hadoud, and M. F. Essghaier. 1994. Ornithological survey of the coast of Libya, July 1993. Report 46. Zeist, The Netherlands: WIWO.

Miller, A. 1983. The Mediterranean Sea. A. Physical aspects. In B. H. Ketchum (ed.). Estuaries and enclosed seas, 219–238. Amsterdam: Elsevier.

Musick, J. A., and C. J. Limpus. 1997. Habitat utilization and migration in juvenile sea turtles. In P. L. Lutz and J. A. Musick (eds.). The biology of sea turtles, 137–163. Boca Raton, Fla.: CRC Press.

Oruç, A., F. Demirayak, and G. Sat. 1997. Trawl fisheries in the eastern Mediterranean and its impact on sea turtles. Istanbul: DHKD.

Peters, A., K. J. F. Verhoeven, and H. Strijbosch. 1994. Hatching and emergence in the Turkish Mediterranean loggerhead turtle Caretta caretta: Natural causes for egg and hatchling failure. Herpetologica 50:369–373.

Pont, S., and F. Alegre. 2000. Work of the Foundation for the Conservation and Recovery of Marine Life. Marine Turtle Newsletter 87:5–7.

RAC/SPA (ed.). 1998. Report. Meeting of experts on the implementation of the action plan for the conservation of Mediterranean marine turtles adopted within MAP. UNEP (OCA) MED WG 145/4. Tunis: RAC/SPA (UNEP).

RAC/SPA (ed.). 1999. Report. Meeting of experts on priority actions for the implementation of the action plan for the conservation of Mediterranean marine turtles. UNEP (OCA) MED WG 152/4. Tunis: RAC/SPA (UNEP).

Ragonese, S., and P. Jereb. 1992. On a nesting of the loggerhead turtle (Caretta caretta L. 1758) along the southern coast of Sicily (Mediterranean Sea). Rapports et Procès-verbaux des réunions de la Commission Internationale pour l'Exploration Scientifique de la Mer Méditerranée 33:305.

Schleich, H. H. 1987. Contributions to the herpe-

tology of Kouf National Park (NE Libya) and adjacent areas. Spixiana 10:37–80.

Schofield, G., and H. Kopsida. 2000. Head injury rehabilitation of sea turtles: The positive side of a negative conundrum. In H. J. Kalb and T. Wibbels (compilers). Proceedings of the 19th annual symposium on sea turtle biology and conservation, 41–43. NOAA Technical Memorandum NMFS-SEFSC-443.

Schroth, W., B. Streit, and B. Schierwater. 1996. Evolutionary handicap for turtles. Nature 384:521–522.

Sella, I. 1982. Sea turtles in the eastern Mediterranean and northern Red Sea. In K. A. Bjorndal (ed.). Biology and conservation of sea turtles, 417–423. Washington, D.C.: Smithsonian Institution Press.

Silberstein, D., and R. Dmi'el. 1991. Loggerhead sea turtle nesting in Israel. Marine Turtle Newsletter 53:17–18.

Storelli, M.M., E. Ceci, and G. O. Marcotrigiano. 1998a. Comparison of total mercury, methylmercury and selenium in muscle tissues and in the liver of Stenella coeruleoalba (Meyen) and Caretta caretta (Linnaeus). Bulletin of Environmental Contamination and Toxicology 61:541–545.

———. 1998b. Distribution of heavy metal residues in some tissues of Caretta caretta (Linnaeus) specimen beached along the Adriatic Sea (Italy). Bulletin of Environmental Contamination and Toxicology 60:546–552.

Stringell, T., D. J. Suggett, and J. D. R. Houghton. 1996. Kefalonian Marine Turtle Project: Expedition report 1996. Isle of Wight: Kefalonian Marine Turtle Project.

Teneketzis, K. 1997. Conservation of Caretta caretta in Lakonikos Bay: Summer management strategy during 1997 [In Greek]. Report to the EC on project LIFE 97NAT/GR. Athens: Sea Turtle Protection Society.

Türkozan, O., and I. Baran. 1996. Research on the loggerhead turtle, Caretta caretta, of Fethiye beach. Turkish Journal of Zoology 20:183–188.

Türkozan, O., I. Baran, H. Durmus, and Y. Kaska. 1998. The loggerhead turtle populations of the southwest beaches of Turkey and protection studies. In S. P. Epperly and J. Braun (compilers). Proceedings of the 17th annual sea turtle symposium, 274–276. NOAA Technical Memorandum NMFS-SEFSC-415.

Vallini, C. In press. Spiaggiamenti di tartaruga comune Caretta caretta (L. 1758) sulle spiagge dei Lidi ferraresi (Mare Adriatico settentrionale). Anni 1996–1997. Milan: Atti Società Italiana di Scienze Naturali.

White, M. G. 1998. Nesting site fidelity of the loggerhead turtle around the Greek island of Kefalonia.
Thesis, University of Wales Bangor, U.K.

Yerli, S., and F. Demirayak. 1996. Marine turtles in
Turkey: A survey on nesting site status. Istanbul:
DHKD.

Yerli, S. V., and M. Dolezel. 1998. The nesting of sea
turtles in Anamur, southeast Turkey: A preliminary study. *In* S. P. Epperly and J. Braun (compilers). Proceedings of the 17th annual sea turtle
symposium, 292–294. NOAA Technical Memorandum NMFS-SEFSC-415.

Chapter 12

Loggerhead Turtles in the Equatorial and Southern Pacific Ocean:

A Species in Decline

—Colin J. Limpus and Duncan J. Limpus

Whereas the loggerhead turtle can be found throughout the tropical and temperate waters of the Pacific Ocean (Dodd 1988), it has a relatively restricted breeding distribution within this ocean basin. Within the Pacific Ocean, breeding is almost totally restricted to the western subtropical and temperate margins in Japan in the north (Kamezaki et al., Chapter 13 this volume) and to eastern Australia and New Caledonia in the south (Figure 12.1).

The Eastern Pacific

Although thousands of loggerhead turtles, including some adult-sized turtles, appear annually in spring and summer in Baja California and Gulf of California waters, none has been reported from this area bearing mature eggs (Marquez 1990). At least some of these immature loggerhead turtles in the eastern Pacific have been genetically identified as originating from nesting beaches in the western South Pacific Ocean (Bowen et al. 1994, 1995). There are no substantiated loggerhead turtle nesting records from the eastern Pacific or central Pacific regions (Pritchard 1979). Cornelius (1982) reported loggerheads breeding from Pacific Panama. However, Argelis Ruiz (pers. comm. July 1983) had no knowledge of the species nesting in Pacific Panama and believed that previous reports were of misidentified olive ridley turtles, *Lepidochelys olivacea*.

The Pacific Island Nations

The most easterly reliable record of loggerhead turtle nesting within the Pacific island nations is from Tokelau, where it was reported in 1981 as an uncommon nesting species and known only from Nukunomu (9.17° S, 171.88° W; Balazs 1983). Guinea (1993) found no evidence of loggerhead turtle nesting in Fiji. McKeown (1977) reported that loggerheads are not known to nest in the Solomon Islands, but Carr

Figure 12.1. Distribution of principal nesting sites for loggerhead turtles in the South Pacific Ocean.

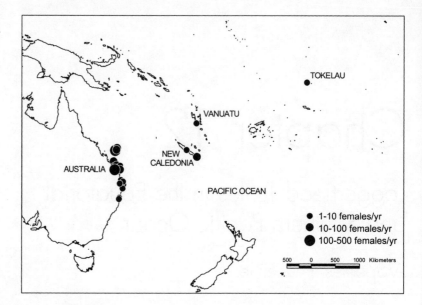

(1952) examined hatchlings from there, indicating that some loggerhead nesting may occur there. In Vanuatu, the status of loggerhead turtle nesting is uncertain because most of the coast has been poorly surveyed for turtle nesting. Unquantified low-density loggerhead turtle nesting was recorded at Malekula in Vanuatu in late 1993 (Atuary 1994). Although Pritchard (1982) provided circumstantial evidence that loggerhead turtle nesting may occur in North New Zealand, there remains no substantiated record of nesting within that country (Gill 1997), where the beaches are expected to have sand temperatures less than 25°C at nest depth. Even if rare nesting did occur on northern New Zealand beaches, it is highly unlikely that the eggs could incubate successfully to produce hatchlings.

New Caledonia

The loggerhead turtle is the most common nesting species in the Île des Pins area (22.6° S, 167.4° E) of southern New Caledonia (Pritchard 1982). However, there has been no quantification of the size of the New Caledonian nesting population. Beloff (pers. comm. 1997) failed to locate regular nesting within the main island of Île des Pins during the 1996–1997 breeding season. His local informants indicated that more substantial loggerhead turtle nesting occurred on the peripheral small coral cays offshore from the main island. The annual nesting population in the Île des Pins area is probably in the range of tens or the low hundreds of nesting females annually. There are no records of loggerhead turtles nesting among the abundant nesting green turtles, *Chelonia mydas*, on the islands within the Recifs d'Entrecasteaux in northern New Caledonia (unpubl. data, Association pour la Sauvegarde de la Nature Neo-Caledonienne).

The distribution of coastal foraging areas that supply turtles to the New Caledonian loggerhead nesting beaches is largely unknown. A small proportion of the loggerhead turtles that live in foraging areas of eastern Australia migrate to breed in New Caledonia: X9334 migrated from its foraging area at Heron Island Reef in the southern Great Barrier Reef and was identified by flipper tags while laying eggs in the Île des Pins (Limpus 1994); T92001 was tracked by satellite telemetry for a breeding migration from its Moreton Bay foraging area in southern Queensland to nesting in the vicinity of Île Neni (21.287° S, 165.737° E) on the mideastern coast of New Caledonia (Limpus and Limpus 2001).

Australia

Until recently, eastern Australia supported one of the major breeding aggregations for loggerhead turtles globally (Limpus 1985). Nesting

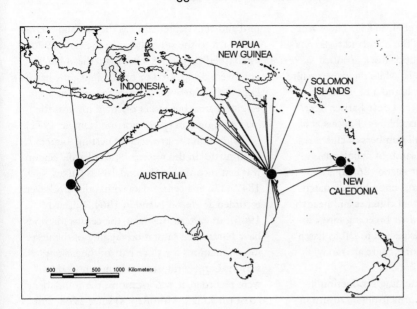

Figure 12.2. Postbreeding migration of adult female loggerhead turtles from Australian and New Caledonian rookeries. The lines link the feeding area capture sites with the respective nesting beaches (solid circles) but are not intended to denote migratory paths. Eastern Australian records are from the Queensland Parks and Wildlife Service turtle database. Western Australian data were supplied by R. Prince (pers. comm.).

occurs annually on effectively all beaches along the mainland and large barrier sand islands from South Stradbroke Island (27.6° S) northwards to Bustard Head (24.0° S) and on islands of the Capricorn Bunker Group (24.2–23.3° S) and Swain reefs (22.0–21.6° S) in the southern Great Barrier Reef and on Bushy Island (21° S) in the central Great Barrier Reef (see Figure 12.1). Within this core area, five principal rookeries account for approximately 70% of the eastern Australian nesting: Mon Repos (24.8° S, 152.45° E) and Wreck Rock (24.32° S, 151.97° E) beaches on the mainland and Wreck Island (23.33° S, 151.95° E), Erskine Island (23.5° S, 151.77° E), and Tryon Island (23.25° S, 151.77° E) in the southern Great Barrier Reef (Limpus and Reimer 1994). Bustard and Greenham (1968), Bustard (1972), Limpus (1971, 1985), and Maloney et al. (1990) provide descriptions of the physical characteristics at a number of these rookeries. Within the core area, loggerhead turtles share their nesting beaches with green turtles and flatback turtles, *Natator depressus*. Low density to sporadic loggerhead turtle nesting occurs outside the core breeding area in New South Wales to as far south as Newcastle (33° S) and in Queensland north on the mainland and continental islands from Bustard Head to approximately the Burdekin River (19.5° S) (Limpus 1985).

Nesting females migrate to these rookeries from feeding areas spread over a 2,600 km radius throughout eastern and northern Australia, eastern Indonesia, Papua New Guinea, the Solomon Islands, and New Caledonia (Figure 12.2; Limpus and Limpus 2001; Limpus et al. 1992). Nesting behavior within this stock has been described by Bustard et al. (1975), and Limpus and Reed (1985) have described site fidelity within the internesting habitat. Limpus et al. (1984) and Limpus (1985) provide a comprehensive description of those demographic parameters usually quantified at a nesting beach: mean curved carapace length is 95.7 cm for nesting females and 96.6 cm for courting males; renesting interval is 14 days; remigration interval is 3.8 years; 3.4 clutches are laid per season; there are 127 eggs per clutch; and incubation period is 8 weeks, but variable between seasons.

As a result of promiscuous mating and associated sperm storage, eggs within a single female's clutch may be fertilized by sperm from more than one male (Harry and Briscoe 1988). Miller (1985) provided a detailed description of loggerhead turtle embryology based on this population. Limpus et al. (1979) identified a critical period during which movement-induced mortality can occur with incubating eggs, and Maloney et al. (1990) have described temperature variation and gas concentrations within incubating clutches. Successful incubation can occur at nest temperatures between 25 and 33°C (Limpus et al. 1985). The pivotal temperature for this stock is 28.7°C (95% confidence limit = 0.6°C; Limpus et al. 1985). The warm brown sand beaches of the mainland rookeries from Mon Repos to Wreck Rock produce mostly female hatchlings, while the cooler white sand beaches of Wreck Island and the other coral cays of the southern Great Barrier Reef produce mostly male hatchlings (Limpus et al. 1983, 1985). The small numbers of clutches laid on the cool white sands of mainland beaches south of Fraser Island (26° S) are expected to produce almost entirely male hatchlings, while the occasional clutches laid near the southern extremity of their breeding range in New South Wales are expected to fail to hatch because sand temperatures there are rarely above 25°C.

Management of hatchling production in eastern Australia relies principally on in situ incubation of naturally laid clutches. Beach hatcheries have been used to a limited extent for some research and education applications. Limpus et al. (1983), Limpus (1973, 1985), and additional unpublished data in the Queensland Parks and Wildlife Service turtle database provide a detailed description of the fate of incubating eggs at a number of the rookeries. The proportion of clutches that successfully incubate to produce hatchlings to the beach surface in the absence of anthropogenic impacts averages about 87% but can be highly variable between seasons, ranging from 91.6% in summers with no cyclones to as low as 17% in extremely severe cyclone seasons. Fox depredation on most of the mainland beaches in the Wreck Rock area was estimated at 90–95% during 1976–1982. Fox baiting programs along these beaches since 1985 have substantially reduced losses from foxes to a nearly negligible level. There are no feral predators of turtles eggs or hatchlings on any of the Great Barrier Reef rookeries. Nesting turtles that dig into existing clutches destroy about 0.4% of the season's egg production. For those clutches that produce hatchlings, approximately 81% of eggs on mainland beaches produce hatchlings to the beach surface. On the southern Great Barrier Reef rookeries, about 65% of eggs produce hatchlings to the beach surface. The reduced incubation success on the islands results mostly from microbial invasion of the eggs. Less than 2% of hatchlings are lost to

bird and crab depredation as the hatchlings cross the beach to the sea. Studies in the early 1970s established that while these loggerhead hatchlings were disoriented by bright lights, the hatchlings did not necessarily move towards the brightest area, but rather oriented towards the lowest bright area on the horizon (Limpus 1971).

Although the presence of nesting loggerhead turtles in the western South Pacific region was first recorded in the mid 1800s (Jukes 1847), the first census data within this stock were recorded at Heron Island in 1964 (Bustard 1966). In eastern Australia, the census methods have focused on saturation tagging of the nesting populations for all or part of the nesting season. Long-term, season-long census data were recorded at two locations, the Bundaberg coast (including Mon Repos) since 1968, and Heron Island since 1974 (Figure 12.3; Limpus 1985; Limpus and Reimer 1994; C. Limpus and D. Limpus, recent unpubl. data). At an additional five sites, tagging census data from mid–breeding-season sampling studies have been recorded since 1977: Wreck Island, Tryon Island, Lady Musgrave Island (23.9° S, 152.38° E), North West Island (23.3° S, 151.7° E), and Wreck Rock (Figure 12.4; Limpus 1985; Limpus and Reimer 1994; C. Limpus and N. McLachlan, recent unpubl. data). In 1977 it was estimated that there were approximately 3,500 loggerhead turtles nesting annually in eastern Australia (Limpus and Reimer 1994). There has been a substantial decline in the annual number of nesting females at all sites since this time (Figures 12.3 and 12.4). It is now estimated that there are less than 500 nesting female loggerhead turtles annually in eastern Australia. This represents an 86% reduction in the size of the annual nesting population in 23 years. Since the age at first breeding for this population is several decades (Limpus and Limpus, Chapter 6 this volume), this magnitude of decline within less than one generation qualifies this major nesting population of the western South Pacific Ocean for a critically endangered rating (IUCN SSC 1994).

Comprehensive habitat protection has been implemented for breeding loggerhead turtles in eastern Australia. Approximately 90% of nesting occurs within national parks or equivalent con-

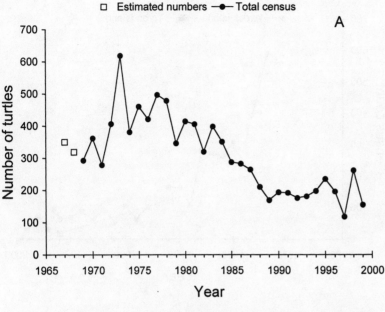

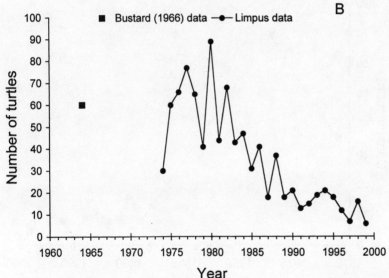

Figure 12.3. Long-term trends in the size of the annual loggerhead turtle breeding population at two eastern Australian rookeries. Data are derived from annual season-long saturation tagging at each site. A. Bundaberg coast. B. Heron Island.

servation areas. Specific recognition is given to the conservation of loggerhead turtles within the management plan for the Capricornia Cays National Park (including the rookeries on Tryon, North West, Wilson, Heron, Erskine, Masthead, and Lady Musgrave islands) and for the Capricornia Cays National Park Scientific (including the rookeries on Wreck, One Tree, Hoskyn, and Fairfax islands) (Anonymous 2000). Of the important nesting areas, only the 22 km of nesting beach at Wreck Rock is not

contained within a conservation management area. The interesting habitat adjacent to the island rookeries of the southern Great Barrier Reef is managed through zoning plans within the Great Barrier Reef Marine Park (Great Barrier Reef Marine Park Act 1975) and state marine parks (Queensland Marine Parks Act 1982) that prohibit deleterious human interactions with the turtles. In 1991 the Woongarra Marine Park was declared, with a zoning plan that excludes trawling from a significant part of

Figure 12.4. Indices of long-term trends in the size of the annual breeding population of loggerheads at five eastern Australian rookeries. Data derived from annual midbreeding season saturation-tagging studies. At each rookery, the saturation tagging was conducted on the same dates each year and provides a count of the number of nesting females encountered as an annual index of nesting population size. A. Wreck Island and Tryon Island (two-week census). B. Lady Musgrave Island (two-week census). C. North West Island (two-week census). D. Wreck Rock (five-week census).

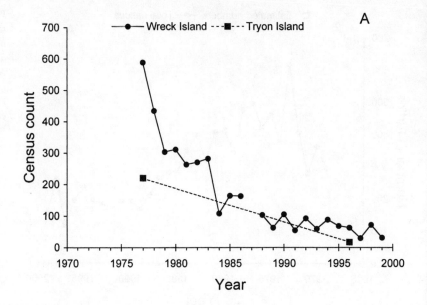

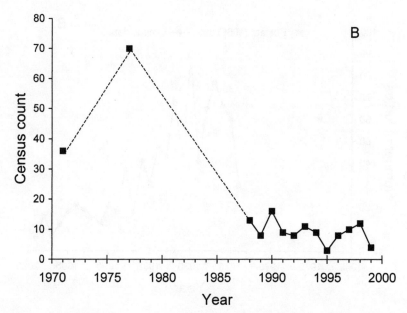

the internesting habitat for the turtles nesting at Mon Repos and adjacent beaches of the Woongarra coast for the duration of the summer nesting season. In May 1999 regulations under the Queensland Fisheries Act were introduced to require year-round compulsory use of turtle exclusion devices on prawn trawls along a 12 km wide, approximately 120 km long stretch of coast encompassing Mon Repos and the Woongarra coast northward to the Wreck Rock beaches. These regulations were extended in December 2000, and turtle excluder devices are now required in all trawl nets in the Queensland east coast trawl fisheries.

Public education relating to turtle conservation has been developed through managed ecotourism focused on the nesting turtles at Mon Repos and Heron Island (Tisdell and Wilson 2001). At the other extreme, some rookeries are totally closed to the public (Wreck, Hoskyn, and Fairfax islands), or open to daytime visitors but closed to the public at night (Erskine and

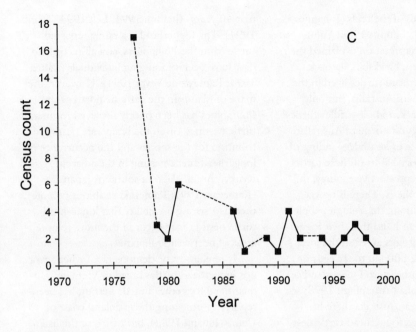

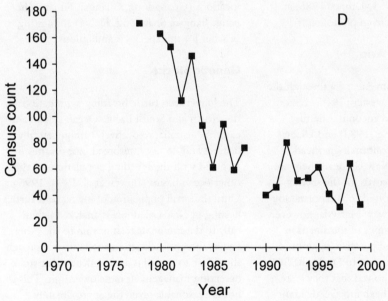

Tryon islands). Mon Repos, the most accessible of the loggerhead turtle rookeries, receives about 25,000 visitors annually. The tourists interact with the nesting turtles and hatchlings through a highly regulated visitor control system under the supervision of Queensland Parks and Wildlife Service (QPWS) guides, interpreters, and research staff (Kay 1995). Tourist visitation to the Mon Repos rookery is estimated to be worth approximately one million dollars annually to the district economy through the associated purchase of accommodation, meals, fuel, and souvenirs (Wilson and Tisdell 2000).

Until recently, indigenous coastal people throughout coastal northern Australia and Torres Strait have identified loggerhead turtles as one of the nesting species in their areas because there was a widespread ancient traditional belief that this species of sea turtle lays its eggs underwater among the corals of the reefs (Johannes and MacFarlane 1991; Limpus 1985; Yunupingu 1998). This interpretation explained their observations that green, hawksbill, flatback, olive ridley, and loggerhead turtles lived in the coastal waters of northern Australia, but only green, hawksbill, flatback, and olive ridley turtles came ashore to lay eggs on northern Australian beaches. In the absence of an understanding of the large-scale migratory habits of these turtles and of marine turtle reproductive ecology, this was a reasonable hypothesis. There is now a clear understanding among the Yolngu people in northeastern Arnhem Land that their loggerhead turtles do not lay eggs at sea in the local waters but migrate > 2,500 km to lay eggs on nesting beaches in southeastern Queensland or central Western Australia (Yunupingu 1998; see Figure 12.2). In tropical Australia there has been only one validated loggerhead turtle nesting attempt north of 20° S (Limpus 1985; at Lizard Island, identified from photograph).

Southeast and East Asia

Traveling northward from Australia through the countries of the tropical western Pacific region, one should not expect to encounter nesting loggerhead turtles. Spring (1982) and Ulaiwi (1997) were unable to confirm loggerhead turtle nesting in Papua New Guinea. There are no confirmed nesting records for the species from Indonesia. Harrisson (1965) reported loggerheads nesting in Sarawak, Malaysia; however, examination by C. J. Limpus of specimens in the Sarawak Museum and putative loggerhead specimens that Harrisson sent to Dr. H. R. Bustard in the early 1970s showed that they were all olive ridleys that had been incorrectly identified. A similar error occurred with olive ridleys nesting at the Sabah Turtle Islands being incorrectly identified as loggerheads (de Silva 1982). However, one of the authors (C. J. Limpus) has identified from photographs beach-washed dead loggerhead turtles at the Sabah Turtle Islands in 1993. These are presumed to have been non-breeding turtles from fisheries bycatch. There are no confirmed loggerhead turtle nesting records from Malaysia, where turtle nesting beaches have been extensively surveyed over the

past 40 years (Ibrahim 1994; Leh 1994; Trono 1994). The loggerhead is a rarely reported turtle from the Philippines, and all records to date have been of foraging individuals (Palma 1994; Ramirez de Veyra 1994). However, the maze of islands in the extreme north of the Philippines has been poorly surveyed for marine turtle nesting. Given the temperate nesting distribution for the species and the occurrence of loggerhead turtle nesting in the adjacent Ryukyu Archipelago of southern Japan (Kamezaki 1991; Kamezaki et al. this volume), there is a strong possibility that loggerhead turtle nesting may occur in the more remote areas of northern Philippines.

It remains to be demonstrated whether or not loggerhead turtles breed in Vietnam. Unquantified loggerhead turtle nesting has been reported from along the mainland coast of China (Huang 1982), but which of the listed locations (Guangdong, Guangxi, Fujian, Zhejiang, Jiangsu, Shandong, Hebei) are nesting beaches for this species is ambiguous.

Genetic Stocks

The loggerhead turtle breeding aggregations in the North and South Pacific Ocean (Japan and eastern Australia, respectively) are genetically distinct and do not interbreed, nor do they interbreed with the breeding populations of the other ocean basins (Bowen et al. 1994, 1995). Until the small population of loggerhead turtles nesting in New Caledonia is analyzed genetically to determine its relationship to the other Pacific Ocean stocks, the conservative approach should be to regard it as an independent stock deserving management in its own right. This is not unreasonable given the approximately 1,300 km of oceanic waters separating the New Caledonian and eastern Australian nesting beaches.

Threats

Heuristic population modeling of the eastern Australian loggerhead turtle stock (Chaloupka and Limpus 1998) indicates that modest levels of mortality from anthropogenic sources superimposed on natural mortality can be expected to have major negative impacts on population size and function. Given that turtle census studies usually occur at the nesting beaches and given the slow growth of wild loggerhead turtles, the difficulty will be identifying the source of problem when its impact eventually is evident at the nesting beaches. The task will be even more complicated if there are competing risks impacting the population.

While loggerhead turtles in the Pacific Ocean basin have not been subjected to widespread, intense harvests such as those that have occurred for green turtles and the hawksbill turtle *(Eretmochelys imbricata)* in this region, there has been a long-term but unquantified harvest of loggerhead turtles and/or their eggs in a number of countries: China (Huang 1982), Papua New Guinea and New Caledonia (Limpus et al. 1992), Fiji (Guinea 1993), and Australia (Limpus 1985). The harvest in Australia has been judged to be of minor consequence for many decades (Limpus and Reimer 1994). In contrast, on the eastern Australian mainland beaches, during the late 1970s and 1980s, introduced red foxes *(Vulpes vulpes)* destroyed a major proportion of loggerhead turtle eggs on these beaches, which have been the primary source of female hatchlings for this stock (Limpus 1985). It is anticipated that this egg loss will seriously impact on recruitment to the loggerhead turtle nesting population in eastern Australia early this century (Chaloupka and Limpus 1998; Limpus and Reimer 1994). Fisheries bycatch (from trawl, gill net, and crab trap fisheries) probably has been the most significant mortality factor operating on loggerhead turtle foraging and internesting populations in coastal waters of the western South Pacific Ocean (Poiner and Harris 1996; Robins 1995,). In eastern Australia, additional mortality results from boat strikes and ingestion of synthetic debris. In Australia the impact of the extensive modification of nesting beaches with coastal development has not been quantified.

Assessment of the conservation status of the loggerhead turtle population nesting in New Caledonian is hindered by a paucity of critical data. There are no census data for any component of this population, the genetic uniqueness or otherwise of the stock has not be determined, and there is an unquantified harvest of loggerhead turtles for local consumption within New Caledonia, even within the Île des Pines area (Pritchard 1982; Beloff, pers. comm. 1997) and in Fiji (Guinea 1993). In addition, the impact of the expanding tourism development on the nesting beaches in the Île des Pines area is unquantified.

There is a high probability that the impact of bycatch mortality within the extensive high seas longline fisheries of the North and South Pacific Ocean may prove to be the greatest threat to the survival of loggerhead turtles in both the North and South Pacific basins. In the absence of temporally and spatially quantified bycatch and mortality rates, it remains difficult to effectively address this problem.

LITERATURE CITED

Anonymous. 2000. Capricornia Cays National Park and Capricornia Cays National Park (scientific) management plan. Brisbane, Australia: QPWS.

Atuary, G. 1994. Report blong totel survey Wiawi (Malekula) 26/11/93 to 3/12/93. Report to South Pacific Regional Environment Programme.

Balazs, G. H. 1983. Sea turtles and their traditional use in Tokelau. Atoll Research Bulletin 279:1–38.

Bowen, B. W., N. Kamezaki, C. J. Limpus, G. R. Hughes, A. B. Meylan, and J. C. Avise. 1994. Global phylogeography of the loggerhead turtle *(Caretta caretta)* as indicated by mitochondrial DNA haplotypes. Evolution 48:1820–1828.

Bowen, B. W., F. A. Abreu-Grobois, G. W. Balazs, N. Kamezaki, C. J. Limpus, and R. J. Ferl. 1995. Trans-Pacific migrations of the loggerhead turtle *(Caretta caretta)* demonstrated by mitochondrial DNA tags. Proceedings National Academy of Science 92:3731–3734.

Bustard, H. R. 1966. Turtle biology at Heron Island. Australian Natural History 15:262–264.

———. 1972. Australian sea turtles—Their natural history and conservation. London: Collins.

Bustard, H. R., and P. M. Greenham. 1968. Physical and chemical factors affecting hatching in the green sea turtle, *Chelonia mydas* (L.). Ecology 49:269–276.

Bustard, H. R., P. Greenham, and C. Limpus. 1975. Nesting behaviour of loggerhead and flatback turtles in Queensland. Proceedings Koninklijke Nederlandse Akademie van Wetenschappen Series C 78:111–122.

Carr, A. 1952. Handbook of turtles. Ithaca, N.Y.: Comstock Publishing Associates.

Chaloupka, M., and C. J. Limpus. 1998. Simulation modeling of trawl fisheries impacts on SGBR loggerhead population dynamics. NOAA Technical Memorandum NMFS-SEFSC 415:26–29.

Cornelius, S. E. 1982. The status of sea turtles along the Pacific coast of middle America. In K. A. Bjorndal (ed.). Biology and conservation of sea turtles, 211–219. Washington, D.C.: Smithsonian Institution Press.

de Silva, G. S. 1982. The status of sea turtle populations in east Malaysia and the South China Sea. In K. A. Bjorndal (ed.). Biology and conservation of sea turtles, 327–337. Washington, D.C.: Smithsonian Institution Press.

Dodd, C. K., Jr. 1988. Synopsis of the biological data on the loggerhead sea turtle Caretta caretta (Linnaeus 1758). USFWS Biological Report 88.

Gill, B. J. 1997. Records of turtles and sea snakes in New Zealand, 1837–1996. New Zealand Journal of Marine and Freshwater Research 31:477–486.

Guinea, M. L. 1993. The sea turtles of Fiji. SPREP Reports and Studies Series 65:1–48.

Harrisson, T. 1965. Notes on marine turtles. 16. Some loggerhead (and hawksbill) comparisons with the green turtle. Journal of the Sarawak Museum 12:419–422.

Harry, J. L., and D. A. Briscoe. 1988. Multiple paternity in the loggerhead turtle (Caretta caretta). Journal of Heredity 79:96–99.

Huang, C. 1982. Distribution of sea turtles in China Seas. In K. A. Bjorndal (ed.). Biology and conservation of sea turtles, 321–322. Washington, D.C.: Smithsonian Institution Press.

Ibrahim, K. B. 1994. Status of marine turtle conservation in Peninsular Malaysia. In A. Nacu, R. Trono, J. A. Palma, D. Torres, and F. Agas (eds.). Proceedings of the first symposium-workshop on marine turtle conservation, 87–104. Manilla: WWF–Philippines.

IUCN Species Survival Commission 1994. IUCN red list categories. Gland, Switzerland: IUCN.

Johannes, R. E., and J. W. MacFarlane. 1991. Traditional fisheries of the Torres Strait Islands. Hobart, Australia: CSIRO Division of Fisheries.

Jukes, J. B. 1847. Narrative of the surveying voyage of the HMS Fly. London: T & L Boone.

Kamezaki, N. 1991. A preliminary report on the distribution of nesting sites of sea turtles in the Ryukyu Archipelago, and their evaluation. Biology Magazine, Okinawa 29:29–35.

Kay, A. 1995. Sea turtle encounters. Brisbane, Australia: QDEH

Leh, C. M. U. 1994. The green turtle conservation program at Sarawak Turtle Islands, 1992. In A. Nacu, R. Trono, J. A. Palma, D. Torres, and F. Agas (eds.). Proceedings of the first symposium-workshop on marine turtle conservation, 151–158. Manilla: WWF–Philippines.

Limpus, C. J. 1971. Sea turtle ocean finding behaviour. Search 2:385–387.

———. 1973. Avian predators of sea turtles in southeast Queensland rookeries. The Sunbird 4:45–51.

———. 1985. A Study of the loggerhead turtle in eastern Australia. Ph.D. Thesis, University of Queensland, Brisbane, Australia.

Limpus, C. 1994. Marine turtles: Ancient mariners in distress. Air Sea Rescue Journal 12:99–104.

Limpus, C. J., and D. J. Limpus. 2001. The loggerhead turtle, Caretta caretta, in Queensland: Breeding migrations and fidelity to a warm temperate feeding area. Chelonian Conservation and Biology 4:142–153.

Limpus, C. J., and P. C. Reed. 1985. The loggerhead turtle (Caretta caretta) in Queensland: Observations on internesting behaviour. Australian Wildlife Research 12:535–540.

Limpus, C. J., and D. Reimer. 1994. The loggerhead turtle, Caretta caretta, in Queensland: A population in decline. In R. James (compiler). Proceedings of the Australian marine turtle conservation workshop, 39–59. Canberra: QDEH and ANCA.

Limpus, C. J., V. Baker, and J. D. Miller. 1979. Movement induced mortality of loggerhead eggs. Herpetologica 35:335–338.

Limpus, C. J., P. Reed, and J. D. Miller. 1983. Islands and turtles: The influence of choice of nesting beach on sex ratio. In J. T. Baker, R. M. Carter, P. W. Sammarco, and K. P. Stark (eds.). Proceedings: Inaugural Great Barrier Reef conference, 397–402. Townsville, Australia: JCU Press.

Limpus, C. J., A. Fleay, and M. Guinea. 1984. Sea turtles of the Capricornia section, Great Barrier Reef Marine Park. In W. T. Ward and P. Saenger (eds.). The Capricornia section of the Great Barrier Reef, 61–78. Brisbane, Australia: Royal Society of Queensland and Australian Coral Reef Society.

Limpus, C. J., P. Reed, and J. D. Miller. 1985. Temperature dependent sex determination in Queensland sea turtles: Intraspecific variation in Caretta caretta. In G. Grigg, R. Shine, and H. Ehmann (eds.). Biology of Australasian frogs and reptiles, 343–351. Sydney: Royal Zoological Society New South Wales.

Limpus, C. J., J. D. Miller, C. J. Parmenter, D. Reimer, N. McLachlan, and R. Webb. 1992. Migration of green (Chelonia mydas) and loggerhead (Caretta

caretta) turtles to and from eastern Australian rookeries. Wildlife Research 19:347–358.

Maloney, J. E., C. Darian-Smith, Y. Takahashi, and C. J. Limpus. 1990. The environment for development of the embryonic loggerhead turtle *(Caretta caretta)* in Queensland. Copeia 1990:378–387.

Marquez, R. 1990. Sea turtles of the world. FAO Fisheries Species Synopsis 125:1–81.

McKeown, A. 1977. Marine turtles of the Solomon Islands. Honiara: Solomon Islands: Ministry of Natural Resources.

Miller, J. D. 1985. Embryology of marine turtles. *In* A. C. Gans, F. Billett, and P. Maderson (eds.). Biology of the *Reptilia*. Vol. 14. Development, 270–328. London: Academic Press.

Palma, J. A. M. 1994. Marine turtle conservation in the Philippines. *In* A. Nacu, R. Trono, J. A. Palma, D. Torres, and F. Agas (eds.). Proceedings of the first symposium-workshop on marine turtle conservation, 105–122. Manilla: WWF–Philippines.

Poiner, I. R., and A. N. M. Harris. 1996. Incidental capture, direct mortality and delayed mortality of sea turtles in Australia's northern prawn fishery. Marine Biology 125:813–825.

Pritchard, P. C. H. 1979. Encyclopedia of turtles. Neptune, N.J.: TFH Publications.

———. 1982. Marine turtles of the South Pacific *In* K. A. Bjorndal (ed.). Biology and conservation of sea turtles, 253–262. Washington, D.C.: Smithsonian Institution Press.

Ramirez de Veyra, R. T. D. 1994. Foreign tag recoveries from the Philippines. Marine Turtle Newsletter 64:6–9.

Robins, J. B. 1995. Estimated catch and mortality of sea turtles from the east coast otter trawl fishery of Queensland, Australia. Biological Conservation 74:157–167.

Spring, C. S. 1982. Status of marine turtle populations in Papua New Guinea. *In* K. A. Bjorndal (ed.). Biology and conservation of sea , 281–290. Washington, D.C.: Smithsonian Institution Press.

Tisdell, C., and C. Wilson. 2001. Wildlife-based tourism and increased support for nature conservation financially and otherwise: Evidence from sea turtle ecotourism at Mon Repos. Tourism Economics 7:233–249.

Trono, R. B. 1994. The Philippines-Sabah Turtle Islands: A critical management area for sea turtles of the ASEAN region. *In* A. Nacu, R. Trono, J. A. Palma, D. Torres, and F. Agas (eds.). Proceedings of the first symposium-workshop on marine turtle conservation, 167–180. Manilla: WWF–Philippines.

Ulaiwi, W. 1997. Marine turtle research and management in Papua New Guinea. *In* Y. S. Noor, I. R. Labis, R. Ounsted, S. Troeng, and A. Abdullah (eds.). Proceeds of the workshop on marine turtle research and management in Indonesia, 111–120. Bogor, West Java, Indonesia: Wetlands International/PHPA/Environment Australia.

Wilson, C., and C. Tisdell. 2000. Sea turtles as a non-consumptive tourism resource especially in Australia. University of Queensland Department of Economics Economic Issues 11:1–23.

Yunupingu, D. 1998. Nhaltjan nguli miwatj Yolngu djaka miyapunuwu: Sea turtle conservation and the Yolngu people of east Arnhem Land. *In* R. Kennett, A. Webb, G. Duff, M. Guinea, and G. Hill (eds.). Marine turtle conservation and management in northern Australia, 9–15. Proceedings of a workshop held at the Northern Territory University, Darwin, 3–4 June 1997. Darwin, Australia: Northern Territory University.

Chapter 13

Loggerhead Turtles Nesting in Japan

—Naoki Kamezaki, Yoshimasa Matsuzawa, Osamu Abe, Hiroshi Asakawa, Takashi Fujii, Kiyoshi Goto, Shinya Hagino, Masao Hayami, Masatoshi Ishii, Toshitaka Iwamoto, Takeshi Kamata, Hiroshi Kato, Jun-ichi Kodama, Yasuo Kondo, Itsuro Miyawaki, Kozo Mizobuchi, Yutaka Nakamura, Yoshito Nakashima, Hiroaki Naruse, Kazuyoshi Omuta, Masamichi Samejima, Hiroyuki Suganuma, Hiroshi Takeshita, Teruhiko Tanaka, Tai-ichiro Toji, Masahiro Uematsu, Akio Yamamoto, Takanobu Yamato, and Ikuo Wakabayashi

Although loggerhead sea turtles are distributed throughout the tropical and temperate waters of the world (Dodd 1988), the loggerhead's breeding distribution within the Pacific Ocean basin is relatively restricted. Within the North Pacific area, loggerhead nesting beaches are found only in Japan, whereas juvenile and some adult-sized turtles are found in the waters near Baja California and within the Gulf of California (Marquez 1990). Bowen et al. (1995) reported on mtDNA analysis that revealed that loggerheads in the North Pacific Ocean are genetically separated from an Australian nesting population.

The principal focus of status assessment in this chapter is on nesting of loggerheads in Japan. The authors feel that until the obstacles to counting sea turtles in the water are sufficiently overcome, these nesting beach assessments will continue to provide the best data on loggerhead abundance.

Nishimura (1967) originally reported that the species of sea turtle known to nest on main-land Japan was the loggerhead, and he compiled loggerhead nesting data from 42 Japanese nesting beaches. However, some of these nesting rookeries have been extirpated since Nishimura's report. Uchida and Nishiwaki (1982) presented a coarsely defined distribution map that indicated the location of loggerhead rookeries in Japan, but this summary did not include beach names. Although sea turtle research and conservation in Japan is growing and is resulting in more widespread beach surveys, only imited reports in Japanese describe the rookeries and the current status of loggerheads in Japan.

In this chapter, the authors introduce a current description of loggerhead rookeries in Japan and summarize population trends based on nesting data from the most consistently monitored beaches. The authors hope to provide a better understanding of the current status of Japanese loggerheads and of threats to their populations.

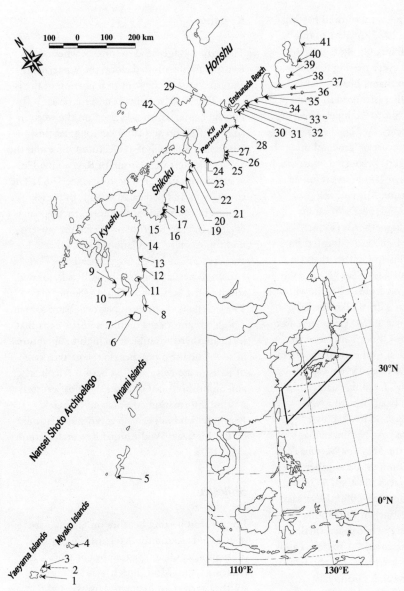

Figure 13.1. Rookeries for loggerhead turtles in Japan. Loggerhead nesting beaches other than those with only sporadic nesting and irregular monitoring: 1. Nishinohama Beach, 2. Ibaruma Beach, 3. Osaki Beach, 4. Gusukube Beach, 5. Itoman Beach, 6. Maehama Beach, 7. Inakahama Beach, 8. Nagahama Beach, 9. Fukiage Beach, 10. Nagasakibana Beach, 11. Shibushi Beach, 12. Nichinan Beach, 13. Miyazaki Beach, 14. Nobeoka Beach, 15. Ohgi Beach, 16. Shimonokae Beach, 17. Okata Beach, 18. Sagasioya Beach, 19. Moto Beach, 20. Kainan Beach, 21. Hiwasa Beach, 22. Kamouda Beach, 23. Minabe Iwashiro Beach, 24. Minabe Senri Beach, 25. Shingu Beach, 26. Kiho Beach, 27. Kumano Beach, 28. Shima Peninsula Beach, 29. Chita Peninsula, 30. Atsumi Beach, 31. Akabane Beach, 32. Toyohashi Beach, 33. Kosai Beach, 34. Hamamatsu Beach, 35. Omaezaki Beach, 36. Sagara Beach, 37. Nijima Island, 38. Izu Peninsula, 39. Izuoshima Island, 40. Boso Peninsula, 41. Kujukuri Beach, and 42. Akashi Beach.

Rookeries

Loggerhead nesting beaches in Japan are widely distributed across 13 degrees of latitude (24° N to 37° N; Figure 13.1). This latitudinal range is similar to that of the North Atlantic population. The authors separate Japanese loggerhead nesting beaches into five geographic areas: the Nansei Shoto Archipelago (Satsunan Islands and Ryukyu Islands), Kyushu, Shikoku, the Kii Peninsula (Honshu), and east-central Honshu and nearby islands.

Nansei Shoto Archipelago (Satsunan Islands and Ryukyu Islands)

Many islands are distributed in the southern ocean area of the Nansei Shoto Archipelago, Japan, between Kyushu and Taiwan. Within this region, the most important loggerhead nesting beaches occur on Yakushima Island. There, Inakahama Beach and Maehama Beach, located on the northwest coast of Yakushima, account for approximately 30% of all loggerhead nesting in Japan (Kamezaki 1989). The Yakushima Sea

Turtle Research Group has monitored nesting on these beaches since 1985. As part of this monitoring, the Yakushima Group tags, identifies, and counts nearly every nesting female that emerges onto Inakahama Beach.

There are many other islands with sandy beaches in the Nansei Shoto Archipelago where loggerhead nesting occurs. At Nagahama Beach, on the western coast of Tanegashima Island, Inatani et al. (2001) reported, with limited data, that more than 100 nests are made per season. At the Amami, Miyako, and Yaeyama island groups, 50–58.5% of sandy beaches were used by loggerheads (Kamezaki 1989, 1991). Nesting beaches are located on the Pacific side of each island, rather than on the sides facing the East China Sea (Kamezaki 1989, 1991). Nesting on Itoman Beach, within the developed southern part of Okinawa Island, has been monitored since 1994 (Wakatsuki and Kobayashi, pers. comm.), but many more females are believed to nest in the northern part of this island (Kikukawa et al. 1996). On Kuroshima Island of the Yaeyama Islands, loggerheads share nesting beaches with green turtles *(Chelonia mydas)* and hawksbills *(Eretmochelys imbricata)*. At Nishinohama Beach on Kuroshima, the Yaeyama Marine Park Research Station has counted the number of nests and emergence tracks since 1975 (Hirate and Iwase 1991; Kondo et al. 2000; Miyawaki 1981). Loggerhead nesting on Kuroshima Island has been decreasing, while green turtle and hawksbill nests have increased. At Ibaruma and Osaki beaches of Ishigakijima Island, the Ishigakijima Sea Turtle Research Group has counted nests and nesting emergences since 1993, and on Gusukube Beach of Miyako Island, the Gusukube Educational Office has monitored nesting between 1992 and 1999 (Gusukube Educational Office 2000).

Although some adult loggerheads migrate through the coastal seas of Taiwan (Cheng and Chen 1997), there are no records of loggerheads nesting on the island. With no information on loggerheads nesting in the Philippines, it appears that the Yaeyama Islands may be the southernmost extent of loggerhead nesting in the western North Pacific.

Kyushu

The major loggerhead nesting beaches of Kyushu are distributed along the western and eastern coasts of the southern portion of the island. The most prominent nesting beach is Fukiagehama, which is located on the western coast of Kyushu and is 35 km long. At this beach, the Kagoshima Prefecture Office and the Sea Turtle Research Group of Kagoshima University have monitored nesting since 1982. The courageous and dedicated actions of these groups in confronting violent sea turtle poachers induced the Kagoshima Prefecture government to establish regulations for sea turtle conservation in 1988. Loggerheads are also known to nest at Nagasakibana Beach, located south of the Satsuma Peninsula (Samejima 1994). The dark sands of Nagasakibana contain a high amount of magnetite, and the eggs that incubate there are subject to high temperatures in situ. The main beaches on the eastern coast of Kyushu are Miyazaki, Nobeoka, Nichinan, and Shibushi. Among these, the most extensive nesting information comes from Miyazaki Beach, which has been surveyed systematically by the Miyazaki Wild Animal Research Group since 1975.

Shikoku

Loggerhead nesting beaches on Shikoku are distributed around the Ashizuri Cape (Ohgi, Shimonokae, Okata, Sagashioya beaches), the Muroto Cape (Moto Beach), and along the southeastern coast (Kainan, Hiwasa, and Kamouda beaches). At Hiwasa Beach (Kondo 1994) and Kamouda beaches (Kamata 1994), nesting attempts have been monitored since the 1950s by the local public school. The resulting half-century data set provides the longest time series of sea turtle nesting numbers in the world.

Kii Peninsula (Honshu)

Although many small beaches are distributed along the coast of the Kii Peninsula (Miyawaki 1998), most loggerhead nesting occurs at

Minabe Senri Beach, where nearly all nesting females are identified by tagging. A similar tagging effort occurs at adjoining Minabe Iwashiro Beach. There has been an obvious decrease in nesting at Minabe Senri Beach (Sato et al. 1997). At Shima Peninsula Beach, loggerhead nests have been counted during each season of the last decade (Wakabayashi 1998); however, monitoring at Shingu Beach, Kiho Beach, and Kumano Beach, has been sporadic.

East-central Honshu and nearby Islands

Other than the Kii Peninsula, the principal nesting beach on Honshu (Japan's main island) is Enshunada Beach, which extends from Atsumi Peninsula to Sagara Beach on Suruga Bay. At this 130 km beach, volunteer groups have counted numbers of nests and nesting attempts on individual stretches including Atsumi, Akabane, Toyohashi, Kosai, Hamamatsu, Omaezaki, and Sagara section beaches. Among these stretches, the Omaezaki section has been monitored the longest, since 1975. Some loggerhead nesting on Honshu occurs on bay beaches that are remote from the ocean, such as Akashi Beach, which is artificially nourished with sand (Kamezaki et al. 1999).

Elsewhere on Honshu and eastern islands, smaller nesting beaches are distributed around the Chita Peninsula, Izu Peninsula, Izuoshima Island, Nijima Island, and Boso Peninsula, which contains Kujukuri Beach. No more than 10 nests per season have been recorded at any of these smaller beaches. Only sporadic nesting of loggerheads has been reported from the beaches of Ibaraki and Fukushima prefectures. These east-central Honshu beaches constitute the northern margin of loggerhead nesting in Japan and correspond in latitude to the northern extent of nesting in the eastern United States (37° N).

Nesting Abundance and Population Trends

As a result of the dedication and hard work of an extensive network involving many independent field teams in Japan, annual census data are available from most nesting beaches. The current population level of Japanese loggerheads is considerably lower than the population levels of other ocean basins. For example, in 1998, 1999, and 2000 seasons, a total of 2,479, 2,255, and 2,589 loggerhead nests, respectively, were recorded on Japanese beaches. Considering multiple renesting in loggerheads, it is probable that there are currently fewer than 1,000 females breeding annually in Japan. Of these total clutches, approximately 75% are deposited on nine major nesting beaches (defined as beaches having at least 100 nests in one season within last decade) and on six submajor nesting beaches (defined as beaches having 10–100 nests in at least one season within last decade). Census data from 12 of these 15 beaches indicate changes in population size over time (Figure 13.2).

Descriptions of the population changes are as follows:

- In the 1990s, there has been a consistent decline in annual nesting, especially in Hiwasa Beach (89% decline) and Minabe (74% decline). For most beaches, the lowest nesting numbers recorded have been during the recent period of 1997–1999.
- In the 1980s, there were increases in nesting numbers. However, nesting at the beginning of the 1980s was in most instances greater than nesting at the same beach some 20 years later at the end of the 1990s.
- There are indications that the 1970s was a period of approximate population stability with respect to breeding numbers.
- For the one population with census data extending back to the 1950s (Kamouda Beach), there is a clear indication that the population has greatly declined.

Given the similarity of population trends across the multiple rookeries for which census data are available, the authors feel that a composite of trends within the above four time periods can be used to describe the long-term trends in loggerhead nesting on Japanese beaches. During the last half of the 20th century, there has been a substantial decline

Figure 13.2. Loggerhead nesting trends in Japan. Census data from six major nesting beaches (Hiwasa, Omaezaki, Minabe Senri, Miyazaki, Inakahama, and Maehama) and six submajor nesting beaches (Kamouda, Nichinan, Shibushi, Nobeoka, Nagasakibana, and Minabe Iwashiro) indicate declines in the Japanese loggerhead population. Gaps in data reporting occur for Hiwasa Beach for 1955–1964 and in 1966, for Shibushi Beach in 1992, and for Minabe Iwashiro Beach in 1997. Hatched bars represent census data based on numbers of emergence tracks; solid bars represent census data based on numbers of nests.

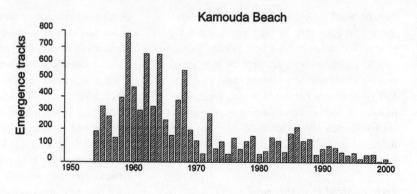

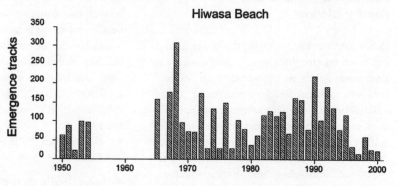

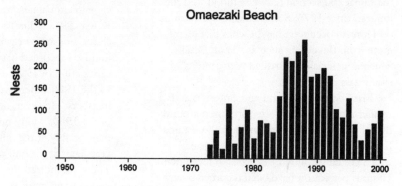

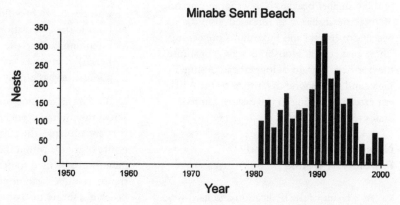

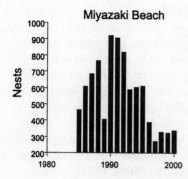

Miyazaki Beach

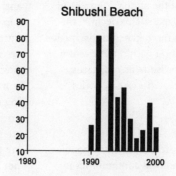

Shibushi Beach

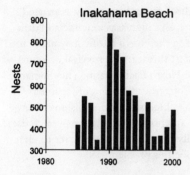

Inakahama Beach

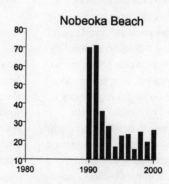

Nobeoka Beach

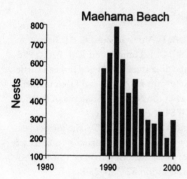

Maehama Beach

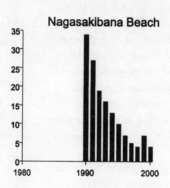

Nagasakibana Beach

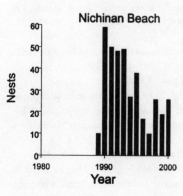

Nichinan Beach

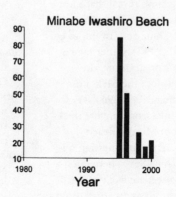

Minabe Iwashiro Beach

(50–90%) in the size of the annual loggerhead nesting population in Japan. This decline, observed over fewer than three generations, qualifies the nesting population within the western North Pacific Ocean for Endangered status, within the 1994 IUCN Red List categories.

Threats

In Japan, loggerhead turtle meat is not popular for food except in some local communities in Kochi and Wakayama prefectures (Sakamoto 1994). Conversely, turtle eggs have been widely consumed in many coastal areas at least during hungry times, and often as a traditional food in some communities. Some Japanese retain the superstition that turtle eggs work as revitalizers or aphrodisiacs, and this misconception provides a demand for poaching and egg selling on the black market. However, egg poaching has nearly disappeared as sea turtle research and conservation efforts have spread throughout Japan.

Egg predation, commonly by raccoon dogs (*Nyctereutes procyonoides*) and weasels (*Mustela itatsi*), is known from some beaches. However, there are no quantitative data to evaluate the negative impact on loggerhead populations. Although the beaches where loggerheads nest in Japan are, extensively eroded due to upstream dams and dredging, and obstructed by seawalls, there have been no quantitative studies to evaluate the impact of those anthropogenic conditions.

An extensive tagging project led by the Sea Turtle Association of Japan since 1990 and other projects by local groups reveal that most females that have concluded their seasonal nesting migrate to the East China Sea (Iwamoto et al. 1985; Kamezaki et al. 1997). Other tag returns come from South Korea, China, the Philippines, and the mouth of the Mekong River, Vietnam (Sadoyama et al. 1996). These results coincide with results from satellite tracking studies of turtles from Minabe Beach (Sakamoto et al. 1997). These postnesting migrations into the East China Sea, where intensive trawl fishing takes place, are likely to put Japanese nesting loggerheads at great risk from trawl capture and drowning mortality.

Other than overseas recapture reports,

many reports of tagged loggerheads came from Japanese coastal waters. Entangling gill nets and entrapping pound nets are common along the coast in Japan, and intensive trawl fisheries for postlarval anchovy are operated offshore of some major rookeries during the summer nesting season. The operation of these coastal fisheries appears to be correlated with sea turtle strandings, and at least 80 mature loggerheads are found stranded every year. This number is not negligible considering the current depleted population level of Japanese loggerheads.

Loggerhead bycatch mortality associated with the extensive high seas longline and driftnet fisheries in the North Pacific may prove to be the greatest threat to the survival of loggerheads in the North Pacific basin. The dramatic decrease in loggerhead nesting in Japan has followed a rise in high seas driftnet fishing. However, in the absence of quantitative bycatch data and mortality rates, it remains difficult to effectively describe this problem.

LITERATURE CITED

Bowen, B. W., A. F. Abre-Grobois, G. H. Balazs, N. Kamezaki, C. J. Limpus, and R. J. Ferl. 1995. Trans-Pacific migrations of the loggerhead turtle demonstrated with mitochondrial DNA markers. Proceedings of the National Academy of Sciences 92:3731–3734.

Cheng I. J., and T. H. Chen. 1997. The incidental capture of five species of sea turtles by coastal set-net fisheries in the eastern waters of Taiwan. Biological Conservation 82:235–239.

Dodd, C. K., Jr. 1988. Synopsis of the biological data on the loggerhead sea turtle *Caretta caretta* (Linnaeus 1758). USFWS Biological Report 88(14): 1–110.

Gusukube Educational Office. 2000. Report of sea turtle research 1992–1999. Gusukube, Japan: Gusukube Town Office.

Hirate, K. and F. Iwase. 1991. The nesting of the sea turtle in the Nishinohama Beach, Kuroshima Island, Yaeyama Group [in Japanese]. Marine Pavilion (Kushimoto Marine Park) 20:14–15.

Inatani, K., J. Sasagawa, and N. Kamezaki. 2001. Nesting status of the loggerhead turtles in the Nagahama Beach of Tanegashima, Japan, with a discussion about the emergence density. Umigame Newsletter of Japan 50:8–13.

Iwamoto, T., M. Ishii, Y. Nakashima, H. Takeshita,

and A. Itoh. 1985. Nesting cycles and migrations of the loggerhead sea turtle in Miyazaki, Japan. Japanese Journal of Ecology 35:505–511.

Kamata, T. 1994. The sea turtles in the Kamouda beach. *In* N. Kamezaki, S. Yabuta, and H. Suganuma (eds.). Nesting beaches of sea turtle in Japan [in Japanese], 59–65. Sea Turtle Association of Japan, Osaka.

Kamezaki, N. 1989. The Nesting of sea turtles in the Ryukyu Archipelago and Taiwan main islands. *In* M. Matsui, T. Hikida, and R. C. Goris (eds.). Current herpetology in East Asia, 342–348. Kyoto: Herpetological Society Japan.

———. 1991. A preliminary report on the distribution of nesting sites of sea turtles in the Ryukyu Archipelago, and their evaluation [in Japanese, with English abstract]. Biology Magazine Okinawa 29:29–35.

Kikukawa, A., N. Kamezaki, K. Hirate, and H. Ota. 1996. Distribution of nesting sites of sea turtles in Okinawajima and adjacent islands of the central Ryukyus, Japan. Chelonian Conservation and Biology 2:99–101.

Kamezaki, N., I. Miyawaki, H. Suganuma, K. Omuta, Y. Nakajima, K. Goto, K. Sato, Y. Matsuzawa, M. Samejima, M. Ishii, and T. Iwamoto. 1997. Post-nesting migration of Japanese loggerhead turtle, *Caretta caretta*. Wildlife Conservation Japan 3:29–39.

Kamezaki N., T. Tochimoto, and R. Iguchi. 1999. Nestings of loggerhead turtles in the Osaka Bay and the adjacent water [in Japanese]. Umigame Newsletter 42:8–9.

Kondo, Y. 1994. Emergence numbers of loggerhead turtles at Hiwasa Beach, Tokushima Prefecture, during 1950–1954. *In* N. Kamezaki, S. Yabuta, and H. Suganuma (eds.). Nesting beaches of sea turtle in Japan [in Japanese], 51–53. Osaka: Sea Turtle Association of Japan, Osaka.

Kondo, T., M. Kotera, Y. Asai, K. Kuroyanagi, K. Nomura, H. Misaki, M. Mori, F. Iwase, F. Sato, and A. Shigei. 2000. Nesting status of sea turtles in the Nishi-no-hama Beach, Kuroshima, Yaeyama Islands 1991–2000. Marine Park Journal 129:3–7.

Marquez, R. M. 1990. Sea turtles of the world. FAO Fisheries Synopsis 125 (11).

Miyawaki, I. 1981. Sea turtles nesting on Kuroshima Island, Yaeyama Islands. Marine Park Journal 53:15–18.

———. 1998. Hearing research about sea turtle nesting in the Wakayama Prefecture. *In* Association for Sea Turtle Information Exchange at Kii Peninsula (ed.). Sea turtles in the Kii Peninsula [in Japanese], 28–36.

Nishimura, S. 1967. The loggerhead turtles in Japan and neighboring waters *(Testudinata, Chelonidae)*. Publication of the Seto Marine Biology Laboratory 15:19–35.

Samejima, M. 1994. The loggerhead turtles in Nagasakibana, the south of Satsuma Peninsula. *In* N. Kamezaki, S. Yabuta, and H. Suganuma (eds.). Nesting beaches of sea turtle in Japan [in Japanese], 37–40. Osaka: Sea Turtle Association of Japan.

Sadoyama, A., N. Kamezaki, and I. Miyawaki. 1996. Recapture of the loggerhead turtle, nested in the Miyakojima Island, Okinawa Archipelago, in the Vietnam. Umigame Newsletter of Japan 29:9.

Sato, K., T. Bando, Y. Matsuzawa, H. Tanaka, W. Sakamoto, S. Minamikawa, and K. Goto. 1997. Decline of the loggerhead turtle, *Caretta caretta*, nesting on Senri Beach in Minabe, Wakayama, Japan. Chelonian Conservation and Biology 2:600–603.

Sakamoto, M. 1994. Turtle dish in Kochi. Folklore 1:144–145.

Sakamoto, W., T. Bando, N. Arai, and Y. Baba. 1997. Migration paths of the adult female and male loggerhead turtles *Caretta caretta* determined through satellite telemetry. Fisheries Science 63:547–552.

Uchida, I., and M. Nishiwaki. 1982. Sea turtles in the waters adjacent to Japan. *In* K. Bjorndal (ed.). Biology and conservation of sea turtles, 317–319. Washington, D.C.: Smithsonian Institution Press.

Wakabayashi, I. 1998. Current status of sea turtle nesting in the Mie Prefecture. *In* Association for Sea Turtle Information Exchange at Kii Peninsula (ed.). Sea turtles in the Kii Peninsula [in Japanese], 37–43.

Chapter 14

Loggerhead Turtles in the Indian Ocean

—Robert Baldwin, George R. Hughes, and Robert I. T. Prince

The occurrence of loggerhead turtles in the Indian Ocean has been long known. Smith (1849) described the species from South Africa in 1849, and in the 1930s, Deraniyagala (1933, 1939) described the Indian Ocean red-brown loggerhead in detail, determining it to be within the subspecies *gigas*. While there appears to be little justification for this status (Hughes 1974), this reference provides early evidence for the occurrence of loggerheads in the northern Indian Ocean, around Sri Lanka. Later work by Loveridge and Williams (1957) and Carr (1952) indicated that loggerheads were distributed along all coasts of Africa and Western Australia, but no quantitative data were available until the late 1960s and early 1970s, when detailed and focused surveys were initiated (McAllister et al. 1965).

Since then, research has provided additional quantitative data on nesting populations (e.g., Govender and Hughes 2001; Prince 1999; Ross 1979; Salm et al. 1993; Tambiah 1989),

and it has been established that loggerhead turtles are distributed throughout the Indian Ocean, found to a greater or lesser degree along most mainland coasts and island groups. Some rare gaps include Mortimer (1990), who makes no reference to loggerheads in Malaysia.

In this chapter, the authors discuss the distribution and abundance of loggerhead turtles within three focal areas: the southwestern, northern, and eastern regions of the Indian Ocean (Figure 14.1). Some of the known nesting sites are described, including broad habitat definitions, conservation status of nesting beaches, and documented or perceived loss/threats to nesting habitat. Reported nesting numbers and trends are discussed, and data on migrations and movements of nesting/foraging individuals are reviewed. From the information presented, the authors make an assessment of general management-related research needs in the Indian Ocean.

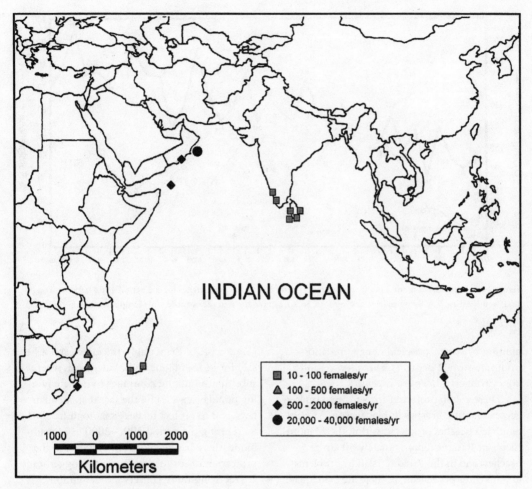

Figure 14.1. Map of the Indian Ocean and known loggerhead nesting sites (after Anonymous 1999).

Southwestern Indian Ocean

Nesting Sites

Loggerhead nesting beaches in the southwestern Indian Ocean are characteristic steep silica sand beaches maintained by medium- to high-energy wave action. Sand grain varies according to position and wave approach, but nesting females show no evidence of selecting nest sites on the basis of sand grain size (Hughes 1974). Human alterations to the beaches, although occasionally catastrophic, are normally of short duration and result in moderate erosion. Such impacts have short-term damaging effects such as washing away clutches of eggs.

The most consistent threat to loggerhead nesting beaches is the possibility of deep-water harbor developments. One such threat in 1978 at Kosi Bay, South Africa, resulted in the translocation of 20,000 eggs per year for 10 years from the study area in Tongaland to the St. Lucia Marine Reserve, 100 km southward.

A new threat of a deep-water harbor development has appeared with proposals to cut into the coast of Mozambique some 30 km north of the Mozambique/South African border. This will effectively split in half the nesting concentration in southern Africa and frustrate conservation efforts in Mozambique to declare a marine reserve from Inhaca Island to the South African border, a reserve that would link Mozambique to the South African marine protected area. Apart from development, other threats to nesting loggerheads are subsistence

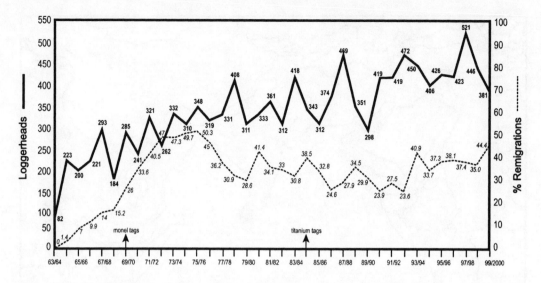

Figure 14.2. Loggerhead nesting population numbers and remigration percentages for the period 1963–1999 at Tongaland, South Africa. The figure reflects nesting on a 56 km sample site that receives the same sampling effort every year.

hunting by coastal people and egg predation from side-striped jackals *(Canis adustus)* and honey badgers *(Mellivora capensis)*.

There are no protected areas focused on loggergead nesting beaches in Madagascar. Mozambique has beaches protected within the Maputo Elephant Reserve (approximately 60 km of beaches) and in the Paradise Islands. Problems in both countries remain, as there are inadequate resources and manpower to ensure protection for nesting females. In South Africa, all nesting beaches are now contained within protected areas. The beaches are inscribed as a Ramsar Convention protected site and, as of 3 December 1999, are contained within the Greater St. Lucia Wetland Park World Heritage Site.

Loggerhead nesting beaches in the southwestern region include the southeastern coast of Africa from the Paradise Islands in Mozambique southwards to St. Lucia in South Africa and to the south and southwestern coasts of Madagascar (see Figure 14.1). The area of highest nesting density is in Tongaland, South Africa, and this area has been the focus of careful protection and research for 38 years. The annual number of individual nesting females recorded in Tongaland since 1963 leaves little doubt that there has been a recovery in the number of nesting females since the inception of the program

(Figure 14.2). Regrettably, the same cannot be said for Mozambique and Madagascar, where subsistence hunting continues to deplete nesting populations despite the fact that adequate laws exist to protect turtles (Rakotonirina 2001).

During the period 1995–2000 in Mozambique, there has been growing interest in the protection of sea turtles. Presently, loggerheads are receiving more conservation attention through tagging programs established with assistance from South Africa.

Estimated Numbers and Trends

Since 1963 an annual survey has been carried out on a 56 km stretch of beach in Tongaland, South Africa (Hughes 1974). Figure 14.2 summarizes the results of this effort, giving the exact number of nesting loggerheads actually encountered during each season. As the effort (twice nightly foot patrols by 22 staff and a double vehicle patrol each night) has remained virtually unchanged for the entire period, it is possible to conclude that the trend in nesting females is upward. For example, the average annual number of nesting females was 256 for the first 10 years (1964–1974) and 428 for the last 10 years (1989–1999), an increase of 40.2% (Hughes 1999).

South of the 56 km study area in South Africa, loggerhead nesting occurs, but fewer females emerge on these beaches; fewer than 100 females per year nest on this approximately 100 km length of coast. This is some three times the number recorded in 1983, but patrols are erratic, and yearly comparisons have only modest value.

Similarly, a month-long program carried out along 30 km of beach centered on Ponto Malongane, Mozambique, 20 km north of the South African border, is now in its fourth year and is recording up to 33 loggerhead females nesting per year. It is too early to identify trends there. Further north in Mozambique there is a less dependable record of seasonal numbers, and likewise, no trends are known. Regrettably, there remain consistent records of nesting turtles being killed in many parts of Mozambique.

Mark-recapture data from over 30 years suggest that the nesting population using the Tongaland beaches is drawn from a population of tens of thousands of breeding females (Govender and Hughes 2001). An extrapolation to cover the total number of loggerheads in the southwestern Indian Ocean would go beyond an intelligent guess until better data exist on the number of nesting females in Mozambique and Madagascar.

Loggerhead nesting grounds are present around Madagascar (Rakotonirina 2001; see Figure 14.1), and it is pleasing to report that there is a growing effort to study and count nesting on the island's southern and southwestern coasts. Numbers of nesting loggerheads appear low, in the order of a few hundred per year. They remain seriously threatened by subsistence harvest of both adults and eggs.

Migration and Movements

Site recoveries of female loggerhead turtles tagged on the Tongaland beaches since 1963 indicate that there is no specific foraging area preferred by Tongaland loggerheads (Figure 14.3). Turtles travel eastwards to Madagascar, northwards to Mozambique, Tanzania, and Kenya, and southwards as far as Cape Agulhas and into the Atlantic Ocean. Although loggerheads probably prefer neritic waters of the re-

gions described, there does not seem to be a favored direction (north, south, or east) of foraging areas from nesting beaches.

The most distant recovery is from the Seychelles, a one-way swim of 3,500 km. Another long-distance recovery from Somalia (3,200 km) is of interest because of the turtle's proximity to loggerheads recovered from the Masirah Island nesting population. Loggerheads are prodigious migrants; even after extensive displacements they appear capable of reorienting and finding their way back to their feeding grounds. Two females were transported from the Tongaland beaches at the end of the 1997 season, fitted with satellite transponders (Telonics ST-6 PTT), and shipped to Madagascar and Réunion, respectively. Both found their way back to Africa and, ultimately, to their feeding grounds (Figure 14.4).

Hatchling Movements and Recovery of Adults Marked as Hatchlings

Each summer in Tongaland, loggerhead hatchlings are marked by clipping their marginal scales. Between the years 1971 and 1978 a single scale was removed, but since 1979 two scales in various combinations have been clipped. Some 314,287 hatchlings have been marked and released since 1971. Recoveries of notched hatchlings reveal that most hatchlings enter the Agulhas current within days of entering the sea and are swept southwards, some even rounding the Cape and entering the Atlantic Ocean. Notched hatchlings have been found at many sites along the eastern and southern coasts and around Cape Agulhas in False Bay, Table Bay, and Ysterfontein, 2,200 km from the release site (Hughes 2001).

Most posthatchlings probably enter the major gyres and the general circulation of the Indian Ocean. There is a paucity of records for juvenile loggerheads that are 10–60 cm carapace length, a size smaller than the subadult (neritic foraging) loggerheads that have returned to the coastal zone (Hughes 1974).

One hundred one nesting females bearing notches have been found since 1988/89 in Tongaland, and the suggested age at first nesting ranges from 10 to 29 years (mean age, 19.5

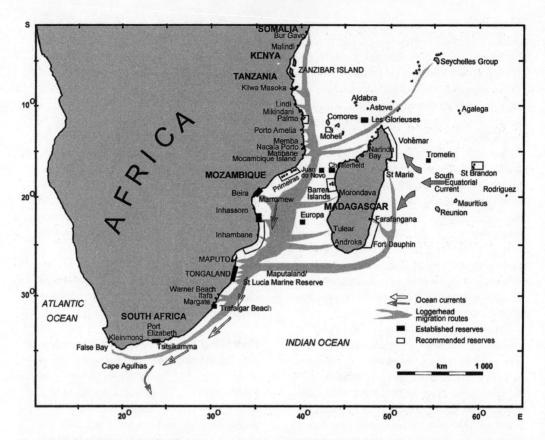

Figure 14.3. Distant recoveries of loggerheads tagged while nesting at Tongaland, South Africa, beaches between 1963 and 2000. Feeding grounds are widely dispersed throughout the western Indian Ocean with no apparent preferred area.

years). Because nesting females are at least 10–30 cm larger than the subadults first encountered on their return to the coastal zone, it is reasonable to assume that the oceanic stage endures from 5 to 15 years. The authors' conclusion from data gathered thus far is that age of first nesting in loggerheads is highly variable and is dependent upon environmental circumstances, but it is certainly not less than 10 years and is perhaps in excess of 20 years. Nesting loggerhead turtles in the southwestern Indian Ocean range in size from 72.8 to 98.5 cm straight carapace length (Hughes 1974).

Northern Indian Ocean

Nesting Sites

It is clear that the largest nesting aggregations for loggerheads in the Indian Ocean occur in the northern region and that in this region, Oman hosts the vast majority of nesting. Log-

gerhead nesting in Oman is exceptional because of its distribution within the tropics. Pritchard (1979), in describing the global tendency for loggerheads to nest north or south of the tropics, noted the unusual distribution for loggerhead nesting in Oman, at 21° N. Elsewhere along the Saudi Arabian coast, Miller (1989) reported loggerheads to be rare and to have no known nesting sites.

Dodd (1988) concluded that loggerhead nesting is rare in the northern Indian Ocean other than in Oman but that Sri Lanka and southern India are confirmed nesting areas. Some loggerhead nesting in the Gulf of Mannar has been reported by Deraniyagala (1939) and Kar and Bhaskar (1982). More recent data indicate widespread nesting in Sri Lanka, although Tambiah (1989) reported that loggerheads were the rarest turtles there.

The concentration of loggerhead nesting in the Arabian region of the northwestern Indian

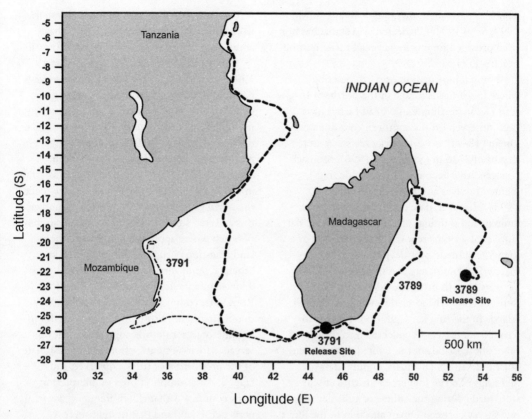

Figure 14.4. Reorientation of satellite-tagged loggerheads that were displaced eastward of their nesting grounds. See text for details.

Ocean occurs on both island and mainland sites in southern Oman (Anonymous 1989a, 1981b; Baldwin 1992; Baldwin and Al-Kiyumi 1996; Ross 1979, 1998; Ross and Barwani 1982; Salm 1991; Salm et al. 1993). The majority of nesting occurs on Masirah Island (21° N, 58° E), on the Al Halaniyat Islands to the south (17° N, 55° E), and on mainland sites south of Masirah Island as far as Khor Khafort near the Oman-Yemen border (Anonymous 1989a, 1989b; Salm 1991; Salm and Salm 1991). It is possible that the mainland Arabian Sea coast of Yemen includes additional nesting beaches. Confirmed nesting in Yemen occurs on Socotra, an island in the eastern Gulf of Aden, south of the Arabian Peninsula (Pilcher and Saad 1999). There is at least one additional record of a loggerhead turtle in the Gulf of Aden, sighted in shallow water (3–4 m deep) off the northern Somali coast (Schleyer and Baldwin 1999). A survey of turtle nesting beaches in this area revealed

probable nesting by this species, based on the evidence of tracks and nests and consultation with local fishers.

Nesting in the Sultanate of Oman occurs mostly in remote, undeveloped areas on exposed beaches, typically consisting of coarse sand and backed by arid coastal plains or low rocky hills. Human development in these areas is generally limited (Anonymous 1989a), with the exception of northern coastal areas of Masirah Island, where human habitation, a military base, and associated infrastructure are sited. This has resulted in minor loss of nesting habitat and numerous threats including artificial lighting, harvesting of eggs, road construction, beach driving, and erosion caused by overgrazing (Baldwin 1992). Loggerhead turtles are additionally threatened in many areas from tourism-related development and in all coastal regions of Oman from fisheries activities, principally from the use of entangling (gill) nets in near-shore areas (Anonymous 1989a; Baldwin 1992; Salm 1991). Protected area status has not been provided for any loggerhead turtle nesting beaches in Oman.

Limited information exists to describe where loggerheads forage in the northern Indian Ocean; feeding loggerhead turtles have been observed off the southern coastline of Oman (18–21° N) over rocky reefs in water depths of 3–26 m (Salm et al. 1993). Stomach contents have been found to include fragmented bivalves and barnacles (Salm et al. 1993). However, data on foraging turtles are limited, and sightings at sea are infrequent. Ballance et al. (1996) report a single sighting of a loggerhead turtle over deep water approximately 120 kilometers east of Masirah Island.

Few records provide evidence for the distribution of loggerhead turtles north of Masirah Island. In the Arabian Gulf, occurrence is inferred from five skulls collected from beaches on offshore islands of the United Arab Emirates at latitude 26° N (Baldwin, unpubl. data). Sightings of seven loggerhead turtles at sea were made during the course of a 30-day seismic survey between Oman and Iran in the Strait of Hormuz in January 2000 (Baldwin and Collins 2000). Sightings at sea off the coast of the capital area of Muscat, Oman (24° N), include one mating pair (Salm et al. 1993) and occasional feeding individuals in shallow reef areas (Baldwin and Al-Kiyumi 1999). Loggerhead turtles in these areas, distant from known nesting grounds in the Arabian Sea, may be part of a foraging population, either feeding in situ or on a migratory route between nesting and feeding grounds.

Estimated Numbers and Trends

Loggerhead nesting at the island of Masirah occurs at astounding densities, ranging 27–102 nesting attempts per kilometer per night (Ross 1998). These densities make it difficult to undertake complete nest counts or to make complete counts of nesting females from tagging efforts. Thus, estimations of annual nesting numbers at Masirah depend upon extrapolations from limited counts of nesting attempts and upon tagging of nesting turtles, with cor-

rections for partial effort. Surveys at Masirah from which reliable estimates of loggerhead abundance can be made have occurred only in 1977–79 and 1991 (Baldwin 1992; Ross 1979, 1998; Ross and Barwani 1982). These surveys have provided broad estimates of nesting abundance that come from two techniques and from multiple years of sampling (Table 14.1). The estimates range from 20,000 to 40,000 loggerhead females nesting annually at Masirah.

Ross (1979, 1998) cited surveys at Masirah in 1977, 1978, and 1979 from which he made the initial estimations of loggerhead abundance there. Aerial surveys identified a 20 km stretch of beach where approximately 85% of the island's nesting occurred. Within this 20 km beach, ground surveys took place on 3 km or 9 km segments during the three years (J. P. Ross, pers. comm.). An assumption held in extrapolating nightly counts of tagged turtles to nightly totals for nesting turtles was that observers had an accurate, effort-derived estimate of the proportion of turtles observed and tagged. An assumption used in interpreting track counts was that clutch frequency was 4.0 nests per female and that nesting success (nests/attempts) was 100% (Ross 1998; J. P. Ross, pers. comm.). A more conservative assumption that 50% of attempts resulted in nests still gives an estimate at the lower end of the range spanning 20,000–40,000 females per year. Both tagging and track count estimations assume that nesting is uniform over the 20 km for which extrapolations are made and that the 120-day nesting season is properly represented.

Baldwin (1992) counted individual turtles on selected high-density nesting beaches on Masirah Island over a one-month period in 1991 and arrived at an estimate of 23,000 nesting females for the season nesting on all of Masirah. The estimate was based on extrapolation of total available nesting habitat, relative nesting density, and estimated seasonal distribution of effort. This estimate falls within the range given by Ross (1998). Although there are limitations to each of the techniques used during the sampling periods, there is general confirmation that annual nesting occurs within the broad range of 20,000–40,000 nesting females per year. Presently, population-specific data on

Table 14.1.
Loggerhead Nesting Abundance and Nesting Trends for the Best-Known Indian Ocean Assemblages

Location	Nesting Loggerheads per Season	Years	Estimation Methods	Data Limitations and Assumptions	Trend in Seasonal Counts
Tongaland, South Africa	428	1963–1999	Saturation tagging	No assumptions	Increasing
Mozambique	> 200	1999	Guesstimate	Irregular studies	Probably decreasing
Madagascar	< 100	1999	Guesstimate	Irregular studies	Probably decreasing
Masirah, Oman	20,000–40,000	1977–1979 1991	Partial tagging and track counts	Various, see text	Unknown
Arabian Sea coast, Oman	500	1989	Nest counts	One survey; assume 4 nests/female	Unknown
Halaniyat Islands, Oman	> 750	1989	Nest counts	One survey; assume 4 nests/female	Unknown
Dirk Hartog Island, Western Australia	800–1,500	1993–2000	Extensive tagging	1995/1996 season not surveyed	Unknown
South Muiron Islands, Western Australia	150–350	1986–1999	Limited to extensive tagging	1994/1995 season not surveyed	Unknown
North West Cape, Western Australia	50–150	1986–2000	Limited to extensive tagging	1994/1995 season not surveyed	Unknown

stock identity, clutch frequency, nesting success, and remigration intervals are lacking. This information is needed to verify the assumptions used to make annual nesting estimates and to extend an assessment of abundance to total numbers of nesting females. Further monitoring will be needed to extend the time series of data so that trends can be detected. Because the broad ranges of total seasonal nesting do not allow annual comparisons, surveys at representative index beach sites may yield the only reliable data for trends in abundance.

Loggerhead turtle nesting is documented on at least 178 beaches in Oman in addition to those on Masirah Island (Salm 1991; Salm et al. 1993). This occurs mostly on the Al Halaniyat Islands (over 3,000 nests per year) and along the mainland Arabian Sea coast (approximately 2,000 nests per year). There are apparently no other data on nesting numbers or trends in the northern Indian Ocean, with the exception of Pilcher and Saad (1999), who report annual nesting of between 50 and 100 loggerheads per year on Socotra Island, Yemen.

Migration and Movements

Information from loggerheads tagged at Masirah shows that nesting turtles migrate north to the Gulf of Kutch and the Gulf of Oman, north and west to the Persian Gulf, and south and west to the Gulf of Aden (Figure 14.5). Given the known ability of these reptiles for remarkable swims, it is likely that their range overlaps with that of the southwestern Indian Ocean population.

Eastern Indian Ocean

Nesting Sites

All known loggerhead nesting sites in the eastern Indian Ocean are found in Western Australia (Dodd 1988). As recently as 1990 (Prince 1994a), little was known of their size or importance. However, studies by Prince (1993, 1994b, 1997, 1998a, 1998b, 1999) have shown that these aggregations are of significant size. The core nesting range of the loggerhead turtle on the Western Australian coast spans approximately 5° of latitude, from the southern limit of the Shark Bay World Heritage Area (26.5° S) northward through Ningaloo Marine

Park coast to the North West Cape and to the nearby Muiron Islands (21.5° S; Figure 14.6a).

Coastal landforms of this Cape Range or Gascoyne coast generally comprise a complex of Holocene calcareous sands, with Pleistocene limestone plus marine Miocene limestone in some places. Seaward, the continental shelf extension of the Phanerozoic sedimentary Carnarvon Basin is relatively narrow, with a minimum width of 40 km just south of North West Cape. Inland, the country is arid, with annual rainfall of approximately 25 cm per year. There are few rivers, and seasonal flow is infrequent. Offshore waters are relatively clear. The exposed western coastline is subject to moderate or high wave energy driven by the strong prevailing southerly winds. Cliffed and rocky shorelines are common. Sheltered embayments are found at Shark Bay and Exmouth Gulf, while the Ningaloo fringing reef tract protects the coast southward from North West Cape (Marine Parks and Reserves Selection Working Group 1994).

The greatest concentrations of loggerhead turtle nesting in Western Australia are found at the beaches of the Muiron Islands and at the northern end of Dirk Hartog Island, which fringes Shark Bay. To a lesser extent, nesting loggerhead turtles also use mainland beaches along parts of the Ningaloo Marine Park coast, including North West Cape. Population studies with tagged adult females are in progress. Current data suggest that Dirk Hartog Island hosts approximately 70–75% of the nesting loggerheads now found in the southeastern Indian Ocean. Many of these turtles forage within Shark Bay, and others in Exmouth Gulf to the north, but some adults range much farther (Figure 14.6a,b).

The principal nesting beaches at Dirk Hartog Island are at its northern extent. Nesting there extends over approximately 4.5 km of predominantly rocky, reefy coast with the sand beaches at the western and eastern ends of this northern coast attracting the greatest concentration of nesting.

Estimated Numbers and Trends

The most reliable loggerhead nesting data within the eastern Indian Ocean come from Dirk Hartog Island, South Muiron Island, and

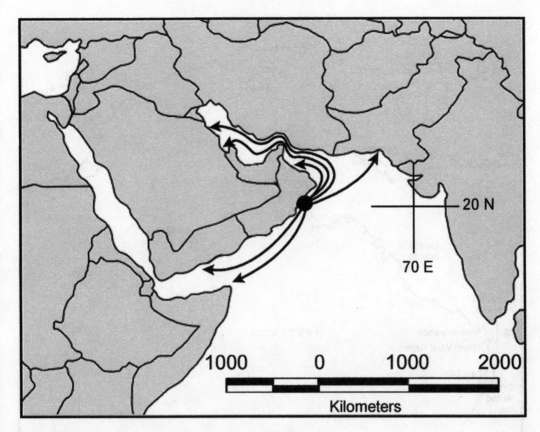

Figure 14.5. Distant recoveries of loggerheads tagged on Masirah Island, Oman.

North West Cape (see Table 14.1). The most extensively nested of these three areas, Dirk Hartog Island, has had six seasons of monitoring between the 1993/94 and 1999/2000 nesting seasons.

The Dirk Hartog Island study was started as a result of information obtained from recreational boaters visiting the island prior to 1993. These initial reports suggested that the island's beaches were at least as important for nesting loggerheads as the South Muiron Island location. The first efforts to tag and release nesting loggerheads at Dirk Hartog Island and to assess the numbers nesting at the peak of season took place during the 1993/94 and 1995/96 seasons. Work during the 1994/95 season was missed, but the effort to tag nesting loggerheads was expanded in 1996/97 and has continued through 1999/2000 at a similar effort level. Observation and tagging of nesting turtles occurs December to March each monitored season, with the greatest concentration of this effort during the January season peak. The short time series and increasing effort do not allow an assessment of trends. Confident assessments indicate that approximately 1,000 or more loggerheads nest annually at the Dirk Hartog Island beaches.

Loggerhead nesting levels at North West Cape and the Muiron Islands during the 1993/94 season indicate the relative importance of South Muiron Island compared with the beaches at the northern end of North West Cape (with a nesting ratio of 10:1); data also indicate that many fewer loggerheads are nesting in this area than at Dirk Hartog Island. These data also represent the returns of a much greater sampling effort than has been mounted at Dirk Hartog Island. But again, there are insufficient data to determine trends in the numbers of loggerhead turtles nesting on these beaches. There is, however, evidence from Japanese fishery bycatch records (Nishimura and Nakahigashi 1990) and recent Australian studies

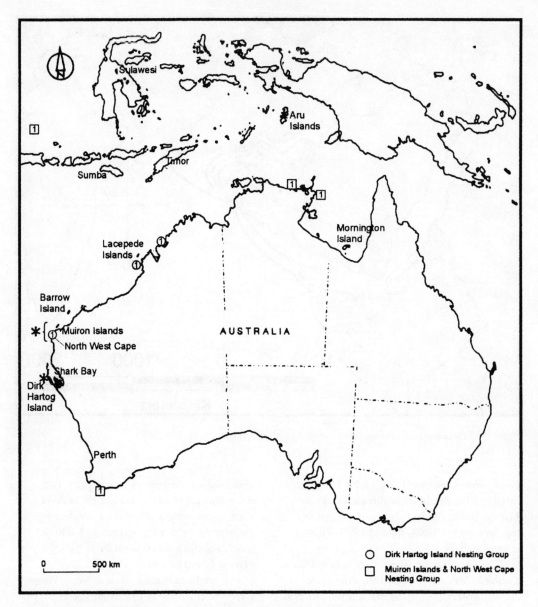

Figure 14.6. Maps showing Western Australian loggerhead turtle nesting sites with population studies in progress (*) and the locations of distant at sea recoveries of tagged female loggerheads from these populations (numbered circles and squares). A. Regional map. B. (facing page) Map of Shark Bay World Heritage Area. Numbers in circles and squares represent numbers of recaptured loggerheads at each site. Turtles from off the east side of Peron Peninsula captured by the rodeo technique; all others captured incidentally by commercial trawl fisheries.

(Poiner et al. 1990; Poiner and Harris 1996) within the range of turtles dispersing from the North West Cape and Muiron Islands region that suggests that this nesting population was depleted before recent beach monitoring commenced. The North West Cape and the mainland nesting beaches of the Ningaloo coast are further known to have a long established population of feral European red fox *(Vulpes vulpes)* that has preyed heavily on eggs (P. Mack, unpubl. work). This longstanding mortality may be one reason for the depletion of the mainland-nesting loggerheads. Dirk Hartog Island and the Muiron Islands are presently fox free.

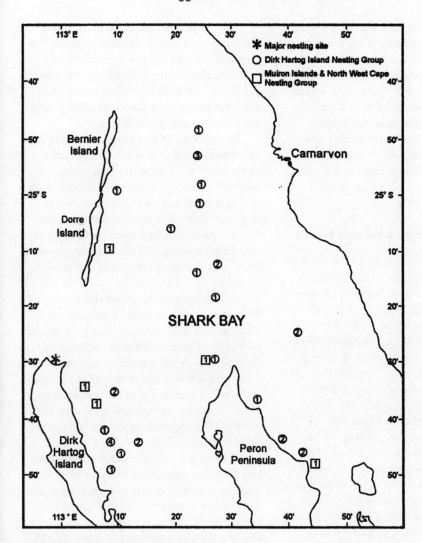

Migration and Movements

The at sea recovery data for adult female logger-head turtles tagged at Western Australia beaches are biased in that nearly all distant records are from reports of third parties. Extensive, directed sampling at sea within the possible foraging range of Western Australian loggerheads has not been possible. These third-party records are, however, sufficiently well dispersed to suggest that there is substantial overlap in the foraging range of turtles from Dirk Hartog Island and North West Cape and Muiron Islands nesting groups. It is also likely that turtles from beaches between these limits share a foraging range.

There are numerous reports of tagged turtles captured at sea within Shark Bay both by the prawn and scallop fisheries and by Simon Fraser University workers using a "turtle rodeo" technique (Heithaus and Frid, pers. comm.) off the eastern side of Peron Peninsula (Figure 14.6b). These tag recoveries suggest that the proportions of tagged turtles caught in each instance are similar to the proportions of female turtles tagged at the two represented nesting beach groups, the Dirk Hartog Island group and the North West Cape and Muiron Islands group.

The three most northerly dispersal locations reported for Western Australian nesting logger-heads are all for Muiron Islands nesting turtles (Figure 14.6a). Two of these are from locations off the north and east Arnhem Land coasts of the Australian Northern Territory, and the third is from Indonesian waters of the Java Sea. These data show that some loggerhead turtles nesting around North West Cape and at the Muiron Islands forage within distant tropical locations, perhaps more so than do loggerheads from the Dirk Hartog Island group. The eastern Arnhem Land coast location for one of these Muiron Island nesting turtles also indicates foraging area overlap between Western Australian and eastern Australian (Queensland) nesting loggerheads (Limpus et al. 1992). There is, however, genetic separation between these groups (Fitzsimmons et al. 1996).

Management Related Research Needs

Although the information presented here is not a comprehensive review of all data available for the Indian Ocean, it is clear that there are many gaps in researchers' knowledge of the abundance and distribution of loggerhead turtles in the region and of the threats to these populations from human activity. The large numbers of nesting loggerheads on Masirah Island suggest that this site is one of two global centers of abundance for loggerhead nesting. Systematic, long-term surveys of nesting at Masirah Island and reliable measures of clutch frequency, nesting success (nests/attempts), and remigration interval are desperately needed for a complete understanding of how many turtles depend on Masirah Island's beaches and how these numbers change with time. Loggerhead nesting elsewhere in Oman needs similar attention. The results of this effort will be instrumental to decisions concerning conservation management planning.

Although Limpus and Limpus (Chapter 12 this volume) refute reports that loggerheads nest in Malaysia, the apparent lack of loggerhead nesting there requires further investigation through dedicated beach surveys and inventories. Surveys could be expanded to include neighboring countries such as Indonesia and Thailand and other Indian Ocean range states for which little or no information is available, including Burma, Bangladesh, Pakistan, Arabian countries, coastal states of northern and eastern Africa, and island nations. Similar research is also needed to provide reliable information on the status of loggerheads in India, Sri Lanka, and Madagascar.

South Africa and Australia have established regular research and monitoring programs that both countries should be encouraged to continue and expand. Implementation of research in other countries should follow consultation with such programs to ensure standard tagging and other research methodology.

Identification of benchmark aquatic habitats and feeding grounds is needed for all Indian Ocean loggerhead populations and more detailed information is required on dispersal from nesting beaches and on migration routes, patterns and movements for different life stages. Genetic studies of loggerheads could facilitate identification of regional population/management units and inform studies of migration, mortality, and other research topics.

Further research on natural and human threats to loggerhead turtles is also needed in all areas. This should include broadscale studies such as those to determine the condition and dynamics of habitats, the effects of coastal development activities and plans, and the temporal and seasonal distribution of fisheries activities, as well as specific studies such as those on the impacts of lighting and on the causes and levels of harvest and bycatch.

The creation of a centralized regional database for the results of relevant research would allow for further analysis of available information and research needs of loggerhead turtles in the Indian Ocean. Such a centralized and accessible source of information would facilitate coordination and cooperation between range states to develop effective regional management strategies.

ACKNOWLEDGMENTS

Thanks are due to numerous workers who have over many years provided baseline data for the Indian Ocean and to the many who have contributed to the awareness of the necessity for loggerhead conservation in the Indian Ocean. In South Africa the work was initiated by the late Mr. Peter Potter of the Natal Parks Board, and over its many years of operation funding has been provided by the Natal Parks Board, the KwaZulu Directorate of Nature Conservation, and their successors, WWF–South Africa and, more recently, Wilderness Safaris. Western Australian data are from the Western Australian Marine Turtle Project, a regional marine wildlife conservation and environmental management program initiated and developed by DCALM, Western Australia, in partnership with the Australian Nature Conservation Agency (now incorporated into Environment Australia). Base funding then available for the North West Cape and Muiron Islands segment was augmented by community contributions made by the North West Cape conservation group CARE, and the Kwinana- Rockingham-Mandurah Branch of the Western Australia Naturalists Club and by industry via participation of Coates' Wildlife Tours. The most recent work at North West Cape and the Muiron Islands has been supported by M. G. Kailis Gulf Fisheries and helped by the DCALM Exmouth District. All work at Dirk Hartog Island has been supported by the World Heritage Management Program and aided by the continuing participation of Craig and Jessie Shankland (James Scheerer Research Charter, Denham). The seasonal fieldwork programs on nesting beaches could not have been done without the substantial help of many volunteers. The many turtle hunters, fisherfolk, and others who have taken the care to ensure that their finds have been reported have provided dispersal data. Oman data are from projects initiated by WWF and IUCN in cooperation with the Omani government.

LITERATURE CITED

Anonymous. 1989a. Oman coastal zone management plan: Dhofar. Vol. 1. Action plan. Gland, Switzerland: IUCN.

———. 1989b. Oman coastal zone management plan: Dhofar. Vol. 2. Resource atlas. Gland, Switzerland: IUCN.

———. 1999. Report of the consultation on needs and mechanisms for regional conservation and management of marine turtles, Perth, Western Australia, 19–22 October 1999.

Baldwin, R. M. 1992. Nesting turtles on Masirah Island: Management issues, options, and research requirements. Report, Ministry of Regional Municipalities and Environment, Oman.

Baldwin, R. M., and A. Al-Kiyumi. 1996. Marine turtles of the Sultanate of Oman. National Report, Northern Indian Ocean, Sea Turtle Workshop and Strategic Planning Session, January 13–18, 1996.

———. 1999. The ecology and conservation status of the sea turtles of Oman. In M. Fisher, S. A. Ghazanfar, and J. A. Spalton (eds.). The natural history of Oman: A *festschrift* for Michael Gallagher, 89–98. Leiden, The Netherlands: Backhuys Publishers.

Baldwin, R. M., and T. Q. C. Collins. 2000. Records of wildlife and observed operational impacts on wildlife. Seismic survey. Block 40. Musandam, Oman. Environmental Observation Report 1. Oman: Triton Oman Resources, Inc.

Ballance, L. T., R. I. Pitman, S. B. Reilly, and M. P. Force. 1996. Report of a cetacean, seabird, marine turtle and flying fish survey of the western tropical Indian Ocean aboard the Research Vessel Malcolm Baldridge, March 21–July 26, 1995. NOAA Technical Memorandum NOAA-TM-NMFS-SWFSC-224.

Carr, A. 1952. Handbook of turtles. Ithaca, N.Y.: Cornell University Press.

Deraniyagala, P. E. P. 1933. The loggerhead turtles (*Carettidae*) of Ceylon. Ceylon Journal of Science 18:61–72.

Deraniyagala, P. E. P. 1939. The tetrapod reptiles of Ceylon. Vol. 1. Testudinates and crocodilians. Colombo: Colombo Museum.

Dodd, C. K., Jr. 1988. Synopsis of the biological data on the loggerhead sea turtle Caretta caretta (Linnaeus 1758). USFWS Biological Report 88.

FitzSimmons, N. N., C. Moritz, C. J. Limpus, J. D. Miller, C. J. Parmenter, and R. Prince, R. 1996. Comparative genetic structure of green, loggerhead, and flatback populations in Australia based on variable mtDNA and nDNA regions. In B. W. Bowen and W. N. Witzell (eds.). Proceedings of the international symposium on sea turtle conservation genetics, 25–32. NOAA Technical Memorandum NMFS-SEFSC-396.

Govender, A., and G. R. Hughes. 2001. Estimating the population size of nesting loggerhead turtles from tagging data. In S. Ciccione, D. Roos, and J.-Y. Le Gall (eds.). Advances in knowledge and conservation of sea turtles in the south-west Indian Ocean, 42–43. IFREMER, La Reunion.

Hughes, G. R. 1974. The sea turtles of southeast Africa 1: Status morphology and distributions. Investigation Report of the Oceanographic Research Institute, Durban, South Africa. 35:1–144.

———. 1999. The Tongaland sea turtle project—1998/1999. Internal Report. Pietermaritzburg, South Africa: KZN Nature Conservation Service.

———. 2001. The loggerhead and leatherback turtles of Tongaland, South Africa, their restoration, their recovery and contribution to local and regional economy. In S. Ciccione, D. Roos, and J-Y Le Gall (eds.). Advances in knowledge and conservation of sea turtles in the southwest Indian Ocean, 30–31. La Reunion: IFREMER.

Kar, C. S., and S. Bhaskar. 1982. Status of sea turtles in the eastern Indian Ocean. In K. A. Bjorndal (ed.). Biology and conservation of sea turtles, 365–372. Washington, D.C.: Smithsonian Institution Press.

Limpus, C. J., J. D. Miller, C. J. Parmenter, D. Reimer, N. McLachlan, and R. Webb. 1992. Migration of green *(Chelonia mydas)* and loggerhead *(Caretta caretta)* turtles to and from eastern Australian rookeries. Wildlife Research 19:347–358.

Loveridge, A., and E. E. Williams. 1957. Revision of African turtles and tortoises of the sub order *Cryptodira*. Bulletin of the Museum of Comparative Zoology, Harvard 155:163–557.

Marine Parks and Reserves Selection Working Group. 1994. A representative marine reserve system for Western Australia. Report of the Western Australian Marine Parks and Reserves Selection Working Group. Perth, Western Australia: DCALM.

McAllister, H. J., A. J. Bass, and H. J. van Schoor. 1965. Marine Turtles on the coast of Tongaland, Natal. Lammergeyer 3:10–40.

Miller, J. D. 1989. An assessment of the conservation status of marine turtles in Saudi Arabia, vol. 1. MEPA Coastal and Marine Management Series 9.

Mortimer, J. A. 1990. Marine turtle conservation in Malaysia. *In* J. I. Richardson, T. H. Richardson, and M. Donnelly (compilers). Proceedings of the 10th annual workshop on sea turtle biology and conservation, 21–23. NOAA Technical Memorandum NMFS-SEFC-278.

Nishimura, W., and S. Nakahigashi. 1990. Incidental capture of sea turtles by Japanese research and training vessels: Results of a questionnaire. Marine Turtle Newsletter 51:1–4.

Pilcher, N. J., and M. A. Saad. 1999. Sea turtles of Socotra. Report to the Senckenberg Research Institute, Frankfurt, Germany.

Poiner, I. R., and A. N. M. Harris. 1996. Incidental capture, direct mortality, and delayed mortality of sea turtles in Australia's northern prawn fishery. Marine Biology 125:813–825.

Poiner, I. R., R. C. Buckorth, and Q. N. M Harris. 1990. Incidental capture and mortality of sea turtles in Australia's northern prawn fishery. Australian Journal of Marine and Freshwater Research 41:97–110.

Prince, R. I. T. 1993. Western Australia Marine Turtle Conservation Project: An outline of scope and an invitation to participate. Marine Turtle Newsletter 60:8–4.

———. 1994a. Status of the Western Australian marine turtle populations: The Western Australian Marine Turtle Project 1986–1990. *In* R. James (compiler). Proceedings of the Australian marine turtle conservation workshop, November 1990, 1–14. Canberra, Australia: ANCA.

———. 1994b. Shark Bay World Heritage Area: An important loggerhead nesting site. Marine Turtle Newsletter 67:5–6.

———. 1997. Dirk Hartog Island loggerhead nesting population study. Report on the 1996/97 seasonal work programme. Perth, Western Australia: DCALM.

———. 1998a. Dirk Hartog Island loggerhead turtle nesting population study. Report on the 1997/98 seasonal work programme. Perth, Western Australia: DCALM.

———. 1998b. North West Cape and Muiron Islands marine turtle nesting population study. Report on the 1997/98 seasonal work programme. Perth, Western Australia: DCALM.

———. 1999. Dirk Hartog Island loggerhead turtle nesting population study. Report on the 1998/99 seasonal work programme. Perth, Western Australia: DCALM.

Pritchard, P. C. H. 1979. Encyclopedia of turtles. Neptune, N.J.: T. F. H. Publications.

Rakotonirina, B. 2001. Sea turtles in Madagascar. *In* S. Ciccione, D. Roos, and J.-Y. Le Gall (eds.). Advances in knowledge and conservation of sea turtles in the southwest Indian Ocean, 38–39. IFREMER, La Reunion.

Ross, J. P. 1979. Sea turtles in the Sultanate of Oman. Manuscript report of IUCN/WWF Project 1320.

———. 1998. Estimations of the nesting population size of loggerhead sea turtles, *Caretta caretta*, Masirah Island, Sultanate of Oman. *In* S. P. Epperly and J. Braun (compilers). Proceedings of the 17th annual sea turtle symposium, 84–87. NOAA Technical Memorandum NMFS-SEFSC-415.

Ross J. P., and M. A. Barwani. 1982. Review of turtles in the Arabian area. *In* K. A. Bjorndal (ed.). Biology and conservation of sea turtles, 373–383. Washington, D.C.: Smithsonian Institution Press.

Salm, R. V. 1991. Turtles in Oman: Status, threats and management options. Manuscript report of IUCN Coastal Zone Management Project CZMP4:F11.

Salm, R., and S. Salm. 1991. Sea turtles in the Sultanate of Oman. Historical Association of Oman.

Salm, R. V., R. A. C. Jensen, and V. A. Papastavrou. 1993. Marine fauna of Oman: Cetaceans turtles, seabirds, and shallow water corals. Gland, Switzerland: IUCN.

Schleyer, M., and R. M. Baldwin. 1999. Biodiversity assessment of the northern Somali coast east of Berbera. Report for IUCN Eastern Africa Programme, Somali Natural Resources Management Programme.

Smith, A. 1849. Appendix to illustrations of the zoology of South Africa. Reptiles. London, U.K.

Tambiah, C. R. 1989. Status and conservation of sea turtles in Sri Lanka. *In* S. A. Eckert, K. L. Eckert, and T. H. Richardson (compilers). Proceedings of the ninth annual workshop on sea turtle conservation and biology, 179–180. NOAA Technical Memorandum NMFS-SEFC 232.

Part Three
Syntheses

Chapter 15

Roles of Loggerhead Sea Turtles in Marine Ecosystems

—Karen A. Bjorndal

The life cycle of the loggerhead is now the best elucidated of all sea turtle species, which is fortuitous, because the loggerhead is the generalist among sea turtle species. In a group of species with specializations verging on the bizarre—the sponge diet of *Eretmochelys imbricata*, the jellyfish diet of *Dermochelys coriacea*, and the mass-nesting *arribadas* of *Lepidochelys*—the loggerhead has taken the middle course in its life cycle, reproductive patterns, and diet.

Throughout their complex life cycle, loggerheads occupy a series of habitats: nesting beach, oceanic, and neritic habitats. Knowledge of the roles that loggerheads play in these habitats is essential to understanding the functioning of these ecosystems. How have ecosystems changed as a result of the depletion or local extinctions of loggerhead populations? What changes will result if loggerhead populations are allowed to decline or if they recover? What ecosystem characteristics are necessary for the recovery of loggerhead populations? How many loggerheads can be supported by ecosystems today, and how do these numbers correspond with recovery goals that have been set for loggerhead populations?

Knowledge of the role of loggerheads within their ecosystems will also improve the ability to predict how environmental changes—either natural or human-induced—will affect loggerhead populations. This understanding would greatly enhance the ability to make informed management decisions. What is the effect of the harvest of horseshoe crabs on loggerhead populations in Chesapeake Bay? What is the effect of the depletion of shark populations on Mediterranean loggerheads? What effect would changes in the designation of allowable use in zones of the Great Barrier Reef have on loggerheads there?

Despite substantial progress in research on the biology of loggerheads, there has been relatively little research on the quantitative interactions of loggerheads with other species and with

Figure 15.1. Basic framework
for the model of the nutri
tional ecology of an organism
that is used in this chapter.

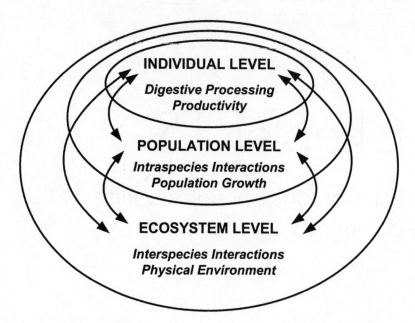

INDIVIDUAL LEVEL

Digestive Processing
Productivity

POPULATION LEVEL

Intraspecies Interactions
Population Growth

ECOSYSTEM LEVEL

Interspecies Interactions
Physical Environment

their environment. Such studies are essential for evaluating the role of loggerheads in ecosystems and for building a quantitative ecological model. In this chapter, a preliminary ecological model of the loggerhead will be constructed as a first step in assessing the role of loggerheads in the ecosystems they inhabit. Current information will be synthesized, new data will be presented, and research needs will be discussed.

The General Model

The basic ecological model developed in this chapter (Figure 15.1) is organized on three levels: individual, population, and ecosystem. As indicated by the arrows, there are interactions within and among all of these levels. Although these interactions may take many forms, the most common currencies of these interactions are energy and nutrients. By tracing the flow of energy and nutrients through these levels, one can quantify the role of loggerheads in their ecosystems. On first consideration, this approach—essentially modeling the nutritional ecology of the loggerhead—may seem a narrow one to some readers. In reality, nutritional ecology provides an all-encompassing approach. Nutrition fuels all biological processes. The flow of energy and the recycling of nutrients are what binds together the components within

ecosystems as well as among ecosystems. For the last several decades, ecologists have used energy as the common currency of ecological systems. More recently, a healthy respect for the role of nutrients has been added. Thus, the development of a model as illustrated in Figure 15.1 complements similar efforts in the field of ecology and may be readily incorporated into models based on a larger scale, such as that of ocean basins. For example, the international program "Ecopath with Ecosim" is based on construction and analysis of mass-balance models and nutrient flow in ecosystems to enhance ecosystem management of marine resources (Polovina 1984; Walters et al. 1997).

To construct such a model, processes within and among the three levels must be quantified. At the individual level (Figure 15.2), digestive processing—primarily intake of food, passage of digesta through the digestive tract, digestion, and development and maintenance of the digestive tract—are key functions to quantify and are closely interrelated. For example, as intake of a given diet increases, passage rate tends to increase, digestion tends to decrease, and gut size may increase. Also at the individual level, digestive processes fuel individual productivity— somatic growth and reproduction.

At the population level, population growth is the major process of concern, with the related

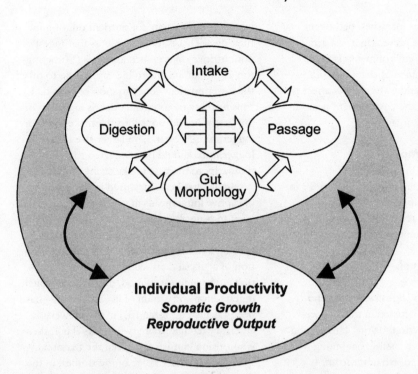

Figure 15.2. The processes at the individual level of the model. Digestive processing is a combination of intake, digestion, passage through the gut, and gut morphology. Digestive processing regulates individual productivity—somatic growth and reproductive output.

population parameters of survivorship, birth rate, immigration, and emigration. Population growth is dependent on individual productivity, and in turn, individual productivity is subject to density-dependent effects imposed by population growth moderated through intraspecific competition.

The complexity of the model increases substantially when the ecosystem level is added (Figure 15.3). Interspecific interactions—preda-

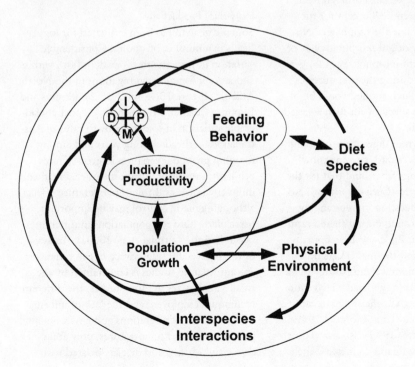

Figure 15.3. The primary pathways within and among the individual, population, and ecosystem levels of the model. Diet species are listed separately from other interspecies interactions because of their central role in this model. Feeding behavior—particularly diet selection—is a critical interface between diet species and digestive processing.

tors, prey, competitors, parasites, pathogens, and commensals—are present in a vast array. Interactions with the environment also take many forms. Environmental characteristics such as temperature and water quality affect the above processes, and the environment is modified by actions of the organism.

The Loggerhead Model

How many of the processes in Figure 15.3 can be quantified for the loggerhead? The current state of knowledge is reviewed below, and important areas for future research are emphasized.

The Individual Level

Gut Morphology and Digestive Processing
Diet species will be discussed in the Loggerheads as Predators section, below. This section deals with digestive processing, beginning with the ingestion of food, of whatever form.

The morphology and histology of the loggerhead digestive tract has been described by Thompson (1980) in a publication with an unfortunately restricted distribution. Thompson (1980) concluded that neither the anatomy nor the histology of the loggerhead differed from those of the "general reptile," except for the cornified papillae that line the esophagus. No study on the plasticity of gut morphology or of the effect of diet on gut morphology in loggerheads was discovered during the literature review for this chapter. Such studies would be of particular interest in a species with such a varied diet as the loggerhead.

Very little is known of digestive processing in loggerheads. In this regard, current knowledge of loggerheads lags far behind that for the herbivorous green turtle (Chelonia mydas). No study on intake and digestion in free-ranging loggerheads was discovered during the literature review for this chapter. Birse and Davenport (1987) found significant thermal effects between 20 and 30°C on intake and passage of an artificial diet in juvenile loggerheads. Digestion has been measured on an artificial diet in captive posthatchlings (McCauley and Bjorndal 1999). McCauley and Bjorndal (1999) also showed that posthatchlings are unable to increase their intake to compensate for nutrient dilution in their diet. That is, posthatchlings that ingest nonnutritive objects such as debris (Witherington 2002) are unable to increase intake to offset the lower nutrient concentration of their diet. This inability to counteract debris ingestion has important implications for sublethal effects for loggerheads. Research on larger size classes of loggerheads should be conducted to determine if capacity to increase intake changes with age.

Intake has been measured in a few studies of captive loggerheads in which growth has also been measured. From data presented in these studies, from fish composition data in Sidwell (1981), and from analyses of nutrient composition of artificial diets, conversion efficiencies—that is, the amount of food, energy or nitrogen ingested for every gram of live mass gain—have been calculated (Table 15.1). The conversion efficiency data illustrate two points. First, there is surprising consistency, given the temporal, spatial, and dietary range of the studies, in the values for those turtles on fish diets and for those turtles on artificial diets. Second, the much lower intakes of artificial diets required to produce a gram of mass gain reflect the importance of balanced diets in loggerhead nutrition.

Individual Productivity
Somatic growth has been evaluated for loggerheads in a number of studies. Considerable variation in growth rates is evident both within and among foraging aggregations in the North Atlantic (Figure 15.4; Table 15.2). Limpus and Limpus (Chapter 6 this volume) report considerable variation in somatic growth rates of Australian loggerheads among years and among foraging grounds. Variation in growth rates is primarily a result of nutrition, either directly or indirectly (such as through temperature effects), although genetic control may be important, particularly between populations in different ocean basins (Bjorndal et al. 2000a). Analysis of the source and significance of the variation among Atlantic studies is constrained by the small sample sizes in most studies, the different techniques employed, and the lack of information on extent of migrations and environmental parameters (water temperatures, prey abundance and quality, and diet) associated with

Table 15.1.

Conversion Efficiencies in Captive Loggerheads Ranging in Size from Post-Hatchlings to 30 kg

| Diet | Temp.(°C) | Conversion Efficiencies (intake per g live mass gain) | | | | Source |
		WM (g)	DM (g)	Energy (kJ)	N(g)	
Fish[a]	21	—	2.4	42.0	0.33	4
Fish[a]	28	11	—	45.4	0.34	2
Fish[a]	24	—	3.3	58.4	0.34	5
Fish[b]	22	15	—	61.0	0.44	1
Artificial[c]	24	—	1.2	15.9	0.12	3
Artificial[d]	27	4.1	1.3	27.0	0.11	6

Source Key: 1. Albert I 1898. 2. Kaufmann 1975. 3. McCauley and Bjorndal 1999. 4. Nuitja and Uchida 1982. 5. Stickney et al. 1973. 6. Swingle et al. 1993.

Note: Values calculated from data presented in each of the studies and from sources described in the footnotes. WM = wet mass; DM = dry mass; N = nitrogen.

[a]Fish species specified; energy and nitrogen from Sidwell (1981).

[b]Fish species not specified; energy and nitrogen estimated from Sidwell (1981); intake and growth during summer months.

[c]Values for 10% dilution diet.

[d]Dry mass, energy, and nitrogen analyzed by Bjorndal for diet sample from M. Swingle; intake and conversion efficiencies averaged for turtles housed at Columbus Zoo and Virginia Marine Science Museum.

each study. Among foraging aggregations in the North Atlantic (Figure 15.4; Table 15.2), one would expect that growth rates would be positively related to water temperature through effects on rates of prey capture, digestive processing, and metabolism. Somatic growth should also be positively related to prey quantity and prey quality; effects of diet quality on growth can be seen in Table 15.1. More northern foraging aggregations with longer seasonal

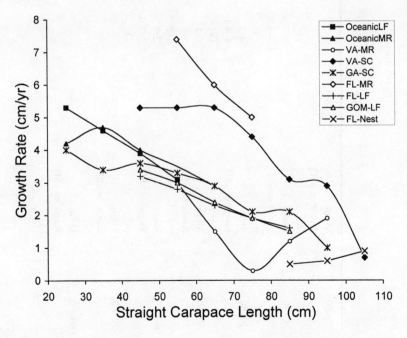

Figure 15.4. Somatic growth curves for loggerheads in the North Atlantic. Data for loggerheads in the Bahamas were omitted (see Table 15.2). LF: length-frequency analysis; MR: mark-recapture data; SC: skeletochronology; FL: Florida; GA: Georgia; GOM: Gulf of Mexico; VA: Virginia.

Table 15.2. Growth Rates for Straight Carapace Length of Noncaptive Loggerheads in North Atlantic Oceanic and Neritic Habitats

Growth Rate (cm/yr)

SCL (cm)		Oceanic Habitat		Neritic Habitat							
		North Atlantic[a]		Virginia[b]		Georgia[c]		Florida		Gulf of Mexico[g]	Bahamas[h]
		LF	MR	MR	SC	SC	MR[d]	MR[e]	LF[f]	LF	MR
20–30	Mean	5.3	4.2	—	—	4.0	—	—	—	—	—
	Range or ±SD	—	—	—	—	3.4–4.9	—	—	—	—	—
	(n)	—	(1)	—	—	(3)	—	—	—	—	—
30–40	Mean	4.6	4.7	—	—	3.4	—	—	—	—	—
	Range or ±SD	—	4.5–5.1	—	—	1.9–7.0	—	—	—	—	—
	(n)	—	(3)	—	—	(10)	—	—	—	—	—
40–50	Mean	3.9	4.0	—	5.3	3.6	—	—	3.2	3.4	15.7
	Range or ±SD	—	3.4–4.6	—	±2.8	2.6–4.3	—	—			14.8–17.2
	(n)	—	(2)	—	(6)	(9)	—	—			(3)
50–60	Mean	3.1	6.1	3.0	5.3	3.3	—	7.4	2.8	3.0	—
	Range or ±SD	—	—	±0.1	±1.4	1.7–5.2	—	±1.4			—
	(n)	—	(1)	(2)	(13)	(8)	—	(2)			
60–70	Mean	—	2.9	1.5	5.3	2.9	—	6.0	2.3	2.4	—
	Range or ±SD	—	2.8–3.0	±1.2	±1.6	2.2–4.1	—	±2.3			
	(n)	—	(2)	(9)	(29)	(6)	—	(7)			
70–80	Mean	—	—	0.3	4.4	2.1	—	5.0	1.9	1.9	5.2
	Range or ±SD	—		—	±2.0	1.6–2.9	—	±3.5			4.6–5.8
	(n)			(1)	(24)	(5)	—	(4)			(2)
80–90	Mean	—	—	1.2	3.1	2.1	0.5	—	1.6	1.5	—
	Range or ±SD			±0.9	±1.2	0.3–4.6	0–1.3	—			—
	(n)			(6)	(2)	(9)	(10)				

90–100	Mean	—	1.9	2.9	1.0	—	0.6
	Range or ±SD	—	—	±0.9	—	—	0–2.2
	(n)	—	(1)	(7)	(1)	—	(54)
100–110	Mean	—	—	0.7	—	—	0.9
	Range or ±SD	—	—	±0.02	—	—	0.2–1.9
	(n)	—	—	(2)	—	—	(4)

Note: CCL = curved carapace length; SCL = straight carapace length; SD = standard deviation; LF = length-frequency analysis; MR = mark-recapture data; SC = skeletochronology.

[a] Bjorndal et al. 2000b; total length-frequency sample = 574; see Bjorndal et al. in press for growth rates based on skeletochronology.

[b] Klinger and Musick 1995.

[c] Parham and Zug 1997; G. Zug, personal communication.

[d] Females measured on nesting beach; modified from Bjorndal et al. 1983.

[e] Mendonça 1981.

[f] Bjorndal et al. 2001; CCL converted to SCL using equation in Bjorndal et al. 2001.

[g] Bjorndal et al. 2001; CCL converted to SCL using equation in Bjorndal et al. 2001.

[h] Great Inagua, Bahamas; Bjorndal and Bolten 1988.

migrations could be expected to have lower growth rates because energy is diverted from growth to migration, unless the extra costs due to migration are offset by greater quantity or quality of prey in northern foraging grounds. Future growth studies should place greater emphasis on associated nutritional and environmental characteristics. When such data are available, they can be incorporated into growth analyses using the generalized additive modeling approach employed by Milani Chaloupka (Bjorndal et al. 2000a; Chaloupka and Limpus 1997; Limpus and Chaloupka 1997). Future research should also evaluate whether polyphasic models are a better representation of loggerhead growth functions (Chaloupka 1998).

Two aspects of the growth data for North Atlantic loggerheads are striking (Table 15.2; Figure 15.4). First is the very rapid growth rates of small loggerheads in the Bahamas. Second, despite the variation reported within and among studies, there is a concordance among mean growth rates reported from the two studies in the oceanic zone and four of the seven studies in neritic foraging grounds (Figure 15.4), although these latter four studies are from widely separated foraging areas (Georgia, Florida, and the Gulf of Mexico). How representative these growth rates are for North Atlantic loggerhead populations will be established as more growth data are collected. The rapid rates reported by Mendonça (1981) for growth of loggerheads in Mosquito Lagoon, Florida, may be an artifact of short growth intervals. Nine of Mendonça's 13 recapture intervals were substantially shorter than 12 months; short recapture intervals, particularly in temperate climates, can generate inaccurate estimates if extrapolated to an annual growth rate.

The two components of individual productivity—growth and reproduction—are integrated. Somatic growth in sexually mature loggerheads is extremely slow (Bjorndal et al. 1983; Frazer and Ehrhart 1985; Limpus and Limpus, Chapter 6 this volume) because available nutrients are diverted away from somatic growth to reproduction. Thus, adult size does not increase substantially after sexual maturity is attained. Within a population, loggerheads achieve sexual maturity at a range of body sizes (Frazer and Ehrhart 1985; Limpus and Limpus,

Chapter 6 this volume); thus, growth rate in immatures is a major determinant of age and size at sexual maturity. A higher plane of nutrition in immature loggerheads, supporting more rapid growth, may well affect future reproductive output by yielding a greater body size at sexual maturity. Larger body size in loggerheads is positively correlated with several measures of reproductive output (Tiwari and Bjorndal 2000; Van Buskirk and Crowder 1994).

Individual reproductive traits (including egg size, clutch size, clutch frequency, hatching success, interbreeding intervals, length of reproductive migrations, and number of reproductive seasons) are some of the most thoroughly quantified demographic parameters for loggerheads (Dodd 1988; Van Buskirk and Crowder 1994). Significant variation in these parameters has been noted both within and among populations (Marcovaldi and Laurent 1996; Margaritoulis et al., Chapter 11 this volume; Tiwari and Bjorndal 2000; Van Buskirk and Crowder 1994). The extent to which nutrition contributes to this variation has not been quantified, but the importance of the energy and nutrient status of sea turtles in determining the allocation of resources to reproduction and the timing of reproduction has been discussed (Bjorndal 1985, 1997). A higher plane of nutrition in adult loggerheads will directly affect reproductive output by increasing the amount of energy and nutrients that can be invested in reproduction.

For loggerheads, nutrient effects are probably greatest for clutch frequency (the number of clutches a female deposits in a breeding season) and the interbreeding interval. Nutrition almost certainly has a smaller effect on clutch size and egg size. A comparison of the reproductive output of green turtles fed a high-protein diet at Cayman Turtle Farm and of wild green turtles feeding on their natural, low-protein diets demonstrated that the greater nutrients available to the farm turtles resulted in greater clutch frequency and shorter interbreeding intervals, but no change in clutch size (Bjorndal 1985).

The Population Level

The current state of knowledge of the dynamics of population growth of loggerhead populations has been thoroughly reviewed (this volume:

Chaloupka, Chapter 17; Heppell et al., Chapter 16). For an ecological model of loggerheads to be developed, researchers need to understand not only population dynamics—a tremendous challenge in itself—but also how demographic parameters are regulated, with emphasis on the extent to which energy and nutrients act as regulating mechanisms. When the mechanisms that regulate population dynamics are understood, the effects of environmental changes—either natural or human-induced—on loggerhead populations can be predicted.

Effects of population density on somatic growth, reproductive output, and population growth have not been quantified in loggerheads. Density-dependent effects would be important additions to population models (this volume: Chaloupka, Chapter 17; Heppell et al., Chapter 16) and are essential to predict how demographic parameters, and thus population dynamics, may change if loggerhead populations are allowed to recover and population densities increase. A density-dependent effect on somatic growth has been evaluated in green turtles (Bjorndal et al. 2000a), and similar effects would be expected in loggerheads. A study currently underway to quantify density-dependent effects on hatchling production of green turtles nesting at Tortuguero, Costa Rica (Tiwari, in prep.), may yield results that can be extrapolated to loggerhead populations.

The Ecosystem Level

Loggerheads as Predators

Loggerheads in both oceanic and neritic habitats are primarily carnivorous, although they do ingest some vegetation (Bjorndal 1997). Witherington (2002) compared lavage samples from 65 posthatchlings inhabiting the surface neritic waters off the coast of Florida with the material surrounding them at time of capture. The posthatchlings had ingested over 100 taxa and had fed selectively—ingesting animal matter to a greater extent than it occurred in the surrounding material. Most animal prey were associated with *Sargassum* communities and were slow moving or attached to *Sargassum* or floating seagrasses (Witherington 2002). In the oceanic zone, loggerheads consume primarily coelenterates and salps, but they also ingest a range of

organisms including the pelagic snail *Janthina* spp., barnacles (*Lepas* spp.), and crabs (Bjorndal 1997). In neritic habitats, loggerheads consume a wide range of invertebrate species, most of which are slow moving or sessile and have hard exoskeletons, but neritic loggerheads continue to ingest coelenterates and salps when available. Lists of prey taxa that clearly reveal the diversity of prey species have been generated —nearly 200 taxa recorded for all life stages (Dodd 1988). In a significant new contribution to the literature on loggerhead diets, Limpus et al. (2001) have described over 94 taxa consumed by loggerheads in neritic habitats in eastern Australia. Recent studies of the diet of Mediterranean loggerheads in neritic habitats (Godley et al. 1997; Laurent and Lescure 1994; Tomas et al. 2001) confirm that loggerheads feed upon a similarly diverse array of taxa with similar characteristics in that region.

Therefore there is good, qualitative information on the diet of loggerheads, although many new prey species will undoubtedly be added in the future, particularly for oceanic stage loggerheads. Quantitative aspects are much weaker. Some studies have quantified the relative proportions of different prey species in the stomach contents of loggerheads (e.g., Limpus et al. 2001; Plotkin et al. 1993), which greatly enhances the understanding of loggerhead foraging beyond lists of prey species or calculations of frequency of occurrence of prey species in loggerhead gut contents.

However, despite the fact that loggerheads have been implicated as major predators on commercially important species, such as the saucer scallop (*Amusium japonicum balloti*) in Australia and the queen conch (*Strombus gigas*) in the Bahamas (Dredge 1985; Iversen et al. 1986), the effect of loggerhead predation on prey species cannot be quantified, nor can the effect of changes in prey populations on loggerhead populations be predicted. Before these effects can be evaluated, two major gaps must be addressed. First, selective feeding must be evaluated in loggerheads—do they exhibit strong feeding selectivity for certain types of prey species or do they feed primarily on the basis of availability in the environment. That is, can the ingestion of prey species be predicted from the relative abundance of prey species in the envi-

244   K. A. Bjorndal

ronment? Selective feeding has received only limited attention. As cited in Limpus et al. (2001), two preliminary studies, one in the Northern Territory, Australia (Conway 1994), and one on the Great Barrier Reef (Moodie 1979), both indicated that the occurrence of prey in the gut contents of loggerheads was not the same as the relative availability of prey. In-depth studies of selective feeding, such as those conducted for green turtles in Australia (Forbes 1996) and hawksbills in the Dominican Republic (León and Bjorndal 2002), are needed. If loggerheads feed selectively, additional studies are needed on how these preferences are established and to what extent they are maintained (Grassman and Owens 1982; Steele et al. 1989).

The second gap, which is even more important for the ecological model, is ignorance of rates of food intake in wild loggerheads. How many conch would a 50 kg loggerhead consume in a day? There are estimates of intake in wild green turtles (summarized in Bjorndal et al. 2000a), but values from herbivorous green turtles cannot be extrapolated to loggerheads. A few studies have measured both intake and growth in captive loggerheads (see Table 15.1), and these values can be used to generate rough estimates of intake in wild loggerheads of known growth rates. For example, the jellyfish *Pelagia noctiluca* is a common prey species of oceanic stage loggerheads in the Atlantic (Bolten and Balazs 1995). The quantity of *P. noctiluca* that would be ingested daily by a loggerhead with a curved carapace length (CCL) of 30 cm growing at the mean rate of 5 cm/year (Bjorndal et al. 2000b) can be estimated as follows. A 5 cm/year growth rate in CCL is equivalent to a 3.5 kg loggerhead gaining 2.2 kg/year or 6 g/day (Bolten et al., unpubl. data). From data presented in Malej et al. (1993) on protein, carbohydrate, and lipid content of *P. noctiluca*, its energy content was calculated as 3.3 kJ/g dry mass. Dry mass of *P. noctiluca* is 6.6%, and nitrogen comprises 1.5% of the dry mass (Malej et al. 1993). From Table 15.1, the mean conversion efficiencies on fish diets are 52 kJ/g mass gain and 0.36 g N/g mass gain, respectively, for energy and nitrogen. The equivalent mean values for the artificial diets are 21 kJ/g mass gain and 0.12 g N/g

mass gain. Therefore, to support growth of 6 g/day, the loggerhead would have to consume 126–312 kJ or 0.72–2.16 g of nitrogen each day. On a diet of *P. noctiluca*, the loggerhead would have to ingest 38–95 g dry mass to meet energy needs or 48–144 g dry mass to meet nitrogen needs. Because *P. noctiluca* is 93.4% water, a loggerhead would have to ingest between 576 and 2,182 g of live *P. noctiluca* each day.

This calculation is necessarily rough. It is offered here as an example of what could be evaluated from the results of well-designed feeding trials with appropriate diets and size classes of loggerheads. Based on the approach used in fish bioenergetics studies (Brett 1995; Stewart et al. 1983), a bioenergetics model for loggerheads that should yield improved estimates is now being developed (Bjorndal and Bolten, in prep.)

Loggerheads as Prey

Loggerheads are preyed upon by a large number of species (Dodd 1988; Stancyk 1982). Risk of predation is assumed to be greatest at early life stages and to decline as loggerheads attain larger sizes and thus outgrow many of their predators. Predation on loggerhead nests is by far the best quantified for any life stage and can vary greatly in extent among regions and annually within the same region (Bouchard and Bjorndal 2000; Foley et al. 2000; Johnson et al. 1996; Marcovaldi and Laurent 1996; Margaritoulis et al., Chapter 11 this volume; Witherington 1986). On many nesting beaches, human activities have resulted in increased predation levels through direct harvest, accidental or intentional releases of introduced species—both wild and domestic—and "subsidizing" natural predator populations. Foxes *(Vulpes vulpes)* intentionally introduced in Australia have depredated a substantial number of loggerhead nests there (Limpus and Reimer 1994). Fire ants *(Solenopsis invicta)* unintentionally introduced in the United States (and the target of massive and as yet unsuccessful eradication programs) kill embryos and preemergent hatchlings. Moulis (1997) reported that fire ants attacked an average of 8% of loggerhead nests over three years on a nesting beach in Georgia. Natural raccoon *(Procyon lotor)* populations in the southeastern United States have increased as a

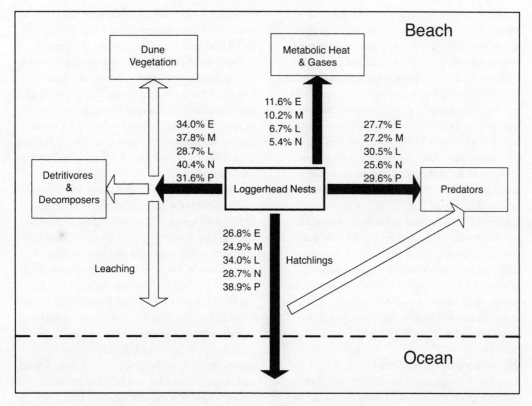

Figure 15.5. Movements of nutrients and energy from loggerhead sea turtle nests in Melbourne Beach, Florida. Values are percentages of energy (E), and each nutrient (M: organic matter; L: lipids; N: nitrogen; P: phosphorus) that followed each pathway. Solid arrows indicate pathways for which values have been determined. Open arrows indicate pathways for which the quantities of nutrients and energy have not been estimated. Modified from Bouchard and Bjorndal (2000).

result of human activities—depletion of raccoon predators and subsidies in the form of food and freshwater supplies. Before control programs were initiated, raccoons depredated over 90% of loggerhead nests in some areas of Florida (McMurtray 1986; Ratnaswamy et al. 1997). A substantial proportion of energy and nutrients contained in loggerhead eggs may be consumed by predators. In 97 loggerhead nests deposited in Melbourne Beach, Florida, 28% of the energy and 26% of the nitrogen contained in the 97 nests were channeled to predators (Figure 15.5; Bouchard and Bjorndal 2000).

Predation on hatchlings as they move across the beach from nest to ocean and as they swim away from shore during their swimming frenzy has been poorly studied. Predation during this interval may well be substantial and could be quantified; research should be directed to this question. Five of 74 hatchling loggerheads tow-

ing small tracking floats (2 of 36 daytime releases and 3 of 38 night releases) were taken by predators (probably fish) off the eastern coast of Florida (Witherington and Salmon 1992). Eleven of 100 hatchlings towing small tracking floats were depredated within 15 minutes of leaving the beach on the eastern coast of Florida, with higher rates recorded at areas with greater nest density (Glenn 1998). These values are substantially lower than predation values obtained for tethered green turtle hatchlings swimming away from Heron Island, Australia (mean = 31%; Gyuris 1994), and from Seligan Island, Malaysia (40–60%; Pilcher et al. 2000), or for leatherback hatchlings (60–71%; Nellis and Henke 2000) leaving St. Croix, U.S. Virgin Islands.

No estimates of predation rate on loggerheads—or any sea turtle—are available once posthatchlings have moved away from shore. Major predators on large size classes of loggerheads are apparently limited to sharks, killer whales *(Orcinus orca)*, and humans, although monk seals *(Monachus monachus)* have preyed upon adult loggerheads in the Mediterranean (Margaritoulis et al. 1996). Tiger sharks *(Galeocerdo cuvier)* are important sea turtle predators and have developed a masticating mechanism and feeding behavior for efficient ingestion of sea turtles (Witzell 1987). White sharks *(Carcharodon carcharias)* can ingest sea turtles essentially intact and may be the primary marine predator of adult chelonians in the Mediterranean (Fergusson et al. 2000). A killer whale consumed a loggerhead in the waters around the Azores (S. Magalhaes and P. Afonso, pers. comm.). Although such predation has apparently not been recorded for loggerheads, adults of other sea turtle species fall prey to crocodiles (reviewed in Ortiz et al. 1997), jaguars *(Panthera onca)*, and pumas *(Felis concolor)* (Chinchilla 1997; Troëng 2000).

Loggerheads as Competitors

The diet of loggerheads overlaps those of other predators, but the extent of overlap and the degree of competition experienced by foraging loggerheads have not been quantified. Substantial diet overlap was reported for juvenile loggerheads and Kemp's ridleys *(Lepidochelys kempii)* in the waters around Long Island, New York (Burke et al. 1993), but larger size classes of these two species were reported to exhibit diet partitioning in Chesapeake Bay (Lutcavage and Musick 1985). Frick et al. (1999) observed loggerheads, leatherbacks, Kemp's ridleys, ocean sunfish *(Mola mola)*, and sharptail molas *(Mola lanceolata)* feeding together on the jellyfish *Stomolophus meleagris* that had formed vast schools in the western Atlantic. On 16 occasions, loggerheads and Kemp's ridleys were observed feeding together on migrating schools of cownose rays *(Rhinoptera bonasus)* by biting off pieces of the rays' wings (Frick et al. 1999).

There is growing concern that the increasing harvests of marine organisms by humans have had or will have a substantial negative effect on marine predator populations through competition for food resources (Pauly et al. 1998; Trites et al. 1997). Such competition is widely accepted as a major cause for the decline

in Steller sea lion *(Eumetopias jubatus)* populations in western Alaska (from 180,000 in 1965 to 50,000 individuals at present). As herring *(Clupea* spp.) populations have declined as a result of harvest by humans, Steller sea lions have had to shift from a diet primarily composed of lipid-rich herring to a diet primarily composed of relatively lipid-poor walleye pollock *(Theragra chalcogramma)* (Calkins et al. 1998; Merrick et al. 1997). Competition for food with humans may also be impeding recovery of Hawaiian monk seals (Antonelis and Ragen 1997).

The potential for similar effects on loggerheads deserves careful consideration (Bjorndal 1997). The diet of loggerheads includes many species that are harvested by humans, and populations of many of those prey species have declined as a result of human harvest. Decreasing food resources for loggerheads could result in sublethal effects in the form of decreased growth rates and reproductive output. Such sublethal effects will be difficult to discern because current knowledge of rates of food intake and rates of growth is so poor. Studies are needed to close these information gaps.

If loggerheads limited by food availability were released from that food limitation—perhaps as a result of migrating to new foraging grounds or of changes in harvest of prey species by humans—compensatory growth may increase productivity. Compensatory growth is realized when an organism that has had poor nutrition—either from limited food quantity or lower food quality—is provided better nutrition. For a period of time, the previously undernourished individual will grow more rapidly than, and obtain the appropriate size-at-age for, an individual that has been maintained on the higher plane of nutrition throughout its life. Compensatory growth has been evaluated in fish, birds, and mammals (Broekhuizen et al. 1994), and in oceanic stage loggerheads (Bjorndal et al., in press).

In contrast, humans have made food resources available to loggerheads that would otherwise be unavailable. Along the southeastern coast of the United States and in the western Mediterranean, nontarget species of fish discarded by commercial fisheries are consumed, sometimes as the primary diet, by loggerheads

(Shoop and Ruckdeschel 1982; Tomas et al. 2001). This discarded fish bycatch represents substantial quantities and may well have a significant impact on the nutrition of loggerheads. How this food subsidy affects loggerhead populations, other than making them more vulnerable to incidental capture in the fisheries by attracting loggerheads into the areas of fishing activity (Shoop and Ruckdeschel 1982), is not known. The shift in nutrient composition from their normal diet to a primarily fish-based diet could have important ramifications.

Interspecific competition is, of course, not limited to food resources. Competition for nest sites on nesting beaches shared with other sea turtle species may well have been substantial in some areas in the past, before sea turtle populations were depleted. Certainly, competition with humans for space on nesting beaches is intense in many areas.

Loggerheads as Substrate for Epibionts

Loggerheads support a vast array of epibionts, apparently the largest and most diverse of any of the marine turtle species (Frick et al. 1998). Extensive species lists have been compiled for several geographic regions. Caine (1986) reported 48 species of epibionts from six phyla from loggerheads nesting in Florida and South Carolina and found that loggerheads nesting north of Daytona Beach, Florida, carried an epibiotic community distinct from that on loggerheads nesting south of Cape Canaveral, Florida. Caine's hypothesis that this distinction reflected discrete loggerhead populations in these two areas was later confirmed by genetic studies (Encalada et al. 1998). A series of studies on the epibionts of loggerheads nesting in Georgia (summarized in Frick et al. 1998, 2000) has yielded 100 species from 13 phyla. Loggerheads nesting at Xcacel, Mexico, carried 37 taxa of algae in total, with up to 12 species on an individual turtle (Senties et al. 1999). Gramentz (1988) found 13 epibiont species on 101 loggerheads in the waters around Malta. Fifteen species of barnacles alone were reported from loggerheads in Queensland waters (Monroe and Limpus 1979).

In addition to species lists, the distribution of epibionts on loggerheads has been evaluated

and shown to exhibit consistent, nonrandom patterns (Frick et al. 1998; Gramentz 1988; Matsuura and Nakamura 1993). These patterns may reflect differential habitat quality—from an epibiont's point of view—over the surface of a loggerhead. Some areas offer epibionts greater protection from the abrasion resulting from contact between a loggerhead and its habitat. Differential water flow over the surface of a loggerhead creates areas that offer greater settlement success or better foraging potential for sessile epibionts.

The extensive species lists provide a solid foundation for studies that evaluate the interactions between loggerheads and the diverse communities of epibionts that they support. Effects of epibionts on loggerheads have not been quantified. Negative effects include tissue damage and increased vulnerability to pathogens caused by burrowing forms (George 1997). Energetic costs of swimming are increased, probably substantially, by the increased drag caused by epibionts. Hydrodynamic effects vary with the quantity and location of epibionts. Logan and Morreale (1994) reported that drag coefficients increased by 0–5% for sea turtles with one barnacle on the rear carapace, 30% with one barnacle on the front carapace, and 1,000% with a heavy epibiotic load over the entire shell.

Beneficial effects of epibionts for loggerheads have not been evaluated. Epibionts could provide some protection from predation by camouflaging the turtle (Frazier et al. 1991), by reinforcing the turtle's protective covering with sharp projections, and by increasing the size of the turtle. As loggerheads increase in size, they become less vulnerable to predation. Would this protection be extended to loggerheads that were larger as a result of epibionts? Epibionts can increase the size of their host considerably. Bolten (unpubl. data) captured a small loggerhead (21.3 cm CCL) in the waters around the Azores that was doubled in mass and volume by the gooseneck barnacles (*Lepas* sp.) attached to it.

The importance of loggerheads to their epibionts is another fertile area for research. Is a loggerhead a higher or lower quality substrate for epibionts than a floating log? The importance of sea turtles in maintaining marine biodiversity through their epibiont communities depends upon the extent to which epibiotic species are endemic to sea turtles and the extent to which sea turtles offer higher quality habitat.

Barnacles of the subfamily Chelonibiinae ("turtle barnacles") are obligate epizoans (Monroe and Limpus 1979; but see Frazier and Margaritoulis 1990) and share a number of characteristics that adapt them to their mobile substrate (Ross and Newman 1967). Within the Chelonibiinae, the genera *Cylindrolepas, Stephanolepas,* and *Stomatolepas* tend to specialize on marine turtles (Ross and Newman 1967). Such specialization incurs risk because the fortunes of the epibiont are tied to the success of its hosts. Ross and Newman (1967) hypothesized that the extinction of the chelonibiine barnacle *Emersonius cybosyrinx,* described from fossils from the Upper Eocene, resulted from the extinction of its host.

Loggerheads may provide a higher quality habitat for the Columbus crab *(Planes minutus)* than floating flotsam. In addition to being a common epibiont of oceanic stage loggerheads, *P. minutus* inhabits a wide range of floating objects. Dellinger et al. (1997) found that *P. minutus* on loggerheads were larger and that a higher proportion of females were brooding eggs than *P. minutus* on flotsam from the same area off Madeira.

Of course, life on a loggerhead is not without risks for epibionts. Epibionts sensitive to desiccation die when females emerge on nesting beaches (Caine 1986) or when loggerheads float with their shells above the surface of the ocean. Carr et al. (1980) reported that epibiotic barnacles were killed when loggerheads buried themselves in mud in Cape Canaveral Channel, Florida.

Loggerheads as Hosts of Parasites and Pathogens

Current knowledge of parasites and pathogens is similar to that of epibionts in that species lists are available (Blair and Limpus 1982; Dodd 1988; Glazebrook and Campbell 1990; Herbst and Jacobson 1995), but there is a dearth of quantitative studies on the effect of these organisms on the flow of energy and nutrients and on the mortality or productivity of sea turtles. Spirorchid trematodes are thought to be the most damaging parasites of loggerheads (George 1997) and may be responsible for significant debilitation and mortality in loggerheads along the Atlantic coast of the United States (Wolke et al. 1982). Fibropapillomatosis, once known only from green turtles, is now known from loggerheads (Herbst and Jacobson 1995). In Florida Bay, Florida, 11% of loggerheads captured from 1990 to 1996 had fibropapillomas (Schroeder et al. 1998); in 2000, 12 of 94 loggerheads captured (13%) exhibited the disease (B. A. Schroeder, pers. comm.). In Moreton Bay, Australia, fibropapillomas were present on 14 of 320 (4.4%) loggerheads captured between 1990 and 1992 (Limpus et al. 1994). No estimate of resulting mortality is available (Herbst 1994).

In the only study of community structure of sea turtle parasites discovered during the literature review for this chapter, Aznar et al. (1998) evaluated the species richness and patterns of species exchange in gastrointestinal helminths from 54 loggerheads from the western Mediterranean. They found low species richness and concluded that constraints to parasite recruitment (ectothermy and nomadic behavior) limited helminth exchange between individual loggerheads and between loggerheads and other marine species.

In recent years, studies of the effects of parasites and pathogens on the fitness and productivity of their hosts have yielded exciting insights (Hochachka and Dhondt 2000; Hudson and Dobson 1998), and the field is rapidly expanding. Similar studies in sea turtles would reveal the biological significance of interactions between sea turtles and their parasites and pathogens.

Loggerheads as Nutrient Transporters

Sea turtles undertake long migrations at various points in their life cycles. All of these migrations result in the transport of nutrients and energy from one area to another. The migration of females from foraging grounds to nesting beaches, however, transports the greatest quantities of nutrients and almost certainly has the greatest ecological significance.

Female loggerheads migrate long distances (this volume: Limpus and Limpus, Chapter 6; Schroeder et al., Chapter 7) from nutrient-rich foraging habitats to relatively nutrient-poor nesting beaches. Because loggerheads apparently feed at most on very limited quantities during their sojourn at the nesting beach (Limpus and Limpus, Chapter 6 this volume; Tanaka et al. 1995), the energy and nutrients contained in the eggs deposited on the nesting beach are derived from the distant foraging grounds. On Melbourne Beach, Florida, the energy and nutrient content of loggerhead eggs were determined, and the amounts incorporated into each of four pathways were quantified (see Figure 15.5; Bouchard and Bjorndal 2000). As can be seen from Figure 15.5, less than a third of the energy and nitrogen deposited in the eggs returned to the ocean in the form of hatchlings. Substantial proportions entered the terrestrial ecosystem. Although the amount of nutrients absorbed by plants was not measured directly, nutrients derived from sea turtle eggs may be an important contribution to the nutrient budget of dune vegetation. Of the 97 nests monitored, 22 had been invaded by plant roots by the end of the incubation period, with roots growing within and around the eggs. In addition, dune vegetation receives nutrients from eggs indirectly in the form of waste products of egg and hatchling predators. Nutrient redistribution by predators has been reported for red foxes (*Vulpes vulpes*) that depredate a large proportion of the loggerhead nests at Dalyan, Turkey, and carry at least some eggs from most of these nests inland and bury them (Macdonald et al. 1994). Most of these cached eggs are later consumed by the foxes, but some are not. By providing nutrients to dune vegetation, loggerheads may help to stabilize the nesting environment upon which they depend for successful reproduction (Bouchard and Bjorndal 2000).

The relative proportions of energy and nutrients that follow the pathways illustrated in Figure 15.5 may change substantially among different loggerhead nesting beaches, among different years on the same beach, and among species of sea turtles. In particular, relative proportions will change substantially with changes in predation pressure. More studies are needed to determine the extent of this variation and, more importantly, the fate of the nutrients in the different pathways.

Loggerheads as Modifiers of Habitats

Loggerheads have direct effects on their physical environment through their foraging activities. When feeding on hard-shelled prey, loggerheads reduce the shells to fragments. These fragments are either discarded at the feeding site or ingested (Limpus et al. 2001) and later deposited with feces, perhaps at a distant location. This reduction in particle size may well have an ecologically significant effect on nutrient recycling in benthic ecosystems by increasing the surface area and thus the rate at which the shells disintegrate.

Infaunal mining—a foraging behavior in which loggerheads excavate trenches by sweeping soft substrate aside with their front flippers to expose infaunal prey—may have substantial effects on substrate characteristics such as compaction, aeration, and nutrient distribution. Infaunal mining was first reported in Australia (Limpus et al. 1994; Preen 1996) and has since been reported for loggerheads in the Mediterranean (Houghton et al. 2000) and inferred from stomach contents from loggerheads along the eastern coast of the United States (Frick et al. 2001).

Hawaiian green turtles transform coral heads to coral rubble (Bennett et al. 2002). In addition to damage done while foraging, green turtles also degrade coral heads by resting adjacent to them and using them as "scratching posts." Loggerheads may have similar impacts on hard-bottom habitats while foraging but are unlikely to affect the habitat to the same degree as green turtles because loggerheads do not exhibit the extensive cleaning and scraping behavior of green turtles, as evidenced by the heavier epibiont loads on loggerheads.

Nesting beach habitats may be held in arrested succession by the activities of nesting sea turtles. Green turtles on Heron Island prevent the establishment of *Pisonia grandis* forests by uprooting seedlings while nesting (Rogers 1989). These activities maintain the open habitat essential for successful reproduction.

Conclusions

Loggerheads are important components of marine ecosystems, and as they grow, they change from important, seasonal prey species for predators on nesting beaches to major predators on benthic invertebrates in neritic habitats. In this chapter, the primary pathways of nutrient and energy exchanges that define the role of loggerheads in ecosystems have been outlined qualitatively. However, the nutrient and energy exchanges have been quantified for only a few of these pathways. Future research should emphasize quantification of these interactions and of environmental parameters associated with loggerhead activities. Such studies would improve quantification of the role of loggerheads in their ecosystems and evaluation of the ecosystem-wide effects of changes in loggerhead populations.

ACKNOWLEDGMENTS

Without Alan Bolten I would not have been able to accomplish the work leading to this chapter; I am grateful for his ideas and encouragement. My graduate students are a constant source of intellectual stimulation, which I appreciate. I thank Mark Swingle of Virginia Marine Science Museum for sending me a sample of his artificial diet for nutrient content analyses and Peter Eliazar for help with literature. I relied heavily on the Online Sea Turtle Bibliography of the Archie Carr Center for Sea Turtle Research for the literature review. I thank George Zug for sharing unpublished data with me, and I thank Michael Frick, Colin Limpus, Jesus Tomas, and Blair Witherington for sharing unpublished manuscripts. I thank the University of Florida and Department of Zoology for support and the academic freedom to pursue my research. Finally, I am grateful to my three open-minded major advisors from my undergraduate, graduate, and postdoctoral studies—John Stephens, Archie Carr, and John Moore—for their encouragement and inspiration.

LITERATURE CITED

Albert I, Prince of Monaco. 1898. Sur le développement des tortues (T. caretta). Societe de Biologie 50:10–11.

Antonelis, G., and T. Ragen. 1997. Habitat conservation and the Hawaiian monk seal. In G. Stone, J. Goebel, and S. Webster (eds.). Pinniped populations, eastern North Pacific: Status, trends, and issues, 142–149. A symposium of the American Fisheries Society 127th annual meeting. Boston, Mass.: New England Aquarium and Monterey Bay Aquarium.

Aznar, F. J., F. J. Badillo, and J. A. Raga. 1998.

Gastrointestinal helminths of loggerhead turtles (Caretta caretta) from the western Mediterranean: Constraints on community structure. Journal of Parasitology 84:474–479.

Bennett, P., U. Keuper-Bennett, and G. H. Balazs. 2002. Changing the landscape: Evidence for detrimental impacts to coral reefs by Hawaiian marine turtles. In A. Mosier, A. Foley, and B. Brost (compilers). Proceedings of the 20th annual symposium on sea turtle biology and conservation, 287–288. NOAA Technical Memorandum NMFS-SEFSC-477.

Birse, R. F., and J. Davenport. 1987. A study of gut function in young loggerhead sea turtles, Caretta caretta L., at various temperatures. Herpetological Journal 1:170–175.

Bjorndal, K. A. 1985. Nutritional ecology of sea turtles. Copeia 1985:736–751.

———. 1977. Foraging ecology and nutrition of sea turtles. In P. L. Lutz and J. A. Musick (eds.). The biology of sea turtles, 199–231. Boca Raton, Fla.: CRC Press.

Bjorndal, K. A., and A. B. Bolten. 1988. Growth rates of juvenile loggerheads, Caretta caretta, in the southern Bahamas. Journal of Herpetology 22:480–482.

Bjorndal, K. A., A. B. Meylan, and B. J. Turner. 1983. Sea turtles nesting at Melbourne Beach, Florida, I. Size, growth and reproductive biology. Biological Conservation 26:65–77.

Bjorndal, K. A., A. B. Bolten, and M. Y. Chaloupka. 2000a. Green turtle somatic growth model: Evidence for density dependence. Ecological Applications 10:269–282.

Bjorndal, K. A., A. B. Bolten, and H. R. Martins. 2000b. Somatic growth model of juvenile loggerhead sea turtles Caretta caretta: Duration of pelagic stage. Marine Ecology Progress Series 202:265–272.

Bjorndal, K. A., A. B. Bolten, B. Koike, B. A. Schroeder, D. J. Shaver, W. G. Teas, and W. N. Witzell. 2001. Somatic growth function for immature loggerhead sea turtles, Caretta caretta, in southeastern U.S. waters. Fishery Bulletin 99:240–246.

Bjorndal, K. A., A. B. Bolten, T. Dellinger, C. Delgado, and H. R. Martins. In press. Compensatory growth in oceanic loggerhead sea turtles: Response to a stochastic environment. Ecology.

Blair, D., and C. J. Limpus. 1982. Some digeneans (Platyhelminthes) parasitic in the loggerhead turtle, Caretta caretta (L.), in Australia. Australian Journal of Zoology 30:653–680.

Bolten, A. B., and G. H. Balazs. 1995. Biology of the early pelagic stage—the "lost year." In K.A. Bjorndal (ed.). Biology and conservation of sea turtles, rev. ed., 575–581. Washington, D.C.: Smithsonian Institution Press.

Bouchard, S. S., and K. A. Bjorndal. 2000. Sea turtles as biological transporters of nutrients and energy from marine to terrestrial ecosystems. Ecology 81:2305–2313.

Brett, J. R. 1995. Energetics. *In* C. Groot, L. Margolis, and W. C. Clarke (eds.). Physiological ecology of Pacific salmon, 3–68. Vancouver: University of British Columbia Press.

Broekhuizen, N., W. S. C. Gurney, A. Jones, and A. D. Bryant. 1994. Modelling compensatory growth. Functional Ecology 8:770–782.

Burke, V. J., E. A. Standora, and S. J. Morreale. 1993. Diet of juvenile Kemp's ridley and loggerhead sea turtles from Long Island, New York. Copeia 1993:1176–1180.

Caine, E. A. 1986. Carapace epibionts of nesting loggerhead sea turtles: Atlantic coast of U.S.A. Journal of Experimental Marine Biology and Ecology 95:15–26.

Calkins, D. G., E. F. Becker, and K. W. Pitcher. 1998. Reduced body size of female Steller sea lions from a declining population in the Gulf of Alaska. Marine Mammal Science 14:232–244.

Carr, A., L. Ogren, and C. McVea. 1980. Apparent hibernation by the Atlantic loggerhead turtle *Caretta caretta* off Cape Canaveral, Florida. Biological Conservation 19:7–14.

Chaloupka, M. Y. 1998. Polyphasic growth in pelagic loggerhead sea turtles. Copeia 1998:516–518.

Chaloupka, M. Y., and C. J. Limpus. 1997. Robust statistical modelling of hawksbill sea turtle growth rates (southern Great Barrier Reef). Marine Ecology Progress Series 146:1–8.

Chinchilla, F. A. 1997. La dieta del jaguar *(Panthera onca)*, el puma *(Felis concolor)* y el manigordo *(Felis pardalis)* (Carnivora: Felidae) en el Parque Nacional Corcovado, Costa Rica. Revista de Biologia Tropical 45:1223–1229.

Conway, S. P. 1994. Diets and feeding biology of adult olive ridley *(Lepidochelys olivacea)* and loggerhead *(Caretta caretta)* sea turtles in Fog Bay (N.T.). Thesis, Northern Territory University, Darwin, Australia.

Dellinger, T., J. Davenport, and P. Wirtz. 1997. Comparisons of social structure of Columbus crabs living on loggerhead sea turtles and inanimate flotsam. Journal of the Marine Biological Association of the United Kingdom 77:185–194.

Dodd, C. K, Jr. 1988. Synopsis of the biological data on the loggerhead sea turtle *Caretta caretta* (Linnaeus 1758). U.S. Fish and Wildlife Service, Biological Report 88(14).

Dredge, M. C. L. 1985. Growth and mortality in an isolated bed of saucer scallops, *Amusium japonicum balloti* (Bernardi). Queensland Journal of Agricultural and Animal Sciences 42:11–21.

Encalada, S. E., K. A. Bjorndal, A. B. Bolten, J. C. Zurita, B. Schroeder, E. Possardt, C. J. Sears, and B. W. Bowen. 1998. Population structure of loggerhead turtle *(Caretta caretta)* nesting colonies in the Atlantic and Mediterranean as inferred from mitochondrial DNA control region sequences. Marine Biology 130:567–575.

Fergusson, I. K., L. J. V. Compagno, and M. A. Marks. 2000. Predation by white sharks *Carcharodon carcharias* (Chondrichthyes: Lamnidae) upon chelonians, with new records from the Mediterranean Sea and a first record of the ocean sunfish *Mola mola* (Osteichthyes: Molidae) as stomach contents. Environmental Biology of Fishes 58:447–453.

Foley, A. M., S. A. Peck, G. R. Harmon, and L. W. Richardson. 2000. Loggerhead turtle *(Caretta caretta)* nesting habitat on low-relief mangrove islands in southwest Florida and consequences to hatchling sex ratios. Herpetologica 56:433–445.

Forbes, G. A. 1996. The diet and feeding ecology of the green sea turtle *(Chelonia mydas)* in an algal-based coral reef community. Ph.D. Dissertation, James Cook University of North Queensland, Australia.

Frazer, N. B., and L. M. Ehrhart. 1985. Preliminary growth models for green, *Chelonia mydas*, and loggerhead, *Caretta caretta*, turtles in the wild. Copeia 1985:73–79.

Frazier, J., and D. Margaritoulis. 1990. The occurrence of the barnacle, *Chelonibia patula* (Ranzani 1818), on an inanimate substratum (Cirripedia, Thoracica). Crustaceana 59:213–218.

Frazier, J. G., I. Goodbody, and C. A. Ruckdeschel. 1991. Epizoan communities on marine turtles: II. Tunicates. Bulletin of Marine Science 48:763–765.

Frick, M. G., K. L. Williams, and M. Robinson. 1998. Epibionts associated with nesting loggerhead sea turtles *(Caretta caretta)* in Georgia, U.S.A. Herpetological Review 29:211–214.

Frick, M. G., C. A. Quinn, and C. K. Slay. 1999. *Dermochelys coriacea* (leatherback sea turtle), *Lepidochelys kempi* (Kemp's ridley sea turtle), and *Caretta caretta* (loggerhead sea turtle): Pelagic feeding. Herpetological Review 30:165.

Frick, M. G., K. L. Williams, D. Veljacic, L. Pierrard, J. A. Jackson, and S. E. Knight. 2000. Newly documented epibiont species from nesting loggerhead sea turtles *(Caretta caretta)* in Georgia, U.S.A. Marine Turtle Newsletter 88:3–5.

Frick, M. G., K. L. Williams, and L. Pierrard. 2001. Summertime foraging and feeding by immature loggerhead sea turtles *(Caretta caretta)* from Georgia. Chelonian Conservation and Biology 4:117–120.

George, R. H. 1997. Health problems and diseases of sea turtles. *In* P. L. Lutz and J. A. Musick (eds.). The biology of sea turtles, 363–385. Boca Raton, Fla.: CRC Press.

Glazebrook, J. S., and R. S. F. Campbell. 1990. A survey of the diseases of marine turtles in northern Australia. 2. Oceanarium-reared and wild turtles. Diseases of Aquatic Organisms 9:97–104.

Glenn, L. 1998. The consequences of human manipulation of the coastal environment on hatchling loggerhead sea turtles *(Caretta caretta)*. *In* R. Byles and Y. Fernandez (compilers). Proceedings of the 16th annual symposium on sea turtle biology and conservation, 58–59. NOAA Technical Memorandum NMFS-SEFSC-412.

Godley, B. J., S. M. Smith, P. F. Clark, and J. D. Taylor. 1997. Molluscan and crustacean items in the diet of the loggerhead turtle, *Caretta caretta* (Linnaeus 1758) (Testudines: Chelonidae) in the eastern Mediterranean. Journal of Molluscan Studies 63:474–476.

Gramentz, D. 1988. Prevalent epibiont sites on *Caretta caretta* in the Mediterranean Sea. Naturalista Siciliano, ser. 4, 12:33–46.

Grassman, M. A., and D. W. Owens. 1982. Development and extinction of food preferences in the loggerhead sea turtle, *Caretta caretta*. Copeia 1982:965–969.

Gyuris, E. 1994. The rate of predation by fishes on hatchlings of the green turtle *(Chelonia mydas)*. Coral Reefs 13:137–144.

Herbst, L. H. 1994. Fibropapillomatosis of marine turtles. Annual Review of Fish Diseases 4:389–425.

Herbst, L. H., and E. R. Jacobson. 1995. Diseases of marine turtles. *In* K. A. Bjorndal (ed.). Biology and conservation of sea turtles, rev. ed., 593–596. Washington, D.C.: Smithsonian Institution Press.

Hochachka, W. M., and A. A. Dhondt. 2000. Density-dependent decline of host abundance resulting from a new infectious disease. Proceedings of the National Academy of Sciences 97:5303–5306.

Houghton, J. D. R., A. Woolmer, and G. C. Hays. 2000. Sea turtle diving and foraging behaviour around the Greek island of Kefalonia. Journal of the Marine Biological Association of the United Kingdom 80:761–762.

Hudson, P. J., and A. P. Dobson. 1998. Prevention of population cycles by parasite removal. Science 393:2256–2258.

Iversen, E. S., D. E. Jory, and S. P. Bannerot. 1986. Predation on queen conchs, *Strombus gigas*, in the Bahamas. Bulletin of Marine Science 39:61–75.

Johnson, S. A., K. A. Bjorndal, and A. B. Bolten. 1996. Effects of organized turtle watches on loggerhead *(Caretta caretta)* nesting behavior and hatchling production in Florida. Conservation Biology 10:570–577.

Kaufmann, R. 1975. Observaciones sobre el crecimiento de tortugas marinas en cautividad. Caldasia 11:139–150.

Klinger, R. C., and J. A. Musick. 1995. Age and growth of loggerhead turtles *(Caretta caretta)* from Chesapeake Bay. Copeia 1995:204–209.

Laurent, L., and J. Lescure. 1994. L'Hivernage des tortues caouannes *Caretta caretta* (L.) dans le sud Tunisien. Revue d'Ecologie (Terre et Vie) 49:63–86.

León, Y. M., and K. A. Bjorndal. 2002. Selective feeding in the hawksbill turtle, an important predator in coral reef ecosystems. Marine Ecology Progress Series 245:249–258.

Limpus, C., and M. Chaloupka. 1997. Nonparametric regression modelling of green sea turtle growth rates (southern Great Barrier Reef). Marine Ecology Progress Series 149:23–34.

Limpus, C. and D. Reimer. 1994. The loggerhead turtle *Caretta caretta*, in Queensland: A population in decline. *In* R. James (compiler). Proceedings of the Australian marine turtle workshop, 39–59. Canberra, Australia: QDEH and ANCA.

Limpus, C. J., P. J. Couper, and M. A. Read. 1994. The loggerhead turtle, *Caretta caretta*, in Queensland: Population structure in a warm temperate feeding area. Memoirs of the Queensland Museum 37:195–204.

Limpus, C. J., D. L. de Villiers, M. A. de Villiers, D. J. Limpus, and M. A. Read. 2001. The loggerhead turtle, *Caretta caretta*, in Queensland: Feeding ecology in warm temperate waters. Memoirs of the Queensland Museum 46:631–645.

Logan, P., and S. J. Morreale. 1994. Hydrodynamic drag characteristics of juvenile *L. kempi*, *C. mydas*, and *C. caretta*. *In* B. A. Schroeder and B. E. Witherington (compilers). Proceedings of the 13th annual symposium on sea turtle biology and conservation, 248–252. NOAA Technical Memorandum NMFS-SEFSC-341.

Lutcavage, M., and J. A. Musick. 1985. Aspects of the biology of sea turtles in Virginia. Copeia 1985:449–456.

Macdonald, D. W., L. Brown, S. Yerli, and A. Canbo-lat. 1994. Behavior of red foxes, *Vulpes vulpes*, caching eggs of loggerhead turtles, *Caretta caretta*. Journal of Mammalogy 75:985–988.

Malej, A., J. Faganeli, and J. Pezdic. 1993. Stable isotope and biochemical fractionation in the marine pelagic food chain: The jellyfish *Pelagia noctiluca* and net zooplankton. Marine Biology 116:565–570.

Marcovaldi, M. A., and A. Laurent. 1996. A six-season study of marine turtle nesting at Praia do Forte, Bahia, Brazil, with implications for conservation and management. Chelonian Conservation and Biology 2:55–59.

Margaritoulis, D., D. Karavellas, and C. Irvine. 1996. Predation of adult loggerheads by Mediterranean monk seals. *In* J. A. Keinath, D. E. Barnard, J. A. Musick, and B. A. Bell (compilers). Proceedings of the 15th annual symposium on sea turtle biology and conservation, 193–196. NOAA Technical Memorandum NMFS-SEFSC-387.

Matsuura, I., and K. Nakamura. 1993. Attachment pattern of the turtle barnacle *Chelonibia testudi-naria* on carapace of nesting loggerhead turtle *Caretta caretta*. Nippon Suisan Gakkaishi 59:1803.

McCauley, S. J., and K. A. Bjorndal. 1999. Conservation implications of dietary dilution from debris ingestion: Sublethal effects in posthatchling loggerhead sea turtles. Conservation Biology 13:925–929.

McMurtray, J. D. 1986. Reduction of raccoon predation on sea turtle nests at Canaveral National Seashore, Florida. Master's Thesis, University of Georgia, Athens.

Mendonça, M. T. 1981. Comparative growth rates of wild immature *Chelonia mydas* and *Caretta caretta* in Florida. Journal of Herpetology 15:444–447.

Merrick, R. L., M. K. Chumbley, and G. V. Byrd. 1997. Diet diversity of Steller sea lions *(Eumetopias jubatus)* and their population decline in Alaska: A potential relationship. Canadian Journal of Fisheries and Aquatic Sciences 54:1342–1348.

Monroe, R., and C. J. Limpus. 1979. Barnacles on turtles in Queensland waters with descriptions of three new species. Memoirs of the Queensland Museum 19:197–223.

Moodie, E. G. 1979. Aspects of the feeding biology of the loggerhead turtle *(Caretta caretta)*. Undergraduate Honors Thesis, James Cook University of North Queensland, Australia.

Moulis, R. A. 1997. Predation by the imported fire ant *(Solenopsis invicta)* on loggerhead sea turtle *(Caretta caretta)* nests on Wassaw National Wildlife Refuge, Georgia. Chelonian Conservation and Biology 2:433–436.

Nellis, D. W., and S. E. Henke. 2000. Predation of leatherback turtle hatchlings by near shore aquatic predators. *In* H. Kalb and T. Wibbels (compilers). Proceedings of the 19th annual symposium on sea turtle biology and conservation, 168. NOAA Technical Memorandum NMFS-SEFSC-443.

Nuitja, I. N. S., and I. Uchida. 1982. Preliminary studies on the growth and food consumption of the juvenile loggerhead turtle (*Caretta caretta* L.) in captivity. Aquaculture 27:157–160.

Ortiz, R. M., P. T. Plotkin, and D. W. Owens. 1997. Predation upon olive ridley sea turtles *(Lepido-chelys olivacea)* by the American crocodile *(Croco-dylus acutus)* at Playa Nancite, Costa Rica. Chelonian Conservation and Biology 2:585–587.

Parham, J. F., and G. R. Zug. 1997. Age and growth of loggerhead sea turtles *(Caretta caretta)* of coastal Georgia: An assessment of skeletochronological age-estimates. Bulletin of Marine Science 6:287–304.

Pauly, D., V. Christensen, J. Dalsgaard, R. Froese, and F. Torres, Jr. 1998. Fishing down marine food webs. Science 279:860–863.

Pilcher, N. J., S. Enderby, T. Stringell, and L. Bateman. 2000. Nearshore turtle hatchling distribution and predation. *In* N. Pilcher and G. Ismail (eds.). Sea turtles of the Indo-Pacific: Research, management, and conservation, 151–166. London, U.K.: Asean Academic Press.

Plotkin, P. T., M. K. Wicksten, and A. F. Amos. 1993. Feeding ecology of the loggerhead sea turtle *Caretta caretta* in the northwestern Gulf of Mexico. Marine Biology 115:1–15.

Polovina, J. J. 1984. Model of a coral reef ecosystem. Part I: The ECOPATH model and its application to French Frigate Shoal. Coral Reefs 3:1–11.

Preen, A. R. 1996. Infaunal mining: A novel foraging method of loggerhead turtles. Journal of Herpetology 30:94–96.

Ratnaswamy, M. J., R. J. Warren, M. T. Kramer, and M. D. Adam. 1997. Comparisons of lethal and non-lethal techniques to reduce raccoon depredation of sea turtle nests. Journal of Wildlife Management 61:368–376.

Rogers, R. W. 1989. The influence of sea turtles on the terrestrial vegetation of Heron Island, Great Barrier Reef. Proceedings of the Royal Society of Queensland 100:67–70.

Ross, A., and W. A. Newman. 1967. Eocene Bal-anidae of Florida, including a new genus and species with a unique plan of "turtle barnacle" organization. American Museum Novitates 2288:1–21.

Schroeder, B. A., A. M. Foley, B. E. Witherington, and A. E. Mosier. 1998. Ecology of marine turtles in Florida Bay: Population structure, distribution, and occurrence of fibropapilloma. *In* S. P. Epperly and J. Braun (compilers). Proceedings of the 17th annual symposium on sea turtle biology and conservation, 265–267. NOAA Technical Memorandum NMFS-SEFSC-415.

Senties G., A., J. Espinoza-Avalos, and J. C. Zurita. 1999. Epizoic algae of nesting sea turtles *Caretta caretta* (L.) and *Chelonia mydas* (L.) from the Mexican Caribbean. Bulletin of Marine Science 64:185–189.

Shoop, C. R., and C. Ruckdeschel. 1982. Increasing turtle strandings in the southeast United States: A complicating factor. Biological Conservation 23:213–215.

Sidwell, V. D. 1981. Chemical and nutritional composition of finfishes, whales, crustaceans, mollusks, and their products. NOAA Technical Memorandum NMFS-F/SEC-11.

Stancyk, S. E. 1982. Non-human predators of sea turtles and their control. *In* K. A. Bjorndal (ed.). Sea turtle biology and conservation, 129–152. Washington, D.C.: Smithsonian Institution Press.

Steele, C. W., M. A. Grassman, D. W. Owens, and J. H. Matis. 1989. Application of decision theory in understanding food choice behavior of hatchling loggerhead sea turtles and chemosensory imprinting in juvenile loggerhead sea turtles. Experientia 45:202–205.

Stewart, D. J., D. Weininger, D. V. Rottiers, and T. A. Edsall. 1983. An energetics model for lake trout, *Salvelinus namaycush*. Application to the Lake Michigan population. Canadian Journal of Fisheries and Aquatic Sciences 40:681–698.

Stickney, R. R., D. B. White, and D. Perlmutter. 1973. Growth of green and loggerhead sea turtles in Georgia on natural and artificial diets. Bulletin of the Georgia Academy of Science 31:37–44.

Swingle, W. M., D. I. Warmolts, J. A. Keinath, and J. A. Musick. 1993. Exceptional growth rates of captive loggerhead sea turtles, *Caretta caretta*. Zoo Biology 12:491–497.

Tanaka, H., K. Sato, Y. Matsuzawa, W. Sakamoto, Y. Naito, and K. Kuroyanagi. 1995. Analysis of possibility of feeding of loggerhead turtle during internesting periods based on stomach temperature measurements. Nippon Suisan Gakkaishi 61:339–345.

Thompson, S. M. 1980. A comparative study of the anatomy and histology of the oral cavity and alimentary canal of two sea turtles: The herbivorous green turtle *Chelonia mydas* and the carnivorous loggerhead turtle *Caretta caretta*. Master's Thesis, James Cook University of North Queensland, Australia.

Tiwari, M., and K. A. Bjorndal. 2000. Variation in morphology and reproduction in loggerheads, *Caretta caretta*, nesting in the United States, Brazil, and Greece. Herpetologica 56:343–356.

Tomas, J., F. J. Aznar, and J. A. Raga. 2001. Feeding ecology of the loggerhead turtle *Caretta caretta* in the western Mediterranean. Journal of Zoology 255:525–532.

Trites, A., V. Christensen, and D. Pauly. 1997. Competition between fisheries and marine mammals for prey and primary production in the Pacific Ocean. Journal of the Northwest Atlantic Fishery Science 22:173–187.

Troëng, S. 2000. Predation of green *(Chelonia mydas)* and leatherback *(Dermochelys coriacea)* turtles by jaguars *(Panthera onca)* at Tortuguero National Park, Costa Rica. Chelonian Conservation and Biology 3:751–753.

Van Buskirk, J., and L. B. Crowder. 1994. Life-history variation in marine turtles. Copeia 1994:66–81.

Walters, C., V. Christensen, and D. Pauly. 1997. Structuring dynamic models of exploited ecosystems from trophic mass-balance assessments. Reviews in Fish Biology and Fisheries 7:139–172.

Witherington, B. E. 1986. Human and natural causes of marine turtle clutch and hatchling mortality and their relationship to hatchling production on an important Florida nesting beach. Master's Thesis, University of Central Florida, Orlando.

———. 2002. Ecology of neonate loggerhead turtles inhabiting lines of downwelling near a Gulf Stream front. Marine Biology 140:843–853.

Witherington, B. E., and M. Salmon. 1992. Predation on loggerhead turtle hatchlings after entering the sea. Journal of Herpetology 26:226–228.

Witzell, W. N. 1987. Selective predation on large cheloniid sea turtles by tiger sharks *(Galeocerdo cuvier)*. Japanese Journal of Herpetology 12:22–29.

Wolke, R. E., D. R. Brooks, and A. George. 1982. Spirorchidiasis in loggerhead sea turtles *(Caretta caretta)*: Pathology. Journal of Wildlife Diseases 18:175–185.

Chapter 16

Population Models for Atlantic Loggerheads:

Past, Present, and Future

—Selina S. Heppell, Larry B. Crowder, Deborah T. Crouse, Sheryan P. Epperly, and Nat B. Frazer

Population models can be useful tools for decision makers because they can quantify the relative effectiveness of different management options (Heppell et al. 2000b). This is particularly critical for long-lived species such as sea turtles, where a scientist's entire career may only span one or two turtle generations. Researchers have modeled the dynamics of a wide range of species and have addressed a variety of management applications, from simple biomass-based models in fisheries (Hilborn and Walters 1992) to population viability analysis (Beissinger and Westphal 1998; Boyce 1992) for endangered species. In all cases, the models serve as hypothesis-testing tools, where a series of potential outcomes is assessed based on a set of parameters and assumptions. While some models attempt quantitative predictions of population dynamics, such as the extinction probabilities in many population viability analyses, these models also serve as heuristic tools to compare the relative magnitude of population changes, even when quantitative predictions are not possible (Groom and Pascual 1998).

Quantitative demographic models require large amounts of data on life-stage–specific survival, growth and fertility, migration, and effects of environmental variability on these parameters (Groom and Pascual 1998). Long-term mark-recapture studies, such as those conducted in Australia (Chaloupka, Chapter 17 this volume), have allowed the construction of statistically based models that can test quantitative hypotheses. But data sets of this quality and magnitude are relatively rare for sea turtles. Population demography for Atlantic loggerheads, which began in the 1970s, continues to suffer from a lack of long-term data on critical demographic rates. These limited data have required simpler models that generally produce qualitative, rather than quantitative, predictions. Although results from analyses of such models require qualitative interpretations due to uncertainty in parameter estimates and simplifying assumptions, they have provided important insights into the relative effects of various management actions and have guided sea turtle management policies in the United States (Heppell et al. 2000b).

Models of the Past

Frazer's Life Tables

Frazer (1983a) constructed a life table for loggerheads for several reasons. First, the life history of loggerheads had never been fully described. He expected that management could be improved if scientists' understanding of the loggerhead's demographic characteristics were synthesized. Second, he believed that the effectiveness of conservation efforts could be evaluated only by comparing future changes with detailed information on the loggerhead's current status. Thus, it seemed prudent to describe their present life-history characteristics in conventional terms so that any subsequent changes might be easily recognized and assessed using standard models. Third, Frazer felt that estimates of age at maturity, survivorship, and fecundity were of intrinsic interest to students of life-history evolution, irrespective of their utility in management and conservation plans. As Wilbur (1975) pointed out, the analysis of long-lived, iteroparous species constituted one of the most serious deficiencies in the study of life-history tactics. Thus, Frazer's (1983a) goal was simply "to describe the loggerhead's life history as completely as possible" by compiling all data available at the time for the western Atlantic. Of necessity, Frazer's (1983a) analyses were fraught with assumptions, as we shall see below.

The most reliable inputs to Frazer's (1983a) analyses were the empirical estimates of adult female survival and fecundity, which were based on a 17-year project at Little Cumberland Island, Georgia, where the beach was patrolled at approximately hourly intervals from dusk until dawn each night of the nesting season. Frazer (1983a, 1983b) estimated adult female survival with and without adjustments for tag loss. The hourly patrols allowed researchers to identify and mark most individual females so clutch frequency could be accurately assessed. Because the researchers transferred eggs from natural nests into a fenced location in a natural sand dune, they also counted eggs to determine clutch sizes (Frazer 1983a; Frazer and Richardson 1985). By eliminating the first five years of tagging data, Frazer (1983a) was able to estimate the reduced clutch size, reduced clutch frequency and smaller body size of "neophytes" (first-time nesters). After five years of saturation tagging on the beach, Frazer assumed that turtles arriving at the site without tags or tag scars were nesting for the first time. Tagging data also allowed Frazer to estimate return or remigration intervals, which were important for assessing age-specific survival and fecundity because not all females appear on the beach each year.

These estimates of adult female survival and fecundity also allowed Frazer to estimate the overall survival rate, from egg to maturity, necessary to maintain either a stable population or a population declining at the observed rate of approximately 3% per year at Little Cumberland Island (Frazer 1983a, 1986). Once this estimate was available, the remaining tasks were to estimate juvenile survival and, hence, determine the shape of the survivorship curve between hatching and adulthood.

At the time there were no reliable means available for aging loggerheads. Frazer (1983a; Frazer and Ehrhart 1985) used information on growth rates of juvenile and adult loggerheads in Florida waters to construct length-at-age growth curves for loggerheads. Unfortunately, no data were available for juveniles smaller than 50 cm in carapace length. Frazer (1983a) rejected the practice of using the size of the smallest known nesting female as indicative of typical size at maturity for the population. In the absence of other data, he had little recourse other than to assume that loggerheads matured at a size slightly smaller than the mean size of nesting females (i.e., the mean size of nesting females minus one standard deviation). This yielded an estimate of 22 years for age at maturity.

Frazer (1983a, 1987) also used the growth curve to assign ages to two groups of juvenile loggerheads: 607 carcasses washed ashore on Georgia beaches and 196 juveniles caught in shrimp trawls in waters off the Atlantic coast of Florida. After assigning ages to the turtles with the growth curve, Frazer (1983a, 1987) conducted a catch-curve analysis to estimate survival of juvenile loggerheads from 8 to 16 years old.

Once estimates were available for logger-heads 8–16 years of age and for nesting females, all that remained was to connect up the survivorship curves by interpolation for those turtles for which no empirical information was available (i.e., from hatchling to age 8 and from age 16 to 22). Frazer (1983a) did this under two scenarios: (1) a stable population and (2) a population declining at a rate of 3% per year, which was the average rate of decline in nesting females appearing on Little Cumberland Island, Georgia, in 1963–1980.

Three major issues merit mention. The first two are vagaries introduced into the life table due to Frazer's simplifying assumption that all loggerheads reach maturity at the same age: (1) the estimate of average fecundity at age 22 is inflated because all females are assumed to nest in the year they attain maturity, and (2) few Little Cumberland loggerheads ever return to nest at an interval of only one year, so the per capita fecundity at age 23 seems unnaturally low (four female hatchlings per year). Lastly, most modern readers will question the wisdom of combining information from the Florida and Georgia loggerhead populations in the western Atlantic. While researchers now know that loggerheads in Florida and those in Georgia probably represent two distinct breeding aggregations (Bowen et al. 1993), the genetic data were not sufficient to discriminate between loggerheads nesting in the two areas when Frazer (1983a) constructed his life tables.

Matrix Models

While Frazer's life table provided the first model for loggerhead life history, it was not clear how it might be used to help managers reverse the declines in loggerhead populations. Various management actions were in place or had been proposed, including nest protection, hatcheries, and fishing gear modification to reduce large turtle mortality in shrimp trawls. Modifications of trawls to release sea turtles were highly controversial among conservationists, managers, and the shrimping industry because it was not clear if these modifications were truly necessary to promote population recovery.

To assess this, Crouse et al. (1987) collapsed Frazer's 54 age-class life table into a 7 × 7

stage-classified transition matrix. This modeling strategy recognized the uncertainty in ages associated with each stage class and the underlying size-based structure of Frazer's life table. In the stage-based model, each row and column of the matrix represented one of Frazer's seven life stages: eggs/hatchlings, small (oceanic) juveniles, large juveniles, subadults, novice breeders, first-year remigrants (the small proportion of females that return to nest in the year following their first nesting migration), and mature breeders. The matrix included three parameters for each stage: P_i, the annual probability of surviving and remaining in a stage; G_i, the annual probability of surviving and growing into the next stage; and F_i, the per capita annual production of daughters (Equation 1). To read the transition probabilities of the matrix, think of individuals growing from a column (j) to a row (i). Reproduction, the production of eggs and hatchlings by females in each stage, occurs in the top row of the matrix. For example, column 3 of the Crouse et al. matrix indicates that, in a given year, 1.5% of large juvenile female turtles grow to become subadults while 66% of them survive but remain in the large juvenile stage (Equation 2). Turtles that die ($100 - 66 - 1.5 = 32.5\%$) "disappear" from the model. Large juveniles do not reproduce, so a zero appears in the top row of the large juvenile column.

$$\begin{bmatrix} P_1 & F_2 & F_3 & F_4 & F_5 & F_6 & F_7 \\ G_1 & P_2 & 0 & 0 & 0 & 0 & 0 \\ 0 & G_2 & P_3 & 0 & 0 & 0 & 0 \\ 0 & 0 & G_3 & P_4 & 0 & 0 & 0 \\ 0 & 0 & 0 & G_4 & P_5 & 0 & 0 \\ 0 & 0 & 0 & 0 & G_5 & P_6 & 0 \\ 0 & 0 & 0 & 0 & 0 & G_6 & P_7 \end{bmatrix} \quad (1)$$

$$\begin{bmatrix} 0 & 0 & 0 & 0 & 127 & 4 & 80 \\ 0.675 & 0.737 & 0 & 0 & 0 & 0 & 0 \\ 0 & 0.049 & 0.661 & 0 & 0 & 0 & 0 \\ 0 & 0 & 0.015 & 0.691 & 0 & 0 & 0 \\ 0 & 0 & 0 & 0.052 & 0 & 0 & 0 \\ 0 & 0 & 0 & 0 & 0.809 & 0 & 0 \\ 0 & 0 & 0 & 0 & 0 & 0.809 & 0.809 \end{bmatrix} \quad (2)$$

Caswell (Caswell 2000; Caswell and Werner 1978) has illustrated many advantages to presenting life table information in matrix form. The eigenvalues and eigenvectors of a transition matrix reveal the asymptotic population growth rate (λ, where ln[λ] = r, the population's intrinsic rate of increase), stable age distribution (w) (the constant proportion of individuals in each stage once the model has reached the equilibrium growth rate, λ, and stage-specific reproductive values (v) (the relative value of current and future reproduction by females in each stage).

Because the model did not incorporate annual variability in vital rates and included a number of uncertainties, using it to predict population size was inappropriate. Instead, Crouse et al. (1987) ran a series of "what if" scenarios to examine the relative impacts of increasing or decreasing the survival rate of each life stage. They found that increasing the annual survival rate of eggs and hatchlings to 100% had virtually no effect on population growth; in spite of an increase in the number of survivors in each annual cohort, the population continued to decline. Increasing the survival rate of small juveniles, large juveniles, subadults, and mature breeders did result in positive population growth. Relative to changes in other model parameters, population growth rate was increased most from a proportional increase in large juvenile annual survival. Thus, through simulation, Crouse et al. (1987) determined the sensitivity of population growth to changes in stage-specific annual survival.

Analytical methods for obtaining similar results were developed by Caswell et al. (1984) and further explored by de Kroon et al. (1986). A proportional sensitivity analysis, called elasticity analysis, is used to calculate the proportional changes in λ expected from proportional changes in each model parameter of a matrix (A). Elasticities ($E_{i,j}$) are easily calculated using the stable age distribution and reproductive value vectors of A:

$$E_{i,j} = \frac{\partial \lambda}{\partial A_{i,j}} \frac{\lambda}{A_{i,j}} = \frac{v_i w_j}{\langle \mathbf{v}, \mathbf{w} \rangle} \tag{3}$$

where $\langle \mathbf{v}, \mathbf{w} \rangle$ is the scalar product of the two eigenvectors, or $\Sigma v_i w_i$ (Caswell 2000). This analysis was applied to the Crouse et al. (1987) model and has been used in subsequent loggerhead models (Crowder et al. 1994; Heppell et al. 1996a). It is one of the most useful results

obtained from a deterministic (i.e., non–time varying) matrix model without density dependence (de Kroon et al. 2000). For management applications, λ is treated as an index, and it is assumed that perturbations that cause large changes in λ are more effective than perturbations that cause small changes in λ.

Stage-classified models are very useful when life stages are based on size or shifts in diet or habitat over the developmental period, but they do not capture population responses to time lags. Late age at maturity in sea turtles makes it particularly important to use an age-classified matrix for population projections, as perturbations that affect one life stage may take years to manifest themselves as population changes in subsequent life stages. An age-based model presented in Crowder et al. (1994) showed that nesting female abundance would not increase exponentially with an increase in survival due to small cohorts that experienced years of heavy shrimping. Transient "waves" in abundance can be expected as cohorts of different sizes reach maturity, even without the added variance expected from environmental stochasticity. Thus, sea turtle population growth rates are notoriously difficult to measure, particularly when censuses are limited to nests and nesting females, and results of conservation actions may not be readily apparent for many years.

Misinterpretations of Matrix Model Results

Unfortunately, model results can be misinterpreted in spite of careful notation of assumptions and caveats. The low elasticities calculated for hatchling loggerheads give the wrong impression that egg and hatchling survival has no impact on population growth. Elasticities are relative measures; what the results actually say is that a proportional increase in egg survival, say 5%, will have a much smaller impact than a 5% increase in large juvenile annual survival (Caswell 2000). These results do not say that eggs are unimportant; obviously, egg survival must be maintained at a high enough level to assure that there will be recruitment to the adult population (Heppell 1997). It may well be that management efforts can increase egg survival and large juvenile survival by different percentages, but the results of Crouse et al. (1987) also show that an increase in egg survival, no matter how large, will fail to prevent population decline in the model. However, an increase in cohort size will increase the population size, at least over the short term. Once the primary anthropogenic mortality sources that are the causes of population decline have been eliminated, boosting the population through larger cohort sizes can be highly beneficial. For example, the current rapid rate of increase observed in Kemp's ridley nests is likely due to a combination of reduced mortality through turtle excluder devices and a much higher egg survival rate than would be expected in an unmanaged population (TEWG 1998).

The life history of loggerheads and other sea turtles gives rise to a common pattern of low hatchling elasticity, high juvenile or subadult elasticity, and somewhat lower adult elasticity (Heppell 1998). In the loggerhead model, the large juvenile stage is eight years in length, whereas the egg/hatchling stage is only one year in length. Thus, an increase in large juvenile survival affects several age classes. In a long-lived, late-maturing species, adults make up a small proportion of the population; thus, a proportional change in the survival rate of adults will have a smaller effect on population growth. This says nothing about the relative value of individual adults versus juveniles. Adult longevity is of critical importance in loggerheads because females must, on average, survive to reproduce several times in order to replace themselves. The "value" of adults is about 600 times that of hatchlings according to the reproductive values calculated by Crouse et al. (1987) and Crowder et al. (1994). The adult reproductive value is also about 100 times that of large juveniles, so the loss of a single adult has a much greater overall effect than the loss of a single juvenile. However, because elasticities measure the proportional effect of a change in the survival rate, which affects all individuals in a stage on a proportional basis, the elasticity of population growth to a change in large juvenile survival is much greater than that expected for the same change in adult survival.

Effects of Model Results on Policy

The loggerhead models provided managers with new insights with which to prioritize management and research activities. Prior to development of the 1987 loggerhead model, management and research tended to focus on the most obvious problems (losses of nests and hatchlings to predators and erosion) or the most accessible life stages (nesting behavior, fecundity, and hatch success). Researchers knew that turtles were caught and drowned incidentally to various fisheries, including shrimp trawl fisheries, but measures to reduce turtle mortality had been unpopular with the industry. Because researchers lacked information on the relative importance to population growth of mortality at different stages, most management efforts focused on the mitigation measures that were easiest to implement: protection of nests and eggs. But this focus relied on the tacit assumption that protecting nests would be adequate to mitigate for incidental losses to fisheries as well as for erosion and nest predation.

The results of Crouse et al. (1987) suggested that this assumption was invalid and provided key information contributing to the National Marine Fisheries Service (NMFS) decision to require turtle excluder devices (TEDs) in certain shrimp trawls at certain times of the year. This decision was tested, first in the courts (Louisiana vs. Verity 681 F. Supplement 1178 and 853 F, 5th Circuit Court 1988) and then in Congress (Public Law 100-478-October 7, 1988; Weber et al. 1995). In each case the science, including the findings of Crouse et al. (1987), was affirmed. A National Research Council panel, mandated by Congress specifically to reevaluate the decision to require turtle excluder devices, noted that ". . . analyses of populations and reproduction (Crouse et al. 1987) are especially useful for making decisions about conservation of sea turtles, because they help to identify life stages in which reduced mortality can have the greatest influence on the maintenance or recovery of endangered or threatened sea turtle populations" (National Research Council 1990:61).

In addition to a new emphasis on reduction of mortality in the older life stages, the models suggested that increasing the survival of the earliest stages (eggs and hatchlings) may be a less effective conservation technique than was previously assumed (Crouse et al. 1987; Crowder et al. 1994; Heppell et al. 1996b). In 1994, the U.S. Fish and Wildlife Service (USFWS) and NMFS reoriented a long-term Kemp's ridley head-start program from rearing hatchlings for release to determining the relative survival of head-started to wild juveniles as a measure of the true effectiveness of head-starting (Eckert et al. 1994).

Finally, while still in the early stages, researchers and agencies have begun documenting and, to some extent, addressing mortality in other life stages. For example, longline fisheries are known to incidentally catch oceanic juvenile loggerheads, which have the second highest elasticity in the original loggerhead models. Pelagic longline takes of loggerheads and other sea turtles occur globally (Aguilar et al. 1995; Johnson et al. 1999; Nishimura and Nakahigashi 1990; National Marine Fisheries Service 2001; Witzell 1999), and the cumulative take of multiple longline fisheries that capture turtles from several life stages may be very high (Crouse 1999; NMFS 2001). Preliminary research has begun to investigate gear modifications that may reduce longline capture rates (Bolten et al. 1994; Ito and Machado 1999), but few changes have been required in the fisheries as yet. Recent court decisions have led to large spatial and temporal closures in the North Pacific to protect sea turtles from bycatch in Hawaii-based longline fisheries (Center for Marine Conservation et al. vs. National Marine Fisheries Service et al. Civil No. 99-00152). Although this case was driven primarily by concerns for the status of Pacific leatherbacks (Crowder 2000; Spotila et al. 2000), the closure will protect loggerheads and three other species of sea turtles as well.

New Information on U.S. Loggerheads

Research over the past 20 years has revealed new information on genetics, growth, the effects of turtle excluder devices, and other aspects of U.S. loggerhead biology. This information has important implications for existing and future population models.

Genetics

Based on mitochondrial DNA, there are at least four genetically distinct loggerhead nesting subpopulations in the western North Atlantic (Bowen 1995; Bowen et al. 1993; Encalada et al. 1998), and possibly there are more (Francisco et al. 1999; TEWG 2000):

1. The northern nesting subpopulation, occurring from North Carolina to northeastern Florida, above 29° N (with approximately 7,500 nests in 1998).
2. The southern Florida nesting subpopulation, occurring from 29° N on the eastern coast to Sarasota on the Gulf coast (with approximately 83,400 nests in 1998).
3. The Florida panhandle nesting subpopulation, occurring at Eglin Air Force Base and the beaches near Panama City, Florida (with approximately 1,200 nests in 1998).
4. The Yucatán nesting subpopulation (Márquez-M. 1990), occurring in Quintana Roo on the eastern Yucatán Peninsula, Mexico (with approximately 1,000 nests in 1998).

Genetic analyses indicate that turtles from several subpopulations mix on foraging grounds. Table 16.1 summarizes the estimated proportional contributions of the four identified subpopulations to foraging-ground assemblages as well as the proportional contributions of Mediterranean haplotypes.

Oceanic Stage Turtles

Loggerhead hatchlings originating from western Atlantic nesting beaches swim offshore into the currents and eddies of the North Atlantic gyre (reviewed by Bolten, Chapter 4 this volume). Small loggerheads have been found in the eastern Atlantic (Bjorndal et al. 1994; Bolten et al. 1994; Carr 1986, 1987; Maigret 1983) and in the Mediterranean Sea (Laurent et al. 1998). After 7–12 years in the oceanic immature life stage (Bjorndal et al. 2000), western Atlantic loggerheads return to nearshore waters and eventually settle into coastal habitats as neritic immatures. This ontogenetic shift is recorded in the growth layers of the humerus bone (Snover et al. 2000).

Growth

Growth rates may be specific to subpopulations (i.e., genetically different groups) and undoubtedly vary by foraging ground. Growth rates of loggerheads in the Bahamas and Florida are reported to be greater than growth rates of loggerheads to the north, where the northern subpopulation is disproportionately represented (Bjorndal and Bolten 1988; Braun-McNeill et al., in review; Klinger and Musick 1995; Mendonca 1981). In the seasonally temperate waters, these animals must migrate, but individual animals repeatedly return to the same developmental habitats in subsequent years. The slower growth rate of northern loggerheads may mean that they mature at a later age than their southern counterparts, and thus the northern subpopulation may be slower to recover than subpopulations with faster individual growth rates (Braun-McNeill et al., in review). Based on growth rates observed in North Carolina (Braun-McNeill et al., in review) and Virginia (Klinger and Musick 1995), the duration of the neritic stage (45–92 cm) would be nearly 25 years, which is much longer than would be estimated based on growth rates observed to the south.

Turtle Excluder Device Effects

The authors have generally assumed that mortality factors affect both juveniles and reproductive adults in proportion to their occurrence in near-shore and inshore neritic habitats; much less is known about the movements and habitats of nonreproductive adults. While turtle excluder devices have likely reduced near-shore mortality in shrimp trawl fisheries in the southeastern United States (Crowder et al. 1995), signs of recovery in the population remain mixed (TEWG 2000). New analyses indicate that current turtle excluder device openings in the southeastern United States are not adequate to release large loggerheads, including all reproductive animals (Epperly and Teas 1999). Turtle excluder devices are now required seasonally in the summer flounder trawl fishery south of Cape Charles, Virginia (61 FR 1846, January 24, 1996), but trawls are also used to fish for other species in waters where logger-

heads occur (flynet trawls, trawls north of Cape Charles, crab trawls, scallop trawls, etc.), and there is no reason to assume they are not taking turtles; limited data suggest some are (S. Epperly, pers. comm.). Likewise, bottom trawl fisheries for shrimp and other target species in other parts of the world are likely to incidentally capture and drown loggerheads and other sea turtle species wherever they coincide.

Updating the Models

Clearly, the "old" models of Frazer, Crouse, Crowder, and Heppell are lacking this new information. There are two alternatives to improving population models for Atlantic loggerheads: (1) use the same basic construct promoted by the earlier matrix models, but update the matrices with new information, or (2) start from scratch, building completely different models that incorporate information that cannot simply be added to the existing models. For this review chapter, the authors decided to examine the effects of increased stage length and potential "turtle excluder device effects" on modified matrix models. The updated models are still largely based on information gathered by Frazer (1983a, 1983b) and therefore best represent the northern nesting subpopulation.

The authors looked at two models with different stage lengths based on new growth rate information (Table 16.2). Model 1 includes the neritic immature stage lengths used in previous loggerhead models but adds one year to the oceanic stage, as predicted by growth estimates from young animals tagged in the Azores (Bjorndal et al. 2000). The age at first nesting in Model 1 is 23 years. Model 2 in composed of longer stage lengths than Model 1. A 10-year oceanic stage is predicted by the outer tail of the growth rate distributions calculated by Bjorndal et al. (2000). The longer neritic immature stages are based on newly calculated growth curves from tagged turtles in North Carolina (Braun-McNeill et al., in review). The age at first nesting in Model 2 is 35 years. The authors feel that the likely range of ages at first nesting for northern loggerheads has been bracketed by these two models, although additional research is needed to improve stage-length estimates.

Table 16.1.
Natal Origin of Foraging-Ground Loggerhead Sea Turtles (Proportional Contribution)

| Foraging Area | Refs. | N | Life Stage(s) | Nesting Subpopulation | | | | | |
| | | | | Western North Atlantic | | | | South Atlantic | Mediterranean |
				Northern	Southern Florida	Florida Panhandle	Quintana Roo, Mexico	Brazil	Greece
Northeastern USA	8	82	Primarily neritic immature	0.25	0.59	0.00	0.16	0.00	0.00
Chesapeake Bay[a]	7	63	Primarily neritic immature	0.54	0.46	—	—	—	—
Pamlico and Core Sounds, North Carolina	1	7	Neritic immature	0.32	0.64	< 0.01	0.03	0.01	0.00
South Carolina[a]	11	33	Neritic immature	0.50	0.50	—	—	—	—
Georgia[a]	10	97	Neritic immature	0.59	0.41	—	—	—	—
Georgia	2	192	Neritic immature	0.24	0.73	—	0.03	0.00	0.00
Hutchinson Island, Florida	12	109	Neritic immature	0.10	0.69	—	0.20	—	—
Florida Bay	9	51	Neritic immature and adult	0.08	0.84	—	0.08	—	—
Mediterranean Sea[a]	4, 5	59	Unknown	—	0.57	—	—	—	0.43
Azores and Madeira	3	183	Oceanic immature	0.19	0.71	0.00	0.11	0.00	0.00

Western Mediterranean	6	Oceanic immature	59	0.02	0.45	—	—	0.53
Eastern Mediterranean	6	Oceanic immature	52	0.02	0.47	—	—	0.51
Eastern Mediterranean	6	Neritic immature and adult	58	—	—	—	—	1.00[b]

Source: Turtle Expert Working Group 2000.

Reference Key: 1. Bass et al. 1998. 2. Bass et al. 1999. 3. Bolten et al. 1998. 4. Bowen 1995. 5. Laurent et al. 1993. 6. Laurent et al. 1998. 7. Norrgard 1995. 8. Rankin-Baransky 1997. 9. Schroeder, unpubl. data. 10. Sears 1994. 11. Sears et al. 1995. 12. Witzell et al., in prep.

Note: Table values are proportional contributions. N = number (in sample).

[a]Studies were conducted before a full complement of genetic analyses of Atlantic nesting beaches was available.

[b]Includes rookeries of Turkey and Cyprus, in addition to Greece.

Table 16.2.
Stage Lengths Used in Updated Loggerhead Matrix Models

	Oceanic Immature 5–45 cm	Small Neritic Immature 45–72 cm	Large Neritic Immature 72–92 cm	Age at 92 cm
Model 1	8 years	6 years	8 years	23 years
Model 2	10 years	11 years	13 years	35 years

Methods

The model framework, as illustrated by the life cycle graph (Figure 16.1), is an adaptation of the five-stage model given by Crowder et al. (1994). Three major changes have been made. Eggs and hatchlings are no longer a separate stage—the survival rate from nest laying to entry into the ocean (0.6747 per year; Frazer 1986) is now included in the fertility term. The model has a prebreeding census, where turtles are "counted" just prior to nesting, requiring that fecundity be multiplied by survival at sea to age one to calculate the fertility term for the matrix (Caswell 2000):

$$F = \text{nests} \times \text{eggs} \times \text{sex ratio} \times \text{survival from egg to age one} \quad (4)$$

Reproduction parameters are the following: nests per female = 4.1; eggs per nest = 115 (TEWG 1998); and sex ratio = 0.5. Survival to age one is a fitted parameter, described below. The second major change in the model is incorporation of a variable remigration interval, based on tag returns at Little Cumberland Island (Richardson et al. 1978). The proportion of females returning to nest after one, two, three, four, or five years is 3%, 56%, 31%, 7%,

and 3%, respectively. Variable remigration intervals can have a major impact on nesting female abundance through time (M. Chaloupka, pers. comm.). All nesting females, regardless of remigration interval, produce the same number of one-year-old female offspring. Finally, the size classes covered by each life stage have been changed from the original models to reflect those size classes defined in an analysis of turtle excluder device effectiveness, where Epperly and Teas (1999) found that larger neritic immatures and adults were probably too large to fit through turtle excluder device openings.

The models are age classified, rather than stage classified, to allow for long time lags in population responses that are caused by delayed maturity and long stage lengths (Crowder et al. 1994). The annual survival rates for each model are based on Frazer (1986) and a model "fit" for oceanic immature annual survival to obtain a pre-1990 population growth rate of –5% per year (Crowder et al. 1994) (Table 16.3). The annual survival rates of each life stage had to be increased somewhat in Model 2 in order to obtain a "reasonable" oceanic survival rate, that is, < 95% per year. The original models by Crouse et al. (1987) and Crowder et al. (1994) used a primary sex ratio of 0.5. Foraging ground stud-

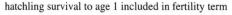

hatchling survival to age 1 included in fertility term

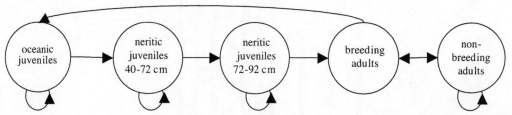

Figure 16.1. Life cycle graph of updated loggerhead matrix models.

Table 16.3.

Annual Survival Rates for Each Stage Used in Updated Loggerhead Matrix Models

	Oceanic Immature 5–45 cm	Small Neritic Immature 45–72 cm	Large Neritic Immature 72–92 cm	Nesting Females 92 cm	Nonnesting Females 92+
Model 1	0.745	0.6758	0.7425	0.8091	0.8091
Model 2	0.875	0.7	0.8	0.85	0.85

ies indicate there is a female bias along the Atlantic coast (Braun-McNeill et al. 2000a, 2000b; Wibbels et al. 1987), but because they are composed of multiple subpopulations, it is difficult to know the sex ratio of any individual population. It is likely that the proportion of females in the southern Florida subpopulation is higher than in the northern subpopulation and that the southern Florida subpopulation dominates the foraging ground studies. To be conservative in their model runs, the authors retained a primary sex ratio of 0.5, which probably more closely approximates the ratio of the northern subpopulation, although no data are available to confirm this.

The authors applied four different turtle excluder device (TED) effectiveness scenarios to the two models: (1) no TEDs (initial population growth = –5% per year), (2) TED-reduced mortality of small neritic immatures only, (3) TED-reduced mortality for small and large neritic immatures, and (4) TED-reduced mortality for neritic immatures and adults (both nesting and nonnesting). In previous models, it was assumed that all neritic turtles would have the same reduction in mortality due to turtle excluder devices (Crowder et al. 1994). According to an analysis of South Carolina strandings by Crowder et al. (1995), the number of dead turtles that stranded on beaches after turtle excluder devices were put in place was reduced by 30–40%. For this analysis, the authors used a mortality (= 1 minus annual survival) reduction of 30% for each affected stage.

Results

Elasticity analysis is a method that compares the potential proportional change in population growth given a proportional change in each annual survival rate (de Kroon et al. 1986, 2000). Elasticities also reveal the proportional contribution of each matrix entry to the population growth rate. The elasticities in an age-based matrix can be added to get the total proportional contribution of survival for a given life stage (Figure 16.2). In age-structured models, the elasticity of λ to changes in immature stage survival is dependent on the number of age classes included in the stage (Caswell 2000; Heppell et al. 2000a). Thus, in Model 1, oceanic immatures and large neritic immatures have the same elasticity, which is higher than those of the other stages. In Model 2, small and large neritic immatures have longer stage lengths than the oceanic stage and, hence, higher elasticities. So stage length is an important factor when comparing the relative contributions of stage-specific survival rates.

Population growth rates, given in proportional change per year, were similar between the two models for each of the four turtle excluder device effectiveness scenarios (Figure 16.3), although greater population growth rates were predicted for Model 1. If turtle excluder devices only reduce the mortality of small neritic immature loggerheads, the population is not expected to increase over the long term. This is likely even if the mortality of small neritic immatures is reduced by a larger percentage, because mortality rates of large neritic immatures and adults would be too high to result in a population increase. Crowder et al. (1994) optimistically applied the same mortality reduction to all neritic stages, represented here by the fourth turtle excluder device effectiveness scenario. As with the original model, a 30% reduction in mortality of neritic immatures and adults

Figure 16.2. Elasticity analysis of two updated loggerhead matrix models, showing the relative proportional contribution of each survival rate to population growth. Stage lengths and survival rates for the two models are given in tables 16.2 and 16.3.

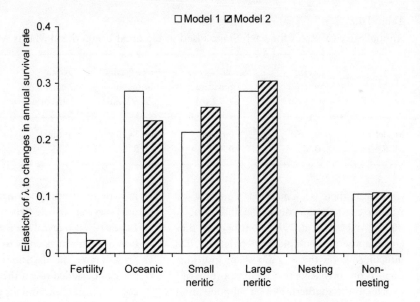

does result in a population increase for both Model 1 and Model 2, but the rate of increase is not large (1–2% per year). The later age at maturity and the longer generation time of Model 2 result in slower population growth.

Using the models given by the turtle excluder device effectiveness scenarios outlined above, the authors plotted the trajectories of nesting female population size through time to show the effects of time lags caused by long stage lengths. All simulations started with a population of 2,000 nesters (1990 estimate; TEWG 1998) and the remaining population at a stable age distribution given by the baseline models (population growth = –5% per year). Because of uncertainties in population distribution and survival rates, these trajectories should be compared qualitatively and not used to predict actual population sizes through time. In both models, the change in nesters exhibits

Figure 16.3. Population growth rates with four turtle excluder device effectiveness scenarios. Turtle excluder devices reduce mortality by 30% for each stage affected: small neritic immature turtles; small and large neritic immatures; and small and large neritic immatures plus adults. None is no turtle excluder devices. Growth rate is expressed as proportional change per year $(\lambda - 1)$.

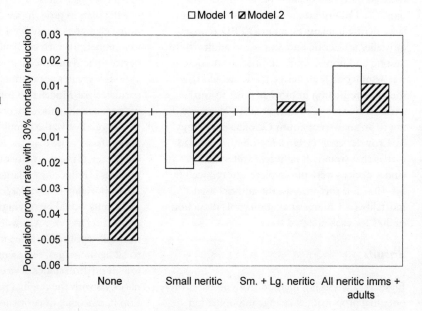

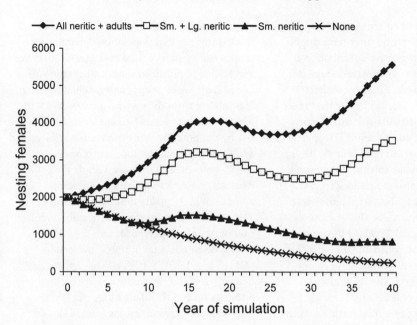

Figure 16.4. Population trajectory predicted by Model 1 with the four turtle excluder device effectiveness scenarios shown in Figure 16.3.

long amplitude "waves" in the population that are caused by shifts in the age distribution following perturbation (turtle excluder device implementation in year 0) (Figures 16.4 and 16.5). The longer time lag of Model 2 (25 years) delays the positive impact of decreased neritic stage mortality, but significant increases in nesting females are predicted after the 40-year simulation period if small and large neritic immatures benefit from turtle excluder devices, or if all three stages benefit.

Conclusions from the Updated Models

The survival rates of the oceanic immature stage and neritic immature stages have a large impact on overall population growth in both of the updated models. Thus, small increases or decreases

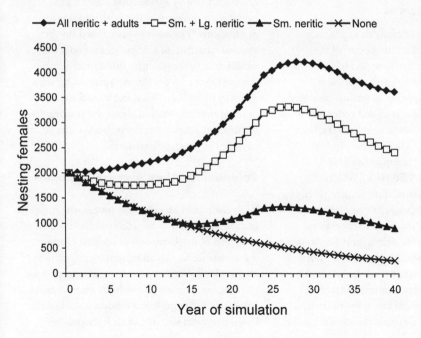

Figure 16.5. Population trajectory predicted by Model 2 with the four turtle excluder device effectiveness scenarios shown in Figure 16.3.

in the annual survival of either of these stages can have a dramatic effect on long-term population growth rates. The relative contribution to population growth of each immature stage depends on its stage length. Elasticity analysis should not be used to simply identify the "most sensitive" life stage, particularly if management policy is based purely on this result (Heppell et al. 2000c). The current estimate of an 8–10-year oceanic stage would make this the "most sensitive stage" in the original matrix models (as shown here in Model 1), but neritic immature growth rates also appear to be slower than previously estimated (Model 2). Until these uncertainties are further researched and a model that incorporates true growth rate variance can be constructed for U.S. loggerheads, updated models like these can only provide a rough comparative analysis of potential turtle excluder device effectiveness.

Time lags caused by late age at first reproduction and a long neritic immature stage will reduce the chances of observing an increase in nesting females for many years. Increases in recruitment to the neritic population are likely to be detected much sooner.

Discussion—Do We Need More Models and Why?

Conservation Concerns

Atlantic loggerheads continue to experience mortality due to human activities at all life stages. Because the loggerhead models have highlighted reductions in survival of both oceanic and neritic juveniles as serious management concerns, identification and reduction of mortality factors for these stages has taken on increased importance. These factors have recently been reviewed for loggerheads in U.S. Atlantic waters (NMFS 2001; TEWG 2000). All of the loggerhead modeling to date points to the oceanic juvenile stage as the first or second most sensitive to increases in mortality. Pelagic longlines, marine debris, and *Sargassum* harvesting are the major known threats. For neritic immature and adult turtles, shrimp, fish, and crab trawls; gill nets; pot lines; incidental hooking; takes by dredges and power plants; collisions with boats; and ingested debris are the

major known threats. While the loggerhead models suggest that population dynamics are most sensitive to increased mortality of juveniles and adults, populations cannot withstand sustained high losses of eggs and hatchlings either. It is unclear from the current models at exactly what point these losses become unsustainable, but by the time they are expressed as reduced adult nesting it may be too late to reverse 25–35 years of such impacts. Clearly the prudent alternative is to protect a significant amount of high quality nesting habitat now. The recovery plan for the U.S. nesting population of Atlantic loggerheads calls for 25% of coastal nesting habitat in public ownership (NMFS and USFWS 1991). While the loggerhead models and this discussion are focused primarily on North Atlantic loggerheads, the general principles and lessons learned should be applicable everywhere.

Incorporating Subpopulation Differences

The large contribution of the southern Florida subpopulation (10 times that of the northern subpopulation) is likely affecting sex ratios and the genetic distribution of loggerheads on foraging grounds. It is also possible that the southern Florida input is "masking" the lack of population recovery in the northern nesting populations. The authors speculated on the general structure of a population model that would take subpopulation differences into account (Figure 16.6). But parameterizing such a model to include this effect would require much more information about the relative proportions of different subpopulations that occur in different geographical areas.

Potential for More Instructive Models

With the rise of modern computers, the information contained in life tables allows the construction of mathematical models to examine the consequences to an imaginary population of altering its survival or fecundity schedules. One can employ a variety of methods from aggregated stage- or age-based models to individual-based and even spatially explicit models

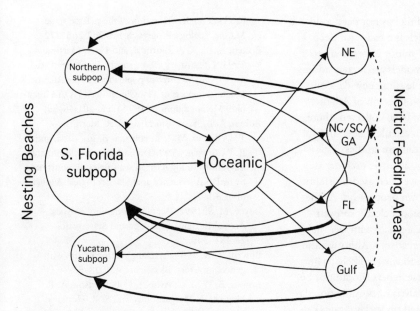

Figure 16.6. Conceptual model for loggerheads that includes subpopulation differences. Arrows denote transitions between life stages and habitats (i.e., migration). Arrow widths denote relative contributions of different feeding areas to nesting populations, determined through genetic analysis. Additional arrows denoting adult migration to and from the nesting beaches are excluded for clarity. NE: northeast; NC: North Carolina; SC: South Carolina; GA: Georgia; FL: Florida; Gulf = Gulf of Mexico.

(DeAngelis and Gross 1992; Tuljapurkar and Caswell 1997). Even simple models have allowed researchers to ask questions about the relative importance of having precise and accurate information about the survival and fecundity of each life stage. That is, one can conduct sensitivity analyses and ask, "For which of the model inputs is it imperative to have more precise or more accurate information?" The models have also allowed researchers to examine the probable outcomes of various management scenarios. Unfortunately, the models will never be better than the information that is put into them. Until new information is gathered and synthesized on the demographic characteristics of loggerheads in the Western Atlantic, little progress will be made in developing more predictive models.

For example, most loggerhead biologists assume that loggerhead hatchlings from the western Atlantic beaches migrate to and inhabit eastern Atlantic areas as developmental habitat before returning to the western Atlantic at about half their adult size. Researchers already know from the work of Bjorndal et al. (2000) that growth rates of juvenile loggerheads in the eastern Atlantic are slower than predicted by the von Bertalanffy growth model. Thus, the age at maturity estimated by Frazer (1983a) and Frazer and Ehrhart (1985) for loggerheads might be much too low. This also calls into serious question the accuracy of the estimates of

juvenile survival rates that were based on using the von Bertalanffy equation to assign ages to juveniles in Frazer's (1983a, 1987) catch-curve analysis. Before further progress can be made with modeling Atlantic loggerhead populations, researchers need information on survival rates for juveniles at sea and new estimates of age at maturity and of adult survival since the initiation of turtle excluder devices.

There is little to be gained from constructing complex models if most of the parameters have no measured means or variances, and results obtained from such models can give a false sense of precision (Caughley 1994). Even heuristic models with a large number of unknowns may produce a myriad of results that are difficult to interpret. TEWG (2000) has made a number of research recommendations, many of which are aimed directly at resolving uncertain model parameters, including subpopulation differences, variable growth rates, and updated survival rate estimates. NMFS recognizes that new and better models can aid population recovery through improved management, but only if the models are based on sound empirical data.

Conclusions

Early sea turtle models by Frazer, Crouse, and Crowder provided important insights, but the fact that research funding has not been available to improve these models is a cause for deep concern. The authors' minor efforts here to improve the existing models are merely adding bells and whistles. While some new data on growth and genetic composition of Atlantic loggerhead stocks have been collected, there have been no efforts to calculate new survival rates through mark-recapture studies. This is especially critical today, as turtle excluder devices are thought to have decreased mortality rates, but by an unknown proportion. As the Crouse et al. (1987) model clearly showed, model results can have a positive impact on policy and population recovery. Although the results from the early models are likely to be qualitatively robust, researchers should not be relying on heuristic analysis of possible population changes today based on survival rates calculated for a single subpopulation 30 years ago.

LITERATURE CITED

Aguilar, R., J. Mas, and X. Pastor. 1995. Impact of Spanish swordfish longline fisheries on the loggerhead sea turtle *Caretta caretta* populations in the western Mediterranean. NOAA Technical Memorandum NMFS-SEFSC-361:1–6.

Bass, A. L., S. P. Epperly, J. Braun, D. W. Owens, and R. M. Patterson. 1998. Natal origin and sex ratios of foraging sea turtles in the Pamlico-Albemarle Estuarine Complex. NOAA Technical Memorandum NMFS-SEFSC-415:137–138.

Bass, A. L., S.-M. Chow, and B. W. Bowen. 1999. Temporal variation in loggerhead strandings from Georgia. Final report to Georgia Department of Natural Resources. Gainesville: Department of Fisheries and Aquatic Sciences, University of Florida.

Beissinger, S. R., and M. I. Westphal. 1998. On the use of demographic models of population viability in endangered species management. Journal of Wildlife Management 62:821–841.

Bjorndal, K. A., and A. B. Bolten. 1988. Growth rates of juvenile loggerheads, *Caretta caretta*, in the southern Bahamas. Journal of Herpetology 22:480–481.

Bjorndal, K. A., A. B. Bolten, J. Gordon, and J. A. Camiñas. 1994. *Caretta caretta* (loggerhead) growth and pelagic movement. Herpetological Review 25:23–24.

Bjorndal, K. A., A. B. Bolten, and H. R. Martins. 2000. Somatic growth model of juvenile logger-

head sea turtles: Duration of the pelagic stage. Marine Ecology Progress Series 202:265–272.

Bolten, A. B., K. A. Bjorndal, and H. R. Martins. 1994. Life history model for the loggerhead sea turtle *(Caretta caretta)* populations in the Atlantic: Potential impacts of a longline fishery. NOAA Technical Memorandum NMFS-SWFC-201:48–55.

Bolten, A. B., K. A. Bjorndal, H. R. Martins, T. Dellinger, M. J. Biscoito, S. E. Encalada, and B. W. Bowen. 1998. Transatlantic developmental migrations of loggerhead sea turtles demonstrated by mtDNA sequence analysis. Ecological Applications 3:1–7.

Boyce, M. S. 1992. Population viability analysis. Annual Review of Ecology and Systematics 23:481–506.

Bowen, B. W. 1995. Tracking marine turtles with genetic markers. BioScience 45:528–534.

Bowen, B. W., J. C. Avise, J. I. Richardson, A. B. Meylan, D. Margaritoulis, and S. R. Hopkins-Murphy. 1993. Population structure of loggerhead turtles *(Caretta caretta)* in the northwestern Atlantic Ocean and Mediterranean Sea. Conservation Biology 7:834–844.

Braun-McNeill, J. B., S. P. Epperly, D. W. Owens, and R. M. Patterson. 2000a. Sex ratios of foraging sea turtles in the Pamlico-Albemarle Estuarine Complex, North Carolina, U.S.A. NOAA Technical Memorandum NMFS-SEFSC-436:121–122.

———. 2000b. Sex ratios of immature sea turtles: Does water temperature make a difference? NOAA Technical Memorandum NMFS-SEFSC-443:127–128.

Braun-McNeill, J., S. P. Epperly, L. Avens, and M. Snover. In review. A preliminary analysis of growth data of juvenile loggerhead *(Caretta caretta)* sea turtles from North Carolina, U.S.A.

Carr, A. 1986. Rips, FADS and little loggerheads. BioScience 36:92–100.

———. 1987. New perspectives on the pelagic stage of sea turtle development. Conservation Biology 1:103–121.

Caswell, H. 2000. Matrix population models, 2nd ed. Sunderland, Mass.: Sinauer Associates, Inc.

Caswell, H., and P. A. Werner. 1978. Transient behavior and life history analysis of teasel (*Dipsacus sylvestris* Huds.). Ecology 59:53–66.

Caswell, H., R. J. Naiman, and R. Morin. 1984. Evaluating the consequences of reproduction in complex salmonid life cycles. Aquaculture 43:123–134.

Caughley, G. 1994. Directions in conservation biology. Journal of Animal Ecology 63:215–244.

Crouse, D. T. 1999. The consequences of delayed maturity in a human-dominated world. American Fisheries Society Symposium 23:195–202.

Crouse, D. T., L. B. Crowder, and H. Caswell. 1987. A stage-based population model for loggerhead sea turtles and implications for conservation. Ecology 68:1412–1423.

Crowder, L. 2000. Leatherback's survival will depend on an international effort. Nature 405:881.

Crowder, L. B., D. T. Crouse, S. S. Heppell, and T. H. Martin. 1994. Predicting the impact of turtle excluder devices on loggerhead sea turtle populations. Ecological Applications 4:437–445.

Crowder, L. B., S. R. Hopkins-Murphy, and A. Royle. 1995. Estimated effect of turtle excluder devices (TEDs) on loggerhead sea turtle strandings with implications for conservation. Copeia 1995:773–779.

DeAngelis, D. L., and L. J. Gross, editors. 1992. Individual-based models and approaches in ecology: Populations, communities and ecosystems. New York: Routledge, Chapman, and Hall.

de Kroon, H., A. Plaisier, J. van Groenendael, and H. Caswell. 1986. Elasticity: The relative contribution of demographic parameters to population growth rate. Ecology 67:1427–1431.

de Kroon, H., J. van Groenendael, and J. Ehrlen. 2000. Elasticities: A review of methods and model limitations. Ecology 81:607–618.

Eckert, S. A., D. T. Crouse, L. B. Crowder, M. Maceina, and A. Shah. 1994. Review of the Kemp's ridley sea turtle headstart experiment. Report to the National Marine Fisheries Service, based on a workshop at Galveston, Texas, 22–23 September 1992. NOAA Technical Memorandum NMFS-OPR-3.

Encalada, S. E., K. A. Bjorndal, A. B. Bolten, J. C. Zurita, B. Schroeder, E. Possardt, C. J. Sears, and B. W. Bowen. 1998. Population structure of loggerhead turtle (Caretta caretta) nesting colonies in the Atlantic and Mediterranean as inferred from mitochondrial DNA control region sequences. Marine Biology 130:567–575.

Epperly, S. P., and W. G. Teas. 1999. Evaluation of TED opening dimensions relative to size of turtles stranding in the Western North Atlantic. NOAA NMFS-SEFSC PRD-98/99-08.

Francisco, A. M., A. L. Bass, and B. W. Bowen. 1999. Genetic characterization of loggerhead turtles (Caretta caretta) nesting in Volusia County. Gainesville: Department of Fisheries and Aquatic Sciences, University of Florida.

Frazer, N. B. 1983a. Survivorship of adult female loggerhead sea turtles, Caretta caretta, nesting on Little Cumberland Island, Georgia, U.S.A. Herpetologica 39:436–447.

———. 1983b. Demography and life history evolution of the Atlantic loggerhead sea turtle, Caretta

caretta. Ph.D. Dissertation, University of Georgia, Athens.

———. 1986. Survival from egg to adulthood in a declining population of loggerhead turtles, Caretta caretta. Herpetologica 42:47–55.

———. 1987. Preliminary estimates of survivorship for loggerhead sea turtles (Caretta caretta). Journal of Herpetology 21:232–235.

Frazer, N. B., and L. M. Ehrhart. 1985. Preliminary growth models for green, Chelonia mydas, and loggerhead, Caretta caretta, turtles in the wild. Copeia 1985:73–79.

Frazer, N. B., and J. I. Richardson. 1985. Annual variation in clutch size and frequency for loggerhead turtles, Caretta caretta, nesting at Little Cumberland Island, Georgia, U.S.A. Herpetologica 41:246–251.

Groom, M. J., and M. A. Pascual. 1998. The analysis of population persistence: An outlook on the practice of viability analysis. In P. L. Fiedler and P. M. Kareiva (eds.). Conservation biology for the coming decade, 2nd ed., 4–27. New York: Chapman and Hall.

Heppell, S. S. 1997. On the importance of eggs. Marine Turtle Newsletter 76:6–8.

———. 1998. Application of life-history theory and population model analysis to turtle conservation. Copeia 1998:367–375.

Heppell, S. S., C. J. Limpus, D. T. Crouse, N. B. Frazer, and L. B. Crowder. 1996a. Population model analysis for the loggerhead sea turtle, Caretta caretta, in Queensland. Wildlife Research (Australia) 23:143–159.

Heppell, S. S., D. T. Crouse, and L. B. Crowder. 1996b. A model evaluation of headstarting as a management tool for long-lived turtles. Ecological Applications 6:556–565.

Heppell, S. S., H. Caswell, and L. B. Crowder. 2000a. Life histories and elasticity patterns: Perturbation analysis for species with minimal demographic data. Ecology 81:654–665.

Heppell, S. S., D. T. Crouse, and L. B. Crowder. 2000b. Using matrix models to focus research and management efforts in conservation. In S. Ferson and M. Burgman (eds.). Quantitative Methods in Conservation Biology, 148–168. New York: Springer.

Heppell, S., C. Pfister, and H. de Kroon. 2000c. Elasticity analysis in population biology: Methods and applications. Ecology 81:605–606.

Hilborn, R., and C. J. Walters. 1992. Quantitative fisheries stock assessment: Choice, dynamics and uncertainty. New York: Chapman and Hall.

Ito, R. Y., and W. A. Machado. 1999. Annual report of the Hawaii-based longline fishery for 1998.

NOAA/NMFS/SWFSC Administrative Report
  H-99-06.

Johnson, D. R., C. Yeung, and C. A. Brown. 1999.
  Estimates of marine mammal and marine turtle
  bycatch by the U.S. pelagic longline fleet in
  1992–1997. NOAA Technical Memorandum
  NMFS-SEFSC-418.

Klinger, R. C., and J. A. Musick. 1995. Age and
  growth of loggerhead turtles (Caretta caretta)
  from Chesapeake Bay. Copeia 1995:205–209.

Laurent, L., J. Lescure, L. Excoffier, B. Bowen,
  M. Domingo, M. Hadjichristophorou, L. Kornaraki, and G. Trabuchet. 1993. Étude génétique
  des relations entre les populations méditer-
  ranéenne et atlantique d'une tortue marine
  (Caretta caretta) à l'aide d'un marqueur mitochondrial. Comptes Rendus de l'Academie des
  Sciences (Paris), Sciences de la Vie, Biologie et
  Pathologie Animale 316:1233–1239.

Laurent, L., P. Casale, M. N. Bradai, B. J. Godley,
  G. Gerosa, A. C. Broderick, W. Schroth,
  B. Schierwater, A. M. Levy, D. Freggii, E. M. Abd
  El-Mawla, D. A. Hadoud, H. E. Gomati,
  M. Domingo, M. Hadjichristophorou, L. Korna-
  raky, F. Demirayak, and Ch. Gautier. 1998.
  Molecular resolution of marine turtle stock com-
  position in fishery bycatch: A case study in the
  Mediterranean. Molecular Ecology 7:1529–1542.

Maigret, J. 1983. Repartition des tortues de mer sur
  les cotes ouest Africaines. Bulletin of the Society
  for Herpetology 1983:22–34.

Márquez-M., R. 1990. FAO species catalogue. Vol. 11.
  Sea turtles of the world, an annotated and illustrated catalogue of sea turtle species known to
  date. FAO Fisheries Synopsis 125.

Mendonca, M. T. 1981. Comparative growth rates of
  wild immature Chelonia mydas and Caretta caretta
  in Florida. Journal of Herpetology 15:447–451.

NMFS and USFWS. 1991. Recovery plan for U.S.
  Atlantic populations of the loggerhead sea turtle
  (Caretta caretta). Silver Spring, Md.: National
  Marine Fisheries Service.

NMFS/SEFSC. 2001. Stock assessments of loggerhead and leatherback sea turtles and an assessment
  of the impact of the pelagic longline fishery on the
  loggerhead and leatherback sea turtles of the western North Atlantic. NOAA Technical Memorandum NMFS-SEFSC-455.

National Research Council. 1990. Decline of sea
  turtles: Causes and prevention. Washington, D.C.:
  National Academy Press.

Nishimura, W., and S. Nakahigashi. 1990. Incidental
  capture of sea turtles by Japanese research and
  training vessels: Results of a questionnaire. Marine
  Turtle Newsletter 51:1–4.

Norrgard, J. 1995. Determination of stock composition and natal origin of a juvenile loggerhead turtle
  population (Caretta caretta) in Chesapeake Bay
  using mitochondrial DNA analysis. M.A. Thesis,
  College of William and Mary, Williamsburg, Va.

Rankin-Baransky, K. C. 1997. Origin of loggerhead
  turtles in the western North Atlantic as determined by mtDNA analysis. M.S. Thesis, Drexel
  University, Philadelphia, Pa.

Richardson, T. H., J. I. Richardson, C. Ruckdeschel,
  and M. W. Dix. 1978. Remigration patterns of
  loggerhead sea turtles (Caretta caretta) nesting on
  Little Cumberland and Cumberland Island, Georgia. Florida Marine Research 33:39–44.

Sears, C. J. 1994. Preliminary genetic analysis of the
  population structure of Georgia loggerhead sea
  turtles. NOAA Technical Memorandum NMFS-
  SEFSC-351:135–139.

Sears, C. J., B. W. Bowen, R. W. Chapman, S. B.
  Galloway, S. R. Hopkins-Murphy, and C. M.
  Woodley. 1995. Demographic composition of
  the feeding population of juvenile loggerhead
  sea turtles (Caretta caretta) off Charleston,
  South Carolina: Evidence from mitochondrial
  DNA markers. Marine Biology 123:869–874.

Snover, M. L., A. A. Hohn, and S. A. Macko. 2000.
  Detecting the precise time at settlement from
  pelagic to benthic habitats in the loggerhead
  sea turtle, Caretta caretta. In H. J. Kalb and
  T. Wibbels (compilers). Proceedings of the 19th
  annual symposium on sea turtle biology and conservation, 174. NOAA Technical Memorandum
  NMFS-SEFSC-443.

Spotila, J. R., R. D. Reina, A. C. Steyermark, P. T.
  Plotkin, and F. R. Paladino. 2000. Pacific
  leatherback turtles face extinction. Nature
  405:529–530.

TEWG. 1998. An assessment of the Kemp's ridley
  (Lepidochelys kempii) and loggerhead (Caretta
  caretta) sea turtle populations in the western
  North Atlantic. NOAA Technical Memorandum
  NMFS-SEFSC-409.

———. 2000. Assessment update for the Kemp's
  ridley and loggerhead sea turtle populations in the
  western North Atlantic. NOAA Technical Memorandum NMFS-SEFSC-444.

Tuljapurkar, S., and H. Caswell (eds.). 1997. Struc-
  tured-population models in marine, terrestrial, and
  freshwater systems. New York: Chapman and Hall.

Weber, M., D. Crouse, R. Irvin, and S. Iudicello.
  1995. Delay and denial: A political history of sea
  turtles and shrimp fishing. Washington, D.C.:
  Center for Marine Conservation.

Wibbels, T., D. W. Owens, Y. A. Morris, and M. S.
  Amoss. 1987. Sexing techniques and sex ratios for

immature loggerhead sea turtles captured along the Atlantic coast of the United States. NOAA Technical Report NMFS-53:65–73.

Wilbur, H. M. 1975. The evolutionary and mathematical demography of the turtle *Chrysemys picta*. Ecology 56:64–77.

Witzell, W. N. 1999. Distribution and relative abundance of sea turtles caught incidentally by the U.S. pelagic longline fleet in the western North Atlantic Ocean, 1992–95. Fisheries Bulletin 97:200–211.

Witzell, W. N., A. L. Bass, M. J. Bresette, D. A. Singewald, and J. C. Gorham. In preparation. Origin of immature loggerhead sea turtles *(Caretta caretta)* from Hutchinson Island, Florida: Evidence from mtDNA markers.

Chapter 17

Stochastic Simulation Modeling of Loggerhead Population Dynamics Given Exposure to Competing Mortality Risks in the Western South Pacific

—Milani Chaloupka

The two most common species of sea turtle resident in southern Great Barrier Reef (sGBR) waters are the green and loggerhead sea turtles (Chaloupka and Limpus 2001). The southern Great Barrier Reef loggerhead stock is the only major breeding population of loggerheads in the South Pacific region (Bowen et al. 1994), with most nesting occurring on coral cays in the southern Great Barrier Reef region or at mainland rookeries on the southern Queensland coast (Limpus et al. 1994). The southern Great Barrier Reef loggerhead stock is exposed to a high risk of incidental capture in Australian coastal fisheries (Poiner and Harris 1996; Slater et al. 1998), and a major decline in nesting activity has been recorded for this stock (Chaloupka and Limpus 2001). The decline in nesting activity was attributed to turtles drowning in the eastern Australian otter trawl fisheries (Heppell et al. 1996), but fox predation of eggs at the mainland rookeries during the 1960s and 1970s has also been implicated (Chaloupka and Limpus 1998). Oceanic southern Great Barrier Reef loggerhead juveniles are also probably exposed to incidental capture in longline fisheries operating in South Pacific waters as has been shown recently for loggerheads in North Atlantic (Witzell 1999) and North Pacific waters (Polovina et al. 2000). The southern Great Barrier Reef loggerhead stock is clearly exposed to several mortality risk factors and is listed as endangered under Australian conservation legislation (Slater et al. 1998).

Yet robust management procedures to support conservation of this endangered stock have not been developed despite the long-term exposure to multiple hazards. The development of such procedures depends in large part on a reasonable understanding of loggerhead demography and application of this information within a risk management framework. Risk comprises the following elements, known as the risk chain (Merkhofer 1987): (1) hazard identification, (2) assessment of the likelihood of exposure to hazards, (3) assessment of the effects of exposure, and (4) social evaluation of the effects. Risk assessment comprises the first three elements of the chain, and simulation modeling is a useful tool to assess risk to population viability given multiple hazards, environmental variability in the key demographic processes, and management uncertainty. Therefore, the author presents a stochastic age-class–structured simulation model of southern Great Barrier Reef loggerhead population dynamics that was used here to (1) assess the long-term viability of the southern Great Barrier Reef stock, given exposure to several competing mortality risk factors, and (2) to support model performance evaluation using robust experimental design procedures.

Methods

Model Description

A simulation model accounting for the population dynamics of loggerhead sea turtles resident in southern Great Barrier Reef waters was developed using a system of ordinary differential equations linked by demographic processes characterized by nonlinear, time variant, distributed delay, and stochastic properties. The demographic parameters were derived from various sources, including a long-term research program on southern Great Barrier Reef loggerheads (Chaloupka and Limpus 2002; Limpus 1992, 1994, 1996; Limpus et al. 1983, 1992, 1994). The demography assumed here was not sex dependent since no sex-specific differences in survival probablilities exist for this stock (Chaloupka and Limpus 2002), and issues such as sex-biased harvesting were not addressed. Spatial structure might be important but was ignored since there is no evidence of any significant dispersal of loggerheads between the foraging grounds of this stock (Limpus 1994; Limpus et al. 1992). Environmental stochasticity was accounted for by sampling the demographic rates from rate-specific probability density functions to reflect the temporal variability observed for several southern Great Barrier Reef loggerhead demographic processes (see Engen et al. 1998 for a useful discussion of environmental and demographic stochasticity).

Model Specification

Demographic Structure

The demographic structure of the model was based on developmental stage, as follows: (1) oceanic juveniles, (2) neritic immatures, and (3) neritic adults. Age is not known directly for southern Great Barrier Reef loggerheads, so developmental-stage– or age-class–based rather than direct age-based demography is assumed in the model. The state variables in the model are the number of male and female loggerheads over time in each of the three stages or age classes that reflect the major ontogenetic phases of loggerhead demography (see Figure 17.1). The three age classes were defined using age-specific growth functions for immatures (see Figure 17.2), estimated age and size at first breeding (see figures 17.2 and 17.3), and size-based reproductive criteria for adults (Limpus et al. 1994).

Age Class Duration

Stage 1 incorporates the oceanic juveniles as well as the first year cohort that comprises eggs, hatchlings, and neonates (Figure 17.1). Eggs hatch after approximately two months, and then the hatchlings escape the nesting beaches to recruit to the sea (Limpus et al. 1994). The hatchlings are then dispersed passively southward as neonates over the next 6–9 months in the eastern Australian current and then dispersed eastwards into the western South Pacific Ocean (Walker 1994). Stage 1 also includes the oceanic juvenile phase that occurs presumably in Pacific gyres or along convergence zones (Polovina et al. 2000). The mean neonate/oceanic juvenile age class duration has been estimated as 10–15 years (Bjorndal et al. 2000b; Chaloupka 1998). Oceanic juveniles then recruit to the neritic immature development habitat (Stage 2) in foraging grounds distributed along the eastern Queensland coastline or Great Barrier Reef region at a median size of approximately 78 cm curved carapace length (CCL).

Neritic immatures then grow slowly from the median recruitment size (78 cm CCL) until the onset of negligible growth and perhaps sexual maturity around a mean size of 94 cm CCL (Figure 17.2a). Neritic immatures from this loggerhead stock display a strong growth spurt

Figure 17.1. Conceptual model. Developmental-stage– and reproductive-status–based life cycle graph or causal loop model (Puccia and Levins 1985) for southern Great Barrier Reef (sGBR) loggerhead turtles resident in sGBR foraging grounds. This is the demographic structure and feedback mechanisms included in the simulation model to explore the population dynamics of the sGBR loggerhead stock subject to three hazards (fox predation, coastal otter trawl fisheries, and distance-water longline fisheries).

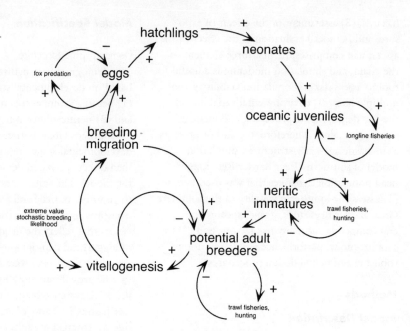

at approximately seven years after recruitment to the neritic habitat (Figure 17.2b). Mean neritic immature age class duration was estimated using a system of Weibull-type growth functions with AR(2) error (Chaloupka 2001b) that fitted well to each longitudinal somatic growth series shown in Figure 17.2a. The mean age-specific growth curve is shown in Figure 17.2b, where the onset of negligible growth is apparent from approximately 12 years after recruitment to the neritic habitat. This suggests that an estimate of the mean immature age class duration is 12 years. Assuming that the oceanic juvenile age class duration is 10–15 years, mean age at maturity is approximately 22–27 years of age for southern Great Barrier Reef loggerheads, which is consistent with skeletochronology-based estimates derived for some southeastern U.S. loggerhead populations (Parham and Zug 1998).

Another means for estimating mean neritic immature age class duration is to use first breeding events observed for individual female loggerheads recorded in the southern Great Barrier Reef loggerhead mark-recapture program (Limpus 1996; Limpus et al. 1994). A range of probability density functions were fitted to age-at-first-breeding events recorded by Limpus (1994, unpubl. updates) for 13 female southern Great Barrier Reef loggerheads monitored an-

nually between 1974 and 1999. Age in this context means years since recruitment to the neritic habitat, so mean age at first breeding provides an estimate of the mean immature age class duration. There were too few data for a goodness-of-fit test, but a Gamma probability density function (Vose 1996) seemed adequate, given visual assessment of the cumulative distribution function of the data. The estimated mean age at first breeding derived from the Gamma probability density function fit was 12.7 years (95% confidence interval: 6–19 years). Given the reasonable fit of the Gamma probability density function, it is appropriate to estimate the discrete Gamma or Erlang probability density function fit to the data to derive an estimate of the number of age subclasses or substages (k) within the immature age class used in the model (see Blythe et al. 1984).

The Erlang probability density function derived from the 13 age-at-first-breeding events is shown in Figure 17.3; the integer parameter (k) reflects the number of substages within the age class, derived as follows:

$$k = \text{integer } (\text{mean}^2/\text{variance}) = \text{integer} \\ (12.7^2/13.4) = 12 \tag{1}$$

suggesting that the neritic immature age class comprises 12 age subclasses, which is similar to

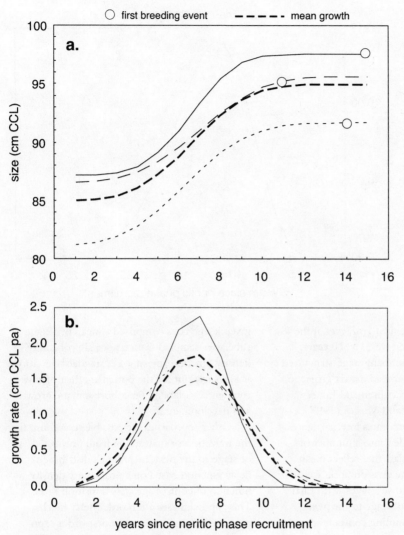

Figure 17.2. Somatic growth model. Somatic growth behavior derived from a longitudinal study for three female loggerheads resident in sGBR waters (Limpus 1994). *Panel a*. Size-at-age function (curve) fitted to growth data and the age at first breeding recorded for each loggerhead. *Panel b*. Age-specific growth rate function for each loggerhead derived from each curve in panel a.

the estimate for mean immature age class duration of 12 years that was derived using the mean somatic growth curve (see Figure 17.2). The significant variation in individual loggerhead growth and age at first breeding presumably reflects individual heterogeneity in growth behavior and temporal variability in food stock dynamics. This behavior can be accommodated in the model by sampling the mean immature age class duration from a probability density function so that growth for a particular immature cohort in a particular year can increase due to increased food availability, which will result in earlier maturation for that cohort into the adult age class.

Age Class Transition Process

The oceanic juvenile and neritic immature age classes were modeled as linear boxcar trains (Goudriaan 1986). Senescence and age-specific demography were not assumed for the adult age class, so a boxcar train for adults was not necessary. A boxcar train ensures minimum development time (aging) within an age class, with age class duration or transit time sampled from a normal probability density function with the relevant parameters; in other words, minimum age class duration can also be time varying. Stage- or age-class–structured models without internal age structure have no delay mechanism, so turtles can enter the stage (age class) in one

Figure 17.3. Erlang probability density function (pdf) fitted to first breeding events recorded by Limpus (1994, unpubl. updates) for 13 female sGBR loggerheads monitored between 1974 and 1999. Immature substages (k) = 12, so a boxcar train used to represent the immature age class comprises 12 slats to ensure developmental delay or aging occurs within the age class.

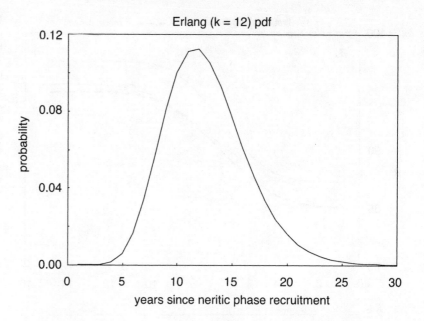

year and exit if alive the next year, even if the stage (age class) duration was, say, 10 years. This is a design defect in many stage-structured models, including loggerhead matrix projection models as discussed in Cochran and Ellner (1992) and Chaloupka and Musick (1997).

A boxcar train incorporates internal age structure by being divided into a number of equal substages (k) or slats that reflect mean age class duration. If age class duration were 10 years, there would be 10 substages, with turtles progressing from one substage to the next within the age class, assuming constant annual survival. Turtles exit the age class and mature to the next age class only from the last substage in the previous age class. This structure ensures that there is a minimum delay from when a cohort of turtles recruits into an age class and when the survivors, after approximately the mean age class duration, mature to the next age class. The boxcar train for the immature age class used here comprises a mean of 12 substages or age subclasses derived from the Erlang probability density function fitted to age at first breeding and from Equation 1, with mean age class duration sampled from a normal probability density function (mean = 12; standard deviation = 2) to account for the potential effect of environmental variability on cohort somatic growth and development. The boxcar train for the oceanic

juvenile age class comprised a mean of 12 age subclasses sampled from a normal probability density function (mean = 12; standard deviation = 1) to account for the potential effect of environmental variability on cohort somatic growth and development.

Other approaches are possible to account for the transition or maturation from one age class or stage to the next, including a distributed delay function based on a probability density function to control age class transition rates. This approach uses a nth order delay mechanism based on a sequence of first-order exponential delay functions (Hamilton 1980). The probability distribution of an nth order delay is obtained by convoluting n independent and identically distributed exponential random variates, with the distribution being an Erlang probability density function (Manetsch 1976). This distributed delay method was used by Chaloupka and Limpus (1998) to model sea turtle population dynamics within a continuous time stochastic simulation modeling framework. Caswell (1989) outlines a similar approach based on negative binomial transition probabilities for a discrete time matrix projection model (see also Lo et al. 1995 for a fisheries example). The boxcar train and distributed delay approaches are both forms of delay mechanisms for use within continuous time simulation modeling frameworks that can yield similar results and are related (Goudriaan 1986). The boxcar train is useful because there is no need to derive empirical estimates of age-class–specific maturation probabilities, which is difficult for sea turtle studies where age is unknown.

Survival Probabilities

Age-class–specific mortality estimates for southern Great Barrier Reef loggerheads were derived from (1) known incubation and hatching-related mortality probabilities (HMP) (= 0.05 ± 0.01; Limpus et al. 1994), (2) proxy hatchling mortality estimates for southern Great Barrier Reef greens (MHM) (= 0.325 ± 0.05; Gyuris 1994), and (3) Cormack-Jolly-Seber statistical modeling of immature and adult loggerhead survival probabilities (Chaloupka 2000; Chaloupka and Limpus 2002). HMP and MHM were sampled in the model from a normal probability density function with the relevant parameters (mean, standard deviation). The annual number of hatchlings recruiting to the oceanic juvenile stage (see Figure 17.1), in the absence of any additional sources of mortality due to egg harvesting, was estimated as follows:

$$\text{HATCHLINGS} = \text{EGGS} \times (1 - \text{HMP}) \times (1 - \text{MHM}) \qquad (2)$$

Environmental stochasticity was included by using the age-class–specific logistic probability density functions derived for both immature and adult age class survival (Chaloupka and Limpus 2002). For instance, adult mortality was derived by sampling the mean annual survival probability from a logistic probability density function (pdf) using an inverse transformation method (see Morgan 1984) with a uniform random variable in the interval [0,1], as follows, with mean adult survival probability ($\phi = 0.875$) and variability (logistic pdf scale = 0.01) sourced from Chaloupka and Limpus (2002):

$$\text{MORTALITY}_{\text{adult}} = 1 - (\phi - \text{scale} \times (\ln(((\text{random } (0,1))^{-1}) - 1))) \qquad (3)$$

Immature age class mortality was derived similarly, using mean immature survival probability ($\phi = 0.859$) and variability (logistic pdf scale =

0.01) sourced from Chaloupka and Limpus (2002). Oceanic juvenile mortality was unknown and so was derived by tuning the model to a stochastic estimate of oceanic mortality that resulted in a fluctuating but stable population. The derived mean annual juvenile survival probability estimate ($\phi = 0.667$) was then sampled from a logistic probability density function, assuming the same scale parameter used for the immature and adult age classes. The distribution of the three age-class–specific survival probabilities realized in the stochastic simulation model based on sampling from these empirically or tuning-derived logistic probability density functions is shown in Figure 17.4a.

Reproductive Output

Clutch size (mean eggs per clutch = 125; standard deviation = 17) was sourced from Limpus (1996) and was consistent with estimates for other loggerhead stocks (van Buskirk and Crowder 1994). There is little evidence for significant seasonal variation in loggerhead clutch size (Frazer and Richardson 1985) and no evidence for significant age-specific variation in loggerhead clutch size (Limpus 1996). Number of clutches laid per season (mean clutches per season = 4; standard deviation = 1) was obtained from Limpus (1996) and is consistent with estimates for other loggerhead stocks (van Buskirk and Crowder 1994). There is some evidence of an age-specific variation in number of clutches laid per season for the southern Great Barrier Reef loggerhead stock (Limpus 1996), but this effect is negligible when discounted for annual survival. Therefore, expected or mean fecundity was derived as follows:

$$\text{FECUNDITY} = \text{EPC} \times \text{CPS} \qquad (4)$$

where EPC (eggs per clutch) and CPS (clutches per season) were sampled independently from normal probability density functions with the relevant parameters (mean, standard deviation), which results in the realized sampling distribution for fecundity shown in Figure 17.4b that is well summarized as a normal probability density function (mean = 500; standard deviation = 143).

Environmental stochasticity was incorpo-

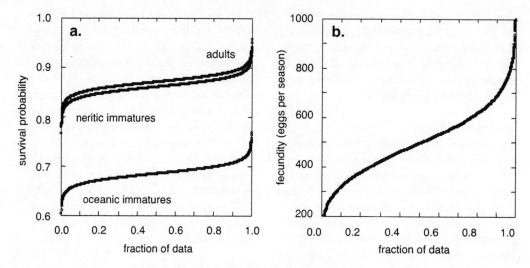

Figure 17.4. Percentile plots of key demographic parameters for the sGBR loggerhead stock showing the distribution of parameter values sampled in simulation model runs assuming a fluctuating but stable population. *Panel a*. Age-class–specific survival probabilities for neritic immatures and adults derived from empirically based logistic probability density functions (pdfs), and oceanic survival probability function derived from model tuning. *Panel b*. The distribution of fecundity sampled in the model (Equation 4), given the mean and variance of clutch size and clutches per season estimated for this stock and assuming that both parameters were adequately sampled from normal probability density functions. Note that the plausible range for mean fecundity is substantial.

rated into the model by using a mean annual breeding probability function derived from selecting the best fit function from a wide range of continuous probability density functions fitted to the breeding probabilities recorded for this stock (Limpus et al. 1994, unpubl. updates). The data comprised 27 estimates of the annual proportion of females breeding or preparing to breed over a 17-year period for the southern Great Barrier Reef population resident in southern Great Barrier Reef waters (1982–1998; Limpus and Reimer 1994) and over a 10-year period for the southern Great Barrier Reef population resident in the Moreton Bay foraging ground (1989–1998; Limpus, unpubl; Limpus et al. 1994). The proportion of southern Great Barrier Reef loggerhead females that are breeding fluctuates significantly from year to year (Limpus et al. 1994), and a right-skewed extreme value probability density function (pdf) (Vose 1996) was found to fit these data well χ^2 = 1.2; p = 0.75) (maximum likelihood estimate of the pdf mode = 0.18; scale = 0.09). The extreme value female breeding probability was sampled in the model using the inverse transformation method and a uniform random variate in the interval [0,1], as follows, which results in

the sampling distribution in the model for female breeding probability (FBP) shown in Figure 17.5a and the lognormal distributed remigration interval shown in Figure 17.5b:

$$FBP = 0.18 - (+0.09) \times \\ (\ln(-\ln(\text{random}(0,1)))) \qquad (5)$$

The primary sex ratio (PSR = 0.50) was obtained from Limpus et al. (1983, 1994). Due to a lack of variability in primary sex ratio, no stochastic effect was included. The sex ratio estimate for the southern Great Barrier Reef stock is not consistent with estimates derived for other loggerhead stocks that display female-biased hatchling sex ratios (Marcovaldi et al. 1997). Annual egg production was then estimated as follows, where FERTILITY = (FBP × FECUNDITY):

$$EGGS = (\text{adult stock size}) \times (PSR) \times \\ (\text{FERTILITY}) \qquad (6)$$

Model Estimation

This model of southern Great Barrier Reef loggerhead population dynamics was implemented

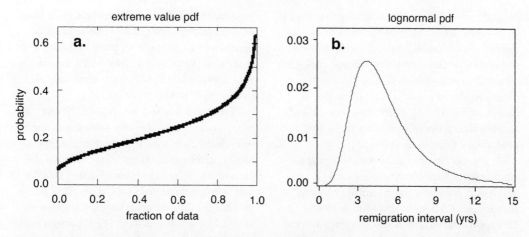

Figure 17.5. Female breeding behavior reflecting significant environmental variability. *Panel a*. Percentile plot showing extreme value distribution of values sampled in the model for the proportion of adult loggerhead females breeding each year. *Panel b*. Sampling distribution of remigration interval derived from simulation model runs, a lognormal probability density distrbution (pdf) (mean ≅ 4 years; 95% confidence interval = 2–9 years) consistent with empirical estimates for this stock (Limpus 1996). The remigration interval is the period between successive nesting seasons, or the inverse of the female breeding probability function shown in Equation 5.

in the iconographic simulation programming language STELLA/iTHINK (see Ruth and Hannon 1997) using the conveyor function to represent the boxcar train structure for the two age-dependent state variables (oceanic juveniles, neritic immatures). The system of ordinary differential equations was solved in STELLA using fourth-order Runge-Kutta numerical integration with integration step or dt = 1 and a one-year sampling period to reflect seasonal loggerhead birth-pulse behavior (Caswell 1989). The model was initialized with a stock of 1,905,500 loggerheads comprising 1,750,000 oceanic juveniles, 140,000 neritic immatures, and 15,500 adults, which is consistent with the relative age class abundance estimates for the southern Great Barrier Reef foraging population of the stock (Chaloupka and Limpus 2001). The expected steady state behavior of the model comprised a similar sex–age class composition and a stock abundance of approximately two million loggerheads.

Model Evaluation

Evaluating model performance is a complex issue that usually requires a pragmatic approach to assessing model verification and validation (Oreskes et al. 1994). Verification concerns the conceptual logic and quality of demographic in-

formation used in the model. The ecological logic used in constructing the southern Great Barrier Reef loggerhead population model is shown in Figure 17.1 and was based on demographic information for this stock derived from a long-term mark-recapture program (Chaloupka and Limpus 2001, 2002; Limpus 1992, 1994, 1996; Limpus et al. 1983, 1992, 1994). There is no reason to consider that the model formalism used here was conceptually incorrect.

Model validation is concerned with evaluating whether the simulation model is acceptable for its intended use given various performance criteria (Rykiel 1996). Model validation was assessed here using two approaches: (1) assessment of model capability to produce outputs that mimic qualitatively a range of empirical information including stock reference behaviors, such as population trends, or time series characteristics, such as reddened spectra (see Cohen 1995) of annual nesting abundance, and (2) parameter sensitivity analysis to identify the demographic parameters that affect model behavior the most and to determine whether those parameters were estimated with reasonable accuracy.

Autoregressive spectral analysis (Bloomfield 1976) was used to derive the spectral properties of the stochastic temporal model output. Spectral color, identified by specific patterns in the spectral density function, is used to identify the scale of environmental variability that might be involved in the temporal fluctuations in ecological series (Cuddington and Yodzis 1999). Cohen (1995) has shown that realistic ecological simulation models should be capable of producing reddened power spectra of model output, and reddened spectra have been found for long time series of annual sea turtle egg production (Chaloupka 2001a).

It is common practice to use individual parameter perturbation to assess sea turtle population model sensitivity to very small parameter changes (see Chaloupka and Musick 1997). This approach has several shortcomings and can result in biased assessments because of nonlinear and parameter interaction effects (Bartell et al. 1986; Breininger et al. 1999; Mills et al. 1999). A more robust approach is based on using experimental or sampling design principles to identify specific parameter combinations to be changed over a realistic ecological range. However, the stochastic simulation model developed here has many parameters, so sensitivity analysis would require an orthogonal factorial sampling design involving many hundreds of thousands of combinations. The number of combinations can be reduced by selecting parameters presumed likely to have a major impact on model behavior.

Survival is considered the most important model parameter for sea turtle population dynamics, while fertility has been considered the least important (Crouse et al. 1987; Crowder et al. 1994; Cunnington and Brooks 1996; Heppell et al. 1996). Therefore, the parameters selected for sensitivity analysis were oceanic juvenile survival probability, adult survival probability, fecundity, and female annual breeding probability. These four parameters were fixed at three levels defined by three empirical percentiles (2.5, 50, 97.5) that summarized the best-fit probability density function for each parameter. Recall that oceanic juvenile and adult survival probabilities were both sampled from logistic probability density functions (Equation 3), fecundity was sampled from a normal probability density function (Equation 4), and female breeding probability was sampled from a right-skewed extreme value probability density function (Equation 5). Sampling a parameter-specific

probability density function at these three levels ensured that an ecologically realistic range of parameter variation was included in model evaluation (Benton and Grant 1996; Breininger at al. 1999) while reducing the factorial combinations to $3^4 = 81$.

Fractional factorial sampling enables further reduction in the number of combinations needed to evaluate the impact of parameter changes on model performance (Henderson- Sellers and Henderson-Sellers 1996; Steinhorst et al. 1978). The simplest fractional factorial sampling design possible for four elements sampled at three levels is a 3^4 fractional factorial (FF3^4) design with one-ninth replication (Cochran and Cox 1957). This particular FF3 design assumes only a main effects model in which all multifactor interactions are confounded with main effects. An FF3^4 design with one-third replication would allow some two-factor effects to be evaluated but requires 27 parameter combinations to be sampled, with most multifactor effects still confounded with the main effects. The FF3^4 one-ninth replication design was used here to evaluate model sensitivity assuming no multifactor effects. This FF3 design requires only nine element combination sets (runs) to estimate the four parameter effects on model performance (Table 17.1). The performance criterion used was mean population growth rate derived for each of the nine FF3 design runs from 100 Monte Carlo trials.

Each run was estimated from 100 Monte Carlo trials sampled over a 200-year interval (1900–2100), with population growth derived as the mean slope of 100 population trajectory slopes. The mean run-specific slopes were estimated using a robust least absolute error (LAE) regression (Judge et al. 1985) of each of the 100 trajectories, with log (total population abundance) as the response variable and simulation year as the independent variable. A four-covariate main effects analysis of variance (ANOVA) accounting for curvilinear functional form was fitted to the Monte Carlo–derived mean for each run using a variance-weighted generalized linear model (McCullagh and Nelder 1989). The FF3^4-ANOVA design and model were estimated using SAS JMP (statistical analysis software) (SAS Institute 1994). The

Table 17.1.

Summary of the FF3[4] Design Used to Assess Southern Great Barrier Reef Loggerhead Population Growth Sensitivity Given an Ecologically Realistic Range of Parameter Variability

Run	Parameter Values				Effect Coding				Mean Slope
	X1	X2	X3	X4	X1	X2	X3	X4	
1	0.63	0.87	491	0.51	1	0	−1	0	0.0107
2	0.67	0.91	491	0.06	−1	1	0	0	−0.0263
3	0.70	0.87	804	0.06	−1	0	1	1	−0.0170
4	0.70	0.83	491	0.21	0	−1	1	0	−0.0022
5	0.63	0.83	235	0.06	−1	−1	−1	−1	−0.1192
6	0.63	0.91	804	0.21	0	1	−1	1	0.0091
7	0.67	0.83	804	0.51	1	−1	0	1	0.0328
8	0.67	0.87	235	0.21	0	0	0	−1	−0.0254
9	0.70	0.91	235	0.51	1	1	1	−1	0.0205

Note: Four demographic parameters were fixed at three levels (−1 = 2.5th percentile, 0 = 50th percentile, 1 = 97.5th percentile) of the parameter-specific probability density function, with other parameters sampled at the nominal value. X1 = mean annual oceanic juvenile survival probability, X2 = mean annual adult survival probability, X3 = mean annual fecundity (eggs per season), X4 = mean annual adult female breeding probability.

model results were summarized using prediction profile plots that are used in quality improvement and industrial studies (Box et al. 1978). A prediction profile plot shows the predicted main effect on long-term model population growth of changing the four parameters.

Results and Discussion

The stochastic simulation model was used to evaluate southern Great Barrier Reef loggerhead stock viability, given (1) competing mortality risk factors and (2) egg harvesting subject to environmental variability and management assessment uncertainty. Firstly, model evaluation was undertaken to establish a reasonable basis for considering that the model was in fact suitable for the intended use. Two forms of model validation were used for this purpose—temporal stochastic behavior and parameter sensitivity analysis.

Model Evaluation

Temporal Stochastic Behavior
The model was used to project the southern Great Barrier Reef loggerhead population over a 200-year period, given the model assumptions, to ensure that this model was capable of producing stationary dynamics and no aberrant temporal behavior. The long-term temporal behavior of the model that results from a single model run is shown in Figure 17.6. The distribution of female breeding probabilities sampled over the 200-year period (1900–2100) is shown in Figure 17.6a and is consistent with empirical estimates for this stock (Limpus et al. 1994). The low and variable female breeding probabilities sampled in the model result in long and variable remigration intervals and, hence, variation in the simulated number of nesting females (Figure 17.6b). This is also consistent with empirical estimates of remigration intervals (Limpus 1996) and annual nesting census records for this stock (Limpus and Reimer 1994). The annual nesting census at the Mon Repos mainland rookery derived from the model over the 200-year sampling period is shown in Figure 17.6c, which shows similar qualitative behavior, in magnitude and frequency of nesting fluctuations, to that which is characteristic of this southern Great Barrier Reef loggerhead stock (Chaloupka and Limpus 2001; Limpus and Reimer 1994).

Figure 17.6. Simulation model behavior. *Panel a.* Simulated female breeding likelihood in percentile plot form, showing median breeding probability of ≈ 0.23 or a remigration interval of ≈ 4.3 years from a single model run. *Panel b.* The nonlinear form that occurs in the simulations between the inverse of breeding probability (remigration interval) and number of breeding females. *Panel c.* Simulated number of female loggerheads nesting each year at the Mon Repos mainland rookery derived from a single model run. *Panel d.* Smoothed periodogram of the square root (annual Mon Repos nesting females) for a 500-year period): Daniell window = c (3,5,7,9); detrend = T; demean = T.

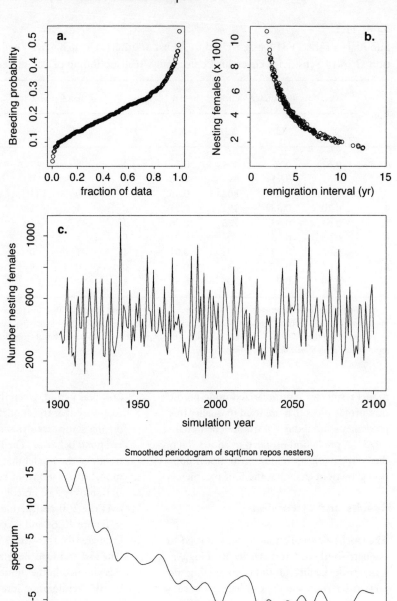

The spectral behavior of the simulated nesting census at the Mon Repos rookery, taken over a 500-year period to ensure adequate capture of low frequency temporal dynamics, is shown in Figure 17.6d. The autoregressive spectral density function shows a predominance of low frequency variability, with a periodogram slope of – 27.1 (LAE linear regression; Judge et al. 1985), which is indicative of dark red or black noise. Cuddington and Yodzis (1999) suggest that population persistence is far more likely in a stochastic environment that comprises very low frequency fluctuations (black noise) rather than low frequency (red noise) or short-term annual fluctuations (white noise). A reddened or black spectrum is consistent with

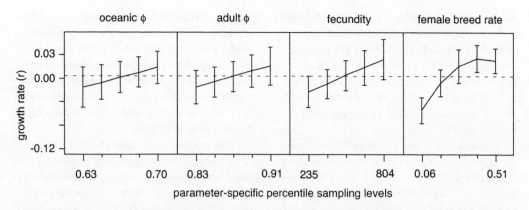

Figure 17.7. Sensitivity model. Prediction profile plot showing the effect of simultaneously changing four key parameters on predicted population growth in accordance with the FF3-ANOVA sampling design (Table 17.1). Solid curves show parameter-specific prediction traces ; error bars show 95% confidence intervals; derived from 100 Monte Carlo trials of mean predicted population growth for each of the nine fractional factorial settings or runs. Dashed line shows predicted population growth at the mean of each parameter.

expectations for population dynamics subject to strong low frequency environmental stochasticity (Cohen 1995). Overall, the simulation model reproduces quite well various empirical estimates of the temporal behavior and demographic characteristics of the southern Great Barrier Reef loggerhead stock and is therefore adequate for assessment of various risks to stock viability.

Parameter Sensitivity Analysis

Model parameter sensitivity was assessed here using a fractional factorial sampling approach with the nine model runs summarized in Table 17.1, enabling a simultaneous assessment of the relative effects of four parameters on southern Great Barrier Reef loggerhead population growth. The variance-weighted FF3-ANOVA model fitted mean population growth well (adjusted R^2 = 0.982) with three significant linear main effects (oceanic juvenile survival, adult survival, and fecundity) and one significant quadratic main effect (for female breeding probability) (Figure 17.7). It is apparent that increasing loggerhead fecundity within feasible bounds results in a similar or greater effect to increasing either oceanic juvenile survival or adult survival. On the other hand, increasing female breeding probability within feasible bounds results in a substantial nonlinear increase in predicted population growth. Clearly, southern Great Barrier Reef population growth

dynamics is just as sensitive to changes in fertility (fecundity, breeding behavior) as it is to changes in age-class–specific survival probabilities.

It is also useful to explore the model sensitivity to specific parameter sets as one means of diagnosing possible reasons for the recorded long-term decline in southern Great Barrier Reef loggerhead population abundance (Chaloupka and Limpus 2001). The different parameter sets have widely differing effects on population growth forecasts. For instance, run 5 indicates that the southern Great Barrier Reef loggerhead stock would be declining at about 12% per year if the four parameters sampled occurred simultaneously at the lowest levels (see Table 17.1). On the other hand, run 7 shows that the population will grow at about 3% per year even if mean adult survival is sampled at the lowest level (2.5 percentile). Run 2 shows that the population would be declining at about 2.6% per year if oceanic juvenile survival were sampled at the lowest level, even if adult survival were sampled at the highest level (see Table 17.1). An ongoing growth rate decline of about 3% per year is consistent with recent southern Great Barrier Reef loggerhead abundance trends based on Horvitz-Thompson-type population abundance estimates derived using sex- and age-class–specific Cormack-Jolly-Seber recapture probabilities (Chaloupka 2000). The southern Great Barrier Reef loggerhead stock has decreased about 3% per year since the 1980s in the southern Great Barrier Reef foraging grounds (Chaloupka and Limpus 2001), while the seasonal nesting population at the Mon Repos rookery has declined significantly since 1985 at 8% per year (Limpus and Reimer 1994) and has continued to do so (Chaloupka and Limpus 2001).

Previous evaluations of sea turtle population dynamics using single-element elasticity analysis (Crouse et al. 1987; Crowder et al. 1994; Cunnington and Brooks 1996; Heppell et al. 1996) have all concluded that fertility has little effect on sea turtle population growth. Pfister (1998) even suggests that the relative unimportance of fertility for population growth is a universal demographic phenomenon. One reason for this discrepancy is that loggerhead fertility is a function of fecundity (Equation 4) and female breeding likelihood (Equation 5), and both display significant variability due to individual heterogeneity or environmental stochasticity (Limpus et al. 1994). On the other hand, age-class–specific survival is restricted to a narrow range of possibilities (see Figure 17.4a; Chaloupka and Limpus 2002). Another reason for the discrepancy is that the female breeding probabilities were sampled from a highly skewed probability density function (extreme value) that reflects the recorded temporal variability in the proportion of females breeding each year due to environmental stochasticity (Limpus et al. 1994). Skewed distributions of demographic rates or probabilities are well known to have a major effect on age-structured population dynamics (Slade and Levenson 1984).

Single-parameter matrix model based elasticity studies evaluate only infinitesimal elasticity effects and so do not account for the magnitude of ecological variability inherent in the demographic processes (Mills et al. 1999). Therefore, single-element elasticity analysis based on the deterministic models commonly used in sea turtle studies can be misleading regarding the importance of demographic parameters. For instance, Breininger et al. (1999), using a stochastic simulation model of Florida scrub-jay population dynamics, found that fertility was of major demographic importance, which was contrary to findings from a single-element elasticity analysis. Bierzychudek (1999) also evaluated the performance of a matrix projection population model and found that model performance was poor compared with population abundance estimates because an ecologically realistic range of parameter variability had not been included in the model, which is similar to the findings of Breininger et al. (1999).

The stochastic simulation based FF3-ANOVA approach adopted here overcomes many limitations of the single-element elasticity approach. The main effects FF3 sampling design used here can be extended to account for higher order element interactions, and criteria other than population growth, such as population persistence indicators, could be used (Akçakaya and Raphael 1998). Overall, assessment of the temporal behavior of the model and parameter sensitivity analysis suggests that this simulation model is adequate for evaluating southern Great Barrier Reef loggerhead population dynamics subject to environmental stochasticity. This is especially so since the model sensitivities were female breeding probability, fecundity, and adult survival probabilities, which are parameters that are reasonably well estimated for this stock.

Competing Mortality Risks Evaluation

The simulation model was used to investigate the potential impact of three mortality risk factors or hazards on the viability of the southern Great Barrier Reef loggerhead stock at all stages of the life cycle (see Figure 17.1). The three hazards evaluated were (1) egg loss at mainland rookeries due to fox predation over a 10-year period (1965–1974), (2) incidental capture of immatures and adults in coastal otter trawl fisheries over a 22-year period (1978–1999), and (3) incidental capture of oceanic juveniles in distance-water longline fisheries over a 33-year period (1967–1999). It has been estimated that approximately 90% of the clutches laid each year from 1965 to the mid-1970s at mainland nesting beaches were lost to fox predation (Chaloupka and Limpus 1998; Heppell et al. 1996). These mainland rookeries account for about 33% of the southern Great Barrier Reef loggerhead egg production (Limpus and

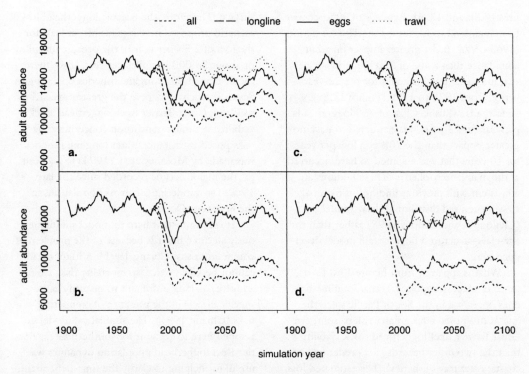

----- all   — — longline   ——— eggs   ········ trawl

Figure 17.8. Evaluation of competing mortality risks on loggerhead population viability. *Panel a*. Mean adult abundance for stock exposed to four risk sets: (1) 90% egg loss per year to foxes (1965–1974), (2) 250 loggerheads drowned per year in trawl fisheries (1978–1999), (3) 2.5% of oceanic juveniles killed per year in longline fisheries (1967–1999), (4) all three hazards combined. *Panel b*. Same as panel a, but with longline mortality of 5% per year. *Panel c*. Same as panel a, but with trawl mortality of 750 loggerheads per year. *Panel d*. Same as panel a, but with trawl mortality of 750 loggerheads per year and longline mortality of 5% per year.

Reimer 1994). Loggerhead mortality due to incidental capture in coastal otter trawl fisheries was evaluated using two simulated loss levels: 250 or 750 loggerheads (immatures and adults) drowned each year between 1978 and 1999. These otter trawl fishery loss scenarios were based on previous scenarios used to evaluate cause-specific loggerhead mortality (Heppell et al. 1996).

The annual loss of 250 southern Great Barrier Reef loggerheads in coastal trawl fisheries is high but plausible (Slater et al. 1998), while the loss of 750 loggerheads is unlikely but was included as a worst-case scenario (Chaloupka and Limpus 1998). The third mortality hazard was due to exposure to oceanic or distance-water longline fisheries that commenced operation in the western South Pacific around 1967 (Lu et al. 1998). Mortality due to incidental capture in longline fisheries was also evaluated using two

simulated loss levels: 2.5% or 5% of oceanic juveniles killed each year for the 33-year period from 1967 to 1999. These longline fishery loss scenarios were based on the incidental capture probabilities estimated for loggerheads in U.S. Atlantic longline fisheries (Witzell 1999) and for oceanic seabirds in Japanese western South Pacific longline fisheries (Gales et al. 1998).

Simulated adult loggerhead abundance over a 200-year period (1900–2100) due to chronic exposure to simulated mortality loss from three competing hazards is shown in Figure 17.8. Egg loss due to fox predation was assumed to be 90% per year in each of the four scenarios (Figure 17.8 a–d), loss due to coastal otter trawl fisheries was 250 loggerheads per year in figures 17.8a and 17.8b and 750 per year in figures 17.8c and 17.8d, while loss due to longline fisheries was 2.5% of the oceanic juveniles per year in figures 17.8a and 17.8c and 5% in figures 17.8b and 17.8d. Egg loss of 90% per year from mainland rookeries for the 10-year period (1965–1974) had a greater impact on adult abundance than a loss of 250 loggerheads per year in coastal trawl fisheries for the 22-year period from 1978 to 1999 (Figure 17.8a). In fact, a trawl fishery loss of 750 loggerheads per year for 22 years was estimated to have no greater impact than the 90% egg loss per year for 10 years that was assumed to have occurred at the mainland rookeries. These findings are consistent with previous findings using an age-class–structured distributed delay model (Chaloupka and Limpus 1998) rather than the age-class–structured boxcar train model developed here.

What is apparent from Figure 17.8 (a–d), given model assumptions, is that longline fisheries operating in the South Pacific since the late 1960s posed a far greater risk to southern Great Barrier Reef loggerhead stock viability than the two other hazards (fox predation and coastal otter trawl fisheries). The estimated loss of 2.5% of oceanic juveniles in the distance-water longline fisheries (figures 17.8a and 17.8c) was equivalent to 35,000 juveniles per year, which is plausible given the estimated 20 million hooks set each year by Japanese and Taiwanese longline fishing fleets operating within the eastern Australian Fishing Zone (AFZ) (Gales et al. 1998; Lu et al. 1998). These are not the only foreign longline fishing fleets operating in the South Pacific Ocean (Lu et al. 1998), so oceanic juvenile loggerheads are most likely exposed to significantly more than 20 million hooks per year in this region.

A loss of 35,000 juveniles exposed to 20 million hooks is a capture probability of about 0.0017, or 1.7 per 1,000 hooks, which is high but consistent with loggerhead capture rates estimated from logbook records for the U.S. Atlantic longline fishery (Witzell 1999) and similar to estimates for incidental catch rates of oceanic seabirds such as albatross in Japanese western South Pacific longline fisheries (Gales et al. 1998). Moreover, loggerheads readily consume baited longline hooks (Witzell 1999) and would be exposed to hooks in these waters for a far longer time than albatross foraging at the surface. Therefore, the oceanic loggerhead loss scenario proposed here is plausible, at least for the loss of 2.5% per year of the oceanic juveniles or about 35,000 juveniles per year. If so, then the distance-water longline fisheries operating in South Pacific waters pose the greatest hazard to southern Great Barrier Reef loggerhead stock viability. A similar conclusion concerning the risks posed by distance-water longline fisheries was made by Moloney et al. (1994) to account for the major decline recorded since the late 1960s for wandering albatross populations in the Southern Ocean.

It was important here to model simultaneously all three hazards because of the problem of competing risks (Chiang 1991). A loggerhead cannot be killed twice, so mortality risks are not additive, making it difficult to quantify cause-specific effects in the presence of competing risks (Chiang 1991). The simulation model developed here to account for southern Great Barrier Reef loggerhead population dynamics was useful for helping to clarify the time-dependent, cause-specific mortality risk effects due to exposure to the three major hazards (see Figure 17.8). For instance, fox predation of eggs at mainland rookeries between 1965 and 1974 reduces hatchling recruitment substantially so that few oceanic juveniles are exposed to the risk of incidental capture in distance-water longline fisheries during that period (Figure 17.9a). Hence, longline-specific mortality declines by approximately 20,000 oceanic juveniles during the early 1970s (Figure 17.9b) despite the continued operation of distance-water fisheries. When fox predation was controlled by the mid-1970s, there was a substantial increase in juvenile mortality caused by increasing exposure to longline fisheries as hatchling recruitment to the oceanic habitat recovered temporarily during the late 1970s to early 1980s (Figure 17.9a).

However, even though fox predation had ceased, there was a further decline in juveniles exposed to longline fishing during the 1990s that resulted from the adult recruitment failure caused by the loss of eggs during the 1960s and early 1970s (Figure 17.9b). The commencement of coastal otter trawl fisheries from 1978 onwards results in a decrease in the number of

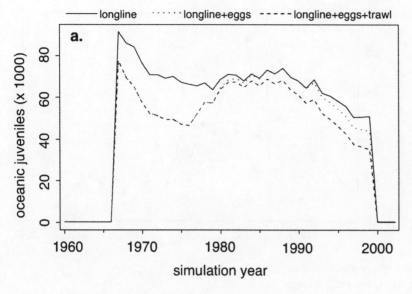

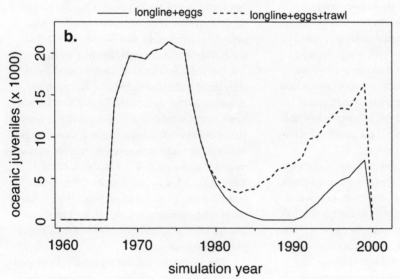

Figure 17.9. Competing mortality risk profiles. *Panel a.* Simulated annual mortality, between 1965 and 1999, of oceanic juvenile loggerheads due to exposure to (1) longline fishing only, (2) combined competing risks effect of longline fishing and fox predation, and (3) combined competing risks effect of all three sources of mortality. *Panel b.* Difference between the longline fishing only scenario, shown in panel a, and (1) the combined effect of longline fishing and fox predation and (2) the combined effect of all three hazards.

oceanic juveniles lost to longline fishing (Figure 17.9b) because fewer breeding females drowning in the otter trawl fisheries means fewer eggs laid and fewer oceanic juveniles available to be caught incidentally in longline fisheries. Meanwhile, the simulated stock was declining by the early 1990s (Figure 17.8), so that the impact of the two remaining hazards (coastal trawl fisheries and pelagic longline fisheries) declines from the mid-1980s (Figure 17.9a) because there are fewer and fewer loggerheads left to die from exposure to either hazard.

The southern Great Barrier Reef loggerhead population resident in southern Great Barrier Reef foraging grounds has declined since the 1980s (Chaloupka and Limpus 2001) and so has the female nesting population at both the mainland (Figure 17.10) and southern Great Barrier Reef rookeries (Limpus and Reimer 1994). The recorded decline in the southern Great Barrier Reef stock has been attributed solely to incidental capture in coastal trawl fisheries (Heppell et al. 1996), but this is unlikely. The southern Great Barrier Reef loggerhead

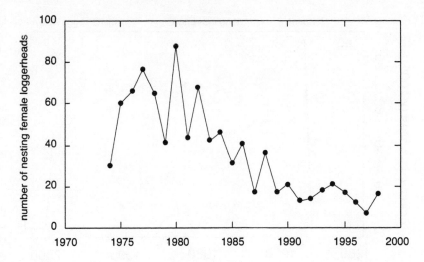

Figure 17.10. Annual census of the number of female loggerheads nesting each season on Heron Island (sGBR foraging grounds) over the last 25 years (1974–1998). The number of nesting loggerheads has declined at around 8% per year since the mid-1980s.

stock has been exposed to three major hazards (foxes, coastal trawl fisheries, and pelagic longline fisheries) at various times over the last 30–40 years, so the impact of all three competing hazards has contributed to the recorded stock decline (Figure 17.10), which appears to be due to chronic adult recruitment failures. Fox predation at the mainland rookeries is now well controlled (Limpus, pers. comm.), and mortality from coastal trawl fisheries is low and likely to be even lower with the proposed adoption of turtle exclusion devices.

On the other hand, the pelagic fisheries operating in the Australian Fishing Zone continue with no risk management strategies in place to reduce loggerhead mortality, while it is this hazard that poses the greatest risk to the long-term viability of this stock, as it does for other marine species such as oceanic seabirds (Gales et al. 1998). Australian monitoring programs operating in the Australian Fishing Zone do not record incidental catch of turtles by foreign longline fisheries (Gales et al. 1998). An expanded Australian Fishing Zone monitoring program is essential to validate the proposed magnitude of oceanic loggerhead loss and confirm the need to develop risk mitigation strategies and conservation policies to protect the declining southern Great Barrier Reef loggerhead stock. Meanwhile, there is some evidence that another longline fishery has developed recently off Chile and is known to incidentally catch southern Great Barrier Reef loggerheads (P. Dutton, pers. comm.).

Conclusion

Sea turtle population dynamics has been evaluated using mainly deterministic modeling approaches (Chaloupka and Musick 1997) that are based on deterministic life history theory. For instance, Spotila et al. (1996) used a discrete-time Euler-Lotka balance equation to diagnose global declines in leatherback populations, and southeastern U.S. loggerhead population dynamics has been assessed using variants of the same stage-structured matrix projection model (Crouse et al. 1987; Crowder et al. 1994; Cunnington and Brooks 1996; Grand and Beissinger 1997). These models were based on limited demographic inputs, and none accounted for temporal variation in the demographic processes.

The stochastic simulation model developed here was based on a comprehensive in-water study of southern Great Barrier Reef loggerhead demography that is subject to environmental stochasticity (Limpus 1994, 1996; Limpus et al. 1994). Moreover, the model was subject to adequate model evaluation and was considered sufficiently robust to support assessment of competing mortality risks to stock viability and for testing the age-class–dependent life-history theory that is applicable for a population subject to fluctuating environments (see Benton and Grant 1996).

However, the model developed here has several limitations in its current form. For instance, demographic stochasticity was not accounted for since small-population effects were not considered, although they could easily be accounted for by using binomial (Akçakaya 1991) or Poisson discrete event sampling (Gustafsson 2000) combined with sampling of the demographic rates from rate-specific probability density functions. Compensatory density-dependent processes were not included due to a lack of evidence concerning the existence and functional form of such processes for southern Great Barrier Reef loggerhead demography, although density-dependent growth was suggested for a population of immature green turtles resident in Bahamian waters (Bjorndal et al. 2000a).

Moreover, Ginsburg et al. (1990) have shown that risk assessment is highly sensitive to the functional form assumed for density-dependent processes and is best ignored if it cannot be reliably estimated. Similarly, neither depensatory density-dependent processes nor Allee effects (Dennis 1989) were considered due to a lack of relevant information for any sea turtle stock. Nonetheless, the model can be readily extended to account for sex dependency, density dependency, and spatial dependency in the demographic processes as relevant information becomes available and where such extension is needed for sex-dependent model application.

The stochastic simulation model was considered suitable for its intended purpose and was used to help diagnose the significant decline in southern Great Barrier Reef loggerhead stock abundance apparent since the 1980s (see Figure 17.10). The decline was attributed to a chronic exposure to three major hazards over the last 30–40 years: fox predation of eggs at the mainland rookeries, incidental drowning of immatures and adults in coastal otter trawl fisheries, and incidental drowning of oceanic juveniles in pelagic longline fisheries operating in South Pacific waters. Southern Great Barrier Reef loggerhead stock viability, unlike that of many other sea turtle populations, is not at risk due to egg harvesting, but it could become so if egg loss to predation by feral animals such as foxes were to become prevalent again, as it was during the late 1960s and early 1970s.

The World Conservation Union (IUCN)

has specified population risk criteria for Red Listing threatened species with the lowest high-risk category ("vulnerable") assigned to a population with an extinction probability > 10% within the next 100 years (Mace and Lande 1991). This risk criterion represents a societal judgment of a species existence value (Merkhofer 1987) where the viability of vulnerable populations is considered doubtful (Mace and Lande 1991). The southern Great Barrier Reef loggerhead stock clearly meets this IUCN risk criterion as the stock is still in decline and at serious risk of extinction due to ongoing exposure to otter trawl fisheries operating in Queensland waters and to pelagic longline fisheries operating in South Pacific waters.

ACKNOWLEDGMENTS

I am especially grateful to Colin Limpus for extensive support and encouragement in completing this work. I also thank Alan Bolten and Karen Bjorndal for constructive comments on the manuscript.

LITERATURE CITED

Akçakaya, H. R. 1991. A method for simulating demographic stochasticity. Ecological Modelling 54:133–136.

Akçakaya, H. R., and M. G. Raphael. 1998. Assessing human impact despite uncertainty: Viability of the northern spotted owl metapopulation in the northwestern U.S.A. Biodiversity Conservation 7:875–894.

Bartell, S. M., J. E. Breck, R. H. Gardner, and A. L. Brenkert. 1986. Individual parameter perturbation and error analysis of fish bioenergetics models. Canadian Journal of Fisheries and Aquatic Sciences 43:160–168.

Benton, T. G., and A. Grant. 1996. How to keep fit in the real world: Elasticity analyses and selection pressures on life histories in a variable environment. American Naturalist 147:115–139.

Bierzychudek, P. 1999. Looking backwards: Assessing the projections of a transition matrix model. Ecological Applications 9:1278–1287.

Bjorndal, K. A., A. B. Bolten, and M. Y. Chaloupka. 2000a. Green turtle somatic growth model: Evidence for density-dependence. Ecological Applications 10:269–282.

Bjorndal, K. A., A. B. Bolten, and H. R. Martins. 2000b. Somatic growth model of juvenile loggerhead sea turtles Caretta caretta: Duration of pelagic stage. Marine Ecology Progress Series 202:265–272.

Bloomfield, P. 1976. Fourier analysis of time series: An introduction. New York: John Wiley and Sons.

Blythe, S. P., R. M. Nisbet, and W. S. C. Gurney. 1984. The dynamics of population models with distributed maturation periods. Theoretical Population Biology 25:289–311.

Bowen, B. W., N. Kamezaki, C. J. Limpus, G. R. Hughes, A. B. Meylan, and J. C. Avise. 1994. Global phylogeography of the loggerhead turtle (Caretta caretta) as indicated by mitochondrial DNA haplotypes. Evolution 48:1820–1828.

Box, G. E. P., W. G. Hunter, and J. S. Hunter. 1978. Statistics for experimenters: An introduction to design, data analysis and model building. New York: John Wiley and Sons.

Breininger, D. R., M. A. Burgman, and B. M. Stith. 1999. Influence of habitat quality, catastrophes and population size on extinction risk of the Florida scrub-jay. Wildlife Society Bulletin 27:810–822.

Caswell, H. 1989. Matrix population models: Construction, analysis and interpretation. Sunderland, Mass.: Sinauer Associates.

Chaloupka, M. 1998. Polyphasic growth in pelagic loggerhead sea turtles. Copeia 1998:516–518.

———. 2000. Capture-recapture modeling of sea turtle population abundance. In K. A. Bjorndal and A. B. Bolten (eds.). Proceedings of a workshop on assessing abundance and trends for in-water sea turtle populations, 16–35. NOAA Technical Memorandum NMFS-SEFSC-445.

———. 2001a. Historical trends, seasonality and spatial synchrony in green turtle egg production. Biological Conservation 101:263–279.

———. 2001b. A system-of-equations growth function for southern Great Barrier Reef green sea turtles. Chelonian Conservation and Biology 4:88–93.

Chaloupka, M., and C. Limpus. 1998. Heuristic modelling of trawl fishery impacts on sGBR loggerhead population dynamics. In S. P. Epperly and J. Braun (compilers). Proceedings of the 17th annual symposium on sea turtle biology and conservation, 26–29. NOAA Technical Memorandum NMFS-SEFSC-415.

———. 2001. Trends in the abundance of sea turtles resident in southern Great Barrier Reef waters. Biological Conservation 102:235–249.

———. 2002. Survival probability estimates for the endangered loggerhead sea turtle resident in southern Great Barrier Reef waters. Marine Biology 140:267–277.

Chaloupka, M. Y., and J. A. Musick. 1997. Age, growth and population dynamics. In P. L. Lutz and J. A. Musick (eds.). The biology of sea turtles, 233–276. Boca Raton, Fla.: CRC Press.

Chiang, C. L. 1991. Competing risks in mortality analysis. Annual Review of Public Health 12:281–307.

Cochran, W. G., and G. M. Cox. 1957. Experimental designs, 2nd ed. New York: John Wiley and Sons.

Cochran, M. E., and S. Ellner. 1992. Simple methods for calculating age-based life history parameters for stage-structured populations. Ecological Monographs 62:345–364.

Cohen, J. E. 1995. Unexpected dominance of high frequencies in chaotic nonlinear population models. Nature 378:610–612.

Crouse, D. T., L. B. Crowder, and H. Caswell. 1987. A stage-based population model for loggerhead sea turtles and implications for conservation. Ecology 68:1412–1423.

Crowder, L. B., D. T. Crouse, S. S. Heppell, and T. H. Martin. 1994. Predicting the impact of turtle excluder devices on loggerhead sea turtle populations. Ecological Applications 4:437–445.

Cuddington, K. M., and P. Yodzis. 1999. Black noise and population persistence. Proceedings of the Royal Society of London, Series B 266:969–973.

Cunnington, D. C., and R. J. Brooks. 1996. Bet-hedging theory and eigenelasticity: A comparison of the life histories of loggerhead sea turtles (Caretta caretta) and snapping turtles (Chelydra serpentina). Canadian Journal of Zoology 74:291–296.

Dennis, B. 1989. Allee effects: Population growth, critical density and the chance of extinction. Natural Resources Modeling 3:481–538.

Engen, S., O. Bakke, and A. Islam. 1998. Demographic and environmental stochasticity—Concepts and definitions. Biometrics 54:39–45.

Frazer, N. B., and J. I. Richardson. 1985. Seasonal variation in clutch size for loggerhead sea turtles, Caretta caretta, nesting on Little Cumberland Island, Georgia, U.S.A. Copeia 1985:1083–1085.

Gales, R., N. Brothers, and T. Reid. 1998. Seabird mortality in the Japanese tuna longline fishery around Australia, 1988–1995. Biological Conservation 86:37–56.

Ginsberg, L. R., S. Ferson, and H. R. Akçakaya. 1990. Reconstructibility of density dependence and the conservative assessment of extinction risks. Conservation Biology 4:63–70.

Goudriaan, J. 1986. Boxcar train methods for modelling of ageing, development, delays and dispersion. In J. A. J. Metz and O. Diekmann (eds.). The dynamics of physiologically structured populations, 453–473. Springer Lecture Notes in Bio-mathematics 68. New York: Springer-Verlag.

Grand, J., and S. R Beissinger. 1997. When relocation of loggerhead sea turtle *(Caretta caretta)* nests becomes a useful strategy. Journal of Herpetology 31:428–434.

Gustafsson, L. 2000. Poisson simulation—A method for generating stochastic variations in continuous system simulations. Simulation 74:264–274.

Gyuris, E. 1994. The rate of predation by fishes on hatchlings of the green turtle *(Chelonia mydas)*. Coral Reefs 13:137–144.

Hamilton, M. S. 1980. Estimating lengths and orders of delays in system dynamics models. *In* J. Randers (ed.). Elements of the system dynamics method, 162–183. Cambridge, Mass.: Productivity Press.

Henderson-Sellers, B., and A. Henderson-Sellers. 1996. Sensitivity evaluation of environmental models using fractional factorial experimentation. Ecological Modelling 86:291–295.

Heppell, S. A., C. J. Limpus, D. T. Crouse, N. B. Frazer, and L. B. Crowder. 1996. Population model analysis for the loggerhead sea turtle, *Caretta caretta*, in Queensland. Wildlife Research 23:143–159.

Judge, G. G., W. E. Griffiths, R. C. Hill, H. Lutke-pohl, and T. C. Lee. 1985. Theory and practice of econometrics, 2nd ed. New York: Wiley and Sons.

Limpus, C. J. 1992. Observations on first breeding by a loggerhead turtle. Marine Turtle Newsletter 56:1–2.

———. 1994. The loggerhead turtle, *Caretta caretta*, in Queensland: Feeding ground selection following her first nesting season. *In* K. A. Bjorndal, A. B. Bolten, D. A. Johnson, and P. J. Eliazar (compilers). Proceedings of the 14th annual symposium on sea turtle biology and conservation, 78–81. NOAA Technical Memorandum NMFS-SEFSC-351.

———. 1996. Changing fecundity with age in Queensland *Caretta caretta. In* J. A. Keinath, D. E. Barnard, J. A. Musick, and B. A. Bell (compilers). Proceedings of the 15th annual symposium on sea turtle biology and conservation, 167–169. NOAA Technical Memorandum NMFS-SEFSC-387.

Limpus, C. J., and D. Reimer. 1994. The loggerhead turtle, *Caretta caretta*, in Queensland: A population in decline. *In* R. James (ed.). Proceedings of the marine turtle conservation workshop, 39–59. Canberra: Australian National Parks and Wildlife Service.

Limpus, C. J., P. Reed, and J. D. Miller. 1983. Islands and turtles: The influence of choice of nesting beach on sex ratio. *In* J. T. Baker, R. M. Carter,

P. W. Sammarco, and K. P. Stark (eds.). Proceedings of the inaugural Great Barrier Reef conference, 397–402. Townsville, Australia: James Cook University Press.

Limpus, C. J., J. D. Miller, C. J. Parmenter, D. Reimer, N. McLachlan, and R. Webb. 1992. Migration of green *(Chelonia mydas)* and loggerhead *(Caretta caretta)* turtles to and from eastern Australian rookeries. Wildlife Research 19:347–358.

Limpus, C. J., P. J. Couper, and M. A. Read. 1994. The loggerhead turtle, *Caretta caretta*, in Queensland: Population structure in a warm temperate feeding area. Memoirs of the Queensland Museum 37:195–204.

Lo, N. C. H., P. E. Smith, and J. L. Butler. 1995. Population growth of northern anchovy and Pacific sardine using stage-specific matrix models. Marine Ecology Progress Series 127:15–26.

Lu, H. J., K. T. Lee, and C. H. Liao. 1998. On the relationship between El Niño/Southern Oscillation and South Pacific albacore. Fisheries Research 39:1–7.

Mace, G. M., and R. Lande. 1991. Assessing extinction threats: Toward a re-evaluation of IUCN threatened species categories. Conservation Biology 5:148–157.

Manetsch, T. J. 1976. Time-varying distributed delays and their use in aggregative models of large systems. IEEE Transactions in Systems Management and Cybernetics 6:547–553.

Marcovaldi, M. A., M. H. Godfrey, and N. Mrosovsky. 1997. Estimating sex ratios of loggerhead turtles in Brazil from pivotal incubation durations. Canadian Journal of Zoology 75:755–770.

McCullagh, P., and J. A. Nelder. 1989. Generalized linear models, 2nd ed. Monographs on Statistics and Applied Probability 37. London: Chapman and Hall.

Merkhofer, M. W. 1987. Decision science and social risk management: Comparative evaluation of cost-benefit analysis, decision analysis and other formal decision-aiding approaches. Dordrecht, Holland: D. Reidel Publishing Company.

Mills, L. S., D. F. Doak, and M. J. Wisdom. 1999. Reliability of conservation actions based on elasticity analysis of matrix models. Conservation Biology 13:815–829.

Moloney, C. L., J. Cooper, P. G. Ryan, and W. R. Siegfried. 1994. Use of a population model to assess the impact of longline fishing on wandering albatross *Diomedea exulans* populations. Biological Conservation 70:195–203.

Morgan, B. J. T. 1984. Elements of simulation. London: Chapman and Hall.

Oreskes, N., K. Shrader-Frechette, and K. Belitz. 1994. Verification, validation, and confirmation of numerical models in the earth sciences. Science 263:641–646.

Parham, J. F., and G. R. Zug. 1998. Age and growth of loggerhead sea turtles (Caretta caretta) of coastal Georgia: An assessment of skeletochronological age-estimates. Bulletin of Marine Science 61:287–304.

Pfister, C. A. 1998. Patterns of variance in stage-structured populations: Evolutionary predictions and ecological implications. Proceedings of the National Academy of Sciences 95:213–218.

Poiner, I. R., and A. N. M. Harris. 1996. The incidental capture, direct mortality and delayed mortality of turtles in Australia's northern prawn fishery. Marine Biology 125:813–825.

Polovina, J. J., D. R. Kobayashi, D. M. Parker, M. P. Seki, and G. H. Balazs. 2000. Turtles on the edge: Movement of loggerhead turtles (Caretta caretta) along oceanic fronts, spanning longline fishing grounds in the central North Pacific, 1997–1998. Fisheries Oceanography 9:71–82.

Puccia, C. J., and R. Levins. 1985. Qualitative modeling of complex systems: An introduction to loop analysis and time averaging. Cambridge, Mass.: Harvard University Press.

Ruth, M., and B. Hannon. 1997. Modeling dynamic economic systems. New York: Springer-Verlag.

Rykiel, E. J. 1996. Testing ecological models: The meaning of validation. Ecology Modelling 90:229–244.

SAS Institute. 1994. SAS JMP: Statistics made visual. Cary, N.C.: SAS Institute, Inc.

Slade, N. A., and H. Levenson. 1984. The effect of skewed distributions of vital statistics on growth of age-structured populations. Theoretical Population Biology 26:361–366.

Slater, J., C. J. Limpus, J. Robins, F. Pantus, and M. Chaloupka. 1998. Risk assessment of sea turtle capture in the Queensland east coast otter trawl fishery. Report prepared for TrawlMAC, QFMA, on behalf of the Great Barrier Reef Marine Park Authority and the QDEH and QDPI, Brisbane, Queensland, Australia.

Spotila, J. R., A. E. Dunham, A. J. Leslie, A. C. Steyermark, P. T. Plotkin, and F. V. Paladino. 1996. Worldwide population decline of Dermochelys coriacea: Are leatherback turtles going extinct? Chelonian Conservation and Biology 2:209–222.

Steinhorst, R. K., H. W. Hunt, G. S. Innis, and K. P. Haydock. 1978. Sensitivity analyses of the ELM model. In G. S. Innis (ed.). Grassland simulation model, 231–255. New York: Springer-Verlag.

van Buskirk, J., and L. B. Crowder. 1994. Life-history variation in marine turtles. Copeia 1994:66–81.

Vose, D. 1996. Quantitative risk analysis: A guide to Monte Carlo simulation modeling. New York: John Wiley and Sons.

Walker, T. A. 1994. Post-hatchling dispersal of sea turtles. In R. James (ed.). Proceedings of the marine turtle conservation workshop, 79–94. Canberra: Australian National Parks and Wildlife Service.

Witzell, W. N. 1999. Distribution and relative abundance of sea turtles caught incidentally by the U.S. pelagic longline fleet in the western North Atlantic Ocean, 1992–1995. Fishery Bulletin 97:200–211.

Chapter 18

Biological Conservation of Loggerheads:

Challenges and Opportunities

—Blair E. Witherington

If understanding the nature of an animal is key to conserving it, then conservationists would seem to have an advantage in their efforts to conserve loggerheads. They are one of the best-known species of sea turtles (the author cites their treatment in this book), and certainly, more is known about the biology of logger-heads than is known about the majority of other organisms that are threatened with extinction (including the many organisms that have yet to be so distinguished). Yet, part of knowing log-gerheads is to understand the difficult, varied, and widespread nature of the threats to their survival. Loggerheads are in trouble, and although an extensive litany of conservation problems can be identified, effective conservation solutions have been elusive.

A great broadening in the understanding of loggerhead life history and threats has occurred within the last two decades (Bjorndal 1995; Carr 1986; Dodd 1988; Lutz and Musick 1997; Meylan and Ehrenfeld 2000; NMFS and USFWS 1991, 1998; NRC Committee on Sea Turtle Conservation 1990; Thorbjarnarson et al. 2000), but much of this understanding is broader than it is deep. Like the other sea turtles, loggerheads spend much of their long lives in inaccessible places and cannot be studied well in an experimental microcosm. Although a conceptual model for loggerhead life stages can be assembled (Figure 18.1), there are critical gaps in quantitative values for age-based survivor-ship. And although there are many pieces of information that compose a picture of loggerhead distribution at sea (e.g., strandings, aerial surveys, and in-water captures), the actual abundance and genetic identity of loggerheads in the water is only beginning to be understood. The places loggerheads can travel to are known (from tag returns and limited remote tracking), but current understanding of the actual migratory routes and behavior of traveling logger-heads remains rudimentary.

Most threats to loggerheads also are known

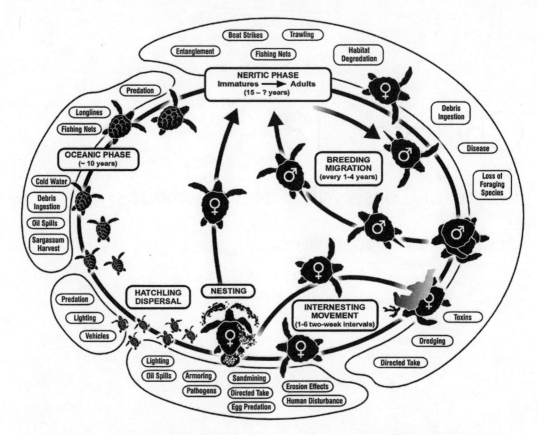

Figure 18.1. A life stage model for the loggerhead sea turtle. Labels on the perimeter of the diagram represent threats to survival that occur during the adjacent life stages represented. Threats are described in the text and by NRC (1990), NMFS and USFWS (1991 and 1998), Lutcavage et al. (1997), Meylan and Ehrenfeld (2000), and Thorbjarnarson et al. (2000).

only in general terms. Like much of the loggerhead life cycle, threats often occur where they cannot be adequately measured. Many threats are well known to occur but remain difficult to quantify in a way that would accurately predict population dynamics.

What seems to be missing from the current understanding of loggerheads is a deeper assessment of their basic biology, an understanding that should include the measurable relationships between loggerheads and other organisms, including humans. Questions in need of additional, population-specific, empirical data include the following: How many live and how many die? At what rates do they feed, grow, and reproduce? What is their value to ecosystems and to human beings? Researchers have learned a lot about loggerheads, but there is still much they need to know.

What researchers know and what they need

to know about loggerheads and the threats to their survival are assessed in this chapter to help guide loggerhead conservation efforts. The author's goal is to compose a portrait of the loggerhead sea turtle from the perspective of a conservationist and to use some of the principal characteristics of loggerheads to frame an outline describing important loggerhead conservation issues. The characteristics focused on are not only those that influence loggerhead population dynamics, but are also those that affect the relationships between loggerheads and humans.

Biological Characteristics and Their Conservation Implications

Loggerheads Are Crusty and Taste Bad

Loggerheads have not been targeted by fisheries to the extent that hawksbills *(Eretmochelys im-*

bricata) and green turtles *(Chelonia mydas)* have. The thickness, plasticity, and beauty of a hawksbill's shell scutes have made them a target of an intense commercial fishery (Meylan and Donnelly 1999). Killing hawksbills for the tortoiseshell industry has brought the hawksbill closer to extinction than any other sea turtle but Kemp's ridley *(Lepidochelys kempii)*. Unlike in hawksbills, the scutes covering the shell of larger loggerheads tend to be biofouled and irregularly deciduous (to most, a bit crusty and flaky). Loggerhead scutes are not as thick those of hawksbills and will often peel apart rather than come free of the turtle in a single piece. Thus, loggerheads are not a source for commercially valuable tortoiseshell and are not commonly stuffed as curios, as green turtles and hawksbills often are.

The assertion that loggerheads taste bad is, of course, a relative statement. It is used to make a comparative distinction between the culinary value put on loggerheads and that put on green turtles by humans. The assertion is not that loggerheads are inedible but that green turtles are a much more sought after species (Bustard 1972; Carr 1952; this volume: Kamezaki et al., Chapter 13; Limpus and Limpus, Chapter 6). Green turtle meat and calipee for turtle soup formed the basis for a vast international trade in green turtles and for an intense green turtle fishery (Thorbjarnarson et al. 2000). Green turtles also have been taken extensively on their nesting beaches, which has been considered the principal reason why many green turtle nesting colonies have been extirpated (Groombridge and Luxmoore 1989; Parsons 1962; Thorbjarnarson et al. 2000).

Unlike the loggerhead's meat, loggerhead eggs are often valued as food. The harvest of loggerhead eggs in the United States was common until the take of eggs was banned in the late 1970s by state and federal laws. But a distinction should be made between the effects of harvesting turtle eggs and those of harvesting turtles that are closer to maturity. Harvesting of population members with the highest reproductive value, such as older juveniles and young adults, has a much greater effect on population growth than does the harvest of turtles as eggs, which have a relatively low reproductive value (Crouse et al. 1987).

Largely due to the harvest of juveniles and adults, green turtles today are greatly reduced from their historical status as possibly the most abundant sea turtle (Groombridge and Luxmoore 1989; Pritchard 1979). Although loggerheads have been, and continue to be, taken sporadically for subsistence use, there has been no prolonged and large-scale commercial harvest of them. Harvesting pressure on the scale of the green turtle harvest would have been devastating to loggerhead populations. With a more limited distribution than that of green turtles, with fewer populations, and with a center of distribution in the developed world, loggerheads could have been quickly overharvested to extinction.

But a lack of historical industrial-scale harvest of loggerheads also means that there is a lack of historical information from fisheries data and trade records. For instance, in the United States, although loggerheads are more abundant than green turtles in coastal waters and, although on nesting beaches loggerheads outnumber green turtles 20 times over (FMRI, Statewide Nesting Beach Survey program, unpubl. data; Meylan et al. 1995), there is little mention of loggerheads in the records of the commercial sea turtle fishery that existed in the United States (principally in Texas and Florida) during the late 19th century (Brice 1896; Doughty 1984). Such fisheries and trade data have been instrumental to understanding the level of regional declines in both hawksbills and green turtles (Groombridge and Luxmoore 1989).

Loggerheads Have Two Centers of Abundance and Many Facets of Diversity

Most of the world's loggerheads nest in two places: southern Florida, in the United States, and on the Island of Masirah, Oman (Dodd 1988). These beaches are the egg baskets for well over half of the reproductive effort of the world's loggerheads. At each nesting area, one can point both to comforting protections and to disturbing troubles.

In Florida, loggerheads and their eggs have been protected from direct harvest since they were listed in 1978 under the Endangered Species Act (although Florida loggerheads have received less extensive legal protections since the 1960s). Following this protection, after a span of time equivalent to a loggerhead generation (approximately 25 years; Bjorndal et al. 2001; Frazer and Ehrhart 1985), the southern Florida population of loggerheads now seems to be showing signs of recovery (TEWG 1998, 2000). It is reasonable to assume that the Endangered Species Act has had a profound, positive influence on loggerhead abundance within the United States.

However, the Florida egg basket is still threatened by several important human effects. Many of these effects are near nesting beaches and are incidental to human activity. Loggerheads in Florida nest on the doorstep of millions of coastal residents. As of 1995, 7.8 million people (over 60% of Florida's population) lived within 8 km of the coast (FCMP 1997). Florida's coastal population is expected to increase by 15% and 13%, respectively, in the next two decades (FCMP 1997), and incidental effects on loggerhead nesting have the potential to increase commensurately.

At Masirah, loggerheads are currently protected both by local laws that prohibit harvest of females on the beach (Baldwin and Al-Kiyumi 1999; Ross and Barwani 1995) and by an Islamic cultural prohibition (haram) against eating meat from animals that crawl on their bellies. This categorization as haram generally benefits sea turtles only when they are on a beach (nesting), although even in the water, loggerheads at Masirah are not targeted for capture to the extent that green turtles are (Baldwin and Al-Kiyumi 1999). Laws on Masirah prohibit the harvest of eggs, although a substantial, but potentially sustainable (< 10% of egg production), subsistence egg harvest continues (R. Baldwin, pers. comm.). Trends in numbers of nesting females at the Masirah nesting beach are uncertain (Baldwin et al., Chapter 14 this volume).

The human population on Masirah is small (10,000–20,000; R. Baldwin, pers. comm.), but the potential exists for tourism development, oil spills, an expansion of military activities, and associated problems with artificial lighting. As in Florida, pressures from human activity on Masirah are increasing.

Unfortunately, conserving most of the world's loggerheads at two principal nesting sites will not sufficiently protect the complete genetic diversity of loggerheads. Much of loggerhead diversity is attributable to turtles that belong to smaller nesting aggregations (reviewed by Bowen, Chapter 4 this volume). Many of these smaller populations are known to be declining (Encalada et al. 1999; this volume: Baldwin et al., Chapter 14; Ehrhart et al., Chapter 10; Kamezaki et al., Chapter 13; Limpus and Limpus, Chapter 12; Margaritoulis et al., Chapter 11). A broad assessment of the global status of loggerheads is that numerous small and genetically diverse populations are also among the most threatened and least stable.

Loggerheads Breed in the Developed World

Loggerheads have the most temperate nesting distribution of all the sea turtles. This distribution intersects with major coastal population centers in the southeastern United States, the northeastern Mediterranean, southern Japan, and others. Many loggerhead nesting beaches serve as either resort or residential areas and are densely developed with accommodations for temporary and permanent residents. This concentration of people at warm temperate coastal sites is formed largely by relatively affluent people seeking a pleasant place to spend their time. In these areas where sand and sea alone are the basis for industry, both real estate prices and the median income of residents are high.

Many incidental effects of humans on loggerhead nesting beaches come both directly and indirectly from development, which includes all manner of anthropogenic structures, objects, and fixtures that are on or near the beach. One of the most important indirect effects of development is the necessity for protecting coastal property against erosion. In protecting property, coastal armoring is often used. Coastal armoring may include walls, rocks, fences, or any other structure meant to retain sand or lessen the erosive effects of water. Armoring structures that are open to the sandy beach frequently prevent turtles from accessing suitable nesting habitat (Mosier 1998).

Coastal armoring is particular to recreational

and residential developments where real estate value is proportional to a property's proximity to the sea—whereas property owners who do not place a premium on ocean views might decide to have their buildings a safer distance from the sea. Coastal property owners on loggerhead nesting beaches have predominantly chosen armoring over retreat from the eroding beach despite the negative effects that armoring has on the beach itself (e.g., increased erosion due to wave scour and interruption of beach-dune sand dynamics; Pilkey and Wright 1988).

Short of armoring, coastal properties are also protected by the construction of artificial beaches in a process often called beach nourishment. It is an involved and expensive endeavor that requires the money and the engineering bravado of an affluent industrial society. Approximately 1.3 billion dollars have been spent to nourish beaches on the U.S. Atlantic coast since 1960, and in recent years (1990–1996) the rate of spending has reached 68 million dollars per year (Valverde et al. 1999). Yet, it is difficult to make a beach that is similar to the one that has eroded away. Hundreds of kilometers of nesting beach have been artificially nourished with highly variable results, including departures from "natural" beaches in sand grain size and sorting, sand color, compaction, beach profile, and formation of escarpments (Crain et al. 1995).

Key differences between artificial beaches and naturally fluctuating beaches are that artificial beaches tend to be wider, flatter, and have more compact sands. Loggerheads do nest on artificial beaches and have been observed to increase nesting activity where nourishment has added sand to areas with little dry beach. However, in comparison to nearby beaches with natural profiles, loggerheads on nourished beaches tend to abandon nesting attempts with greater frequency (Herren and Ehrhart 2000; Steinitz et al. 1998). The altered profile and frequent formation of midbeach escarpments on nourished beaches (Crain et al. 1995; Herren and Ehrhart 2000; Steinitz et al. 1998) combined with the sensitivity of loggerheads to beach slope when they are selecting a nest site (Wood and Bjorndal 2000) may explain why some turtles abandon their attempts to nest on these beaches. Hatching success in nests, which is highly variable under any set of conditions and is subject to scores of effects from many phenomena, has not been shown to be profoundly influenced by incubation within nourished sands (but note a significant effect measured by Herren and Ehrhart 2000).

Another incidental effect of human presence on nesting beaches comes from artificial lighting. Light from artificial sources that is visible from a nesting beach can discourage loggerheads from nesting (Witherington 1992) and can lead hatchlings to their deaths (Witherington and Martin 2000). In Florida alone, data on hatchling disorientation rates (Witherington et al. 1996) and hatchling production (FMRI, Index Nesting Beach Survey program, unpubl. data) suggest that approximately one million loggerhead hatchlings have their seaward orientation disrupted by lighting and that mortality from this may reach the hundreds of thousands.

The artificial lighting of nesting beaches is generally commensurate with the density of electrified development. However, there are solutions to lighting problems that do not preclude people from using the beach and from lighting their property—solutions generally referred to as light management. On most of the nesting beaches of Florida, residents of local communities have enacted light management ordinances that prohibit lighting from being visible from the beach during the nesting season (but allow lighting that is hidden from the beach). Acceptance of these sea turtle protection laws has been broad, and enforcement is meaningful, although by no means complete.

Little Loggerheads Spend a Long Time as Oceanic Drifters

Young loggerheads spend approximately a decade (estimated range 7–12 years; Bolten, Chapter 4 this volume) in a pelagic and largely oceanic phase. This oceanic phase begins when loggerheads disperse from nesting beaches and escape from what is believed to be a gauntlet of numerous littoral and neritic predators (Stancyk 1995; Witherington and Salmon 1992). Although the rate of predation on small loggerheads is thought to lessen as they reach oceanic waters (deeper than 200 m), additional mortality may occur as turtles disperse into waters too cold for survival (Lohmann and Lohmann, Chapter 3 this volume).

An important consideration for stage-based mortality is that the number of loggerhead deaths in a stage is equal to risk of death multiplied by exposure time. Mortality in oceanic juveniles may occur at a lower rate than in hatchlings but for a far longer period of time (Heppell et al., Chapter 16 this volume). This concept of risk and exposure is especially important when anthropogenic threats at sea are considered. One of these threats is exposure to marine debris. Oceanic loggerheads forage within areas of surface downwelling where advection assembles not only the floating organisms on which turtles feed but also a beguiling assortment of plastics and tar (Witherington 2000, 2002). In lines of surface downwelling in the Atlantic Ocean off Florida nesting beaches, 15–17% of posthatchling (weeks old) loggerheads were found to have consumed plastics, and 20–63% had consumed tar (Witherington 2000, 2002). And of 83 posthatchling loggerheads that had begun feeding and had washed ashore dead during storm events in Florida, 83% had consumed plastic (Witherington, unpubl. data). Ingestion of plastics and tar by sea turtles is believed to have both lethal and sublethal effects (Carr 1987; McCauley and Bjorndal 1999). The exposure to this hazard over years spent in the open ocean would be expected to kill far more loggerheads than if the threat occurred during a shorter life stage.

The areas of downwelling (often oceanic frontal boundaries) where loggerheads spend much of their first decade are also zones of concentrated fishing activity. Longlines (numerous baited hooks on short lines attached to a single long main line) are often set at downwellings in order to capitalize on concentrations of commercially valuable fishes such as swordfish (*Xiphias gladius*) and tunas (*Thunnus* spp.). Young loggerheads bite the longline baits, become hooked, and frequently drown (reviewed in Balazs and Pooley 1994). Sea turtles (many or most being loggerheads) incur mortality from longlines set in the U.S. Atlantic and Gulf of Mexico, the eastern Atlantic near the Azores, the Mediterranean, the northern Pacific, and the tropical Pacific (Balazs and Pooley 1994; Bolten et al. 1998). The extensive Japanese tuna longline fleet alone is estimated to kill more than 12,000 sea turtles annually in the western Pacific and the South China Sea (Nishimura and Nakahigashi 1990). In comparison to efforts to reduce turtle mortality from shrimp trawling (discussed below), the development of methods and technology to reduce longline mortality has just begun.

Loggerheads Migrate

Loggerheads move great distances during their lives, which makes it difficult to count and study them. Much of this migration takes place in complex, stage-specific and population-specific patterns and in regions of ocean that are not readily accessible to researchers (see Figure 18.1). Hatchling loggerheads disperse from beaches into the open ocean and occupy entire ocean basins during a decade-long, oceanic developmental stage. These oceanic juveniles then recruit into neritic habitats, but in a manner that is likely to be highly variable in space and time. Then, as older neritic-stage juveniles, loggerheads may move hundreds of kilometers between foraging grounds and further separate themselves relative to age (or they might stay near the same foraging grounds for life; Limpus and Limpus, Chapter 6 this volume). And upon reaching adulthood, loggerheads from the same foraging area may make migrations to different nesting beaches, or from different foraging areas to the same nesting beach.

Knowing the migratory tendencies of loggerheads helps researchers understand the importance of assessing the identity of the turtles they study and wish to conserve. A single foraging area may contain loggerheads that originate from several geopolitically separate nesting beaches. Within such a foraging area, assessments of loggerhead abundance, collection of demographic information, quantification of threats, and efforts to reduce threats would all apply fractionally to the proportions of the populations represented. Mixed-stock assessments for loggerheads have just begun to uncover loggerhead identities at some foraging grounds in the southeastern United States

(Bowen 1995; Sears et al. 1995) and in the open Pacific (Bowen et al. 1995) and Atlantic oceans (Bolten et al. 1998).

Because of their migrations, loggerheads are international animals. In an example of the extent to which this is true, Bowen and Karl (1997) describe the migrations of loggerheads that emerge as hatchlings on beaches in southern Japan, travel the expanse of the Pacific Ocean (where they are known from incidental captures in international driftnet and longline fisheries), forage as neritic juveniles off Baja California, and return across more than 10,000 km of Pacific Ocean to nest on Japanese beaches.

Large, Valuable Loggerheads Have a Coastal Distribution

Large juvenile and adult loggerheads are largely benthic foragers that are distributed in coastal and neritic waters (this volume: Hopkins-Murphy et al., Chapter 5; Limpus and Limpus, Chapter 6; see also Figure 18.1). These older loggerheads are among the few that have survived the high mortality of egg, hatchling, and oceanic stages and have reached a stage where they have a decent chance to live until they reproduce. Given these differing odds for survival, older juveniles and young adults are likely to have a much greater reproductive contribution than are turtles in other stages (Crouse et al. 1987). This reproductive value—which is essentially an age-specific expectation of future offspring (Pianka 1994)—is an important assessment for loggerhead conservationists because it offers a way to translate the deaths of turtles in specific life stages into effects on the population.

The coastal and neritic distribution for reproductively valuable loggerheads has great consequences, in that this distribution overlaps that of penaeid shrimps and other commercially harvested species. Within these areas, commercial bottom trawling for shrimp has expanded rapidly in the last half of the 20th century (NRC 1990). Presently, the seven species of shrimp captured in bottom trawls within U.S. waters have the highest product value of any U.S. commercial fishery.

In trawling nets for shrimp, loggerheads are caught incidentally and drowned. The magnitude of this incidental loggerhead mortality during decades of shrimping, especially in the southeastern United States and the Gulf of Mexico (NRC 1990) and in northeastern Australia (Poiner and Harris 1996), is critical to understanding the present status of loggerheads. That is, it is reasonable to assume that loggerhead stocks subjected to this mortality are greatly depleted from historical levels. The assumption seems justified for the stocks of loggerheads where mortality from bottom trawling is best understood, in the southeastern United States and the Gulf of Mexico. Loggerheads foraging in this region—a number that may approach one-half of the world's loggerheads—have been exposed to decades of bottom trawling that has killed the most reproductively valuable members of the population at an annual rate estimated to range higher than the total annual number of breeding females from these stocks (NRC 1990).

The principal conservation tool currently in place to reduce sea turtle mortality from trawling is the turtle excluder device (TED). Turtle excluder devices are additions to trawling nets that divert turtles and other large objects from the net bag where shrimp and other small items collect (NRC 1990). Turtle excluder devices allow most loggerheads that have been overcome by a bottom trawl to escape the net after a period of time. These devices were developed through cooperation among shrimpers, the U.S. National Marine Fisheries Service, and Sea Grant and were introduced as a sea turtle conservation tool in 1977. Turtle excluder devices have been required on U.S. shrimping vessels since regulations were implemented during the period 1989–1992 (TEWG 1998). Turtle excluder devices are also used on vessels from Belize, Colombia, Costa Rica, Ecuador, El Salvador, Guatemala, Guyana, Honduras, Indonesia, Mexico, Nicaragua, Panama, Thailand, Trinidad and Tobago, and Venezuela (C. Oravetz, pers. comm.).

Compelling the use of turtle excluder devices is likely to have been the most important action ever taken to conserve loggerheads. However, recent evidence indicates that trawling with turtle excluder devices still results in some turtle mortality (Crowder et al. 1995; Poiner and Harris 1996). The mortality may come from the drowning of stressed turtles that are repeatedly captured and excluded from nets during periods of high-density trawling efforts and from a tendency for larger turtles to become stuck in turtle excluder device escape openings that are too small (Epperly and Teas 1999). Modifications to turtle excluder devices are recommended (Epperly and Teas 1999), and selective zone closures are held out (NRC 1990) as additional measures necessary to protect sea turtles from trawling mortality.

Additional threats from fisheries that occur in the shallow waters where loggerheads forage include bottom trawling for flounder *(Paralichthys)* and other fishes, gill netting, setting of pound nets, and lobster *(Panulirus)* and crab (Xanthidae and Portunidae) trapping. Each of these techniques is used to catch species that are smaller than loggerheads but occupy the same areas. Mortality to loggerheads occurs when they are kept from surfacing due to underwater entrapment in trawls or from entanglement in netting or trap buoy lines. The propensity for loggerheads to become entangled in netting and lines makes lost or discarded fishing gear an important drowning threat. Other threats occurring in shallow water include collisions with boats, injury from suction dredging of channels, and the use of explosions to remove oil platforms and other structures (NRC 1990).

Loggerheads Are Late Bloomers

Loggerheads reach sexual maturity in 12–37 years (Bjorndal et al. 2001; Frazer and Ehrhart 1985; Heppell et al. 1996). This long maturation period has important consequences for assessments of loggerhead population dynamics (Heppell et al., Chapter 16 this volume). One consequence of a multiple-decade maturation period is that any increase in survival among young loggerheads—such as might result from the reduction of a particular source of mortality—will take decades of time to show up as increases in the number of adult turtles and in subsequent net reproduction. Time that stretches into decades amounts to an important human limitation. It is a period that spans the

careers of biologists and that may surpass political terms, changes in government, and the attention span of organizations. The result is that evidence from loggerhead conservation efforts will seldom manifest quickly enough to help justify the continuance of conservation programs.

Another consequence of late maturation is that disturbing trends in population dynamics will not be readily evident at the place where researchers have their most reliable counts of loggerheads—on nesting beaches. While researchers diligently monitor nesting activity, the results of even a profound threat may remain obscure for decades during which the threat occurs. This would certainly be the case for extensive egg predation or egg harvest. One hundred percent mortality at the egg stage could continue for decades (even as increases in numbers of nesting females might be seen) before nesting numbers would begin to plummet. This lag time between population changes and nesting beach evidence will vary with the age of the population segment affected by change. The fact that nesting numbers respond so sluggishly to changes in younger members of the population should always be given as a caveat when the meaning of nesting number changes is discussed.

The late maturation of loggerheads confounds a conservation strategy that is purely reactionary; that is, initiating action only when loggerheads seem to be declining or discontinuing action when numbers appear to increase. The most successful loggerhead conservation efforts are likely to be anticipatory, requiring liberal estimates of threats, conservative estimates of survivorship, and occasional extrapolation from scarce data.

Loggerheads Have Charisma

Loggerheads go through a cute phase as young turtles, and even older loggerheads evoke positive emotional responses from most people. Sea turtles as a group seem to fit the set of characteristics that people consider to be either cute (in hatchlings: large heads and eyes relative to body size, rounded features, hyperactivity) or otherwise charismatic (in older turtles: large size, a nonthreatening nature, mysterious, ancient). These appearance traits and human perceptions directly affect human relationships with loggerheads and provide an important basis for public incentives to conserve loggerheads and other "charismatic megafauna" (Wilson and Peter 1988). Granted, conservation incentives based on charisma do not rely on evidence from ecological modeling or on philosophical proofs of intrinsic value, nor does the argument to conserve charismatic organisms benefit from sound science or from the logic of metaethical analysis. Yet, the charisma phenomenon exists, and its effects are widespread.

Charismatic traits may provide the most compelling inspiration for most people to want to save loggerheads. Part of capitalizing on this inspiration is to understand the charisma effect, from both stoic and emotional perspectives, when making conservation decisions. For instance, understanding the benefits of fostering an affinity for loggerheads can help conservationists manage the demand for human access to them. One form of human access is through turtle watches, in which visitors to a nesting beach sit behind a turtle at night to watch her nest. Stoic views of this interaction often emphasize only conservation actions that would reduce effects on the nesting turtle, to the extent that limits are placed on the number of people participating in turtle watches. Alternatively, a more emotional view might emphasize an effort to maximize the positive experiences of the turtle watchers so as to make them active sea turtle conservation constituents. In another example, emotional perspectives on research activity might help to reveal the importance of an effort like the satellite telemetry of a single aberrant turtle (e.g., a turtle rehabilitated from injury). Justifiably, the information gathered from the research may have little application toward understanding the behavior of turtles in the wild and may be too limited to allow conclusions on postrehabilitation survivorship. However, the orchestrated broadcast of tracking information from such a turtle (e.g., through the Internet and other media) might yield great conservation benefits in the form of newly inspired conservationists.

However, there are pitfalls to allowing the charisma of loggerheads to guide conservation efforts. The affinity generated by charisma often makes people focus on individuals rather than on populations. Thus, the welfare of a single injured loggerhead may receive great attention, while the comparatively mundane task of mitigating the threat that caused the injury is ignored. Both biological guidance and recognition of emotional concerns are critical to effective loggerhead conservation decisions.

Challenges and Opportunities

Consequences of loggerhead biology bring about both challenges and opportunities. It may be useful to think of these challenges to be overcome and opportunities to be seized as guides for conservation tasks. Below, the author discusses a number of these points that he feels are likely to be among the most important for loggerhead conservation both now and in the future.

Challenges

Unknown Baselines and Baseline Shift
One challenge to loggerhead conservation is uncertainty over the historical abundance of loggerheads. This knowledge would serve to root assessments of loggerhead status and guide expectations for loggerhead recovery. Although specific baselines of historical loggerhead abundance are largely a mystery, there is general evidence from every ocean basin where loggerheads occur that populations have recently declined (this volume: Baldwin et al., Chapter 14; Ehrhart et al., Chapter 10; Kamezaki et al., Chapter 13; Limpus and Limpus, Chapter 12; Margaritoulis et al., Chapter 11). Even at the best-known nesting beaches, however, nearly all of the data on loggerhead abundance are limited to the previous 35 years. Without a historical baseline for loggerhead numbers, conservationists are left with a latter-day baseline that is likely to represent an already depleted set of populations. Warnings of this "shifting baseline syndrome" have been sounded as a pitfall for sea turtle conservation (Jackson 1997).

Specific tasks that would address the challenge of unknown baselines are to make the most of archeological information and historical records and to fully elucidate genetic diversity in loggerhead groups. Many beaches within the nesting range of loggerheads may have sites with archeological remains of adult turtles that would indicate extirpated rookeries. Likewise, a thorough review of historical records and interviews with people having cultural knowledge may help piece together a more complete picture of past ranges and abundance. Furthermore, in the genetics of extant loggerheads, researchers may begin to answer the question of whether small but genetically diverse populations were once much larger.

Vanishing Nesting Beaches

Decades from now, the limitation of loggerhead nesting sites is likely to be much closer to crisis. Sea levels are rising (Titus and Narayanan 1996). From a broad model based on expert sea level predictions, Titus and Narayanan report projections with 50% probability that global sea level will rise at least 45 cm (with landward erosion averaging 67.5 m) by the year 2100.

To be sure, there have been many fluctuations in sea level during the past million years (Haq et al. 1987). Throughout these changes, the sands between vegetated dune and water have had a mobile, wavelike persistence; thus, loggerhead nesting habitat has persisted as well. However, a present-day problem for loggerheads is that tomorrow's nesting beaches lie in the sands beneath the foundations of valuable human structures. Throughout the lengthy period during which humans will cope with sea level rise, continued artificial beach building, coastal armoring, and eventual crumbling of structures and roadways, will severely hamper loggerhead nesting. In many areas, loggerheads will only be able to nest if there is a large-scale removal of structures and hard debris.

However, within the long-term trend in sea level rise, conservationists will need to deal with shorter periods of beach erosion and bouts of environmental alteration. Short-term erosion of beaches is created by natural events (e.g., storms, currents), is exacerbated by anthropogenic structures (e.g., jetties), and is often dealt with by engineering efforts on the beach (e.g., building of groins, armoring, and artificial beaches). Engineering of the beach and dune system affects many loggerhead beaches and is likely to affect additional beaches long before

profound effects from sea level rise are seen (Pilkey and Wright 1988).

Although "vanishing beaches" is meant to describe habitat loss, some loss of nesting habitat can be said to come from human alterations that actually make beaches more conspicuous: for example, when beaches are illuminated with artificial lighting. Apart from effects on hatchlings leaving nests, light pollution also alters beaches so as to make them unsuitable for nesting (Witherington 1992). The effects of this environmental alteration may explain the shunning of densely developed areas by loggerheads in Florida (Witherington and Martin 2000).

Tasks to address the challenge of vanishing beaches should include both nesting beach preservation and nesting beach management. Present-day actions to place nesting beaches into protected public ownership will largely determine where successful loggerhead nesting will occur in the future. Aside from this preparation for a bleak future, many tasks having more immediate results also are at hand. Loggerheads continue to nest on developed beaches where the effects of human occupation could be understood and managed better. Nesting beach research and management tasks should include (1) understanding how to artificially build a beach most suitable for sea turtles and managing beach nourishment projects with these standards in mind, (2) understanding the effects of different coastal armoring structures and prohibiting armoring that reduces nesting habitat, (3) establishing setback rules that minimize the erosion threat for new structures, (4) moving erosion-threatened buildings and other structures away from the beach, and (5) restricting the visibility of artificial lighting to areas landward of the beach.

Identifying Loggerheads

Knowing loggerhead identities will help to prevent the decline of more vulnerable stocks that are distributed within less vulnerable stocks. The tasks under this challenge are (1) to obtain representative samples of genetic information from loggerheads on all nesting beaches and (2) to perform mixed-stock assessments of loggerheads assembled at principal foraging areas, of stranded loggerheads, and of loggerheads known to have been taken by specific threats (e.g., as recorded by fisheries observers). Both maternally inherited (mtDNA) and biparentally inherited (nDNA) genetic markers would provide important stock information from these groups (FitzSimmons et al. 1999; Taylor 1995). Bowen (Chapter 1, this volume) outlines the present completeness of this effort.

Counting Loggerheads

Like other sea turtles, loggerheads are easiest to count on nesting beaches. Yet, regular, standardized surveys do not occur in many places where loggerheads nest, including the important beaches of Masirah, Oman, which may host nearly half of the world's loggerheads. A principal task under this challenge is to work within the limited resources of beach surveyors to implement representative surveys at index beaches. Representative nesting indices, however limited they may be, will be critical to accurately estimating loggerhead abundance and to assessments of trends in nesting numbers, both between beaches and over time (Schroeder 1994).

Loggerheads are most difficult to count in the water, which is where they spend the vast majority of their lives. But knowing the abundance of loggerheads in the water is critical to an adequate model of their demography, and it is imperative to recognizing alarming changes in populations before it is too late. The challenge of counting loggerheads in the water can be met by continuing long-term in-water capture programs with an emphasis on catch-per-effort estimates. These programs differ greatly in technique, water conditions, and scope, but each has the potential to provide stage-specific, location-specific, and identity-specific estimates of relative loggerhead abundance over time (Bjorndal and Bolten 2000).

Some technological advances in aerial survey and vessel survey methods for sea turtles are likely to occur. Tasks to explore the suitability of water-penetrating technologies such as the airborne imaging LIDAR (Light Detection and Ranging; Churnside et al. 1998) and both active and passive acoustic imaging (Epifanio et al. 1999; Rees 1998) may result in important turtle-

counting methods. These methods could complement existing, long-term, in-water programs and allow a translation of catch-per-effort into estimated abundance.

Managing Incidental Take from Fisheries

Loggerheads will continue to be incidentally killed as a result of fisheries. One of the greatest ongoing challenges to loggerhead conservationists is to reduce this mortality as much as is both technically and politically possible. Tasks under this challenge might be guided by what has been learned from the ongoing case study of turtle excluder device implementation (NRC 1990; Crowder et al. 1995). Mirroring the tasks in turtle excluder device implementation, tasks in reducing mortality from other fisheries include the development of mortality-reducing fisheries technologies in conjunction with, or initiated by, the fishing industry in which the mortality occurs. Some examples of mortality-reducing technologies might include improved turtle excluder device designs, reduced-fouling longline hooks, and longline baits that are less attractive to turtles. An additional lesson from the turtle excluder device saga is that technological solutions are not likely to be complete, making it necessary to strategically limit fisheries that take loggerheads. Some season and zone closures based on the intersection of fishing effort and turtle abundance may always be needed.

Another lesson from turtle excluder device implementation describes the importance of selling ideas and methods to the people who will use them. New mortality-reducing ideas, technologies, and methods may require both positive and negative incentives for their success. For instance, turtle excluder devices have been introduced to shrimpers not only as a way to avoid broader season and zone closures but also as a device to decrease unwanted bycatch, to reduce damage to shrimp, to lower fuel costs, and to improve the consumer image of the product they sell.

Patience

Conserving an animal with a long generation time challenges one's patience. Both the rewards of conservation efforts and the alarms from conservation problems are likely to develop slowly.

This challenge of patience is best met with persistence. Programs to monitor loggerheads on nesting beaches and in the water and efforts to conserve loggerheads and their habitat should be long-term, if not continuous, efforts.

Nesting beaches, especially, are both sluggish sentinels of conservation problems and suspect bearers of good news. Conclusions drawn from increases in abundance on nesting beaches measured over less than a decade are likely to be premature, yet declines measured over such a short period may actually foretell a disastrous trend. This treatment of short-term nesting beach news seems like cheating—where good news is mistrusted and bad news generates concern. But the prudence of such a policy lies more in the consequences of error than in its probability.

The reluctantly reaffirmed faith that is required for loggerhead conservation can be likened to the faith that inspires good automobile maintenance. Although the regular changing of engine oil is unlikely to yield any short-term benefit, its value to long-term engine life is critical. And although a prudent automobile owner monitors the oil pressure gauge carefully for problems, it would be foolish to depend on it as an indicator of when maintenance is due because a warning from the oil gauge could very well mean that it is too late.

Frustration and Allocation of Effort

Loggerhead conservation challenges can frustrate. Solutions to the sources of loggerhead mortality and habitat loss shown in Figure 18.1 have a wide range of difficulty. For instance, there are anthropogenic sources that can be readily mitigated with sufficient effort (e.g., artificial lighting effects), there are natural sources that also can be readily mitigated (e.g., egg predation), and there are both anthropogenic and natural sources that have difficult solutions and unlikely prospects for elimination (e.g., non–point-source dumping of plastics, oceanic loggerhead predation, and cold water mortality from dispersal toward the poles).

In the public mind, the frustration that comes from an inability to solve one conservation problem can detract from efforts to solve another. For instance, the public may question

why resources are spent on nesting beach conservation in a home country when hatchlings that leave those beaches suffer high mortality at sea from debris ingestion. Or in a more localized example, the people of one community may question whether they should have a light management law to protect sea turtles when a nearby city makes no effort to control its lighting. Loggerhead conservationists presenting arguments to the public for conservation action and allocation of funding may need to emphasize that logic favors decisions to increase, rather than decrease, local conservation efforts when global threats become large.

What should be done and what can be done to conserve loggerheads can confuse the allocation of conservation efforts. Many individuals, organizations, and countries will not be able to focus all of their loggerhead conservation resources onto the most critical problems (e.g., onto the greatest source of mortality at the most reproductively valuable life stage). Loggerhead conservation must also be guided by opportunity, found either in readily applied solutions or in the abilities of individuals to effect positive changes. For example, artificial lighting on a given beach may cause moderate mortality to a stage that is relatively low in reproductive value (hatchlings), but if the solution to the problem can be readily identified (light management) and implemented by local conservation interests (through education, incentives, and local government action), then the allocation of effort to this problem makes sense.

International Cooperation

One of the greatest challenges to loggerhead conservation is in fostering and maintaining international cooperation. Each stock of loggerheads is shared by multiple nations and is located for long periods of time within international waters. One important task under this challenge is to identify loggerheads by their nations of stewardship. In an example presented by Bowen (Chapter 1 this volume), genetic markers show that hatchlings dispersing from Japanese beaches develop as oceanic juveniles in the North Pacific, where many are killed by longline and driftnet fisheries mounted from multiple nations; juveniles move into neritic habitats in Mexico; and adults return to Japan to nest. Steward-specific loggerhead identifications like this clearly determine the stakeholders who have an interest in solving a conservation problem. Knowing whose loggerheads are affected by whom helps avoid the "tragedy of the commons" that may otherwise occur in international waters (Hardin 1968).

Opportunities

Strange-Bedfellow Coalitions

An underutilized opportunity lies in recruiting sea turtle conservation efforts into coalitions with similar interests. These coalitions need not have loggerhead conservation as their principal agenda. Because loggerheads, humans, and many other animals often suffer the same ills, efforts on the behalf of one group may greatly help another. Given this opportunity, there are a number of partnering tasks that loggerhead conservationists should pursue. Some examples include partnerships with astronomers and power companies to solve light pollution problems (with a mutual goal of effective light management); with coastal tourism councils to solve beach erosion problems (with a mutual goal of avoiding harmful coastal armoring); with the property insurance industry to reduce the need for erosion control efforts (with a mutual goal of increased setbacks for coastal development); with sport-fishing organizations to reduce bycatch mortality from longline fisheries (with a mutual goal to reduce multispecies hooking mortality); and with a broad spectrum of conservation, packaging industry, and oil transport industry groups to solve problems with marine debris (with a mutual goal to reduce illegal dumping).

Wealthy Admirers

Many potential stewards of loggerheads have the economic wherewithal to actively conserve them. A principal task for loggerhead conservationists is to inspire this stewardship. But even the uninspired can be convinced that loggerheads should be conserved if the cost of conservation is low and the relative sacrifice they must make is minimal. Few in the developed world will need to forgo a food source or endure profound changes in lifestyle in order to conserve loggerheads. Metaphorically, these are people who do not need to be convinced not to eat the daisies, but just to mind their steps through the garden so as not to trample them.

Although the developed world tends to be heavy footed in the metaphorical garden, the economic resources there have the potential to greatly offset this tendency. Some examples of loggerhead conservation benefits from robust economies include transfers of turtle excluder device (TED) technology to developing nations, broadening of international research and monitoring efforts, and decisions made by economically powerful consumers not to purchase products or receive services that harm loggerheads. Although the world trade aspects of conservation consumerism are complex (as in the regulation of shrimp imports according to country-specific TED use; Crouse 1999), consumer decisions at the individual level are simpler and can be effective as long as consumers are accurately informed.

Loggerhead Charisma

Charisma influences the conservation attention that loggerheads get. They are not as difficult to sell as a tiny animal with beady eyes and noxious habits might be. Rather than apologize for this extra consideration, loggerhead conservationists should seize upon it. One important task under this opportunity is to facilitate loggerheads' selling themselves, especially to children. Introducing loggerheads and their conservation to educational programs is an opportunity that should not be missed.

Although conservation resources are not fixed, they are scarce. In the midst of this scarcity, charismatic megafauna such as loggerheads receive resources and attention that are disproportional to their ecological value (but, arguably, proportional to their perceived value). Recognizing this, an additional task for loggerhead conservationists may be to present loggerheads as conservation catalysts. Loggerheads represent more than themselves when the horseshoe crabs (*Limulus*) they eat require protection from overharvest and habitat loss, when the *Sargassum* community they inhabit is threatened by surface pollutants, and when the beaches on which they nest are receding into the concrete foundations of coastal buildings. As a poster species, loggerheads have a great deal to contribute toward conserving the web of less conspicuous, noncharismatic organisms that actually run the world.

Conclusions

1. Loggerheads are long-lived, late-maturing animals that are threatened by prolonged exposure to varied threats. Threats occur throughout individual population ranges, which can span entire ocean basins.
2. Loggerheads are threatened with extinction. Although two large centers of abundance exist, there are many additional smaller populations with valuable levels of genetic diversity, and many of these smaller populations are believed to be in decline.
3. The distribution and habits of loggerheads make them particularly vulnerable to incidental mortality from commercial fisheries and from numerous human activities, both on nesting beaches and at sea.
4. The nonconsumptive value of loggerheads to humans generally outweighs their consumptive value throughout most of their global distribution. This nonconsumptive value is the basis for important loggerhead conservation opportunities.
5. The challenges and opportunities presented by the consequences of loggerhead biology, economics, and sociology compel ongoing conservation tasks that include:

- Elucidate meaningful baselines for loggerhead abundance and refine goals for loggerhead recovery.
- Prepare for continued sea level rise and chronic erosion of loggerhead nesting habitat.
- Identify genetic stocks where loggerheads nest, forage, migrate, and are threatened by mortality.
- Manage incidental loggerhead mortality from fisheries by recognizing intersections of loggerhead distribution with fishing activities; by selective temporal and spatial closures of fisheries; and by the development,

use, and multinational transfer of mortality-reducing methods and technology.
- Maintain long-term loggerhead conservation programs that are guided by local opportunity in addition to global need.
- Develop effective coalitions comprising diverse groups with mutual goals that forward the needs of loggerhead conservation.
- Inspire and guide the present and future members of a loggerhead conservation constituency.

ACKNOWLEDGMENTS

I thank Karen Bjorndal, Allen Foley, Judy Leiby, Anne Meylan, Buddy Powell, and Jim Quinn for their helpful comments on the draft manuscript, and I am grateful to Dawn Witherington for drafting the figure.

LITERATURE CITED

Balazs, G. H., and S. G. Pooley (eds.). 1994. Research plan to assess marine turtle hooking mortality: Results of an expert workshop held in Honolulu, Hawaii, November 16–18, 1993. NOAA Technical Memorandum NOAA-TM-NMFS-SWFSC-201.

Baldwin, R. M., and Al-kiyumi. 1999. The ecology and conservation status of the sea turtles of Oman. In M. Fisher, S.A. Ghazanfar, and J. A. Spalton (eds.). The natural history of Oman: A festschrift for Michael Gallagher, 89–98. Leiden, The Netherlands: Backhuys Publishers.

Bjorndal, K. A. (ed.). 1995. Biology and conservation of sea turtles, rev. ed. Washington, D.C.: Smithsonian Institution Press.

Bjorndal, K. A., and A. B. Bolten (eds.). 2000. Proceedings of a workshop on assessing abundance and trends for in-water sea turtle populations. NOAA Technical Memorandum NMFS-SEFSC-445.

Bjorndal, K. A., A. B. Bolten, B. Koike, B. A. Schroeder, D. J. Shaver, W. G. Teas, and W. N. Witzell. 2001. Somatic growth function for immature loggerhead sea turtles, Caretta caretta, in southeastern U.S. waters. Fishery Bulletin 99:240–246.

Bolten, A. B., J. A. Wetherall, G. H. Balazs, and S. G. Pooley (compilers). 1996. Status of marine turtles in the Pacific Ocean relevant to incidental take in the Hawaii-based pelagic longline fishery. NOAA Technical Memorandum NMFS-SWFSC-230.

Bolten, A. B., K. A. Bjorndal, H. R. Martins, T. Dellinger, M. J. Biscoito, S. E. Encalada, and B. W. Bowen. 1998. Transatlantic developmental migrations of loggerhead sea turtles demonstrated by mtDNA sequence analysis. Ecological Applications 8:1–7.

Bowen, B. W. 1995. Tracking marine turtles with genetic markers: Voyages of the ancient mariners. BioScience 45:528–534.

Bowen, B. W., and S. A. Karl. 1997. Population genetics, phylogeography, and molecular evolution. *In* P. L. Lutz and J. A. Musick (eds.). The biology of sea turtles, 29–50. CRC Marine Science Series. Boca Raton, Fla.: CRC Press.

Bowen, B. W., F. A. Abreu-Grobois, G. H. Balazs, N. Kamezaki, C. J. Limpus, and R. J. Ferl. 1995. Trans-Pacific migrations of the loggerhead turtle (*Caretta caretta*) demonstrated with mitochondrial DNA markers. Proceedings of the National Academy of Sciences of the 92:3731–3734.

Brice, J. J. 1896. The fish and fisheries of the coastal waters of Florida. Report of the U.S. Commission on Fisheries and Fish 22:263–342.

Bustard, H. R. 1972. Australian sea turtles: Their natural history and conservation. London: Collins.

Carr, A. F. 1952. Handbook of turtles: The turtles of the United States, Canada and Baja California. Ithaca, N.Y.: Comstock Publishing Associates.

———. 1986. Rips, FADS, and little loggerheads. Bioscience 36:92–100.

———. 1987. The impact of nondegradable marine debris on the ecology and survival outlook of sea turtles. Marine Pollution Bulletin 18:352–356.

Churnside, J. H., J. J. Wilson, and C. W. Oliver. 1998. Evaluation of the capability of the experimental oceanographic fisheries lidar (FLOE) for tuna detection in the eastern tropical Pacific. NOAA Technical Memorandum ERL ETL-287. Boulder, Colo.: Environmental Technology Laboratory.

Crain, D. A., A. B. Bolten, and K. A. Bjorndal. 1995. Effects of beach nourishment on sea turtles: Review and research initiatives. Restoration Ecology 3:95–104.

Crouse, D. 1999. Guest Editorial: The WTO shrimp/turtle case. Marine Turtle Newsletter no. 83:1–3.

Crouse, D. T., L. B. Crowder, and H. Caswell. 1987. A stage-based population model for loggerhead sea turtles and implications for conservation. Ecology 68:1412–1423.

Crowder, L. B., S. R. Hopkins-Murphy, and J. A. Royle. 1995. Effects of turtle excluder devices (TEDs) on loggerhead sea turtle strandings with implications for conservation. Copeia 1995:773–779.

Dodd, C. K., Jr. 1988. Synopsis of the biological data on the loggerhead sea turtle *Caretta caretta* (Linnaeus 1758). USFWS Biological Report 88–14.

Doughty, R. W. 1984. Sea turtles in Texas: A forgotten commerce. Southwestern Historical Quarterly 88:43–70.

Encalada, S. E., J. C. Zurita, J. C., and B. W. Bowen. 1999. Genetic consequences of coastal development: The sea turtle rookeries at X'cacel, Mexico. Marine Turtle Newsletter no. 83:8–10.

Epifanio, C. L., J. R. Potter, G. B. Deane, M. Readhead, and M. J. Buckingham. 1999. Imaging in the ocean with ambient noise, the ORB experiments. Journal of the Acoustical Society of America 106:3211–3225.

Epperly, S. P., and W. G. Teas. 1999. Evaluation of TED opening dimensions relative to size of turtles stranding in the western North Atlantic. NMFS SEFSC Contribution PRD-98/99-08.

FCMP. 1997. Florida assessment of coastal trends. Report to FCMP, Florida Department of Community Affairs.

FitzSimmons, N., C. Moritz, and B. W. Bowen. 1999. Population identification. *In* K. L. Eckert, K. A. Bjorndal, F. A. Abreu-Grobois, and M. Donnelly (eds.). Research and management techniques for the conservation of sea turtles, 72–79. IUCN/SSC Marine Turtle Specialist Group Publication no. 4.

Frazer, N. B., and L. M. Ehrhart. 1985. Preliminary growth models for green, *Chelonia mydas*, and loggerhead, *Caretta caretta*, turtles in the wild. Copeia 1985:73–79.

Groombridge, B., and R. Luxmoore. 1989. The green turtle and hawksbill (Reptilia: Cheloniidae): World status, exploitation and trade. Lausanne, Switzerland: CITES Secretariat.

Haq, B. U., J. Hardenbol, and P. R. Vail. 1987. Chronology of fluctuating sea levels since the Triassic. Science 238:1156–1167.

Hardin, G. 1968. The tragedy of the commons. Science 162:1243–1248.

Heppell, S. S., C. J. Limpus, D. T. Crouse, N. B. Frazer, and L. B. Crowder. 1996. Population model analysis for the loggerhead sea turtle, *Caretta caretta*, in Queensland. Wildlife Research 23:143–159.

Herren, R. M., and L. M. Ehrhart. 2000. The effect of beach nourishment on loggerhead nesting and reproductive success at Sebastian Inlet, Florida. *In* H. J. Kalb and T. Wibbels (compilers). Proceedings of the 19th annual symposium on sea turtle biology and conservation, 221–224. NOAA Technical Memorandum. NMFS-SEFSC-443.

Jackson, J. B. C. 1997. Reefs since Columbus. Coral Reefs 16:S23–S32.

Lutcavage, M., P. Plotkin, B. Witherington, and P. Lutz. 1997. Human impacts on sea turtle survival. *In* P. Lutz and J. Musick (eds.). The biology of sea turtles, 387–409. Boca Raton, Fla.: CRC Press.

Lutz, P. L., and J. A. Musick (eds.). 1997. The biology of sea turtles. CRC Marine Science Series.

Boca Raton, Fla.: CRC Press.

McCauley, S. J., and K. A. Bjorndal. 1999. Conservation implications of dietary dilution from debris ingestion: Sublethal effects in post-hatchling loggerhead sea turtles. Conservation Biology 13:925–929.

Meylan, A. B., and M. Donnelly. 1999. Status justification for listing the hawksbill turtle (Eretmochelys imbricata) as critically endangered on the 1996 IUCN Red List of Threatened Animals. Chelonian Conservation and Biology 3:200–224.

Meylan, A. B., and D. Ehrenfeld. 2000. Conservation of marine turtles. In M. W. Klemens (ed.). Turtle conservation, 96–125. Washington, D.C.: Smithsonian Institution Press.

Meylan, A., B. Schroeder, and A. Mosier. 1995. Sea turtle nesting activity in the state of Florida 1979–1992. Florida Marine Research Publications no. 52.

Mosier, A. E. 1998. The impact of coastal armoring structures on sea turtle nesting behavior at three beaches on the east coast of Florida. Unpublished Master's Thesis, University of South Florida, Tampa.

Nishimura, W., and S. Nakahigashi. 1990. Incidental capture of sea turtles by Japanese research and training vessels: Results of a questionnaire. Marine Turtle Newsletter 51:1–4.

NMFS and USFWS . 1991. Recovery plan for U.S. population of loggerhead turtle (Caretta caretta). Washington, D.C.: NMFS.

———. 1998. Recovery plan for the U.S. Pacific populations of the loggerhead turtle (Caretta caretta). Silver Spring, Md.: NMFS.

NRC, Committee on Sea Turtle Conservation. 1990. Decline of the sea turtles: Causes and prevention. Washington, D.C.: National Academy Press.

Parsons, J. J. 1962. The green turtle and man. Gainesville: University of Florida Press.

Pianka, E. R. 1994. Evolutionary ecology, 5th ed. New York: Harper Collins.

Pilkey, O. H., and H. L. Wright III. 1988. Seawalls versus beaches. In N. C. Kraus and O. H. Pilkey (eds.). Journal of Coastal Research, Special Issue no. 4, 41–66.

Poiner, I. R., and A. N. M. Harris. 1996. Incidental capture, direct mortality and delayed mortality of sea turtles in Australia's northern prawn fishery. Marine Biology (Berlin) 125:813–825.

Pritchard, P. C. H. 1979. Encyclopedia of turtles. Neptune, N.J.: T. F. H. Publications.

Rees, C. D. 1998. Active towed-array acoustic system design study for yellowfin tuna in the Eastern Tropical Pacific Fishery Area. NOAA-TM-NMFS-SWFSC-251.

Ross, J. P., and M. A. Barwani. 1995. Review of sea turtles in the Arabian area. In K. A. Bjorndal (ed.). Biology and conservation of sea turtles, rev. ed., 373–383. Washington, D.C.: Smithsonian Institution Press.

Schroeder, B. A. 1994. Florida index nesting beach surveys: Are we on the right track? In K. A. Bjorndal, A. B. Bolten, D. A. Johnson, and P. J. Eliazar (compilers). Proceedings of the fourteenth annual symposium on sea turtle biology and conservation, 132–133. NOAA Technical Memorandum NMFS-SEFSC-351.

Sears, C. J., B. W. Bowen, R. W. Chapman, S. B. Galloway, S. R. Hopkins-Murphy, and C. M. Woodley. 1995. Demographic composition of the feeding population of juvenile loggerhead sea turtles (Caretta caretta) off Charleston, South Carolina: Evidence from mitochondrial DNA markers. Marine Biology (Berlin) 123:869–874.

Stancyk, S. E. 1995. Non-human predators of sea turtles and their control. In K. Bjorndal (ed.). Biology and conservation of sea turtles, 139–152. Washington, D.C.: Smithsonian Institution Press.

Steinitz, M. J., M. Salmon, and J. Wyneken. 1998. Beach renourishment and loggerhead turtle reproduction: A seven-year study at Jupiter Island, Florida. Journal of Coastal Research 14:1000–1013.

Taylor, B. L. 1995. Defining "populations" to meet management objectives for marine mammals. SWFSC Administrative Report LJ-95-03:1–22.

TEWG. 1998. An assessment of the Kemp's ridley (Lepidochelys kempii) and loggerhead (Caretta caretta) sea turtle populations in the western North Atlantic. NOAA Technical Memorandum NMFS-SEFSC-409.

———. 2000. Assessment update for the Kemp's ridley and loggerhead sea turtle populations in the western North Atlantic. NOAA Technical Memorandum NMFS-SEFSC-444.

Thorbjarnarson, J. B., C. J. Lagueux, D. Bolze, M. W. Klemens, and A. B. Meylan. 2000. Human use of turtles: A worldwide perspective. In M. W. Klemens (ed.). Turtle conservation, 33–84. Washington, D.C.: Smithsonian Institution Press.

Titus, J. G., and V. Narayanan. 1996. The risk of sea level rise: A delphic Monte Carlo analysis in which twenty researchers specify subjective probability distributions for model coefficients within their respective areas of expertise. Climatic Change 33:151–212.

Valverde, H. R., C. Trembanis, and O. H. Pilkey. 1999. Summary of beach renourishment episodes on the U.S. east coast barrier islands. Journal of Coastal Research 15:1100–1118.

Wilson, E. O., and F. M. Peter (eds.). 1988. Biodiversity. Washington, D.C.: National Academy Press.

Witherington, B. E. 1992. Behavioral responses of nesting sea turtles to artificial lighting. Herpetologica 48:31–39.

———. 2000. Habitats and bad habits of young loggerhead turtles in the open ocean. *In* F. A. Abreu-Grobois, R. Briseño-Dueñas, R. Marquez-Millan, and L. Sarti-Martinez (compilers). Proceedings of the 18th international sea turtle symposium, 34–35. NOAA Technical Memorandum MFS-SEFSC-436.

Witherington, B. E., and R. E. Martin. 2000. Understanding, assessing, and resolving light-pollution problems on sea turtle nesting beaches, 2nd rev. ed. FMRI Technical Report TR-2.

Witherington, B. E., and M. Salmon. 1992. Predation on loggerhead turtle hatchlings after entering the sea. Journal of Herpetology 26:226–228.

Witherington, B. E., C. Crady, and L. Bolen. 1996. A "Hatchling Orientation Index" for assessing orientation disruption from artificial lighting. *In* J. A. Keinath, D. E. Barnard, J. A. Musick, and B. A. Bell (compilers). Proceedings of the 15th annual symposium on sea turtle biology and conservation, 344–347. NOAA Technical Memorandum NMFS-SEFSC-387.

Witherington, B. E. 2002. Ecology of neonate loggerhead turtles inhabiting lines of downwelling near a Gulf Stream front. Marine Biology (Berlin) 140:843–853.

Wood, D. W., and K. A. Bjorndal. 2000. Relation of temperature, moisture, salinity, and slope to nest site selection in loggerhead sea turtles. Copeia 2000:119–128.

Index